SECOND EDITION

DIVERSITY
IN SPORT ORGANIZATIONS

DISCARDED

George B. Cunningham

TEXAS A&M UNIVERSITY

Consulting Editor, Sport Management Series

Packianathan Chelladurai

Holcomb Hathaway, Publishers

Scottsdale, Arizona

Library of Congress Cataloging-in-Publication Data

Cunningham, George B.
  Diversity in sport organizations / George B. Cunningham. — 2nd ed.
    p. cm.
  ISBN 978-1-934432-09-9
1. Sports administration—United States.   2. Sports--Management.   I.
Title.
  GV713.C86 2011
    796.06'9—dc22
                                                        2010042646

DEDICATION

For Melissa, Harper, and Maggie.

Holcomb Hathaway, Publishers, Inc.
8700 E. Via de Ventura Blvd., Suite 265
Scottsdale, Arizona 85258
480-991-7881
www.hh-pub.com

10 9 8 7 6 5 4 3 2 1

ISBN 978-1-934432-09-9

Brief Contents

Preface   xvii

PART I   FOUNDATIONS OF DIVERSITY   1

1   Overview of Diversity   3

2   Theoretical Tenets of Diversity   27

3   Prejudice and Discrimination   49

PART II   FORMS OF DIVERSITY   67

4   Race   69

5   Sex and Gender   101

6   Age   133

7   Mental and Physical Ability   153

iii

8 Appearance 175

9 Religious Beliefs 195

10 Sexual Orientation 213

11 Social Class 237

PART III **MANAGING WORKPLACE DIVERSITY** 261

12 Legal Aspects of Diversity 263

13 Managing Diverse Organizations 289

14 Managing Diverse Groups 315

15 Diversity Training 339

Author Index 365
Subject Index 371

Contents

Preface xvii • *Acknowledgments xix* • *About the Author xx*

PART I   FOUNDATIONS OF DIVERSITY   1

1   Overview of Diversity   3

Learning Objectives   3
Diversity Challenge   3

DEFINITIONS   4
   Diversity   4
   Diversity Management   6

FORMS OF DIVERSITY   7
   Surface-Level Diversity   8
   Deep-Level Diversity   8

ALTERNATIVE PERSPECTIVES: *Classifying Diversity   9*
   Interdependence of Surface- and Deep-Level Diversity   9

UNDERSTANDING THE EMPHASIS ON DIVERSITY   10
   Changing Demographics   10
   Changing Attitudes Toward Work   14
   Changes in the Nature of Work   15
   Legal Mandates   16

ALTERNATIVE PERSPECTIVES: *Social Responsibility for Diversity   17*
   Social Pressures   17
   Potential Negative Effects of Diversity   17

DIVERSITY IN THE FIELD: *Communication Barriers   18*
   Value-in-Diversity Hypothesis   18

PROFESSIONAL PERSPECTIVES: *The Importance of Diversity in Sport   19*

PUTTING IT ALL TOGETHER   20

Chapter Summary   20

Questions for Discussion   21

Learning Activities   21

Reading Resources   22

References   22

2 Theoretical Tenets of Diversity   27

Learning Objectives   27

Diversity Challenge   27

DEFINING THEORY   28

Practicality   29

PROFESSIONAL PERSPECTIVES: *The Importance of Theory   30*

THEORIES USED TO UNDERSTAND DIVERSITY   30

Managerial Theories   31

Sociological Theories   34

ALTERNATIVE PERSPECTIVES: *Black Feminist Theory   37*

PROFESSIONAL PERSPECTIVES: *Participatory Action Research   38*

Social Psychological Theories   38

DIVERSITY IN THE FIELD: *Overcoming Dissimilarity   41*

ALTERNATIVE PERSPECTIVES: *Ways of Studying Diversity   42*

Chapter Summary   43

Questions for Discussion   43

Learning Activities   44

Reading Resources   44

References   45

3 Prejudice and Discrimination   49

Learning Objectives   49

Diversity Challenge   49

PREJUDICE   50

Definition   51

Explicit and Implicit Prejudice   51

DIVERSITY IN THE FIELD: *Racism in Soccer   52*

Outcomes of Prejudice   53

DISCRIMINATION   54

Definitions   54

ALTERNATIVE PERSPECTIVES: *Discrimination Based on Language   56*

Theoretical Explanations for Discrimination   56

DIVERSITY IN THE FIELD: *Limited Access to Participation   57*

ALTERNATIVE PERSPECTIVES: *Questioning Different Work Experiences 58*

Discrimination Outcomes   58

PROFESSIONAL PERSPECTIVES: *Discrimination in the Hiring Process   59*

Chapter Summary   61

Questions for Discussion   62

Learning Activities   63

Reading Resources   63

References   63

PART II   FORMS OF DIVERSITY   67

Race   69

Learning Objectives   69

Diversity Challenge   69

DEFINING RACE, ETHNICITY, AND MINORITY GROUP   71

DIVERSITY IN THE FIELD: *Defining Ourselves in Terms of Race?   72*

GENERAL RACIAL TRENDS   72

RACE IN THE EMPLOYMENT CONTEXT   73

Earnings   73

Representation of Racial Minorities   74

DIVERSITY IN THE FIELD: *Underrepresentation of African Americans as High School Coaches   77*

Occupational Segregation   78

Reasons for Racial Minority Underrepresentation   79

PROFESSIONAL PERSPECTIVES: *Creating and Maintaining Networks   85*

Race and Employee Outcomes in Other Contexts   87

PROFESSIONAL PERSPECTIVES: *Knowing the Language   88*

THE INFLUENCE OF RACE ON PARTICIPATION IN SPORT   88

Sport and Leisure Participation   89

Positions Played on Athletic Teams   89

ALTERNATIVE PERSPECTIVES: *Is It Really Stacking?*   *90*

    Stereotypes and Attitudes   90

DIVERSITY IN THE FIELD: *Stereotypes About Athletic Performance*   *90*

    Athlete Treatment   91

RACE ISSUES BEYOND UNIVERSITY ATHLETICS   91

    Marketing and Spectator Consumption   91

    International Sport   92

    Sport Experiences of Native Persons   92

DIVERSITY IN THE FIELD: *Native American Mascots*   *93*

Chapter Summary   *93*

Questions for Discussion   *94*

Learning Activities   *95*

Reading Resources   *95*

References   *96*

5 Sex and Gender   101

Learning Objectives   *101*

Diversity Challenge   *101*

PROFESSIONAL PERSPECTIVES: *Using Sexist Language*   *103*

SEX AND GENDER   103

    Gender Identity   104

DIVERSITY IN THE FIELD: *Hitting "Like a Girl"*   *107*

    Gender in the Sport Context   107

MEN AND WOMEN IN THE WORKPLACE   108

    Participation in the Workforce   108

    Earnings   109

    Representation in Management and Leadership Positions   111

    Reasons for Underrepresentation   113

ALTERNATIVE PERSPECTIVES: *Women and Transformational Leadership*   *114*

ALTERNATIVE PERSPECTIVES: *Effects of Discrimination*   *116*

DIVERSITY IN THE FIELD: *Elite Athletes as Mothers*   *117*

PROFESSIONAL PERSPECTIVES: *Women's Work Experiences in Mexico*   *119*

    Section Summary   119

SEX, GENDER, AND SPORT PARTICIPATION   119

THE INTERSECTION OF GENDER AND RACE   120

    Earnings   121

Representation in Management and Leadership Positions   121

Sport Participants   122

THE MARKETING OF SPORT   123

Motives for Sport Consumption   124

Consumption of Women's Sports   124

Customer Service   124

Promoting Sport   125

Chapter Summary   125

Questions for Discussion   127

Learning Activities   127

Reading Resources   127

References   128

6 Age   133

Learning Objectives   133

Diversity Challenge   133

BACKGROUND AND KEY TERMS   134

DIVERSITY IN THE FIELD: *Bridge Employment in College Athletics   136*

AGE AND OTHER DIVERSITY DIMENSIONS   136

AGE AND EMPLOYMENT   137

Stereotypes   137

ALTERNATIVE PERSPECTIVES: *Age and Performance   139*

Age, Opportunities, and Work Experiences   141

DIVERSITY IN THE FIELD: *Youth Movement in the NFL   142*

PROFESSIONAL PERSPECTIVE: *Training Employees over Age 50   143*

DIVERSITY IN THE FIELD: *Age Discrimination in College Athletics   144*

Moderators   144

ALTERNATIVE PERSPECTIVES: *Caring for the Elderly   145*

Effects of Age in Work Groups   146

SPORT AND LEISURE PARTICIPATION   147

DIVERSITY IN THE FIELD: *Influence of Age on Sport Consumption   147*

Chapter Summary   148

Questions for Discussion   149

Learning Activities   149

Reading Resources   149

References   150

Mental and Physical Ability   153

Learning Objectives   153

Diversity Challenge   153

DEFINITION, INCIDENCE, AND HISTORICAL BACKGROUND   155

EDUCATIONAL AND WORK OPPORTUNITIES   157

   Education   158

   Work   158

   Pay   158

WORK EXPERIENCES   159

   Supervisor Relationship   159

   Performance Expectations   160

ALTERNATIVE PERSPECTIVES: *Disability and Performance   160*

   Accommodations   160

   Antecedents of Discrimination   161

   Moderating Variables   164

DISABILITY SPORT   165

   Issues Related to Disability Sport   167

PROFESSIONAL PERSPECTIVES: *Trends and Issues in Disability Sport   167*

MEDIA AND CONSUMERS   168

Chapter Summary   169

Questions for Discussion   170

Learning Activities   170

Reading Resources   170

References   171

Appearance   175

Learning Objectives   175

Diversity Challenge   175

WEIGHT   177

   Background and Key Terms   177

   Effects of Weight in the Workplace   178

ALTERNATIVE PERSPECTIVES: *Who Is Stigmatized?   179*

DIVERSITY IN THE FIELD: *Weighing the Coaching Options   180*

DIVERSITY IN THE FIELD: *Anti-Fat Attitudes Toward Customers   181*

   Weight and Fitness Promotion   181

ALTERNATIVE PERSPECTIVES: *Dove Body Lotion*   *182*

    Weight and Physical Activity Participation   182

HEIGHT   **183**

    Key Terms   183

    Effects of Height in the Workplace   183

ATTRACTIVENESS   **185**

    Background Information   185

    Attractiveness in the Workplace   187

DIVERSITY IN THE FIELD: *Attractiveness and the Promotion of Sport*   *188*

    Attractiveness and Physical Activity   189

DIVERSITY IN THE FIELD: *Women's Headscarves and Their Sport Participation*   *189*

Chapter Summary   *190*

Questions for Discussion   *190*

Learning Activities   *191*

Reading Resources   *191*

References   *192*

Religious Beliefs   195

Learning Objectives   *195*

Diversity Challenge   *195*

BACKGROUND AND KEY TERMS   **196**

    The Emphasis on Religion   197

RELIGION IN THE WORKPLACE   **198**

    Strategic Decisions   198

DIVERSITY IN THE FIELD: *Church-Organized Sport Leagues*   *199*

    Ethical Behavior   200

    Leadership   201

    Stress   202

    Religion as a Source of Categorization   203

DIVERSITY IN THE FIELD: *Religion and Soccer*   *204*

RELIGION AND SPORT PARTICIPATION   **204**

    Influence on Sport Participation   204

ALTERNATIVE PERSPECTIVES: *Some Sports Are Tolerated*   *205*

    Athletes' Use of Religion   205

ALTERNATIVE PERSPECTIVES: *Sport as Religion*   *206*

DIVERSITY IN THE FIELD: *Costs of Prayer*   *207*

Chapter Summary *208*

Questions for Discussion *209*

Learning Activities *209*

Reading Resources *209*

References 210

10 Sexual Orientation 213

Learning Objectives *213*

Diversity Challenge *213*

KEY TERMS AND HISTORICAL CONTEXT **215**

ALTERNATIVE PERSPECTIVES: *Determining Sexual Orientation Through Implicit Tests* *216*

SEXUAL PREJUDICE **217**

Background and Key Terms 217

Prevalence of Sexual Prejudice 218

DIVERSITY IN THE FIELD: *Sexual Prejudice Toward Coaches* *219*

Motivations for Negative Behaviors and Attitudes 220

Effects of Sexual Prejudice 220

SEXUAL ORIENTATION AND WORK **221**

Differential Work Experiences 221

Sexual Orientation Disclosure 225

ALTERNATIVE PERSPECTIVES: *Negative Outcomes of Revealing at Work?* *229*

Marketing to Customers Who Are LGB 229

PROFESSIONAL PERSPECTIVES: *Olivia Cruises and Resorts* *230*

SEXUAL ORIENTATION AND SPORT PARTICIPATION **230**

Chapter Summary *232*

Questions for Discussion *232*

Learning Activities *233*

Reading Resources *233*

References *234*

11 Social Class 237

Learning Objectives *237*

Diversity Challenge *237*

BASIC CONCEPTS **239**

Socioeconomic Status 240

Social Class   242

CLASSISM   243

Cognitive Distancing   244

Interpersonal Distancing   245

Institutional Distancing   245

DIVERSITY IN THE FIELD: *Inequitable Wage Distributions in College Athletics   247*

DIVERSITY IN THE FIELD: *Housing and the Olympics   250*

ALTERNATIVE PERSPECTIVES: *Are There Benefits to Displacement?   251*

PROFESSIONAL PERSPECTIVES: *Alternate Conceptions of Social Class   254*

SPORT AND SOCIAL MOBILITY   256

Chapter Summary   256

Questions for Discussion   257

Reading Resources   258

References   258

PART III   MANAGING WORKPLACE DIVERSITY   261

12 Legal Aspects of Diversity   263

Learning Objectives   263

Diversity Challenge   263

EVOLUTION OF EMPLOYMENT DISCRIMINATION LAW   265

Title VII of the Civil Rights Act of 1964   265

Griggs v. Duke Power Co.   265

Albemarle Paper Co. v. Moody   266

Price Waterhouse v. Hopkins   266

Wards Cove Packing Co. v. Atonio   266

Civil Rights Act of 1991   267

EQUAL EMPLOYMENT OPPORTUNITY LEGISLATION   267

Race   268

Sex   269

Religion   272

Age   272

Ability   273

DIVERSITY IN THE FIELD: *ADA Compliance in Fitness Organizations   274*

Obesity   274

DIVERSITY IN THE FIELD: *Casey Martin and the PGA*   *275*

Sexual Orientation   275

Section Summary   277

EMPLOYMENT DISCRIMINATION CLAIMS   277

Employee Perspective   277

Employer Perspective   278

TITLE IX   278

History of Title IX   279

Title IX Compliance   281

DIVERSITY IN THE FIELD: *The Influence of Title IX on Physical Education and Recreation   282*

Title IX Outcomes   283

PROFESSIONAL PERSPECTIVES: *Title IX   284*

Chapter Summary   285

Questions for Discussion   286

Learning Activities   286

Reading Resources   286

References   287

Managing Diverse Organizations   289

Learning Objectives   289

Diversity Challenge   289

PROFESSIONAL PERSPECTIVES: *Potential Unintended Effects of Diversity Management Programs   291*

DIVERSITY MANAGEMENT STRATEGIES   291

DIVERSITY IN THE FIELD: *A Little Diversity Management Would Have Helped   292*

DeSensi's Model   292

Doherty and Chelladurai's Model   293

Fink and Pastore's Model   294

Chelladurai's Model   296

ALTERNATIVE PERSPECTIVES: *The False Hope of Competency   297*

SPORT INDUSTRY SUPPORT FOR DIVERSITY MANAGEMENT   298

Racial and Gender Report Card   298

Diversity in Athletics Award   300

DIVERSITY MANAGEMENT PROCESSES   302

Factors Influencing Change   302

Implementing Change *304*

Commitment to and Behavioral Support of Diversity *307*

DIVERSITY AND LEADERSHIP **308**

Knowledge of Cultural Differences *308*

Increased Self-Awareness *309*

Multicultural Skills *309*

Chapter Summary *310*

Questions for Discussion *311*

Learning Activities *311*

Reading Resources *312*

References *312*

Managing Diverse Groups 315

Learning Objectives *315*

Diversity Challenge *315*

THE CONTACT HYPOTHESIS **316**

Conditions of Contact *317*

Intergroup Anxiety *319*

Influence of Status *320*

Contact Hypothesis Limitations *320*

SOCIAL CATEGORIZATION STRATEGIES FOR REDUCING BIAS **321**

Decategorization *322*

ALTERNATIVE PERSPECTIVES: *Cross-Categorization Strategies for Managing Diverse Groups* *323*

Recategorization *325*

PROFESSIONAL PERSPECTIVES: *Recategorization on a Soccer Team* *327*

Intergroup Contact *329*

INTEGRATED MODEL **330**

General Principles *330*

Moderators *331*

Chapter Summary *332*

Questions for Discussion *333*

Learning Activities *333*

Reading Resources *334*

References *334*

Diversity Training   339

Learning Objectives   339

Diversity Challenge   339

PREVALENCE OF DIVERSITY TRAINING   341

EFFECTS OF DIVERSITY TRAINING   341

    Positive Effects   341

    Negative Effects   342

    Making Sense of the Effects   343

DESIGNING AND DELIVERING EFFECTIVE DIVERSITY TRAINING PROGRAMS   344

    Needs Analysis   345

DIVERSITY IN THE FIELD: *How a Needs Analysis Shows the Need for Diversity Training   346*

    Pre-Training Conditions   347

    Training Methods   350

    Post-Training Conditions   353

ALTERNATIVE PERSPECTIVES: *Evaluating Diversity Training Effectiveness   356*

GENERAL PRINCIPLES   357

PROFESSIONAL PERSPECTIVES: *Diversity Behind the Face   358*

Chapter Summary   359

Questions for Discussion   360

Learning Activities   360

Reading Resources   361

References   361

Author Index   365

Subject Index   371

Preface

iversity has been, and will continue to be, one of the most important issues managers encounter, and this is particularly true with sport and physical activity. The United States continues to become more diverse, both in terms of demographics and attitudes, and this diversity is evident in the organizational context, where dissimilarities among employees are now commonplace. These differences are important because they impact opportunities not only for employment but also for sport and physical activity participation. Following diversity-related legal requirements, or failing to do so, can have meaningful implications for an organization. The specific diversity management strategies used by an organization can influence employee attitudes, group processes, and the organization's overall effectiveness. Consequently, understanding the effects of diversity and the strategies to effectively manage those differences is of paramount importance. The purpose of the second edition of *Diversity in Sport Organizations* is to provide students with such an understanding.

I have divided the book into three parts. Part I provides an overview of diversity. Chapter 1 defines diversity and diversity management, and then analyzes why diversity warrants attention by students and managers. The focus of Chapter 2 is on the theoretical tenets of diversity, with a focus on the three primary theoretical approaches to the study of diversity—managerial, sociological, and social psychological—as well as the practical implications associated with each. Chapter 3 addresses prejudice and discrimination, the theoretical tenets undergirding those constructs, and their associated outcomes.

Part II is devoted to the various forms of diversity. Specifically, I focus on race (Chapter 4), sex and gender (Chapter 5), age (Chapter 6), mental and physical ability (Chapter 7), appearance (Chapter 8), religious beliefs (Chapter 9), sexual orientation (Chapter 10), and social class (Chapter 11). In this second edition, I devote an entire chapter to each diversity dimension (a change from the first edition); in doing so, I am better able to flesh out diversity-related issues in sport and physical activity.

Part III focuses on effectively managing diversity in organizations. I outline diversity-related laws in Chapter 12 and discuss how those laws influence employment decisions and sport opportunities. In Chapters 13 and 14, I highlight several diversity management strategies that can be used to effectively manage dissimilar employees. The emphasis in the former chapter is on organization-wide strategies, while the focus in the latter is on smaller groups. Finally, Chapter 15 is devoted to diversity training. Here, I underscore the importance of this training and provide the steps to design, implement, and evaluate effective diversity training programs.

The book is intended for upper-level undergraduate and graduate students. Teachers, coaches, managers, marketers, and administrators also will benefit from the text's information. Because the sport industry is composed of many segments, examples are drawn from a bevy of sources—professional sports, university athletics, fitness organizations, physical education, recreation and leisure settings, and nonprofit entities such as the YMCA.

The Book's Special Features

- **Diversity Challenge.** Each chapter opens with a Diversity Challenge, a real-life scenario introducing the chapter's topic. It is followed by a series of questions to prompt students to think about the issues raised.

- **Diversity in the Field.** These sidebars use real-life examples to help readers comprehend chapter concepts.

- **Professional Perspectives.** These recurring boxes reflect interviews of leading professionals with responsibilities in sport and leisure (e.g., a sport industry employment recruiter, professors, an elementary school principal, a university president, a president of a cruise line) and provide students with practical, informed opinions on the chapter content.

- **Alternative Perspectives.** Because so many topics and issues are subject to varying opinions, I have included Alternative Perspectives boxes to provide readers with additional sides of a discussion.

- **Questions for Discussion, Learning Activities, Supplementary Readings, and Web Resources.** Each chapter concludes with student activities and sources of additional information. Many of the Learning Activities are designed for students to explore in small groups. The Supplementary Readings are annotated, and the Web Resources augment chapter material by providing links to professional associations, electronic methods of testing prejudicial attitudes, and resources for diversity training, among others.

- **Ancillaries.** An Instructor's Manual, a PowerPoint presentation, and a test-bank (new to this edition) are available for instructors who adopt this text for course use.

- **HHP Sport Management Community site.** This site, at www.hhpcommunities. com/sportmanagement, highlights the connections between the various subject areas in the sport management curriculum. It is a convenient resource for updating class discussions with interesting news and author commentaries related to the topics in HHP textbooks and for communicating with HHP authors and other instructors.

I am excited about diversity and what it means for sport, sport organizations, and people associated with the sport industry. I hope I have reflected this enthusiasm in the text and that this enthusiasm is passed on to instructors and readers. I welcome your comments and look forward to any and all feedback. Please contact me in care of Holcomb Hathaway, Publishers, at feedback@hh-pub.com.

Acknowledgments

I would like to thank the wonderful colleagues and students with whom I have worked. In particular, I enjoyed my collaborative efforts with Dr. Michael Sagas, Dr. Janet Fink, and Dr. John Singer. A large debt of gratitude is owed to all of my students, especially Melanie L. Sartore, Jacqueline McDowell, Claudia Benavides-Espinoza, and E. Nicole Melton. They were a joy to work with, and they also reviewed the book and provided helpful and constructive feedback along the way. I am grateful to my doctoral advisor, Packianathan Chelladurai, for his guidance in my professional preparation and for encouraging me to write this book.

I appreciate the very helpful comments and suggestions offered by the reviewers: Roxanne Allen, McNeese State University; Debra Blair, Temple University; Elaine Blinde, Southern Illinois University Carbondale; Glenna Bower, University of Southern Indiana; Willie Burden, Georgia Southern University; Eddie Comeaux, University of Kentucky; Alison Doherty, The University of Western Ontario; Courtney Flowers, University of West Georgia; JoAnne Graf, Florida State University; Christy Greenleaf, University of North Texas; C. Keith Harrison, University of Central Florida; Louis Harrison, University of Texas at Austin; Lori Head, Idaho State University; Nancy Lough, University of Nevada, Las Vegas; Fritz Polite, University of Tennessee; Cecile Reynaud, Florida State University; Karen Rickel, Gonzaga University; Claudia Santin, Concordia University Chicago; Melanie Sartore, East Carolina University; Brian Sather, Eastern Oregon University; John Singer, Texas A&M University; Jennifer Spry-Knutson, Des Moines Area Community College; Ellen Staurowsky, Ithaca College; and Eli Wolff, Center for the Study of Sport in Society, Northeastern University. Their input during the writing process was very helpful.

I also thank Colette Kelly, Gay Pauley, and others at Holcomb Hathaway, Publishers. I enjoyed working with them and will forever be indebted to them for the opportunity they have provided.

Finally, to those most important in my life: I thank my Lord and Savior, Jesus Christ, for his love, mercy, and grace. I am also thankful for my family: my wife, Melissa, and our two girls Harper and Maggie. They are my everything.

About the Author

 eorge B. Cunningham (Ph.D., The Ohio State University) is a professor of Sport Management in the Department of Health and Kinesiology at Texas A&M University. He also serves as the Director for the Laboratory for Diversity in Sport—a lab dedicated to producing and disseminating research related to all forms of diversity in the sport context. Author of over 120 articles and book chapters, Cunningham focuses his research in the areas of diversity, group processes, and employee attitudes. Within the diversity domain, he investigates the underrepresentation of various groups in leadership positions, the impact of dissimilarity on subsequent outcomes and behaviors, and strategies for capitalizing on the positive effects of diversity. His research has been published in various journals, including those in the sport domain (e.g., *Journal of Sport Management*, *Journal of Sport and Exercise Psychology*, and *Sociology of Sport Journal*), the area of social psychology (e.g., *The Journal of Social Psychology*, *Journal of Applied Social Psychology*, *Sex Roles*, and *Group Dynamics*), and in various management journals (e.g., *Organizational Analysis*, *Journal of Business and Psychology*), among others. Cunningham is a Research Fellow of the North American Society for Sport Management and also served as President of that organization.

Cunningham and his wife, Melissa, have two daughters, Harper and Maggie. His free time is spent with his family, swimming, or playing golf.

PART I

Foundations of Diversity

CHAPTER 1
Overview of Diversity   3

CHAPTER 2
Theoretical Tenets of Diversity   27

CHAPTER 3
Prejudice and Discrimination   49

1

1

Overview of Diversity

 ennis, a sport played in various venues such as private clubs, schools, parks, and recreational facilities, provides its participants with the strenuous exercise needed to maintain a healthy lifestyle. Hispanics, however, are relatively unlikely to play tennis—they represent less than 10 percent of all participants. Participant numbers are even lower for members of other racial minority groups. Relative to Whites, Hispanics are more likely to play at recreational facilities (rather than private clubs), to begin playing tennis at a later age, and to have different motivations to participate. Because the discretionary income of Hispanics is generally lower than that of Whites, they also have fewer opportunities to participate in tennis. These differences are important because the Hispanic population is the fastest growing minority group in the United States and is the largest minority group in Texas, New Mexico, and California, states where minority group members represent the majority of the states' citizens.

Recognizing this apparent contradiction, the United States Tennis Association (USTA) has embarked on a number of initiatives designed to attract and recruit athletes to the sport. For instance, the organization offers a multicultural excellence program grant aimed at developing racial minority tennis players. As another example, the Texas Section of the USTA makes special efforts to target Hispanics and entice them to participate in tennis by using such strategies as increasing the availability of public courts, emphasizing the sport's health benefits, and advertising and promoting the sport in Spanish. Regardless of the strategy used, attracting Hispanics and members of other racial minority groups to tennis is essential to the sport's growth and survival.

Information adapted from: ■ Caldwell, A. A. (2005, August 11). Minorities become majority in Texas. *The Eagle*, pp. A7, A9 ■ Fitzgerald, M. P., Fink, J. S., & Riemer, H. A. (2002). *USTA Texas Section marketing research report: Implications for growing tennis membership.* Austin, Texas: Authors; www.usta.org.

LEARNING OBJECTIVES

After studying this chapter, you should be able to:

■ Define diversity and diversity management.

■ List and explain the different forms of diversity.

■ Discuss the different factors that led to an increased interest in diversity.

3

DIVERSITY CHALLENGE   **R E F L E C T I O N**

Imagine that you are the manager of the Texas Section of the USTA, then answer the following questions:

1. What strategies would you use to attract Hispanics and other minorities to tennis?
2. What are specific marketing or promotional activities that could be developed?
3. What changes are needed at an organizational level to attract minority participants?

Diversity is one of the most important topics in the context of sport and physical activity today. As the opening scenario illustrates, the United States' population is changing; therefore, organizations and the people who work in them must also change. Although the scenario focuses on current racial changes, other changes are also occurring, including those based on sex, age, beliefs, attitudes, and preferences. Due to these changes, managers must now implement alternative marketing and promotional activities to attract diverse participants and spectators and must structure their organizations so they are open to all people, irrespective of their demographic characteristics, preferences, or beliefs. Managers, athletic administrators, coaches, and others in the sport industry should be aware of the legal implications associated with having a diverse workforce and how various mandates and laws influence the human resource decisions they make. Because diversity is now a central issue for persons in sport organizations, it is crucial that they understand the underlying dynamics and effects of diversity and implement strategies to maximize the benefits of having a diverse workforce.

This chapter provides an overview of diversity. The first section examines several definitions of diversity and diversity management, developing from them the definitions used throughout the text. This is followed by a discussion of the various forms of diversity and the ways in which people can differ. The third section identifies and analyzes the seven factors that contribute to the current interest in and importance of diversity. Finally, the last section provides a brief overview of the major diversity-related issues discussed in subsequent chapters.

Definitions

This section considers several definitions of diversity and diversity management in order to develop the working definitions used in the text.

Diversity

To begin developing a working definition of *diversity,* consider the following definitions used by others in this field:

Diversity "is defined as real or perceived differences among people that affect their interactions and relationships (Bell, 2007, p. 4).

Diversity "refers to differences between individuals on any attribute that may lead to the perceptions that another person is different from self" (van Knippenberg, De Drue, & Homam, 2004, p. 1008).

Diversity is the "distribution of personal attributes among interdependent members of a work unit" (Jackson, Joshi, & Erhardt, 2003, p. 802).

Diversity refers to "differences among people that are likely to affect their acceptance, work performance, satisfaction, or progress in an organization" (Hayes-Thomas, 2004, p. 12).

Diversity is an "aggregate group level construct that represents differences among members of an interdependent work group with respect to a specific personal attribute" (Joshi & Roh, 2007, p. 3).

Diversity is "any characteristic used to differentiate one person from others" (Joplin & Daus, 1997, p. 32).

We can draw several points from these definitions. First, most of the definitions consider the group or dyad (i.e., two people working together, such as a supervisor and subordinate) as a requisite condition. People must be able to compare their attributes to the characteristics of others in the dyad or group. Without an ability to compare, people do not know if they are similar to or different from others. Thus, we can say that diversity is a dyadic or group-related topic.

Second, diversity is concerned with differences among people (Bell, 2007); therefore, a truly diverse group has various characteristics. For example, some may consider a group of five African Americans working in a sport marketing firm to be diverse because the group is composed entirely of members of a racial minority. However, if the definitions we cited earlier are applied, the group is actually homogeneous, not diverse, because each member is an African American. Another group in the same sport marketing firm has as its members two Hispanics, one White, one African American, and one Asian American. Clearly, with respect to race, this group has a broader array of attributes, as persons from four racial backgrounds are included. Relative to the group of five African Americans, the latter group is more racially diverse because it reflects more racial differences.

Third, note that van Knippenberg et al. (2004) and Bell (2007) assert that differences between a person and other members of the group or dyad may lead to perceptions of being different. Others have also noted that actual differences may lead to perceptions of being different (Riordan, 2000), and they reason that perceptions of being different have a greater impact on subsequent outcomes than the actual differences themselves. Refer again to the two groups in the sport marketing firm discussed previously. The members of the all–African American group, because they are all racially similar to one another, are likely to *perceive* themselves as similar to one another as well. Because the Asian American in the second group is racially different from four other members, this person is likely to *perceive* herself to be racially different from others in the group. Thus, actual differences result in perceptions of dissimilarity.

Finally, diversity is related to various work outcomes (Hayes-Thomas, 2004). These outcomes can occur at the individual level, such as the satisfaction a physical education student has with his teacher or the performance an employee realizes at work, and at the group level, including the conflict, cohesion, or creativeness of the group. Diversity also impacts organizational outcomes such as product innovation, personnel turnover, and organizational effectiveness. The benefits and possible shortcomings of diversity are discussed in greater detail later in this chapter and throughout the text.

Using the discussion and the previous definitions, diversity can be defined as *the presence of differences among members of a social unit that lead to perceptions of such differences and that impact work outcomes.* This definition highlights (a) the presence of differences, (b) the dyadic or group nature of diversity, (c) the manner in which actual differences can influence perceptions of such heterogeneity, and (d) the impact diversity has on subsequent outcomes.

Finally, Prasad, Pringle, and Konrad (2006) argue that a discussion of power differences among social groups is critical to the understanding of diversity. As DiTomaso, Post, and Parks-Yancy (2007) note, "group differences are rarely sustained if they are just different (e.g., blue eyes and brown eyes)" (p. 475); rather, some diversity forms are more meaningful than others as a result of the socially constructed power differences among group members, the historical context, and the political nature of organizations (Cunningham & Singer, 2009). Notice that, although power is not explicitly mentioned in the definition (nor in DiTomaso et al.'s), the effects are readily observable. Differences among group members are unlikely to result in perceptions of such differences (Bell, 2007; van Knippenberg et al., 2004) unless there are socially constructed meanings attached to the characteristics in question. Objective differences in race should result in greater perceptual differences than corresponding differences in eye color. Power is also a contributing factor to the relationship between diversity and subsequent work outcomes. For instance, group members from disadvantaged groups often have their ideas discounted by majority group members (DiTomaso et al., 2007). Collectively, this evidence points to the important role of power in discussions of diversity—a point elaborated upon in subsequent chapters.

Diversity Management

In addition to defining diversity, it is also necessary to define *diversity management.* Consider first how other authors define diversity management:

> Diversity management is "an organizational practice which seeks to redress employees' negative responses to differences associated with age, gender, race, class, occupation, and religion, as well as physical ability and sexual orientation" (Lorbiecki, 2001, p. 345).

> Managing diversity is "creating a climate in which the potential advantages of diversity for organizational or group performance are maximized while the potential disadvantages are minimized" (Cox & Beale, 1997, p. 2).

> Diversity management "is the proactive management technique designed to utilize employee differences in order for an organization to glean a competitive advantage in the marketplace" (Fink & Pastore, 1999, p. 313).

Diversity management is "the purposeful use of processes and strategies that make . . . differences among people into an asset rather than a liability for the organization" (Hayes-Thomas, 2004, p. 12).

Several conclusions about diversity management can be drawn from these definitions. First, diversity management is generally considered to be proactive and management-initiated (Fink & Pastore, 1999; Hayes-Thomas, 2004). This differs from reactive measures organizations may take to respond to federal or state initiatives, such as affirmative action guidelines. Rather, diversity management is viewed as a purposeful, proactive strategy organizations use to realize a competitive advantage and organizational effectiveness.

Second, diversity management is aimed at improving the interactions among persons within a social unit who differ in some way (Lorbiecki, 2001). Although diversity has many benefits to the individual, group, and organization, dissimilarities among interacting people can also lead to friction, process losses, and other negative outcomes. The purpose of diversity management, therefore, is to minimize these potential pitfalls.

Finally, diversity management is a strategic action aimed at maximizing the benefits that diversity can bring to the social unit (Cox & Beale, 1997; Hayes-Thomas, 2004). Just as organizations, departments, or teams set strategic objectives and initiatives to accomplish tasks and achieve goals, diversity management is a deliberate plan established to realize the benefits of diversity. Diversity can bring tangible benefits to an organization and serve as a source of competitive advantage (Robinson & Dechant, 1997); however, for these benefits to be realized, managers must be strategic in their policy and decision-making process. When managers fail to adopt an effective strategy or when they treat diversity as a "problem to be dealt with," the advantages diversity can bring to a social unit are not likely to materialize (Fink & Pastore, 1999). Thus, as Hayes-Thomas (2004) notes, effective diversity management entails making "differences among people into an asset rather than a liability for the organization" (p. 12).

Using the previous definitions and the discussion, diversity management may be defined as *a proactive, strategic action aimed at capitalizing on the benefits diversity can bring to an organization.* This definition highlights the strategic nature of diversity management and requires a proactive, rather than reactive, management plan that emphasizes the advantages of diversity and seeks to eliminate potential pitfalls.

Because people differ in so many ways, it is useful to classify the types of differences. The next section discusses the various forms of diversity.

Forms of Diversity

Much of the early work in diversity focused on demographic attributes such as sex, race, or age. However, as our definition of diversity illustrates, limiting the examination only to demographic differences results in an overly narrow approach to the study of diversity. Rather, diversity entails all the ways in which people can differ, including dissimilarities based on demographics, culture, language, physical and mental ability, education, preference, attitudes, and beliefs.

Harrison, Price, and Bell (1998) identified two forms of diversity: surface-level and deep-level (see Exhibit 1.1).

exhibit **1.1** Forms of diversity.

- **Surface-level diversity:** differences among individuals based on readily observable characteristics such as age, sex, race, and physical ability.

- **Deep-level diversity:** differences among individuals based on psychological characteristics.

  - **Information diversity:** those differences based on knowledge and information, oftentimes resulting from variations in education, functional background, training, and organizational tenure.

  - **Value diversity:** those differences in values, attitudes, beliefs, and preferences.

Adapted from Harrison, Price, & Bell (1998) and Jehn, Northcraft, & Neale (1999).

Surface-Level Diversity

Surface-level diversity includes those dimensions that are readily observed—dissimilarities based on sex, race, age, and in some cases, physical ability and language. These variations are important because people make judgments as to how similar they are to others based on these characteristics. For example, when people enter a classroom, aerobics class, or workplace, they make almost instantaneous assessments of their similarity, or lack thereof, to others in the social unit with respect to demographic attributes. An African American coach who enters a room of White coaches almost instantly knows that she is racially different from the others. Surface-level diversity is also important because demographic attributes are permanent and potentially strong sources of member identity.

Similarly, cues about these differences are continually present in face-to-face interactions because of others' outward appearance. For example, members of face-to-face teams have a constant reminder of how other team members vary with respect to age, sex, race, and the like; as a result, the perceptions of difference are continually reinforced.

Deep-Level Diversity

The second form of diversity identified by Harrison et al. (1998) is termed *deep-level diversity*—dissimilarities among people based on psychological characteristics such as attitudes, beliefs, values, culture, or preferences. In general, deep-level differences become apparent only through interaction with others. Consider once again the previous example of the African American coach in the room of Whites. If the African American coach engages in conversation with others in the room, she might learn that some have values, attitudes, and beliefs similar to hers. Thus, even though the coaches may differ in surface-level characteristics, they may be quite similar with respect to deep-level characteristics. As this example illustrates, people can be different on one level, but similar on another.

Deep-level diversity can be divided into two categories, as identified by Jehn, Northcraft, and Neale (1999): information diversity and value diversity.

Information diversity. Information diversity refers to differences based on knowledge or information that members bring to an organization or group. Members may vary in their functional background, level of education, amount of training, or tenure in the organization. For example, sport organization executive boards are frequently comprised of members from various business sectors in the community, including banking, coaching, and marketing. Thus, the board members bring a variety of experiences and sources of information to the board, thereby increasing the level of information diversity.

Value diversity. The second category of deep-level diversity is value diversity. A group has high value diversity when there are variations in members' attitudes toward work, personal preferences, or beliefs. These differences may be based on personality attributes, such as conscientiousness, or personal traits such as the value one attaches to sport and physical activity. Suppose some members of an athletic department place top priority on education and moral citizenship, while others value individual and team performance. In this case, employees' attitudes toward athletics differ; thus, that athletic department is characterized by value diversity.

alternative
P E R S P E C T I V E S

Classifying Diversity. Chelladurai (2009) adopted an alternative approach to classifying the forms of diversity. His first form is based on appearance and visible features—age, sex, or race—and this form is synonymous with Harrison et al.'s notion of surface-level diversity. A second form is based on behavioral preferences; for example, food or dress preferences. Because these differences are readily observed, this is a form of surface-level diversity. Third, Chelladurai identified value and attitudinal differences. This form is more akin to the deep-level diversity that comes to light only after interacting with others. Finally, Chelladurai proposed that people could also vary based on their cognitive orientations and individual skills, also considered deep-level differences that can be discerned only through observing an individual's task performance.

Interdependence of Surface- and Deep-Level Diversity

Thus far, I have discussed surface- and deep-level diversity as independent concepts. In reality, the two may be intertwined. In many cases, surface-level demographics might be representative of more deep-level characteristics. For example, a person, Jim, born in the 1930s is likely to have certain life experiences, expectations, preferences, and values that are quite different from a person, Jackson, born in the 1980s. Jim lived through World War II, the Korean War, and the Vietnam War, worked in an era prior to the advent of computers and the Internet, and experienced a host of civil rights movements. These experiences, and others like them, shaped his values, beliefs, and attitudes. Jackson, on the other hand, has not experienced as many wars, considers workplace technologies a fact of life, and knows only of workplaces governed by equal employment opportunity laws. As with Jim, these factors shaped Jackson's values, beliefs, and attitudes. Thus, Jim and Jackson, who differ in the surface-level characteristic of age, are likely to vary in their deep-level characteristics as well.

A number of studies have demonstrated the link between surface- and deep-level diversity (Cunningham, 2006; Thomas, Ravlin, & Wallace, 1996). One example is seen in Cunningham's (2007) research of track and field coaches. In his first study, he found that both the age and racial diversity of the coaching staff were positively associated with coaches' perceptions of diversity. Racial diversity had a stronger effect, however, probably because of the historical significance of race. He then conducted a second study, also of track and field coaches, to understand the effects of such perceptions. Cunningham found that perceptions of surface-level diversity were reliably associated with perceptions of deep-level diversity. Coaches who believed their staffs were high in deep-level diversity also expressed less coworker satisfaction and greater intentions to leave the staff. Collectively, these studies demonstrate that people take cognitive stock of their coworkers' characteristics and form impressions of the group (i.e., perceptions of group diversity) that can influence their work experiences.

Understanding the Emphasis on Diversity

This next section considers why the topic of diversity is so important and receives such interest. The literature on diversity points to seven specific factors: changing demographics, changing attitudes toward work, changes in the nature of work, legal mandates, social pressures, potential negative effects of diversity, and the value-in-diversity hypothesis (see Exhibit 1.2). Each of these factors is discussed in greater detail.

Changing Demographics

The most important factor spurring interest in diversity is the changing demographic makeup of the workforce. In the United States, significant changes in the

exhibit **1.2**   **Factors contributing to interest in, and importance of, diversity.**

Changing demographics: increases in the median age, proportion of racial minorities, and women in the workforce.

Changing attitudes toward work: changes in the commitment and loyalty to employers and work–family conflict.

Changes in the nature of work: increases in the number of organizations that structure work around teams, the impact of globalization, and the frequency of mergers and acquisitions.

Legal mandates: federal and state laws that require equal employment opportunities for all persons, irrespective of demographic characteristics or background.

Social pressures: the notion that organizations have a moral and ethical obligation to have a diverse workplace.

Potential negative effects of diversity: diversity can potentially lead to negative outcomes such as low satisfaction, high conflict, and poor team performance.

Value-in-diversity hypothesis: diversity can positively influence desired individual, group, and organizational outcomes.

racial, sex, and age composition of the country took place during the 20th century, and demographics are projected to continue changing. Shifts were also seen in socioeconomic status. Demographic changes in the population correspond to changes in the workforce, thus making diversity an organizational reality. These changes prompted managers and other professionals to take note of diversity and to devise strategies to manage such differences. I examine specific demographic shifts in further detail below.

Racial minority representation

From 1980 to 2000, the Hispanic population in the United States doubled. Significant growth occurred for other racial groups as well, as evidenced in Exhibit 1.3. By 2050, the minority population is expected to be 235.7 million of a total U.S. population of 429 million; thus, racial minorities will represent roughly 55 percent of the population. Whites are expected to comprise 46.3 percent of the population in 2050, down from 64.7 percent in 2010. The Hispanic population is projected to increase significantly, representing about one of three Americans by 2050. The proportion of African Americans is expected to decrease slightly (from 12.2 to 11.8 percent), while Asian Americans' share of the population is expected to increase from 4.5 to 7.6 percent. These changes are expected to be reflected in the workforce, and as a result, employees of sport and physical activity organizations will grow more racially diverse. Consequently, people are likely to be working with, working for, or supervising someone who is racially different.

Projected racial changes in the U.S. population.   *exhibit* **1.3**

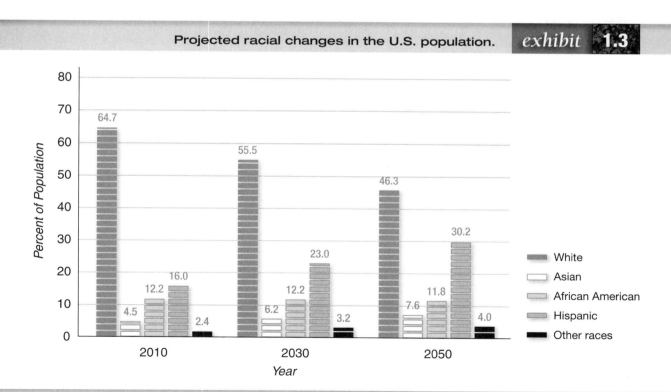

Furthermore, potential customers will also become more racially diverse; therefore, managers will have to devise strategies aimed at attracting those customers to their goods and services.

Median age

Changes in the median age of the U.S. population have also been dramatic. According to the U.S. Census Bureau, at the beginning of the 20th century, the median age was 22.9 years. This figure increased over the 100-year span such that by the year 2000, over half of the U.S. population was over 35.3 years of age. Much of that change is a result of the large number of babies born in the 1940s and 1950s—the baby boom generation. As the baby boomers have grown older, so too has the overall population. The population of persons age 65 and older grew tenfold in the 20th century; furthermore, projections indicate the U.S. population will continue to grow older into the 21st century, so that by 2050, one in five people will be over age 65 (see Exhibit 1.4). Not only is the nation growing older but people are also working to a later age, resulting in greater age diversity within all organizations, including those for sport and physical activity, and an older potential consumer base. Just as strategies are needed to attract persons from different racial groups to purchase an organization's goods and services, so too is there a need to devise plans to draw older customers to the organization.

exhibit **1.4** **Projected changes in percentages of various age ranges in the U.S. population.**

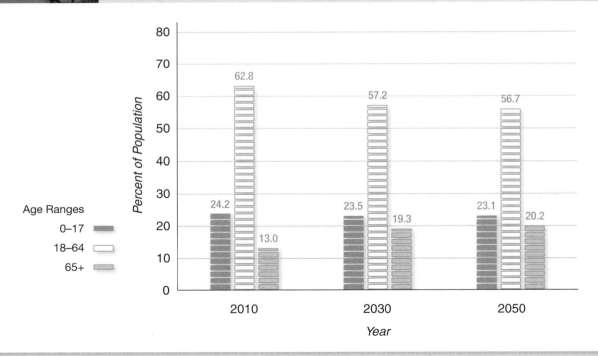

Age Ranges

0–17
18–64
65+

Sex composition

Sex composition of the United States has also changed, though not as dramatically as the shifts in age and race. The U.S. Census Bureau reports that the U.S. population shifted from majority male at the beginning of the 20th century to majority female by the century's midpoint. At the end of the 20th century, women still outnumbered men (see Exhibit 1.5). Although women continue to enter the workforce in increasing numbers, they are still less likely to be members of the workforce than men. It should be noted, however, that the magnitude of the difference in the proportion of men and women in the workforce has decreased over time (see also Tsui & Gutek, 1999). As with the other forms of diversity, the increase in the proportion of working women means sex diversity in all types of organizations has increased as well.

Socioeconomic status

Changes also have occurred with respect to socioeconomic status. Data from the U.S. Census Bureau indicate that in 1967, the mean income in 2008 dollars of the primary householder was $39,899, a figure that increased to $50,132 by 2008. In isolation, these figures do not tell us much, as they simply indicate that people make more money over time, something that could be attributed to inflation. However, other data indicate that the share of aggregate income is increasingly unevenly dispersed. In 1967, the top 5 percent of all households possessed a 17.2 percent share of aggregate income. By 1980, the share had actually dropped to 16.5 percent. However, since that time, the share of aggregate income held by the top 5 percent increased. By 2008, the top 5 percent of all households possessed 21.5 percent of

Change in the proportion of the sexes in the U.S. population. *exhibit* **1.5**

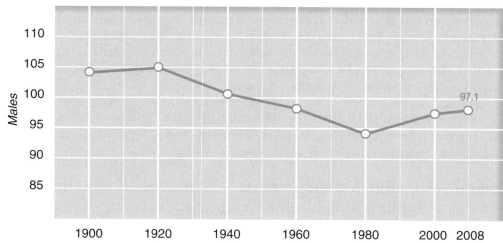

Males per 100 Females

U. S. Census Bureau data.

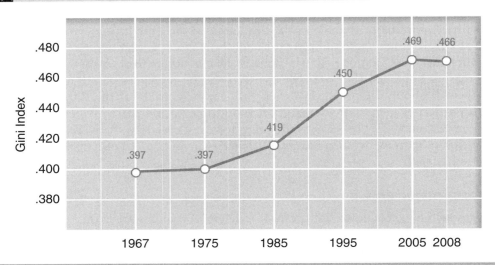

exhibit **1.6**   Income changes in the U. S. population.

U. S. Census Bureau data.

the aggregate income. The Gini Index, a measure that summarizes the dispersion of income over the entire income distribution, also increased during that time. This increase means that the income is increasingly being received by one group of people (see Exhibit 1.6). As this exhibit indicates, the socioeconomic status of the U.S. population has changed over time, with the distribution of wealth growing increasingly inequitable.

Global changes

Such changing demographics occurred in other areas of the world as well. Canada witnessed an increase in the proportion of native persons and other racial minorities during the last 20 years (Haq, 2004). New Zealand also witnessed increased racial diversity, primarily due to immigration from Asian countries (Haq, 2004). Further, the populations of a large number of European nations, as well as Japan and Australia, continue to increase in median age (Haq, 2004). In the UK, estimates suggest that women will account for 90 percent of the increase in the British workforce in the next 10 years (Hewitt, 2002), and by 2008, over 70 percent of women were employed (Record number of women employed, 2008). These figures indicate that increasing diversity is occurring globally.

Changing Attitudes Toward Work

Just as the demographic composition of the workforce has changed, so too have employees' attitudes toward work (Mathis & Jackson, 2006; Ployhart, Schneider, & Schmitt, 2006). Employees are no longer likely to spend an entire career with a single organization, moving up through the ranks as they progress in tenure and skills. Rather, employees are now likely to move from one organization to another several times during their working years either by choice or as a result of changes outside their control, such as downsizing, mergers, and so forth. The average person is likely to follow a number of career paths before retirement. As a result, employees may identify less with an organization, and their job satisfaction may be affected. In general, employees' loyalties and commitments to their employers have decreased.

In addition to a more mobile workforce, a significant portion of the U.S. workforce now works part-time rather than full-time. This is meaningful because part-time workers have different attitudes about their work than their full-time counterparts (Korman, 1999; Thorsteinson, 2003). For example, Thorsteinson reports that full-time employees strongly identify with their jobs and report higher pay satisfaction than their part-time counterparts.

Finally, increases in the number of women in the workforce, the number of dual-career families, and the number of single parents have resulted in greater emphasis being placed on balancing work and family life (Dixon & Bruening, 2005). The conflict between those two roles, termed *work–life balance* (sometimes also called work–family conflict), results in role conflicts and tensions in the workplace that would otherwise not be present.

New and evolving employee attitudes toward work increase the number of perspectives and variety of beliefs held in the workplace. Such changes result in greater deep-level diversity within organizations. Whereas demographic changes have increased the surface-level diversity in organizations, changes in attitudes and preferences have increased the deep-level diversity.

Changes in the Nature of Work

The third reason diversity has become such a major issue for sport managers is related to changes in the nature of work. Many organizations are now structured around work teams (Marks, Mathieu, & Zaccaro, 2001). Interdependence among employees has increased, and consequently, people work more closely with their colleagues than they have in the past. When people work closely with one another, variations in talents, values, perspectives, and attitudes come to the forefront (DiTomaso et al., 2007). Furthermore, differences between people, whether deep- or surface-level, are continually reinforced by constant face-to-face interaction. These factors can influence the way work is experienced (Doherty & Chelladurai, 1999; Thomas, 1996).

Globalization has also influenced diversity within organizations. Many sport organizations, including pro sports, are recruiting employees and athletes from around the world (see Exhibit 1.7 for a Major League Baseball breakdown). The proportion of foreign students enrolled in U.S. universities and participating in collegiate athletics is also growing (Ridinger & Pastore, 2000). It is incumbent upon administrators, professors, and coaches to understand the cultures and backgrounds of the student-athletes in order to aid foreign students to make the transition. Although many of these students return to their native countries upon graduation, others seek to remain and work in this country.

At the same time, sport organizations are striving to broaden the products and services they offer to an international market. For instance, the National Football League (NFL) annually plays regular season games in cities outside the United States, including Toronto and London. The National Basketball Association (NBA) has teams in both Canada and the United States and intends to expand to Europe

exhibit **1.7** **MLB players from around the world.**

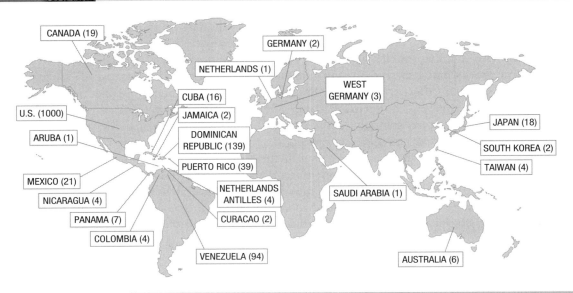

CANADA (19)
GERMANY (2)
NETHERLANDS (1)
WEST GERMANY (3)
CUBA (16)
JAMAICA (2)
U.S. (1000)
JAPAN (18)
ARUBA (1)
SOUTH KOREA (2)
DOMINICAN REPUBLIC (139)
TAIWAN (4)
PUERTO RICO (39)
MEXICO (21)
NETHERLANDS ANTILLES (4)
SAUDI ARABIA (1)
NICARAGUA (4)
PANAMA (7)
CURACAO (2)
COLOMBIA (4)
VENEZUELA (94)
AUSTRALIA (6)

Data from Baseball Almanac. Major League Baseball Players by Birthplace During the 2009 Season. www.baseball-almanac.com/players/birthplace.php?y=2009. Retrieved 5/17/2010.

(Stern lays out vision for NBA expansion in Europe, 2008). Understanding different cultures and customs is of paramount importance for an effective expansion into foreign markets.

Organizational diversity is also impacted by mergers and acquisitions. Mergers and acquisitions are commonplace in the business world, and the sport industry is no exception. For example, in 2003, NIKE purchased Converse for $200 million. Reebok spent roughly the same amount of money to buy The Hockey Company in April of 2004 (Rovell, 2005). In 2006, adidas purchased Reebok for $3.8 billion. Such mergers have a bearing on diversity. When organizations join together, so do members of formerly different entities. Individuals with a great variety of backgrounds and experiences are expected to work effectively with one another. Information diversity increases in the workplace, which can be a positive change, but employee differences and differing organizational identities may make a true merging of talents difficult to accomplish (van Kippenberg, van Kippenberg, Monden, & de Lima, 2002). In general, mergers serve to increase deep-level diversity within organizations.

Legal Mandates

Legal mandates also spur interest in diversity. Diversity-related laws are discussed in greater detail in Chapter 12, so their significance is only briefly discussed here. Civil rights legislation passed in the 1960s and later in the 1990s made discriminatory practices based on race, national origin, sex, age, and so forth illegal and mandated equal employment opportunities for all persons. These laws also required that wages be based on work qualifications rather than personal demographics. As might be expected, such laws have changed the way human resource decisions are made, and they generally serve to increase diversity within organizations.

Within the realm of sport, recreation, and physical education, Title IX represents the most significant legislation passed during the 20th century. This law requires that all persons, regardless of their sex, be afforded equal opportunities to participate in federally funded educational activities. As discussed in subsequent chapters, the law has had a tremendous impact on participation opportunities for girls and women.

Social Pressures

Social pressures are another factor thought to influence the interest in diversity—specifically the notion that there is a moral or ethical obligation for diversity within organizations. For example, Doherty and Chelladurai (1999) outlined how an organizational culture of diversity is likely to result from a sense of social responsibility to treat all employees fairly. Furthermore, DeSensi (1995) argued for an increase in the appreciation of and value placed on employee differences. For many adopting this perspective, social responsibilities with respect to diversity should be the primary focus of diversity initiatives. Proponents of this perspective also may take umbrage at the term "managing diversity" because the term connotes "using" people to achieve organizational goals. This "using" of people stands in contrast to valuing and understanding employee differences in order to further benefit the employee and company (Prasad, Pringle, & Konrad, 2006). These social pressures have led to an increase in the diversity within organizations, especially with respect to surface-level differences.

alternative
P E R S P E C T I V E S

Social Responsibility for Diversity. Although many argue that there is a social or ethical responsibility to achieve diversity, others suggest that such arguments are not pertinent in an organizational context (Fink & Pastore, 1999; Robinson & Dechant, 1997). These authors submit that alternative, business-case arguments provide a more compelling reason for diversity than do social or ethical arguments, especially within for-profit organizations. Robinson and Dechant suggest that empirical data showing how diversity helps the business "bottom line" provide a much more persuasive case for diversity than the social responsibility argument. Fink and Pastore, in their study of sport organizations, take a similar stance; they note that "while it would be wonderful for all of those in positions of power to realize the moral and social advantages of diversity, it may not be a realistic goal. Thus, for diversity initiatives to be truly embedded within the organization, those in power must be convinced of diversity's relationship to organizational effectiveness" (p. 314). Herring's (2009) research supports these contentions, as he found that for-profit businesses that increased their racial and gender diversity also saw increases in a host of outcomes, including sales revenue, market share, and customer growth.

Potential Negative Effects of Diversity

Although diversity does lead to positive outcomes, this is not always so. Thus, a sixth reason for the increased attention on diversity is the potential for negative effects of such heterogeneity. For some, diversity initiatives such as diversity management strategies, equal employment opportunity laws, and affirmative action mandates are seen as unfair, a form of reverse discrimination. Tsui and Gutek (1999) reported the negative feelings some employees felt toward diversity issues. As one employee noted, "minorities receive special attention. It is difficult to fire them because HR gets involved to minimize litigation. Managers do not want the hassle" (p. 2).

These negative attitudes are not felt only by Whites. Fitzgerald Hill, a former head football coach at San Jose State University and current president of Arkansas

DIVERSITY *in the field*

Communication Barriers. Much of the research concerning the negative effects of diversity has focused on the organizational setting; however, these effects can be observed in all contexts. An example can be found among Little League baseball teams in Methuen, MA. In the summer of 2005, the Methuen team was playing Seekonk in Lakeville. Methuen was leading the contest 3–1 when the coach, Domingo Infante, gave instructions to his pitcher in Spanish. After the ensuing play, the umpire called a time-out, briefly spoke to a Little League official, and then ruled that only English could be spoken during the game. At the time, there were no rules dictating the language to be spoken during the contest. A spokesperson for the League explained: "It appears the umpire was concerned that the coach or manager may have been using a language other than English . . . to communicate potentially 'illegal' instructions to his players." The Methuen coaches criticized the ruling, arguing that it demoralized the players, ultimately leading to a loss. A formal protest was denied, and the umpire did not face disciplinary action ("Ump's language," 2005). The implication here is, of course, that those who are not speaking English must be trying to break the rules and gain an unfair advantage. Interestingly, it is acceptable in baseball to use signs and hand motions—a nonverbal form of communication that only team members can understand—to provide instructions. Even though the League rules do not ban other languages, teams who use languages other than English may be penalized, such as occurred in Methuen; thus, the players, coaches, and team are penalized for being different.

Baptist College, found that coaches belonging to racial minorities often felt they were pigeon-holed into certain positions. As one research participant explained, Black coaches are "hired to fill a quota, recruit the black athletes and become their mentor" (as cited in Brown, 2002). Thus, there is the perception among some African American coaches that, although they may have some access to certain positions, they are hired only to fulfill requirements or quotas set by organizations or legal mandates. Other research found that members of racial minorities have negative attitudes toward diversity initiatives when they perceive plans to achieve racial diversity as providing them an unwanted advantage (Highhouse et al., 1999).

People who are different from other members of a social unit generally have negative experiences in that unit (see Mannix & Neale, 2005; van Knippenberg & Schippers, 2007). This is true whether the differences are surface- or deep-level. A feeling of being different can have a negative impact on the attitudes people have toward the group or organization as well as on the group's ability to function. For example, consider Catherine, a female Asian American sport marketer who believes she is different from other employees with whom she works because of her race and the value she places on work and family. To the extent that these differences are meaningful to Catherine, she is unlikely to integrate well with her coworkers or have a positive experience in the workplace. On the other hand, if Bill, a White male in the same organization, feels that he is similar in demographics and values to others in that organization, then his experiences are likely to be positive. The same would also hold true for other demographics and deep-level differences, such as sexual orientation or religious beliefs.

As the examples illustrate, diversity can have a negative effect on organizational functioning. Because diversity is an organizational reality, managers have a responsibility to understand the potential for negative effects and to devise methods and processes to eliminate them.

Value-in-Diversity Hypothesis

The notion that diversity adds value to an organization represents the final factor that has led to an increase in the interest in diversity. To the extent that people can show that diversity brings real, tangible benefits to a group or organization, the value-in-diversity hypothesis (Cox, Lobel, & McLeod, 1991) is likely to result in the greatest acceptance of diversity by group or organization members.

Robinson and Dechant (1997) present several ways in which diversity might benefit an organization, the first of which is cost savings. Specifically, these authors contend that effectively managing a diverse workforce will result in lower turnover costs, a decrease in absenteeism, and a reduction in lawsuits. Indeed, business strategies, such as effective diversity management, that can reduce human resource costs and litigation fees are likely to be valued by any organization.

Second, Robinson and Dechant (1997) argue that effective diversity management plans will allow companies to successfully compete for talented human resources. They note, "winning the competition for talent means attracting, retaining, and promoting excellent employees from different demographic groups" (p. 24). Alternatively, if the available talent pool is limited only to persons from a certain demographic group (e.g., White, able-bodied, Protestant, heterosexual males), then a company is severely limiting the potential pool of human resources. Effective diversity management efforts not only attract diverse persons to the organization but also help to retain them. If employees believe that there are equal opportunities for training, development, and advancement, irrespective of individual differences, this bodes well for the employee retention process.

Organizational diversity can also potentially drive business growth (Robinson & Dechant, 1997). One way business growth occurs is through improved marketplace understanding. For example, when NASCAR sought to increase the diversity of its spectators, it turned to former NBA great and successful entrepreneur Ervin "Magic" Johnson for help. NASCAR chief operating officer George Pyne noted, "Magic will help NASCAR achieve its goals to better educate new audiences and facilitate greater participation among the industry and communities of color" (as cited in "Magic," 2004). Other ways in which diversity spurs business growth include increased creativity and innovation, improved problem solving, enhanced leadership capabilities, and enhanced global technologies. The manner in which diversity influences these important outcomes is discussed in detail throughout this book.

The benefits to, or valued outcomes for, an organization (e.g., cost savings, increased pool of talented human resources, competitive advantage) far outweigh any potential negative effects. Refer to the Professional Perspectives box for further discussion on why diversity is important within the context of sport and physical activity.

PROFESSIONAL PERSPECTIVES

The Importance of Diversity in Sport. Peter Roby served as Director of the Center for Sport in Society, an entity that was created based on the idea that "sport can play an important role in helping to create social change," and is currently the athletic director at Northeastern University. According to Roby, there are several reasons why diversity has become such a major issue in sport and physical activity. Primarily, he suggests that sport highlights differences among people, differences based on sex, age, race, religion, life experiences, and learning style. Roby explains that "there is a lot that people can benefit from as a result of being exposed to difference." In addition, "with regard to sport in particular, one of the values that we see in sport is how much it acts as a great common denominator—how it brings people from different backgrounds together under the common umbrella of sport." Sport serves as an educational tool—what people learn about diversity in the context of sport can be applied to their everyday lives on a daily basis.

Putting It All Together

As the preceding discussions illustrate, diversity has become a central topic within organizations for sport and physical activity. The world around us has become more heterogeneous, with respect to demographic characteristics and attitudes, beliefs, and preferences, and the way work is accomplished has also changed. Legal and social pressures to diversify, as well as the evidence that diversity can both negatively and positively influence organizational outcomes, have all increased the interest in, and attention paid to, diversity.

The purpose of this text is to provide readers with an overview, understanding, and analysis of diversity in sport organizations. In Part I, I discuss the theoretical tenets of diversity (Chapter 2) and discrimination and prejudice (Chapter 3). I provide definitions and key points, discuss the theoretical tenets behind those constructs, and outline the effects that discrimination and prejudice have on persons in the workplace.

Part II is devoted to the various diversity forms. I examine the various ways in which people differ, and how these differences influence people's lives and work experiences, as well as organizational initiatives and functioning. In doing so, I focus on race (Chapter 4), sex and gender (Chapter 5), age (Chapter 6), mental and physical ability (Chapter 7), appearance (Chapter 8), religious beliefs (Chapter 9), sexual orientation (Chapter 10), and social class (Chapter 11).

Part III is devoted to strategies that can be used to create a diverse workplace and to capitalize on the positive effects of diversity. In this section, I first examine legal aspects of diversity (Chapter 12), such as those dealing with equal employment opportunity, sexual harassment, persons with disabilities, and gender equity. Chapter 13 then provides an overview of various strategies that can be used to manage diversity at the department and organization levels. Chapter 14 examines diversity at the group level and how interactions and relationships among dissimilar people can be improved. Finally, in Chapter 15, I examine diversity training, the methods of conducting such training, and the influence of training on subsequent outcomes.

CHAPTER *summary*

This chapter provided an opening glimpse of diversity in organizations. As seen in the Texas Section of the USTA Diversity Challenge, diversity is an important issue for all persons involved in sport and physical activity. In light of the ongoing changes in the workforce, coupled with other pressures to achieve diversity, diversity will continue to be at the forefront for years to come. After reading the chapter, you should be able to do the following:

1. Define diversity and diversity management.

Diversity is the presence of differences among members of a social unit that lead to perceptions of such differences and that impact work outcomes. Diversity management is a proactive, strategic process designed to capitalize on the benefits diversity can bring to an organization.

2. List and explain the different forms of diversity.

Two forms of diversity were identified (Harrison et al., 1998): surface-level diversity, which is related to observable characteristics, and deep-level diversity, which is related to differences in psychological characteristics. Deep-level diversity is further broken down into information diversity, or those differences based on the knowledge and information members bring to the organization or group, and value diversity, which is related to differences in the values, attitudes, and preferences of group members (see Jehn et al., 1999).

3. Discuss the different factors that led to an increased interest in diversity.

The factors that have made diversity such an important topic include: (a) changing demographics in the workforce, (b) changing attitudes of organizational employees, (c) changes in the nature of work, (d) legal mandates, (e) social pressures, (f) the potential negative effects of diversity, and (g) the positive impact diversity can have on a group, department, or organization.

QUESTIONS *for discussion*

1. Why is it important to understand diversity and the influence of diversity in the sport and physical activity context?

2. Based on your experiences, how much emphasis is placed on diversity by managers and other personnel of sport organizations? Why is this so?

3. What are some potential pitfalls of diversity in the work context?

4. In what ways does diversity benefit people in sport organizations?

5. Some people raised concerns about the term "diversity management." What are some of those concerns, and what are the merits of each? Should these concerns change the management of diverse organizations?

6. Consider the various ways in which people differ. Are some forms of diversity more important than others? Would you expect some forms of diversity to have a stronger impact on attitudes and beliefs, or others to have a stronger impact on job performance? Why or why not?

7. Changes in workforce demographics represent one of the major factors that has led to an increase in diversity. Suppose that a workgroup is demographically different (i.e., members from different races, sexes, ages, and so forth), but they all have the same attitudes, values, and beliefs. If the members all think and act in a similar fashion, is the group still considered diverse?

LEARNING *activities*

1. Several demographic trends were noted in this chapter. Visit the U.S. Census Bureau website (www.census.gov) and gather data concerning other demographic and population trends. Also search for similar websites giving information about other countries. How do the trends in the United States and in other countries differ? How are they the same?

2. Many people oppose diversity in the workplace or in educational settings. What are some of their arguments, and what are counterarguments you can use to alleviate these concerns? Divide into small groups, with each group adopting a particular position. Be prepared to present your position to the class.

READING *resources*

SUPPLEMENTARY READINGS

Bell, M. P. (2007). *Diversity in organizations.* Mason, OH: Thomson South-Western. (A diversity textbook with a business management focus; the author devotes considerable attention to race and ethnicity, as well as addressing other topics.)

Brooks, D., & Althouse, R. (2007). *Diversity and social justice in college sports: Sport management and the student athlete.* Morgantown, WV: Fitness Information Technology. (An edited text that focuses on a host of diversity-related issues in college sports, with a particular focus on race.)

Stockdale, M. S., & Crosby, F. J. (Eds.). (2004). *The psychology and management of workplace diversity.* Malden, MA: Blackwell. (An edited text that contains essays from leading diversity scholars in the field; addresses issues related to the need for diversity, diversity management, and strategies for an inclusive workplace, among others.)

WEB RESOURCES

- Center for the Study of Sport in Society (www.sportinsociety.org): organization devoted to the study of sport in society; focuses on issues concerning race and disability, among others.
- Diversity, Inc. (www.diversityinc.com): site devoted to diversity in the general organizational context.
- U.S. Census Bureau (www.census.gov): provides demographic data for the United States across a variety of contexts.

references

Bell, M. P. (2007). *Diversity in organizations.* Mason, OH: Thomson South-Western.

Brown, G. T. (2002). Diversity grid lock. *The NCAA News.* Retrieved February 15, 2003, from www.ncaa.org/news/2002/20021028/active/3922n01.html.

Chelladurai, P. (2009). *Managing organizations for sport and physical activity: A systems perspective* (3rd ed.). Scottsdale, AZ: Holcomb Hathaway.

Cox, T., Jr., & Beale, R. L. (1997). *Developing competency to manage diversity: Readings, cases, & activities.* San Francisco: Berrett-Koehler.

Cox, T. H., Lobel, S. A., & McLeod, P. L. (1991). Effects of ethnic group cultural differences on cooperative and competitive behavior. *Academy of Management Journal, 34,* 827–847.

Cunningham, G. B. (2006). The influence of demographic dissimilarity on affective reactions to physical activity classes. *Journal of Sport and Exercise Psychology, 28,* 127–142.

Cunningham, G. B. (2007). Perceptions as reality: The influence of actual and perceived demographic dissimilarity. *Journal of Business and Psychology, 22,* 79–89.

Cunningham, G. B., & Singer, J. N. (2009). *Diversity in athletics: An assessment of exemplars and institutional best practices.* Indianapolis, IN: National Collegiate Athletic Association.

DeSensi, J. T. (1995). Understanding multiculturalism and valuing diversity: A theoretical perspective. *Quest, 47,* 34–43.

DiTomaso, N., Post, C., & Parks-Yancy, R. (2007). Workforce diversity and inequality: Power, status, and numbers. *Annual Review of Sociology, 33,* 473–501.

Dixon, M. A., & Bruening, J. (2005). Perspectives on work-family conflict: A review and integrative approach. *Sport Management Review, 8,* 227–254.

Doherty, A. J., & Chelladurai, P. (1999). Managing cultural diversity in sport organizations: A theoretical perspective. *Journal of Sport Management, 13,* 280–297.

Fink, J. S., & Pastore, D. L. (1999). Diversity in sport? Utilizing the business literature to devise a comprehensive framework of diversity initiatives. *Quest, 51,* 310–327.

Haq, R. (2004). International perspectives on workplace diversity. In M. S. Stockdale & F. J. Crosby (Eds.), *The psychology and management of workplace diversity* (pp. 277–298). Malden, MA: Blackwell.

Harrison, D. A., Price, K. H., & Bell, M. P. (1998). Beyond relational demography: Time and the effects of surface- and deep-level diversity on work group cohesion. *Academy of Management Journal, 41,* 96–107.

Hayes-Thomas, R. (2004). Why now? The contemporary focus on managing diversity. In M. S. Stockdale & F. J. Crosby (Eds.), *The psychology and management of workplace diversity* (pp. 3–30). Malden, MA: Blackwell.

Herring, C. (2009). Does diversity pay? Race, gender, and the business case for diversity. *American Sociological Review, 74,* 208–224.

Hewitt, P. (2002, May 29). The way we work now: A shift in demographics and culture means Britain's labor market must become far more flexible. *The Guardian,* p. 19.

Highhouse, S., Stierwalt, S. L., Bachiochi, P. D., Elder, A. E., & Fisher, G. G. (1999). Effects of advertised human resource management practices on attraction of African American applicants. *Personnel Psychology, 52,* 425–442.

Jackson, S. E., Joshi, A., & Erhardt, N. L. (2003). Recent research on team and organizational diversity: SWOT analysis and implications. *Journal of Management, 29,* 801–830.

Jehn, K. A., Northcraft, G. B., & Neale, M. A. (1999). Why differences make a difference: A field study of diversity, conflict, and performance in workgroups. *Administrative Science Quarterly, 44,* 741–763.

Joplin, J. R. W., & Daus, C. S. (1997). Challenges of leading a diverse workforce. *Academy of Management Executive, 11*(3), 32–37.

Joshi, A., & Roh, H. (2007). Context matters: A multilevel framework for work team diversity research. *Research in Personnel and Human Resources Management, 26,* 1–48.

Korman, A. K. (1999). Motivation, commitment, and the "new contracts" between employers and employees. In A. I. Kraut & A. K. Korman (Eds.), *Evolving practices in human resource management: Responses to a changing world* (pp. 23–40). San Francisco: Jossey-Bass.

Lorbiecki, A. (2001). Changing views on diversity management: The rise of the learning perspective and the need to recognize social and political contradictions. *Management Learning, 32,* 345–361.

Magic Johnson to help NASCAR diversity efforts. (2004, May 20). SI.com. Retrieved September 2, 2005, from http://sportsillustrated.cnn.com/2004/racing/05/20/bc.rac.lgns.nascarmagicjohnson.r/index.html.

Mannix, E., & Neale, M. A. (2005). What differences make a difference? The promise and reality of diverse teams in organizations. *Psychological Science in the Public Interest, 6,* 31–55.

Marks, M. A., Mathieu, J. E., & Zaccaro, S. J. (2001). A temporally based framework and taxonomy of team processes. *Academy of Management Review, 26,* 356–376.

Mathis, R. L., & Jackson, J. H. (2006). *Human resource management* (11th ed.). Mason, OH; Thomson South-Western.

Ployhart, R. E., Schneider, B., & Schmitt, N. (2006). *Staffing organizations: Contemporary practice and theory* (3rd ed.). Mahwah, NJ: Lawrence Erlbaum.

Prasad, P., Pringle, J. K., & Konrad, A. M. (2006). Examining the contours of workplace diversity: Concepts, contexts, and challenges. In A. M. Konrad, P. Prasad, & J. K. Pringle (Eds.), *Handbook of workplace diversity* (pp. 1–22). Thousand Oaks, CA: Sage.

Record number of women employed. (2008). http://news.bbc.co.uk/2/hi/uk_news/7638056.stm. Retrieved 5/17/2010.

Ridinger, L. L., & Pastore, D. L. (2000). A proposed framework to identify factors associated with international student-athlete adjustment to college. *International Journal of Sport Management, 1,* 4–24.

Riordan, C. M. (2000). Relational demography within groups: Past developments, contradictions, and new directions. In G. R. Ferris (Ed.), *Research in personnel and human resources management* (Vol. 19, pp. 131–173). Greenwich, CT: JAI Press.

Robinson, G., & Dechant, K. (1997). Building a business case for diversity. *Academy of Management Executive, 11*(3), 21–31.

Rovell, D. (2005, August 3). Reebok, Adidas have plenty issues to solve. *ESPN.* Retrieved September 1, 2005, from http://sports.espn.go.com/espn/columns/story?columnist=rovell_darren&id=2123332.

Stern lays out vision for NBA expansion in Europe. (March 27, 2008). http://sports.espn.go.com/nba/news/story?id=3315819. Retrieved 5/17/2010.

Thomas, D. C., Ravlin, E. C., & Wallace, A. W. (1996). Effect of cultural diversity in work groups. In P. A. Bamberger, M. Erez, & S. B. Bacharach (Eds.), *Research in the sociology of organizations* (Vol. 14, pp. 1–33). London: JAI Press.

Thomas, R. R. (1996). *Redefining diversity.* New York: AMACOM.

Thorsteinson, T. J. (2003). Job attitudes of part-time vs. full-time workers: A meta-analytic review. *Journal of Occupational and Organizational Psychology, 76,* 151–177.

Tsui, A. S., & Gutek, B. A. (1999). *Demographic differences in organizations: Current research and future directions.* New York: Lexington Books.

Ump's language ban incites protest: Little Leaguers told to stop speaking Spanish on the field. (2005, July 29). SI.com. Retrieved July 29, 2005, from http://sportsillustrated.cnn.com/2005/more/07/29/ll.spanish.ap/indiex.hrml?cnn=yes.

van Knippenberg, D., De Drue, C. K. W., & Homan, A. C. (2004). Work group diversity and group performance: An integrative model and research agenda. *Journal of Applied Psychology, 89,* 1008–1022.

van Knippenberg, D., & Schippers, M. C. (2007). Work group diversity. *Annual Review of Psychology, 58,* 515–541.

van Kippenberg, D., van Kippenberg, B., Monden, L., & de Lima, F. (2002). Organizational identification after a merger: A social identity perspective. *British Journal of Social Psychology, 41,* 233–252.

Theoretical Tenets of Diversity

DIVERSITY ▼ CHALLENGE

Diversity education is a critically important component both in academic institutions and in organizations. These educational efforts can have an impact on people's diversity-related knowledge, attitudes, and behaviors. And, although many diversity trainers meaningfully influence the students or employees with whom they interact, few have had a more significant impact on the field than Taylor Cox, Jr. and R. Roosevelt Thomas. In praise of Cox, other diversity educators commented, "His research, teaching, consulting, and professional advocacy helped to establish a foundation for educators, practitioners, and researchers seeking to understand and manage diversity in organizations." In a similar way, Thomas has been described as a "thought leader" on the issue of diversity and someone who is "a pioneer in the field."

Given this praise, many diversity educators have sought to understand the approach Cox and Thomas use in their diversity training efforts. A common theme in these assessments is Cox and Thomas's emphasis on theory as a foundation. Cox effectively melds theory and research into his practice as a diversity consultant. In fact, one of his more influential books is titled *Cultural Diversity in Organizations: Theory, Research, & Practice.* His colleagues laud his ability to educate others about how to "become competent, thoughtful leaders of diversity-based organizational change"—something that he is able to do by incorporating theory and research into his work.

Thomas follows a similar approach is his diversity education efforts. He is weary of organizational leaders who want quick-fix solutions, or what he refers to as "the five to do's," without first understanding the basic theoretical background. In commenting on this need, he notes, "quite frankly, we have to be careful about giving people skills and tactics without the conceptual underpinning." He further argues that diversity education is best delivered when there is a "theoretical integration" of the diversity literature. Thus, while diversity

LEARNING OBJECTIVES

After studying this chapter, you should be able to:

- Understand what a theory is and why theory is important in understanding diversity.

- Discuss the different classes of theory used to understand diversity.

- Discuss how the different theories can be applied to diversity issues within organizations for sport and physical activity.

education should include a host of characteristics (e.g., role playing, practical examples, and case studies), the leaders in the field also suggest that diversity theory should provide *the foundation* for these efforts.

Information gathered from: ■ Avery, D. R., & Thomas, K. M. (2004). Blending content and contact: The roles of diversity curriculum and campus heterogeneity in fostering diversity management competency. *Academy of Management Learning & Education, 3,* 380–396 ■ Bell, M. P., Connerley, M. L., & Cocchiara, F. K. (2009). The case for mandatory diversity education. *Academy of Management Learning and Education, 8,* 597–609 ■ Blake-Beard, S. D., Finley-Hervey, J. A., & Harquail, C. V. (2008). Journey to a different place: Reflections on Taylor Cox, Jr.'s career and research as a catalyst for diversity education and training. *Academy of Management Learning & Education, 7,* 394–405 ■ Johnson, C. D. (2008). It's more than the five to do's: Insights on diversity education and training from Roosevelt Thomas, a pioneer and thought leader in the field. *Academy of Management Learning & Education, 7,* 406–417.

DIVERSITY CHALLENGE **R E F L E C T I O N**

1. In your experience, what are people's attitudes toward theory?

2. Thomas noted that managers often want the quick fixes without understanding the underlying principles of the issue. Why do you think this is the case?

3. What steps could be taken to make people more amenable to theory?

s the Diversity Challenge illustrates, experts and "thought leaders" in the field consider a strong theoretical grounding as central in understanding diversity's effects. According to Cox and Thomas, this foundation helps people understand the underlying concepts related to the issues at hand. Whether people want to understand why discrimination is occurring in the workplace, why there are likely more similarities than differences among their personnel, the manner in which they can leverage employee differences to realize organizational performance gains, or some other diversity matter, they first need a theoretical base on which to draw.

Given this perspective, the purpose of this chapter is to provide an overview of the theories that undergird our discussion of diversity. To do so, I begin by defining the term theory and explaining why theory is important in the study of diversity. Next, I discuss the three major categories of theories used to study and understand diversity, briefly outlining the specific theories within each category and the major tenets or propositions put forth by each. I also describe the application of each theory category to diverse organizations.

Defining Theory

o develop a definition of *theory*, consider the following definitions used by others in the field:

Theory is "a set of interrelated constructs (concepts), definitions, and propositions that present a systematic view of phenomena by specifying relations among variables, with the purpose of explaining and predicting phenomena" (Kerlinger & Lee, 2000, p. 11).

Theory "is a statement of relations among concepts within a set of boundary assumptions and constraints. It is no more than a linguistic device used to organize a complex world" (Bacharach, 1989, p. 496).

Theory is "any coherent description or explanation of observed or experienced phenomena" (Gioia & Pitre, 1990, p. 584).

We can draw several conclusions from these definitions. First, theory primarily consists of constructs and propositions (Bacharach, 1989; Kerlinger & Lee, 2000). For our purposes, it may be useful to consider a *construct* as a variable of interest, such as deep-level diversity or job satisfaction, and a *proposition* as the expected relationships among the constructs. For example, it may be proposed that people who are different from others in their work group have low job satisfaction.

Second, theory contains boundary conditions (Bacharach, 1989). Think of *boundary conditions* as assumptions about values, space, and time. Boundary conditions place "if–then" conditions or caveats on the expected relationships among the constructs set forth in the propositions. Using the previous deep-level diversity and job satisfaction constructs, we might expect that if people interact closely with one another, then their relationships are stronger than relationships between group members who rarely work with one another (i.e., high-task interdependence versus low task interdependence; see Doherty & Chelladurai, 1999). Thus, the negative relationship between deep-level dissimilarity and job satisfaction (i.e., the proposition that specifies the relationship between the constructs) may be dependent upon the level of task interdependence in the group (i.e., the boundary condition).

Third, and perhaps most important, theory organizes, explains, and predicts (Bacharach, 1989; Gioia & Pitre, 1990; Kerlinger & Lee, 2000). As Bacharach notes, "the primary goal of theory is to answer the questions of *how, when,* and *why,* unlike the goal of description, which is to answer the question of *what*" (p. 498, emphasis in original). Continuing with the previous example, we might explain that dissimilarity leads to low job satisfaction because dissimilar people are often considered to be in the out-group and receive less trust, liking, and so forth than in-group members (see Riordan, 2000). These unpleasant work experiences may then translate into low satisfaction. Further, the relationship may be amplified for people who must work closely with others (high interdependence), because the differences are reinforced by the continued interaction (Doherty & Chelladurai, 1999). Explaining *why, how,* and *when* phenomena are likely to occur provides a richer understanding than simply describing *what.*

Practicality

Having defined theory, we next consider its usefulness in everyday life and in understanding diversity. As Lewin (1952) correctly noted, "there is nothing more practical than a good theory." Indeed, the ultimate effectiveness of a theory can be assessed by its usefulness and practicality (Bacharach, 1989). Coakley (2004) further suggests that "the best theories are those we understand so clearly that they help us make sense out of the social world" (p. 34). Good theories help us to make better sense of the world around us and, in doing so, cognitively simplify our social surroundings.

PROFESSIONAL
P E R S P E C T I V E S

The Importance of Theory. Sally Shaw is a lecturer of Sport Management at the University of Otago in New Zealand. Shaw's research focuses primarily on gender and power relations in organizations for sport and physical activity. In commenting on her definition of theory, Shaw explained that "theory can be anything from a conversation in a pub to a highly developed, scientific set of ideas." To Shaw, understanding theory and its contributions is important because theory represents "a way of interpreting, or understanding, and of critiquing our social world and the ideas that go into that process." In short, theory is a "way to try to understand the world."

To further illustrate, consider Sue, an employee of our company, who is dissatisfied with her job. Understanding *why* she feels the way she does, *how* that state of being arose, and *when* it occurred can help her and us resolve the situation. If we stop at the *what* of the situation (i.e., Sue is dissatisfied), we would not be able to remedy the situation or predict when it may occur again in the future. Because one of the goals of theory is to aid in prediction—by explaining why, how, and when—we are able to better understand *why* phenomena occur and make educated predictions about *how* and *when* they might occur in the future. These predictions enable us to take steps to reduce activities that might lead to negative outcomes, such as Sue's dissatisfaction, and capitalize on activities that might result in desired outcomes, such as commitment or high work performance from Sue. Further, we might be able to take steps to ensure that her dissatisfaction does not occur in the future or in others. Thus, the practicality and utility of good theory is far-reaching.

Theories Used to Understand Diversity

Given the importance of theory, the next section examines several theories that are used to understand the effects of diversity. In general, the theories fall into one of three categories based on their focus: managerial, sociological, and social psychological. An overview of the three theory classes is provided in Exhibit 2.1. Not all proposed theories are included in this chapter; rather, I discuss those theories that have received the most attention in the diversity literature.

exhibit **2.1**   **Theories of diversity.**

MANAGERIAL:
- *Focus:* the impact of diversity on group/organizational processes and performance
- *Theories:* intervening process, information/decision-making, and resource-based

SOCIOLOGICAL:
- *Focus:* issues, such as structural determinants, power, and conflict, and how they influence diversity and persons who are different from the majority
- *Theories:* functionalism, conflict, critical, and interactionist

SOCIAL PSYCHOLOGICAL:
- *Focus:* how being different from (or similar to) others in a dyad or group influences subsequent affective reactions and behaviors
- *Theories:* social categorization framework and similarity-attraction paradigm

Managerial Theories

Managerial theories related to diversity focus primarily on group and organizational functioning. These theories may attempt to explain the impact of diversity on group processes, such as conflict or cohesion, and on group outcomes, such as creativity and decision-making comprehensiveness. They may also focus on the organization and how diversity can influence the competitive advantage an organization is able to realize. Several theories fall under the managerial class and are described below.

Intervening process theory

Pelled (1996) developed the intervening process theory to outline the manner in which various types of demographic diversity influence conflict within the group (i.e., the intervening processes) and subsequent outcomes. Pelled categorized demographic variables along two dimensions: (a) level of visibility, or the degree to which the form of diversity is easily recognized and observed by group members; and (b) job relatedness, or the extent to which the form of diversity influences the skills and competencies related to cognitive tasks.

The form of diversity within each could be either high or low (e.g., high visibility or low job relatedness). Pelled then used these dimensions to classify the types of demographic variables:

- Low visibility–low job relatedness: no demographic characteristics
- High visibility–low job relatedness: age, sex, and race
- Low visibility–high job relatedness: organizational tenure, education, and functional background
- High visibility–high job relatedness: group tenure

Pelled (1996) also identified two forms of conflict: affective and substantive. *Affective conflict* represents those tensions raised as a result of emotional clashes among group members that are characterized by fear, distrust, and general negative affect. Such conflict is thought to give rise to negative outcomes such as member turnover. *Substantive conflict,* on the other hand, refers to differences in opinion among group members as to how to complete tasks, the importance of certain goals, and appropriate courses of action. This form of conflict is more productive, as it gives rise to divergent views and alternative ways of completing tasks. Therefore, substantive conflict is thought to be positively associated with group performance in cognitive tasks.

In integrating this information, *intervening process* theory holds that the different forms of diversity will have predictable effects on group conflict (see Exhibit 2.2). First, highly visible demographic diversity variables such as age, sex, and race are expected to positively influence affective conflict. This effect is thought to arise from the strong emotions associated with being different from others based on race, age, or sex. Second, demographic variables associated with high job relatedness are believed to have a positive impact on substantive conflict, sometimes referred to as task conflict. Variations in how long one has worked in a group or in an occupation, in education, and in functional background are likely to result in a variety of conflicting perspectives related to how tasks should be completed, which goals a group should adopt, and so forth. Given these divergent perspectives, substantive conflict is likely to be present, increasing the breadth of decision making, the number of opinions, and

exhibit 2.2 Integration of the form of diversity, demographic variables, and form of conflict in intervening process theory (Pelled, 1996).

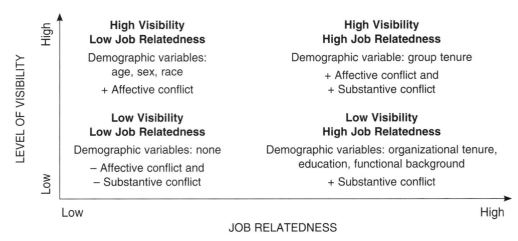

so forth, thereby improving subsequent task performance. In sum, diversity in highly visible demographic characteristics is thought to result in affective conflict, which is then expected to influence outcomes such as turnover. Diversity in highly job-related characteristics is believed to positively influence substantive conflict and result in more positive group processes and outcomes. A 1999 study by Pelled, Eisenhardt, and Xin demonstrated general empirical support for these propositions.

Information/decision-making theory

Similar to the intervening process theory, the *information/decision-making* theory holds that diversity should augment the information and perspectives available in the group, thereby allowing for greater decision-making capabilities (see Gruenfeld, Mannix, Williams, & Neale, 1996; Phillips, Northcraft, & Neale, 2006; for similar predictions, see van Knippenberg, De Dreu, and Homan's, 2004, Categorization-Elaboration Model). These two theories are similar to the extent that diversity in demographics, education, functional background, and so forth is thought to increase the number of perspectives and ideas in the group. However, the information/decision-making theory departs significantly from intervening process theory regarding the manner in which diversity influences performance. Specifically, this theory explains such an influence based on demonstrating that people are more likely to associate and converse with people who are similar to themselves (discussed in further detail in the social psychological theory section). This is important for diverse groups because individuals in such groups have access to information from others similar to themselves outside the group. The information obtained from these outside persons is then brought back to the group and used to complete group tasks. Because diverse groups may have access to a greater variety of perspectives, their decision making will be enhanced, leading to better performance than their more homogeneous counterparts (see Ancona & Caldwell, 1992).

To illustrate, consider a group with high age-diversity tasked with developing a new clothing line for Titleist, a major manufacturer of golf products. The group consists of two members in their twenties, two in their forties, and two in their sixties. Given that people in different age cohorts are also likely to have varying life experiences and preferences, these six persons have different ideas, perspectives, and beliefs about which products should be introduced. However, each pair from the three divisions also has access to persons from their social networks and the ideas and perspectives these people have to offer. Thus, Susan, a group member in her twenties, may discuss the project with her colleagues of similar age. They may have their own ideas about how the task should be completed and which products should be introduced. Susan then takes these ideas back to the original group and presents them to her group members. If all of the group members speak with members from their specific social networks and age cohorts and bring ideas back to the group, then the number of ideas and perspectives available to the group increases dramatically. Clearly, this synergistic effect improves the number of alternatives from which the group could choose, ultimately aiding their decision-making process and overall performance.

Resource-based theory

The final theory in the managerial class is the *resource-based* view (Barney, 1991). According to this theory, firms have various resources, including physical capital (e.g., technology, equipment, or physical structure), organizational capital (e.g., the firm's structure and planning mechanisms), and human capital (e.g., the personnel within the organization, along with the training, experience, and capital they possess). To the extent that these resources are *valuable, rare,* and *difficult to imitate,* the firm realizes a competitive advantage. Some researchers argue that organizational diversity represents such a resource (Cunningham & Sagas, 2004; Richard, 2000). As Richard, Murthi, and Ismail (2007) note, "the most valuable natural resource in the world is not oil, diamonds, or even gold; it is the diverse knowledge, abilities, and skills that are immediately available from cultural diversity" (p. 1213). Consider that:

- diverse groups have greater decision-making capabilities,
- diverse organizations are relatively rare, and
- it is difficult, if not impossible, to duplicate the effects of a diverse workforce without actually having a diverse workforce.

Research demonstrates support for the belief that diversity gives an organization a competitive advantage. For example, Cunningham and Sagas (2004) found that racial diversity on coaching staffs was related to greater success for the athletic team. In a different context, Richard (2000) found that racial diversity in banks was related to greater financial performance when the bank followed a growth strategy. These positive effects are also seen over the long term (Richard et al., 2007). As these examples illustrate, diversity, because it is a rare and valued resource, brings benefits to groups and organizations.

Implications

The managerial theories have several implications for persons managing diverse groups or organizations. As all three theories illustrate, diversity increases the decision-making ability of groups. According to the intervening process and the information/decision-making theories, decision-making capabilities improve as a result of increases in the informational diversity of the social units. However, in drawing from Richard's (2000; Richard et al., 2007) work, it is also possible that demographic diversity provides such benefits. The underlying assumption is that people who are dissimilar bring different sources of information, varying ideas, and an array of perspectives to the group (van Knippenberg et al., 2004). If creativity and breadth of decision making are desired, then group members should be persons from different educational, work, or perhaps racial backgrounds. This practice is often applied to committees, task forces, and other short-term work groups that are responsible for creating policy, developing new product lines, and the like.

Second, although there are many benefits attendant to diversity, there is also the possibility that increased diversity can bring negative outcomes such as affective conflict. As Pelled (1996) noted, highly visible sources of diversity are more likely to be associated with this detrimental form of conflict than with the less visible forms of diversity. Managers are then faced with a quandary, especially when it comes to racial diversity. This form of diversity can bring real benefits to a group or an organization (Cunningham & Sagas, 2004; Richard, 2000), but it can also be associated with potentially high levels of affective conflict within that unit (Pelled, 1996). Furthermore, high levels of affective conflict may counteract the otherwise positive effects of substantive conflict (Pelled, 1996). Managers must competently handle the various affective conflicts within their social units. How to do so is discussed in Chapters 13 and 14.

Sociological Theories

Some researchers have adopted theories using a more sociological slant in order to study diversity. *Sociological* theories focus on issues such as power and conflict as they relate to diversity in society and organizations. These theories also tend to focus on more macro issues such as the impact of societal norms, institutional practices, and organizational policies on persons with diverse backgrounds. Eitzen and Sage (2009) outlined four theories that are used to study and understand diversity from a sociological perspective: functionalism, conflict, critical, and interactionist. These theories are discussed next.

Functionalism theory

According to Eitzen and Sage (2009), *functionalism* "attributes to societies the characteristics of cohesion, consensus, cooperation, reciprocity, stability, and persistence" (p. 10). Society is viewed as a system of parts working together in harmony because there is general congruence among the parts concerning the goals and values of society. As a part of society, sport is seen as something that brings people together, socializes youth who participate in it, and serves as a model for success and the achievement of excellence.

As an example, research by Brown et al. (2003) found that participation in sport helped to reduce racial tensions that otherwise might have been present. As the authors of this study of intercollegiate athletes noted, "the use of integrated, organized team sports could be one way to help alleviate interracial tensions by urging individuals to shift the relative weight attached to being White or Black to the identity of teammate" (p. 177). In this way, sport is viewed as something that has the potential to unify people across racial boundaries.

In a similar way, Hums and MacLean (2009) suggested that high school sports provide a number of functional benefits by:

- promoting character development, leadership skills, citizenship, and personal responsibility among youth,
- offering opportunities for cross-cultural contact among participants, and
- strengthening connections both within and between communities.

From this perspective, sport is something that offers a host of advantages for its participants and the communities in which it is housed.

Conflict theory

Seen as an opposite of functionalism, *conflict* theory focuses on social processes that result in disharmony, social discord, and conflict (Eitzen & Sage, 2009). Political power and the distribution of wealth are also influential in conflict theory. Drawing heavily from the writings of Karl Marx, this theory holds that people tend toward competition, not cooperation, and this competition leads to disharmony among groups. Social structures and class differences play an important role in this theory because those who are privileged (i.e., the upper class) are thought to use their status to maintain power and advantage within society, often at the expense of others (e.g., the lower class). This may be achieved explicitly, such as through a show of force, or more implicitly, such as through the media, schools, or other institutions.

People who adopt this approach to the study of diversity examine such issues as the underrepresentation of women and racial minorities in leadership positions or the resistance on the part of university athletic programs to follow gender equity laws (Eitzen & Sage, 2009). Acosta and Carpenter (2010), for example, have tracked the underrepresentation of women in coaching and leadership positions for over three decades. Their work is discussed in greater detail in Chapter 5.

Other research has studied the influences of class on the extent to which one can participate in or watch sport and leisure events (McGraw, 1998). A greater appreciation of this issue can be garnered by considering the average cost of attending professional sports in North America (see Exhibit 2.3). According to the

The cost of enjoying sport, per four attendees.						*exhibit* **2.3**	
SPORT	TICKET	SODA	HOT DOG	PARKING	TOTAL	SEASON TOTAL	PERCENT OF INCOME
Major League Baseball	$101.72	$13.92	$14.80	$12.50	$142.94	$11,578.14	22.25%
National Basketball Association	$197.88	$14.76	$15.88	$13.13	$241.65	$9,907.65	19.04%
National Football League	$288.80	$15.20	$16.52	$21.75	$342.27	$2,738.16	5.26%
National Hockey League	$198.64	$13.84	$14.56	$12.20	$239.24	$9,808.84	18.85%

Team Marketing Report (www.teammarketing.com) and U. S. Census Bureau (www.census.gov) data. Prices for MLB, NBA, and NFL based on 2008 data. Prices of tickets, sodas, and hot dogs are based on four persons. Total price is based on attending a single game. Percent of income is based on attending all home games (MLB, 81; NBA, 41; NFL, 8; and NHL, 41) and using $52,029 as the median income.

Team Marketing Report's Fan Cost Index, in 2008 the mean cost for a family of four to attend a professional sport event ranged from $142.94 (MLB) to $342.27 (NFL). According to the U.S. Census Bureau, the median U.S. household income in that year was $52,029. By synthesizing these data, we see that attending all eight home games of an NFL team would account for roughly 5 percent of that household's income. Even more staggering, attending all 81 home games of an MLB team requires spending approximately 22 percent of the household income. These figures indicate that few households with an annual income of $52,029 can afford to spend from 5 to 22 percent of that income on sport events. Therefore, it can be argued that sport, and more specifically spectator sport, is structured in such a way that only individuals with incomes well above the median level can afford to purchase tickets and regularly attend major events. Also, consider the move in 2010 by most games in the college Bowl Championship Series (BCS) from network TV (ABC) to cable TV (ESPN).

Critical theory

Critical theories are the third type of sociological theories used to study diversity in the sport and physical activity context (Eitzen & Sage, 2009). *Critical* theories seek to understand power and explain how power operates within social entities. These theories also emphasize human agency—the choices people make concerning their actions and behaviors. Three theories are subsumed under this general heading: hegemony theory, feminist theory, and critical race theory.

Hegemony theory. *Hegemony* theory concentrates on the political, economic, and cultural patterns of power and dominance in a society. As Sage (1998) explains, "hegemony theory sensitizes us to the role dominant groups play in American government, economic system, mass media, education, and sport in maintaining and promoting their interests" (p. 10). This social dominance provides privilege to certain persons or groups at the expense of others, such as men over women, rich over poor, and Whites over racial minorities. Researchers applying this perspective examine how sport is related to race, gender, social class, and the production and control of resources (e.g., Whisenant, Pedersen, & Obenour, 2002).

Feminist theory. Most of the gender-related research in sport and physical activity has adopted a feminist approach. *Feminist* theory makes two basic assumptions. First, people's experiences, both within and outside the workplace, are gendered in nature. According to Birrell (2000), when people speak of sport as a gendered activity, they mean that sport "is an activity that not only welcomes boys and men more enthusiastically than girls and women but also serves as a site for celebrating skills and values clearly marked as 'masculine'" (p. 61).

The second assumption is that because women have been oppressed and devalued in many contexts, there is a need to develop strategies to change those conditions (Coakley, 2004; Eitzen & Sage, 2009). By reversing the oppression of women, it is expected that women will become empowered and be able to transform their environments. Research examples in the sport realm include studies related to homophobia, the belittlement of women's accomplishments and activities, and the underrepresentation of women in leadership roles (e.g., Knoppers, 1992).

Critical race theory. Critical race theory represents the third critical theory that is often used to examine diversity issues in sport and leisure. As the name suggests, *critical race* theory places the issue of race at the forefront in studies of organizational, political, educational, and other social issues (Hylton, 2009; Ladson-Billings & Tate, 1995; Tate, 1997). Tate (1997) outlines the theory's five key suppositions (see also Singer, 2005a). According to these authors, critical race theory:

1. Argues that racism is endemic in the United States. Specifically, the theory presumes that racism is a central part of U.S. society, embedded in the social institutions, laws, and culture.

2. Borrows from several different disciplines and "ways of knowing," including liberalism, feminism, and critical legal studies. Doing so allows for broader perspectives and a more gestalt-like analysis of the intersection of race and society.

3. Questions civil rights legislation and the effectiveness of such mandates, arguing that they are often undermined before they can be fully implemented. Furthermore, any progress that has been made in terms of equal employment opportunity legislation is seen as having been too slow.

4. Questions the notions of meritocracy, neutrality, color-blindness, and objectivity; these terms and ideas are viewed only as smoke screens for the self-interests of the powerful in society—the self-interests of Whites. As Singer (2005a) notes, "Whites will tolerate or encourage racial advances for people of color only when they also promote White self-interest" (p. 468).

5. Supports context-specificity and relative truths, as opposed to a single truth being applicable in all situations across all contexts (see also Ladson-Billings & Tate, 1995). In this way, this theory emphasizes storytelling as a "way of knowing" and a manner by which oppressed persons can have their voices heard.

Several studies in the sport management literature highlight the efficacy of using critical race theory. Singer (2005b) incorporated focus groups and interviews to understand the racism perceived by African American university football players. Using this technique, he was able to help the athletes develop strategies to overcome such barriers and to improve their overall experiences. Hylton (2005) used critical race theory to argue that sport and leisure managers should consider race, racism, and race equality when developing their policies and structures.

In addition, see the Alternative Perspectives box for a discussion of a different perspective—one that focuses on how gender and race intersect.

Interactionist theory

Unlike the previous theories that focus predominantly on structural forces such as culture or social class, *interactionist* theory aims to understand

alternative **PERSPECTIVES**

Black Feminist Theory. Many discussions of race fail to acknowledge women, just as discussions of gender fail to acknowledge women of color (Bruening, 2005). One perspective that addresses this shortcoming is black feminist theory. This is a critical theory that focuses on the intersection of race, gender, and class while putting the voices and experiences of African American women at the center of analysis. The theory recognizes that they are subjugated based on multiple identities (i.e., race, gender, class), and as a result, stresses the need for African American women to be self-determined and self-defined in the face of these oppressions (Collins, 2000). Many authors have found this perspective to be helpful in their quest to explain and understand the experiences of female athletes, coaches, and administrators of color (see Bruening, 2005; McDowell & Cunningham, 2009).

PROFESSIONAL
PERSPECTIVES

Participatory Action Research. In addition to the theories highlighted in the text, others have proven helpful in the study of diversity. One such theory is called *participatory action research* (PAR), a subset of the larger sociological critical theories. PAR can be defined as collective inquiry in which researchers and participants are partners in examining a practice they consider problematic with the goal of changing or improving it. Wendy Frisby, Chair of Women's Studies at the University of British Columbia, found this framework to be particularly useful in her research of women living below the poverty line. As Frisby explains, PAR is committed to the practical side of research. "It gets us thinking about how we can improve policies and practices" within the domain of sport and physical activity. The word "participatory" is key to the theory. According to Frisby, "one way of building theory is to work with people who are the intended beneficiaries of our research." In the case of Frisby's studies, this means working with women who live below the poverty line to develop strategies aimed at improving the conditions of their lives, including increasing their level of physical activity. Because Frisby works with the women in a co-collaborator role, she can ask research questions that are relevant to the women's daily lives. The knowledge developed from this collaboration is much richer than would otherwise be possible because it is co-produced by Frisby and the women with whom she is working.

how people give meaning to their lives. From this perspective, there is not a single reality or truth; rather, people define their own reality based on their interactions with others and through cultural influences. The process by which this reality is created is referred to as the social construction of reality (Eitzen & Sage, 2009). For example, the meanings we place on gender or race are socially constructed, and they may mean slightly different things to different people, depending on the experiences of each person. From a research perspective, the primary goal is to understand how people give meaning to their lives—something that is accomplished through observation and interviews that, for example, ask about how sport socializes youth or what meanings gays and lesbians place on their role as athletes (see Anderson, 2005).

Implications

Sociological theories used to understand diversity have several implications for managers of sport and physical activity organizations. First and foremost is the recognition of the structural factors that influence people who are different from the majority. Because these societal determinants have a negative influence on such persons, it is necessary to critically analyze sport, sport organizations, and the people within them. To do so, we might ask questions such as

- Why are sport organizations structured the way they are and who benefits from this arrangement?
- How do power arrangements impact people within sport organizations?

Sociological theory provides us with a means of answering these questions. Looking critically at these issues is an important step in remedying inequities within sport organizations.

Second, sociological theories put such issues as gender and race in the forefront. Whereas managerial theories explain the relationship between diversity and important organizational outcomes, sociological theories allow us to consider how personal demographics influence the manner in which people behave, the way organizations operate, and societal and cultural expectations. Sociological theories provide a different perspective from which we can understand diversity in sport organizations.

Social Psychological Theories

Whereas managerial theories focus on how diversity can bring value to the organization and sociological theories predominantly focus on structural issues related to diversity, *social psychological* theories focus on the individual in relation to others. Specifically, these theories focus on how being similar to, or different from, others in a social unit impacts subsequent affect and behaviors. Whereas sociological theories tend to focus on macro issues such as the impact of societal norms, institutional practices, and organizational policies on persons with diverse backgrounds, social psychological theories focus on the individual within social contexts. Sociological theories place an emphasis on society and culture, while social psychological theories emphasize the individual within these contexts. Two major frameworks are included in this general class of theories: the social categorization framework and the similarity-attraction paradigm, which are discussed next.

Social categorization framework

Most of the research adopting a compositional or relational perspective draws from the social categorization framework (see Riordan, 2000). Two theories contribute to this framework: *social identity* theory (Tajfel & Turner, 1979) and *self-categorization* theory (Turner, Hogg, Oakes, Reicher, & Wetherell, 1987). According to these two theories, people classify themselves and others into social groups. The classification can be based on a myriad of characteristics, including those based on surface-level attributes (e.g., age, sex), deep-level characteristics (e.g., liberal, conservative), or other memberships (Catholic, Protestant). Thus, people define themselves and others in terms of a social identity. People similar to the self are considered in-group members, while those who differ from the self are considered out-group members. In general, people hold more positive attitudes toward in-group members than they do toward their out-group counterparts. Therefore, there is likely to be an intergroup bias in which affective reactions and helpful behaviors toward in-group and out-group members differ. Within the group setting, this creates an "us and them" dynamic. These social categorizations and related biases will be used in subsequent interactions (Tsui & Gutek, 1999): attitudes formed toward out-group members in one situation are likely to be applied toward persons of the same social category in similar situations in the future. This is likely to take place because the categorization process leads to the formation of stereotypes about in-group and out-group members; thus, as Tsui and Gutek (1999) explain, "without categorization, stereotyping does not occur" (p. 48). However, just because categorization takes place does not necessarily mean that the stereotype process will ensue.

When discussing the categorization process, it is important to distinguish between social categorization and intergroup bias because the two are not the same. *Social categorization* simply refers to the perceptual grouping of people into social units. *Intergroup bias*, on the other hand, refers to the more favorable attitudes, perceptions, and behaviors directed toward in-group members relative to out-group members. Making such a distinction is important, because any negative effects of diversity observed from a social categorization are linked to intergroup biases and not the social categorization process, per se (van Knippenberg et al., 2004).

These theoretical tenets are paramount to the discussion of diversity. As Tsui, Egan, and O'Reilly (1992) suggest, the formation of in-groups and out-groups is central to the tendency of people to prefer working in groups of persons similar to the self. In a similar way, Williams and O'Reilly (1998), after reviewing over 40 years of diversity research, argued that the social categorization process is fundamental to the potentially negative effects of diversity in work groups and in organizations.

Let us consider two very different examples to illustrate the way that social categorization can influence how people interact with one another. The first example involves fans at a sporting event. As you enter the stands, you will see many fans around you. Some may be wearing gear with your team's logo and name, while others may be wearing hats and shirts representative of the opposing team. When you initially see all of the fans, you will immediately classify them as similar to or different from the self based on their apparel. People wearing your team's clothes might be considered in-group members (i.e., people similar to you), while those wearing the opposing team's apparel might be considered out-group members (i.e., people different from you). To the extent that being a fan of your team is an important part of who you are, you might prefer to sit close to other in-group members rather than out-group members. If you have ever sat in an opposing team's cheering section during an athletic contest, you can appreciate how different and perhaps uncomfortable that experience was.

The second example is set in the workplace. If you work in a group of seven persons and five of them are of a race different from yours, then to the extent that race is a source of social categorization, you are surrounded by more out-group members than in-group members. Research shows that when this happens, it is possible that your experiences will be less positive than if you were surrounded by predominantly in-group members (Williams & O'Reilly, 1998). In both examples, the social categorization process is the impetus behind subsequent attitudes and behaviors. Exhibit 2.4 illustrates these trends.

exhibit **2.4**   **The effects of social categorization on fan and employee reactions.**

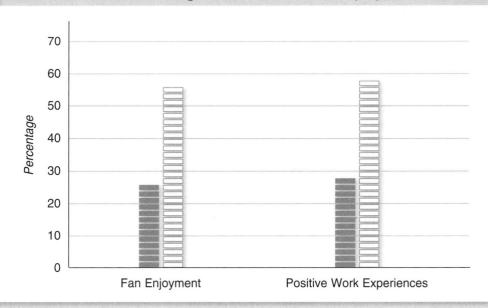

Data from Williams & O'Reilly, 1998.

Similarity-attraction paradigm

According to the *similarity-attraction paradigm* (Byrne, 1971), people who are similar to one another also demonstrate high interpersonal attraction and liking toward one another. The similarities might lead them to believe that they share common life experiences, have similar values and beliefs, and view their social worlds in a similar fashion. Thus, surface-level similarities are seen as resulting in perceptions that more deep-level similarities exist as well (Chattopadhyay, 1999). People who find they share certain deep-level similarities might make assumptions as to the congruence of other deep-level characteristics as well. As a result of this perceived similarity and increased liking, people are likely to have more positive affective and behavioral reactions when they are similar to their colleagues than when they differ.

Note that though the intervening mechanisms may differ, the end predictions that arise from the social categorization framework and the similarity-attraction paradigm are essentially the same (Tsui & Gutek, 1999). The social categorization framework holds that dissimilarity will lead to categorization, stereotyping, and ultimately poor work experiences. According to the similarity-attraction paradigm, dissimilarity results in a lack of perceived deep-level differences, a decrease in liking and communication, and ultimately, poor work experiences. Dissimilarity from others should result in poorer affective and behavioral reactions than similarity.

Implications

What is important for sport organization managers to understand is that being different, with respect to either surface- or deep-level characteristics, may be stressful or burdensome for an employee. As a result, communication among group members, helping behaviors, and positive affective reactions are likely to suffer. Of course, these outcomes are not necessarily consistent across all contexts; see the Diversity in the Field box.

Social psychological theories allow us to understand diversity beyond the organizational context. Specifically, these theories can be applied to employee–customer relationships, coach–player relationships, or any other dyadic or group relationship involving employees and persons outside the organization. For example, customer satisfaction can be dependent upon, at least in part, the (dis)similarity between the customer and the service provider (Cunningham & Sagas, 2006). Knowing this, managers can take steps to mitigate the potentially negative effects of employee–customer dissimilarity. Social psychological theories can have a meaningful influence on the way we understand diversity as well as the methods we take to manage differences in sport organizations.

DIVERSITY *in the field*

Overcoming Dissimilarity. One of the many ways that people can differ is in their country of origin. This is the case with Israel and Pakistan. Indeed, these two countries, with different religious and political ideologies, are often at odds with one another concerning various issues. These differences made the relationship between Aisam-Ul-Haq Qureshi of Pakistan and Amir Hadad of Israel all the more noteworthy, as the two men paired to play tennis doubles at the 2002 Wimbledon. These players not only faced potential difficulties playing together but they were also subjected to pressures from their homelands. Qureshi was threatened with a ban if he continued to play with Hadad; however, the quest to excel on the court served as an overriding factor. As Qureshi noted, "If I believe that I can win at the Grand Slams and the big events with Amir then I'll stay and play with him." Hadad voiced similar sentiments, as he added, "I chose to play with him because of his talent, his skills as a tennis player, and I also like him as a person." Clearly, tennis served as a catalyst for the two players (Newbery, 2002).

alternative
PERSPECTIVES

Ways of Studying Diversity. Now that we have examined how theories can be used to understand diversity, let us examine from a different perspective how researchers study diversity. Researchers generally employ either the categorical, compositional, relational, or diversity management approach when they study diversity (Cunningham & Fink, 2006; Tsui & Gutek, 1999).

■ **Categorical approach:** When examining diversity using a categorical approach, the focus is on comparing the experiences and behaviors of members of one social unit (e.g., demographic group or work group) to those of another social unit—for example, comparing the recreational experiences of poor and elite class youth. According to research conducted using this approach, personal characteristics provide important cues about how people will behave, what their attitudes will be toward certain other people, and how they will be treated in the organizational context. This approach is widespread in the study of diversity in sport, with findings illustrating that people's experiences can vary based on their gender, age, race, class, and education. Despite its prevalence, the approach does have its limitations. An underlying assumption of the categorical approach is that all (or most) members of a social category have similar experiences, but this idea is unfounded in many situations. In fact, there are cases in which within-group variance is greater than between-group variance.

■ **Compositional approach:** The compositional approach to the study of diversity focuses on the social unit, such as a work group, athletic team, or physical education class. This approach is used to study the processes and outcomes of a diverse social unit and compare them with those of a homogeneous social unit. As group members bring different life experiences to the group and also have varying social networks, diversity can bring about greater decision making, creativity, and productivity. These differences can also be a source of strife, however, and result in process losses and employee turnover. Despite the efficacy of the compositional approach in understanding group dynamics and performance, the approach is not without its limitations. First, this approach ignores the characteristics of individuals. Because the group is the focus, the effects of individual characteristics within the group are not considered.

Second, the approach assumes that characteristics of the group affect all group members the same; however, not all people are affected in the same way by being different.

■ **Relational approach:** The relational approach to the study of diversity focuses on individual characteristics in relation to those of the group. In doing so, the approach combines both the categorical *and* compositional approaches. The categorical approach is captured by considering individual characteristics; consideration of group characteristics captures the compositional approach. The fundamental premise of the relational approach is that the relationship between an individual's characteristics and those of the group will influence the behaviors, attitudes, and performance of that individual. For instance, researchers have shown that people who differ from others in a group have less satisfaction with the group, do not integrate well into the team, and sometimes perform less well than their counterparts. As with the other approaches, the relational approach is not without its limitations. The main drawback is its focus solely on employee characteristics (both as individuals and as a group) without considering other contextual determinants.

■ **Diversity management strategy approach:** Researchers adopting this approach to the study of diversity seek to understand how organizations capitalize on the benefits diversity can bring and the methods managers can use to leverage the beneficial effects and mitigate the potential drawbacks. This research tradition has shown that diversity management strategies focusing on inclusion result in a number of organizational benefits, including employee satisfaction and performance gains. These effects are particularly strong when an inclusive strategy is coupled with high employee diversity. This approach to the study of diversity has two potential limitations. First, most of the approaches focus on describing diversity in organizations instead of developing strategies that managers, educators, and coaches can use to better manage their workplaces. Obviously, developing such strategies would have more pragmatic value. Second, many of the current strategies have not been empirically tested. A key component of a strategy's validity is testability. If a strategy cannot be tested, then its ultimate utility is questionable.

CHAPTER *summary*

This chapter focused on various theories and how they can be used to better understand diversity in sport organizations. As illustrated in the Diversity Challenge, understanding the basic theories that undergird diversity is crucial in fully understanding this complex topic. The theories we use to understand diversity influence the questions we ask, the focus of our examination, and the way we see the world in general. After reading the chapter, you should be able to do the following:

1. **Understand what a theory is and why theory is important in understanding diversity.**

Using various early definitions (Bacharach, 1989; Gioia & Pitre, 1990; Kerlinger & Lee, 2000), the term *theory* was defined as a set of propositions concerning relationships among constructs, bound by assumptions of value, space, and time, with the purpose of organizing, explaining, and predicting social phenomena. Theory is important because of its practicality and its utility in helping managers understand their complex social surroundings.

2. **Discuss the different classes of theory used to understand diversity.**

Three classes of theory are used to study diversity: managerial, sociological, and social psychological. Managerial theories focus on the impact of diversity on organizational outcomes. Sociological theories focus on structural issues, power, and conflict, and how these factors influence diversity and persons who differ from the majority. Finally, social psychological theories focus on how being (dis)similar from others in social settings influences an individual's affect and behavior.

3. **Discuss how the different theories can be applied to diversity issues within organizations for sport and physical activity.**

The implications of each theory class for sport managers was discussed. The managerial theories illustrated the need to recognize how the various types of diversity influence outcomes (e.g., the influence of job-related aspects of diversity on substantive conflict). The sociological theories require managers to ask questions about how organizational factors, such as power structure, influence the experiences of persons different from the majority. Finally, social psychological theories suggest that managers should pay attention to the composition of work groups and employee–customer relationships, as surface- and deep-level differences within these relationships can lead to negative outcomes.

QUESTIONS *for discussion*

1. Some readers may express an aversion to a discussion of theory. Prior to studying this chapter, what were your attitudes toward theory? After reading the chapter, identify several benefits of studying theory.
2. Several definitions of theory were discussed in this chapter. What is a definition you can use that would allow you to describe what a theory is?
3. How do issues of power in organizations influence people who differ from the majority?

4. Social psychological theories suggest that being different from others in a dyad or group will negatively influence subsequent affective reactions and behaviors. How might a manager reduce these negative effects?

5. Four approaches to the study of diversity were identified. Which approach makes the most sense to you? Why?

LEARNING *activities*

1. Some people believe that students should not be taught theory, because it has limited applicability to workplace settings. Divide into groups and argue the pros and cons of understanding theory and theoretical principles as they apply to diversity in sport organizations.

2. Visit a local sport organization and ask the manager, employees, and athletes how diversity impacts the workplace, group dynamics, and overall outcomes for the organization. Then, compare their responses with the theoretical tenets outlined in this chapter.

3. Visit your school's athletic department and ask administrators and student-athletes how diversity impacts the department, group dynamics, and outcomes. Then compare their responses with the theoretical tenets outlined in this chapter.

READING *resources*

SUPPLEMENTARY READINGS

Coakley, J., & Dunning, E. (Eds.). (2000). *Handbook of sports studies*. Thousand Oaks, CA: Sage. (An edited book that contained chapters on a number of theoretical approaches to the study of sport; also contains chapters focusing on a host of diversity dimensions, as well as discussions of sport around the world.)

Cox, Jr., T. (1994). *Cultural diversity in organizations: Theory, research and practice*. San Francisco, CA: Berrett-Koehler. (Applies teaching, research, and consultation expertise to explore the dynamics behind diversity in the organizational context; useful for organizational development initiatives.)

Giulianotti, R. (2004). *Sport and modern social theorists*. Basingstoke, UK: Palgrave MacMillan. (Examines the contributions of major social theorists to our critical understanding of modern sport; includes contributions from Marx, Weber, Durkheim, Adorno, Gramsci, Habermas, Merton, C. Wright Mills, Goffman, Giddens, Elias, Bourdieu, and Foucault.)

WEB RESOURCES

- Gender and Diversity in Organizations (http://division.aomonline.org/gdo/): a division of the Academy of Management; provides diversity resources related to research and teaching.

- Laboratory for Diversity in Sport (www.diversityinsport.com): provides overview of research initiatives as well as other diversity-related Internet sources.

- North American Society for the Sociology of Sport (www.nasss.com): provides a resource center and directory of experts in several diversity-related areas.

references

Acosta, R. V., & Carpenter, L. J. (2010). *Women in inter-collegiate sport: A longitudinal study—33-year update—1977–2010.* Unpublished manuscript, Brooklyn College, Brooklyn, NY.

Ancona, D. G., & Caldwell, D. F. (1992). Demography and design: Predictors of new product team performance. *Organization Science, 3,* 321–341.

Anderson, E. (2005). *In the game: Gay athletes and the cult of masculinity.* Albany: State University of New York Press.

Bacharach, S. B. (1989). Organizational theories: Some criteria for evaluation. *Academy of Management Review, 14,* 496–515.

Barney, J. (1991). Firm resources and sustained competitive advantage. *Journal of Management, 17,* 99–120.

Birrell, S. (2000). Feminist theories for sport. In J. Coakley and E. Dunning (Eds.), *Handbook of sports studies* (pp. 61–76). Thousand Oaks, CA: Sage.

Brown, K., Brown, T. N., Jackson, J. S., Sellers, R. S., Keiper, S., & Manuel, W. J. (2003). There's no race on the playing field: Perceptions of racial discrimination among White and Black athletes. *Journal of Sport & Social Issues, 27,* 162–183.

Bruening, J. E. (2005). Gender and racial analysis in sport: Are all the women White and all the Blacks men? *Quest, 57,* 330–349.

Byrne, D. (1971). *The attraction paradigm.* New York: Academic Press.

Chattopadhyay, P. (1999). Beyond direct and symmetrical effects: The influence of demographic dissimilarity on organizational citizenship behavior. *Academy of Management Journal, 42,* 273–287.

Coakley, J. (2004). *Sports in society: Issues and controversies* (8th ed.). New York: McGraw-Hill.

Collins, P. (2000). *Black feminist thought: Knowledge, consciousness, and the politics of empowerment* (2nd ed.). New York: Routledge.

Cunningham, G. B., & Fink, J. S. (2006). Diversity issues in sport and leisure: Introduction to a special issue. *Journal of Sport Management, 20,* 455–465.

Cunningham, G. B., & Sagas, M. (2004). People make the difference: The influence of human capital and diversity on team performance. *European Sport Management Quarterly, 4,* 3–22.

Cunningham, G. B., & Sagas, M. (2006). The role of perceived demographic dissimilarity and interaction in customer service satisfaction. *Journal of Applied Social Psychology, 36,* 1654–1673.

Doherty, A. J., & Chelladurai, P. (1999). Managing cultural diversity in sport organizations: A theoretical perspective. *Journal of Sport Management, 13,* 280–297.

Eitzen D. S., & Sage, G. H. (2009). *Sociology of North American sport* (8th ed.). Boulder, CO: Paradigm Publishers.

Gioia, D. A., & Pitre, E. (1990). Multiparadigm perspectives on theory building. *Academy of Management Review, 15,* 584–602.

Gruenfeld, D. H., Mannix, E. A., Williams, K. Y., & Neale, M. A. (1996). Group composition and decision making: How member familiarity and information distribution affect process and performance. *Organizational Behavior and Human Decision Processes, 67,* 1–15.

Hums, M. A., & MacLean, J. C. (2009). *Governance and policy in sport organizations* (2nd ed.). Scottsdale, AZ: Holcomb Hathaway.

Hylton, K. (2005). "Race," sport and leisure: Lessons from critical race theory. *Leisure Studies, 24,* 81–98.

Hylton, K. (2009). *"Race" and sport: Critical race theory.* New York; Routledge.

Kerlinger, F. N., & Lee, H. B. (2000). *Foundations of behavioral research* (4th ed.). Fort Worth, TX: Harcourt College Publishers.

Knoppers, A. (1992). Explaining male dominance and sex segregation in coaching: Three approaches. *Quest, 44,* 210–227.

Ladson-Billings, G., & Tate, W. F., IV. (1995). Toward a critical race theory of education. *Teachers College Record, 97*(1), 47–68.

Lewin, K. (1952). *Field theory in social science: Selected theoretical papers by Kurt Lewin* (p. 169). London: Tavistock.

McDowell, J., & Cunningham, G. B. (2009). The influence of diversity perspectives on Black female athletic administrators' identity negotiations outcomes. *Quest, 61,* 202–222.

McGraw, D. (1998, July 13). Big league troubles. *U.S. News & World Report, 125*(2), 40–46.

Newbery, P. (2002). Pakistani doubles star defiant. BBC Sports Online. Retrieved September 30, 2005, from http://news.bbc.co.uk/sport1/tennis/Wimbledon/2079170.stm.

Pelled, L. H. (1996). Demographic diversity, conflict, and work group outcomes: An intervening process theory. *Organization Science, 7,* 615–631.

Pelled, L. H., Eisenhardt, K. M., & Xin, K. R. (1999). Exploring the black box: An analysis of work group diversity, conflict, and performance. *Administrative Science Quarterly, 44,* 1–28.

Phillips, K. W., Northcraft, G. B., & Neale, M. A. (2006). Surface-level diversity and decision-making in groups: When does deep-level similarity help? *Group Processes & Intergroup Relations, 9,* 467–482.

Richard, O. (2000). Racial diversity, business strategy, and firm performance: A resource-based view. *Academy of Management Journal, 43,* 164–177.

Richard, O. C., Murthi, B. P. S., & Ismail, K. (2007). The impact of racial diversity on intermediate and long-term performance: The moderating role of environmental context. *Strategic Management Journal, 28,* 1213–1233.

Riordan, C. M. (2000). Relational demography within groups: Past developments, contradictions, and new directions. In G. R. Ferris (Ed.), *Research in personnel and human resources management* (Vol. 19, pp. 131–173). Greenwich, CT: JAI Press.

Sage, G. H. (1998). *Power and ideology in American sport: A critical perspective* (2nd ed.). Champaign, IL: Human Kinetics.

Singer, J. N. (2005a). Addressing epistemological racism in sport management research. *Journal of Sport Management, 19,* 464–479.

Singer, J. N. (2005b). Understanding racism through the eyes of African American male student-athletes. *Race, Ethnicity, & Education, 8,* 365–386.

Tajfel, H., & Turner, J. C. (1979). An integrative theory of intergroup conflict. In W. G. Austin & S. Worchel (Eds.), *The social psychology of intergroup relations* (pp. 33–47). Monterey, CA: Brooks/Cole.

Tate, W. F. (1997). Critical race theory and education: History, theory, and implications. In M. Apple (Ed.), *Review in research education 2* (pp. 191–243). Washington, DC: American Educational Research Association.

Tsui, A. S., Egan, T. D., & O'Reilly, C. A., III (1992). Being different: Relational demography and organizational attachment. *Administrative Science Quarterly, 37,* 549–579.

Tsui, A. S., & Gutek, B. A. (1999). *Demographic differences in organizations: Current research and future directions.* New York: Lexington Books.

Turner, J., Hogg, M. A., Oakes, P. J., Reicher, S. D., & Wetherell, M. S. (1987). *Rediscovering the social group: A self-categorization theory.* Oxford, UK: B. Blackwell.

van Knippenberg, D., De Dreu, C. K. W., & Homan, A. C. (2004). Work group diversity and group performance: An integrative model and research agenda. *Journal of Applied Psychology, 89,* 1008–1022.

Whisenant, W. A., Pedersen, P. M., & Obenour, B. L. (2002). Success and gender: Determining the rate of advancement for intercollegiate athletic directors. *Sex Roles, 47,* 485–491.

Williams, K. Y., & O'Reilly, C. A., III (1998). Demography and diversity in organizations: A review of 40 years of research. In B. M. Staw and L. L. Cummings (Eds.), *Research in organizational behavior* (Vol. 20, pp. 77–140). Greenwich, CT: JAI Press.

3

Prejudice and Discrimination

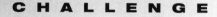

LEARNING OBJECTIVES

After studying this chapter, you should be able to:

- Define and discuss the major tenets of prejudice.

- Understand the differences between explicit and implicit prejudice.

- Define discrimination and identify its two forms.

- Discuss the prevalence of discrimination in the sport context.

- Understand why discrimination occurs.

- Discuss the effect of discrimination on subsequent work outcomes.

Serena Williams is one of the top tennis players in the world. By the time she was 28 years old, she had already won 23 career Grand Slams (the most prestigious tournaments in tennis), which included 11 singles titles, 2 mixed doubles, and 10 in women's double. These feats put her as one of the game's greatest of all time. In recognition of her accomplishments, she was named the Female Athlete of the Year in 2002 by the Associated Press. She is also active in the community, where she volunteers in schools, conducts tennis clinics for at-risk youth, and helps fund programs that aid academically challenged students.

But, it was not her amazing tennis accomplishments or her philanthropic activities that made headlines in 2009; instead, Williams was soundly panned by the press and sports personalities for her outburst at the U.S. Open. During one of her matches, Williams perceived that a line judge had ruled incorrectly on a call. As a result, she became angry with the judge, yelling profanities at her for a long period of time. As a result of the outburst, Williams was fined $10,000 immediately after the tournament. She was then fined another $82,000 months after the incident (once it was reviewed more thoroughly by tennis authorities) and placed on probation. The $92,000 (combined fine) was the largest fine ever levied against a tennis player.

In commenting on the nature of the fines, Williams readily admitted that she was wrong to behave as she did. She also pointed out, however, the inequitable nature of the punishment, especially when considering the behavior of male tennis players. Though similar outbursts from men are more common, they are rarely fined for their inappropriate displays. Male players who have yelled similar curse words at line judges have been fined—but only $10,000, little more than a tenth of what Williams was fined. Another player was fined less than half of what Williams was after a member from his camp *physically attacked* an official. In fact, John McEnroe was wildly popular in the 1980s, in part because of outbursts similar to those of Williams. In commenting on the differential treatment she received compared with the treatment McEnroe and other men who act like him receive, Williams noted, "Is it because they are all HE's and not a SHE like me? It is indeed a massive difference. Being American I guess the 1st amendment, freedom of speech, does not apply to a SHE in this case? In any event the Grand Slam Committee, ITF, and its staff did not hesitate to call, send a note, text, nor write letters after this incident. Ironic is it not?"

Information adapted from: ■ Williams, S. (2009, December). To be honest, I believe I reached my boiling point. Retrieved online January 13, 2010, from http://globalgrind.com/channel/gossip/content/1204284/I-Want-To-Speak-About-My-Recently-Dubbed-Outburt/ ■ www.serenawilliams.com.

DIVERSITY CHALLENGE REFLECTION

1. In your estimation, was Williams' fine justified?
2. Why do you think men who behave similarly to Williams are not punished as harshly?
3. Can you think of other instances in sport where women and men are treated differently for the same behaviors?

s Serena Williams' situation seems to illustrate, even 40 years after major civil rights legislation (e.g., the Civil Rights Act of 1964) and gender equity mandates (Title IX of the Education Amendments of 1972) were passed, gender biases still exist. Such practices, however, are not limited to the professional tennis domain; many instances of prejudice and discrimination have been documented in other areas of the sport industry, including university athletics and high school sports. Furthermore, women are not the only people who face discrimination; rather, anyone who is not a White, Protestant, able-bodied, heterosexual male may face inequitable treatment in sport organizations (Fink, Pastore, & Riemer, 2001). There is considerable evidence that facing such discrimination can have a negative impact on an individual's work experiences, career progress, and even life satisfaction (see Button, 2001). The purpose of this chapter, therefore, is to explore the issues of differential treatment in the sport industry.

Prejudice

his section provides an overview of prejudice and discusses both explicit and implicit prejudicial attitudes. In doing so, the theoretical tenets and outcomes associated with these constructs are presented.

Definition

There are various definitions of *prejudice*. Allport (1954), for instance, suggested that prejudice represents an "antipathy based upon faulty and inflexible generalization" (p. 9). Crandall, Eshleman, and O'Brien (2002) defined prejudice as "a negative evaluation of a group or of an individual on the basis of group membership" (p. 359). Finally, Gaertner and Dovidio (2000) considered prejudice to represent "an unfavorable attitude toward another group, involving both negative feelings and beliefs" (Gaertner & Dovidio, 2000, p. 15). Collectively, these definitions suggest that prejudice represents negative attitudes toward members of a social group that are maintained over time.

Indeed, when most people think of what it means to be prejudiced, definitions similar to the ones provided above are likely to come to mind. That said, there are potential limitations with this perspective. Perhaps the most noteworthy is that not all forms of prejudice are the result of negative attitudes (Brewer, 1999; Dovidio, Glick, & Rudman, 2005). Certainly there are cases where prejudice is the result of disdain or dislike toward another person or group, but there are also instances where very positive attitudes are directed toward the persons facing prejudice. For instance, although Whites' attitudes toward racial minorities have improved over time (thereby signaling positive attitudes), there is still considerable evidence of prejudice and discrimination in housing, hiring, and other contexts (Rudman, 2004a). These dynamics could be due to the mismatch between the stereotype of the individual and the role in which the person is situated (Eagly & Diekman, 2005). For instance, women in medical fields might be viewed positively (doctors are generally held in high esteem), though not as positively as their male counterparts (because the stereotypical doctor is a man, not a woman). In this case, these women would still face prejudice. Similar patterns would be expected regarding other persons occupying non-stereotypical roles (e.g., a team chaplain who is gay). These examples also demonstrate that prejudice is contextual in nature and therefore is a more subtle concept than is commonly thought (Eagly & Diekman, 2005).

The aforementioned definitions also mask that there are different forms of prejudice, as is discussed next.

Explicit and Implicit Prejudice

Researchers (e.g., Son Hing, Chung-Yan, Hamilton, & Zanna, 2008) have identified two primary forms of prejudice, explicit and implicit, which are outlined in the following sections.

Explicit prejudice

Explicit prejudicial attitudes are those negative attitudes toward persons different from the self that people consciously and deliberately maintain (Dovidio, Kawakami, & Beach, 2001). This perspective is consistent with the definitions offered earlier in the chapter. As an example, people who express explicit racial prejudice might (a) attribute negative characteristics, such as laziness, to African Americans; (b) direct negative attitudes (e.g., antagonism) toward the group racial minorities; or (c) promote mandates that limit African Americans' opportunities, such as those related to housing or employment (Gaertner & Dovidio, 2000). For example, members of the Ku Klux Klan

DIVERSITY
in the field

Racism in Soccer. Racism is present in all parts of the sport world, and soccer (football) is no exception. Norway's John Carew and Daniel Braathen, for example, faced considerable racist abuse by Slovenian fans as Norway battled Slovenia in a World Cup qualifying match in September of 2005 ("Carew," 2005). Unfortunately for these two players, there is little they can do while playing on the field; however, team and stadium officials can take steps to curb such abuse. Benjamin Davis-Todd, who hurled racist insults toward a Peterborough United player during a match in 2005, was banned from Lincoln City games for three years ("Match," 2005). In addition to the fines and court costs he was ordered to pay, Davis-Todd was prohibited from visiting any town or city where Lincoln City or the English national team was playing while the ban was in place. Apparently, the court action had an effect on Davis-Todd. After the court case concluded, he noted, "I'm very sorry for what I did. I'm embarrassed not only for myself but for my family as well. I've been going to watch Lincoln City my whole life, so I'm absolutely gutted that I can't go to matches anymore." Perhaps penalties such as these will curb the abusive insults racial minorities hear while participating in soccer.

are generally expected to hold such attitudes and therefore express explicit prejudice. See the Diversity in the Field box for other examples.

Explicit prejudice against people is normally deemed socially unacceptable, though there are some exceptions. In drawing from Sherif and Sherif's (1953) group norm theory, Crandall et al. (2002) argued that the expression of prejudice was socially constructed to correspond with the values, attitudes, and norms of a given context or society. In this case, the expression of prejudice is sometimes socially acceptable. As an example, the authors found that prejudice against rapists, child abusers, and thieves was seen as acceptable, while similar attitudes expressed toward racial minorities and persons with disabilities were not. This linkage has obvious ramifications, because if people believe it is socially permissible to express prejudice against a particular group, then it is also likely tolerable to discriminate against those persons, too. Crandall et al. found evidence to suggest as much, as the acceptability of prejudice predicted the acceptability of discrimination (e.g., housing, employment) among groups such as rapists, drug users, and ex-convicts.

The acceptability norms also influence people's reactions to hearing prejudicial comments. Cunningham, Ferreira, and Fink (2009) examined this issue in their study of people's responses to prejudicial comments heard at sporting events. They argued that sport was a context that tended to privilege men and masculinity (see also Messner, 2002), and as such, sexist comments might not be met with disdain. On the other hand, racist comments were predictably deemed offensive because of the social norms against expressing such views (Dowden & Robinson, 1993). Consistent with these predictions, participants viewed racist comments (i.e., "Of course we lost. The other team had more Black players than we do.") as more offensive than sexist comments (i.e., "Of course we lost. We played like a bunch of girls."). The negative reactions to racist comments were heightened when the comments were expressed by a White person, as was the aversion to sexist comments when the comments were uttered by a male. Participants were also asked to explain why they responded as they did. One person noted, "I think that saying that playing like a bunch of girls is not very offensive because girls' basketball is not even close to the level that men's basketball is, even though it is sexist I do not find it offensive" (p. 68).

Implicit prejudice

By contrast with explicit prejudice, implicit prejudice reflects "evaluations that (a) have an unknown origin (i.e., people are unaware of the basis of their evaluation);

(b) are activated automatically; and (c) influence implicit responses, namely uncontrollable responses and ones that people do not view as an expression of their attitudes and thus do not attempt to control" (Wilson, Lindsey, & Schooler, 2000, p. 104). Whereas people are consciously aware of and can monitor their explicit prejudices, people's implicit prejudices are unconsciously harbored and, as a result, cannot be controlled (Rudman, 2004b). Thus, they represent latent, underlying evaluations of a given social group.

Implicit prejudice operates at the subconscious level, but that does not mean people are unaware of the possibility of expressing that prejudice. For instance, Rudman and Borgida (1995) conducted a study in which a group of men were primed with commercials depicting women as sex objects while another group did not see these pictures and served as a control group. The men who saw the pictures displayed more negative implicit attitudes toward women than those in the control group, and treated female job applicants as sex objects. After the study, the men reported that they were not aware of the influence of the primes; as a result, they were unable to control or check their behaviors. In discussing this study, Rudman (2004a) noted that although the men were unaware of the primes, they were likely aware that they were capable of potentially objectifying women. Thus, "what is implicit is the effect of the priming manipulation on their subsequent thoughts and actions" (p. 135). For additional information related to implicit prejudices, see the accompanying sidebar.

AVERSION RACISM

One of the most well-researched forms of implicit prejudice is what Gaertner and Dovidio (2000; Dovidio & Gaertner, 2004) refer to as aversive racism. Aversive racists are socially liberal and endorse egalitarian values. Despite these good intentions, aversive racists unconsciously harbor feelings of uneasiness toward racial minorities and try to avoid interacting with them. Their actions toward racial minorities are thought to be predicated by the situation: they will behave in ways that do not reflect poorly on the self. That is, if the situation clearly calls for a prescribed course of action, and not following that course would reflect negatively on the individual, then aversive racists are likely to treat racial minorities in a positive manner; however, when the normative structure is weak or when guidelines for appropriate behaviors are vague, then discrimination is likely to occur.

A number of studies have demonstrated the negative effects of aversive racism. One example comes from Dovidio and Gaertner's (2000) research in job selection. When job applicants were highly qualified, or when the applicant clearly lacked the requisite credentials, there was no discrimination against African Americans. However, when the qualifications were less obvious, thereby making the selection decision more ambiguous, Whites recommended other Whites more frequently than they did African Americans. Similar effects have been observed with the help provided to others (Frey & Gaertner, 1986) and legal decisions (Knight, Guiliano, & Sanchez-Ross, 2001), to name a few.

Outcomes of Prejudice

Both explicit and implicit prejudices result in biases expressed toward the targeted social groups. Of course, the nature of the biases might differ. For persons with explicit prejudices, the bias is likely to be overt and potentially hate-driven. For example, the racial slurs hurled at Jackie Robinson or the death threats sent to Hank Aaron (both African American Hall of Fame baseball players) were likely made only by explicit racists, not by people with egalitarian values who did not consider themselves as prejudiced (i.e., aversive racists). Similarly, hate crimes directed toward gay, lesbian, bisexual, and transgendered individuals are committed by people with explicit sexual prejudice (Herek, 2009). In other cases, such as when underrepresented groups are passed over in job interviews, both explicit and implicit prejudices could be to blame (see Dovidio & Gaertner, 2004; Rudman, 2004a).

Finally, recall from previous sections that not all prejudice is the result of negative attitudes; rather, in some cases, people have positive evaluations of out-group members, but their attitudes toward in-group members are simply more positive (Brewer, 1999). Regardless of the underlying mechanisms, bias still exists. For example, that male coaches are more likely to hire other men than they are to hire women (Lovett & Lowry, 1994; Stangl & Kane, 1991) could be attributed to potentially negative attitudes men harbor toward women coaches (see Acosta & Carpenter, 1985, 1988). From another perspective, it is possible that male administrators have positive attitudes toward women coaches, but their positive attitudes toward male coaches are stronger than those felt toward women. Drawing from the existing literature (e.g., Gaertner & Dovidio, 2000; Son Hing et al., 2008), we might expect that when social forces to hire a woman are weak (i.e., the applicants all have similar qualifications), the male athletic director may be more likely to hire the male coach. On the other hand, when social forces to hire the woman are strong (i.e., the woman applicant is clearly more qualified), the male administrator will select the woman. Of course, perceptions of qualifications may be tempered by the gendered nature of the selection process (e.g., Knoppers, 1992). Nevertheless, it does show that the same outcome—the woman not receiving the coaching position—may be due to different underlying motivations and mechanisms than people have traditionally assumed.

Discrimination

This section begins by defining discrimination, including the two forms—access and treatment—the construct can take. The discussion then turns to theoretical explanations of why discrimination exists. This section concludes with the identification of discrimination outcomes.

Definitions

Allport (1954) defined *discrimination* as a behavior that "comes about only when we deny to individuals or groups of people equality of treatment which they may wish" (p. 51). Though related, prejudice and discrimination are conceptually distinct. According to Abercrombie, Hill, and Turner (2000), "prejudice, often the object of psychological study, is contrasted with *discrimination,* which refers to the outcome of social processes which disadvantage social groups" (p. 276, emphasis in original).

Greenhaus, Parasuraman, and Wormley (1990) identified two types of discrimination: access and treatment (see Exhibit 3.1). *Access discrimination* prevents members of a particular social category from obtaining a job or entering a profession. This form of discrimination takes place while people are looking for a job or when they are moving from one job to another.

Treatment discrimination occurs once people are employed. As Greenhaus et al. explain, this form of discrimination "occurs when subgroup members receive fewer rewards, resources, or opportunities on the job than they legitimately deserve on the basis of job-related criteria" (pp. 64–65). As this definition illustrates, the differences in treatment are the result of membership in a specific social category (e.g., being a woman), rather than poor performance at work. As previously noted, Fink et al. (2001) found that employees who are different from the majority in the

Forms of discrimination.   *exhibit* **3.1**

ACCESS DISCRIMINATION:

- *Definition:* denies one access to an organization, job, or profession based on membership in a social category
- *Theoretical perspective:* social categorization framework
- *Example:* an African American who is more qualified than the other applicants is denied a managerial position

TREATMENT DISCRIMINATION:

- *Definition:* members of a specific social category have less-positive work experiences and receive fewer opportunities and rewards than they legitimately deserve based on job-related criteria
- *Theoretical perspectives:* critical theories, social categorization framework
- *Example:* an African American who performs better than her colleagues receives the lowest performance evaluation

sport context are likely to face difficult work experiences. Research in this area generally supports their thesis.

Access discrimination

Several studies have demonstrated the existence of access discrimination in the sport and recreation context. Both Stangl and Kane (1991) and Lovett and Lowry (1994) found that women coaches faced discrimination in the hiring process, so that men (the persons who make the majority of the personnel decisions in this context) were more likely to hire other men than to hire women. In a similar vein, Cunningham and Sagas (2005) found that African Americans faced access discrimination in the men's basketball context. These authors also found that the prevalence of discrimination was accentuated on staffs with a White head coach, relative to those with an African American head coach (see also Hamilton, 1997, for similar effects in professional basketball). Longley (2000) found that French Canadians were underrepresented, both as players and as front-office personnel, on English Canadian NHL teams, relative to their U.S. counterparts. Cunningham, Sartore, and McCullough (2010) observed that, relative to their heterosexual counterparts, job applicants presumed to be gay, lesbian, or bisexual were denied access to fitness club positions. Other research has demonstrated that persons with disabilities (Hums, Moorman, & Wolff, 2003) and persons from a lower socioeconomic class are often denied access to sport and recreational opportunities. Finally, although research in other areas is lacking, it is reasonable to assume that other persons, such as religious minorities, may also face similar discriminatory practices.

Treatment discrimination

Research suggests that treatment discrimination is widespread in the sport context. The research conducted among coaches illustrates this point. With respect to gender, various studies have shown that women, relative to men, face limited opportunities

Discrimination Based on Language. Discussions of discrimination are often related to differential access and treatment based on membership in a social group. For example, lesbian coaches might face more discrimination than their heterosexual counterparts. However, discrimination can also stretch beyond the way people look, their personal beliefs, or their sexual orientation. Others might face discrimination because of their language. Language discrimination is denying people access to particular opportunities or treating people differently in the workplace solely because of their native tongue or a specific characteristic of their speech. For example, requiring that only English be spoken in the workplace is likely to be considered language discrimination. Various U.S. Supreme Court decisions, dating back as early as 1926, have established the illegality of such actions. Furthermore, plaintiffs have successfully sued under Title VII of the Civil Rights Act of 1964. It is important to remember that discrimination is based not only on physical characteristics, beliefs, or preferences but also on the language people use.

American Civil Liberties Union (www.aclunc.org/language/lang-report.html).

for advancement, both in their careers and within their organizations (e.g., Knoppers, Meyer, Ewing, & Forrest, 1991; Whisenant, 2003). Men are more likely than women to reap the rewards of extra training, education, and social contacts in the industry (Cunningham & Sagas, 2002; Sagas & Cunningham, 2004). Furthermore, women often encounter more negative work experiences than men (e.g., Inglis, Danylchuk, & Pastore, 2000). Given this differential treatment, it should not be surprising that women in the sport industry often have career goals and outcomes that differ from those of men. For example, research has shown that women coaches, relative to men, are likely to leave the profession at an earlier age (Cunningham & Sagas, 2003) and have fewer career advancement goals (e.g., Cunningham & Sagas, 2002; Cunningham, Doherty, & Gregg, 2007).

Treatment discrimination is not limited only to women, however. With respect to race, research has shown that athletes of color face unique experiences on university campuses (Bruening, Armstrong, & Pastore, 2005). Among coaches, racial minorities are likely to perceive fewer advancement opportunities and to receive fewer promotions (Sagas & Cunningham, 2005). In addition, various studies have indicated that gays and lesbians face negative attitudes from others in the sport industry (Gill, Morrow, Collins, Lucey, & Schultz, 2006) and encounter treatment discrimination in the workplace (Krane & Barber, 2005; Sartore & Cunningham, 2009). The general pattern of these studies supports the contention of Fink et al. (2001) that persons who are different from the majority often face discriminatory practices within the sport context.

Theoretical Explanations for Discrimination

With this background, the discussion turns to explanations of why discrimination exists. As was done previously, we examine theoretical perspectives related to access and treatment discrimination separately.

Theories related to access discrimination

Although several theories could be used to understand access discrimination, social psychological theories (see Chapter 2) seem to have the most explanatory power. Access discrimination is concerned with persons who differ from the majority being denied access to certain positions, organizations, or occupations (Greenhaus et al., 1990). When considering this lack of access, it is useful to identify those who are denying the access to such people. Who are the decision makers and persons in charge of personnel decisions? As previously noted, within the sport context, these persons most often include men who are White, Protestant, able-bodied, and heterosexual (Fink et al., 2001). We can then use this information to make predictions about personnel decisions. Drawing from both the social categorization framework (Tajfel & Turner, 1979; Turner, Hogg, Oakes, Reicher, & Wetherell, 1987) and similarity-attraction paradigm (Byrne, 1971), it might be expected that decision makers will select people who are similar to themselves. In this case, the people similar to the self are other White men who are able-bodied, heterosexual, and Protestant. This demographic profile mirrors that of most of the personnel in sport organizations today.

If we assume that people will hire others who are like them, then that also is true for persons who are not in the majority. Women who are in power, for example, will be more likely to hire other women. Using other demographic or deep-level characteristics to replace "women" in the previous example produces the same results. Current research supports this contention: Among NCAA Division I athletic departments, the proportion of women serving as head coaches of women's teams increases from 43.9 percent to 50.0 percent when the athletic director (the person charged with hiring decisions) is a woman (Acosta & Carpenter, 2008). Similar findings result when race is considered: Among NCAA Division I basketball teams, the proportion of African American assistant coaches increases from 30 percent to 45 percent when the head coach is an African American (Cunningham & Sagas, 2005).

DIVERSITY *in the field*

Limited Access to Participation. Many times, access discrimination is discussed in terms of the limited opportunities persons from certain groups have to obtain particular jobs or work in a certain profession. However, people can also face access discrimination when it comes to participation in sports. Because athletes such as Jackie Robinson broke the "color barrier" over 50 years ago, many may assume that denying people access to participation opportunities based on their demographic characteristics is a thing of the past. However, this is not the case. For example, in the country club context, Augusta National, which hosts the Masters golf tournament, still denied membership to women as of 2010. In a similar way, Shoal Creek did not admit persons of color as club members until its discriminatory admissions practices came under fire when the club hosted the 1990 PGA Championship (Daddario & Wigley, 2006). Such discriminatory practices are not limited to country clubs or to the exclusion of women and persons of color. Fernwood Women's Health Club is an organization designed as women-only fitness clubs. Other organizations, such as Fitness Etcetera for Women, have similar policies. As these examples illustrate, access discrimination occurs not only in sport organizations but also in country clubs and fitness organizations.

These studies illustrate that all people, irrespective of their demographic characteristics, are likely to hire similar others. One way to reduce or eliminate access discrimination, therefore, is to change the sport organizations' power structure—an argument also advanced by some sociological theorists (see Chapter 2). If more women, racial minorities, or others who are different from the traditional majority are placed in decision-making roles, then the proportion of those persons in all levels of sport organizations is likely to increase.

Theories related to treatment discrimination

Several theories have been adopted to explain the incidence of treatment discrimination; however, critical theories (see Chapter 2) remain the most often used. Feminist theory focuses on the gendered nature of organizations. In the context of many sport organizations, this means the organizational structures, the jobs within these organiza-

alternative
P E R S P E C T I V E S

Questioning Different Work Experiences. Much of the literature in sport and leisure suggests that women have poorer work experiences than their male counterparts, thereby suggesting that they encounter treatment discrimination. Some studies, however, do not support this trend. Specifically, within the context of women's university athletics, several studies have shown that women coaches perceive more opportunity for advancement than do the men. For example, Sagas, Cunningham, and Ashley (2000) asked assistant coaches of women's teams who had applied for head coaching positions why they did not receive the positions. Men were much more likely to indicate that discriminatory hiring practices prevented them from obtaining the position. That is, in the minds of these assistant coaches, administrators sought a woman for the position, not a man. Similar sentiments have been expressed by coaches in the field. In 2005, Michael Cox filed a discrimination lawsuit against Boston University, claiming that he did not receive a coaching position for the women's ice hockey team, because he was a man (Levenson, 2005). Thus, although there is considerable evidence to suggest that women face treatment discrimination in sport and leisure, it is also possible that men, in some instances, also face differential treatment based on their sex. People adopting this perspective fail to take into account that power (which men possess in sport) is a requisite condition for discrimination to take place.

tions, and the activities within these entities are all defined in such a way that hegemonic masculinity is enhanced (Knoppers, 1992). Applying the feminist theory, sport organizations are places where men and the activities in which men participate are valued and celebrated, thereby privileging men and dominant forms of masculinity. As a result, women in these organizations face poorer work experiences than their male counterparts, and the activities in which they engage may be less valued.

Critical race theory is also used to explain discrimination in sport. Recall that one of the central tenets of this theory is that racism is endemic in society (Hylton, 2009; Singer, 2005). Researchers who adopt this theory argue that racism is a central part of U.S. society, enmeshed in the society's institutions, legal system, and culture. This position supports the argument that the discrimination experienced by racial minorities is due, at least in part, to the racist institutions and systems present in American society.

Although most research adopts a sociological approach to the study of treatment discrimination, recent research suggests that a social psychological approach can also be embraced (Sartore, 2006). Such an approach is especially useful when considering the presence of discrimination in work dyads, such as supervisor–subordinate pairs. It is assumed that managers (or coaches) categorize their subordinates into in-groups and out-groups based, at least in part, on the surface- or deep-level similarity to the self. In-group members, relative to their out-group counterparts, are then afforded greater trust, respect, and positive affect. In an organizational setting, such positive attitudes toward in-group members may also mean more challenging and meaningful work assignments, greater access to information, and more positive work experiences in general. Because most managers in sport organizations are White, able-bodied, Protestant, heterosexual men (Fink et al., 2001), people with similar characteristics are likely to be considered in-group members and have pleasant work experiences, while people with different characteristics are more likely to have poor work experiences.

Discrimination Outcomes

This section discusses how discrimination influences subsequent outcomes both for those who experience the differential treatment and for those who do not. The effects of access and treatment discrimination are addressed separately, though it is acknowledged that the two can interact and influence one another.

Outcomes related to access discrimination

Because access discrimination denies people, based on their personal characteristics, the opportunity to obtain a particular job, enter an organization, or pursue a career in a certain profession (Button, 2001; Greenhaus et al., 1990), one of the most obvious outcomes is the limitation placed on the kinds of jobs and careers one can pursue. There is a strong history of excluding people who do not fit the "typical" profile of a sport organization employee. As one example, an Asian American has never served as a head coach for a Division I-A football team. For current assistant coaches in the profession, the message is clear: unless you are White, the chances of obtaining a head coaching position are slim. Although the focus here is on race and coaching, the same is true for others who differ from the majority—women, persons with disabilities, and so forth.

Access discrimination influences those who encounter it directly; for example, the woman who is denied a managerial role because of her sex (see the Professional Perspectives box for other examples). However, a history of access discrimination in a particular profession or industry also influences people who have not yet entered the field—namely, students. There is a growing body of literature that suggests that when people anticipate substantial barriers in a profession, they are unlikely to choose that career path (see Bandura, 2000; Lent, Brown, & Hackett, 1994). For example, if a student is considering entering the sport management profession, but observes that people with characteristics similar to hers face considerable discrimination and are not afforded an opportunity to progress, then it is unlikely that she will pursue that career. Instead, she may choose a career path that is more inviting to persons similar to her, and presumably then, to her as well (for an example, see Cunningham, Bruening, Sartore, Sagas, & Fink, 2005). Thus, access discrimination influences not only those who experience it but also those who may consider that career path.

PROFESSIONAL PERSPECTIVES

Discrimination in the Hiring Process. Becky Heidesch is the founder and CEO of Women's Sports Services (WSS), an organization specializing in job placement for women, minorities, and professional athletes. According to Heidesch, the sports industry, like many others, is one that has traditionally been dominated by White males. Recently, however, this field has been making inroads when it comes to diversifying the workforce. This progress grew from an awareness that a diverse staff can help a firm identify with and relate to people from different backgrounds. Although a push for greater diversity is evident, there are still many instances of discrimination, particularly among women and racial minorities. Those are not the only persons facing such barriers, however. As Heidesch notes, "certainly we see age discrimination across the board." Such discrimination often arises from perceptions among sport organization decision makers that older employees might not fit into the organization's culture. Discrimination can also take place based on the applicant's attractiveness. Heidesch notes that attractiveness plays a meaningful role in certain positions, such as those related to public relations, marketing, and advertising. Physical appearance is particularly important anytime a person represents the company in public.

Outcomes related to treatment discrimination

Button (2001) argues that treatment discrimination can impact both tangible and subtle outcomes. Tangible outcomes include the job assignments one receives, the opportunities for development and training, the number and size of the raises one receives, and the number of promotions one is given. Subtle outcomes, although more difficult to quantify or observe, are equally as important. Such outcomes include differences in integrating into the workgroup, the support received from supervisors, and the discretion to execute job activities.

One of the primary ways treatment discrimination occurs is through performance appraisals (Ilgen & Youtz, 1986; Stauffer & Buckley, 2005). Unfair ratings have important implications for an employee's development, particularly the raises and promotions received. Recognizing the potential for bias in performance appraisals, Sartore (2006) drew from organizational psychology, social psychology, human resource management, and sociology literature to develop a conceptual model explaining how treatment discrimination, as manifested through performance appraisals, can influence subsequent work-related outcomes. This model is described next (see also Exhibit 3.2).

Using the social categorization framework (Tajfel & Turner, 1979; Turner et al., 1987), Sartore (2006) argues that the categorization of persons into in-groups and out-groups will influence performance appraisals in such a manner that the performance ratings of in-group members will be higher than those of out-group members. This effect has been demonstrated in various contexts over many years (see Stauffer & Buckley, 2005). Sartore then suggests that this performance appraisal bias will result in self-limiting behavior. Self-limiting behavior refers to the decrease in abilities and loss of motivation that occur over time as a result of negative performance feedback. One's ability is likely to diminish because poor performance appraisals result in being assigned less meaningful work and being offered fewer training opportunities. Thus, opportunities to develop skills and abilities decrease. Motivation decreases because continual negative performance feedback may deplete an employee's confidence and reduce the overall effort put forth to complete a task. We might expect that if people perceive that discrimination is the cause of the poor appraisal, they may become less motivated because they feel helpless to alter or control the situation.

As might be expected, when self-limiting behavior occurs, subsequent task performance becomes poor. When employees lose opportunities to develop their skills, lack confidence in their abilities, and demonstrate a lack of motivation, their

exhibit **3.2** The effects of performance appraisal bias.

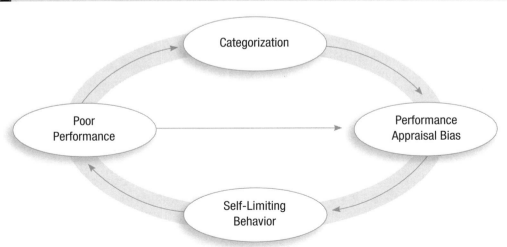

performance is likely to diminish. Recognizing this relationship, Sartore (2006) proposes that self-limiting behavior is negatively related to task performance.

The subsequent poor performance has two expected outcomes: additional poor performance appraisals and stereotype confirmation. The former outcome is straightforward because poor performance should result in a poor evaluation. With respect to the latter outcome, recall that out-group members were initially given poor performance evaluation scores not so much because of their actual job performance but because they were different from the rater. These differences translated into negative attitudes toward such employees, or at the very least, less positive attitudes than were afforded in-group members. Thus, when out-group members subsequently perform poorly because of self-limiting behavior, this simply serves to reinforce initial stereotypes about that person.

Sartore (2006) further suggests that these relationships can be influenced by various factors such as the amount of time the rater and ratee spend with one another, how closely the two work with one another, the extent to which the dissimilarities that lead to categorization are important to the rater, and the extent to which the rater and ratee consider themselves as belonging to a single, common in-group. Notwithstanding these potential caveats, Sartore correctly argues that rater–ratee differences can have a negative impact not only on immediate outcomes, such as the raise received, but also on more long-term outcomes as motivation, confidence, and performance. Furthermore, the categorization is not limited to demographic attributes; research has shown that rater–ratee deep-level characteristic differences can also result in biased performance appraisals (Antonioni & Park, 2001).

CHAPTER *summary*

This chapter has focused on discrimination and prejudice. As illustrated in the Diversity Challenge, these phenomena still play a major role in the context of sport and physical activity. Specifically, prejudice and discrimination influence the people who join an organization; the structure and policies an organization implements; the processes within the workplace; and various outcomes for individuals, groups, and organizations. After reading the chapter, you should be able to:

1. Define and discuss the major tenets of prejudice.

Prejudice has traditionally been defined as negative attitudes toward members of a social group. Contemporary research suggests that negative attitudes are not always a requisite condition, however, because people can experience prejudice even when others view them in a positive light.

2. Understand the differences between explicit and implicit prejudice.

Explicit prejudice represents those negative attitudes that people consciously and deliberately maintain. Implicit prejudice is a latent evaluation of social groups that elicits subtle or unconscious responses over which people do not have cognitive control.

3. Define discrimination and identify its two forms.

Drawing from Allport (1954), discrimination was defined as a behavior that "comes about only when we deny to individuals or groups of people equality of treatment which they may wish" (p. 51). Greenhaus et al. (1990) further differentiated between two forms of discrimination: access and treatment.

4. Discuss the prevalence of discrimination in the sport context.

Research and anecdotal evidence both suggest that discrimination is widespread in the sport industry. With respect to access discrimination, people are denied access to certain positions within sport organizations or to participation opportunities in sport and recreation based on their personal demographics. With respect to treatment discrimination, research shows that people who differ from the typical majority profile in an industry are less likely to be rewarded for their career investment and success and generally have less-positive work experiences.

5. Understand why discrimination occurs.

Several theoretical perspectives may explain discriminatory behavior. The social categorization framework is useful in understanding access discrimination: in-group members are thought to be favored for positions over their out-group counterparts. On the other hand, critical theories, such as feminist theory and critical race theory, have most often been used to explain treatment discrimination. Although most research adopts a sociological approach when examining the issue of treatment discrimination, other research uses the social categorization framework to compare the different experiences of in-group and out-group members.

6. Discuss the effect of discrimination on subsequent work outcomes.

Several outcomes are associated with discrimination. First, when people are denied access to a particular job, organization, or profession based solely on personal characteristics, they are denied the opportunity to pursue the vocation of their choice. Treatment discrimination results in such negative outcomes as decreased training opportunities, poorer job assignments, lack of work group integration, and weakened support from supervisors.

QUESTIONS *for discussion*

1. What are the major differences between traditional and aversive racism? What are examples of each?
2. Which form of prejudicial attitude is most prevalent in sport today? Are some sectors of sport and physical activity more likely to see certain types of prejudice than others? Why do you think this is the case?
3. With federal, state, and local statutes mandating equal employment opportunities, is discrimination still a problem? Why or why not?
4. What are the major distinctions between access and treatment discrimination?
5. Which form of discrimination has the more harmful effect? Why?
6. Several theories are used to understand why discrimination occurs. Which of the theories allows for the best explanation and why?

LEARNING *activities*

1. Visit the Project Implicit website (https://implicit.harvard.edu/implicit/) and test your aversive, or implicit, attitudes toward various targets (e.g., age, race, disability).
2. Search the Web for recent examples of discrimination and prejudice in the context of sport and physical activity. Based on your search results, which group or groups are most likely to face discrimination?

READING *resources*

SUPPLEMENTARY READINGS

Brown, R., & Gaertner, S. (Eds.). (2001). *Blackwell handbook of social psychology: Intergroup processes.* Malden, MA: Blackwell. (Edited collection of essays related to intergroup processes; contains specific sections of prejudice and changing intergroup processes.)

Colella, A., & Dipboye, R. (Eds.). (2005). *Discrimination at work: The psychological and organizational bases.* Mahwah, NJ: Lawrence Erlbaum Associates. (Edited volume with a focus on explaining discrimination, understanding discrimination against particular groups, and discussing the practical implications for reducing such behaviors.)

Dovidio, J. F., Glick, P., & Budman, L. A. (Eds.). (2005). *On the nature of prejudice: Fifty years after Allport.* Malden, MA: Blackwell. (An edited collection of essays from the leading social psychologists in the field; focuses on the contributions of Allport's original work related to prejudice; provides updates to the theory and directions for future inquiry.)

WEB RESOURCES

- Human Rights and Equality Commission (www.hreoc.gov.au/index.html): Australian agency aimed at eliminating discrimination in various contexts, including sport.
- Institute for Diversity and Ethics in Sport (www.bus.ucf.edu/sport/cgi-bin/site/sitew.cgi?page=/ides/index.htx): provides reports concerning diversity and discrimination in the university athletics and professional sport settings.
- Project Implicit (https://implicit.harvard.edu/implicit/): provides an electronic demonstration of how to test for implicit attitudes.

references

Abercrombie, N., Hill, S., & Turner, B. S. (2000). *The Penguin dictionary of sociology* (4th ed.). New York: Penguin Books.

Acosta, R. V., & Carpenter, L. J. (1985). Status of women in athletics: Changes and causes. *Journal of Physical Education, Recreation, and Dance, 56*(8), 33–37.

Acosta, R. V., & Carpenter, L. J. (1988). *Perceived causes of declining representation of women leaders in intercollegiate sports—1988 update.* Unpublished manuscript, Brooklyn College, Brooklyn, NY.

Acosta, R. V., & Carpenter, L. J. (2008). *Women in intercollegiate sport: A longitudinal study—thirty-one year update—1977–2008.* Unpublished manuscript, Brooklyn College, Brooklyn, NY.

Allport, G. W. (1954). *The nature of prejudice.* Cambridge, MA: Addison-Wesley.

Antonioni, D., & Park, H. (2001). The effects of personality similarity on peer ratings of contextual work behaviors. *Personnel Psychology, 54,* 331–360.

Bandura, A. (2000). Exercise of human agency through collective self-efficacy. *Current Directions in Psychological Science, 9*(3), 75–78.

Brewer, M. B. (1999). The psychology of prejudice: Ingroup love or outgroup hate? *Journal of Social Issues, 55,* 429–444.

Bruening, J. E., Armstrong, K. L., & Pastore, D. L. (2005). Listening to voices: The experiences of African American female student athletes. *Research Quarterly for Exercise and Sport, 76,* 82–100.

Button, S. B. (2001). Organizational efforts to affirm sexual diversity: A cross-level examination. *Journal of Applied Psychology, 86,* 17–28.

Byrne, D. (1971). *The attraction paradigm.* New York: Academic Press.

Carew and Braathen abused by Slovenian fans. (2005, September 7). Retrieved September 30, 2005, from www.farenet.org/news_article.asp?intNewsID=461.

Crandall, C. S., Eshleman, A., & O'Brien, L. (2002). Social norms and the expression and suppression of prejudice: The struggle for internalization. *Journal of Personality and Social Psychology, 82,* 359–378.

Cunningham, G. B., & Sagas, M. (2002). The differential effects of human capital for male and female Division I basketball coaches. *Research Quarterly for Exercise and Sport, 73,* 489–495.

Cunningham, G. B., & Sagas, M. (2003). Occupational turnover intent among coaches of women's teams: The role of organizational work experiences. *Sex Roles, 49,* 185–190.

Cunningham, G. B., & Sagas, M. (2005). Access discrimination in intercollegiate athletics. *Journal of Sport and Social Issues, 29,* 148–163.

Cunningham, G. B., Doherty, A. J., & Gregg, M. J. (2007). Using social cognitive career theory to understand head coaching intentions among assistant coaches of women's teams. *Sex Roles, 56,* 365–372.

Cunningham, G. B., Ferreira, M., & Fink, J. S. (2009). Reactions to prejudicial statements: The influence of statement content and characteristics of the commenter. *Group Dynamics: Theory, Research, & Practice, 13,* 59–73.

Cunningham, G. B., Sartore, M. L., & McCullough, B. P. (2010). The influence of applicant sexual orientation and rater sex on ascribed attributions and hiring recommendations of personal trainers. *Journal of Sport Management, 24,* 400–415.

Cunningham, G. B., Bruening, J., Sartore, M. L., Sagas, M., & Fink, J. S. (2005). The application of social cognitive career theory to sport and leisure career choices. *Journal of Career Development, 32,* 122–138.

Daddario, G., & Wigley, B. J. (2006). Prejudice, patriarchy, and the PGA: Defensive discourse surrounding the Shoal Creek and Augusta National controversies. *Journal of Sport Management, 20,* 466–482.

Dovidio, J. F., & Gaertner, S. L. (2000). Aversive racism and selection decisions: 1989 and 1999. *Psychological Science, 11,* 315–319.

Dovidio, J. F., & Gaertner, S. L. (2004). Aversive racism. *Advances in Experimental Social Psychology, 36,* 1–52.

Dovidio, J. F., Glick, P., & Rudman, L. A. (2005). Introduction: Reflecting on *The Nature of Prejudice:* Fifty years after Allport. In J. F. Dovidio, P. Glick, & L. A. Rudman (Eds.), *On the nature of prejudice: Fifty years after Allport* (pp. 1–16). Malden, MA: Blackwell.

Dovidio, J. F., Kawakami, K., & Beach, K R. (2001). Implicit and explicit attitudes: Examination of the relationship between measures of intergroup bias. In R. Brown and S. L. Gaertner (Eds.), *Blackwell handbook of social psychology: Intergroup processes* (pp. 175–197). Malden, MA: Blackwell.

Dowden, S., & Robinson, J. P. (1993). Age and cohort differences in American racial attitudes: The generational replacement hypothesis revisited. In P. M. Sniderman, P. E. Tetlock, & E. G. Carmines (Eds.), *Prejudice, politics, and the American dilemma* (pp. 86–103). Stanford, CA: Stanford University Press.

Eagly, A. H., & Diekman, A. B. (2005). What is the problem? Prejudice as an attitude-in-context. In J. F. Dovidio, P. Glick, & L. A. Rudman (Eds.), *On the nature of prejudice: Fifty years after Allport* (pp. 19–35). Malden, MA: Blackwell.

Fink, J. S., Pastore, D. L., & Riemer, H. A. (2001). Do differences make a difference? Managing diversity in Division IA intercollegiate athletics. *Journal of Sport Management, 15,* 10–50.

Frey, D., & Gaertner, S. L. (1986). Helping and the avoidance of inappropriate interracial behavior: A strategy which perpetuates a non-prejudiced self-image. *Journal of Personality and Social Psychology, 50,* 1083–1090.

Gaertner, S. L., & Dovidio, J. F. (2000). *Reducing intergroup bias: The common ingroup identity model.* Philadelphia, PA: Psychology Press.

Gill, D. L., Morrow, R. G., Collins, K. E., Lucey, A. B., & Schultz, A. M. (2006). Attitudes and sexual prejudice in sport and physical activity. *Journal of Sport Management, 20,* 554–564.

Greenhaus, J. H., Parasuraman, S., & Wormley, W. M. (1990). Effects of race on organizational experiences, job performance, evaluations, and career outcomes. *Academy of Management Journal, 33,* 64–86.

Hamilton, B. H. (1997). Racial discrimination and professional basketball salaries in the 1990s. *Applied Economics, 29,* 287–296.

Herek, G. M. (2009). Sexual stigma and sexual prejudice in the United States: A conceptual framework. In D. A. Hope (Ed.), *Contemporary perspectives on lesbian, gay, and bisexual identities* (pp. 65–111). New York; Springer.

Hums, M. A., Moorman, A. M., & Wolff, E. A. (2003). The inclusion of the Paralympics in the Olympic Amateur

Sports Act: Legal and policy implications for integration of athletes with disabilities into the United States Olympic Committee. *Journal of Sport and Social Issues, 27,* 261–275.

Hylton, K. (2009). *"Race" and sport: Critical race theory.* New York: Routledge.

Ilgen, D. R., & Youtz, M. A. (1986). Factors affecting the evaluation and development of minorities in organizations. In K. Rowland & G. Ferris (Eds.), *Research in personnel and human resource management: A research annual* (pp. 307–337). Greenwich, CT: JAI Press.

Inglis, S., Danylchuk, K. E., & Pastore, D. L. (2000). Multiple realities of women's work experiences in coaching and athletic management. *Women in Sport and Physical Activity Journal, 9*(2), 1–26.

Knight, J. L., Guiliano, T. A., & Sanchez-Ross, M. G. (2001). Famous or infamous? The influence of celebrity status and race on perceptions of responsibility for rape. *Basic and Applied Social Psychology, 23,* 183–190.

Knoppers, A. (1992). Explaining male dominance and sex segregation in coaching: Three approaches. *Quest, 44,* 210–227.

Knoppers, A., Meyer, B. B., Ewing, M., & Forrest, L. (1991). Opportunity and work behavior in college coaching. *Journal of Sport and Social Issues, 15,* 1–20.

Krane, V., & Barber, H. (2005). Identity tensions in lesbian intercollegiate coaches. *Research Quarterly for Exercise and Sport, 76,* 67–81.

Lent, R. W., Brown, S. D., & Hackett, G. (1994). Toward a unifying social cognitive theory of career and academic interest, choice, and performance [Monograph]. *Journal of Vocational Behavior, 45,* 79–122.

Levenson, M. (2005, July 5). BC coach alleges gender bias at BU: Files complaint over hockey job. *The Boston Globe.* Retrieved September 2, 2005, from www.boston.com/ sports/colleges/womens_hockey/articles/2005/07/05/ bc_coach_alleges_gender_bias_at_bu/.

Longley, N. (2000). The underrepresentation of French Canadians on English Canadian NHL teams: Evidence from 1943–1998. *Journal of Sports Economics, 1,* 236–256.

Lovett, D. J., & Lowry, C. D. (1994). "Good old boys" and "good old girls" clubs: Myth or reality? *Journal of Sport Management, 8,* 27–35.

Messner, M. A. (2002). *Taking the field: Women, men, and sports.* Minneapolis: University of Minnesota Press.

Rudman, L. A. (2004a). Social justice in our minds, homes, and society: The nature, causes, and consequences of implicit bias. *Social Justice Research, 17,* 129–142.

Rudman, L. A. (2004b). Sources of implicit attitudes. *Current Directions in Psychological Science, 13*(2), 79–82.

Rudman, L. A., & Borgida, E. (1995). The afterglow of construct accessibility: The behavioral consequences of priming men to view women as sex objects. *Journal of Experimental Social Psychology, 31,* 493–517.

Sagas, M., & Cunningham, G. B. (2004). Does having the "right stuff" matter? Gender differences in the determinants of career success among intercollegiate athletic administrators. *Sex Roles, 50,* 411–421.

Sagas, M., & Cunningham, G. B. (2005). Racial differences in the career success of assistant football coaches: The role of discrimination, human capital, and social capital. *Journal of Applied Social Psychology, 35,* 773–797.

Sagas, M., Cunningham, G. B., & Ashley, F. B. (2000). Examining the women's coaching deficit through the perspective of assistant coaches. *International Journal of Sport Management, 1,* 267–282.

Sartore, M. L. (2006). Categorization, performance appraisals, and self-limiting behavior: The impact on current and future performance. *Journal of Sport Management, 20,* 535–553.

Sartore, M. L., & Cunningham, G. B. (2009). Sexual prejudice, participatory decisions, and panoptic control: Implications for sexual minorities in sport. *Sex Roles, 60,* 100–113.

Sherif, M., & Sherif, C. W. (1953). *Groups in harmony and tension.* New York: Harper.

Singer, J. N. (2005). Addressing epistemological racism in sport management research. *Journal of Sport Management, 19,* 464–479.

Son Hing, L. S., Chung-Yan, G. A., Hamilton, L. K., & Zanna, M. P. (2008). A two-dimensional model that employs explicit and implicit attitudes to characterize prejudice. *Journal of Personality and Social Psychology, 94,* 971–987.

Stangl, J. M., & Kane, M. J. (1991). Structural variables that offer explanatory power for the underrepresentation of women coaches since Title IX: The case of homologous reproduction. *Sociology of Sport Journal, 8,* 47–60.

Stauffer, J. M., & Buckley, R. M. (2005). The existence and nature of racial bias in supervisory ratings. *Journal of Applied Psychology, 90,* 586–591.

Tajfel, H., & Turner, J. C. (1979). An integrative theory of intergroup conflict. In W. G. Austin & S. Worchel (Eds.), *The social psychology of intergroup relations* (pp. 33–47). Monterey, CA: Brooks/Cole.

Turner, J., Hogg, M. A., Oakes, P. J., Reicher, S. D., & Wetherell, M. S. (1987). *Rediscovering the social group: A self-categorization theory.* Oxford, UK: B. Blackwell.

Whisenant, W. A. (2003). How women have fared as interscholastic athletic administrators since the passage of Title IX. *Sex Roles, 49,* 179–184.

Wilson, T. D., Lindsey, S., Schooler, T. Y. (2000). A model of dual attitudes. *Psychological Review, 107,* 101–126.

PART II

Forms of Diversity

CHAPTER 4
Race   69

CHAPTER 5
Sex and Gender   101

CHAPTER 6
Age   133

CHAPTER 7
Mental and Physical Ability   153

CHAPTER 8
Appearance   175

CHAPTER 9
Religious Beliefs   195

CHAPTER 10
Sexual Orientation   213

CHAPTER 11
Social Class   257

Race

During the 1980s, Dexter Manley played professional football for the NFL's Washington Redskins. He was selected for the Pro Bowl based on his accomplishments as a defensive end and won two Super Bowl rings while playing with the Redskins. Despite these achievements, and having received a college degree from Oklahoma State University, Manley was illiterate until age 30. Manley's situation was not an isolated incident. Another player, Kevin Ross, was functionally illiterate but played four seasons at Creighton University. He was admitted to the university even though he scored only 9 of 36 on the ACT entrance exam. While attending the university, other students took his exams for him, and the athletic department hired a secretary to complete his homework assignments.

Dexter Manley and Kevin Ross are but two examples of racial minority players being used for their athletic talents so a university may benefit. In both cases, the players were streamlined into "easy" classes and had their assignments completed for them. After their eligibility was exhausted, the benefits stopped. Even though the NCAA and the U.S. Department of Education passed new rules concerning the academic progress of student-athletes, the abuses have continued. In a 2001 report, the NCAA analyzed graduation rates for men's basketball players who entered school between 1990 and 1994—the equivalent of five straight recruiting classes. The NCAA study showed that 36 of the 323 Division I schools did not graduate *a single* African American athlete during that time. That some of the athletic programs were run by African American head coaches, such as Nolan Richardson at the University of Arkansas, indicates that the problem is not limited to those programs run by White head coaches.

Information adapted from: ■ Moore, K. (2004, July 1). Tackling illiteracy: Former Washington Redskin Pro Bowl defensive end Dexter Manley keynote speaker, The Connection Newspapers, retrieved November 21, 2005, from www.connectionnewspapers.com/article.asp?archive=true&article=34303&paper=62&cat=109 ■ Outside the lines: Unable to read (2002, May 17), ESPN: Page 2, retrieved November 22, 2005, from http://sports.espn.go.com/page2/tvlistings/show103transcript.html ■ Richardson: "I'm supposed to make a difference" (2002, February 28), ESPN.com, retrieved November 22, 2005, from http://espn.go.com/nbc/s/2002/0228/1342915.html.

R E F L E C T I O N

1. How frequently are cases similar to those of Dexter Manley or Kevin Ross seen today?

2. Is a university "exploiting" a student-athlete if the school provides a scholarship in exchange for the basketball services? Explain your answer.

3. Why do you think graduation rates of African American athletes are lower than those of White athletes competing in similar sports?

4. Are you surprised that some of the programs that graduated none of their African American athletes were run by African American head coaches? Why or why not?

s the Diversity Challenge illustrates, issues of race are still a very important part of sport and physical activity. From an employment standpoint, race can impact the type of job one fills, access to certain jobs, the rate of promotion, and the representation in certain positions. From an athletic standpoint, one's race can influence the sports in which one participates, the positions played, and the treatment received while participating. Even decades after federal legislation outlawing racial discrimination, race influences nearly every aspect of sport and physical activity in some form or fashion.

The purpose of this chapter is to examine the categorical effects of race in greater detail by focusing on the experiences of racial minorities relative to those of Whites. The decision to focus the discussion in this manner was made for two reasons. First, racial oppression was historically a significant factor in the United States. Feagin (2006, p. 2) claims that with its slavery ties (and despite founding documents purporting equality), the United States represents "the only major Western country that was explicitly founded on racial oppression." Similarly, critical race theorists support the case that racial bias is still present today and evidenced in many countries' cultures and major institutions (Hylton, 2009; Ladson-Billings & Tate, 1995; Tate, 1997; for a gripping historical account of the power of institutionalized racism, see Zinn, 2003). These viewpoints suggest that the experiences of racial minorities, as persons who have traditionally been subjugated to discrimination, should be different from those of Whites. Given this, it is instrumental to consider the experiences of racial minorities relative to those of Whites.

In addition, while this discussion will attempt to examine the experiences of all racial minorities, I focus predominantly on African Americans for several reasons. First, although Whites have historically discriminated against every other race, research indicates that discrimination against African Americans has been most insidious (e.g., Agyemang, DeLorme, & Singer, 2010), most egregiously but not limited to slavery and post–Civil War discrimination (i.e., Jim Crow laws) (Sage, 2000; Zinn, 2003). Second, many athletes in high-profile sports are African American, therefore bringing them and their experiences to the fore. Third, and perhaps a function of the first two points, most (though certainly not all) race-related research in sport has focused on the experiences of African Americans. Because of these factors, the discussion here will focus primarily on African Americans. I have provided this rationale in the hope that readers will recognize this focus is a reflection of historical context and available research, and not intended as a dismissal of the experiences of other racial minorities in sport.

In the first section, I define race, ethnicity, and minority group. The influence of race on general employment trends, such as occupational segregation and wages earned, is discussed next, followed by an examination of the factors that influence the underrepresentation of racial minorities in coaching and leadership positions within the sport industry. The chapter concludes with an examination of race with respect to athletic participation.

Defining Race, Ethnicity, and Minority Group

To begin, it is important to understand the definitions of three key terms: race, ethnicity, and minority group (see Thomas & Dyall, 1999). Though race and ethnicity are used interchangeably at times, there are definite distinctions between them. As Eitzen and Sage (2009) explain, "race is a social category regarded as distinct because the members supposedly share some genetically transmitted traits" (p. 291). As this definition of *race* implies, classifying people into different races is based on biological characteristics and on one race's presumed genetic dissimilarity to another. *Ethnicity*, on the other hand, refers to the cultural heritage of a particular group of people, and as such, moves away from attempting to classify people based on biological characteristics (Coakley, 2009; Eitzen & Sage, 2009). Ethnic groups share a common culture, such as a language or dialect, a specific custom, or a shared history (Eitzen & Sage, 2009). Members of a specific ethnic group (e.g., Italian Americans, Irish Americans) share a way of life and have a common commitment to a specific set of norms, ideals, and values structuring that way of life.

Some researchers question the scientific merit of the concept of race, suggesting that such classifications lack validity (Abercrombie, Hill, & Turner, 2000; Littlefield, Lieberman, & Reynolds, 1982). In fact, there are many more similarities than differences among people who are supposed to be from different races. Nevertheless, there are many reasons why its use continues. First, though classifications based on race have little scientific merit from a biological standpoint, there are social meanings attached to the term. As Coakley (2009) explains, the concept of race is ultimately based on socially constructed meanings associated with biological characteristics. In this way, race is a cultural creation. Second, the meanings people attach to race have substantial implications for everyone. The way people are treated, the social systems that are created, and privileges afforded to members of certain social groups are often centered around race. This is consistent with critical race theory, which supposes that racial issues are at the forefront of organizational, political, educational, and other social issues (Hylton, 2009; Ladson-Billings & Tate, 1995; Tate, 1997). It is therefore important to consider race, the meanings people attach to race, and various theories about race in our study of sport and physical activity. For further discussion of how people racially classify themselves, see the Diversity in the Field box on the following page.

DIVERSITY
in the field

Defining Ourselves in Terms of Race? The manner in which people define themselves is complex. For instance, some people consider themselves to be members of a single race while others identify as biracial or multiracial. Consider Tiger Woods, who coined the term "Cablinasian" to refer to his multiple racial identities: Caucasian, Black, (American) Indian, and Asian (see Agyemang et al., 2010). In recognizing this possibility, the 2010 U.S. Census allowed people to mark several racial categories on their census forms to capture precisely how they saw themselves. It is important that people not only be able to accurately identify themselves but, as research suggests, it is also equally important for others to recognize that identity—a process called self verification (Swann, Polzer, Seyle, & Ko, 2004). Within the work setting, others' recognition of important personal identities has been linked with a host of positive outcomes, such as high employee satisfaction and low turnover.

Finally, we must understand the use of the term "minority." A *minority group* is a collection of individuals who share common characteristics and face discrimination in society because of their membership in that group (Coakley, 2009). As Coakley notes, a minority group is simply a "socially identifiable population that suffers disadvantages due to systematic discrimination and has a strong sense of social togetherness based on shared experiences of past and current discrimination" (p. 285; see also Bell, McLaughlin, & Sequeira, 2004). Within the context of this study of sport and physical activity, all members of non-White racial groups, such as African Americans, Hispanics, and so forth, are being considered as racial minorities.

General Racial Trends

To better understand the influence of race in society and the workplace in general, recall from Chapter 1 that the proportions of racial minorities in the United States are increasing, and consequently, the proportion of Whites is decreasing. According to U.S. Census Bureau estimates, though Whites represented 64.7 percent of the population in the year 2010, by 2050, they will account for only 46.3 percent. This growth is particularly evident in several states throughout the United States where minorities are the majority (i.e., California, Hawaii, New Mexico, and Texas). Other nations, such as Canada and New Zealand, have recently witnessed a sizeable growth in the proportion of some racial minority groups as well.

Though racial minorities represent a substantial proportion of the population, their treatment is often poor. In the United States, consider the history of slavery, laws in the 19th and 20th centuries legalizing segregation, the occurrence of race riots such as those in Los Angeles in the 1990s, the continued discrimination in certain sectors of society such as housing, and the increased incidence of hate crimes. According to the U.S. Census Bureau, Hispanics, African Americans, and Native Americans are less likely to graduate from high school or from college than are Whites. With regard to health, research shows that, compared with Whites, African Americans live shorter lives, have almost twice the number of infant mortalities, have lower self-reports of their health, and have a higher incidence of various illnesses, including hypertension, AIDS, diabetes, and certain forms of cancer (Adler & Rehkopf, 2008; Schnittker & McLeod, 2005). Although socioeconomic status has some bearing on these findings, the research found that race also has independent effects (e.g., Williams, 1997). And while there are some variations, there are similar trends for Hispanics and Native Americans (cf., Schnittker & McLeod, 2005). Thus, consistent with Coakley's (2009) definition, racial minorities are likely to be disadvantaged in society in general.

Race in the Employment Context

The negative impact of racism seen in society at large is also observed in the employment context. In the following section, I outline how racism influences earnings, positions held, and employment decisions, and also provide a framework for understanding why these effects take place.

Earnings

U.S. Census Bureau data provide considerable evidence of the earnings differences among various racial groups. As of 2002, African Americans and Hispanics were much more likely to live in poverty (24.1 and 21.8 percent, respectively) than were Asians (10.3 percent) or Whites (8.0 percent). Another indicator of earnings differences is the median household income and how such incomes vary based on the householder's race. Incomes were highest for Asian householders ($51,908) and lowest for African American householders ($29,423). Whites ($45,367) and Hispanics ($33,676) fell in between those two median incomes. Not surprisingly, the same pattern emerges when we examine the median income across the races (see Exhibit 4.1). Asians reported the highest median income ($52,285), followed by Whites ($46,900), Hispanics ($33,103), and African Americans ($29,177). These data also indicate that Whites are much more likely to earn at least $50,000 (47.4 percent) than Hispanics (31.6 percent) or African Americans (27.2 percent) (see Exhibit 4.2). These figures demonstrate the influence of race on monies earned, as in each case, Hispanics and African Americans earned less than their White counterparts.

Median incomes by racial group. *exhibit* **4.1**

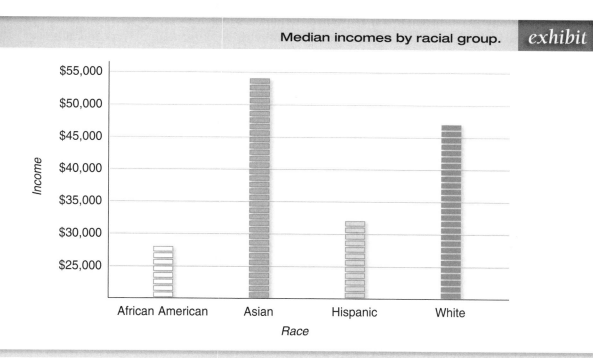

U. S. Census Bureau data.

exhibit **4.2**   **Percentage of persons earning at least $50,000 by racial group.**

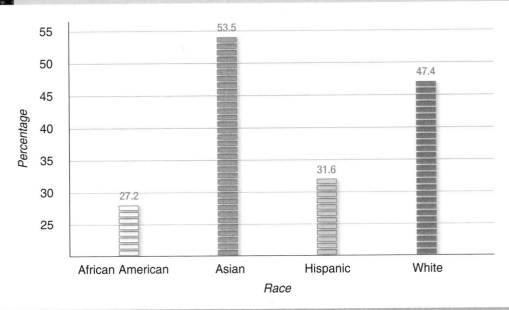

U. S. Census Bureau data.

Differences in compensation are also observed in the sport context. For example, Hamilton (1997) examined the salaries of NBA players for the 1994–1995 season. No racial differences were present when looking at all players and all salary ranges. However, a more in-depth analysis revealed that, among the players receiving the highest salaries, the average White high earner earned 18 percent more than his African American counterpart. Further analyses revealed that the general manager's race (i.e., the person who negotiates the salaries) *did not* influence compensation levels. Similar results have been observed across a variety of sports and among professional sport team coaches (Pattnayak & Leonard, 1994).

Representation of Racial Minorities

The representation of racial minorities in sport organizations is mixed and depends largely on the context (i.e., professional sport versus university athletics) and the particular race. Lapchick's *Racial and Gender Report Card* is a publication devoted to tracking the representation of women and minorities in various sport entities. Grades are assigned to the professional leagues and university athletics based on the proportion of persons of color in the league or university relative to their representation in the general U.S. population. In his *2008 Report Card,* Lapchick assigned the following grades:

- National Basketball Association = A+
- National Football League = B+
- Major League Baseball = A−

- Major League Soccer = A
- Women's National Basketball Association = A
- University Athletics = C+

In many cases, Lapchick notes differences within a specific context. For example, within university athletics, Lapchick wrote that Whites domination of key positions negatively influences the representation of racial minorities; however, this was not evident in other sport contexts.

Coaches at the pro and collegiate levels

Lapchick's work is widely cited in both the popular media, such as ESPN, and in academic works, and his work has made a substantial contribution to the field. It is possible, however, that Lapchick's assessments are overly generous. Recall that grades in the *Report Card* are assigned based on the representation of persons of color in the league or university relative to the proportion of those persons in the general population. This rationale is based on affirmative action guidelines set by the federal government. However, from a practical standpoint, not all people in a population have an equal chance to enter a particular league or sport, especially as a coach. Rather, many researchers argue that former players represent the largest pool of potential coaches (e.g., Everhart & Chelladurai, 1998). Research continues to support this contention, and most present coaches once participated in university athletics (Cunningham & Sagas, 2002). Therefore, the comparison should be to the proportion of racial minorities who played that sport (Cunningham & Sagas, 2005), not to the proportion of racial minorities in the general U.S. population. When this approach is adopted, a much different picture emerges related to coaches.

Using professional sports as an example (see Exhibit 4.3), in the NBA, persons of color represented 80 percent of all the players during the 2007–2008 season. This percentage has remained relatively stable over the years—persons of color representing 79 percent of the players in the 1993–1994 season, for example. Despite the large proportion of racial minorities as players, they represented only 40 percent of the head coaches and 42 percent of the assistant coaches. Of course, many factors contribute to the selection of head coach, of which only one may be previous playing experience. There are some head coaches, such as Laurence Franks of the New Jersey Nets, who did not play at the professional level. However, such a large difference in the proportion of minority players relative to the proportion of minority coaches suggests that racial identity may play a role in selecting head and assistant coaches.

The numbers are even more disproportionate when we examine other sports. In the NFL, racial minorities represented 69 percent of the participants during the 2007 season—but only 19 percent of the head coaches and 36 percent of the assistant coaches (Lapchick, 2008). During the 2006–2007 academic year, racial minority athletes represented over 40 percent of all football players (DeHass, 2008), yet they constituted only 11 percent of the head coaches and 23 percent of the assistant coaches (DeHass, 2007). This trend is also seen in the high school ranks, as evidenced in the Diversity in the Field box on page 77.

Considered together, these figures represent a mixed picture with respect to coaching. On the one hand, basketball, both at the professional and university

Representation of racial minority players and coaches in the 2007–2008 season.

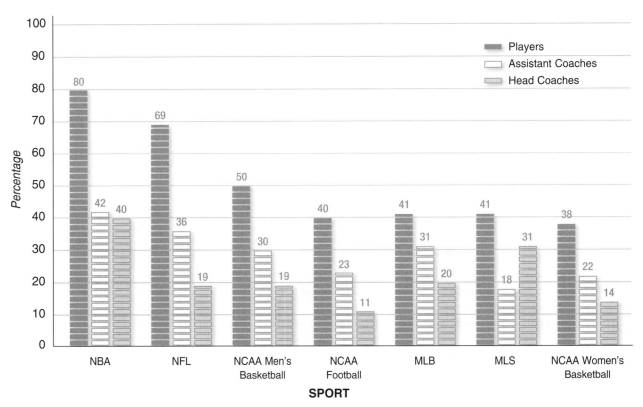

Data from DeHass, 2007, 2008; and Lapchick, 2008.

levels, appears to be relatively open to racial minorities. However, a closer examination of the proportions suggests that relative to the pool of potential coaches (i.e., the athletes), the proportions of racial minorities in coaching positions are lower than might be expected. These differences are further amplified when we consider other sports such as professional and university football. Overall then, it can be argued that minorities are underrepresented in coaching positions.

Administration

In the previous section, I suggested that past playing experience was often a requisite qualification for becoming a coach of a particular team. The same is not necessarily true for administrative positions. Understanding how to navigate the intricacies of a salary cap, knowing how to market a particular product, making personnel decisions, and so on require business acumen more than previous playing experience. Theo Epstein, who is the general manager of the Boston Red Sox, and Jon Daniels, who serves in a similar role for the Texas Rangers—neither of whom had profes-

DIVERSITY
in the field

Underrepresentation of African Americans as High School Coaches. The underrepresentation of African Americans as football head coaches is widely documented in the college and professional ranks. The problem also exists at the high school level—sometimes to a greater degree than in other contexts. Matt Wixon of the *Dallas Morning News* documented this trend (Wixon, 2006). Specifically, Wixon found that although minorities might have access to positions in inner-city schools, they are often not afforded opportunities in suburban schools. In 2002, of the 66 Class 5A and 4A (the two largest classifications in Texas) football teams in the Dallas area, only 4 were led by an African American. The numbers grew even bleaker in 2006, as only 3 of 72 teams had an African American head coach.

Coaches and athletic directors in the area surveyed by Wixon pointed to several contributing factors. Mike Robinson, an African American head coach at Hillcrest, said that "It wasn't what you've done or what you know. It's who you know." Garland ISD athletic director Homer Johnson acknowledged this possibility when he suggested that some coaches do not get hired because the athletic directors do not know them that well.

Others suggested that African American coaches lack experience. Joe Barnett, the Irving ISD athletic director, suggested that "sometimes maybe they [African Americans] don't have the experience because they haven't been given the opportunity somewhere else. It's hard to get that experience if you don't get hired. It's a Catch-22."

Although the lack of experience may impede the progress of some coaches, there are other instances where very qualified assistant coaches were not afforded the chance to become a head coach. Dallas Carter football coach Allen Wilson is one such example. Despite serving as an assistant coach on two state championship teams and having 19 years of experience, Wilson has repeatedly been denied a head coaching position.

The effects of continually being passed over for head coaching positions can have a harmful effect on African Americans. Kendall Miller, an African American who serves as the offensive coordinator at Lincoln High School, has applied for five positions over the past two years, only to be passed over each time. He suggested that there is a "feeling of restriction" when it comes to the schools at which one can become a head coach. He explained that "after a while, it makes you think, 'Why go through with it?' because you've seen the track record. But at the same time, you have to make yourself go through with it because you don't want to allow the excuse, 'Well, they're not applying.'" Thus, despite the lack of opportunity, these African American high school coaches continue to press forward in their quest for head coaching opportunities.

sional playing experience—both exemplify this point. Therefore, all persons have as much of an opportunity to be an administrator of a sport organization as they do in any other organization. Because the opportunity is available to everyone, it is possible to use the proportion of racial minorities in the general U.S. population (35.3 percent in 2010) as a comparison marker when examining the proportion of minorities in administrative positions in sport organizations.

Even using this more conservative comparison point, the data still suggest that minorities are underrepresented in administrative positions. As shown by the following statistics, the majority of the senior administrators in all professional leagues and university athletics are White (DeHass, 2007; Lapchick, 2008):

- National Basketball Association: 77 percent
- National Football League: 83 percent

- Major League Baseball: 93 percent
- Major League Soccer: 92 percent
- Women's National Basketball Association: 79 percent
- National Collegiate Athletic Association: 90 percent

These figures illustrate that Whites are overrepresented as senior administrators within sport organizations (77–93 percent) relative to what is expected based on their proportion in the general U.S. population (64.7 percent). As with the coaching positions, racial minorities are underrepresented as senior administrators.

Occupational Segregation

According to Cokley, Dreher, and Stockdale (2004), *occupational segregation* is "the extent to which individuals of various racial/ethnic backgrounds are disproportionately represented in various occupational groupings" (p. 170). The U.S. Census Bureau developed a taxonomy of six occupational groups:

1. management and professional;
2. service;
3. sales and office;
4. farming, fishing, and forestry;
5. construction, extraction, and maintenance; and
6. production, transportation, and material moving.

These six groups are further broken down into 509 occupational categories. For purposes of this discussion, we will examine the influence of race on the proportion of people only in the six major occupational categories.

Data from the 2000 Census indicate that there are differences in the positions people hold based on their race. For example, both African Americans and Hispanics are most likely to hold sales or office jobs (27.3 and 23.1 percent, respectively), while Whites are most likely to hold management, professional, and related positions (36.6 percent). Only 25.2 percent of African Americans and 18.1 percent of Hispanics reported having a management-type job. Furthermore, African Americans (22.0 percent) and Hispanics (21.8 percent) were more likely than Whites (12.8 percent) to hold service jobs.

This disproportion, or occupational segregation, also occurs in the sport context. Using football as an example, racial minorities are likely to coach running backs and wide receivers (Anderson, 1993) and unlikely to serve as a coordinator of the defense or offense (DeHass, 2007). There is also some sentiment among minority football coaches that they are hired primarily to aid in the recruitment of minority athletes, not necessarily for their coaching expertise (Brown, 2002). There is also evidence that this trend is continuing, as African American coaches are more likely to be hired to positions with a high concentration of African American athletes (i.e., running back, wide receiver, and defensive back; Cunningham & Bopp, 2010). Similar findings occur in the basketball context. Research shows that on basketball coaching staffs, Whites are significantly more likely to hold the first assistant position than African Americans; the second assistant position is more likely to be filled by an African American (Cunningham & Sagas, 2004a).

Similar trends exist among university athletic administrators. Data from the NCAA (DeHass, 2007) indicate that racial minorities are more likely to hold positions that involve contact with athletes, such as academic advisor (26.3 percent) or life skills coordinator (25.1 percent), than they are to hold positions dealing with budgetary or administrative duties. Only 12.7 percent of all business managers and 10.0 percent of all head athletic directors are racial minorities. Together, these data suggest that persons of color are likely to be "pigeonholed" into certain types of jobs, both in the coaching and administrative areas. Indeed, qualitative research suggests that administrators are aware of this occupational segregation process and point to discrimination, dubious hiring practices, a lack of career role models, and limited social networks as explanations for this occurrence (McDowell, Cunningham, & Singer, 2009).

Reasons for Racial Minority Underrepresentation

This section examines the reasons for racial minority underrepresentation. The discussion here focuses on the underrepresentation in coaching positions, though many of the identified factors can be used to explain the underrepresentation in administrative positions.

Cunningham (2010) suggested that the underrepresentation of racial minorities in coaching positions could best be understood from a multi-level perspective, taking into account factors at the macro- (i.e., institutionalized practices, political climate, stakeholder expectations), meso- (i.e., prejudice on the part of decision makers, discrimination, leadership prototypes, organizational culture of diversity), and micro-levels (i.e., head coaching expectations and intentions, occupational turnover intentions). Consistent with a systems theory approach (Chelladurai, 2009; Kozlowski & Klein, 2000), the factors at each level are also thought to influence one another. An illustrative summary is presented in Exhibit 4.4, and the model's underlying tenets are presented in the following sections.

Multi-level explanation for the underrepresentation of African American coaches.

exhibit **4.4**

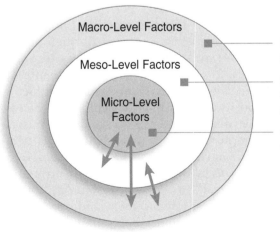

(institutionalized practices, political climate, stakeholder expectations)

(prejudice on the part of decision makers, discrimination, leadership prototypes, organizational culture of diversity)

(head coaching expectations and intentions, occupational turnover intentions)

Adapted from Cunningham (2010).

Macro-level factors

Macro-level explanations for the under-representation of African American head coaches focus on those elements external to the specific athletic department but which still exert considerable influence on that entity. Cunningham (2010) identified three such factors: institutionalized practices, political climate, and stakeholder expectations.

Institutionalized practices. Activities are said to be institutionalized when, as a result of habit, history, and tradition, they become standardized and unquestionably accepted as "the way things are done" (Scott, 2001). Because of various legitimizing factors, over time, sport organizations are likely to adopt similar institutional practices and activities, thereby coming to resemble one another (see Kikulis, 2000; DiMaggio & Powell, 1983). As sport organizations continue to adhere to these institutionalized ways of doing things, the practices become further embedded, habituated, and perpetuated. Thus, they become the "obvious" or "normal" way in which organizational activities are completed. As Zucker (1987) noted, institutional activities "are maintained over long periods of time without further justification or elaboration, and are highly resistant to change" (p. 446).

In many ways, racism in the United States is institutionalized. Recall from the discussion earlier in the chapter that the United States is the only Western country whose origins are directly linked with racial prejudice and oppression (Feagin, 2006) and consequently, as Feagin argues, racism has been systemic in the country. Such a perspective is also congruent with critical race theory, which holds that racism is embedded into the fabric of U.S. society (Ladson-Billings & Tate, 1995; Tate, 1997). Indeed, the ways in which public schools are organized and financed, the prevalence of racial profiling among many enforcement agencies, informal job selection processes favoring "fit" over qualifications, health care provisions, the organization of the U.S. legal system, and even the notion of meritocracy all operate in ways that privilege Whites while casting persons of color as "others" (Applebaum, 2003; Coates, 2003; McIntosh, 1990; Williams, 2004).

Sport is not exempt from institutionalized racism (Hylton, 2009; Long, Robinson, & Spracklen, 2005; Singer, 2005a, 2005b). Racist ideologies that promote Whites as smarter, more ethical, and better leaders than persons of color are perpetuated on a continual basis (Coakley, 2009). These stereotypical prejudices have been intact for centuries (Rader, 1999) and are transmitted through media outlets (Buffington, 2005; Woodward, 2004) and expressed to others through language and socialization tactics (Coakley, 2009). As a result, the racism that continues to persist in sport denigrates and subjugates African American athletes and coaches (Sailes, 2000), limits the positions to which athletes have access (Sack, Singh, & Thiel, 2005), and most relevant to the current discussion, thwarts racial minority coaches' opportunities and advancement (Anderson, 1993; McDowell & Cunningham, 2007). Not surprisingly, Yale head football coach Tom Williams, an African American, described the painfully slow pace of diversity-related change in university athletics as "glacial" (as cited in Robinson, 2009). All of these factors have served to limit the career advancement and opportunities of African Americans, thereby resulting in their underrepresentation in head coaching positions.

Political climate. The political climate is another societal factor thought to influence the representation of coaches of color (Cunningham, 2010). The prevailing political climate of an administration or time, coupled with the accompanying social dynamics, influence sport in a number of ways, including the public funding of sport facilities (Crompton, 1995), the empowerment (or lack thereof) of unions (Abercrombie et al., 2000), educational opportunities (West & Currie, 2008), and diversity-related activities and initiatives. As legislative examples, the Civil Rights Act of 1964, which, among other achievements, guaranteed employment protection for women and racial minorities in the United States, and the Voting Rights Act of 1965, which ensured the voting privileges of racial minorities, were both signed into law under President Lyndon Johnson, who was a member of the more progressive Democrat party. On the other hand, some conservative presidencies have been marked by attempts to reduce equal opportunities; for example, federal administrators sought to limit the scope of Title IX, which mandates equal opportunities for girls and women in federally funded educational activities, during both President Ronald Reagan's and President George W. Bush's administrations.

The political environment also impacts equal employment opportunities and the enforcement of laws governing such activities (Marshall, 2005; Ogmundson, 2005; Saguy, 2002). For instance, enforcement of equal employment legislation and fair labor practices is thought to be more stringent when the political climate is more progressive than conservative. Cunningham and Benavides-Espinoza (2008) found support for this contention in their analysis of sexual harassment, as the claims filed with federal agencies mirrored the political environment in the United States during that time. In discussing the nature of their findings, the authors concluded that "the actions and social policies of the President of the United States may set the tone for the political environment, and in a related way, the emphasis on civil rights" (p. 781).

In drawing from this literature, Cunningham (2010) argued that the political climate is also likely to influence the proportion of racial minority head coaches. In more progressive environments, opportunities for coaches of color should increase, while the same is not necessarily the case in conservative political environments. Anecdotal evidence supports this contention: at Ivy League schools, which are located in the more progressive East Coast of the U.S., nearly 50 percent (7 of 16) of the football and men's basketball coaches are African American—a percentage far greater than any other athletic conference (Robinson, 2009). Time will tell if the election of Barack Obama, a Democrat and a person of color, as the 45th President of the United States will result in greater opportunities for racial minorities in coaching and leadership positions.

Stakeholder expectations. Stakeholder expectations represent a third macro-level factor influencing the underrepresentation of racial minorities in coaching positions (Cunningham, 2010). Stakeholders are key constituent groups who are both influenced by and can influence organizational activities (Freeman, 1984). Within university athletics, stakeholders might include coaches, administrators, faculty, athletes, alumni, boosters, community members, and so on. From a strategic management perspective, gaining insights into and addressing the perceptions, needs, and wants of key strategic stakeholder groups can result in optimal organization-environment fit, thereby increasing the success the organization enjoys.

Alumni and boosters represent two stakeholder groups that have particular influence on athletic department operations, including personnel decisions. As one key indicator of how influential these stakeholders are, consider that nearly a quarter (24 percent) of all revenues at NCAA Football Bowl Subdivision athletic departments came from alumni and booster donations (Fulks, 2008). This amounts to roughly $8.5 million in annual monies. This money is rarely altruistically donated; instead, it comes with strings attached (Sperber, 2000). Indeed, given their tremendous financial influence, the persuasive power of alumni and boosters is undeniable.

Economic reliance on alumni and boosters influences employment decisions because there is a perceived need to have employees with whom these stakeholders can identify. This perceived need is most heightened when hiring coaches, particularly those who coach football—a sport that has been referred to as the "front porch" of an institution (Beyer & Hannah, 2000). As Michael Rosenberg of the *Detroit Free Press* (2004) noted:

> It is largely about money. It is about a face to show the alumni, especially the ones with big wallets. College coaches don't just coach; they are, in many ways, the public faces of their schools. And if the big donors don't like a coach because of his weight/accent/skin color, schools will stay away.

Lapchick drew similar conclusions:

> I have had discussions with people in searches for coaches and athletic directors that the final decision was made to hire a White male because they were afraid their alumni, who also happen to be strong boosters of the football program, would not contribute nearly as much or as readily to an African American athletic director or football coach. (as cited in Wong, 2002, p. 1)

These quotations illustrate the need for boosters to (a) identify with the head coaches and (b) to give large sums of money to support the department's activities, two factors that may result in preference for White coaches over coaches of color.

Meso-level factors

Meso-level factors operate at the organizational level, influencing ways in which decisions are made, the structures in place, and the internal processes. Cunningham (2010) suggested that four meso-level factors influenced the underrepresentation of racial minority coaches: prejudice, discrimination, leadership prototypes, and organizational cultures of diversity.

Prejudice. As noted in Chapter 3, prejudice can take two primary forms: explicit and implicit. Although it still exists, explicit racial prejudice is seen as socially unacceptable, and people's willingness to publicly express such hatred has decreased over time (Campbell, 1947; Dowden & Robinson, 1993). In its place is implicit prejudice, and more specifically, aversive racism (Dovidio & Gaertner, 2004; Gaertner & Dovidio, 2000). Aversive racists are people who consciously and sincerely support egalitarian ideals and do not believe that they personally harbor prejudiced feelings toward racial minorities; nonetheless, these persons unconsciously have feelings of unease toward historically disadvantaged groups and therefore seek to avoid interracial interactions. When such interactions are unavoidable, aversive racists will experience anxiety and discomfort and will also try to end the interaction as quickly as possible. Finally, aversive racists' behaviors differ from those of "old fashioned" racists. Unlike the "old fashioned" racist, who will openly discriminate, aversive racists will not discriminate in situations with strong social norms or when the discriminatory acts could be attributed to the self. Rather, aversive racists will tend to discriminate when the normative structure is weak, when there are vague guidelines for the appropriate course of action, and when a negative response can be attributed to a factor other than race (Gaertner & Dovidio, 2000, 2005). This dynamic is what Son Hing Chung-Yan, Hamilton, and Zanna (2008) refer to as the attributional-ambiguity effect.

As noted in Chapter 3, while the underlying processes might differ, one outcome of both aversive and "old fashioned" racism is the same: truncated career opportunities of racial minorities. Research from Dovidio and Gaertner (2000) shows that aversive racists discriminate against racial minorities in subtle ways during the selection process—a finding that has remained over time. Hodson, Dovidio, and Gaertner (2002) showed how this takes place. Specifically, they found that the differences in recommendations were based on the way the raters viewed the supporting materials. When prejudiced Whites reviewed the minority's materials, they were likely to weigh the weaker portions of the packet (e.g., standardized test scores) as more meaningful and important than they did when reviewing the Whites' packets. Thus, the standards shifted to accommodate the racially biased decision in such a way that the rater would not be viewed negatively. Similar findings have been observed with legal decisions made by jurors (Hodson, Hooper, Dovidio, & Gaertner, 2005).

Cunningham (2010) pointed to these findings to buttress his argument that prejudice limits the number of coaches of color. Specifically, when job applicants are clearly qualified or clearly unqualified, racial bias is unlikely to influence the decision. However, most coaching searches are not this unequivocal. On any given search, many coaches (sometimes hundreds) apply, and these persons have varying strengths and weaknesses—opening the door to ambiguous interpretation, which is only heightened by a lack of standardized selection procedures. This situation neatly fits the conditions enabling aversive racism to manifest: when the normative structure is weak, guidelines for apposite behavior are ambiguous, and potentially controversial decisions can be justified with other supporting evidence (Dovidio & Gaertner, 2004; Gaertner & Dovidio, 2000). Thus, the prevailing norms, processes, and structures for hiring coaches of university athletic teams create situations ripe for aversive racism to prevail and for African Americans to continue to be underrepresented in those employment roles.

Discrimination. Cunningham (2010) further argues that discrimination will limit the representation of racial minorities in the coaching ranks. Recall from Chapter 3 that Greenhaus, Parasuraman, and Wormley (1990) identified two forms of discrimination: access discrimination, which prevents members of a particular group from entering a particular job, organization, or profession, and treatment discrimination, which "occurs when subgroup members receive fewer rewards, resources, or opportunities on the job than they legitimately deserve on the basis of job-related criteria" (Greenhaus et al., 1990, pp. 64–65).

The data presented in Exhibit 4.3 illustrate that African Americans have limited access to coaching positions across a variety of sports, and one might conclude from these data alone that access discrimination is present. What the statistics do not convey, however, is whether or not access to the coaching positions is dependent upon the race of the head coach. This is an important distinction because access discrimination is concerned with limiting opportunities for members of historically underrepresented groups (Greenhaus et al., 1990); thus, if access discrimination is truly present, then differences should be observed between the racial compositions of the coaching staffs guided by Whites and those guided by African Americans.

Cunningham and Sagas (2005) provided evidence of this in their study of men's basketball coaching staffs. In drawing from the notion that former players represent the best pool of potential coaches, they compared the proportion of assistant coaches of color on the staff to the corresponding percentage of all former men's basketball players who had graduated (48 percent). Their results were telling. Overall, African Americans represented only 33 percent of all assistant coaches— a proportion significantly less than the 48 percent standard. The results varied considerably, however, when the race of the head coach was taken into account. African Americans comprised just 30 percent of the coaches on staffs headed by a White head coach but represented 45 percent of the coaches on staffs headed by an African American. This pattern suggests that the underrepresentation of African Americans was due to their lack of access to coaching positions when the head coach was White. Equally striking, among the staffs guided by a White head coach, *one in six* (or 16.2 percent) did not have any assistant coaches of color.

These findings inform our discussion of head coaches, too. When the race of the person charged with making personnel selections influences the race of those hired to the staff, this is particularly meaningful in discussions about head coaches. After all, 90 percent of all athletic directors are White (DeHass, 2007), and thus, pro-similarity bias is likely to be highly prevalent when hiring head coaches. There is some evidence to support this latter point, and as a participant in one qualitative study noted, "Administrators hire White coaches because the vast majority of administrators are White" (as cited in Brown, 2002). Powell (2008) advanced similar arguments, albeit from a different perspective: "As long as blacks are unable to hold true power in sports, the issue of hiring will remain" (p. 213). Collectively, these dynamics limit the access racial minorities have to head coaching positions.

Treatment discrimination also negatively affects coaches of color. The available research suggests that racial minority coaches face open hostility from opposing team players (Lawrence, 2004), are valued more for their ability to recruit and associate with athletes (most of whom are African American) than for their coaching talents (Brown, 2002; Cunningham & Bopp, 2010), and do not receive just returns for the networks they have developed or the experience and education they have accumulated (Sagas & Cunningham, 2005; Sartore & Cunningham, 2006; for additional information related to the importance of networks, see the Professional Perspectives box).

Furthermore, the failures of minority coaches are often painted as indicative of all minority coaches, while the same is not true for Whites (Wojciechowski, 2008). In commenting on this dynamic, Wojciechowski wrote that "the trickle-down effect is that skittish university presidents and athletic directors can use those failures as an excuse not to hire head coaches." In the same article, University at

Buffalo athletic director Warde Manuel further noted the apparent contradiction by adding, "If a White person is not successful in a particular position, that doesn't mean that another White person would not be successful" (as cited in Wojciechowski, 2008). The differential treatment of, and adjustable standards applied to, African Americans is characteristic of treatment discrimination (Greenhaus et al., 1990) and perpetuates their underrepresentation.

Leadership stereotypes. In addition to prejudice and discrimination, leadership stereotypes are also thought to negatively impact racial minorities' job prospects (Cunningham, 2010). According to leadership categorization theory (Lord & Maher, 1991), people develop mindsets of who they think is a typical leader, and they use these ideas to develop ideas about prototypical leaders. They then use these prototypes when evaluating potential leaders: those who possess the "typical" characteristics are considered a good fit, and those who do not have those characteristics receive negative evaluations.

Rosette, Leonardelli, and Phillips (2008) drew from this perspective to investigate the intersection of race and leadership. These authors suggested that "at least in the United States, a central characteristic of leadership is 'being White' and accordingly, evaluators will perceive that White leaders are more prototypical business leaders than are leaders who are racial minorities" (p. 759). There is some evidence to support as much. People consistently see Whites in leadership positions within business and the public sector. This pattern has been consistently observed throughout U.S. history, where political (44 of the 45 presidents) and business leaders (e.g., John D. Rockefeller, Steve Jobs, Warren Buffett) have predominantly been White. This historical conditioning shapes how people perceive potential leaders and who they think should hold leadership roles. Indeed, Rosette et al. found that Whiteness was seen as a prototype for business leaders—though not necessarily for everyday employees—and White leaders were considered to be more effective than leaders of color, especially when the organization's success was attributed to the leader.

In drawing from this work, Cunningham (2010) suggested that coaches of color might be *perceived* as ill-suited for head coaching roles. These expectations are influenced by the color of people who have historically been seen in these roles and who are therefore believed best suited to handle these responsibilities (Rosette et al., 2008). Consider, for instance, that Whites have historically held the primary leadership and coaching positions on athletic teams (for recent trends, see DeHass, 2007), and, as former head coach Fitz Hill has commented "You say you're trying to find the best person for the job, but when you do that you don't have a qualified

PROFESSIONAL PERSPECTIVES

Creating and Maintaining Networks. Gary Sailes is an applied sport sociologist who has considerable experience consulting with athletes and teams. His expertise and primary research interests are in the area of racial issues in university and professional sports. When asked what racial minorities could do to advance in the profession, Sailes indicated that networking was most important. "People hire people who they know. It's that simple. I don't care if you're Black, White, male, female, ethnic minority, or majority, people hire who they know. So you have to get yourself out there and meet the people who are doing the hiring," Sailes explained. Networking provides many advantages. It affords more visibility and provides greater access to information. In addition, Sailes believes that because networking allows people to know the applicant on a more personal level, any personal biases held by the decision maker may be overcome. As he notes, "This will go a long ways toward your advancement."

African American picture that comes to mind" (as cited in Brown, 2002). Thus, the historical trends shape people's perceptions about who *can* and *cannot* fill particular roles, and they continue to contribute to an underrepresentation of African American head coaches.

Organizational culture. Cunningham (2010) suggested that organizational culture represented the final meso-level factor influencing racial minorities' coaching opportunities. According to Schein (1990), organizational culture refers to the basic assumptions and beliefs in the workplace that are passed down over time and considered valid by most of the employees. It is manifested through observable artifacts, values, and basic assumptions. In short, the culture represents the underlying values of a workplace.

Organizational culture can have a meaningful impact on employee experiences and organizational performance (see Cunningham, 2009). Indeed, research suggests that athletic departments characterized by a culture of diversity and inclusion are likely to have diversity enmeshed into all organizational activities, likely to create mentoring and development opportunities, and likely to have proactive top management leadership who engage in bold recruitment and attraction strategies (Cunningham & Singer, 2009). Such workplaces stand in stark contrast to those with a culture of similarity (e.g., Doherty & Chelladurai, 1999; Fink & Pastore, 1999)—those with closed membership, homologous leadership teams, unstructured hiring and promotion standards, and a view of diversity as a liability rather than an asset. Indeed, cultures of diversity and inclusion are needed to address the underrepresentation of African American head coaches.

Micro-level factors

In addition to macro-level and meso-level factors, micro-level factors, or those pertaining to the individual, also influence the underrepresentation of racial minority coaches. These are manifested in head coaching expectations and intentions and in turnover intentions (Cunningham, 2010).

Head coaching expectations and intentions. Social cognitive career theory holds that people's career choices are shaped by a myriad of factors, including perceived barriers, supports, self-efficacy, and outcome expectations (Lent, Brown, & Hackett, 1994). This framework has proved helpful in understanding if and when athletes choose to pursue coaching after graduation. Various studies have shown that student-athletes of color foresee considerable barriers in the coaching profession, that their race will hinder their advancement, and that they will have few professional role models on which to lean for support (Cunningham, 2004; Cunningham & Singer, 2010; Kamphoff & Gill, 2008). Nevertheless, racial minority student athletes still anticipate high levels of satisfaction and strong intentions to enter the profession (Cunningham & Singer, 2010). Their desire stems from the belief that although discrimination will persist, the benefits of coaching (e.g., remaining involved in the sport, mentoring other student athletes) outweigh the costs.

Assistant coaches of color have expressed similar outlooks when asked about their head coaching prospects. Across a number of studies and samples, African Americans have indicated that they experience racial discrimination, have truncated advancement opportunities, and enjoy less career satisfaction than their counterparts (Cunningham & Sagas, 2004b, 2007; Cunningham, Bruening, & Straub, 2006; Sagas & Cunningham, 2005). These effects are especially pronounced among football coaches, and there is little doubt why, when one considers the sparse representation African Americans have had as head coaches of that sport (see Exhibit 4.3).

Despite these poor work experiences, racial minority assistant coaches, like the student-athletes they coach, have persistently expressed firm intentions to pursue and apply for head coaching intentions (Cunningham et al., 2006). Thus, despite the data suggesting that doing so might be a fruitless endeavor, coupled with a history of facing prejudice and discrimination during their career, racial minorities continue to pursue leadership positions. As one coach commented, "after a while, it makes you think, 'Why go through with it?' because you've seen the track record. But at the same time, you have to make yourself go through with it because you don't want to allow the excuse, 'Well, they're not applying'" (as cited in Wixon, 2006).

Turnover intentions. Finally, although limited advancement opportunities and repeated discrimination do not quell minority coaches' aspirations to be a head coach, there is some evidence that these factors do contribute to their career longevity. Across a number of studies in different contexts, racial minorities indicate that they plan on leaving coaching earlier than Whites (Cunningham & Sagas, 2004b, 2007; Cunningham et al., 2006, Cunningham, Sagas, & Ashley, 2001). A number of factors contribute to this trend, including health concerns (Cunningham et al., 2006), a lack of time with family (Cunningham et al., 2006), a lack of advancement opportunities (Cunningham & Sagas, 2004b, 2007), low career satisfaction (Cunningham & Sagas, 2004b, 2007), and treatment discrimination (Cunningham & Sagas, 2007).

Racial differences in occupational turnover can have serious repercussions, not the least of which is a potential supply-side shortage of African Americans to fill head coaching positions. As Tsui and Gutek (1999) articulated, "small effects could accumulate and lead to non-trivial consequences. For example, a small tendency for the most different groups to leave can, over time, result in increasingly more homogeneous groups as one moves up the organizational hierarchy" (p. 40). The data presented in Exhibit 4.3 support this contention: In most coaching contexts, the proportion of African Americans trends negatively the higher up the organizational hierarchy they move (i.e., from player to assistant coach to head coach). When the differential turnover rate is coupled with the macro- and meso-level factors already working against their advancement, a picture explaining the underrepresentation of African Americans in coaching positions becomes crystallized.

Race and Employee Outcomes in Other Contexts

Thus far, the focus has been primarily on employees in the university athletics context. Though many of the overall trends are similar to those experienced by coaches and administrators, it is also useful to consider the effects of race on employees in other contexts, such as professors of color in higher education. Lavigne (2003) demonstrated that the proportion of racial minorities in faculty positions lags behind national population trends. In a similar way, Turner, Myers, and

PROFESSIONAL
P E R S P E C T I V E S

Knowing the Language. Buffy Filippell is the President of Teamwork Online, LLC, an organization aimed at identifying and recruiting individuals for jobs in the sport industry. According to Filippell, sport organizations are making concerted efforts to diversify. As she explains, "There is a real push on behalf of the professional sports organizations that I'm familiar with to really try to reach out and capture as many diverse candidates and female candidates as possible." This push is much more intense than in years past. In addition to demographic diversity, sport organizations are increasingly looking to employ people who know a variety of languages. Filippell explains that for some sport organizations in the southwestern and western areas of the United States, such as Arizona and California, it is imperative that an employee be bilingual because much of the customer base is primarily Spanish-speaking. Thus, many forms of diversity are needed to ensure that sport organizations operate effectively and efficiently.

Creswell (1999) found that African Americans, Native Americans, and Latinos are underrepresented in faculty positions and that they receive poorer compensation than Asians or Whites. The same is true for faculty in kinesiology and physical education programs. Hodge and Stroot (1997) found that encountering racism is a fact of life among African American graduate students and faculty members in physical education programs. The racism is believed to manifest from the White undergraduate students, faculty members, and persons in the community. In a different study, Burden, Harrison, and Hodge (2005) interviewed nine African American physical education faculty members concerning the faculty members' experiences on primarily White campuses. In framing their study from a critical race theory perspective, these authors found that the faculty members experienced social isolation, were perceived as intellectually inferior, and were marginalized. These studies, and others like them, paint a consistent picture of racial minority faculty members facing considerable obstacles on university campuses.

Issues of race are also prevalent among people working in the recreation profession. Allison and Hibbler's (2004) qualitative study of recreational professionals illustrates this point. Professionals in their study argued that the racial makeup of the community in which the recreational agency operates should inform hiring decisions. As one professional noted, "I'm not saying that if you're in a barrio that's 95 percent Hispanic, that every single staff person should be Hispanic, but you should have a good representation of Hispanics on that staff" (p. 269). Similar sentiments were expressed concerning the language spoken (see the Professional Perspectives box). The professionals also noted that if there was a desire to design a program emphasizing diversity, it was left to the agency's racial minority members to design the program. Such programs were seldom seen as central or integral to the agency's functioning.

The Influence of Race on Participation in Sport

Race plays an influential role among sport participants, just as it does in sport and physical activity organizations. It influences the kinds of sports in which people participate, the positions they play on athletic teams, the stereotypes and attitudes toward athletes, athletes' treatment, and athletes' careers. Each of these issues is discussed in turn (see Exhibit 4.5).

| The influence of race on participants' experiences. | *exhibit* 4.5 |

Sport and leisure participation:

■ Race influences the amount of participation and in which sport one participates. Other factors that contribute to sport and leisure participation include socioeconomic status and cultural norms.

Positions played on athletic teams:

■ Racial minorities are overrepresented in some positions and underrepresented in others, a phenomenon known as stacking.

Stereotypes and attitudes:

■ People develop stereotypes about sport participants related to their cognitive and "natural" athletic abilities.

Athlete treatment:

■ Racial minority athletes are often treated differently than their White counterparts in such areas as academic advising, graduation rates, treatment by administrators and coaches, opportunities for sport participation, and life after sports.

Sport and Leisure Participation

Historically, slavery, racism, and segregation limited the participation of racial minorities in sport. More recently, race influences sport participation primarily through two dynamics: social class and cultural norms. First, one's discretionary income influences the amount of time spent working or engaged in other activities, including sport and exercise. As previously noted, many racial minorities have less discretionary income than Whites, and this difference corresponds to the differing participation levels between the two groups (Hibbler & Shinew, 2002). Second, the prevailing cultural norms influence sport participation by sending signals about what is popular and appropriate (Eitzen & Sage, 2009). These norms influence why some sports (e.g., snow skiing) are more popular among some groups (i.e., Whites) than other sports.

Positions Played on Athletic Teams

Race influences the positions employees hold in organizations, and it influences the positions athletes play on teams. This phenomenon, called *stacking*, occurs when "minority athletes are overrepresented in some playing positions and underrepresented in others" (Sack et al., 2005, pp. 300–301). Research demonstrates that stacking exists across a variety of contexts, including baseball (Gonzales, 1996), rugby (Hallinan, 1991), and hockey (Lavoie, 1989; see also the Alternative Perspectives box).

Why stacking occurs, however, is less clear. From one perspective (i.e., social closure theory), decision makers intentionally discriminate against athletes of color, ensuring that the high-status jobs are reserved for Whites. From the human capital perspective, however, positions are assigned based on the skills and abilities athletes possess. Sack and colleagues (2005) tested these two theories in the MLB context. As expected, most (71 percent) of the African Americans played in the outfield,

alternative
P E R S P E C T I V E S

Is It Really Stacking? Although many studies support the existence of stacking in various sport contexts, others question the premise behind stacking. Chelladurai (2009) argues that *geographically* central positions, such as the center or quarterback position in football, are not necessarily *functionally* central positions. Rather, it is primarily those who play wide receiver or running back who are charged with advancing the ball downfield for a touchdown. The other team positions play only a supporting role. From this perspective, the wide receiver and running back positions are the team's key positions. As Chelladurai (2009) notes, "the assertion that there is discrimination against black players in football cannot be sustained by these data. In fact, it can be argued that it is whites who are precluded from the functionally central positions" (p. 418).

DIVERSITY
in the field

Stereotypes About Athletic Performance. Stereotypes about the athletic performance of African Americans is nothing new, and they continue today. For example, in October of 2005, Fisher DeBerry, the head football coach at the Air Force Academy, attributed his team's loss to Texas Christian University (TCU) to the fact that TCU had more African Americans who "can run very, very well." He further noted that he planned to make a concerted effort to recruit more African Americans to his team, commenting, "it just seems to be that way, that Afro-American kids can run very, very well. That doesn't mean that Caucasian kids and other descents can't run, but it's very obvious to me they [African American kids] run extremely well."

Source: DeBerry, 2005.

compared with the relatively few Whites (25 percent) or Hispanics (36 percent). After accounting for variations in speed and power, the effects of race on playing position still existed, albeit in a reduced fashion. These findings support the social closure theory by suggesting that baseball managers might be "assigning disproportionate numbers of African Americans to the outfield because of racial prejudice or for other reasons that have little to do with the skills the players bring to the league" (p. 313).

Stereotypes and Attitudes

Race also influences people's stereotypes about athletes and the attitudes athletes have about their abilities. Many athletes face the "dumb jock" stereotype, but this is a particularly prevalent indignity experienced by African Americans. Research suggests that White college students (a) perceive they perform better academically than African American athletes, (b) view African American athletes as academically unprepared to enter the university context, and (c) anticipate that African American athletes' academic performance will be poor (Sailes, 1993). The notion of African Americans as "dumb jocks" is accompanied by stereotypes about their "natural" athletic abilities (Sailes, 2000; see also the Diversity in the Field box). Perceptions such as these serve to detract from the hard work and dedication African Americans exude in order to achieve high athletic performance.

In a similar way, Stone, Lynch, Sjomeling, and Darley (1999) found that racial stereotypes influenced actual athletic performance. The researchers asked students to participate in a golf activity and varied the information provided concerning the task. The results were striking. African Americans who were told that the task related to "sports intelligence" performed much more poorly than African Americans who did not receive such information. On the other hand, Whites performed poorly when they were told that the task involved an assessment of "natural athletic ability." These results suggest that athletic participants take cognitive stock of racial stereotypes and that such stereotypes influence their subsequent performance. Similar effects have been found with intellectual performance (Nguyen & Ryan, 2008).

Athlete Treatment

A fourth way that race influences sport participation is in the treatment of athletes, and this is manifested in several ways. First, African American athletes believe they are treated differently, from an academic standpoint, than Whites (Singer, 2005b). For instance, while Whites are free to choose their majors, African Americans frequently convey that they are funneled into a limited number of majors. Second, African Americans consistently have lower graduation rates than Whites, something that could be related to the previous point concerning different academic treatment. Third, racial minorities report being treated differently than Whites by coaches and administrators (Singer, 2005b). This is manifested in drug testing and feelings of exploitation, among other things. Finally, members of racial minorities often believe that available opportunities, both in their current sport participation and in their life after sport, are limited (Singer, 2005b). Not only is stacking present (as discussed earlier) but also racial minorities receive less praise than Whites for similar athletic accomplishments.

Race Issues Beyond University Athletics

uch of the discussion thus far has focused on the influence of race on coaches, administrators, and players in the university athletics setting. As might be expected, race significantly influences sport and physical activity in other contexts. These contexts are examined below.

Marketing and Spectator Consumption

Research by Armstrong and Peretto Stratta (2005) illustrates that race plays a significant role in the area of marketing and spectator consumption. These authors examined the preferences and behaviors of consumers who attended women's professional basketball games in two markets—one for a team in the Midwest and the other for a team in the South. Although there were many similarities between White and African American spectators, there were also differences. Promotional giveaways were more important in influencing African Americans to attend the events than in influencing Whites. The authors also found variations in the level of spectator consumption. In the Midwest market, the team had a relatively even racial composition and had an all-White coaching staff. Whites and African Americans did not differ in the frequency of their game attendance for the Midwest team. However, the team located in the South was predominantly African American, including the team's star player, the head coach, and most of the front office personnel. In this market, African Americans attended games at a higher frequency than Whites. Further, the proportion of African American fans at these games (53 percent) was almost twice the proportion seen in the city's general population (26 percent). These findings support previous research in other areas—people of all races will consume products designed for the general public at equal rates; however, products geared primarily for an African American market will be consumed primarily by African Americans (Gouke, 1987). Race plays an influential role not only in who responds to promotional activities but also in how the sport is perceived and the frequency of attendance.

Some companies and sport sponsors make efforts to target specific racial groups. For example, MasterCard used television, print, and electronic advertising to target the growing Hispanic population during its "Memorable Moments" campaign that was associated with MLB (McKelvey, McDonald, & Cramer, 2005). Advertisements aired on Spanish-language television stations such as ESPN Desportes while print ads ran in *MLB en Espanol* magazine. An advertisement also was posted on a special Spanish website, along with links that sent the consumers to mastercardespanol.com. These efforts were geared toward attracting Hispanic consumers to the MasterCard brand, using sport to achieve this end.

As another example, the Detroit Pistons hosted "Hispanic Night" when they battled the San Antonio Spurs on February 21, 2010. For every ticket sold, the Pistons donated $5 to the Detroit Hispanic Development Corporation—an organization devoted to making life-changing differences in the lives of Hispanics in Detroit.

International Sport

As noted in Chapter 1, sport is a worldwide phenomenon, and many sport organizations can be considered multinational in nature. Those professional leagues that traditionally play games only in the United States are now venturing into other countries. The NBA, for example, considers China a viable alternative for expansion (Howard & Crompton, 2004). China is the largest country in the world (population 1.3 billion), has 7 percent annual economic growth, and has high brand awareness of NBA players among its youth. Therefore, the NBA believes there are many opportunities for product sales and television revenues within China.

Although there are intriguing business opportunities in China as well as other countries, cultural and ethnic dissimilarities present potential hurdles. According to Ordish (2005), brand management and protection of intellectual property rights are primary concerns for managers entering the Chinese sport market. For example, China maintains a "first-to-file" trademark registration system, meaning that companies should file papers early and also register the Chinese versions of their trademarks. Another consideration for sport marketers involves negotiations with individual athletes. Because most Chinese athletes are supported by state-run sport organizations, the state retains the right to manage the athlete's commercial ventures. This was a hard lesson learned for Tian Lang, the 2000 and 2004 Olympic diving champion. Tian entered a sponsorship agreement with Emperor Entertainment Group without permission from the state. Afterward, Tian was expelled from the national diving team and placed on a provincial squad, bringing into doubt his participation in future Olympics. Further, the sponsor lost not only the sponsorship but also the money it had already paid Tian. As this situation illustrates, sport marketers must negotiate with the athlete, the team, and the state (Ordish, 2005).

Sport Experiences of Native Persons

The sport experiences of native persons (i.e., aboriginal peoples, indigenous peoples, First Nations) are often quite different from the experiences of persons of other races (Paraschak, 1997). Paraschak examined sporting events of native persons in southern and in northern Canada and found variations among the events. Native persons in the northern part of Canada were largely isolated from Euro-Canadians and, consequently, were more in tune with their traditions and "native-derived lifestyle" (p. 16). Not surprisingly, sport events held in this region reflected a particular lifestyle, and the activities were structured according to tribal values and traditions. This sport structure stood in contrast to the structure that existed for native persons in southern Canada. Native persons in this region had close interaction with Euro-Canadians, had largely adopted the Euro-Canadian way of life, and were considered "others" in that area. Because they could not maintain government support for their sport events, they were forced to develop a self-funded sport system—a system that largely reflected the ideals and policies of Euro-Canadians.

Robidoux's research (2004) on race relations in Southern Alberta, Canada, further exemplifies these points. Robidoux found that native persons frequently faced antagonistic environments while participating in sport, and Euro-Canadians sometimes viewed them in a negative light. Youth hockey participants in Robidoux's study told of being called a variety of racial slurs, such as "wagon burners" and "prairie niggers," by both the opposing players and those players' parents. On the other hand, Euro-Canadian hockey participants and their parents objected to the highly physical style of the native person teams and often advocated segregation. As one parent of a Euro-Canadian player noted, "Sportsmanship on the part of the Kaini team was non-existent. . . . Perhaps these teams should make up their own league with their own 'rules' and be forced to travel long distances for competition" (p. 29). These studies illustrate the sometimes unique experiences of native persons participating in sport and the need for administrators and coaches to make sport accessible to *all* persons, irrespective of their race.

In addition to examining the sport experiences of Native persons, others have focused on the use of Native Americans as mascots. The Diversity in the Field box explores this issue.

For more information on the controversial use of Native American mascots in intercollegiate athletics, see Covell and Barr (2010).

DIVERSITY *in the field*

Native American Mascots. Many high school, collegiate, and professional teams continue to use Native American mascots, logos, and imagery. The Washington Redskins are one example. To some, Native American mascots are representative of the bravery and fierceness that they want associated with their teams. Others disagree and suggest that such practices are offensive and demeaning to Native Americans (see Staurowsky, 2007). In line with the latter perspective, in 2005, the NCAA ruled that teams using Native American mascots could not participate in postseason competitions, because the mascots were "hostile and abusive." As a result, several schools decided to change their mascots (e.g., the Midwestern State University switched from the Indians to the Mustangs), while others kept the name but removed the imagery (e.g., the University of Illinois' athletic teams are still referred to as the Illini, but the school no longer uses the Native American mascot, Chief Illiniwek). Florida State University was granted a waiver because the Seminole Tribe of Florida endorsed the mascot's use (for an overview, see Covell & Barr, 2010). However, not all Seminoles were pleased with the decision, including members of the Seminole Nation of Oklahoma. General Council member David Narcomey responded to the NCAA ruling by expressing the following: "I am deeply appalled, incredulously disappointed. . . . I am nauseated that the NCAA is allowing this 'minstrel show' to carry on this form of racism" (Weinberg, 2005).

CHAPTER *summary*

This chapter focused on the categorical effects of race in sport and physical activity organizations. As illustrated in the Diversity Challenge, race has a substantial impact on the way people are treated while participating in sport and leisure activities. The same is also true for employees because race influences the way people are treated, people's behaviors in relation to their work and to others, and the aspirations people possess. After reading the chapter, you should be able to:

1. **Define race, ethnicity, and minority group, and describe the differences among these concepts.**

Though sometimes used interchangeably, the concepts of race and ethnicity have distinct meanings. Race refers to a social category used to differentiate people based on supposed genetic differences. Ethnicity, on the other hand, refers to the cultural heritage of a particular group of people, with an emphasis on the common culture certain groups of people share. Finally, a minority group is a collection of persons who share common characteristics and face discrimination in society because of their membership in that group.

2. **Discuss the experiences of racial minorities in the employment context, including variations in wages earned, access to positions, and treatment on the job.**

Relative to Whites, most racial minorities earn less money, have limited access to positions in sport organizations, and, when they do have access to positions, are segregated into stereotypical and peripheral job roles.

3. **Discuss the underrepresentation of racial minorities in the sport industry, and identify factors that contribute to the underrepresentation.**

Racial minorities are underrepresented in both coaching and administrative positions. Macro- (i.e., institutionalized practices, political climate, stakeholder expectations), meso- (i.e., prejudice on the part of decision makers, discrimination, leadership prototypes, organizational culture of diversity), and micro-levels (i.e., head coaching expectations and intentions, occupational turnover intentions) all impact this phenomenon.

4. **Understand the influence of race on the experiences of sport and physical activity participants.**

Race affects sport participation primarily through two dynamics: socioeconomic status and cultural norms. The positions people play in sport are also influenced by their race, a phenomenon known as stacking. Both social closure theory and human capital theory have been used to understand the stacking process. There is evidence that participants of color are treated differently than their White counterparts, both in sport and leisure and team participation. Beyond university athletics, race plays a role in sport marketing and consumption, international sport, and the experiences of native persons. Research suggests that native persons engage in forms of physical activity unique to their culture, and there is also evidence that they face hostile environments when participating in sport against Whites.

QUESTIONS *for discussion*

1. What are the primary distinctions between race and ethnicity? Which term do you prefer and why?

2. Though the proportion of racial minorities in various countries is increasing, they continue to be disadvantaged in several areas. What are some of the reasons for this differential treatment?

3. Various factors were identified to help explain the underrepresentation of racial minorities in the coaching profession. Which of these factors is most important and why?

4. Discuss the various ways that race influences sport and leisure participation.

5. Two theories—social closure theory and human capital theory—help explain stacking. In your opinion, which theory provides the best explanation of why stacking occurs, and why?

6. Race influences the treatment of sport participants in several ways. Which of the factors identified in the chapter has the largest impact on sport participants? Why?

LEARNING *activities*

1. What is the best comparison point to use when discussing the representation of racial minorities in coaching positions? What are the pros and cons of the different benchmarks discussed in the chapter (e.g., the composition of the general population versus the composition of the pool of former athletes)? Divide into two groups, with each group adopting one perspective, and discuss.

2. Using the Web, identify mandates in different countries that address either racial equality in general or racial equality in the sport and physical activity context.

READING *resources*

SUPPLEMENTARY READINGS

Brooks, D., & Althouse, R. (Eds.). (2000). *Racism in college athletics: The African American athlete's experience* (2nd ed.). Morgantown, WV: Fitness Information Technology. (Edited collection of essays concerning the intersection of race and university athletics; touches on issues such as stacking, opportunities, and the intersection of gender and race, among others.)

Feagin, J. R. (2006). *Systemic racism: A theory of oppression.* New York: Routledge. (Provides a historical overview of race and racism in the United States; focuses on the racial realities held by members of different racial groups.)

West, C. (1994). *Race matters.* New York: Vintage Books. (Analysis of race issues in the United States, including leadership, affirmative action, sexuality, and the legacy of Malcolm X, among others.)

WEB RESOURCES

- Black Athlete (www.blackathlete.net): site devoted to issues and controversies concerning African American athletes of all ages and skill levels.
- Black Coaches and Administrators (www.bcasports.org): contains several resources, including the annual Hiring Report Card for college football teams.
- Commission for Racial Equality (www.cre.gov.uk/): British association aimed at achieving racial equality in several contexts, including sport and physical activity.

references

Abercrombie, N., Hill, S., & Turner, B. S. (2000). *The Penguin dictionary of sociology* (4th ed.). New York: Penguin Books.

Adler, N. E., & Rehkopf, D. H. (2008). U.S. disparities in health: Descriptions, causes, and mechanisms. *Annual Review of Public Health, 29*, 235–252.

Agyemang, K., DeLorme, J., & Singer, J. N. (2010). Race and ethnicity in American sport. In G. B. Cunningham & J. N. Singer (Eds.), *Sociology of sport and physical activity* (pp. 261–288). College Station, TX: Center for Sport Management Research and Education.

Allison, M. T., & Hibbler, D. K. (2004). Organizational barriers to inclusion: Perspectives from the recreation profession. *Leisure Sciences, 26*, 261–280.

Anderson, D. (1993). Cultural diversity on campus: A look at intercollegiate football coaches. *Journal of Sport and Social Issues, 17*, 61–66.

Applebaum, B. (2003). White privilege, complexity, and the social construction of race. *Educational Foundations, 17*(4), 5–19.

Armstrong, K. L., & Peretto Stratta, T. M. (2005). Market analyses of race and sport consumption. *Sport Marketing Quarterly, 13*, 7–16.

Bell, M. P., McLaughlin, M. E., & Sequeira, J. M. (2004). Age, disability, and obesity: Similarities, differences, and common threads. In M. S. Stockdale & F. J. Crosby (Eds.), *The psychology and management of workplace diversity* (pp. 191–205). Malden, MA: Blackwell.

Beyer, J. M., & Hannah, D. R. (2000). The cultural significance of athletics in U.S. higher education. *Journal of Sport Management, 14*, 105–132.

Brown, G. T. (2002). Diversity grid lock. *The NCAA News.* Retrieved February 15, 2003, from http://www.ncaa.org/news/2002/20021028/active/3922n01.html.

Buffington, D. (2005). Contesting race on Sundays: Making meaning out of the rise in the number of Black quarterbacks. *Sociology of Sport Journal, 21*, 19–37.

Burden, J. W., Jr., Harrison, L., Jr., & Hodge, S. R. (2005). Perceptions of African American faculty in kinesiology-based programs at predominantly White American institutions of higher education. *Research Quarterly for Exercise and Sport, 76*, 224–237.

Campbell, A. A. (1947). Factors associated with attitudes toward Jews: In T. Newcomb & E. Hartley (Eds.), *Readings in social psychology* (pp. 518–527). New York: Holt.

Chelladurai, P. (2009). *Managing organizations for sport and physical activity: A systems perspective* (3rd ed.). Scottsdale, AZ: Holcomb Hathaway.

Coakley, J. (2009). *Sports in society: Issues and controversies* (10th ed.). New York: McGraw Hill.

Coates, R. D. (2003). Introduction: Reproducing racialized systems of social control. *American Behavioral Scientist, 47*, 235–239.

Cokley, K., Dreher, G. F., & Stockdale, M. S. (2004). Toward the inclusiveness and career success of African Americans in the workplace. In M. S. Stockdale & F. J. Crosby (Eds.), *The psychology and management of workplace diversity* (pp. 168–190). Malden, MA: Blackwell.

Covell, D., & Barr, C. A. (2010). *Managing intercollegiate athletics.* Scottsdale, AZ: Holcomb Hathaway.

Crompton, J. L. (1995). Economic impact analysis of sports facilities and events: Eleven sources of misapplication. *Journal of Sport Management, 9*, 14–35.

Cunningham, G. B. (2004). Already aware of the glass ceiling: Race related effects of perceived opportunity on the career choices of college athletes. *Journal of African American Studies, 7*(1), 57–71.

Cunningham, G. B. (2009). The moderating effect of diversity strategy on the relationship between racial diversity and organizational performance. *Journal of Applied Social Psychology, 36*, 1445–1460.

Cunningham, G. B. (2010). Understanding the under-representation of African American coaches: A multilevel perspective. *Sport Management Review, 13*, 395–406.

Cunningham, G. B., & Benavides-Espinoza, C. (2008). A trend analysis of sexual harassment claims: 1992–2006. *Psychological Reports, 103*, 779–782.

Cunningham, G. B., & Bopp, T. D. (2010). Race ideology perpetuated: Media representations of newly hired football coaches. *Journal of Sports Media, 5*(1), 1–19.

Cunningham, G. B., Bruening, J. E., & Straub. T. (2006). Examining the under-representation of African Americans in NCAA Division I head-coaching positions. *Journal of Sport Management, 20*, 387–417.

Cunningham, G. B., & Sagas, M. (2002). The differential effects of human capital for male and female Division I basketball coaches. *Research Quarterly for Exercise and Sport, 73*, 489–495.

Cunningham, G. B., & Sagas, M. (2004a). Examining the main and interactive effects of deep- and surface-level diversity on job satisfaction and organizational turnover intentions. *Organizational Analysis, 12*, 319–332.

Cunningham, G. B., & Sagas, M. (2004b). Racial differences in occupational turnover intent among NCAA Division IA assistant football coaches. *Sociology of Sport Journal, 21*, 84–92.

Cunningham, G. B., & Sagas, M. (2005). Access discrimination in intercollegiate athletics. *Journal of Sport and Social Issues, 29*, 148–163.

Cunningham, G. B., & Sagas, M. (2007). Perceived treatment discrimination among coaches: The influence of race and sport coached. *International Journal of Sport Management, 8,* 1–20.

Cunningham, G. B., Sagas, M., & Ashley, F. B. (2001). Occupational commitment and intent to leave the coaching profession: Differences according to race. *International Review for the Sociology of Sport, 16,* 131–148.

Cunningham, G. B., & Singer, J. N. (2009). *Diversity in athletics: An assessment of exemplars and institutional best practices.* Indianapolis, IN: National Collegiate Athletic Association.

Cunningham, G. B., & Singer, J. N. (2010). "You'll face discrimination wherever you go": Student athletes' intentions to enter the coaching profession. *Journal of Applied Social Psychology, 40,* 1708–1727.

DeBerry, F. (2005, Oct. 26). DeBerry cites lack of minority players for struggles. ESPN.com. Retrieved February 2, 2006, from http://sports.espn.go.com/ncf/news/story?id=2203926.

DeHass, D. (2007). *2005–06 ethnicity and gender demographics of NCAA member institutions' athletics personnel.* Indianapolis, IN: The National Collegiate Athletic Association.

DeHass, D. (2008). *1999–00 —2006–2007 student-athlete race and ethnicity report.* Indianapolis, IN: The National Collegiate Athletic Association.

DiMaggio, P. J., & Powell, W. W. (1983). The iron cage revisited: Institutional isomorphism and collective rationality in organizational fields. *American Sociological Review, 48,* 147–160.

Doherty, A. J., & Chelladurai, P. (1999). Managing cultural diversity in sport organizations: A theoretical perspective. *Journal of Sport Management, 13,* 280–297.

Dovidio, J. F., & Gaertner, S. L. (2000). Aversive racism and selection decisions: 1989 and 1999. *Psychological Science, 11,* 319–323.

Dovidio, J. F., & Gaertner, S. L. (2004). Aversive racism. *Advances in Experimental Social Psychology, 36,* 1–52.

Dowden, S., & Robinson, J. P. (1993). Age and cohort differences in American racial attitudes: The generational replacement hypothesis revisited. In P. M. Sniderman, P. E. Tetlock, & E. G. Carmines (Eds.), *Prejudice, politics, and the American dilemma* (pp. 86–103). Stanford, CA: Stanford University Press.

Eitzen D. S., & Sage, G. H. (2009). *Sociology of North American sport* (8th ed.). Boulder, CO: Paradigm Publishers.

Everhart, B. C., & Chelladurai, P. (1998). Gender differences in preferences for coaching as an occupation: The role of self-efficacy, valence, and perceived barriers. *Research Quarterly for Exercise and Sport, 68,* 188–200.

Feagin, J. R. (2006). *Systemic racism: A theory of oppression.* New York: Routledge.

Fink, J. S., & Pastore, D. L. (1999). Diversity in sport? Utilizing the business literature to devise a comprehensive framework of diversity initiatives. *Quest, 51,* 310–327.

Freeman, R. E. (1984). *Strategic management: A stakeholder approach.* Boston, MA: Pitman/Ballinger.

Fulks, D. L. (2008). *Revenues/expenses: 2004–06 NCAA revenues and expenses of Division I intercollegiate athletics programs report.* Indianapolis, IN: National Collegiate Athletic Association.

Gaertner, S. L., & Dovidio, J. F. (2000). *Reducing intergroup bias: The Common Ingroup Identity Model.* Philadelphia, PA: Psychology Press.

Gaertner, S. L., & Dovidio, J. F. (2005). Understanding and addressing contemporary racism: From aversive racism to the common ingroup identity model. *Journal of Social Issues, 61,* 615–639.

Gonzales, G. L. (1996). The stacking of Latinos in Major League Baseball: A forgotten minority? *Journal of Sport and Social Issues, 20,* 134–160.

Gouke, C. G. (1987). *Blacks and the American economy.* Needham Heights, MA: Ginn Press.

Greenhaus, J. H., Parasuraman, S., & Wormley, W. M. (1990). Effects of race on organizational experiences, job performance, evaluations, and career outcomes. *Academy of Management Journal, 33,* 64–86.

Hallinan, C. (1991). Aborigines and positional segregation in the Australian Rugby League. *International Review for the Sociology of Sport, 26,* 69–81.

Hamilton, B. H. (1997). Racial discrimination and professional basketball salaries in the 1990s. *Applied Economics, 29,* 287–296.

Hibbler, D. K., & Shinew, K. J. (2002). Interracial couples' experience of leisure: A social network approach. *Journal of Leisure Research, 34,* 135–156.

Hodge, S. R., & Stroot, S. A. (1997). Barriers and support structures perceived by African American and Caucasian physical educators during their career development. *Equity & Excellence in Education, 30*(3), 52–60.

Hodson, G., Dovidio, J. F., & Gaertner, S. L. (2002). Processes in racial discrimination: Differential weighting of conflicting information. *Personality and Social Psychology Bulletin, 28,* 460–471.

Hodson, G., Hooper, H., Dovidio, J. F., & Gaertner, S. L. (2005). Aversive racism in Britain: Legal decisions and the use of inadmissible evidence. *European Journal of Social Psychology, 35,* 437–448.

Howard, D. R., & Crompton, J. L. (2004). *Financing sport* (2nd ed.). Morgantown, WV: Fitness Information Technology.

Hylton, K. (2009). *"Race" and sport: Critical race theory.* New York: Routledge.

Kamphoff, C., & Gill, D. (2008). Collegiate athletes' perceptions of the coaching profession. *International Journal of Sports Science & Coaching, 3,* 55–71.

Kikulis, L. M. (2000). Continuity and change in governance and decision making in national sport organizations: Institutional explanations. *Journal of Sport Management, 14,* 293–320.

Kozlowski, S. W. J., & Klein, K. J. (2000). A multilevel approach to theory and research in organizations: Contextual, temporal, and emergent processes. In K. J. Klein & S. W. J. Kozlowski (Eds.), *Multilevel theory, research, and methods in organizations: Foundations, extensions, and new directions* (pp. 3–90). San Francisco: Jossey-Bass.

Ladson-Billings, G., & Tate, W. F., IV. (1995). Toward a critical race theory of education. *Teachers College Record, 97*(1), 47–68.

Lapchick, R. E. (2008). *2008 Racial and Gender Report Card.* Accessed November 9, 2005, from http://www.tidesport.org/RGRC/2008/2008_RGRC.pdf.

Lavigne, P. (2003, August 6). Measuring minority advances. *The Dallas Morning News,* pp. 12A, 13A.

Lavoie, M. (1989). Stacking, performance differentials, and salary discrimination in professional hockey. *Sociology of Sport Journal, 6,* 17–35.

Lawrence, S. M. (2004). African American athletes' experiences of race in sport. *International Review for the Sociology of Sport, 40,* 99–110.

Lent, R. W., Brown, S. D., & Hackett, G. (1994). Toward a unifying social cognitive theory of career and academic interest, choice, and performance. *Journal of Vocational Behavior, 45,* 79–122.

Littlefield, A., Lieberman, L., & Reynolds, L. T. (1982). Redefining race: The potential demise of a concept in physical anthropology. *Current Anthropology, 23,* 641–655.

Long, J., Robinson, P., & Spracklen, K. (2005). Promoting racial equality within sports organizations. *Journal of Sport & Social Issues, 29,* 41–59.

Lord, R., & Maher, K. (1991). *Leadership and information processing.* New York: Unwin Hyman.

Marshall, A. M. (2005). *Confronting sexual harassment: The law and politics of everyday life.* Burlington, VT: Ashgate.

McDowell, J., Cunningham, G. B., & Singer, J. N. (2009). The supply and demand side of occupational segregation: The case of an intercollegiate athletic department. *Journal of African American Studies, 13,* 431–454.

McIntosh, P. (1990). White privilege: Unpacking the invisible knapsack. *Independent School, 49,* 31–36.

McKelvey, S., McDonald, M., & Cramer, R. (2005). MasterCard and Major League Baseball: Metrics for evaluating a most "memorable" promotion. *Sport Marketing Quarterly, 14,* 253–261.

Nguyen, H. D., & Ryan, A. M. (2008). Does stereotype threat affect test performance of minorities and women? A meta-analysis of experimental evidence. *Journal of Applied Psychology, 93,* 1314–1334.

Ogmundson, R. (2005). Does it matter if women, minorities and gays govern? New data concerning an old question. *Canadian Journal of Sociology, 30,* 315–324.

Ordish, R. (2005). Sports marketing in China: An IP perspective. *The China Business Review, 32*(6), 34–37.

Paraschak, V. (1997). Variations in race relations: Sporting events for native peoples in Canada. *Sociology of Sport Journal, 14,* 1–21.

Pattnayak, S. R., & Leonard, J. E. (1994). Explaining discrimination in the National Football League: A study of coaches' salaries. *Sociological Viewpoints, 10,* 35–44.

Powell, S. (2008). *Souled out? How Blacks are winning and losing in sports.* Champaign, IL: Human Kinetics.

Rader, B. G. (1999). *American sports: From the age of folk games to the age of televised sport* (4th ed.). Upper Saddle River, NJ: Prentice Hall.

Robidoux, M. A. (2004). Narratives of race relations in Southern Alberta: An examination of conflicting sporting practices. *Sociology of Sport Journal, 21,* 287–301.

Robinson, J. (2009, January 8). Yale hires new coach and racial issue fades for the Ivys. *New York Times.* Retrieved June 2, 2009, from http://www.nytimes.com.

Rosenberg, M. (2004). Two few: Of 117 football coaches, two are black; it's called institutional racism. *Detroit Free Press.* Accessed November 14, 2005, from http://www.freep.com/cgi-bin/forms/printerfriendly.pl.

Rosette, A. S., Leonardelli, G. J., & Phillips, K. W. (2008). The White standard: Racial bias in leader categorization. *Journal of Applied Psychology, 93,* 758–777.

Sack, A. L., Singh, P., & Thiel, R. (2005). Occupational segregation on the playing field: The case of Major League Baseball. *Journal of Sport Management, 19,* 300–318.

Sagas, M., & Cunningham, G. B. (2005). Racial differences in the career success of assistant football coaches: The role of discrimination, human capital, and social capital. *Journal of Applied Social Psychology, 35,* 773–797.

Sage, G. (2000). Introduction. In D. Brooks & R. Althouse (Eds.), *Racism in college athletics: The African American athlete's experience* (2nd ed., pp. 1–12). Morgantown, WV: Fitness Information Technology.

Saguy, A. C. (2002). International crossways: Traffic in sexual harassment policy. *The European Journal of Women's Studies, 9,* 249–267.

Sailes, G. A. (1993). An investigation of campus typecasts: The myth of black athletic superiority and the dumb jock stereotype. *Sociology of Sport Journal, 10,* 88–97.

Sailes, G. A. (2000). The African American athlete: Social myths and stereotypes. In D. Brooks and R. Althouse (Eds.), *Racism in college athletics: The African American athlete's experience* (pp. 53–63). Morgantown, WV: Fitness Information Technology.

Sartore, M. L., & Cunningham, G. B. (2006). Stereotypes, race, and coaching. *Journal of African American Studies, 10*(2), 69–83.

Schein, E. (1990). Organizational culture. *American Psychologist, 45,* 109–119.

Schnittker, J., & McLeod, J. D. (2005). The social psychology of health disparities. *Annual Review of Sociology, 31,* 75–103.

Scott, W. R. (2001). *Institutions and organizations* (2nd ed.). Thousand Oaks, CA: Sage.

Singer, J. N. (2005a). Addressing epistemological racism in sport management research. *Journal of Sport Management, 19,* 464–479.

Singer, J. N. (2005b). Understanding racism through the eyes of African American male student-athletes. *Race Ethnicity and Education, 8,* 365–386.

Son Hing, L. S., Chung-Yan, G. A., Hamilton, L. K., & Zanna, M. P. (2008). A two-dimensional model that employs explicit and implicit attitudes to characterize prejudice. *Journal of Personality and Social Psychology, 94,* 971–987.

Sperber, M. (2000). *Beer and circus: How big-time college sports is crippling undergraduate education.* New York: Henry Holt & Co.

Staurowsky, E. J. (2007). "You know, we are all Indian": Exploring White power and privilege in reactions to the NCAA Native American mascot policy. *Journal of Sport & Social Issues, 31,* 61–76.

Stone, J., Lynch, C. I., Sjomeling, M., & Darley, J. M. (1999). Stereotype threat effects on Black and White athletic performance. *Journal of Personality and Social Psychology, 77,* 1213–1227.

Swann, W. B., Jr., Polzer, J. T., Seyle, D. C., & Ko, S. J. (2004). Finding value in diversity: Verification of personal and social self-views in diverse groups. *Academy of Management Review, 29,* 9–27.

Tate, W. F. (1997). Critical race theory and education: History, theory, and implications. In M. Apple (Ed.), *Review in research education 2* (pp. 191–243). Washington, DC: American Educational Research Association.

Thomas, D. R., & Dyall, L. (1999). Culture, ethnicity, and sport management: A New Zealand perspective. *Sport Management Review, 2,* 115–132.

Tsui, A. S., & Gutek, B. A. (1999). *Demographic differences in organizations: Current research and future directions.* New York: Lexington Books.

Turner, C. S. V., Myers, S. L., Jr., & Creswell, J. W. (1999). Exploring underrepresentation: The case of faculty of color in the Midwest. *The Journal of Higher Education, 70,* 27–59.

Weinberg, S. (2005, August 24). NCAA lets FSU keep "Seminoles." *USA Today.* Retrieved December 30, 2005 from http://www.keepmedia.com/pubs/USATODAY/2005/08/24/977842?extID=10032&oliID=213.

West, A., & Currie, P. (2008). School diversity and social justice: Policy and politics. *Educational Studies, 34,* 241–250.

Williams, D. R. (1997). Race and health: Basic questions, emerging directions. *Annals of Epidemiology, 7,* 322–333.

Williams, J. (2004). *50 facts that should change the world.* New York: The Disinformation Company, Ltd.

Wixon, M. (2006, May 17). Black coaches see dearth of opportunity in suburbs: High schools diverse, but few land top football jobs. *Dallas Morning News.* Retrieved May 17, 2006, from www.dallasnews.com/cgi-bin/bi/gold_print.cgi.

Wojciechowski, G. (2008, November 11). Number of African American coaches remains unconscionable. *ESPN.com.* Retrieved June 2, 2009, from http://sports.espn.go.com/espn/print?id=3695007&type=Columnist&imagesPrint=off.

Wong, E. (2002). The mystery of the missing minority coaches. *New York Times Online.* Retrieved January 15, 2002, from https://www.patrick.af.mil/deomi/Library/EOReadFile/ Affirmative%20Action/Spring02/The%20Mystery%20of%20the%20Missing%20Minority%20Coaches.pdf 151.

Woodward, J. R. (2004). Professional football scouts: An investigation of racial stacking. *Sociology of Sport Journal, 21,* 356–375.

Zinn, H. (2003). *A people's history of the United States: 1492–present.* New York: HarperCollins.

Zucker, L. G. (1987). Institutional theories of organizations. *Annual Review of Sociology, 13,* 443–464.

5

Sex and Gender

 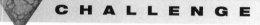
LEARNING OBJECTIVES

istorically, sport was created by men, for men. As a result, it seems as though all things male and masculine are privileged in sport. Despite advances made through Title IX legislation, an imbalance toward males can still be seen in participation rates, monies devoted to sport teams on university campuses, the media coverage of women's and men's sporting events, prize monies at major sport events, and leadership opportunities. Furthermore, the activities in which girls and boys compete are differentially valued. Physical activity in which young girls engage is often seen as frivolous, leading to girls discarding such activities by the time they reach adolescence; on the other hand, physical activities in which boys typically engage are valued by society and have become the foundation of institutionalized sport.

These imbalances make the accomplishments of Nancy Lieberman all the more impressive. Lieberman dominated women's basketball for years. She was a 1976 Olympian, contributed to two national championships while attending the Old Dominion University, was the 1984 MVP of the Women's American Basketball Association, and at age 50, was the oldest person to ever play in the Women's National Basketball Association (WNBA). After her playing career, Lieberman served as head coach and general manager of the WNBA's Detroit Shock and also served as President of the Women's Sports Foundation.

Lieberman's accomplishments also reach beyond women's basketball. She is recognized as the only woman ever to play in an all-male league, the United States Basketball League (1986–1987). In 2009, Lieberman was named head coach of an NBA Development League team in Frisco, Texas. In that capacity, she become the first woman to serve as head coach of a men's professional basketball team, a feat described by the Women's Sports Foundation as her "most historic achievement." Commenting on the achievement, Lieberman noted "I can't look at anything as daunting because then it becomes over-

After studying this chapter, you should be able to:

- Understand the meaning of sex and gender and the differences between the two concepts.

- Discuss the differing experiences men and women have in the workplace.

- Be familiar with the influence of sex and gender on sport participation.

- Discuss the intersection of gender and race.

- Understand the influence of sex and gender on the marketing of sport.

whelming. I look at it as an unbelievable opportunity to do something positive for the sport I love. I've been on every level of this. I'm certainly used to being the first female or the only female to do something. It's second nature to me."

Compiled/adapted from: ▪ www.nancylieberman.com ▪ www.womenssportsfoundation.com ▪ Sefko, E. (2009, November). Lieberman calls chance to coach NBA Development League team "an unbelievable opportunity." *Dallas Morning News*. Retrieved November 6, 2009, from www.dallasnews.com ▪ Young, I. M. (2010). The exclusion of women from sport: Conceptual and existential dimensions. In P. Davis & C. Weaving (Eds.), *Philosophical perspectives on gender in sport and physical activity* (pp. 13–20). New York: Routledge.

DIVERSITY CHALLENGE   R E F L E C T I O N

1. Some suggest that men are privileged in sport while women are disadvantaged. Do you agree with this perspective? Why or why not?

2. Nancy Lieberman was the first coach of a men's professional basketball team. Do you think this accomplishment will open opportunities for women in basketball or other sports? Why or why not?

The representation of women in key leadership positions is just one of many topics concerning women and men in sport organizations that continues to be hotly debated. Research and anecdotal evidence related to sex and gender in the workplace is abundant, but data concerning the extent to which women and men differ in that environment are mixed. Some research suggests that women and men do not differ in work-related outcomes. Other studies, however, have found differences in the way women and men experience work, the wages earned, the occupational status, and the attitudes toward work and careers. Therefore, managers must be cognizant of the potential for one group (e.g., women) to experience work in a more negative fashion than another group (e.g., men).

This chapter examines the experiences of women and men in sport organizations. In the first section, the concepts of sex, gender, and gender role identities are presented. This is followed by a discussion of the experiences of men and women in the workplace. Next, I explore the experiences of sport participants and whether such experiences differ between women and men. This discussion is followed by an examination of the intersection between race and gender and, finally, the influence of gender in sport marketing efforts.

Before proceeding, it is important to note the intersection between many of the topics discussed in this chapter and those in Chapter 10 (sexual orientation). For instance, there is considerable evidence that women face discrimination in the workplace, and this limits their career progression—a topic discussed in subsequent sections. There is also evidence that women face discrimination when others perceive them to be lesbian. For instance, rival coaches will try to "use" a coach's lesbian status against her when recruiting potential athletes. So as not to create redundancy, I limit the latter discussion and related topics to Chapter 10.

Sex and Gender

Though the terms are often used interchangeably, this text makes distinctions between sex and gender (see Exhibit 5.1). According to Powell and Graves (2003), *sex* is a biological classification of individuals based on their physiological properties and reproductive apparatus. Males and females have different sex organs and physical characteristics that distinguish them from a scientific standpoint. *Gender*, on the other hand, is related to the social roles expected of men and women. Discussions of gender focus on the roles, attitudes, behaviors, and interests perceived to be appropriate for, or typical of, members of one sex relative to members of another. Such discourse usually focuses on notions of femininity and masculinity, in which masculinity is associated with aggressiveness and independence while femininity is affiliated with warmth, dependence, and gentleness (Abercrombie, Hill, & Turner, 2000; for further discussion, see Unger, 1979).

The distinction between sex and gender is further clarified by considering the following. Sex differences represent variations that have biological foundations. For instance, exercise physiologists who find that male and female mice respond differently to various exercise regimens are finding sex differences. These represent physiological responses that are independent of social constructions about what it means to be a woman or man. On the other hand, gender differences arise from the social conditions placed on women and men and are not rooted in the

PROFESSIONAL PERSPECTIVES

Using Sexist Language. A topic associated with gender issues concerns the use of sexist language—the use of false generics such as "mankind," for example, and the use of "girl" to refer to an adult woman. Sexist language implies that the masculine is the norm, and it perpetuates male privilege in society. Research on this topic in the sport realm has largely been spearheaded by Parks and Roberton (1998a, 1998b, 2000, 2002, 2004). Their research shows that males generally endorse the use of sexist language more so than women and that the difference is relatively large, with Cohen's d values ranging from .72 to 1.43. The authors examined qualitative responses (e.g., "a woman . . . will never be one hundred percent equal to a man. It is a concept that needs to be faced" and "if women want to be men, have them get a sex change") to determine why there is such a difference.

Other research by Parks and Roberton shows that attitudes toward women in general mediate the relationship between one's sex and the endorsement of sexist language. Using their findings, they concluded that sexist language may be important, from a symbolic standpoint, to people who either consciously or unconsciously believe that men are superior to women. The question, then, is how is the use of sexist language to be reduced or eliminated? Their research indicates that emphasizing the harmful effects the use of such language may have on others will make people more aware of the words they use, and they may make greater efforts to reduce the use and endorsement of sexist language.

Defining sex and gender. *exhibit* **5.1**

Though often used interchangeably, sex and gender are distinct terms.

- **Sex:** a biological classification of individuals based on their physiological properties and reproductive apparatus.

- **Gender:** the social roles expected of men and women, including expectations related to attitudes, behaviors, and interests perceived to be appropriate for, or typical of, men and women. (The gender roles people adopt are influenced by at least three factors: parents, schools, and the media.)

biology of the individual. For instance, women and men differ in the stress that work places on one's family and life (Dixon & Bruening, 2005)—something that is at least partly attributable to the varying societal expectations of women and men in the workplace and at home. The same can be said for girls' and women's interest in sport: though some suggest that girls and women are simply "made differently" than boys and men and therefore do not have an innate interest in sport, gender socialization and opportunities to participate in such endeavors actually account for many if not most perceived differences (for an overview, see Messner & Solomon, 2007).

Some may question whether the distinction between sex and gender really matters. For example, if one discusses "gender differences" in personality, height, or any other immutable characteristic, is this incorrect or inappropriate? Furthermore, do people really make these distinctions, or is this simply something with which academics concern themselves? Pryzgoda and Chrisler (2000) examined these very questions through a survey of 137 college students. They asked participants to write down what they thought of when seeing the word "gender." The majority of the respondents (66.8 percent) indicated that they thought of biological terms, such as "sex," "male/female," or "boy/girl." Participants were also asked to provide definitions of the term *gender*. The most common responses included "male/female" (34.8 percent) and "sex" (34.8 percent), while references to masculinity and femininity were included approximately 12 percent of the time. Though used somewhat interchangeably from a definitional standpoint, participants did make distinctions when completing sentences. Most participants selected "sex" to complete sentences related to biological features (e.g., "The _____ of the cat is male," p. 567) and "gender" to complete socially cued sentences (e.g., "Masculine is an adjective that best describes a person's _____," p. 567). Two exceptions occurred with the following sentences: "The girl's gender is _____," and "The boy's gender is _____" (p. 567). With both sentences, participants were as likely (if not more so) to choose a biological descriptor (e.g., female) as the socially constructed descriptor (e.g., feminine). Pryzgoda and Chrisler concluded that people may use gender to describe both anatomical and behavioral characteristics but will otherwise make distinctions between the terms. Overall, these results indicate that, in most situations, people do make a distinction between sex and gender.

Gender Identity

For many years, gender identity was considered a dichotomous construct, with masculinity and femininity believed to be opposites (Powell & Graves, 2003). If a person was considered to be highly masculine, then he or she would have to be low in femininity and vice versa. These dissimilarities were thought to mirror sex differences in such a way that men were highly masculine and women were highly feminine. A male who demonstrated feminine qualities (e.g., dependence, gentleness) was considered abnormal, as was a female demonstrating masculine characteristics (e.g., aggressiveness, independence).

Bem (1974, 1977) provides an alternative view of gender identity (see also Spence & Helmreich, 1978). Rather than viewing masculinity and femininity as being at opposite ends of a single construct, she suggests that the two concepts are distinct: one could conceivably rank high on both attributes, low on both, or somewhere in between. Using this reasoning, Bem developed the Bem Sex-Role Inventory, consisting of 20 items measuring masculinity, 20 items measuring femininity, and 20 items disguising the purpose of the instrument. To complete the questionnaire, respondents rate themselves in relation to traditional concepts of masculinity and femininity. Based on their responses, people could then be classified into one of four categories:

- *Masculine:* high masculinity, low femininity
- *Feminine:* low masculinity, high femininity
- *Androgynous:* high masculinity, high femininity
- *Undifferentiated:* low masculinity, low femininity

Bem's notion of androgyny, which comes from the Greek words *andr* (meaning man) and *gyne* (meaning woman), was unique to the gender identity literature. People with androgynous characteristics were thought to have more desirable outcomes, such as high self-esteem and greater confidence, than people in other categories.

The relationship between gender identity and various outcomes has been reported at length in the sport literature. The research indicates that athletes have higher masculine and lower feminine gender orientations than nonathletes (Lantz & Schroeder, 1999). Furthermore, those persons with a feminine gender orientation who participate in highly competitive sports have low levels of athletic competence and poor perceptions of their own self-worth (Bowker, Gadbois, & Cornock, 2003). This pattern is true for both males and females. These results are consistent with the notion that sport has traditionally been considered a masculine domain; as such, people with gender orientations that are not masculine may not remain engaged in competitive sports for long. These people may have more pleasant and positive experiences in less competitive or more socially oriented sport settings (Bowker et al., 2003).

More recently, Woodhill and Samuels (2003) conducted a more in-depth analysis of gender roles. Although androgyny was initially thought to be an ideal gender role that balances the best attributes of both masculinity and femininity (Bem, 1975), these authors convincingly argue that gender roles can be both positive and negative. Consider the following: an elite level swim coach with high levels of independence, ambition, compassion, and tolerance would fit desirable masculine (the first two characteristics) and feminine (the latter two characteristics) gender roles and be considered *positively* androgynous. Another swim coach has the following characteristics: high levels of both selfishness and submissiveness, characteristics that are negative attributes of masculinity and femininity, respectively. The latter swim coach is considered *negatively* androgynous. The same distinctions can be made for people with only feminine, or only masculine, characteristics. The demarcation of gender roles in this manner is useful when examining various outcomes such as overall well-being. Woodhill and Samuels, for example, found that positively androgynous people scored higher on indicators of mental health and well-being than persons who were negatively androgynous, negatively masculine, negatively feminine, or undifferentiated androgynous. Thus, the gender roles one adopts can have a meaningful impact on a variety of outcomes, including sport participation and overall well-being.

Origins of gender socialization

As previously noted, because ideas about gender and gender roles are influenced by societal forces, there are several factors that influence one's gender role identity: parents, schools, and the mass media (Powell & Graves, 2003). Each factor is discussed in turn.

Parents. Parents play an influential part in children's gender role identity development. Parents who believe that women and men should enjoy equal opportunities in the "adult world" are more likely to encourage their children to deviate from traditional gender stereotypes (Eccles, Jacobs, & Harold, 1990). The parents' working status also influences gender role identities because working mothers are more likely to have daughters who embrace egalitarian views toward gender roles than stay-at-home mothers. These effects are less substantial on the attitudes sons hold toward gender roles (Hoffman & Youngblood, 1999). Research shows that both parents, but especially fathers, are likely to encourage gender-stereotypical behavior for both boys and girls, promote activities requiring motor skills for boys, and discourage aggressive behavior among girls (Lytton & Romney, 1991). This is consistent with other studies that show the father plays a significant role in the development of attitudes toward sport participation for both girls and boys. Furthermore, the lack of a female parent who has participated, or is participating in sport potentially conveys to children that sport is an exclusively male domain (Shakib & Dunbar, 2004). Finally, parents are also likely to purchase different types of toys for their male and female children, further reinforcing gender stereotypes (Pomerleau, Boldue, Malcuit, & Cossette, 1990).

Schools. Schools also influence the development of gender roles. Powell and Graves (2003) outline how girls generally perform better academically than boys in school—a trend that exists in all academic areas, including math and science, across all ages, and through all levels of education. The grade differences are not necessarily the result of varying cognitive ability; rather, they are the result of the girls' superior work habits and study skills. Ironically though, boys receive more attention, both positive and negative, in the classroom than girls. They are called on more often, praised more, criticized more, and have more ideas that are both rejected and accepted. Though girls volunteer to answer questions more often than boys do, they are called on less frequently and are afforded less time to provide answers. Powell and Graves maintain that the cumulative effects of these practices lead to lower self-esteem among girls than boys, findings that have been substantiated in empirical studies (Kling, Hyde, Showers, & Buswell, 1999). The lower self-esteem among girls negatively influences their choice of academic course work, the degrees they seek, and the career paths they pursue.

Mass media. Media, television, print, radio, and the Internet have a significant influence on individuals and on the culture, prompting some to suggest that they "have become one of the most powerful institutional forces for shaping values and attitudes in modern culture" (Kane, 1988, pp. 88–89). The media have an effect on how we think, influence our attitudes toward various topics, and shape our perceptions of the roles men and women should play in society. The same is true in sport, as research on the coverage of sport teams and participants demonstrates. Such coverage often produces inequitable and biased representation: The media generally portray sport as a masculine venture (Cramer, 1994; Tuggle, 1997). Women participating in traditionally "feminine" sports such as golf or swimming are featured more frequently than women competing in "masculine" sports such as rugby (Fink & Kensicki, 2002; Lumpkin & Williams, 1991). When women do receive media or press coverage, they are likely to be depicted as sex symbols and/or in supportive rather than participating roles (e.g., cheering the contestants; Cuneen & Sidwell, 1998; Fink & Kensicki, 2002; Tuggle, 1997). Other research indicates that women and women's teams receive considerably less coverage than men and men's teams. This pattern exists across a variety of mass media, including sport magazines (Fink & Kensicki, 2002; Kane, 1988), newspapers (Wann, Schrader, Allison, & McGeorge, 1998), television (Tuggle, 1997), the Internet (Sagas, Cunningham, Wigley, & Ashley, 2000), and publications from professional organizations, such as the *NCAA News* (Cunningham, Sagas, Sartore, Amsden, & Schellhase, 2004; Shifflett & Revelle, 1994).

DIVERSITY *in the field*

Hitting "Like a Girl." Gender stereotypes play just as much a role in the sports world as they do in any other part of society, if not more so. Phrases such as "you throw like a girl" are sometimes bandied among male participants with the intention of belittling someone.

Similar stereotypes were at work during a golf tournament in November, 2005. Fred Funk, Tiger Woods, Annika Sorenstam, and Fred Couples were all competing in a tournament together. Woods told Funk that he (Funk) would never hear the end of it if Sorenstam hit the ball farther than he did, even on one hole. However, that is just what happened on the third hole. Afterward, Funk wore a pink skirt over his pants for the remainder of the hole (Van Sickle, 2005). It didn't matter that Sorenstam had more career wins and had earned more prize money than Funk. She was a woman and hit the ball farther, so he attempted to deflect the focus from his shortcoming by wearing the skirt for the remainder of the hole. This is but one of many examples illustrating the way gender roles influence sport and sport participants.

Gender in the Sport Context

As this examination of gender identity demonstrates, gender plays a significant role for all people in all walks of life, including sport and physical activity. Parents, schools, and the media all significantly influence the gender roles girls and boys adopt. These gender roles are then used to define behaviors and participation in other areas of life, including sport and leisure. For example, girls' and women's participation in some sports thought to be masculine in nature, such as football or rugby, is limited. On the other hand, their participation in sports that are thought to be feminine in nature, such as gymnastics, often outnumbers the participation by boys, even though boys generally have greater participation in all sports than girls (Carpenter & Acosta, 2005). These trends illustrate the gender roles adopted in the sport domain, especially with respect to choices in sport participation.

Gender stereotypes are seen throughout other areas of sport, including the workplace (discussed later), commercials, events, and facilities. Commercials promoting the beginning of the 2005 NHL season illustrate this point: The commercials showed a bare-chested hockey player sitting on a bench, with the sounds of drums and sabers rattling in the background. He is approached by a woman clothed only in a bra and gauzy robe who proceeds to help clothe him in his shoulder pads and jersey. Although some see this as nothing more than a way to grab the viewers' attention, others disagree, suggesting that the advertisement depicts the woman as a "sexual ornament" ("Deeply," 2005). Another example is found in the University of Iowa's visitor's locker room at Kinnick Stadium: it has pink walls, carpet, showers, and lockers. Football officials contend that pink was used because the color is believed to have a calming effect on the opposing teams. Others see it differently, suggesting that the use of pink is demeaning and perpetuates negative stereotypes about women. After raising these objections, one professor on the campus received death threats ("Color," 2005). As these examples demonstrate, gender stereotypes are seen in many aspects of sport and influence people's behaviors, attitudes, and beliefs.

Women and Men in the Workplace

We next turn our attention to women and men in the workplace, examining the differences and similarities between women and men in workforce participation, earnings, and representation in management and leadership positions. We also consider several potential reasons for the underrepresentation of women in top-level positions. Each topic is discussed below.

Participation in the Workforce

There are variations in the proportion of women and men in the workplace, though the extent of the differences has narrowed over time. According to the U.S. Census Bureau, 19 percent of women and 80 percent of men were members of the U.S. labor force in 1900. By 1950, the proportion of women in the labor force had risen to 31 percent, while the proportion of men remained constant at 80 percent. By the year 2000, the gap had narrowed even further, as 60 percent of women and 75 percent of men were members of the U.S. labor force. To examine these figures from a different perspective, in 1900, four out of five women *did not* work, while in 2000, three out of five women *were* members of the labor force (see Exhibit 5.2). This general trend is mirrored in the sport and physical activity context (Eitzen & Sage, 2009).

Note that the proportion of women choosing to enter the workforce coincides with the changing attitudes toward gender roles. In the early 20th century, "appropriate" gender roles called for women to raise their children and work in the home, focusing on domestic duties. Women who worked outside the home during this time were seen as challenging traditional gender roles. However, several legislative, political, and societal factors slowly helped to change these stereotypes. The ratification of the 19th Amendment (granting women the right to vote), World Wars I and II (resulting in women working in factories in the place of men away at war), the women's movements in the 1960s and 1970s, the Civil Rights Act of 1964, and Title IX (discussed at length in Chapter 12) all influenced women's participation in the workforce and in sport. These changes challenged stereotypes, altered the perceptions about what a woman could do and who she should be, granted women rights not previously enjoyed in the workplace, and ultimately allowed women the right to choose to work away from home and participate in organized sport activities.

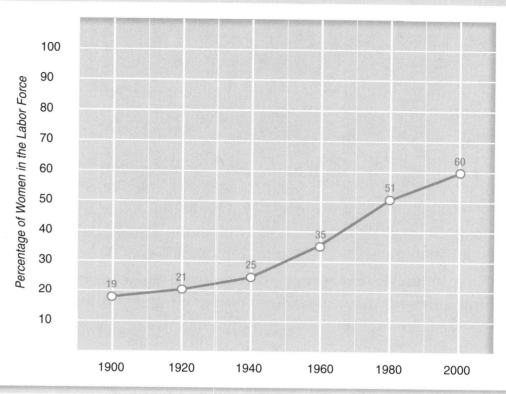

Percentage of women in the labor force since 1900.   *exhibit* **5.2**

U.S. Census Bureau data.

Earnings

Despite the increased representation of women in the workforce, men have traditionally received larger salaries than women—a trend that continues today. The U.S. Census Bureau reports that in 2008 the real median earnings of men over age 15 was $46,367, while the median earnings for women over age 15 was $35,745. Thus, women earned 77 percent of what men did. This variation could be a function of the type of job that men and women hold. Exhibit 5.3 provides the 2004 median weekly earnings of full-time women and men across several occupations. The data indicate that men continue to receive greater weekly earnings than women. Among persons in management occupations, men earn $1,215 a week and women earn $871. Among educators, men earn $227 more a week than women ($956 and $729, respectively). A similar trend is present for recreation and fitness workers, where men earn $585 a week and women earn $473. Comparable findings have been reported across a variety of countries, including Australia (Eastough & Miller, 2004) and Great Britain (Ward, 2001). These data also show that discrepancies in the amount of pay increase as one earns more money: women earn 81 percent of what men earn in recreation and fitness jobs but only 72 percent of what men earn in management positions.

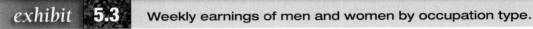

exhibit 5.3 Weekly earnings of men and women by occupation type.

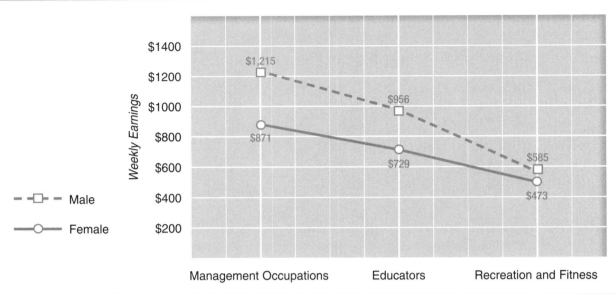

U.S. Census Bureau data.

There are discrepancies between salaries of men and women in sport organizations, but the picture is more complex. Consider the salaries of university basketball coaches. Among coaches of women's teams, women head coaches earn more than men (Humphreys, 2000); however, this statistic is only related to the coaches of women's teams. Coaches of men's basketball teams earn almost double what coaches of women's teams earn. This is significant because in practice, the coaching positions for men's teams are reserved for men, but the same is not true for coaching positions of women's teams. Therefore, the women's earning potential is substantially less than the men's, and this same trend generally exists throughout university sports.

Consider the following example at the University of Texas, as outlined by Zimbalist (1999). Jody Conradt was hired as the head coach of the women's basketball team in 1976, and since that time, she amassed a .771 winning percentage. The women's games regularly drew between 7,000 and 8,000 fans, among the top 10 in attendance in the nation. In the early 1990s, she was appointed athletic director for women's sports at the university while still fulfilling her head-coaching duties. Her total compensation package for the 1998–1999 academic year was $237,235—substantially less than the compensation of Rick Barnes ($800,000), the head coach of the men's team with a .601 career winning percentage (.170 points lower than Conradt's). Note that Barnes did not fill two jobs, as did Conradt, yet he still received a compensation package worth more than three times Conradt's.

Some assert that because men's sports generate greater revenues, the coaches of those teams (men) should receive more compensation. Sport economist Andrew Zimbalist (1999) showed that this is not necessarily true, because the coaches of men's teams earn greater salaries than what would be expected if the compensation were based on the revenue generated by their teams. Zimbalist suggests that differences in men's and women's salaries are a function of social factors (i.e., discrimination), not economic rationale.

It is interesting that these salary discrepancies between women and men do not necessarily result in outrage by women. Parks, Russell, Wood, Roberton, and Shewokis (1995) describe a phenomenon known as the "paradox of the contented working women," in which women receive lower pay than their male counterparts yet are equally, if not more, satisfied with their compensation than the men. This is especially prevalent among women working in male-dominated professions. In the 1995 Parks et al. study of intercollegiate athletic administrators, the authors found that the men earned $6,000 more on average than the women. Despite this difference, job satisfaction among men and women in their sample was the same. To explain their findings, Parks et al. suggest that "contemporary female administrators working in a male-dominated environment may incorrectly consider themselves to be 'pioneers' involved in 'men's work'" (p. 77), or they may simply not be aware of the salary discrepancies.

Representation in Management and Leadership Positions

Women have historically been underrepresented in organizational management and leadership positions. As recently as 1972, women filled only 17 percent of all management positions. Times changed, however, and by 1995, women filled 42.7 percent of all management positions (Stroh, Langlands, & Simpson, 2004). These data suggest that women are making strides within organizational settings. A closer look at the data, however, reveals that women continue to be severely underrepresented in top management positions. A study of Fortune 500 companies conducted by the Catalyst Institute (2008) found that women represented only 15.4 percent of all corporate officer positions and only 6.2 percent of the top-earning positions. Seventy-five of the companies had *no* women corporate officers.

Similar trends are apparent in sport organizations. Women represent only 25 percent of the commissioners for the Australian Sports Commission (Australian Sports Commission, 2010) and 44 percent of the executive board members in Sport England (Sport England, 2010). Within North America, women represent only 10 percent of the NCAA Division I Board of Directors (National Collegiate Athletic Association, 2010) and only 27 percent of the directors of the Coaching Association of Canada (Coaching Association of Canada, 2010).

Women are also underrepresented as coaches. In 1972, women constituted over 90 percent of the coaches of NCAA women's teams. As a result of Title IX being enacted that same year, the coaching compensation and the prestige associated with coaching women's teams gradually increased. Consequently, being a coach of a women's team served as a viable alternative for men, and they steadily began to occupy a larger proportion of the coaching positions for women's teams (Acosta & Carpenter, 2010). By 1978, the percentage of women serving as the head coach of an NCAA women's team had dropped to 58.2 percent. In 2010, women represented less than half (42.6 percent) of the head coaches of women's teams—one of the lowest percentages ever recorded (Acosta & Carpenter, 2010; see Exhibit 5.4). There is evidence this trend may be continuing. Of the 270 new coaching jobs of

exhibit **5.4**   **Percentage of women coaching women's teams.**

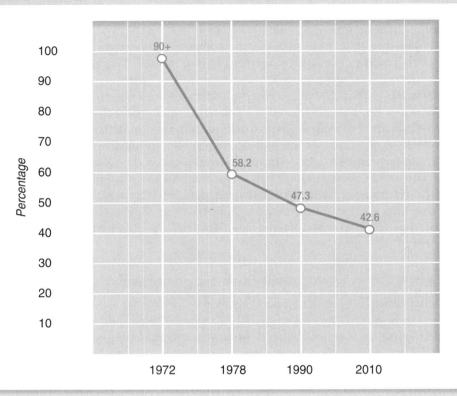

Data from Acosta and Carpenter, 2010.

women's teams to open between 2002 and 2004, men received approximately 53 percent (Acosta & Carpenter, 2004). Canada has also witnessed an influx of male coaches of women's teams to an even greater extent than NCAA teams (Danylchuk & MacLean, 2001).

This underrepresentation of women in management and leadership positions is referred to as the "glass ceiling" (see Stroh et al., 2004). This concept describes the invisible, but certainly real, barrier that limits the upward progression of women in the organizational context. In addition to the glass ceiling, women also encounter "glass walls" (akin to the occupational segregation discussed in Chapter 4). Glass walls prevent people from moving laterally within an organization or profession. For example, women are often employed in the administrative ranks of university athletic departments in positions called the Senior Woman Administrator. They are rarely seen in management positions in development or those that oversee men's sports, even though men are routinely charged with overseeing women's sports (see DeHass, 2007). Rather, these positions, which have high prestige and may be considered a requisite stepping-stone to becoming a head athletic director, are generally reserved for men. These ideas are consistent with the notion of male hegemony, one of the critical theories discussed in Chapter 2.

Reasons for Underrepresentation

The quest to understand why women are underrepresented in management positions has been the objective of much research, both within and outside the sport context. Using this literature, we can identify three basic categories of factors that influence this phenomenon: stereotypes, structural forces, and personal characteristics (see Exhibit 5.5). These are discussed in the subsections that follow.

Stereotypes

Stereotypes influence the advancement of women in an organization in several ways. Specifically, they influence people's attitudes about whether women exhibit leadership characteristics and the job types considered appropriate for women.

Leadership. In her classic work, Schein (1973, 1975) compiled a list of 92 attributes believed to distinguish women and men, thus serving as the basis for gender stereotypes. She asked a sample of middle managers to rate how those 92 characteristics fit women in general, men in general, and effective middle managers. As expected, she found that the characteristics believed to embody the successful middle manager were closely aligned with those thought to be representative of a man in general. This was true for both male and female respondent managers in her sample. Thus, to think of a successful manager was to think of a man, not a woman.

More recent research shows that people associate masculine characteristics with successful managers and that people are more likely to use masculine, rather

Factors that influence the underrepresentation of women in coaching positions.	*exhibit* **5.5**

Gender stereotypes:

- *Leadership:* Effective leaders are thought to possess masculine characteristics.
- *Job type:* Coaching is considered a profession best suited for men.

Structural forces:

- *Discrimination:* Athletic administrators favor men over women in the hiring process.
- *Social networks:* Women's social networks are not as strong as the "old boys club" with which men are associated.
- *Nature of the coaching profession:* The work-family conflict associated with coaching may have a stronger impact on women than it does on men.

Personal characteristics:

- *Attitudes about being a head coach:* Women have less positive attitudes about becoming a head coach than men.
- *Intention to become a head coach:* Women have less desire than men to become a head coach.
- *Occupational turnover:* Women leave coaching at an earlier age than men, thereby creating a shortage of qualified women coaches.

alternative PERSPECTIVES

Women and Transformational Leadership. The conventional thinking about the issue of who makes an effective leader has traditionally favored men. This is due to the link between gender stereotypes and the perceived qualities of good leaders. Recent leadership theory, however, questions these perceptions. Many researchers believe transformational leaders are the best type for an organization. *Transformational leaders* have charisma and provide inspirational motivation, intellectual stimulation, and individualized consideration. Because some of these attributes are thought to be consistent with feminine gender stereotypes, it is possible that women are more likely to be transformational leaders than men. Organizations led by transformational leaders are likely to achieve high levels of effectiveness and a committed workforce. Doherty (1997) found that coaches rated female administrators as demonstrating greater charisma and more individualized consideration. This finding suggests that, contrary to traditional stereotypes, women may be as suited as men to lead groups and organizations, if not more so.

than feminine, pronouns when describing an ideal manager (Knoppers & Anthonissen, 2008). An earlier study by Shaw and Slack (2002) of sport national governing bodies in England had anticipated these findings. They found that female leaders were usually described in terms of their elegance and style, without mention of their leadership qualities. On the other hand, male leaders were noted for their vision and revolutionary style. Managers' behaviors are also cast in gender stereotypes. Shaw and Hoeber (2003) found that people within sport organizations believe that "a strong man is direct and a direct woman is a bitch" (p. 347). See the Alternative Perspectives box for a further discussion of this issue.

As might be expected, these stereotypes can negatively influence women's career advancement. If organizational decision makers associate "being a manager" with "being a man," then women are at a distinct disadvantage in the hiring process. To the extent that primary decision makers hold such perceptions, stereotypes will limit the advancement of women (see also Sartore & Cunningham, 2007).

Job type. Gender stereotypes concerning the type of jobs and activities considered appropriate for men and women also influence the proportion of women in leadership positions. The U.S. Census Bureau data document sex differences in occupational employment. For example, the top occupations employing men in 2004 included truck drivers, managers of retail sales workers, retail salespersons, and general laborers. On the other hand, the top occupations employing women in 2004 included secretaries, elementary and middle school teachers, registered nurses, cashiers, and retail salespersons. Note that only one occupation, retail salesperson, appears on both lists.

This pattern suggests that some job types are considered masculine in nature, and thus more suitable for men, while others are considered feminine and more appropriate for women. The gendering of jobs and activities also occurs within the sport and physical activity industry. Shaw and Slack (2002) found that men hesitated to fill some positions, such as regional development officer, in the sport organizations they studied because of the positions' legacy as "women's work" (p. 93). Similarly, Knoppers (1992) argues that coaching is associated with masculine qualities and perceived as a position for men. This stereotype remains even though many coaching activities, such as nurturing athletes, facilitating their play, and providing them with individualized consideration, are more associated with the feminine nature than the masculine. Burton, Barr, Fink, and Bruening (2009) found evidence of this persisting stereotype when participants in their study associated "masculine" with "managerial" roles, which, stereotypically, were those most associated with men's activities and considered to be most important for top leadership roles. As these authors noted, if masculine managerial activities are considered most important for holding leadership in sport organizations, then women are likely to be deemed incapable of holding that position.

Structural forces

Structural forces refer to established forces, either in the coaching profession or in individual athletic departments, that serve to constrain the advancement of women. These forces include discrimination, social networks, and the nature of the coaching profession, as discussed below.

Discrimination. Much research points to discrimination, both access and treatment, as one cause of the underrepresentation of women in coaching (Knoppers, 1992; Lovett & Lowry, 1994; Lowry & Lovett, 1997; Stangl & Kane, 1991). For examples in the leisure industry, see Aitchison, Jordan, and Brackenridge (1999). This discrimination takes several forms. Organizational decision makers could prefer men over women when filling coaching vacancies. In the athletics context, this means that athletic directors, most of whom are men, prefer other men to serve as coaches. This rationale is consistent with the social categorization framework and is supported by earlier studies. Acosta and Carpenter (2010) report that in Division I athletic departments run by a male, women represent 43.8 percent of the coaches of women's teams. This figure is less than the 46.2 percent of women coaching women's teams when the athletic director is female. When there are no women in an athletic department's administrative structure, women represent 38.1 percent of the coaches of women's teams.

Others adopt a different approach, suggesting that power is at the heart of the matter (Sartore & Cunningham, 2007). Mary Jo Kane, director of the Tucker Center for Research on Girls and Women in Sport at the University of Minnesota, commented on the status of women coaching women's teams: "I think it can be summed up in one word: power. The stakes have gotten higher—there's money, scholarships, TV contracts. It's a new career for men, and men have taken it over" (as cited in Anderson, 2001, p. 88). Consistent with the previous discussion of gender stereotypes, Kane also suggests, "I think there is still some deep-seated cultural assumption that if you want to take your program big time, you want to get a *real* coach, so you should get a male coach" (as cited in Anderson, 2001, p. 88). Thus, gender stereotypes may lead organizational decision makers to consciously decide to hire men over women, thinking that men are more likely to have "what it takes" to be a successful coach.

Treatment discrimination also influences the underrepresentation of women in coaching positions. Because current women coaches are treated differently, there are variations in the career outcomes achieved by men and women. A study by Cunningham and Sagas (2002) lends credence to this position. These authors surveyed male and female assistant coaches of men's and women's university athletics teams and found that the women had more valued human capital investments (e.g., playing experience, playing honors) than the men. In fact, 25 percent of all the men in the sample never played university athletics, compared with only 3.3 percent of women without such experience. Nevertheless, the men had longer coaching tenures and more of the desired attitudes toward coaching (e.g., head coaching intentions) than the women. The authors reason that although women had greater human capital, they

alternative
PERSPECTIVES

Effects of Discrimination. Many discussions of discrimination assume that the effects are uniform—that they impact all people the same. This is not necessarily the case, however. People who are not accustomed to facing discrimination, and are otherwise privileged, might experience discrimination more negatively than those more accustomed to discriminatory treatment. Cunningham and Sagas (2007) found evidence for this in their study of assistant coaches of women's teams. For men in their study, discriminatory treatment negatively impacted their career satisfaction and ultimately their occupational turnover intentions. For women, these effects were not observed. These findings are consistent with those from Tsui, Egan, and O'Reilly (1992), who found that being different affected subsequent outcomes more for Whites and for men than for other persons—a concept called *nonsymmetrical effects.*

did not receive the return on such investments that men did. Therefore, their attitudes toward the profession were not as positive as the men's attitudes. This reasoning is supported by various studies both in (Sagas & Cunningham, 2004) and out of the sport context (Kirchmeyer, 1998). To explain this pattern, Kirchmeyer notes, "low returns for female managers can be explained by perceptual distortions and cognitive biases among employers that lead to discriminatory practices" (p. 675). Thus, differences in the return on human capital investments that are associated with differences in sex negatively influence women's advancement in the coaching profession.

While we might implicitly think that felt discrimination impacts people similarly, this is not necessarily the case. See the Alternative Perspectives box for a discussion of this issue.

Social networks. The underrepresentation of women can also be attributed to dissimilarities in the social networks of male and female coaches (Kilty, 2006). Social networks serve many important functions, including providing access to information, mentoring, and supporting upward mobility (Seibert, Kraimer, & Liden, 2001). People who are successful in forming social networks are likely to have greater career success than those who cannot form such alliances. Furthermore, people who have networks comprised of demographically similar others are likely to enjoy greater career success than those whose social networks are comprised of demographically different people (Seibert et al., 2001). This presents a quandary for women, especially in the sport context, considering that access to demographically similar social networks may be limited. That is, if coaching is considered a male domain and men are more likely to be coaches than are women, then men have a better chance of having other men in their social network than women do of having other women in their network. The effect is especially telling when we consider those people in the network who are in high organizational positions, such as an athletic director.

What impact does a social network have on female coaches? The answer is: a substantial one. Many point to the "good old boys" network prevalent in the sport context (for an example, see Lovett & Lowry, 1994) as a reason for the underrepresentation of women in coaching and leadership positions. Christine Grant, formerly women's athletic director at the University of Iowa, speaks to this issue: "I don't think there is a concerted effort to go and get qualified women. If you want well-qualified women candidates, you have to get on the phone and do your homework. Male athletic directors apparently aren't doing that. When they hire male coaches, they are on the phone with their buddies finding out what their recommendations are" (as cited in Anderson, 2001, p. 88). Thus, consistent with Grant's position, when it comes to coaching, or being considered for a coaching position, "who you know" might be just as important as "what you know."

Nature of the coaching profession. Coaching requires 12- to 15-hour workdays, extensive travel to games and events, and countless hours spent watching game films, practicing, and recruiting quality players. The coaching profession demands that time spent performing other life activities such as those related to friends and family must be reduced, given half-heartedly, or put on hold for another time. As Dixon and Bruening (2005) note, women are more likely than men to experience stress resulting from conflicts between time spent at work and time spent with family, a phenomenon known as *work–family conflict*. As previously discussed, gender stereotypes call for the woman to spend more time than the man on family and domestic duties. Thus, women are more likely than men to have to choose between coaching and family or find a compromise between the two (but see also Greenhaus & Powell, 2006, for a discussion of work–family enrichment). These factors contribute to their overall well-being and desire to remain in coaching (Allen & Shaw, 2009; Kilty, 2006). See also the Diversity in the Field box for additional information pertaining to how work–family conflict influences elite athletes.

Women who do balance these roles either have support from friends and family or wait until later in life to begin a family. For Purdue swim coach Cathy Wright-Eger, the answer is a strong support network that includes parents, in-laws, sisters, and friends who all help with family issues while she is away coaching (Anderson, 2001; see also Bruening & Dixon, 2008). Pat Summitt, the women's basketball coach at the University of Tennessee, also notes the potential stress: "for women who are trying to balance family and a coaching career, it is very difficult" (Anderson, 2001, p. 91). Summitt did not have her son until she was 38—after she was well-established in the coaching profession and could afford a full-time nanny. Of course, not all coaches are as successful as Summitt, have her financial security ($1.4 million annual salary), or can afford a full-time nanny. Thus, discussions on how women can successfully manage their coaching life and their family life continue.

DIVERSITY *in the field*

Elite Athletes as Mothers. Many elite athletes are also parents. For instance, Ken Griffey, Jr. played Major League Baseball with his father, Ken Griffey. However, just as observed in coaching, the potential strain created by balancing the time needed to be a parent with the time needed to be an elite athlete is often greater for women than it is for men. For instance, Lorena Ochoa, the number-one-ranked female golfer in the world, retired from golf at age 28 in 2010, citing the desire to spend more time raising her children. Other elite athletes, such as tennis's Lyndsay Davenport, have also retired or taken extended leaves of absence in order to spend time with their children. Elite male athletes do not make similar career choices, however, and this may be due, in part, to the variations in gender stereotypes for women and men.

Palmer and Leberman (2009), in noting this trend, interviewed elite female athletes to understand how they balance family and sport obligations. The authors found that the athletes in their study managed the multiple roles and potential constraints (e.g., guilt, lack of time) by emphasizing the centrality of sport to their sense of self. The women also pointed to the importance of strong social networks, as well as concerted efforts to integrate the two roles. Based on their study, Palmer and Leberman discussed the importance of developing practices and policies that allow mothers to achieve and sustain elite status.

Personal characteristics

Personal characteristics such as attitude toward being a head coach, intention to become a head coach, and likelihood to leave the coaching profession influence women's underrepresentation. When discussing these factors, it is important to remember that personal characteristics are substantively influenced by gender, societal expectations, and structural forces. Some factors, such as personality, are considered fairly stable over time and are at least partially due to genetics. Other characteristics (e.g., self-efficacy, outcome expectations, and head coaching aspirations), however, are shaped largely by personal experiences; the influence of family, friends, and coworkers; and societal expectations and stereotypes. As Sartore & Cunningham (2007) note, "the response to the social and cultural forces that function to shape one's self (i.e., multiple identities) may result in the unconscious manifestation of self-limiting behaviors" (pp. 245–246). Thus, discussing the personal characteristics is not a "blame the victim" approach (Knoppers, 1987; Staurowsky, 1996); rather, not discussing such factors paints an incomplete picture of the phenomenon.

Attitudes about being a head coach. Research documents sex differences in attitudes toward being a head coach. For example, Sagas, Cunningham, and Ashley (2000) surveyed 112 assistant coaches (72 women, 40 men) of a variety of NCAA Division I athletic teams. They asked the coaches to indicate why they would not seek head coaching positions. The women in the sample listed the following as the most important factors: (a) they enjoy their current coaching situation and do not want to leave, (b) there is too much pressure to win as a head coach, (c) there is less stress associated with being an assistant coach, and (d) loyalty to their current team or head coach. Because the men in the sample had no aversion to being a head coach (a point discussed in the next section), they did not respond to these items. Other coaches express similar sentiments. Mickie DeMoss, a former head coach at the University of Florida and current associate coach at Tennessee, notes, "women establish relationships where they are, and there's a greater sense of loyalty with women than with men. If they get comfortable somewhere, that means more to women than to men" (as cited in Anderson, 2001, p. 90). The negative attitudes some women have toward being a head coach prevent them from seeking those positions.

Intention to become a head coach. An aspiration for career advancement is one of the most fundamental antecedents to progressing in one's career. Without such an aspiration, one is unlikely to make the human and social capital investments necessary to become a manager, to seek such a position, or to ultimately be promoted. Using this rationale, Cunningham and associates examined head coaching intentions among assistant coaches across a variety of contexts (Cunningham & Sagas, 2002; Cunningham, Doherty, & Gregg, 2007; Cunningham, Sagas, & Ashley, 2003; Sagas, Cunningham, & Ashley, 2000), as have other authors (e.g., Kilty, 2006). The findings reliably show that women have less desire to become a head coach and are less likely to apply for such a position. Sagas, Cunningham, and Ashley found that 92.5 percent of men in their sample had a desire to become a head coach, compared with 68.1 percent of women. These findings were replicated in several studies and hold for both American (Cunningham & Sagas, 2002; Cunningham et al., 2003) and Canadian (Cunningham et al., 2007) coaches. Consistent with these findings, Sagas, Cunningham, and Ashley (2000) also found men were more likely than women to have sought head coaching positions in the past (37.5 percent versus 15.2 percent).

That female assistant coaches have less desire to become a head coach than do men is one of the more salient factors influencing the underrepresentation of women in head coaching positions. If men are more likely to search for head coaching positions and express a greater desire to obtain such a position in the future, then the representation of women in head coaching positions is going to continue to lag behind that of men.

Occupational turnover. Differences in occupational turnover also influence the underrepresentation of women in head coaching positions. In a study by Sagas et al. (2000), 68 percent of the women in the sample reported that they planned to leave the profession before age 45, a substantially higher percentage than men (15 percent) expressing similar plans. Subsequent research supports this finding among both assistant coaches (Cunningham & Sagas, 2002, 2003; Cunningham et al., 2003) and head coaches (Sagas & Ashley, 2001; Sagas & Batista, 2001). These findings are also consistent with research in other contexts, such as high school sports (Hart, Hasbrook, & Mathes, 1986). The problem associated with gender differences in occupational turnover is exacerbated when we consider that the vacancies are likely to be filled by men (Acosta & Carpenter, 2004; Hart et al., 1986).

Section Summary

Several factors contribute to the underrepresentation of women in coaching positions. Stereotypes about what women should do, who they should be, and what characteristics a successful coach should possess all work against women. When organizational decision makers, most of whom are male, seek to hire others who are demographically similar to themselves, the opportunity for women to be seriously considered is significantly reduced. Finally, women are not only less likely to seek head coaching positions but also more likely to leave coaching at an earlier age than men, thereby creating a supply-side shortage of women coaches.

Sex, Gender, and Sport Participation

The discussion now turns to participation in sport and physical activity. Research shows few gender differences in physical activity levels among infants. However, as people grow older, differences emerge: in the toddler, youth, young adult, adult, and older populations, men are more physically active than women (Carron, Hausenblas, & Estabrooks, 2003).

PROFESSIONAL PERSPECTIVES

Women's Work Experiences in Mexico. Although much of the research related to women in the sport industry takes place in the United States or Canada, it is also useful to consider women's work experiences in other countries such as Mexico. Gabriela Deyanira Martinez Garcia, who served as the women's athletic coordinator at Universidad Autonoma de Nuevo Leon from 2003 to 2005, explains that, in general, "women are not given the opportunity to hold decision-making positions in sports organizations either in universities, government, or any other organization." These limited opportunities are largely the result of men holding the power positions within sport organizations and selecting other men to fill vacancies. Garcia also notes that many men "consider that women have no right to be in leadership positions. The predominance of 'machismo' is the main factor why women are relegated and faced with limitations to do their work." (Note that machismo is a strong sense of masculine pride or an exaggerated masculinity considered to be present in many Latin cultures.) She further notes that, although attitudes toward women are slowly changing, it will be a long time before women obtain decision-making positions based on their experiences and knowledge rather than the politics involved.

Several reasons account for the sport participation differences between women and men. As previously noted in the discussion of gender stereotypes, parental influences, schools, and the mass media all serve to portray sport and physical activity as more appropriate for males than for females. In the early 1970s, *Sports Illustrated* columnists Bil Gilbert and Nancy Williamson noted, "there may be worse (more socially serious) forms of prejudice in the United States, but there is no sharper example of discrimination today than that which operates against girls and women who take part in competitive sports, wish to take part, or might wish to if society did not scorn such endeavors" (as cited in Eitzen & Sage, 2009, p. 317). Given these stereotypes, it is easy to understand why girls and women chose not to participate in sport in the past.

However, over time, female involvement in sport has increased substantially. Coakley (2009) points to five factors that influenced this increase:

1. Females have far more opportunities for sport participation today than ever before. Females have many sport and physical activity alternatives from which to choose.

2. Government mandates increased sport opportunities for girls and women. Most notably, Title IX requires equal opportunities for males and females participating in federally funded educational activities, including physical education courses and athletics. Title IX prohibits schools from offering sport opportunities and activities for one group (i.e., boys) and not the other (i.e., girls) in nearly all situations. Title IX is discussed at length in Chapter 12.

3. The global women's movement promotes the precept that females are most complete as human beings when they develop their mental *and* physical abilities.

4. The health and fitness movement, which emphasizes the positive health benefits associated with physical activity participation, increased the awareness and appreciation of physical activity and sport, with an associated increase in those activities.

5. Increased media coverage of girls and women participating in sport prompted others to participate. Now, young girls have role models to show them that females can not only participate in sport but also excel in it. These media images are powerful and inspiring, resulting in an increase in the interest in sport and physical activity among females.

The Intersection of Gender and Race

Thus far, the experiences of women and men have been discussed in general terms. However, not all men and not all women have similar experiences in sport or sport organizations. Rather, other factors such as race may significantly influence one's experiences in the workplace. The effects of gender and race are not merely additive: they are qualitative, in that women of color are likely to have experiences that differ from those of men of color or White women. This section examines the intersection of gender and race among persons in the sport context. (For further discussion of this issue, see Bruening, 2005.)

Earnings

Gender and race interact to influence people's earnings. As previously indicated, men generally earn more than women, and Whites generally earn more than racial minorities. Examination of the data from the U.S. Department of Labor reveals other interesting patterns. As of 2008, among men, African Americans and Hispanics earn 75 percent and 67.8 percent of what Whites earn, respectively. The variations are less pronounced among women, though the general pattern still remains. African American women earn 84.7 percent of what White women earn, while Hispanic women earn only 76.6 percent.

An examination of gender differences within each race yields interesting findings as well. According to the U.S. Department of Labor (2009), in 2008 white women earned 79.3 percent of what White men earned. The gap between earnings was less pronounced among African American men and women (89.3 percent) and also Hispanic men and women (89.6 percent). Of course, Asian and White men earned the most among all people compared in this analysis, so that may contribute to these differences. Nevertheless, the figures reported here do illustrate how race and sex interact to influence earnings. See Exhibit 5.6.

Representation in Management and Leadership Positions

As previously noted, women are generally underrepresented in management and leadership positions. The underrepresentation increases further when considering

Median weekly earnings of full-time wage and salary workers, by sex, race, and Hispanic or Latino ethnicity, 2008 annual averages. *exhibit* **5.6**

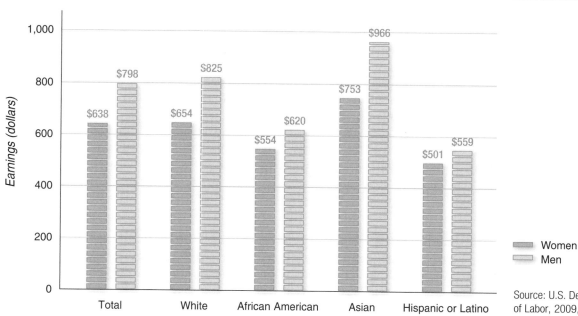

Source: U.S. Department of Labor, 2009, p. 4.

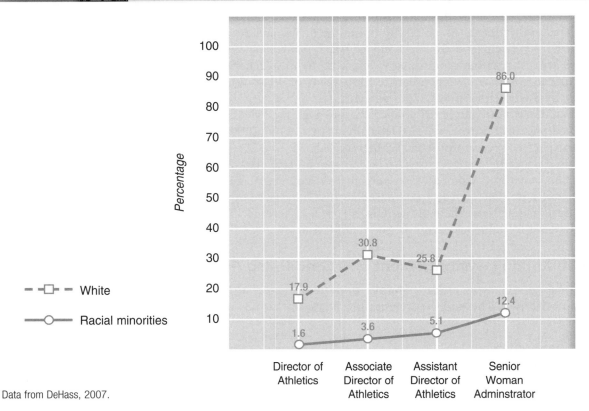

exhibit **5.7**   Racial differences in the representation of women in administrative positions within university athletics.

Data from DeHass, 2007.

women of color (see Exhibit 5.7). For example, in the Australian Sports Commission, Sport England, the NCAA, and the Coaching Association of Canada, the proportion of White women far outnumbers that of minority women. On many of these boards, women of color are not represented at all. The same is true within university athletic departments. According to DeHass (2007), White women constitute 86.0 percent of the Senior Woman Administrators, compared with only 12.4 percent for women of color. These figures demonstrate that racial minority women face particularly challenging obstacles in the workplace, both in their compensation and in their advancement up the organizational hierarchy.

Sport Participants

Women of color are more likely to have poor health (e.g., be overweight) and less likely to be physically active than White women (see Armstrong, 2001; Henderson & Ainsworth, 2001). Because physical activity improves one's health, several studies examined factors that influence participation in sport and recreational programs by racial minority women. Henderson and Ainsworth (2001), in their qualitative study of African American and Native American women, identified several factors that influenced physical activity levels. Job demands, family expectations and needs, economic constraints, and the lack of available facilities and opportunities were listed for women of both races as the major constraints to physical activity participation. Armstrong (2001) reports that the results of a nationwide research project consisting of mostly African American women indicate that lack of motivation, lack of time, lack of energy, and prohibitive costs are the top barriers to being physically active. Interestingly, younger women were more likely to cite these constraints than their older counterparts. In both studies, those women who participated in sport and recreational activities cited strong support networks. The support comes from friends, family, or other community members. Finally, in both studies, walking was reported as the most popular physical activity. As Henderson and Ainsworth (2001) note, walking was appealing because of its accessibility to all persons, the social and/or solitary dimensions of the activity, and the thinking that it is "not really exercise" (p. 28).

Using another perspective, the Women's Sports Foundation (Butler & Lopiano, 2003) commissioned a study to examine the influence of Title IX on men and women across races who participated in university athletics. The study was commissioned because anecdotal evidence suggested that women of color had not benefited from Title IX to the extent that White women had. The results indicate that this is not the case. Since 1971, the number of women of color participating in university athletics increased 995 percent, a figure much larger than the corresponding increase for White women (320 percent). Women of color also receive a percentage of the scholarship monies (19.5 percent) above what might be expected based on their proportion among all female athletes (14.8 percent). Finally, although women athletes of color graduate at lower rates than White women athletes (55 percent versus 68 percent), this proportion is substantially higher than the proportion of minority women who graduate in the general student body (49 percent).

Based on this data, Butler and Lopiano arrived at several conclusions. First, claims that people of color are disadvantaged as a result of Title IX seem unfounded. Second, based on the representation of female athletes of color across all sports and their experiences while participating in those sports, gender and race discrimination are still present in the context of university athletics. Third, patterns of racial inequality are present in most women's sports, as clustering effects (i.e., the overrepresentation of athletes of color in some sports, but underrepresentation in others) are present in 20 of 25 (80 percent) of women's sports. Finally, there is no overt evidence of graduation rate or scholarship bias for athletes of color: female athletes of color receive a greater proportion of scholarship dollars than would be expected based on their participation rates and also graduate at higher rates than their racially similar peers in the general student body. Overall then, Title IX can be seen as benefiting, not hurting, racial minority women who participate in university athletics.

The Marketing of Sport

he influence of sex and gender is evident in the marketing of sport and physical activity. Marketing efforts traditionally have been geared toward attracting the "average fan" to the event—that is, the efforts have been aimed at men (Fink, Trail, & Anderson, 2002). Today, women represent a growing segment of the fan base. Further, research shows that, relative to men, women are more likely to purchase team merchandise and remain loyal to the team in the future (Fink et al., 2002). Nevertheless, research suggests that women and men have different motivations for attending events and react differently to services provided at the event. Thus, it is important to understand these differences in order to implement more effective and efficient marketing efforts.

Motives for Sport Consumption

Several studies examined the differing reasons women and men have for attending events. Swanson, Gwinner, Larson, and Janda (2003) argue that gender stereotypes guide motivations for sport consumption. They predicted that men, who are thought to be more aggressive and success oriented, might value those activities that are high in entertainment value, stimulate them, and provide a sense of self-worth when the team succeeds. On the other hand, women, with their presumed emphasis on feminine qualities such as communal concerns, might be more apt to seek activities that are family oriented. These predictions were largely supported: men's attendance was primarily guided by the motivation to be emotionally aroused at the event (a concept known as eustress). Women, on the other hand, were motivated to attend sport events primarily for group affiliation reasons. Other researchers obtained similar results (Wann, 1995; Wann, Schrader, & Wilson, 1999).

Consumption of Women's Sports

Other studies examined the reasons for attending women's sport events. Funk, Ridinger, and Moorman (2003) studied people who chose to attend women's professional basketball games. In addition to those motives identified in other sport contexts, the authors uncovered unique motivations for attending women's events, including players serving as role models, the need to support opportunities for women to compete in sports, and the perception of women's sports as a wholesome environment. The former two variables were especially influential in explaining the level of team support among the fans. As Funk et al. note, both of these factors could be leveraged by sport marketers to increase sport consumption among women, both young and old.

Customer Service

Team success is one of the most reliable indicators of fan loyalty; however, not all teams can be successful. As such, other factors such as customer service satisfaction become important in gaining consumer trust and loyalty. Trail, Anderson, and Fink (2002) found that women rated several service quality factors as more important than men did, including the cleanliness of the facilities, the quality of the restrooms, the audio experience, and the quality of the service personnel. These findings are consistent with research outside the sport context that shows that some service provider characteristics, such as the appropriateness of the attire, have a stronger influence on women's affective reactions than on men's (Shaoa, Baker, & Wagner, 2004). These results suggest that gender likely influences the relationship between event factors other than performance and satisfaction with the event. Specifically, these factors may be more important to the formation of women's satisfaction with the event than men's satisfaction.

Promoting Sport

Finally, other studies examined gender issues in relation to promoting sport events. Fink, Cunningham, and Kensicki (2004) drew from the match-up hypothesis, which suggests that advertising endorsers are more effective when there is a match between them and the product. They examined the influence of athlete attractiveness and expertise in an advertisement promoting women's softball. Results from their experiment indicate that both attractiveness and expertise influence the fit of the endorser. Specifically, participants who believed the athlete was attractive and that she had a high level of expertise also believed that she was an appropriate endorser of the athletic event. Such perceptions about endorser fit are important because they influence both positive attitudes toward the event and the intention to purchase tickets for the event. As expected, athlete expertise influences perceptions of endorser fit, and highly skilled athletes, such as Serena Williams, are likely to be more effective endorsers of an athletic event than less skilled athletes. The fact that attractiveness—an attribute that has nothing to do with how masterful a sport is played—also positively influences perceptions about endorser fit is explained by gender stereotypes demanding that women maintain their femininity and beauty while participating in sports. Promoters of sport events remain mindful of this stereotype, as evidenced by the popularity of some attractive but not highly successful athletes as event promoters (e.g., Anna Kournikova).

A follow-up study from Cunningham, Fink, and Kenix (2008) shed further light on these dynamics. Whereas Fink et al. focused on the effects of attractiveness and expertise in a sex-inappropriate sport (i.e., softball), Cunningham et al. focused on the effects of these attributes among spectators of tennis—a sex-appropriate sport. Their results pointed to the interactive effects of attractiveness and expertise. As might be expected, when an athlete was perceived to be unattractive, a highly skilled athlete was seen as a better fit than a less skilled counterpart. However, a different pattern emerged for athletes perceived to be highly attractive. Among these persons, the skill level did not matter: less skilled attractive athletes were seen as just as good a fit for promoting the tournament as were highly skilled athletes. These findings suggest that, at least in sex-appropriate sports such as tennis, attractiveness is seen as a requisite condition. In this way, women have come to be valued as much for their physical characteristics as their athletic talent.

CHAPTER *summary*

This chapter focused on the experiences of men and women in the sport context. The Diversity Challenge demonstrated the substantial influence of sex and gender on who participates in sport, the allocation of resources, and attitudes toward sport. The same is also true in the workplace: work experiences, compensation, access to managerial and leadership positions, and attitudes toward their careers differ as between women and men. After reading the chapter, you should be able to:

1. Understand the meaning of sex and gender and the differences between the two concepts.

Sex refers to the biological characteristics, such as reproductive organs, that distinguish women and men. Gender, on the other hand, refers to the social roles expected of women and men, with an emphasis on the concepts of masculinity and femininity. Though the two terms are sometimes used interchangeably, especially when referring to biological differences (e.g., "his gender is male"), they have separate meanings and connotations.

2. Discuss the differing experiences men and women have in the workplace.

Across a variety of contexts, research shows that, relative to men, women are less likely to be members of the workforce, receive less compensation for their work, and are less likely to be in upper-echelon management positions. These trends are present in the sport and physical activity context as well. Considerable research examined why women are underrepresented in management and leadership positions, revealing three possible explanations: stereotypes, structural forces, and personal characteristics.

3. Be familiar with the influence of sex and gender on sport participation.

Women are generally less physically active than their male counterparts. This is due, in large part, to gender stereotypes emanating from various socialization agents (e.g., parents, school, media). More recently, women's participation in sport has increased, largely due to five factors: (1) increased opportunities, (2) governmental mandates, (3) the global women's movement, (4) the health and fitness movement, and (5) increased media coverage of women's sport.

4. Discuss the intersection of gender and race.

Research shows that women are generally disadvantaged relative to men and that racial minorities are generally disadvantaged relative to Whites. For women of color, these effects are magnified in such a way that their experiences, both in the general workplace and in sport, are considered to be poorer than people from other social groups. Relative to others, women of color receive the lowest salaries and are least likely to hold management positions. These effects are also seen among sport participants, and these women often face unique challenges when seeking physical activity participation opportunities. Nevertheless, participation opportunities for women of color have increased substantially as a result of Title IX.

5. Understand the influence of sex and gender on the marketing of sport.

Though sport marketing efforts traditionally have been geared toward a "male" prototype, there is a growing recognition that women and consumers of women's sports have unique motivations, wants, and desires when it comes to sport consumption. From a customer service perspective, the factors that women value in the service exchange often vary from those of men. Finally, research shows that gender stereotypes probably influence marketing and promotion efforts, as evidenced by the research suggesting that female spokespersons for athletic events are generally better received when they are highly qualified *and* highly attractive.

QUESTIONS *for discussion*

1. What are the primary gender stereotypes associated with women and men? Are those stereotypes still observable today?

2. What are the primary factors that influence the formation of gender stereotypes? Which is likely to have the strongest impact?

3. What is the influence of gender stereotypes on participation in sport and physical activity?

4. Why are gender differences in earnings still present today? Are they more likely to be seen in one context than in another?

5. Women are underrepresented in top management positions. What are some of the reasons for this phenomenon?

6. Several potential explanations for the underrepresentation of women in management and leadership positions were discussed in the chapter. Which is the most important in explaining this phenomenon? Why?

7. Why does the participation of women in sport and physical activity lag behind that of men? What steps can sport managers take to reverse this trend?

8. This chapter suggested that women of color have experiences in sport and in the workplace that are unique to them. Why is this the case?

9. Are the experiences of all women of color likely to be the same? If not, why and what are examples of where this would not be the case?

LEARNING *activities*

1. Suppose you are involved in searching for a coach for a women's team at your university. What emphasis would you put on the gender of the coach in the hiring process? What about the assistant coaches? Divide into two groups and discuss.

2. Search online for the presence of female administrators in national sport organizations such as United States Basketball.

READING *resources*

SUPPLEMENTARY READINGS

Konrad, A. M. (2006). *Cases in gender and diversity in organizations.* Thousand Oaks, CA: Sage. (Provides real-life cases related to workplace discrimination, sexual harassment, work–life balance, organizational diversity programs, cross-cultural diversity, and entrepreneurship.)

Messner, M. (2002). *Taking the field: Women, men, and sports.* Minneapolis: University of Minnesota Press. (Argues that sport largely retains and continues its longtime conservative role in gender relations; considers the influences of the daily routines of sport participants, structural foundations in place, and the mass media.)

Powell, G. N., & Graves, L. M. (2003). *Women and men in management* (3rd ed.). Thousand Oaks, CA: Sage. (Comprehensive overview of the issues surrounding women in the workplace; examines historical aspects, sex and gender, and the influence of sex and gender on employment decisions, leadership, and career aspirations.)

Reynaud, C. (2005) *She can coach!* Champaign, IL: Human Kinetics. (Provides an insider's view of such topics as professional foundation and conduct, personal investment and self-direction, program implementation and management, relationship building, and promotional activities through the words and experiences of 20 successful female coaches in 13 different sports.)

WEB RESOURCES

- National Association of Collegiate Women Athletic Administrators (www. nacwaa.org)
- National Association for Girls & Women in Sport (www.aahperd.org/nagws/template.cfm): division of the American Alliance for Health, Physical Education, Recreation, and Dance; good resource site.
- Women's Sports Foundation (www.womenssportsfoundation.org): provides a wide range of resources related to girls' and women's participation in sport.

references

Abercrombie, N., Hill, S., & Turner, B. S. (2000). *The Penguin dictionary of sociology* (4th ed.). New York: Penguin Books.

Acosta, R. V., & Carpenter, L. J. (2004). *Women in intercollegiate sport: A longitudinal study—twenty-seven year update—1977–2004.* Unpublished manuscript, Brooklyn College, Brooklyn, NY.

Acosta, R. V., & Carpenter, L. J. (2010). *Women in intercollegiate sport: A longitudinal study—thirty-three year update—1977–2010.* Unpublished manuscript, Brooklyn College, Brooklyn, NY.

Aitchison, C., Jordan, F., & Brackenridge, C. (1999). Women in leisure management: A survey on gender equity. *Women in Management Review, 14*(4), 121–127.

Allen, J. B., & Shaw, S. (2009). Women coaches' perceptions of their sport organization's social environment: Supporting coaches' psychological needs? *The Sport Psychologist, 23,* 346–366.

Anderson, K. (2001, January/February). Where are all the women coaches? *Sports Illustrated for Women, 3*(1), 86–91.

Armstrong, K. L. (2001). Black women's participation in sport and fitness: Implications for sport marketing. *Sport Marketing Quarterly, 10,* 9–18.

Australian Sports Commission. (2010). *Board of the Australian Sports Commission.* Retrieved January 24, 2010, from www.ausport.gov.au.

Bem, S. L. (1974). The measurement of psychological androgyny. *Journal of Consulting and Clinical Psychology, 42,* 155–162.

Bem, S. L. (1975). Sex role adaptability: One consequence of psychological androgyny. *Journal of Personality and Social Psychology, 31,* 634–643.

Bem, S. L. (1977). On the utility of alternative procedures for assessing psychological androgyny. *Journal of Consulting and Clinical Psychology, 45,* 196–205.

Bowker, A., Gadbois, S., & Cornock, B. (2003). Sports participation and self-esteem: Variations as a function of gender and gender role orientation. *Sex Roles, 49,* 47–58.

Bruening, J. E. (2005). Gender and racial analysis in sport: Are all the women White and all the Blacks men? *Quest, 57,* 330–349.

Bruening, J. E., & Dixon, M. A. (2008). Situating work-family negotiations within a life course perspective: Insights on the gendered experiences of NCAA Division I head coaching mothers. *Sex Roles, 58,* 10–23.

Burton, L. J., Barr, C. A., Fink, J. S., & Bruening, J. E. (2009). "Think athletic director, think masculine?": Examination of the gender typing of managerial subroles within athletic administration positions. *Sex Roles, 61,* 416–426.

Butler, J. A., & Lopiano, D. (2003). *The Women's Sports Foundation report: Title IX and race in intercollegiate sport.* East Meadow, NY: Women's Sports Foundation.

Carpenter, L. J., & Acosta, R. V. (2005). *Title IX.* Champaign, IL: Human Kinetics.

Carron, A. V., Hausenblas, H. A., & Estabrooks, P. A. (2003). *The psychology of physical activity.* New York: McGraw-Hill.

Catalyst Institute. (2008). *2008 Catalyst Census of women corporate officers and top earners of the* Fortune 500. New York: Author.

Coaching Association of Canada. (2010). *Board of directors.* Retrieved January 24, 2010, from www.coach.ca/eng/.

Coakley, J. (2009). *Sports in society: Issues and controversies* (10th ed.). New York: McGraw-Hill.

Color controversy at Iowa: Prof. threatened for criticizing pink locker room. (2005, September 28). SI.com. Retrieved September 28, 2005, from http://sportsillustrated.cnn.com/2005/football/ncaa/09/28/bc.fbc.bigtennotebook.ap/index.html.

Cramer, J. A. (1994). Conversations with women journalists. In P. J. Creedon (Ed.), *Women, media, and sport: Challenging gender values* (pp. 159–180). Thousand Oaks, CA: Sage.

Cuneen, J., & Sidwell, M. J. (1998). Gender portrayals in *Sports Illustrated for Kids* advertisements: A content analysis of prominent and supporting models. *Journal of Sport Management, 12,* 39–50.

Cunningham, G. B., Doherty, A. J., & Gregg, M. J. (2007). Using social cognitive career theory to understand head coaching intentions among assistant coaches of women's teams. *Sex Roles, 56,* 365–372.

Cunningham, G. B., Fink, J. S., & Kenix, L. J. (2008). Choosing an endorser for a women's sporting event: The interaction of attractiveness and expertise. *Sex Roles, 58,* 371–378.

Cunningham, G. B., & Sagas, M. (2002). The differential effects of human capital for male and female Division I basketball coaches. *Research Quarterly for Exercise and Sport, 73,* 489–495.

Cunningham, G. B., & Sagas, M. (2003). Occupational turnover intent among coaches of women's teams: The role of organizational work experiences. *Sex Roles, 49,* 185–190.

Cunningham, G. B., & Sagas, M. (2007). Perceived treatment discrimination among coaches: The influence of race and sport coached. *International Journal of Sport Management, 8,* 1–20.

Cunningham, G. B., Sagas, M., & Ashley, F. B. (2003). Coaching self-efficacy, desire to head coach, and occupational turnover intent: Gender differences between NCAA assistant coaches of women's teams. *International Journal of Sport Psychology, 34,* 125–137.

Cunningham, G. B., Sagas, M., Sartore, M. L., Amsden, M. L., & Schellhase, A. (2004). Gender representation in the *NCAA News:* Is the glass half full or half empty? *Sex Roles, 50,* 861–870.

Danylchuk, K. E., & MacLean, J. (2001). Intercollegiate athletics in Canadian universities: Perspectives on the future. *Journal of Sport Management, 15,* 364–379.

Deeply offensive to me: Martha Burk protests new NHL advertising campaign. (2005, September). SI.com. Retrieved September 23, 2005, from http://sports illustrated.cnn.com/2005/hockey/nhl/09/23/burk.ads.ap/index.html.

DeHass, D. (2007). *2005–06 ethnicity and gender demographics of NCAA member institutions' athletics personnel.* Indianapolis, IN: The National Collegiate Athletic Association.

Dixon, M. A., & Bruening, J. E. (2005). Perspectives on work–family conflict in sport: An integrated approach. *Sport Management Review, 8,* 227–253.

Doherty, A. J. (1997). The effect of leader characteristics on the perceived transformation/transactional leadership and impact on interuniversity athletic administrators. *Journal of Sport Management, 11,* 275–285.

Eastough, K., & Miller, P. W. (2004). The gender wage gap in paid- and self-employment in Australia. *Australian Economic Papers, 43,* 257–276.

Eccles, J. S., Jacobs, J. E., & Harold, R. E. (1990). Gender role stereotypes, expectancy efforts, and parents' socialization of gender differences. *Journal of Social Issues, 46,* 183–201.

Eitzen, D. S., & Sage, G. H. (2009). *Sociology of North American sport* (8th ed.). Boulder, CO: Paradigm.

Fink, J. S., Cunningham, G. B., & Kensicki, L. J. (2004). Utilizing athletes as endorsers to sell women's sport: Attractiveness versus expertise. *Journal of Sport Management, 18,* 350–367.

Fink, J. S., & Kensicki, L. J. (2002). An imperceptible difference: Visual and textual constructions of femininity in *Sports Illustrated* and *Sports Illustrated for Women. Mass Communication & Society, 5,* 317–339.

Fink, J. S., Trail, G. T., & Anderson, D. F. (2002). Environmental factors associated with spectator attendance and sport consumption behavior. Gender and team differences. *Sport Marketing Quarterly, 11,* 8–19.

Funk, D. C., Ridinger, L. L., & Moorman, A. M. (2003). Understanding consumer support: Extending the Sport Interest Inventory to examine individual differences among women's professional sport consumers. *Sport Management Review, 6,* 1–31.

Greenhaus, J. H., & Powell, G. N. (2006). When work and family are allies: A theory of work–family enrichment. *Academy of Management Review, 31,* 72–92.

Hart, B. A., Hasbrook, C. A., & Mathes, S. A. (1986). An examination of the reduction in the number of female interscholastic coaches. *Research Quarterly for Exercise and Sport, 57,* 68–77.

Henderson, K. A., & Ainsworth, B. E. (2001). Researching leisure and physical activity with women of color: Issues and emerging questions. *Leisure Sciences, 23,* 21–34.

Hoffman, L. W., & Youngblood, L. M. (1999). *Mothers at work: Effects on children's well-being.* Cambridge, UK: Cambridge University Press.

Humphreys, B. R. (2000). Equal pay on the hardwood: The earnings gap between male and female NCAA Division I basketball coaches. *Journal of Sports Economics, 1,* 299–307.

Kane, M. J. (1988). Media coverage of the female athlete before, during, and after Title IX: *Sports Illustrated* revisited. *Journal of Sport Management, 2,* 87–99.

Kilty, K. (2006). Women in coaching. *The Sport Psychologist, 20,* 222–234.

Kirchmeyer, C. (1998). Determinants of managerial career success: Evidence and explanation of male/female differences. *Journal of Management, 24,* 673–692.

Kling, K. C., Hyde, J. S., Showers, C. J., & Buswell, B. N. (1999). Gender differences in self-esteem: A meta-analysis. *Psychological Bulletin, 125,* 470–500.

Knoppers, A. (1987). Gender and the coaching profession. *Quest, 39,* 9–22.

Knoppers, A. (1992). Explaining male dominance and sex segregation in coaching: Three approaches. *Quest, 44,* 210–227.

Knoppers, A., & Anthonissen, A. (2008). Gendered managerial discourses in sport organizations: Multiplicity and complexity. *Sex Roles, 58,* 93–103.

Lantz, C. D., & Schroeder, P. J. (1999). Endorsement of masculine and feminine gender roles: Differences between participation in and identification with the athletic role. *Journal of Sport Behavior, 22,* 545–556.

Lovett, D. J., & Lowry, C. D. (1994). "Good old boys" and "good old girls" clubs: Myth or reality? *Journal of Sport Management, 8,* 27–35.

Lowry, C. D., & Lovett, D. J. (1997). Women coaches: Does when dictate why they leave? *Applied Research in Coaching and Athletics Annual, 1997,* 35–53.

Lumpkin, A., & Williams, L. D. (1991). An analysis of *Sports Illustrated* feature articles, 1954–1987. *Sociology of Sport Journal, 8,* 16–32.

Lytton, H., & Romney, D. M. (1991). Parents' differential socialization of boys and girls: A meta-analysis. *Psychological Bulletin, 109,* 267–296.

Messner, M. A., & Solomon, N. M. (2007). Social justice and men's interests: The case of Title IX. *Journal of Sport and Social Issues, 31,* 162–178.

National Collegiate Athletic Association. (2010). *Division I board of directors.* Retrieved January 4, 2010, from www.ncaa.org.

Palmer, F. R., & Leberman, S. I. (2009). Elite athletes as mothers: Managing multiple identities. *Sport Management Review, 12,* 241–254.

Parks, J. B., & Roberton, M. A. (1998a). Contemporary arguments against nonsexist language: Blaubergs (1980) revisited. *Sex Roles, 39,* 445–461.

Parks, J. B., & Roberton, M. A. (1998b). Influence of age, gender, and context on attitudes toward sexist/nonsexist language: Is sport a special case? *Sex Roles, 38,* 477–494.

Parks, J. B., & Roberton, M. A. (2000). Development and validation of an instrument to measure attitudes toward sexist/nonsexist language. *Sex Roles, 42,* 415–438.

Parks, J. B., & Roberton, M. A. (2002). The gender gap in student attitudes toward sexist/nonsexist language: Implications for sport management education. *Journal of Sport Management, 16,* 190–208.

Parks, J. B., & Roberton, M. A. (2004). Attitudes toward women mediate the gender effect on attitudes toward sexist language. *Psychology of Women Quarterly, 28,* 233–239.

Parks, J. B., Russell, R. L., Wood, P. H., Roberton, M. A., & Shewokis, P. A. (1995). The paradox of the contented working woman in intercollegiate athletics administration. *Research Quarterly for Exercise and Sport, 66,* 73–79.

Pomerleau, A., Boldue, D., Malcuit, G., & Cossette, L. (1990). Pink or blue: Environmental stereotypes in the first two years of life. *Sex Roles, 22,* 359–367.

Powell, G. N., & Graves, L. M. (2003). *Women and men in management* (3rd ed.). Thousand Oaks, CA: Sage.

Pryzgoda, J., & Chrisler, J. C. (2000). Definitions of gender and sex: The subtleties of meaning. *Sex Roles, 43,* 553–569.

Sagas, M., & Ashley, F. B. (2001). Gender differences in the intent to leave coaching: The role of personal, external, and work-related variables. *International Journal of Sport Management, 2,* 297–314.

Sagas, M., & Batista, P. J. (2001). The importance of Title IX compliance on the job satisfaction and occupational turnover intent of intercollegiate coaches. *Applied Research in Coaching and Athletics Annual, 16,* 15–43.

Sagas, M., & Cunningham, G. B. (2004). Does having the "right stuff" matter? Gender differences in the determinants of career success among intercollegiate athletic administrators. *Sex Roles, 50,* 411–421.

Sagas, M., Cunningham, G. B., & Ashley, F. B. (2000). Examining the women's coaching deficit through the perspective of assistant coaches. *International Journal of Sport Management, 1,* 267–282.

Sagas, M., Cunningham, G. B., Wigley, B. J., & Ashley, F. B. (2000). Internet coverage of university softball and baseball Web sites: The inequity continues. *Sociology of Sport Journal, 17,* 198–205.

Sartore, M. L., & Cunningham, G. B. (2007). Ideological gender beliefs, identity control and self-limiting behavior within sport organizations. *Quest, 59,* 244–265.

Schein, V. E. (1973). The relationship between sex role stereotypes and requisite management characteristics. *Journal of Applied Psychology, 57,* 95–100.

Schein, V. E. (1975). Relationships between sex role stereotypes and requisite management characteristics among female managers. *Journal of Applied Psychology, 60,* 340–344.

Seibert, S. E., Kraimer, M. L., & Liden, R. C. (2001). A social capital theory of career success. *Academy of Management Journal, 44,* 219–237.

Shakib, S., & Dunbar, M. D. (2004). How high school athletes talk about maternal and paternal sporting experiences: Identifying modifiable social processes for gender equity physical activity interventions. *International Review for the Sociology of Sport, 39,* 275–299.

Shaoa, C. Y., Baker, J., & Wagner, J. A. (2004). The effects of appropriateness of service contact personnel dress on customer expectations of service quality and purchase intention. The moderating influences of involvement and gender. *Journal of Business Research, 57,* 1164–1176.

Shaw, S., & Hoeber, L. (2003). "A strong man is direct and a direct woman is a bitch": Gendered discourses and their influence on employment roles in sport organizations. *Journal of Sport Management, 17,* 347–375.

Shaw, S., & Slack, T. (2002). "It's been like that for donkey's years": The construction of gender relations and the cultures of sports organizations. *Culture, Sport, Society, 5,* 86–106.

Shifflett, B., & Revelle, R. (1994). Gender equity in sports and media coverage: A review of the NCAA News? *Journal of Sport and Social Issues, 18,* 144–150.

Spence, J. T., & Helmreich, R. L. (1978). *Masculinity and femininity: Their psychological dimensions, correlates, and antecedents.* Austin: The University of Texas Press.

Sport England. (2010). *Our executive team.* Retrieved January 24, 2010, from www.sportengland.org.

Stangl, J. M., & Kane, M. J. (1991). Structural variables that offer explanatory power for the underrepresentation of women coaches since Title IX: The case of homologous reproduction. *Sociology of Sport Journal, 8,* 47–60.

Staurowsky, E. J. (1996). Blaming the victim: Resistance in the battle over gender equity in intercollegiate athletics. *Journal of Sport and Social Issues, 20,* 194–210.

Stroh, L. K., Langlands, C. L., & Simpson, P. A. (2004). Shattering the glass ceiling in the new millennium. In M. S. Stockdale & F. J. Crosby (Eds.), *The psychology and management of workplace diversity* (pp. 147–167). Malden, MA: Blackwell.

Swanson, S. R., Gwinner, K., Larson, B. V., & Janda, S. (2003). Motivations of college student game attendance and word-of-mouth behavior: The impact of gender differences. *Sport Marketing Quarterly, 12,* 151–162.

Trail, G., Anderson, D., & Fink, J. S. (2002). Examination of gender differences in importance and satisfaction with venue factors at intercollegiate basketball games: Effects of future spectator attendance. *International Sports Journal, 6,* 1–14.

Tsui, A. S., Egan, T. D., & O'Reilly, C. A., III. (1992). Being different: Relational demography and organizational attachment. *Administrative Science Quarterly, 37,* 549–579.

Tuggle, C. A. (1997). Differences in televised sports reporting of men's and women's athletics: ESPN SportsCenter and CNN Sports Tonight. *Journal of Broadcasting and Electronic Media, 41*(1), 14–24.

Unger, R. K. (1979). Toward a redefinition of sex and gender. *American Psychologist, 34,* 1085–1094.

U.S. Department of Labor. (2009). Highlights of women's earnings in 2008, p. 4. Retrieved May 26, 2010, from http://www.bls.gov/cps/cpswom2008.pdf.

Van Sickle, G. (2005, November). *Funk-y bunch: Skirt-wearing underdog brings life to Skins Game.* SI.com. Retrieved January 5, 2006, from http://sportsillustrated.cnn.com/2005/writers/gary_van_sickle/11/27/skins.game/index.html.

Wann, D. L. (1995). Preliminary validation of the sport fan motivation scale. *Journal of Sport and Social Issues, 19,* 377–397.

Wann, D. L., Schrader, M. P., Allison, J. A., & McGeorge, K. K. (1998). The inequitable newspaper coverage of men's and women's athletics at small, medium, and large universities. *Journal of Sport and Social Issues, 22,* 79–87.

Wann, D. L., Schrader, M. P., & Wilson, A. (1999). Sport fan motivation: Questionnaire validation, comparisons by sport, and relationship to athletic motivation. *Journal of Sport Behavior, 22,* 114–140.

Ward, M. (2001). The gender salary gap in British academia. *Applied Economics, 33,* 1669–1681.

Woodhill, B. M., & Samuels, C. A. (2003). Positive and negative androgyny and their relationship with psychological health and well-being. *Sex Roles, 48,* 555–565.

Zimbalist, A. (1999). *Unpaid professionals.* Princeton, NJ: Princeton University Press.

6

Age

P hysical inactivity rates in the United States have steadily risen over time, to the detriment of the country and its citizens. In fact, the World Health Organization estimates that over 60 percent of the population does not achieve the minimum recommendations for daily physical activity. According to the American Heart Association, a lack of physical activity is associated with a host of health problems, including heart disease, high blood pressure, diabetes, obesity, and low levels of "good" cholesterol. The price of inactivity goes beyond the individual's well-being; there are also monetary costs. In fact, in 2000, inactivity contributed to $75 billion in healthcare costs in the United States, alone.

Most people do not engage in the recommended levels of physical activity, and participation levels continually decrease as a person ages. This is particularly noteworthy in Western countries, where the average age continues to increase. Thus, left unchanged, the current physical activity patterns will only be exacerbated over time.

Of course, physical inactivity is not characteristic of all persons, even all seniors. Rather, a number of persons age 50 and higher are very active, as evidenced by their participation in the Senior Games. This is an event, held every two years, that affords persons age 50 to 100+ the opportunity to competitively participate in 18 medal sport events (e.g., archery, race walking) and 7 exhibitions (e.g., fencing, sailing). The 2009 Games were held in the San Francisco Bay Area. The Games were hailed as the largest multisport event in Bay Area history, with more than 10,000 athletes, 2,000 volunteers, and 20,000 visitors. The economic impact was estimated to be $35 million. Phil Godfrey, President and CEO of the National Senior Games Association, remarked: "For two wonderful weeks here in the San Francisco Bay Area, our athletes have fulfilled their dreams, enjoyed the venues, the competition and the many activities of the San Francisco peninsula. More importantly they showed the world what can happen when you take charge of your life and exercise on a regular basis."

LEARNING OBJECTIVES

After studying this chapter, you should be able to:

- Discuss the various ways in which age and age diversity are conceptualized.

- Provide an overview of how age is related to stereotypes, work experiences, and opportunities.

- Analyze the intersection of age and sport and leisure participation.

Information adapted from: ■ In the news. (2009). *2009 Summer National Senior Games.* Retrieved October 29, 2009, from http://www.2009seniorgames.org ■ Physical activity. (2009). *American Heart Association.* Retrieved October 29, 2009, from http://www.americanheart.org ■ Physical activity. (2009). *World Health Organization.* Retrieved October 29, 2009, from http://www.who.int.

DIVERSITY CHALLENGE   **R E F L E C T I O N**

1. Despite the many benefits of regular physical activity, participation rates decrease with age. Why is this the case?

2. Organizations like the Senior Games not only address the problem of physical inactivity but also have the potential to impact other outcomes. What are some of these, and why are these effects observed?

3. What can sport managers do to increase the physical activity levels of seniors?

 s the Diversity Challenge illustrates, one's age plays a meaningful role in a number of areas, including sport and physical activity participation. This is also the case within sport organizations, where age influences the opportunities people have, their interactions with their coworkers and supervisors, and how they relate to others in groups. Indeed, Posthuma and Campion (2009) outlined three specific reasons for the analysis of age in the workplace. First, the average employee age for persons in the United States and other industrialized nations is increasing (see also Haq, 2004; Feyrer, 2007); therefore, people are more likely than ever before to work with someone who differs in age, and age stereotypes might be more prevalent than in the past. Second, in order to spur economic growth, there is a need for older workers to remain in organizations longer than they have in the past (Feyrer, 2007). Their activity in the workforce will not only result in more contributions to retirement systems but will also reduce the strain on such programs. Finally, despite the aforementioned points, there is evidence that age discrimination is more prevalent than it has ever been before (Lieber, 2007). Despite these pressures, there is little attention paid by researchers and sport managers to age and age diversity in the employment context.

The purpose of this chapter, therefore, is to remedy this situation. To do so, I first provide an overview of key terms and statistics related to age. The discussion then moves to an analysis of the intersection of age and employment. Subsumed in this section is an overview of age-related stereotypes, the impact of these stereotypes on subsequent work-related outcomes, and important moderators. In the final section, I examine how age influences sport and leisure participation.

Background and Key Terms

 o an 18-year-old employee, a colleague who is 35 may seem old. That same 35-year-old may consider herself young, especially in relation to others or when contemplating she has lived less than half her expected lifespan. Thus, in some respects, what qualifies as "old" is in the eye of the beholder. On the other hand, there are specific criteria in some areas of sport, such as federal anti-discrimination statutes and sport organization policies, that provide specific guidelines. For instance, the Age Discrimination in Employment Act (discussed in detail in Chapter 12) sets 40 as the age when people become "protected" from various organizational practices. It is illegal to hire and fire employees based simply on their age; therefore, from this perspective, we can consider persons 40 or older as "older" employees. A different standard is observed among some sport organizations. Entities such as the Champions Golf Tour or the Senior Games use age 50 as the minimum age for participation in their events. Alternatively, one has to be at least 19 to participate in the NBA. Finally, we can also consider generational differences in our discussions of age, and this is illustrated in Exhibit 6.1.

U.S. Census Bureau estimates suggest that the average age of U.S. residents will continue to increase this century—a trend observed in other industrialized countries around the world (Haq, 2004). In 2008, 44.13 million persons were age 65 or older, which represented 14 percent of the population. As the Baby Boomers continue to age, this proportion will grow accordingly. In 2030, all Baby Boomers will be at least age 65, which will mean that roughly one in five (21.6 percent) people in the United States will be expected to fall into this age group. This proportion is expected to increase, and by 2050, a quarter of all residents are expected to be age 65 or older. Of course, as one age group increases its proportion in the total population, others must decrease. This pattern is observed among persons age 18 to 64 years (i.e., the years in which people have traditionally worked): the proportion of persons in this age group is expected to decrease from 63 percent of the population in 2008 to 57 percent in 2050.

The aging of the U.S. population coincides with an increased proportion of employees who choose to work past the traditional retirement age (i.e., 65 years). Mehrotra and Wagner (2009) point to several factors influencing this trend. First, in an effort to promote longer employment tenures, Social Security was altered so that those who work past the typical retirement age receive increased monthly Social Security benefits. Second, since most working employees receive health insurance coverage through the workplace, there is an incentive to remain employed until at least age 65, at which point people become eligible for Medicare. Third, many workers express concerns about having available funds after retirement. Only 52 percent

---

Generational differences. *exhibit* **6.1**

The generation to which one belongs is based on the year of her or his birth. Although the exact years might differ depending on who is asked, Chamberlain (2009) suggests that generations typically can be categorized in the following way:

- Traditionalists or veterans: before 1946
- Baby boomers: 1946 to 1964
- Generation X: 1965 to 1980
- Generation Y: after 1980

DIVERSITY
in the field

Bridge Employment in College Athletics. According to Bell, "bridge employment occurs when workers have retired from long-term jobs, but have not fully withdrawn from the workforce" (2007, p. 321). She notes that bridge employees bring many benefits to the workplace, including being more flexible and having considerable expertise and knowledge accrued from a lifetime of employment.

Bridge workers are commonly hired to part-time positions. This is particularly the case with many game-day service positions for college athletic departments. Bridge employees often serve as ushers, as security, as guest services personnel, or in other capacities. Cunningham and Mahoney's (2004) research also suggests that bridge employees in this context are particularly loyal and committed to the workplace. They found that the average person in their study had worked for the university for over 7 years, and some for up to 30 years. They also demonstrated high levels of commitment to the athletic department and were eager to engage in training exercises that they thought would benefit the delivery of the sport product. Thus, consistent with Bell's (2007) contention, bridge employees in this context added considerable value to the workplace.

of retirees receive some form of pension income, meaning that nearly half of the retired workforce lives off personal savings and Social Security benefits. These dynamics make working longer, and therefore accruing more Social Security benefits and greater savings, an appealing option. Next, many older workers continue to work as a way to stay active and engage in meaningful activities (see also the Diversity in the Field box for a discussion of bridge employment). Fifth, compared with generations past, older workers today are healthier and can therefore remain engaged in the workforce for longer periods of time. Sixth, the United States is now primarily a service economy, which means that only a small portion of jobs require strenuous physical labor. Instead, most work now requires only light physical exertion, which means that the physical demands of work do not limit older persons from participating. Finally, many of the Baby Boomers are more educated than older employees have been in the past, and this is particularly the case for women. This education is important because labor force participation rates increase threefold for persons over age 50 who have a college degree, relative to those who dropped out of high school. Collectively, all these factors tend to keep older persons in the workforce for longer periods of time, and as a consequence, age diversity within sport organizations is increasing.

Age and Other Diversity Dimensions

As the U.S. population and the population in the workforce age, the fact that age intersects with other diversity dimensions is an important consideration. For instance, elderly minorities face circumstances that are much different from circumstances faced by Whites. This is due primarily to differential opportunities they had during their youth. Mehrotra and Wagner (2009) explain that elderly persons of color who were born in the United States have experienced both racial and school segregation, low social class, and truncated access to healthcare. During their youth, most persons of color were denied access to schools, housing, and hospitals. Collectively, these factors have negatively influenced their overall health and well-being today, especially by comparison with persons who did not experience such discrimination.

Age has also been shown to intersect with two dimensions of socioeconomic status: education and poverty (Mehrotra & Wagner, 2009). Approximately 10 percent of all elderly Hispanics and African Americans have not completed high school. This obviously impacts the job one obtains and one's earning potential, and this is evidenced in poverty rates: 23.7 percent of African Americans age 65 or older and 19.5 percent of Hispanics age 65 or older live below the poverty level. These numbers are considerably higher than the corresponding percentages among Asians (14.1 percent) and Whites (8.0 percent). Chapter 11 provides a complete overview of issues related to socioeconomic status and social class. The accompanying sidebar also provides a discussion of the educational attainment of younger persons.

Research also suggests that people's sex impacts the aging population (Mehrotra & Wagner, 2009). Because of a host of factors, including health-related habits and the work in which they are engaged, women generally outlive men. As a result, the gap in the population ratio (the number of men for every hundred women) grows wider with age group. Improvements have been made over time, however. In 1990, the male to female ratio for persons over age 65 was 67, meaning that for every 100 women, there were 67 men. In 2000, the ratio had increased to 70, in 2008, 72, and U.S. Census Bureau estimates suggest that the ratio will increase to 79 by 2050. Despite these improvements, "the fact remains that a very large proportion of older women today will outlive their spouses and face challenges of later life alone" (Mehrotra & Wagner, 2009, p. 18).

EDUCATIONAL ATTAINMENT AMONG YOUNG ADULTS

Age diversity discussions revolve primarily around persons 65 years and older. However, age diversity is encompassing of all individuals, both young and old. As such, it is also important to consider the educational attainment of young adults, especially when considering the linkage between education, job type, and income. Andrew Sum, from the Center for Labor Market Studies at Northeastern University, provided such an analysis and also examined differences between native-born and foreign-born. His data focused on persons age 18 to 24 who were out of school. Among native-born young adults, 19.5 percent dropped out of high school, 45.0 percent were high school graduates, and 35.5 percent completed some college or graduated from college. These proportions were quite different from foreign-born young adults. Among this group of people, 45.0 percent dropped out of high school, 32.0 percent graduated high school, and 23.0 percent completed some college or graduated from college. Thus, foreign-born young adults are more than twice as likely to drop out of high school than their native-born counterparts. As immigrants represent an increasing proportion of the U.S. population, sport managers must find methods to educate their future workforce.

Age and Employment

Given the increased age diversity in organizations, including those in sport, it is hardly surprising that one's age influences work experiences and outcomes. This section focuses on age-related stereotypes, the manner in which those stereotypes influence people's work, and moderators of those relationships. The focus is primarily on older employees, and this is due to the aging of the U.S. population and workforce, as previously outlined. It is important to note, however, that age stereotypes also exist for younger employees, thereby having the potential to negatively affect their work as well. Thus, where the supporting literature is available, those dynamics are also highlighted.

Stereotypes

According to Hamilton and Sherman (1994), workplace age stereotypes represent beliefs and expectations about employees based on the person's age or presumed age. These stereotypes then influence a host of outcomes, including the way people interact with their coworkers, the way supervisors relate to their subordinates, and *exhibit* **6.2**   **Age-related stereotypes in the workplace.**

Age-related stereotypes represent beliefs or expectations about employees based on their age or presumed age. Common stereotypes include:

1. Poor performance: the belief that older employees perform at lower levels than their counterparts.
2. Resistance to change: the belief that older employees are adverse to change and set in their ways.
3. Ability to learn: the belief that older employees are less able to learn new materials or techniques.
4. Shorter tenure: the belief that older employees will remain in the organization for a shorter time than younger employees.
5. More costly: the belief that older employees cost more to the organization because of salaries, healthcare, and retirement costs.
6. More dependable: the belief that older employees are more responsible and trustworthy than their younger counterparts.

the presumed quality that service providers offer, to name a few. In their comprehensive review of the literature, Posthuma and Campion (2009) identified several age-related stereotypes, each of which is outlined in Exhibit 6.2 and below.

Poor-performance stereotype

Perhaps the most common stereotype of older employees is that their job performance is expected to lag behind that of their younger counterparts (Gordon & Arvey, 2004). These stereotypes might be based on a number of factors, including the belief that older employees have low mental ability, cannot handle stress, or are less competent.

Though performance stereotypes exist, the empirical research suggests that such beliefs are unfounded. Instead, these studies suggest that, in many cases, performance actually increases with age (Rosen & Jerdee, 1988; Waldman & Avolio, 1986). Some suggest that the performance differences are a function of the speed at which it takes young and old workers to complete a task. Research does suggest that young workers are quicker in completing tasks, but they also tend to make more mistakes. Thus, when performance is viewed as a multidimensional construct (i.e., taking into account time spent on the task and the accuracy of the results), older and younger workers are equally productive (Prenda & Stahl, 2001). For instance, young sales representatives might make more calls, but older representatives might be more thorough when making the calls.

Ng and Feldman (2008) provided the most comprehensive examination of this issue to date when they analyzed the effects of age on a host of performance indicators. To do so, they aggregated the results across 380 different studies with thousands of participants. They found that age was unrelated to core task performance, or the degree to which the employees effectively accomplished their primary job tasks. Age was also not associated with creativity, as younger and older (i.e., those over 40) persons were found to be equally creative. Despite these two null findings, the authors observed that age was positively associated with a number of performance dimensions, including organizational citizenship behaviors (i.e., engagement in extra-role behaviors) and safety performance. Older workers were also found to express less workplace aggression, have less on-the job substance use, and be absent less frequently. The only negative performance indicator was with respect to training performance, as older workers performed slightly worse in their training programs than their younger counterparts. Collectively, these findings suggest that, if anything, older workers are more productive than younger ones.

These findings have led some to suggest that there is greater variability in performance *within* age groups than *between* them (Posthuma & Campion, 2009). The Alternative Perspectives box provides another view of the relationship between age and performance.

Resistance-to-change stereotype

The next stereotype is that older workers, relative to their younger counterparts, are generally resistant to change (Posthuma & Campion, 2009). This aversion to change could be a function either of people being set in their ways or being hesitant to engage in training to learn new skills. In a classic study illustrating this point, Rosen and Jerdee (1976) found that students thought older workers would be unreceptive to changing their negative job behaviors and would be less motivated to adapt to new technologies in the workplace. Not surprisingly, students were likely to favor young employees in promotions, training, and job transfers. A follow-up study (Rosen & Jerdee, 1977) using a sample of *Harvard Business Review* readers confirmed this pattern of findings, thereby eliminating concerns that the findings were observed only among college students.

These stereotypes have remained over time, too. Weiss and Maurer (2004), in a study conducted nearly three decades after Rosen and Jerdee's, found that students still believed older workers would be unwilling to change their negative work habits. Despite the widespread and lasting nature of this stereotype, there has been no systematic investigation into its validity (Posthuma & Campion, 2009).

Lower-ability-to-learn stereotype

Another stereotype negatively affecting senior employees is the belief that they have low capacities to learn to use new tools, procedures, or materials (Posthuma & Campion, 2009). A qualitative study from Brooke and Taylor (2005) illustrates this point. In one organization where they conducted their research, new technologies had been implemented, resulting in a large portion of the workforce, most of whom were old-

alternative **PERSPECTIVES**

Age and Performance. According to Thomas, Mack, and Montagliani (2004), empirical studies do not support the stereotypes that older employees are less qualified or less productive than their younger counterparts. Several indices such as job performance, capacity to learn, and overall competence are either unrelated to age or have a very small association. Most older employees possess several qualities that younger employees do not, such as a wealth of knowledge and experience accumulated over their lifetime. Those who have been with an organization for a number of years have accumulated institutional knowledge—a knowledge base of organizational practices and policies that reflect why particular decisions and changes were made. Thus, older employees are the living history of their organization. This sense of history is important because, as philosopher George Santayana noted, "Those who do not remember their past are condemned to repeat their mistakes."

er, being displaced. There was a prevailing belief that young employees were better suited to adapt to these new technologies than their older counterparts. For instance, older workers commented that their coworkers saw them in a negative light and incapable of being able to handle new technologies. The stereotypes negatively affected not only older employees but also the effectiveness of the workplace. In analyzing their findings, Brooke and Taylor concluded that "the redeployment of older workers to positions using new technologies was impeded by a perception that younger workers were more able to make skills transitions. Such age-bound assumptions, however, led to mismanagement between the actual skills required and the age segmentation of the labour force" (p. 421).

Shore and Goldberg (2005) provide a detailed description of the different types of learning and how they are impacted by age. Specifically, as one ages, there are corresponding performance decrements in information processing speed, work memory, and attentional abilities. However, intellectual abilities that involve verbal skills are not affected by age, and other forms of intelligence do not regress until late in life, past one's working age. Based on this evidence, Shore and Goldberg concluded that "these results do not suggest that older workers are less able to learn; rather, they underscore the need for organizations to consider different training and development approaches as people age in order to optimize learning" (p. 214).

Shorter-tenure stereotype

A fourth stereotype negatively affecting older workers is the belief that they will leave the organization sooner than their younger counterparts (Posthuma & Campion, 2009). If this does occur, then the organization will be forced to spend the considerable monies needed to recruit, attract, retain, and train a new employee, all of which can costs thousands of dollars. Further, current training efforts, which also cost considerable resources, are thought to be lost on older employees, when compared with their younger counterparts, because employers might not reap their return on investment.

Despite these sentiments, the empirical evidence does not support this stereotype (Hedge, Borman, & Lammlien, 2006). As noted in Chapter 1, the notion that people remain with a sport organization for their whole career has increasingly become outdated (Korman, 1999). Instead, employees are likely to move from one organization to another several times throughout their career. Thus, the notion that younger employees will remain in the organization longer than older employees is unfounded. Furthermore, the benefits of training are often realized in the short term, thereby making concerns related to training and older employee tenure misplaced.

More-costly stereotype

Another stereotype negatively affecting the opportunities and experiences of older workers is that they are overly expensive to the organization (Posthuma & Campion, 2009). Older workers, relative to younger ones, are generally paid higher wages, might be ill more frequently and therefore use more benefits, and are closer to retirement. These stereotypes lead to the perceptions that older employees have limited economic value (Ostroff & Atwater, 2003). Managers often rate older workers as having low economic worth, and these considerations are often at the forefront when making decisions to lay off older employees (Finkelstein & Burke, 1998). In fact, Finkelstein and Burke found that in 68 of 100 comparisons of young and old job prospects, the younger applicant was viewed as more economically viable. Despite the prevalence of this stereotype, there is little empirical evidence to support the notion that younger employees are the better economic alternative for an organization (Posthuma & Campion, 2009).

Dependability stereotype

The final age-related stereotype, dependability, actually serves to benefit older workers to the detriment of their younger counterparts (Posthuma & Campion, 2009). Specifically, older workers are considered to be loyal, trustworthy, stable, and committed to the workforce. They are also less likely to steal from their employer or to be absent from work (Hedge et al., 2006). Younger employees, on the other hand, are sometimes seen as irresponsible, unreliable, and not loyal to the workplace (Bell, 2007). As with the other stereotypes, many of these beliefs have not been subjected to empirical scrutiny.

Age, Opportunities, and Work Experiences

People's age not only affects the stereotypes they encounter but also impacts their job opportunities and work experiences (see Exhibit 6.3 for a summary). Each of these areas is outlined in the following sections.

Selection

Older employees are routinely disadvantaged in the selection process (Perry & Parlamis, 2007). For instance, experimental studies have demonstrated that when people have to decide between two equally qualified job applicants, they will routinely choose the younger of the two (Finkelstein & Burke, 1998). Older workers also have to search longer for jobs than their younger counterparts, and when they do obtain a position, they often have to take a pay cut. To illustrate, people age 25 to 35 spend approximately 13 weeks searching for a job, while people over age 54 spend 18 weeks, or 38 percent longer, on their job hunt (Shore & Goldberg, 2005).

There are a number of factors that influence the relationship between age and selection. One is the type of job for which one applies. Shore and Goldberg (2005)

The influence of age on work opportunities and experiences.   *exhibit* **6.3**

A person's age has the potential to influence various opportunities and experiences encountered in the workplace, including:

1. Selection
2. Training and development
3. Mentoring
4. Performance and promotion potential
5. Exiting the organization

suggest that in some cases, prototype matching takes place, so that a job applicant's age is compared with the age of the general or prototypical person currently in the position. Note too that these prototypes are linked with the prevalent stereotypes associated with age. "Old" jobs are those in which experience and tenure are valued, physical labor is kept to a minimum, and people oversee "big picture" operations. These might include being a head coach or coordinator or a manager of a sports store. "Young" jobs are those in which high energy is needed, people are able to handle a number of tasks simultaneously, and familiarity with new technologies is valued. These might include jobs in marketing and promotions or a job as a sports information director. See also the Diversity in the Field box for additional information related to prototype matching.

Training and development

A second area in which age influences people's work is in the training and development they receive. With rapidly changing technologies and workplace dynamics, effective training and development of employees is essential for workplace competitiveness. The same is true for individual employees, as failing to update one's skills can have serious, negative career consequences. Despite the advantages of training, there is considerable evidence that older workers do not receive the needed training. In fact, employees age 55 to 64 receive just one third the training of persons age 35 to 44 (Bell, 2007). This could be due to stereotypes about their ability to learn and their motivation to adapt to new techniques and strategies, both of which were outlined previously in the chapter. These factors influence a sport organization's willingness to provide development opportunities for older workers.

From a different perspective, some authors have suggested that differences in training are a function of employee choices: older employees choose to not participate in the development opportunities provided (for an overview, see Perry & Parlamis, 2007). Older employees might already have the skill sets that elementary training offers. Consistent with this perspective, Simpson, Greller, and Stroh (2002) observe that involvement in general skills training declines with age. However, this is not the case for all training, and older employees were found to be likely to participate in training of specific occupational skills, such as courses that focused on career- or job-related activities. As an example illustrating these points, an older high school coach might not express interest in training for general skills, such as PowerPoint development (i.e.,

DIVERSITY
in the field

Youth Movement in the NFL. Traditionally, National Football League coaches have had to pay their dues as an assistant coach for many years before even being considered as a head coach. This requisite maturation process meant that a head coach who was age 45 was considered young. But, times have changed. In 2009, Eric Mangini (age, 38; Cleveland Browns), Mike Tomlin (age, 37; Pittsburgh Steelers), Raheem Morris (age, 33; Tampa Bay Buccaneers), and Josh McDaniels (age, 33; Denver Broncos) were all guiding professional football teams, and Tomlin's team won the Super Bowl in 2008. According to Jeffri Chadiha, an ESPN columnist, three factors contribute to this trend. First, many owners and general managers believe that younger coaches can relate better to the current players. Further, coordinator positions, which are oftentimes seen as the pre-requisite for becoming a head coach, are increasingly going to coaches younger than age 40. Finally, financial considerations (young, first time coaches are paid less than older, veteran coaches) and philosophical issues (general managers might be averse to strong-minded, veteran coaches) contribute to the trend as well. Collectively, these factors mean that, in today's NFL "young coaches suddenly seem far more attractive." Thus, at least with some teams, the prototypical NFL coach is young, not old.

general or generic skills), but might be quite interested in attending a basketball coaching workshop (i.e., occupation-specific skills). The Professional Perspectives box offers additional considerations related to training older employees.

Mentoring

Age also influences the mentoring one receives. Traditionally, people have assumed that mentors were older than their protégés, ideally by half a generation (Levinson, Darrow, Klein, Levinson, & McKee, 1978). This is reasonable, as traditionally, older persons would have spent more time in the organization, accrued considerable business acumen, and accordingly, be well-suited to provide career- and organization-related guidance. However, as the age of the average employee has increased, these dynamics are no longer always applicable; instead, employees considered "older" now need mentoring, both formally and informally.

Recall from previous discussions about prototype matching that people have preconceptions about who is suitable for certain positions or roles within the workplace. These dynamics are also applicable to mentoring: research suggests that younger employees are sometimes perceived to be better suited as protégés, and as a result, have better mentoring relationships than older employees. As an example, Finkelstein, Allen, and Rhoton (2007) gathered data from over 600 non-faculty personnel at a large university in the United States. They found that older employees, relative to their younger counterparts, were more likely to be mentored through informal relationships and were less likely to receive career mentoring. Furthermore, the older employees' relationships with their mentors were shorter than younger employees' relationships.

PROFESSIONAL PERSPECTIVES

Training Employees Over Age 50. According to a 2008 AARP study (see www.aarp.org), most employees age 50 or older enjoy the training and development opportunities afforded them, and when the programs are offered, these employees participate in large numbers. The study also indicated that education influenced participation: persons with a four-year college degree were 70 percent more likely to have taken employee-based training over the previous two years than employees with a high school degree or less. In response to these findings, Deborah Russell, AARP's Director of Workforce Issues, said: "For employees to be successful in recruiting and retaining 50-plus workers, they will need to consider ongoing training as a key strategy. Ongoing training and development is what mature workers view as a top attraction in an ideal workplace."

Furthermore, the type of training offered has been found to make a meaningful difference in its effectiveness. Callahan, Kiker, and Cross (2003) found that a combination of training approaches, such as using lectures, modeling, and active participation, improved the training performance of older workers. Additionally, training that occurred in small groups and that allowed for self-pacing was also linked with training effectiveness. Thus, it is important for sport organizations not only to offer training and development opportunities but also to consider the method and structure of the training in order to maximize the benefits of such programs.

Performance and promotion potential

As previously noted, one of the most prevalent age-related stereotypes is that performance declines with age. If this is the case, all else equal, a 50-year-old should perform more poorly than a 30-year-old. However, as we have stated, the empirical evidence simply does not support this contention. In fact, when considering performance as a multidimensional construct, the data suggest that age is positively associated with a number of performance indicators (Ng & Feldman, 2008).

Despite these findings, the negative stereotypes persist, and they affect the promotion potential of older workers. That is, older workers are seen as having little promise or potential for advancement. These effects are especially pronounced when there is a mismatch between the employee and his supervisor. Shore, Cleveland, and Goldberg (2003) report that "employees who are older than their managers suffer negative consequences when examining data most relevant to their careers—promotability, managerial potential, and development" (p. 535). This could be due to the effects of supervisor-subordinate dissimilarity or because of career timetable effects. The latter occurs when people are promoted more slowly than others in their peer group, thereby giving the impression that they are lagging behind (Lawrence, 1988). As an example, a 55-year-old employee of Foot Locker who works for a 35-year-old manager might be seen as "lagging behind" in her career, and the manager's ratings of her career potential and promotion potential are likely to reflect such perceptions.

Exiting the organization

Employees can exit the organization in one of three ways: voluntary turnover, involuntary turnover (i.e., layoffs, downsizing, firing), and retirement. Researchers have found that there is no relationship between age and voluntary turnover (Healy, Lehman, & McDaniel, 1995). Thus, contrary to popular stereotypes, younger and older employees are equally likely to quit in favor of another job. There are differences, however, in layoffs because older employees are frequently targeted. Perry and Parlamis (2007) note that this is due to negative age-related stereotypes and the fact that older workers are more likely than younger ones to occupy mid-level managerial positions that are so often the target of corporate layoffs. Being targeted in corporate downsizing is particularly troubling for employees over age 50 because it substantially reduces their future employment opportunities (Chan & Stevens, 2001). The Diversity in the Field box provides an example of how age influences exit from sport organizations.

DIVERSITY *in the field*

Age Discrimination in College Athletics. In 1998, Joe Moore, a former offensive line coach for Notre Dame, won an age discrimination suit against the university after it was found that he was wrongfully terminated. Bob Davie, the coach at the time, replaced Moore after telling assistants that he needed someone younger for the job. As a result, Moore was awarded twice the amount of back pay he was due ($85,870.56).

Moderators

Thus far, I have focused on age-related stereotypes and the degree to which age impacts work experiences and outcomes. Although age independently and directly influences these outcomes, a number of factors (i.e., moderators; see Chapter 2) also may modify this influence. These moderators include an employee's age relative to coworkers, type of job, and human resource practices. See also the Alternative Perspectives box for other age-related factors that influence employee well-being.

The first moderator refers to an employee's age relative to his or her coworkers and supervisor. Recall from Chapter 2's discussion of relational diversity that people generally prefer to be around others who are similar to the self; thus, people who differ from others in a dyad or group are likely to be negatively affected. Research suggests that this is the case with age, too. For instance, the social norms and historical precedents in some organizations question the appropriateness of a manager who is "too young." Perry, Kulik, and Zhou (1999) report that tensions might arise when employees have a manager who is the same age as their children, if not younger. They found that those employees who were older than their upper-level supervisor were likely to miss work more often than those who did not have such incongruence.

The type of job held might also correlate with the prevalence of stereotypes or affect age-related outcomes in the workplace. This is consistent with the notion of prototype matching previously discussed. A study from Perry, Kulik, and Bourhis (1996) produced an interesting finding. They asked study participants to evaluate applicants for two types of jobs: a salesperson selling stamps and coins (i.e., an "old-type job") and a salesperson selling records and CDs (i.e., a "young-type job"). They found that participants preferred young people over their older counterparts for the young-type job but that there were no age preferences for the old-type job. This effect was heightened when considering the age bias of the evaluator: highly biased evaluators showed a strong preference for younger employees in young-type jobs. This finding suggests that people seek congruence between the type of job and the job holder, particularly in the case of young-type jobs.

Finally, human resource practices might influence the effects of age on stereotypes and work outcomes. Posthuma and Campion (2009) outlined several such approaches:

alternative
PERSPECTIVES

Caring for the Elderly. Although most research related to the categorical effects of age focuses on the employee's age, some research shows that the age of an employee's dependents can also influence important outcomes. Kossek, Colquitt, and Noe (2001) examined the effects of caregiving for elderly dependents (e.g., parents, in-laws) on subsequent employee well-being and performance. The authors note that many cultures call for the separation of children from their parents in order for the children to form a personal identity independent of their parents. When these children are then required to care for their elderly parents, it produces a potential stressor, and the clear separation of identity becomes muddled or lost completely. This situation can have a negative effect on the employee both at home and in the workplace. For example, Kossek et al. found that employees who cared for elderly dependents performed poorly at work and reported lower well-being, relative to those who did not. Furthermore, home and family care decisions were more likely to have a negative impact on the employee when the organizational climate (or atmosphere) discouraged the sharing of family concerns. These findings show that the age of employees' dependents can influence the manner in which work is experienced.

1. Using job-specific information in making decisions concerning selection and promotions can help eliminate age bias and stereotyping. Skill is much more important than age in predicting job performance; thus, focusing on applicant skill sets, rather than their age, should result in fair and effective selection processes.

2. Training and development efforts help managers avoid stereotyping workers by (a) highlighting the prevalence of stereotyping and the ways in which it is manifested and (b) elucidating the many benefits that workers of all ages bring to the organization.

3. Viewing older workers as a source of competitive advantage reduces negative work experiences. Consider, for instance, that older workers bring a wealth of institutional knowledge and expertise to the workplace—an understanding of situations that arises only from experience. Thus, older employees potentially bring benefits to the organization that their younger counterparts cannot.

4. Research suggests that adding complexity, rather than reducing it, improves employees' cognitive functioning and, as a result, their job performance. Managers should not be tempted to simplify an older employee's job when they are concerned that the person is losing his cognitive abilities.

Effects of Age in Work Groups

Thus far, the discussion has focused on the individual employee's work experience and, in some cases, how differing from others in a dyad or group might influence subsequent outcomes. Age and, more specifically, the age dispersion within a group can also influence that entity's processes and outcomes. In drawing from social psychological theories, it might be expected that age dissimilarity would negatively impact the group because people prefer to be around others similar to the self (Byrne, 1971; Tajfel & Turner, 1979; Turner, Hogg, Oakes, Reicher, & Wetherell, 1987). The evidence generally supports this.

Cunningham (2007), in his study of track and field coaching staffs, found that actual group age diversity was positively associated with perceptions of such differences but that perceived age diversity was negatively related to the presence of a common group identity (i.e., the belief that members of the coaching staff all belonged to a single, common group). Research in other contexts supports these findings. Lichtenstein, Alexander, Jinnett, and Ullman (1997) found that age diversity was negatively associated with various indicators of team consideration, including overall team functioning.

Such poor group dynamics are likely to result in undesirable social outcomes. Research consistently shows that age diversity in a group is associated with greater turnover among the group members (Jackson, Brett, Sessa, Cooper, & Peyronnin, 1991; Wiersema & Bird, 1993). One exception is the Cunningham and Sagas (2004) study, though they examined the degree to which age diversity would influence turnover in the coaching profession specifically—not just in organizations in general.

Although age has some impact on a group's social outcomes, the same is not always true for effectiveness. Zenger and Lawrence (1989) found that age diversity is negatively associated with the amount of technical communication among group members. The more people differed with respect to age, the less they discussed a project's technical aspects, both with one another and with people outside the group. However, this study is the exception, as a myriad of other studies show that age diversity does not influence communications in the group (e.g., Simons, Pelled, & Smith, 1999) or the group's overall effectiveness (e.g., Wiersema & Bantel, 1992).

An exception to this generalization might be when effectiveness is contingent upon contacts outside the organization. Siciliano (1996) studied the effects of a variety of diversity variables on the ability of YMCA boards to raise funds. She found that age diversity was positively associated with the level of donations the YMCAs received. It is possible that people of varying ages also have social contacts of varying ages. A board with members all in their 50s might focus on generating donations from people who are also in their 50s, thereby limiting the number of potential donors. Conversely, a board with members whose ages range from 30 to 75 might have social contact with people in the same age range. This group's number of potential donors would be higher, as would the overall donation amount.

Sport and Leisure Participation

Age also influences people's sport and leisure participation. Carron, Hausenblas, and Estabrooks (2003) report that as people grow older, they tend to exercise less. In fact, there is a 50 percent decrease in physical activity levels between the ages of 6 and 16. This trend continues over time, and as a result, many people get little to no physical activity after age 50 (Ruuskanen & Puoppila, 1995). Carron et al. offer two explanations for this occurrence. First, advancing age is associated with a number of ailments such as cardiovascular disease and arthritis. These impairments are likely to make it more difficult for older persons to engage in mild or moderate forms of physical activity. Second, the lack of physical activity could be a generational effect. People born in the early part of

the 20th century may possess different attitudes toward physical activity and exercise than those born in the latter part of the century. Later generations might be more aware of the physical and mental benefits of sport and exercise and thus be more willing to participate. According to this line of reasoning, the physical activity levels in later generations should decrease less than in earlier generations as these people grow older. Only time will tell if this reasoning is correct.

Researchers have also shown that age is associated with the sports people prefer to watch, as seen in the Diversity in the Field box.

Age also influences participation in leisure time activities. Leisure is different from sport in that the former refers to "an inherently satisfying activity that is characterized by the absence of obligation. Free time alone is not necessarily leisure. Instead, the key variable is how a person defines tasks and situations to create intrinsic meaning. Thus, leisure implies feeling free and satisfied" (Mehrotra & Wagner, 2009, p. 295). According to Wink (2007), retirees engage in a number of leisure activities, including reading or writing, exercising, traveling, listening to music, and participating in religious and spiritual activities. Thus, contrary to beliefs about retirees becoming disengaged, research indicates that they actually lead busy, active lives.

One of the most popular leisure activities in which retirees engage is volunteering. This is particularly the case for persons over age 65, who spend twice as much time volunteering as persons under age 50. They participate in these activities for a host of reasons, including the need to keep

DIVERSITY *in the field*

Influence of Age on Sport Consumption. Discussions of the influence of age on sport consumption often center around Generation Y consumers (Bennett, Henson, & Zhang, 2003; Stevens, Lathrop, & Bradish, 2005). These persons are highly sought after by sport marketers because of the size of the generation (78 million in the United States) and their spending habits. The spending potential of this generation is expected to reach $300 billion.

Because of these characteristics, many efforts have been made to examine their preferences, attitudes, and behaviors. Stevens et al. (2005) found that persons in this demographic favored purchasing sports apparel and athletic shoes, and that the same-sex parent played an influential role in purchase decisions. Additional research from Bennett et al. (2003) showed that Generation Y consumers are Internet-savvy and are likely to watch at least two hours of television daily. In terms of their sport preferences, Generation Y consumers most prefer to watch football, soccer, and track and field. Interestingly, these persons also prefer action sports, such as those found at the X-Games, over more traditional sport forms, such as baseball, basketball, and hockey. They are also more likely to watch the X-Games or Gravity Games on television than they are to watch the World Series or the World Cup (Bennett et al., 2003). These findings suggest that the popularity of extreme or action sports may continue to grow, especially when considering the size and spending potential of Generation Y sport consumers.

active, to meet others, to provide themselves with a sense of satisfaction, and to become identified with the entity for which they are volunteering. In fact, people who volunteer are generally happier and healthier than their counterparts who do not (Mehrotra & Wagner, 2009).

The level and type of volunteerism varies by race. Mehrotra and Wagner (2009) note that "volunteering as a way to help others through informal social networks is common in minority communities" (p. 298). Among African Americans, service to one's church allows for a way to incorporate hard work into leisure experiences and service to the community. Asians have been found to volunteer the most in Asian organizations that reinforce their cultural value systems. Native Americans volunteer in ways that provide mutual assistance to others, such as providing food and shelter to elderly individuals. Finally, Hispanic communities tend to concentrate their volunteer efforts on services that provide neighborhood assistance, care for the elderly, and mutual aid.

CHAPTER *summary*

The purpose of this chapter was to examine the effects of age on people's work and their sport and leisure activities. Research strongly suggests that age has a meaningful impact on the stereotypes people encounter, the way in which they experience work, and the opportunities they have. As the Diversity Challenge illustrated, age is usually associated with a decrease in physical activity levels but it does not always have to be; rather, a number of seniors actively participate in sport and physical activity as well as leisure-time activities. After reading this chapter, you should be able to:

1. **Discuss the various ways in which age and age diversity are conceptualized.**

Age and age diversity can be discussed in many ways. According to anti-discrimination laws, people are protected from various organizational practices at age 40. Sport organizations, such as the Senior Games or the Champions Tour, set age 50 as the minimum for participation. Finally, others discuss age in terms of generational differences.

2. **Provide an overview of how age is related to stereotypes, work experiences, and opportunities.**

Age is associated with stereotypes (e.g., poor performance, resistance to change, limited ability to learn, short tenure, more cost, and more dependability) and work experiences and opportunities (e.g., selection, training, performance and promotion potential, and exit from the organization). These effects are moderated by the employee's age relative to coworkers and her or his supervisor, the type of job held, and the sport organization's human resource practices. Age differences within a group influence the internal processes and group outcomes.

3. **Analyze the intersection of age and sport and leisure participation.**

Participation in sport and exercise generally decreases with age. Leisure participation, especially volunteering, increases with age, particularly after age 65.

QUESTIONS *for discussion*

1. What are the reasons for people choosing to work past retirement age? Which of these is the most important? Why?
2. What are the common age-related stereotypes, and which of these is most prevalent? Why?
3. Most of the research related to age diversity focuses on older employees. Do younger employees also face age-related stereotypes? If so, what are they?
4. Research suggests that older employees learn differently than their younger counterparts. Knowing this, what are steps managers can take to facilitate older employees' learning in the workplace?
5. Age diversity is positively associated with the ability of nonprofit boards to raise funds. Why is this the case? How would this influence personnel decisions?
6. How might a sport manager design a volunteer program that would attract older adults of various races?

LEARNING *activities*

1. There are a number of human resource practices in which sport organizations can engage that help mitigate the incidences of age discrimination. In groups, develop a list of such practices as they relate to selection and promotion.
2. Using the Internet, identify sport organizations and sport events targeted toward senior athletes. Based on your search, how would you characterize the available sport and physical activity opportunities for seniors?
3. Research either local or national sport organizations to determine if they attempt to attract or use the services of older volunteers.

READING *resources*

SUPPLEMENTARY READINGS

Beatty, P. T., & Visser, R. M. S. (Eds.) (2005). *Thriving in an aging workforce: Strategies for organizational and systemic change.* Malabar, FL: Krieger. (This edited text focuses on the way in which age intersects with seven organizational issues: selection, training, career development, employee relations, health, pensions, and retirement.)

Gregory, R. F. (2001). *Age discrimination in the American workplace: Old at a young age.* New Brunswick, NJ: Rutgers University Press. (Provides an overview of discriminatory practices aimed at older workers; also addresses ways that older employees can respond to such acts.)

Mehrotra, C. M., & Wagner, L. S. (2009). *Aging and diversity: An active learning experience* (2nd ed.). New York: Routledge. (Offers a comprehensive overview of how age influences a number of life activities, including work, leisure participation, and retirement.)

WEB RESOURCES

- Administration on Aging (http://www.aoa.gov/AoARoot/Index.aspx): Part of the Department of Health and Human Services; provides up-to-date statistics on older Americans across a number of subject areas.

- National Senior Games Association (www.nsga.com): contains information about the National Senior Games, competitive sport events for persons age 50 or older.
- Wi$eUp (http://wiseupwomen.tamu.edu): With a focus on Generation X and Generation Y women, this site promotes financial well-being through educational efforts and by encouraging women to develop responsible saving habits.

references

Bell, M. P. (2007). *Diversity in organizations.* Mason, OH: Thomson South-Western.

Bennett, G., Henson, R. K., & Zhang, J. (2003). Generation Y's perceptions of the action sports industry segment. *Journal of Sport Management, 17,* 95–115.

Brooke, L., & Taylor, P. (2005). Older workers and employment: Managing age relations. *Ageing & Society, 25,* 415–429.

Byrne, D. (1971). *The attraction paradigm.* New York: Academic Press.

Callahan, J. S., Kiker, D. S., & Cross, T. (2003). Does method matter? A meta-analysis of the effects of training method on older learner training performance. *Journal of Management, 29,* 663–680.

Carron, A. V., Hausenblas, H. A., & Estabrooks, P. A. (2003). *The psychology of physical activity.* New York: McGraw-Hill.

Chadiha, J. (2009, September). Youth might dictate new hiring model: Finances, philosophies, and power among reasons to opt for young head coaches. *ESPN.com.* Retrieved November 11, 2009, from http://sports.espn.go.com/nfl/columns/story?columnist=chadiha_jeffri&page=hotread1/youngcoaches.

Chamberlain, J. (2009). Overgeneralizing the generations: As workplaces become increasingly age-diverse, psychologists are working to help people of all ages to work together. *Monitor.* Retrieved October 27, 2009, from www.apa.org.

Chan, S., & Stevens, A. H. (2001). Job loss and employment patterns of older workers. *Journal of Labor Economics, 19,* 484–521.

Cunningham, G. B. (2007). Opening the black box: The influence of perceived diversity and a common in-group identity in diverse groups. *Journal of Sport Management, 21,* 58–78.

Cunningham, G. B., & Mahoney, K. L. (2004). Self-efficacy of part-time employees in university athletics: The influence of organizational commitment, valence of training, and training motivation. *Journal of Sport Management, 18,* 59–73.

Cunningham, G. B., & Sagas, M. (2004). Group diversity, occupational commitment, and occupational turnover intentions among NCAA Division IA football coaching staffs. *Journal of Sport Management, 18,* 236–254.

Feyrer, J. (2007). Demographics and productivity. *Review of Economics and Statistics, 38,* 545–557.

Finkelstein, L. M., Allen, T. D., & Rhoton, L. A. (2007). An examination of the role of age in mentoring relationships. *Group & Organization Management, 28,* 249–281.

Finkelstein, L. M., & Burke, M. J. (1998). Age stereotyping at work: The role of rater and contextual factors on evaluations of job applicants. *Journal of General Psychology, 125,* 317–345.

Gordon, R. A., & Arvey, R. D. (2004). Age bias in laboratory and field settings: A meta-analytic investigation. *Journal of Applied Social Psychology, 34,* 468–492.

Hamilton, D. L., & Sherman, J. W. (1994). Stereotypes. In R. S. Wyer & T. K. Srull (Eds.), *Handbook of social cognition* (2nd ed., vol. 2, pp. 1–68). Mahwah, NJ: Lawrence Erlbaum.

Haq, R. (2004). International perspectives on workplace diversity. In M. S. Stockdale & F. J. Crosby (Eds.), *The psychology and management of workplace diversity* (pp. 277–298). Malden, MA: Blackwell.

Healy, M. C., Lehman, M., & McDaniel, M. (1995). Age and voluntary turnover: A quantitative review. *Personnel Psychology, 48,* 335–344.

Hedge, J. W., Borman, W. C., & Lammlein, S. E. (2006). *The aging workforce: Realities, myths, and implications for organizations.* Washington, DC: American Psychological Association.

Jackson, S. E., Brett, J. F., Sessa, V. I., Cooper, D. M., & Peyronnin, K. (1991). Some differences make a difference: Individual dissimilarity and group heterogeneity as correlates of recruitment, promotions, and tenure. *Journal of Applied Psychology, 76,* 675–689.

Korman, A. K. (1999). Motivation, commitment, and the "new contracts" between employers and employees. In A. I. Kraut & A. K. Korman (Eds.), *Evolving practices in human resource management: Responses to a changing world* (pp. 23–40). San Francisco: Jossey-Bass.

Kossek, E. E., Colquitt, J. A., & Noe, R. A. (2001). Caregiving decisions, well-being, and performance: The effects of place and provider as a function of dependent type and work–family climates. *Academy of Management Journal, 44,* 29–44.

Lawrence, B. S. (1988). New wrinkles in the theory of age: Demography, norms and performance ratings. *Academy of Management Journal, 31,* 309–337.

Lichtenstein, R. A., Alexander, J. A., Jinnett, K., & Ullman, E. (1997). Embedded intergroup relations in interdisciplinary teams: Effects on perceptions of team integration. *Journal of Applied Behavioral Science, 33,* 413–434.

Lieber, L. D. (2007). As average age of the U.S. workforce increases, age-discrimination verdicts rise. *Employment Relations Today, 34,* 105–110.

Mehrotra, C. M., & Wagner, L. S. (2009). *Aging and diversity: An active learning experience* (2nd ed.). New York: Routledge.

Ng, T. W. H., & Feldman, D. C. (2008). The relationship of age to ten dimensions of job performance. *Journal of Applied Psychology, 93,* 392–423.

Ostroff, C., & Atwater, L. E. (2003). Does whom you work with matter? Effects of referent group gender and age composition on managers' compensation. *Journal of Applied Psychology, 88,* 725–740.

Perry, E. A., & Parlamis, J. D. (2007). Age and ageism in organizations: A review and consideration of national culture. In A. M. Konrad, P. Prasad, & J. K. Pringle (Eds.), *Handbook of workplace diversity.* Thousand Oaks, CA: Sage.

Perry, E. L., Kulik, C. T., & Bourhis, A. C. (1996). Moderating effects of personal and contextual factors in age discrimination. *Journal of Applied Psychology, 81,* 628–647.

Perry, E. L., Kulik, C. T., & Zhou, J. (1999). A closer look at the effects of subordinate–supervisor age differences. *Journal of Organizational Behavior, 20,* 341–357.

Posthuma, R. A., & Campion, M. A. (2009). Age stereotypes in the workplace: Common stereotypes, moderators, and future research directions. *Journal of Management, 35,* 158–188.

Prenda, K. M., & Stahl, S. M. (2001). The truth about older workers. *Business and Health, 19,* 30–35.

Rosen, B., & Jerdee, T. H. (1976). The influence of age stereotypes on managerial decisions. *Journal of Applied Psychology, 61,* 428–432.

Rosen, B., & Jerdee, T. H. (1977). Too old or not too old? *Harvard Business Review, 55,* 97–106.

Rosen, B., & Jerdee, T. H. (1988). Managing older workers' careers. *Research in Personnel and Human Resource Management, 6,* 37–74.

Ruuskanen, J., & Puoppila, I. (1995). Physical activity and psychological well-being among people aged 65–84 years. *Age and Aging, 24,* 292–296.

Shore, L. M., Cleveland, J. N., & Goldberg, C. B. (2003). Work attitudes and decisions as a function of manager age and employee age. *Journal of Applied Psychology, 88,* 529–537.

Shore, L. M., & Goldberg, C. B. (2005). Age discrimination in the workplace. In R. L. Dipboye & A. Collela (Eds.), *Discrimination at work: The psychological and organizational bases* (pp. 203–225). Mahwah, NJ: Lawrence Erlbaum.

Siciliano, J. I. (1996). The relationship of board member diversity to organizational performance. *Journal of Business Ethics, 15,* 313–332.

Simons, T., Pelled, L. H., & Smith, K. A. (1999). Making use of difference: Diversity, debate, and decision comprehensiveness in top management teams. *Academy of Management Journal, 42,* 662–673.

Simpson, P. A., Greller, M. M., & Stroh, L. K. (2002). Variations in human capital investment activity by age. *Journal of Vocational Behavior, 61,* 109–138.

Stevens, J., Lathrop, A., & Bradish, C. (2005). Tracking Generation Y: A contemporary sport consumer profile. *Journal of Sport Management, 19,* 254–277.

Sum, A. M. (2003). *Leaving young workers behind.* Special Report, Institute for Youth, Education, and Families. National Leagues of Cities. Retrieved October 29, 2009, from http://www.nlc.org/ASSETS/AFD99C532A024FC0BC27480FDEDCFBDA/iyefdyleavingwork.pdf.

Tajfel, H., & Turner, J. C. (1979). An integrative theory of intergroup conflict. In W. G. Austin & S. Worchel (Eds.), *The social psychology of intergroup relations* (pp. 33–47). Monterey, CA: Brooks/Cole.

Thomas, K. M., Mack, D. A., & Montagliani, A. (2004). The arguments against diversity: Are they valid? In M. S. Stockdale & F. J. Crosby (Eds.), *The psychology and management of workplace diversity* (pp. 31–51). Malden, MA: Blackwell.

Turner, J., Hogg, M. A., Oakes, P. J., Reicher, S. D., & Wetherell, M. S. (1987). *Rediscovering the social group: A self-categorization theory.* Oxford, UK: B. Blackwell.

Waldman, D. A., & Avolio, B. J. (1986). A meta-analysis of age differences in job performance. *Journal of Applied Psychology, 71,* 33–38.

Weiss, E. M., & Maurer, T. J. (2004). Age discrimination in personnel decisions: A reexamination. *Journal of Applied Social Psychology, 34,* 1551–1562.

Wiersema, M. F., & Bantel, K. (1992). Top management team demography and corporate strategic change. *Academy of Management Journal, 35,* 91–121.

Wiersema, M. F., & Bird, A. (1993). Organizational demography in Japanese firms: Group heterogeneity, individual dissimilarity, and top management team turnover. *Academy of Management Journal, 36,* 996–1025.

Wink, P. (2007). Everyday life in the third age. In J. B. James & P. Wink (Eds.), *Annual review of gerontology and geriatrics: The crown of life: Dynamics of the early postretirement period* (Vol. 26, pp. 243–261). New York: Springer.

Zenger, T. R., & Lawrence, B. S. (1989). Organizational demography: The differential effects of age and tenure distributions on technical communication. *Academy of Management Journal, 32,* 353–376.

7

Mental and Physical Ability

LEARNING OBJECTIVES

Erik Weihenmayer is an accomplished mountain climber who has scaled what is referred to as the Seven Summits, or the highest mountains on each of the Earth's seven continents. Unlike others who have accomplished this rare feat, Weihenmayer is blind. In fact, he is the only person who is blind ever to climb Mount Everest. Interestingly, this fact altered how people view his achievements. As Weihenmayer described, "When I was learning how to climb mountains as a blind person, I had a lot of encouragement from experts. But after I summited Mount Everest, these people weren't ready to accept what I had done at face value. Some said I must have cheated; one even claimed I had an unfair advantage: 'I'd climb Mount Everest too if I couldn't see how far I had to fall.'"

Weihenmayer is not the only athlete with a disability who has encountered skepticism about his accomplishments. Oscar Pistorius, who was born without fibulas, had his lower legs amputated at age 1. This did not slow Pistorius, however, and he participated in water polo, rugby, and tennis throughout his teenage years. He later turned to sprinting events and now holds the double-amputee world records for the 100-, 200-, and 400-meter races. He then began competing against able-bodied runners and beat most of his competitors. He placed sixth in the 2005 South African national championships and finished second in the 2007 event. At this point, his athletic achievements started to come under fire. Specifically, his critics began to call into question the J-shaped prosthetics he wears while competing, arguing that they give him an advantage other runners cannot realize. LaShawn Merritt, a top 400-meter runner, commented: "I guess he worked really hard to get here, so he should run. But I feel like if he was running the same times I was, it would not be even. There's a lot we have to deal with that he doesn't." Echoing these concerns, the International Association of Athletics Federations (IAAF), track's international governing body, ruled in January 2008 that Pistorius could not

After studying this chapter, you should be able to:

- Provide a definition of disability and an overview of the historical background related to mental and physical ability.

- Discuss the work experiences of, and educational and work opportunities for, persons with disabilities.

- Describe the state of disability sport and the key issues in that context.

- Discuss the way in which the media and advertisers depict persons with disabilities.

compete in the Olympics, because of the supposed advantage his prosthetics give him. This ruling was subsequently overturned by the Court of Arbitration for Sport (CAS) when researchers from Southern Methodist University demonstrated that the energy costs and fatigability Pistorius experiences is similar to that of intact-limb runners. Given the CAS ruling, Pistorius was able to try out for the 2008 South African Olympic team, barely missing the time needed to make the team. He told reporters that his sights were set on the 2012 London Games.

In response to Pistorius's success, Weihenmayer commented that it is important to remain cognizant that Pistorius's training and effort, not his prosthetics, allowed him to succeed. Weihenmayer said, "we mustn't lose sight of what makes an athlete great. It's too easy to credit Pistorius's success to technology. Through birth or circumstance, some are given certain gifts, but it's what one does with those gifts, the hours devoted to training, the desire to best the best, that is at the true heart of a champion."

Information adapted from: ■ Ebenezer, S. (2008, June 1). Oscar Pistorius' Olympic quest opens ethical debate over use of prosthetics. *New York Daily News*. Retrieved October 8, 2009, from http://nydailynews.com. ■ Southern Methodist University. (2009, August 4). Oscar Pistorius: Amputee sprinter runs differently. *ScienceDaily*. Retrieved October 8, 2009, from http://www.sciencedaily.com/releases/2009/06/090629132200.htm. ■ Weihenmayer, E. (2008, April 25). Oscar Pistorius. *Time*. Retrieved October 8, 2009, from www.time.com.

DIVERSITY CHALLENGE   R E F L E C T I O N

1. Does the use of prosthetics provide an unfair advantage for sprinters? How does the use of prosthetics differ from other medical treatment such as a golfer getting Lasik eye surgery or a pitcher getting Tommy John surgery (i.e., ulnar collateral ligament reconstruction)?

2. Is it conceivable that, if there were an advantage, athletes would choose to amputate their legs so they too could wear the prosthetics?

3. What are other cases in sport where one's disability could be seen as an advantage?

 s the Diversity Challenge illustrates, perceptions of performance are often shaped, at least in part, by a person's physical and mental ability. LaShawn Merritt's comments are particularly telling. Note that he "guessed" that Pistorius worked really hard, even though Pistorius had placed second in national events and was the world record holder in several double-amputee categories. It is unlikely that Merritt would question the work ethic of able-bodied runners. Merritt went on to suggest that he would dismiss Pistorius's times if they were ever to equal or better his own. These comments suggest that Merritt did not lend credence to the idea that a double-amputee could ever do something as well as he, an able-bodied runner, could. Comments such as those advanced by LaShawn Merritt are not uncommon; instead, persons with disabilities are often stereotyped as being less skilled and less capable than others. These stereotypes then subsequently influence the opportunities and experiences persons with disabilities have in work organizations.

The purpose of this chapter is to examine these issues in further depth. Specifically, I first provide a definition of disability and offer a brief historical overview of issues related to mental and physical disabilities. This is followed by a discussion of the educational and work opportunities for persons with disabilities, and then by an overview of the state of disability sport and the primary issues affecting athletes in that context. In the final section, I discuss how the media and advertisers depict persons with disabilities.

Definition, Incidence, and Historical Background

Determining what constitutes a *disability* is often difficult. For some impairments, such as a complete lack of sight or the ability to hear, the existence of the disability is clear. For others, such as a partial hearing loss or the beginning stages of arthritis, there is more debate. The Americans with Disabilities Act (discussed in more detail in Chapter 12) governs what constitutes a disability within the employment context. From a legal perspective, people are considered to have a disability when they have a mental or physical impairment that largely restricts one or more major life activities, when there is a recorded history of such, or when they are considered to have such impairment. A major life activity, as defined in the ADA, is an activity that is fundamental to human life—"caring for oneself, performing manual tasks, walking, seeing, hearing, speaking, breathing, learning, and working" (ADA, 1985). In practical terms, mental and physical aspects of disability are varied. Generally, physical conditions include diabetes, cancer, and AIDS, among others, and mental disabilities include retardation, dyslexia, and emotional illness, among others.

In 2000, the U.S. Census Bureau (www.census.gov) reported that 49.7 million Americans age 5 or older reported having a disability or long-lasting condition. This represented 19.3 percent of the population, meaning that one in five people had a disability. Within this population:

- 9.3 million people reported a disability pertaining to their sight or hearing (i.e., a sensory disability).
- Many (21.2 million) people had a disability that substantially limited their physical activities, such as walking, climbing stairs, or carrying objects.
- 18.2 million persons age 16 or older had a disability that made it difficult for them to leave the house to visit the doctor or shop.

The incidence of disability is not evenly distributed across the population, however. For instance, disability rates rise with age and are higher for men than they are for women (see Exhibit 7.1). The relationship between age and disability can be largely explained by disease: as one's age increases, so too does the incidence of heart disease, hypertension, and diabetes. These and other health problems can lead to weight gain, obesity, or other physical disabilities (Bell, McLaughlin, & Sequeira, 2004). This trend is particularly troubling, considering that the mean age in most industrialized nations

exhibit **7.1**   **Disability rates based on age and sex.**

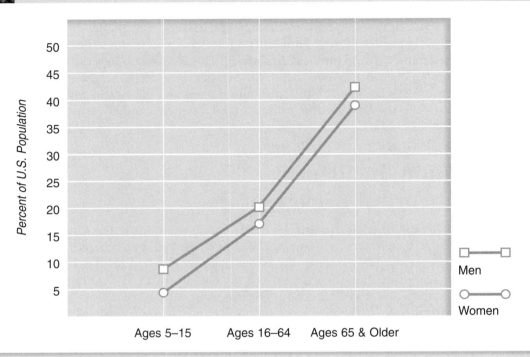

Source: U.S. Census Bureau.

around the world has increased and will continue to do so (Haq, 2004). In addition, you can review Exhibit 7.2 (Pittz, 2005) on the intersection of disability with race.

These dynamics also illuminate what Bell et al. refer to as the "permeable boundaries" of disability. Many diversity forms cannot be changed (e.g., race) but one's disability status can change: an individual can become ill or have an accident and thereby be considered a person with a disability. An example of the changeable nature of this type of physical diversity is illustrated by the career of Michael Teuber of Germany. Teuber was an avid, able-bodied wind surfer and snowboarder. After an automobile accident, however, he had limited use of his legs—about 65 percent of their previous capacity. He began mountain biking for rehabilitation reasons and soon became an avid cyclist. This love of cycling led him to compete, and he has done quite well. In fact, Teuber is a Paralympic world champion; a European cycling champion; and a winner of other medals in various forms of cycling, including road racing, trail racing, and pursuit racing (DePauw & Gavron, 2005).

It is important to note, however, that while some disabilities are permeable, others are not. For people born with disabilities, those disabilities are likely to be permanent and thus socially constructed, much like race and gender.

From a historical perspective, negative perceptions of persons with disabilities have persisted over time. As Bell (2007) explains, these perceptions are manifested in stereotypes, distancing, and language (see the accompanying box). In former times and in various cultures, persons with disabilities were consid-

| Intersection of disability with race. | *exhibit* **7.2** |

When discussing disability, it is important to remember that the incidence of various illnesses and disabilities *are not* equally dispersed among racial groups; rather, racial minorities are more likely to face health challenges than Whites. Recent research revealed the following:

- Compared with Whites, African Americans are 10% more likely to get cancer and 30% more likely to die from cancer.

- 25% of Native American and Alaskan Native children and 20% of African American children suffer from asthma.

- Hispanics, African Americans, and Native Americans are three times more likely than Whites to receive late or no prenatal care. This corresponds with the high infant mortality rate among racial minorities relative to Whites.

- Hispanics, African Americans, and Native Americans are more likely to have diabetes and die from the illness than Whites.

- In some parts of the United States, Native Americans can expect to live only into their 50s, while the life expectancy for Whites is in the 70s.

Adapted from Pittz, 2005.

ered undesirable, defective, and unwanted. As a result, efforts were often made to alienate persons with disabilities: babies with club feet were abandoned to die in ancient Greece. Schools would separate children with sensory impairments from their peers, similar to the way people were segregated based on their race. Sometimes people found it necessary to hide their disabilities; a famous politician had an agreement with the press not to be photographed using a cane, for example. Finally, people's language, such as use of the terms "cripple," "deaf and dumb," or "crazy" reflect commonly held negative perceptions of persons with disabilities. This is further illustrated by the more recent use of the term "retarded" to refer to persons who are perceived as unusual, silly, or out of the ordinary.

LANGUAGE AND DISABILITY

As with any discussion of diversity, the language we use is of considerable importance. Some scholars, such as Thomas and Smith (2009), use the term "disabled people" while others, such as Legg, Fay, Hums, and Wolff (2009) opt for the term "persons with disability." In this book, I opt for the latter, people-first approach. As DePauw and Gavron (2005) correctly note, doing so recognizes persons as individuals first rather than placing the focus on their disability.

Educational and Work Opportunities

Research suggests that opportunities afforded to persons with mental and physical disabilities differ from opportunities afforded to their able-bodied counterparts. These differences are reflected in their education, work, and pay.

Education

According to U.S. Census Bureau data, persons with work disabilities (i.e., conditions that affect their ability to work at a job or business) are less educated than their peers. For instance, 25.8 percent of persons with work disabilities do not have a high school diploma. This proportion is considerably higher than the corresponding percentage for persons without work disabilities (17.6 percent). Similarly, persons with work disabilities are less than half as likely to earn a four-year degree as are their counterparts (11.8 percent and 25.2 percent, respectively). Exhibit 7.3 offers a detailed account of the intersection of disability status and educational attainment.

Work

Persons with disabilities tend to lag in their education, and they also face obstacles in securing work. Results from a Harris Poll (Taylor, 2000) showed that less than one in three (31 percent) of all persons with disabilities are employed either full time or part time. Furthermore, 56 percent of persons who have a disability and indicate that they can work are gainfully employed. This is considerably lower than the comparable proportion (81 percent) in the overall U.S. population (Taylor, 1998). U.S. Census Bureau (www.census.gov) statistics provide a similar pattern of findings. The latter dataset also reveals that persons with disabilities are much more likely to work part time than to have a full-time position.

Pay

Persons with disabilities are not only underemployed relative to the rest of the population but also they are paid less. In fact, persons with disabilities earn, on average, 23.72 percent less than their able-bodied counterparts. Critics could argue that persons with disabilities should be paid less because they are less educated than their able-bodied counterparts. However, even with equal levels of education, wage disparities exist. According to the U.S. Census Bureau, the mean earnings for a person without a disability and who has earned a bachelor's degree or greater is $69,617. This is 33 percent higher than what a person with a disability and similar educational attainment earns ($53,243). As seen in Exhibit 7.4, these disparities are present across all levels of educational attainment.

 **7.3**   **Intersection of disability status and educational attainment.**

	PERSONS WITH A WORK DISABILITY	PERSONS WITHOUT A WORK DISABILITY
No high school degree	25.8%	17.6%
High school degree	37.6%	29.6%
Associate's degree or some college	24.7%	27.6%
Four-year degree or more	11.8%	25.2%

Source: U.S. Census Bureau.

| | Earnings differences between workers with and without disabilities. | *exhibit* **7.4** |

EDUCATIONAL ATTAINMENT	EMPLOYEES WITHOUT DISABILITIES	EMPLOYEES WITH DISABILITIES	PERCENT DIFFERENCE
12th grade or less, no diploma	$25,281	$20,781	21.65%
High school graduate	$34,153	$31,726	7.65%
Associate's degree or some college	$40,935	$37,415	9.41%
Bachelor's degree or more	$69,617	$52,243	33.25%
Total	$46,609	$37,672	23.72%

Source: U.S. Census Bureau.

Work Experiences

In addition to facing considerable access discrimination, persons with disabilities routinely encounter treatment discrimination when at work (see also Chapter 3). This discrimination manifests primarily in having poor relationships with supervisors, low performance expectations, and negative attitudes toward accommodations.

Supervisor Relationship

Leader-member exchange theory suggests that leaders develop unique relationships with their various subordinates (Graen & Uhl-Bien, 1995). High-quality relationships are marked by mutual trust, obligation, support, and respect. On the other hand, low-quality relationships are characterized by a relatively low level of mutual influence. As might be expected, employees' relationships with their supervisors impact a number of work-related decisions, including the type of job assignment received, pay, and opportunity for promotion. These dynamics are important because research suggests that persons with disabilities have poorer quality relationships with their supervisors than do their peers.

Colella and Varma's (2001) work illustrates this point. They collected data from 220 employees (32 of whom reported having a disability) and their supervisors ($n = 41$; none of whom reported having a disability). They found that, on average, supervisors had closer, better relationships with their able-bodied subordinates than with their subordinates with disabilities. There was one caveat, however: employee behaviors influenced the relationships. Specifically, when employees engaged in behaviors that endeared them to the supervisor, such as rendering favors or expressing opinion similarity, they experienced enhanced leader-member exchange. This effect was particularly strong for employees with disabilities, thereby leading Colella and Varma to conclude that, unlike their colleagues, persons with disabilities "must take it upon themselves to make others comfortable and initiate interaction" (p. 313, see also Jones et al., 1984).

Performance Expectations

There are a number of negative stereotypes concerning persons with disabilities, including beliefs that they

- do not have the requisite skills to perform their work effectively;
- increase the time demands placed on their supervisors;
- increase healthcare costs for the rest of the workplace; and
- have poor emotional adjustment, including being overly bitter, nervous, and depressed (for an overview, see Stone-Romero, Stone, & Lukaszewski, 2007).

Ren, Paetzold, and Colella (2008) examined this phenomenon by aggregating the results from 51 experimental studies. Consistent with Stone-Romero et al.'s contention, Ren et al. found that people routinely expected poorer performance from persons with disabilities than from able-bodied persons. They concluded that "these results may stem from perceptions of the individual with a disability as unsuitable for employment because of stigmatized views of the disability itself or because of negative perceptions regarding the ability of a person with a disability to perform a job" (p. 199). Interestingly, though these perceptions persist, there is considerable evidence to the contrary, as illustrated in the Alternative Perspectives box.

Such perceptions have many work-related implications. For instance, coworkers might be reluctant to work with persons with disabilities for fear that the collective work performance might suffer. Supervisors might hold similar perceptions—something that would contribute to the low-quality relationships people with disabilities have with their supervisors (Colella & Varma, 2001). Finally, negative perceptions of work competencies probably explain why persons with disabilities are assigned low-level jobs, are isolated from their coworkers, and receive little mentoring (Stone-Romero & Stone, 2005), even though mentoring is so critical to one's career success.

Accommodations

A third way in which people with disabilities face discrimination is in the reactions to their requests for accommodations. The Americans with Disabilities Act (ADA) requires organizations with at least 15 employees to make "reasonable accommodation" for a person with a disability as long as the accommodation does not place undue hardship on the organization (discussed later in Chapter 12). Such an accommodation for an employee who is hard of hearing might be a requirement that her manager face her and speak loudly when addressing her. A person who uses a wheelchair might need a taller desk (or blocks under his current desk) because his knees hit the current desk.

alternative **PERSPECTIVES**

Disability and Performance. Although ableism does exist, Thomas, Mack, and Montagliani (2004) note that some firms have found that persons with disabilities are a major asset: they often express greater loyalty to the organization, thereby decreasing the costs associated with turnover (i.e., recruitment and training of new employees). Pizza Hut, for example, found that employees with disabilities had half the turnover rate of other employees. Furthermore, despite stereotypes related to performance decrements, empirical research shows that the performance of persons with disabilities is on a par with, or above that of, employees without disabilities. For example, DuPont found that persons with disabilities, compared with other employees, achieved greater performance levels, were absent less often, and paid greater attention to safety issues (Thomas et al., 2004). These data suggest that persons with disabilities are more likely to be an asset, not a liability, to an organization.

The ADA places the responsibility for requesting the accommodation on the employee. Interestingly, research suggests that two of every three employees with a disability withhold requests for accommodations at least once each year, and about 60 percent withhold requests each quarter (Baldridge, 2001). Why would people withhold their requests, especially when they are permissible under the law? The negative reactions to such requests provide part of the answer. For example, Baldridge (2005) found that people with supportive supervisors and coworkers are unlikely to withhold their requests. On the other hand, those without such support may not make the requests. As one participant in his study noted, "I hardly ever make requests to my new supervisor because she is so hostile. In her mind, any accommodation is unreasonable" (p. 2). In a different study, Florey and Harrison (2000) found that managers responded negatively when they received a request from people perceived to be responsible for their disability. They also found that managers responded favorably to requests from persons whose previous performance had been high. Finally, McLaughlin, Bell, and Stringer (2004) observed that requests from people who are highly stigmatized (e.g., those with AIDS) were met with negative attitudes and were perceived as unfair, particularly when compared with requests from people with less-stigmatized disabilities, such as cerebral palsy. Collectively, these studies provide an understanding of why and when persons with disabilities will request accommodations.

Antecedents of Discrimination

The aforementioned studies have highlighted how persons with disabilities face both access and treatment discrimination. Given these effects, it is also instructive to consider antecedents of that discrimination—that is, the factors that influence the disparaging treatment of persons with disabilities. I outline three antecedents here: stigma, pity, and anxiety.

Stigma

According to Paetzold, Dipboye, and Elsbach (2008), stigma "represents an attribute that produces a social identity that is devalued or derogated by persons within in a particular culture at a particular point in time" (p. 186). Stigmas are socially constructed and specific to a particular context. A characteristic that is stigmatizing in one context might not be viewed as such in another. Stigmatized persons are seen as different from what is "normal" or typical and come to be viewed as aberrant or deviant (McLaughlin et al., 2004; see also Goffman, 1963).

Jones et al. (1984) provide a framework for understanding how persons with disabilities might become stigmatized. Specifically, they argue for six major dimensions of stigma, each of which can be rated from low to high:

1. Disruptiveness, or the degree to which the disability influences social interactions or communications among people;
2. Origin, or the degree to which one is seen as responsible for her or his disability;
3. Aesthetic qualities, or the extent to which the disability negatively influences one's attractiveness;
4. Course, or the extent to which the disability is transient or permanent;

5. Concealability, or the degree to which the disability can be plainly observed by others; and

6. Peril, or the degree to which one's disability could cause others harm.

The concept of stigma is important in our discussions of disability because, according to McLaughlin et al. (2004), stigma is thought to be the most proximal antecedent of discrimination. From this perspective, it is not one's disability, *per se*, that affects people's attitudes and behaviors. Instead, a stigma is attached to certain disabilities, and the reactions to that stigma influence subsequent bias and discrimination (for similar reasoning, see Stone & Colella, 1996). As McLaughlin et al. note, "it is the perceived attributes or consequences that people associate with disability (which vary across disability types) that influence acceptance" (p. 308).

In drawing from the work of Jones et al. (1984) and McLaughlin et al. (2004), several points become clear. First, the concept of stigma helps explain why some disabilities are met with greater resistance than others. Consider, for instance, that persons with HIV/AIDS might be seen as responsible for contracting the illness (high in origin), have their physical appearance negatively affected by the disease (high in aesthetics), are affected by the illness for the remainder of their life (high in course), and might be seen as a risk to others (high in peril). These perceptions are different from perceptions of a person who suffered from a stroke: the person did not cause the illness (low in origin), physical appearance may or may not be affected (moderate level of aesthetics), negative physical effects might be overcome through rehabilitation (low in aesthetics), they might not be affected for the rest of their life (low in course), and others cannot catch a stroke from the person (low in peril). Thus, a person with HIV/AIDS is likely to be more stigmatized than one who recently suffered a stroke, and the bias and discrimination affecting those two would vary accordingly. Second, the definition of stigma also helps explain why *ableism*, or discrimination against persons with disabilities, varies by context. For instance, people with mental disabilities might be viewed less warmly in the youth sport context, where their disability might impede their performance relative to others, than they would in the Special Olympics setting, where mental disabilities are a part of participation. Note here that the mental disability has remained constant while the stigma attached to it and subsequent bias and discrimination have not.

Pity

Fiske, Cuddy, Glick, and Xu (2002) suggested that stereotypes are captured by two different perceptions: warmth and competence. Perceptions of these two attributes can be low or high such that a 2 × 2 matrix is formed, e.g., high warmth, high competence; low warmth, high competence; and so on (see Exhibit 7.5). In building from this framework, the authors conducted a series of studies with numerous participants from diverse backgrounds. Their findings were telling. Persons from groups that are privileged and have traditionally held in-group status in the United States (e.g., Whites, Christians) were considered both warm and competent. These people were also generally admired. These perceptions differed from those of other groups, including persons with mental and physical disabilities, as these persons were consistently rated as high in warmth but low in competence. Persons with disabilities were also likely to be pitied but not admired or envied.

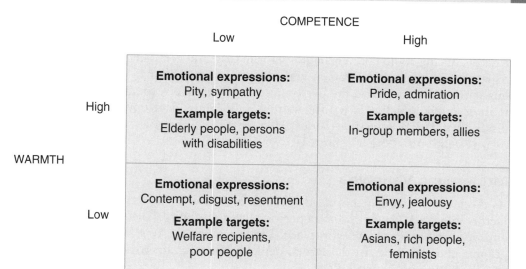

exhibit **7.5**

A classification of stereotypes based on warmth and competence (based on Fiske et al., 2002).

COMPETENCE

	Low	High
WARMTH High	**Emotional expressions:** Pity, sympathy **Example targets:** Elderly people, persons with disabilities	**Emotional expressions:** Pride, admiration **Example targets:** In-group members, allies
WARMTH Low	**Emotional expressions:** Contempt, disgust, resentment **Example targets:** Welfare recipients, poor people	**Emotional expressions:** Envy, jealousy **Example targets:** Asians, rich people, feminists

Colella and Stone (2005) have echoed these findings in suggesting that many people feel both compassion and pity when seeing or interacting with someone with a disability. Compassion represents an awareness of another's distress, coupled with the desire to lend aid (Lazarus & Lazarus, 1994). This differs from pity, which can be considered as feeling sorry for another person. Compared to compassion, pity is more condescending and is often accompanied by the view that the person with a disability is inferior (Colella & Stone, 2005). Given these differences, Colella and Stone suggest that people with disabilities are more likely to face bias and discrimination when people view them with pity rather than compassion.

In building from this literature, it is clear that pity toward persons with disabilities can have negative effects. Fiske et al. (2002) argued that pity was an inherently mixed emotion because it combined sympathy and superiority. Thus, while people who feel pity might express compassion for persons with disabilities (i.e., awareness that they do have a disability and the potential distress that it might cause), they also view such people as inferior and subordinate. In the workplace, such prejudice might result in low leader-member exchange relationships or low performance expectations, both of which were outlined previously.

Anxiety

Anxiety represents a third antecedent to bias and discrimination. As Stone and Colella (1996) explain, this anxiety, which is thought to be implicit in nature, can take two forms: aesthetic anxiety, which is brought on by fears of persons whose appearance deviates from the "norm" in society, and existential anxiety, which refers to the fear brought on when one is reminded of one's own vulnerability by seeing the person with the disability. For instance, encounters with a person in a wheelchair might elicit concerns of one's own vulnerability and the potential loss of mobility. When encountering persons with mental disabilities, there might be an uncertainty about how to act or inability to predict behaviors, thereby provoking stress or anxiousness.

When people experience anxiety, they are likely to distance themselves from the anxiety-producing stimulus, which in this case is the person with the disability. This distancing could take a behavioral form. Coworkers might express a reluctance to work with or near the person with the disability, or human resource personnel might refrain from hiring the person at all. Alternatively, the distancing could be more strongly affective in nature, so that a disdain is developed for persons with disabilities. This is sometimes observed in reactions to persons with HIV/AIDS and their relegation to "other" status.

Moderating Variables

As discussed previously, not all disabilities are viewed the same; rather, a host of factors influence whether or not a person with a disability will experience prejudice and discrimination in the workplace. These include the type of disability, demographic characteristics of the target, demographic characteristics of the perceiver, and the nature of the workplace.

Type of disability

Researchers have found that persons react more negatively to some disabilities than to others. As previously noted, these differences are probably a function of the stigma attached to specific disabilities (Jones et al., 1984; McLaughlin et al., 2004). Persons who are thought to pose a risk to others or who are perceived as being responsible for their disability are likely to be viewed more negatively than their counterparts. Thus, a person who is quadriplegic due to illness is likely to be seen in a more positive light than is a person who is quadriplegic because of an automobile accident that occurred while driving under the influence. In a similar way, a person who is deaf since birth is probably viewed more positively than another person whose deafness is due to listening to too much loud music or not wearing ear plugs on a job with constant loud noise. It is interesting to note that in both examples, the disability type is the same (i.e., both persons are either quadriplegic or deaf), but the reactions vary based on the perceived cause.

Demographics of the target

The demographic characteristics of the person with the disability might also impact the bias and discrimination faced. This is particularly the case with sex, as having a disability might run counter to cultural norms about men and masculinity (Stone & Colella, 1996). Stereotypical traits of persons with disabilities, such as a lack of strength, run counter to the corresponding supposed traits of men (e.g., rugged, strong). They do not necessarily diverge, however, from prevailing stereotypes of women (e.g., fragile, timid). Consequently, people's reactions to men with disabilities are likely to be more negative than they are to women. Illustrative of these dynamics, Ren et al. (2008) found empirical evidence that women with disabilities were more likely than men with comparable disabilities to receive a hiring recommendation.

Demographics of the perceiver

The demographics of the perceiver might also influence the incidence of discrimination. Specifically, persons who are not part of the dominant group in the workforce, such as women, racial minorities, and sexual minorities, might express more empathy than their dominant counterparts toward persons with disabilities. All of these persons are likely to experience prejudice and discrimination in the workplace, and as a result, they might be able to identify with one another. As evidence of this in the literature, Olkin and Howson (1994) found that women expressed more positive attitudes toward persons with disabilities than did men. In another study, McLaughlin et al. (2004) found significant effects associated with both sex and race: women and racial minorities viewed persons with disabilities more favorably than did their male, White counterparts.

Nature of the workplace

Finally, the human resource system in the workplace might also influence whether or not persons with disabilities face prejudice and discrimination (Bell, 2007). This can be seen in the selection process, compensation and benefits, training, and performance evaluations:

- *Selection.* Organizations should use the job description in selecting persons who are able to effectively perform the job, with or without reasonable accommodations. Indeed, "having and using a job description can help organizations in selecting appropriately in all situations (not just with applicants with disabilities)" (Bell, 2007, p. 361).
- *Compensation.* Persons with disabilities should be paid based on the worth of the job, coupled with their education, experience, and skills. Disability status *should not* be considered in the compensation process.
- *Training and development.* Persons with disabilities should be provided all of the opportunities other employees are afforded. Not doing so is illegal and thwarts the career advancement opportunities they might enjoy.
- *Performance evaluation.* All employees should be evaluated on a regular basis, irrespective of their disability. Job performance standards should be explicitly outlined and used as the criteria. Failure to fairly and accurately evaluate performance not only hurts the employee's development but also is deleterious to the organization.

Disability Sport

Athletes with disabilities have increasingly excelled in sport and physical activity. The Diversity Challenge illustrates this point, as Oscar Pistorius excelled in national-level track competitions, finishing as high as second place in 2007. Pistorius's case is not an anomaly. DePauw and Gavron (2005) point out that elite performances by athletes with disabilities are often comparable to their able-bodied counterparts. Consider, for instance, that athletes with cerebral palsy bench press over 400 pounds, and athletes with other physical impairments have bench pressed over 600 pounds in competition! Harry Cordellos, who is blind, has successfully run over 100 marathons, including a 2:57:42 finish at the prestigious Boston Marathon. He has also competed in the Iron Man Triathlon and a grueling 100-mile race in San Francisco. As a final example, Jim Abbott was born with one hand but pitched in Major League Baseball from 1988 to 1998.

As these examples illustrate, a number of athletes with disabilities have competed skillfully and successfully against their able-bodied counterparts. For others, there is a substantial enough difference created by the disability that competing against athletes without disabilities creates an uneven playing field. Therein rests the need for disability sport, or "sport that has been designed for or is specifically practiced by athletes with disabilities" (DePauw & Gavron, 2005, p. 80). This definition includes sports designed specifically for persons with disabilities, such as goal ball for athletes who are blind; sports that able-bodied persons practice that are altered or modified to include athletes with disabilities, such as wheelchair basketball; and sports that require little or no modification, such as swimming.

As Legg et al. (2009; see also Hums & MacLean, 2009) note, many of the advancements of disability sport can be traced to the efforts of neurosurgeon Sir Ludwig Guttman. During and after World War II, sport and exercise was used in rehabilitation efforts for wounded soldiers. Guttman recognized the effectiveness of this approach, particularly in reducing boredom during the rehabilitation process. Thus, in 1944 he opened the Spinal Injuries Center at Stoke Mandeville Hospital in England, with a particular emphasis on sport. Within four years, sport as a form of rehabilitation had grown into a competitive venture with patients in different wards competing against one another. This soon blossomed into an international competition when a team from The Netherlands competed in 1952. The official title of the competition was the Stoke-Mandeville Games. The event grew in such magnitude that by 1960, the first Paralympic Games were staged in Rome. Since that time, the Paralympic Games have been staged in tandem with the Olympic Games every four years. To illustrate the growth of the Games, 400 athletes from 23 countries competed in 1960. In 2004, nearly 3,700 athletes representing 136 different countries competed in the Athens Games.

Of course, the Paralympics represents just one of many forms of disability sport (see Exhibit 7.6 for additional information).

exhibit **7.6**   **Large-scale disability sport events.**

- *Paralympic Games:* a showcase of elite athletes with disabilities, including visual impairments, cerebral palsy, amputations, spinal cord injuries, and (on a limited basis) athletes with mental impairments; includes both winter and summer contests.

- *Deaflympics:* elite competition for athletes who are deaf. The first summer Deaflympics were held in 1924 in Paris, with the winter Deaflympics added in 1949.

- *Special Olympics:* sport opportunities for persons with cognitive and developmental disabilities; focus on development and social interaction of the athletes and not elite competition.

Information gathered from Hums & MacLean, 2009; www.specialolympics.org; www.deaflympics.com.

Issues Related to Disability Sport

DePauw and Gavron (2005) addressed three issues related to persons with disabilities in the sport context: attitudes toward athletes with disabilities, barriers to inclusion, and accessibility. Each issue is discussed below. For related information, see the Professional Perspectives box. Also note that, although the discussion focuses on disability sport, some persons with disabilities are also involved in mainstream sport, such as NCAA able-bodied teams.

Attitudes toward athletes with disabilities

Historically, athletes with disabilities were marginalized or excluded because sport traditionally required some form of physical prowess not possessed or not perceived to be possessed by those with physical impairments. This perception has been reinforced over time and perpetuated by parents, friends, schools, and more recently, the media. Because of this perception, people have generally viewed disability sport as second class or illegitimate, with the result that athletes with disabilities receive less media coverage, fewer rewards, and fewer opportunities for participation (DePauw & Gavron, 2005).

Barriers to inclusion

The negative perceptions of disability sport and its athletes have resulted in several barriers to inclusion, including a lack of:

- organized sport programs devoted to disability sport,
- informal sport experiences for children who are disabled,
- access to training programs and qualified, highly trained coaches,
- access to sport facilities, and
- financial resources for specialized equipment.

Although various statutes reduced these barriers somewhat, they still exist and curb participation in disability sport (DePauw & Gavron, 2005).

Accessibility

The lack of accessibility comes in several forms. First, limited access to adapted equipment serves to make sport participation impossible for many disability-sport athletes. Second, even though current statutes require facilities to be accessible to persons with disabilities, many are not. Third, there is limited information, relatively

PROFESSIONAL PERSPECTIVES

Trends and Issues in Disability Sport. Eli Wolff is a two-time Olympic soccer athlete, a graduate of Brown University, and current director of the Disability Sport Program at the Center for the Study of Sport in Society. According to Wolff, one of the major issues in the area of disability sport today is the inclusion and integration of persons with disabilities within the fabric of mainstream sport. How do mainstream sport organizations at every level of sport actually embrace disability sport opportunities? The answer, according to Wolff, is that full integration and inclusion is still a ways away. Wolff also points to two primary barriers for persons with disabilities who wish to participate in sport: attitudes toward such participation and the portrayal of disability sport in the media. Wolff notes that there is a misconception about "what it means to be a person with a disability in sport." Too often, people pity disability sport athletes rather than recognizing their efforts as athletes. The same trend occurs in the media, where athletes with disabilities are often portrayed as sources of inspiration for others. This stands in contrast to focusing on the athletes' accomplishments and athletic prowess. Seeking to overcome such barriers, Wolff argues that an awareness of these issues needs to be raised. People in the media, athletes, coaches, and supporters all need to know that the status quo is not how disability sport "has to be."

speaking, about which disability-sport opportunities exist. Persons with disabilities often have to make concerted efforts to track down the information from physical educators, sport managers, or park and recreation specialists. Finally, because there is a lack of coaches to guide the athletes, many are self-coached. For the most part, athletes without disabilities do not face these challenges to their participation in sport (DePauw & Gavron, 2005).

Media and Consumers

In this final section, we examine the ways in which persons with disabilities are depicted in the media and portrayed by advertisers. Research has consistently shown that persons with disabilities are underrepresented in print and television media. As an example, the BBC broadcast more than 500 hours of the 2000 Olympic Games but devoted only 10 hours to the Paralympic Games that same year (Brittain, 2004). Athletes describe the limited coverage they do receive as fleeting, and the Paralympics and its participants receive no attention after the 2 or 3 weeks following the closing ceremonies. The lack of coverage by the BBC is particularly perplexing when considering that it is a federally funded broadcast; thus, a lack of commercial viability (which is sometimes claimed as the reason for the lack of coverage) is not applicable. Brittain notes that "by failing completely to give any coverage to these championships, the media effectively reinforced the message that disability sport, even at the world championship level, is neither interesting nor worthy of attention" (p. 448).

Persons with disabilities not only receive little media attention, but the coverage they do receive is often condescending and trivializing. Thomas and Smith (2009) note that the media frequently depict persons with disabilities as passive objects of charity. The stereotypical representations serve to evoke fear and pity. The media is also more likely to focus on athletes' disabilities than their athletic prowess. Stories often concentrate on how the athlete overcame obstacles (i.e., disabilities) and demonstrated so much courage. These patronizing portrayals, which serve to perpetuate stereotypes of these athletes as objects of pity, are notably absent in media coverage of able-bodied athletes, where the focus is instead on their athletic ability and performance on the field.

Similar to media depictions, marketers, including those who focus their efforts in the sport context, largely ignore persons with disabilities in their market segmentation efforts. A casual perusal of the sport marketing literature shows efforts to segment fans and consumers based on age, sex, race, and other characteristics, hoping to understand the preferences, attitudes, and purchase intentions of people within each demographic category. Why greater efforts have not been made to better understand consumers with disabilities or to market directly to these persons is unclear. After all, roughly 20 percent of the U.S. population has a disability, and the spending potential of these persons is substantial. Recognizing this void, Stephens and Bergman (1995) identified five guidelines for marketing to consumers with disabilities, with the intent of helping marketers conform to the spirit of the Americans with Disabilities Act and potentially improve the effectiveness of their marketing efforts. Exhibit 7.7 provides a summary of these guidelines.

Guidelines for marketing to consumers with disabilities.	*exhibit* **7.7**

- Remember that different disabilities result in different consumer needs.
- Use language that connotes respect.
- Depict persons with disabilities in a deferential and accurate way.
- Be cognizant of your own biases about the quality of others' lives.
- Train employees to show respect to persons with disabilities.

Stephens and
Bergman (1995).

Although sport marketers typically opt not to use persons with disabilities in their commercials, Toyota was a sponsor of the 2004 Paralympic Games. The purpose of a Toyota advertisement was to convey the message that although the athletes had disabilities, they were still elite in their field. To express this idea, the advertisement showed an athlete running, with the lower half of the screen blacked out so the athlete appeared able-bodied. The voice-over commentary indicated that the athlete was winning. The full screen was then revealed, showing that the athlete possessed some form of disability. *B&T Weekly,* an Australian publication devoted to advertising, marketing, and media, noted that the advertisement was well received and had the "wow factor" often sought when developing advertisements ("Simple," 2005).

CHAPTER *summary*

The purpose of this chapter was to outline the effects of mental and physical ability in the workplace and sport. As the case of Oscar Pistorius in the opening Diversity Challenge illustrates, ability influences people's opportunities and experiences. After reading this chapter, you should be able to:

1. **Provide a definition of disability and an overview of the historical background related to mental and physical ability.**

People are considered to have a disability if they have a mental or physical impairment that limits one or more major life activities. Historically, people with disabilities have faced discrimination and been ostracized from others.

2. **Discuss the work experiences of, and educational and work opportunities for, persons with disabilities.**

Persons with disabilities are less educated than their able-bodied counterparts. Even when educational levels are equal, persons with disabilities are less likely to be employed and are paid less. They also face discrimination, as evidenced by poor relationships with their supervisors, low performance expectations, and negative attitudes toward requests for accommodations.

3. **Describe the state of disability sport and the key issues in that context.**

Opportunities to participate in disability sport have grown substantially. Nevertheless, there are several issues affecting its delivery, including negative attitudes toward athletes with disabilities, barriers to inclusion, and lack of accessibility.

4. **Discuss the way in which the media and advertisers depict persons with disabilities.**

Persons with disabilities are underrepresented in media coverage, and when they do receive attention, it is often in stereotypical ways. Similarly, advertisers often fail to effectively market to persons with disabilities, thereby missing out on a viable sport consumer segment.

QUESTIONS *for discussion*

1. A brief historical overview of issues related to mental and physical disabilities was provided. Are some of the ways that persons with disabilities historically faced discrimination still present today? What are examples?

2. Identify some of the factors that may influence requests for accommodation by persons with disabilities in the workplace. What might be done to overcome some of the potential barriers?

3. Why are the athletic accomplishments of persons with disabilities brought into question by able-bodied athletes?

4. Disabilities are stigmatized in several ways. Which of the dimensions of stigma, as identified by Jones et al., is most influential?

5. What might be some ways sport managers could market directly to individuals with disabilities?

LEARNING *activities*

1. Using the Internet, identify sport organizations and sport events targeting athletes with disabilities. Based on your search, how would you characterize the available sport and physical activity opportunities for persons with disabilities?

2. Using the Internet, identify common requests for accommodations and the price incurred to the sport organization for making such accommodations. Was the price more or less than what was anticipated? What impact would the accommodation have on the organization?

READING *resources*

SUPPLEMENTARY READINGS

DePauw, K. P., & Gavron, S. J. (2005). *Disability sport* (2nd ed.). Champaign, IL: Human Kinetics. (Provides a historical account of disability sport and athletes with disabilities; also addresses the current challenges and controversies surrounding disability and sport.)

Hums, M. A., & MacLean, J. C. (2009). *Governance and policy in sport organizations* (2nd ed.). Scottsdale, AZ: Holcomb Hathaway. (Provides an overview of governance and policy issues in sport, with one of the most comprehensive treatments of the Paralympics in the literature.)

Thomas, N., & Smith, A. (2009). *Disability, sport and society: An introduction.* New York: Routledge. (Provides an overview of the theories and policies related to disability and sport, with a particular emphasis on sport in the UK.)

WEB RESOURCES

- National Disability Sports Alliance (www.ndsaonline.org): organization that serves as the governing body for competitive sport for persons with disabilities.

- International Paralympic Committee (www.paralympic.org): serves as the official website of the Paralympic movement.

- Global Disability Research in Sport and Health Network (www.disability researchinsportandhealth.ca/): an organization comprised of researchers focusing on disability issues in the sport and physical activity context.

references

Americans with Disabilities Act, 45 C.F.R. 843(j)(2)(i) (1985).

Baldridge, D. C. (2001). *The everyday ADA: The influence of requestors' assessments on decisions to ask for needed accommodation.* Unpublished doctoral dissertation, University of Connecticut.

Baldridge, D. C. (2005). Withholding accommodation requests: The role of workgroup supportiveness and requester attributes. *Academy of Management Proceedings, 2005,* D1–D6.

Bell, M. P. (2007). *Diversity in organizations.* Mason, OH: Thomson South-Western.

Bell, M. P., McLaughlin, M. E., & Sequeira, J. M. (2004). Age, disability, and obesity: Similarities, differences, and common threads. In M. S. Stockdale & F. J. Crosby (Eds.), *The psychology and management of workplace diversity* (pp. 191–205). Malden, MA: Blackwell.

Brittain, I. (2004). Perceptions of disability and their impact upon involvement in sport for people with disabilities at all levels. *Journal of Sport and Social Issues, 28,* 429-452.

Colella, A., & Stone, D. L. (2005). Workplace discrimination toward persons with disabilities: A call for some new research directions. In R. L. Dipboye & A. Colella (Eds.), *Discrimination at work: The psychological and organizational bases* (pp. 227–253). Mahwah, NJ: Lawrence Erlbaum.

Colella, A., & Varma, A. (2001). The impact of subordinate disability on leader-member exchange relationships. *Academy of Management Journal, 44,* 304–315.

DePauw, K. P., & Gavron, S. J. (2005). *Disability sport* (2nd ed.). Champaign, IL: Human Kinetics.

Fiske, S. T., Cuddy, A. J. C., Glick, P., & Xu, J. (2002). A model of (often mixed) stereotype content: Competence and warmth respectively follow from perceived status and competition. *Journal of Personality and Social Psychology, 82,* 878–902.

Florey, A. T., & Harrison, D. A. (2000). Responses to informal accommodation requests from employees with disabilities: Multistudy evidence on willingness to comply. *Academy of Management Journal, 43,* 224–233.

Goffman, E. (1963). *Stigma: Notes on the management of spoiled identity.* New York: Simon and Schuster.

Graen, G. B., & Uhl-Bien, M. (1995). Relationship-based approach to leadership: Development of leader-member-exchange (LMX) theory of leadership over 25 years: Applying a multi-level multi-domain perspective. *Leadership Quarterly, 6,* 219 – 247.

Haq, R. (2004). International perspectives on workplace diversity. In M. S. Stockdale & F. J. Crosby (Eds.), *The psychology and management of workplace diversity* (pp. 277–298). Malden, MA: Blackwell.

Hums, M. A., & MacLean, J. C. (2009). *Governance and policy in sport organizations* (2nd ed.). Scottsdale, AZ: Holcomb Hathaway.

Jones, E., Farina, A., Hastorf, A., Markus, H., Miller, D., Scott, R., & de Sales-French, R. (1984). *Social stigma: The psychology of marked relationships.* San Francisco: W. H. Freeman.

Lazarus, R. S., & Lazarus, B. N. (1994). *Passion and reason: Making sense of emotions.* New York: Oxford University Press.

Legg, D., Fay, T., Hums, M. A., & Wolff, E. (2009). Examining the inclusion of wheelchair events within the Olympic Games 1984–2004. *European Sport Management Quarterly, 9,* 243–258.

McLaughlin, M. E., Bell, M. P., & Stronger, D. Y. (2004). Stigma and acceptance of persons with disabilities. Understanding aspects of workforce diversity. *Group & Organization Management, 29,* 302–333.

Olkin, R., & Howson, L. J. (1994). Attitudes toward and images of physical disability. *Journal of Social Behavior and Personality, 9,* 81–96.

Paetzold, R. L., Dipboye, R. L., & Elsbach, K. D. (2008). A new look at stigmatization in and of organizations. *Academy of Management Review, 33,* 186–193.

Pittz, W. (2005). *Closing the gap: Solutions to race-based health disparities.* Oakland, CA: Applied Research Center & Northwest Federation of Community Organizations.

Ren, L. R., Paetzold, R. L., & Colella, A. (2008). A meta-analysis of experimental studies on the effects of disability on human resource judgments. *Human Resource Management Review, 18,* 191–203.

Simple and effective Paralympic campaign. (2005, January 14). *B&T Weekly, 54* (2502), 22.

Stephens, D. L., & Bergman, K. (1995). The Americans with Disabilities Act: A mandate for marketers. *Journal of Public Policy & Marketing, 14,* 164-168

Stone, D. L., & Colella, A. (1996). A model of factors affecting the treatment of disabled individuals in organizations. *Academy of Management Review, 21,* 352–401.

Stone-Romero, E. F., & Stone, D. L. (2005). How do organizational justice concepts relate to discrimination and prejudice? In J. Greenberg & J. A. Colquitt (Eds.), *Handbook of organizational justice* (pp. 439–467). Mahwah, NJ: Lawrence Erlbaum.

Stone-Romero, E. F., Stone, D. L., & Lukaszewski, K. (2007). The influence of disability on role-taking in organizations. In A. M. Konrad, P. Prasad, & J. K. Pringle, (Eds.), *Handbook of workplace diversity* (pp. 401–430). Thousand Oaks, CA: Sage.

Taylor, H. (1998, October 14). Americans with disabilities still persuasively disadvantaged on a broad range of key indicators. *The Harris Poll.* Retrieved October 13, 2009, from www.louisharris.com?harris_poll/index.asp?PID=152.

Taylor, H. (2000, October 7). Conflicting trends in employment of people with disabilities 1986–2000. *The Harris Poll.* Retrieved October 13, 2009, from www.louisharris.com?harris_poll/index.asp?PID=121.

Thomas, K. M., Mack, D. A., & Montagliani, A. (2004). The arguments against diversity: Are they valid? In M. S. Stockdale & F. J. Crosby (Eds.), *The psychology and management of workplace diversity* (pp. 31–51). Malden, MA: Blackwell.

Thomas, N., & Smith, A. (2009). *Disability, sport and society: An introduction.* New York: Routledge.

8

Appearance

The fitness industry is a multibillion-dollar segment of the U.S. economy and makes substantial economic contributions in countries worldwide. For example, Gold's Gym, founded in Venice Beach, California, in 1965, now has over 600 gyms in 25 countries around the world. Bally Total Fitness has over 400 gyms located in such countries as the United States, Canada, South Korea, China, and the Bahamas. The focus of these organizations, and others like them, is to help people reach their fitness goals. For many people, the goal is losing weight or increasing overall health and fitness levels. Therefore, these gyms are open to all types of customers, young and old, fit and unfit.

Although fitness organizations are open to a diverse membership, they may not always be so open to diversity among their employees. There may be a bias in favor of hiring individuals who appear fit over those who do not appear fit, suggesting the existence of anti-fat attitudes. Jennifer Portnick's situation supports this contention. Standing 5'8" and weighing 240 pounds, Portnick participated in high-impact aerobics for 15 years. Given her stamina and demonstrated excellence in the activity, her instructor, Kristi Howard, encouraged her to seek an aerobics certification with Jazzercise. Howard noted, "She has everything it takes. Jennifer is very healthy. She is not pooped out and sucking for air in class."

However, Ann Rieke, district manager for Jazzercise, saw things differently and denied Portnick's request for certification. Rieke wrote that although she believed Portnick "will be a fabulous instructor someday," she did not currently have the "fit appearance" needed to be a Jazzercise instructor. She further suggested that Portnick, who is primarily a vegetarian, change her diet and try body sculpting. After receiving Portnick's protest, Maureen Brown, the director for programs and services for Jazzercise, agreed with Rieke's initial conclusion. She indicated to Portnick that "a Jazzercise applicant must have a higher muscle-to-fat ratio and look leaner than the public. People must believe

After studying this chapter, you should be able to:

- Understand key terms and different standards related to appearance.

- Discuss the influence of weight, height, and attractiveness on how people are viewed by others.

- Highlight the influence of appearance on exercise participation and physical activity promotion.

175

Jazzercise will help them improve, not just maintain their level of fitness. Instructors must set the example and be the role models for Jazzercise enthusiasts."

After Brown's decision, Portnick obtained certification through the Aerobics and Fitness Association of America and currently teaches six high-energy, low-impact classes a week. She also filed a discrimination suit against Jazzercise, arguing that she did not receive certification because the company's decision was based on her physical characteristics, not on her qualifications as a potential aerobics instructor. The suit was dismissed when Jazzercise agreed to eliminate the fit appearance as a prerequisite for the company's instructors and franchisees.

Information adapted from: ■ Fernandez, E. (2002, February). *Teacher says fat/fitness can mix: S.F. mediates complaint Jazzercise showed bias.* SFGate.com. Retrieved January 18, 2006, from www.sfgate.com/cgi-bin/article.cgi?file=/ chronicle/archive/2002/02/24/MN187100.DTL ■ Portnick's Complaint (2002, May 20). *People, 57,* 139 ■ www.bally fitness.com; www.goldsgym.com.

DIVERSITY CHALLENGE   R E F L E C T I O N

1. How much should a fitness instructor's appearance influence customers' perceptions of the instructor's capabilities and ability to train them?

2. Should a fitness organization such as Jazzercise be able to select their employees and trainers based, at least in part, on the applicant's physical characteristics? Why or why not?

3. If you believe fitness organizations should be able to choose to hire only those people who appear physically fit, should this same standard apply to all organizations? Why or why not?

4. What are other situations where employee physical characteristics might be considered a prerequisite to holding a particular position?

Discussions of diversity often focus on race, gender, or age, with some discussions also centering on class or more deep-level characteristics. Appearance is rarely considered. However, as the Diversity Challenge illustrates, the way people look has the potential to influence a host of outcomes, including their opportunities to lead fitness classes. Indeed, researchers have shown that one's appearance can impact a constellation of outcomes, including career aspirations, work experiences, and interactions with others. The effects of appearance are also observed in advertisements and promotions, where slim, and often athletically built persons are used to endorse fitness organizations and related products.

The purpose of this chapter is to explore the influence of appearance in greater depth. I begin with a discussion of issues related to one's weight, focusing on key terms, the influence of weight on work experiences and opportunities, the focus on weight loss among health professionals, and the impact of weight on sport and exercise behavior. In the next section, I turn the attention to height. Though limited research is devoted to this topic, the existing literature does show that height influences people's attraction to others, their work outcomes, and their career success—all of which are discussed in turn. In the final section, I highlight the influence of physical attractiveness on people's employment experiences and how attractiveness affects the marketing of sport.

Weight

In this section, I provide an overview of the diversity research related to weight. In doing so, I introduce key terms, discuss the effects of weight in the workplace, and offer an analysis of the effects of weight on fitness promotion and sport participation.

Background and Key Terms

Terminology related to weight varies depending on the context. *Obese, obesity,* and *overweight* are general terms but are also used by clinicians and public health professionals as biomedical terms with specific meanings. For instance, some consider people to be obese when they have an excessive amount of body fat relative to lean muscle, but others consider people to be obese who are at least 20 percent above their recommended body weight (Bell, McLaughlin, & Sequeira, 2004). The Centers for Disease Control (CDC) considers people to be overweight when they have a body mass index (BMI) over 25.0 and to be obese when the BMI is over 30.0. The mathematical formula for BMI is: BMI = (weight in pounds / height in inches^2) $\times$ 703. A person who is 5'9" and weighs 210 pounds has a BMI of 31.01 [(210/4761) $\times$ 703] and is considered obese according to the CDC's definition.

Of course, the BMI does not account for those people who have considerable muscle mass and therefore weigh more. They may be considered obese when in fact they are not. This is perhaps best illustrated by separate reports released in 2005 indicating that a majority of NFL players and a number of NBA players are considered obese according to the BMI formula (Kava, 2005). At that time defensive end Jevon Kearse had about 5 percent body fat, indicating that he was very lean. At 6'4" and 265 pounds, however, Kearse is considered obese according to his BMI [(265/5776) $\times$ 703 = 32.25]. Dr. Ruth Kava, Director of Nutrition at the American Council on Science and Health, explains that the BMI is used as an index for sedentary people. For professional athletes, or those with an active lifestyle, the index is less useful (Kava, 2005).

While biomedical terms are frequently used, some criticize their usage. Activists argue that use of terms such as "obese" and "overweight" assumes that there is a "normal" weight—a point they dispute (Solovay, 2000). As Bell (2007) explains, many of these standards were based on data obtained from insurance companies, who used middle-class Whites as the standard. Obviously, what is "normal" or the standard for middle-class Whites might be very different for other groups. They further argue that people clinically categorized as overweight might be much healthier than persons who are thin due to unhealthy practices (e.g., anorexia). Given these concerns, activists will often use terms such as *fat, fatness,* and *corpulent* (Duncan, 2008).

This debate highlights the difficulties and ambiguity surrounding issues related to weight. Nevertheless, there is general consensus among national and international agencies, such as National Institutes of Health, the World Health Organization, and the Centers for Disease Control, that there is a continuum from normal, overweight, obese, to morbidly obese and that health outcomes grow progressively worse toward the high end of that continuum. Furthermore, Bell (2007) correctly notes that "for the average person, exactly where she or he falls on an inexact continuum is not the critical issue. Being fat is negative in employment contexts; being very fat is more negative, yet a prospective employer will not generally be concerned with or consider whether an applicant is specifically overweight or obese in making negative judgments" (p. 403).

According to the World Health Organization (www.who.int), obesity is increasing globally. In 2009, more than 1 billion people worldwide were overweight, with at least 300 million of them considered clinically obese; and although there is considerable consternation about the obesity rates in Western countries like the United States, obesity is also regularly observed in developing countries. Some countries such as China and Japan have 5 percent obesity rates, but other countries have much higher rates. In Samoa, for instance, three of every four people are considered obese.

The World Health Organization points to several factors that contribute to obesity, including diet, activity level, and genetics. People have moved away from consuming fresh foods, fruits, and vegetables and, instead, now consume processed foods that lack complex carbohydrates but are high in saturated fats and sugars. Urbanization and modernization impact physical activity levels. Where people might have performed manual labor in the past, in today's service-and-information economy, jobs require comparatively minimal levels of energy expenditures. City infrastructures often encourage people to take cars or public transportation rather than walk or ride a bicycle. Finally, genetics influence people's weight. Studies of adopted children who were separated from their biological parents early in life suggest that the adoptees' weight is closely associated with that of their biological parents. There is no association, however, among the weight of the adoptees and that of their adoptive parents (Stunkard et al., 1986).

Effects of Weight in the Workplace

As illustrated in the Diversity Challenge, one's weight has the potential to influence a number of work outcomes. Weight stigma and anti-fat attitudes are often determinative factors in these poor work experiences (Sartore & Cunningham, 2007; see also the Alternative Perspectives box for a different viewpoint related to weight stigma). In many respects, American society is fixated on physical appearance and beauty, and people who do not fit the ideal are relegated to "other" status. Common stereotypes directed toward people who are fat include the perception of them as unattractive, unkempt, and even disgusting (Bellizzi & Hasty, 2000; Roehling, 1999) and the belief that they are incompetent, lazy, and lacking self-discipline (Paul & Townsend, 1995).

Research suggests that these stereotypes are commonly held among sport and health promotion professionals. For instance, Schwartz, Chambliss, Brownell, Blair, and Billington (2003) found that health profession-als *who specialized in obesity* expressed high levels of implicit anti-fat bias and also endorsed implicit stereotypes of people who are fat being stupid, in-dolent, and worthless. Not all health professionals in their study expressed such viewpoints; rather, older persons, men, persons who had high BMI scores, those who had obese friends, and persons who understood the experiences of obese persons all expressed less prejudice than their counterparts. Dimmock, Hallett, and Grove (2009) observed similar findings in their study of fitness center employees. Though participants did not express overt, explicit anti-fat attitudes, they did have implicit anti-fat biases, as measured by implicit at-titudes tests (see Chapter 3). Greenleaf and Weiller (2005) found that physical educators held moder-ate anti-fat attitudes and tended to consider weight to be largely a function of personal control. Final-ly, although the aforementioned studies focus on practicing professionals, there is also evidence that students aspiring to work in the sport and fitness industry also endorse anti-fat beliefs (Chambliss, Finley, & Blair, 2004; Duncan, 2008). One student in Duncan's analysis, when asked to respond to the notion that people who are fat are abused by so-ciety, wrote, "In a way it makes me feel bad for people that are fat. But then again I don't feel bad because most of the fat people aren't trying to do anything about it. But honestly, it's hard to hear people actually say that . . . [they] can't help being fat, it runs in their family. They should do something about their body, stop eating so much and exercise three to four times a week" (p. 2).

These anti-fat attitudes have a damaging effect on people's work experiences, particularly in industries that put a premium on appearance, as sport does (see the Diversity in the Field box on the next page). In this context, the "ideal" body type is lean and muscular (Vogel, 1999), and people who deviate from that standard are viewed negatively. Consider, for instance, the case of a fitness club. Job applicants who are considered to be overweight might be viewed as a bad fit for the organiza-tion and ill-equipped to instruct others on how to lead healthy lifestyles. Of course, people can be unhealthy and have low BMI scores, just as they can be healthy and have higher BMI scores; nevertheless, the anti-fat attitudes and stereotypical norms both serve to disadvantage people who do not fit the "ideal" body type. As a result, persons considered to be overweight suffer discrimination in the selection process, in promotions received, and in performance evaluations (Rudolf, Wells, Weller, & Baltes, 2009). Given this level of discrimination, it is hardly surprising that persons considered to be overweight have less career success than their counterparts. Gort-maker, Must, Perrin, Sobol, and Dietz's (1993) longitudinal study of over 10,000 randomly selected participants illustrates this point. Women considered to be over-

alternative PERSPECTIVES

Who Is Stigmatized? Many researchers suggest that bias expressed toward people who are overweight is due to stigma (e.g., Sartore & Cunningham, 2007). From this perspective, people who deviate from what is "normal" are viewed in a negative light. Bell and McLaughlin (2007) note, however, that this reasoning is not applicable in the United States. In this context, the majority of people are considered overweight, and thus, what is "typical" or "normal" should reflect this reality. In this case, people who are particularly thin are the ones who should be stigmatized, and they are the ones who differ from the typical majority. The authors note that "this does not appear to be happening, which calls into question the ap-plicability of the deviation from the standard as a major cause of stigmatization. What appears to occur is that stigmatization occurs when the target (job applicant, for example) *deviates from an ideal or preferred* target rather than from the normal target" (p. 467, emphasis original).

DIVERSITY
in the field

Weighing the Coaching Options. There are several requisite qualifications for being a head coach in the NFL, including success as an assistant coach or administrator, leadership qualities, and quality coaching contacts. In addition to these qualities, Charlie Weis believed that most owners sought a coach with a certain body type. Therefore, the overweight Weis opted for gastric bypass surgery, a risky procedure designed to reduce the size of the stomach to allow for weight loss. Unfortunately for Weis, the surgery almost killed him. In fact, a Catholic priest gave last rites two days after the surgery. Weis ultimately recovered and went on to help the New England Patriots win a Super Bowl as their offensive coordinator. He served as head coach of the Notre Dame Fighting Irish from 2005 to 2009. That he went to such lengths to obtain a head coaching position demonstrates two points: (1) there is the very strong perception that people who are overweight or obese do not have access to head coaching positions, and (2) people will go to great lengths to realize their dream of becoming a head coach (Mortensen, 2002).

weight had less formal education, earned $7,000 less per year, and had 10 percent higher rates of poverty than their counterparts. Similar trends were observed for men, though to a lesser degree.

Sartore and Cunningham's (2007) series of experimental studies also sheds light on these dynamics. In their research, participants viewed applications for a position at a fitness club. The material contained a picture of the applicant (either thin or fat) and the relevant experience (either poorly or highly qualified). Across three studies, applicants considered to be overweight were ascribed negative attributions (e.g., lazy, unkempt), considered a poor fit for the job, and given negative hiring recommendations. These effects remained across different qualification levels. In fact, unqualified thin applicants were sometimes viewed as a better fit for the organization than were their highly qualified fat counterparts. Given the results, Sartore and Cunningham argued that fitness club managers should seek to eliminate such biases, and by doing so, "managers can not only provide opportunities for nonstereotypical, qualified applicants, but they can also expose fitness customers and clients to new ideas of what group fitness instructors and personal trainers can look like" (p. 189).

While employees who are perceived to be overweight experience discrimination, the same is also true for customers, as evidenced in the Diversity in the Field box on the facing page.

Moderators

As with most issues, the aforementioned effects are not uniform across all situations. Instead, researchers have found that demographics, the type of job, and applicant qualifications all potentially serve as moderators.

Demographics. With respect to demographics, women are more negatively affected than men by perceptions of being overweight. Roehling, Roehling, and Pichler (2007) found that women classified as very obese were 16 times more likely than men to report weight-based discrimination in the workplace. Women's wages are also more negatively affected than men's by being classified as overweight (Gortmaker et al., 1993). These findings suggest that it is less appropriate for a woman to be considered overweight than it is for a man (see also Pingitore et al., 1994). Race also affects reactions to weight differences, as Whites are less tolerant of large body sizes than are African Americans (Hebl & Heatherton, 1998), a finding that could be due to the notion that African Americans are exposed to role models that have larger frames (Parker et al., 1995). The weight-by-race interaction impacts a number of outcomes. For instance, Wade and Di-Maria (2003) found that White thin women were viewed as more attractive, friendly, and successful than their larger counterparts. The opposite trend occurred for African Americans: heavier women were perceived as friendlier and more trustworthy than thin African American women. Finally, Finkelstein, Frautschy Demuth, and Sweeney (2007) observed weight-by-race effects in the employment context: White thin women were rated more favorably than White heavier women, but no differences were observed among African American women of varying body types.

Type of job. The type of job also affects such ratings. People who are obese are more likely to be hired for jobs that do not require face-to-face interaction, such as inside telephone sales, than jobs that require such interaction (Bellizzi & Hasty, 1998). These findings are consistent with Rudolph et al.'s (2009) study, which found weight bias to have more impact in sales positions than in managerial positions.

Qualifications. Finally, the qualifications of applicants have been shown to moderate the effects

DIVERSITY *in the field*

Anti-Fat Attitudes Toward Customers. Research by Shapiro and King of Rice University shows that the general treatment of consumers who are obese is substantially poorer than the treatment of those whose weight is normal (Reyes, 2005). They designed a study in which 10 young women donned "fat suits" to make them appear heavier than they really were. The women shopped at various stores in the Houston area and noted the responses they received from the salespersons. In general, salespeople spent little time with the women who were overweight and, in some cases, even wondered aloud why shoppers who are overweight would bother patronizing a particular store. The researchers also found that the treatment the women received was better if they were drinking a diet cola or discussing weight loss. Reflecting on their findings, Shapiro noted that "obesity instantly gets you second-class treatment . . . it was distressing—an eye-opening experience" (as cited in Reyes, 2005, p. 125).

of weight on subsequent job-related outcomes. In general, better qualifications of people who are thin give rise to more favorable ratings, but the same is not the case for applicants perceived to be overweight. In the latter case, both highly qualified and unqualified applicants face barriers to employment. This is particularly the case in the sport context, where a premium is placed on appearance (Sartore & Cunningham, 2007). In other settings, the effects are more nuanced, and weight bias is likely to appear only when people are marginally qualified for the job (Finkelstein et al., 2007). In such a case, people can justify their discrimination by pointing to other factors (e.g., the applicant did not have enough experience), whereas such excuses are not available when the applicant is highly qualified.

Weight and Fitness Promotion

In addition to influencing people's experiences in the workplace, issues related to weight, and more specifically weight loss, impact health promotion. The increased number of people medically classified as overweight or obese has resulted in a number of programs designed to increase people's physical activity levels (for an overview, see Lox, Martin Ginis, & Petruzzello, 2010). Indeed, the World Health Organization's promotion and support of regular physical activity is key in these weight-loss efforts.

Health and fitness clubs also play a potentially key role in this area. Research suggests that the way these clubs position themselves and promote the benefits of physical activity influences people's subsequent exercise intentions. Specifically, Woods, Cunningham, and Greenleaf (2010) conducted an experimental study in which participants viewed an advertisement for a new fitness club and then reported their reactions to the club and their interest in joining. The advertisements were varied by the focus (appearance: "look better instantly and get your best body ever," or wellness: "learn fitness and nutrition strategies; acquire life-long wellness") and the sex of the model. Their results showed that people agreed more with the fitness club's culture when there was a wellness focus rather than an appearance focus in the advertisement, irrespective of model's sex in the advertisement. Participant agreement with the club culture was then reliably associated with their interest in joining the club.

These findings suggest that the dominant theme among most fitness clubs—that is, if you exercise then you will lose weight—is potentially misguided. A different, better approach would be to focus on how membership in a club can result in being healthy, irrespective of one's weight. The same is true for the models used in advertisements—the fit, athletic models used predominantly by sport marketers in their advertisements. What is interesting, however, is that these marketing efforts may not effectively reach the primary target audience or the people who need sport and exercise the most—those who are overweight or obese. Recall from Chapter 2 that the social categorization framework for understanding diversity holds that people will have positive attitudes toward and trust those people who are similar to them (in-group members). If that is true, then use of thin models with well-defined muscles to attract people to a fitness club will be most effective for those people who already embody those characteristics. Persons who are overweight or obese may view those product endorsers as out-group members; hence, the positive attitudes toward, and the trust afforded to, such endorsers are likely to be low. Building from this argument, for more effective ads, sport and fitness organizations should use models who represent all body types. Of course, drawing from the matchup hypothesis literature, the product endorsers should still demonstrate some level of physical fitness. See the Alternative Perspectives box for an example of such an advertising campaign.

Weight and Physical Activity Participation

Carron, Hausenblas, and Estabrooks (2003) report that women and men considered to be overweight are less likely to exercise and participate in other physical activities than other persons. The same is not necessarily true for children, however, and past research has yielded equivocal findings related to the activity levels of children of varying body types (Carron et al., 2003).

Persons thought to be overweight may choose not to exercise because they are self-conscious about others seeing them participate, especially when the

alternative PERSPECTIVES

Dove Body Lotion. Companies often use ultra-thin models to advertise skin care or beauty products to entice consumers to purchase the products. In 2004, Dove began an ad campaign, called *Campaign for Real Beauty,* for their hand and body lotions. The women in the advertisements are of varying ages, races, heights, and body types. Some are pregnant, some are curvaceous, others are thin. By incorporating "real women with real bodies and real curves," Dove sought to broaden the definition of beauty. Olphie Camacho, Unilever de Puerto Rico general manager, praised the ad campaign. "It's positive, it's powerful, it's empowering women," she noted. The impetus for the campaign resulted, in part, from research Dove conducted. Dove found that people viewed the models most often used in commercials for beauty products as setting "an unrealistic standard for beauty." This empirical research was supported by comments women had provided Dove for years. The campaign using models with "real bodies" has been wildly successful across the United States, Europe, and Latin American (Albanese, 2005).

activities are difficult for them to complete (Carron et al., 2003). This seems understandable, especially if many of the other participants have lean or muscular body types. Some people experience social physique anxiety, which is felt when they believe others are evaluating their body type (Carron et al., 2003). Those who experience such anxiety are likely to exercise in private (e.g., in their home) or wear loose fitting clothes. Social physique anxiety also influences the choice of activities. For example, Crawford and Eklund (1994) found that women with social physique anxiety were likely to have a positive attitude toward aerobics classes that did not emphasize the female physique.

On a different note, the female athlete triad represents another weight-related issue stemming from sport participation. According to the Female Athlete Triad Coalition (www.femaleathletetriad.org), the female athlete triad is a syndrome consisting of three conditions: eating disorder, amenorrhea, and osteoporosis. The eating disorder occurs when female athletes try to lose weight as a way of improving their performance or of addressing body-image dissatisfaction. Amenorrhea refers to menstrual disturbances (e.g., an athlete missing her period for three months or more). This is the most serious element of the triad and could result from decreases in estrogen stemming from energy deficiency (i.e., the athlete's caloric intake does not match the energy burned through participation). The third element, osteoporosis (i.e., weakening of the bones), occurs with low estrogen and poor nutrition. All of these conditions can vary in severity, and women can exhibit one, two, or all three of them. In seeking to address the female athlete triad, most health professionals emphasize nutrition and the need for healthy eating habits.

Height

he purpose of this section is to offer an overview of height. Specifically, I first define key terms and then highlight the effects of height in the workplace.

Key Terms

The average height for women and men varies depending on time (people have grown taller over time) and location. According to McDowell, Fryar, Ogden, and Flegal (2008), the average height for adult women in the United States is 5'3", while the average height for adult men is 5'9" (see Exhibit 8.1). Only 5 percent of women are above 5'8", while the corresponding height for men is 6'2". Among women and men, Whites and African Americans are about two inches taller than Hispanics. Given these figures, discussions of "taller" people refer to people whose height is above the national average.

Effects of Height in the Workplace

The impact of height has been studied in a number of areas outside the organizational context. For instance, researchers have shown that women generally prefer taller men rather than shorter ones (Swami, Furnham, Balakumar, Williams, Canaway, & Stanistreet, 2008). Unlike weight, on which researchers have steadily focused their efforts in order to understand that diversity dimension's effects in *exhibit* **8.1**   Average height (in inches) for U.S. adults.

GROUP	MEAN	5TH PERCENTILE	50TH PERCENTILE	95TH PERCENTILE
Women				
All races	63.8	59.3	63.8	68.2
Whites	64.2	59.9	64.2	68.4
African Americans	64.1	59.7	64.0	68.4
Hispanics	62.1	59.0	62.1	66.2
Men				
All races	69.4	64.4	69.4	74.3
Whites	69.9	65.4	69.8	74.5
African Americans	69.8	65.1	69.7	76.6
Hispanics	67.0	62.5	65.0	71.6

Source: McDowell et al. (2008).

the workplace, height has received relatively scarce attention from organizational scientists. Much of the research that focused on height was conducted in the early-to-mid 1900s, where researchers investigated the effects of height on a number of attributes, particularly leadership and performance (Collins, 1955; Garrison, 1933; Kitson, 1922). The link between height and leadership does have some anecdotal support: consider, for instance, that for over 100 years, there has not been a single U.S. president whose height was below the national average. That said, leadership theories generally moved from the study of immutable individual characteristics to a more behavioral and contingency focus (Robbins, & Judge, 2007).

Despite the lack of work in the area, there is some compelling evidence that height does make a difference for people and their careers. Judge and Cable (2004) provide the strongest and most comprehensive evidence. These authors suggested that physical height is positively associated with social esteem and self-esteem—that is, people have higher regard for taller people, and taller people are also likely to have greater self-confidence and perceptions of self-worth. Both of these factors are thought to influence various measures of performance: people who are confident and who are well thought of by others generally perform well. Finally, those who perform well in their tasks are more likely than their peers to ascend into leadership positions and be well-compensated.

Judge and Cable (2004) then conducted a number of studies to test their theoretical model. In the first study, they aggregated findings from past studies to examine the overall relationship among the variables. As expected, they found that height is positively associated with social esteem, ascension into leadership positions, and performance. In the next set of analyses, the authors analyzed longitudinal data collected from over 4,000 people to examine the effects of height on earnings. After controlling for the possible confounding effects of gender, weight, and age, they found that taller people earn appreciably more than their shorter counterparts. For instance, a person standing 72 inches tall is expected to earn

$5,525 more per year than was a person who was 65 inches tall. Over a 30-year career, this amounts to $165,750 in earnings, without even taking interest into account. Subsequent analyses showed that the effect of height on income did not vary for women or men and had remained constant over time.

Gladwell (2007) also addressed this issue in his book, *Blink*. Specifically, he collected data from about half of the Fortune 500 companies, asking each about the characteristics of its CEO. He found that the average male CEO was just under six feet tall, nearly three inches taller than the national average. He also observed that 58 percent of the male CEOs were over six feet tall—a proportion substantially higher than the 14.5 percent U.S. average. Even more remarkable, even though only 3.9 percent of all U.S. men are 6'2" or taller, nearly a third of the Fortune 500 CEOs reached this mark. Finally, although millions of U.S. men stand below 5'6", only 10 male CEOs in his sample were this height.

Gladwell (2007) points to implicit biases that favor taller people in explaining his findings. Consider, for instance, that the average height for entry level employees is likely to mirror that of the U.S. population, which is 5'9". As we progress up the managerial ranks, however, the average height increases, and male CEOs are three inches taller than the national average. This is not because people explicitly think taller people are better; rather, people subconsciously associate height and stature with power and leadership—a relationship observed throughout nature. Gladwell explains, "Most of us, in ways that we are not entirely aware of, automatically associate leadership ability with imposing physical stature. We have a sense of what a leader is supposed to look like, and that stereotype is so powerful that when someone fits it, we simply become blind to other considerations" (p. 88).

These findings have potential consequences for other diversity dimensions. Few people would suggest that people are explicitly biased against short people. After all, it would be preposterous to promote people merely because they are tall. However, although explicit attitudes might not be at work, the evidence suggests that implicit attitudes are. Similarly, some argue that stereotypes and biases against women, racial minorities, or sexual minorities (i.e., gays, lesbians, and bisexuals) are a thing of the past. However, if implicit biases contribute to people ascending to leadership positions based on something as innocuous as height, then how much more likely is it that other implicit biases would favor historically dominant groups, such as men, heterosexuals, or Whites?

Attractiveness

In the final section, I provide an overview of the research related to attractiveness. As with the other sections, I first give an overview of key concepts. The discussion then moves to an analysis of how attractiveness influences both people's work experiences and their sport participation.

Background Information

People's attractiveness has been shown to influence how they are treated by others and the career success they enjoy (see the box on page 187 for an overview of the factors influencing perceptions of facial attractiveness). Langlois, Kalakanis,

Rubenstein, Larson, Hallam, and Smoot's (2000) impressive study aptly demonstrates these effects. They aggregated the results from over 1,800 studies that covered a 67-year time frame (1932–1999) and observed the following:

■ Contrary to the notion that different cultures have distinct ideas about what is attractive, their analysis showed that both within and across cultures, there was agreement about who is attractive and who is not. This effect held for both children and adults. Similarly, they observed uniformity in attractiveness ratings across ethnicities. These findings led Langlois et al. (2000) to conclude "that beauty is not simply in the eye of the beholder" (p. 399).

■ Attractive and unattractive people are judged differently. Relative to their unattractive counterparts, attractive children are perceived to be more positively adjusted and to display greater interpersonal competence, while attractive adults are thought to have more social appeal, be better adjusted, and be more interpersonally competent.

■ Attractive children and adults are treated better than their less attractive counterparts on a constellation of outcomes, including positive interactions, allocation of rewards, attention, and provision of help and cooperation.

■ Behavioral differences are also present. Attractive children have been shown to be better emotionally adjusted, display greater intelligence, and to be more popular than their unattractive counterparts. Differences in adults were observed for occupational success, physical health, social skills, mental health, and intelligence.

Why are these effects observed? That is, why are attractive people judged and treated differently? Dipboye (2005) suggests that cognitive, affective, organizational, and behavioral antecedents could all be factors explaining this phenomenon.

Cognitive sources of bias occur due to the categorization process (Dipboye, 2005). A diversity form is likely to be a source of categorization (and potentially bias) when it is easily accessible and recognized by others, and this is certainly the case with appearance. In fact, research suggests that appearance is frequently used when describing someone (Fiske & Cox, 1979). People then use these easily accessible characteristics to categorize the self and others into social groups—that is, into ingroups and out-groups. This categorization process is guided by their implicit theories regarding appearance. As Langlois et al.'s study illustrates, people are likely to evaluate perceived attractive others in a positive light, resulting in a "beautiful is good" connection (see also Eagly, Ashmore, Makhijani, & Longo, 1991). As a consequence, attractive people are attributed positive characteristics and often considered a better fit for a position or entry into the organization than their less attractive counterparts.

There may be affective sources of attractiveness bias, causing people to *feel* differently toward attractive and unattractive targets (Dipboye, 2005). From this perspective, people feel drawn to attractive people, without mediating mental processes. Consider, for instance, that even infants as young as three months old have demonstrated a preference for faces typically considered to be attractive over faces considered unattractive (Langlois, Ritter, Roggman, & Vaughn, 1991). The sight of a beautiful face has also been shown to activate reward centers in the brain (see Rhodes, 2006). From this perspective, preference for attractive people is not simply a function of the categorization process; it proceeds from emotional responses that the perceiver might be unaware of or even unable to control (Dipboye, 2005).

Additionally, organizational and social factors might influence attractiveness bias (Dipboye, 2005). In this case, the bias would be a function of the social norms in place. Suppose, for instance, that a particular sport club had always hired young, attractive men as administrators. This norm would in turn influence who was believed to be suitable for other openings in the club.

Finally, attractiveness bias might be a function of behaviors (Dipboye, 2005). As previously noted, people are likely to ascribe positive characteristics to an attractive person. When they do this, certain behaviors are also likely to follow. People are more likely to treat in a positive manner someone who is considered smart, out-going, and sociable (i.e., characteristics ascribed to attractive people) than they are someone to whom they do not attribute these characteristics. These dynamics can result in a host of differences in work outcomes, including performance appraisals and assessment of promotion potential, to name a few.

Attractiveness in the Workplace

The positive effects of being attractive are also observed in the workplace. Hosoda, Stone-Romero, and Coats (2003) examined this issue in their meta-analysis of 68 different experimental studies that had previously been published (1975–1998) in psychology, management, and economics journals. They found that attractiveness is positively associated with a host of work outcomes, including selection, performance appraisals, and promotion. The effects exist for both women and men and for the type of job considered. There were two factors that influenced the results, however: the amount of job-relevant information provided and the time at which the study was conducted. With respect to the first moderator, they found that the attractiveness bias is strongest when the job-relevant information is weak (e.g., when information about the needed background or qualifications is ambiguous). This finding, particularly relevant in the selection process, suggests that if raters do not have much information on which to base their conclusion, or if the information is ambiguous, then attractiveness plays a key role; on the other hand, when an applicant is clearly unqualified or clearly qualified, the effects of attractiveness are diminished. With respect to time, Hosoda et al. found that the effect size (i.e., strength of association between attractiveness and work outcomes, expressed as d) decreased in each time frame they examined: 1975–1979 ($d = .54$), 1980–1984 ($d = .48$), 1985–1989 ($d = .38$), 1990–1994 ($d = .37$), and 1995–1999 ($d = .19$).

WHAT MAKES PEOPLE'S FACES BEAUTIFUL?

Are there characteristics that make someone's face beautiful? According to psychologist Gillian Rhodes, there are. Rhodes identified three specific characteristics: averageness, symmetry, and sexual dismorphism. With respect to the first characteristic, contrary to what people might expect, the evidence suggests that the more average a face—that is, those with few distinctive features—the more beautiful it is perceived. Thus, typical faces, which more closely resemble the population average, have consistently rated higher in attractiveness than have very distinct faces. With respect to the second characteristic, research indicates that symmetrical faces are preferred over asymmetrical ones. These effects remain irrespective of the person's sex or race, or the sex of the rater. Finally, sexual dismorphism refers to the characteristics generally observed among men and women. For instance, after puberty, testosterone in men stimulates growth of the jaw bone, cheek bones, brow ridge, facial hair, and the center of the face. Growth in these areas is inhibited in women due to an increase in estrogen. The presence of estrogen also increases the lip size of women relative to men. These dynamics potentially result in a typically masculine look in some men and a typically feminine look in some women. Research suggests that femininity among women is associated with attractiveness, as is masculinity among men—though to a lesser extent.

Adapted from Rhodes (2006).

DIVERSITY *in the field*

Attractiveness and the Promotion of Sport. Athlete endorsers are often used to promote a variety of products and services, including sport events. According to si.com, in 2007 Michelle Wie earned a little over $735,000 in earnings from her performance in golf tournaments. That same year, she earned over $19.5 million in endorsement monies, over *25 times* the amount earned on the course. Unfortunately, Wie is the exception rather than the norm. Although athletes are used as endorsers in 11 percent of all television commercials, women are used only 3 percent of the time (Turner, Bounds, Hauser, Motsinger, Ozmore, & Smith, 1995).

A number of researchers have examined factors that influence the commercial effectiveness of female athlete endorsers. To do so, they have drawn largely from the match-up hypothesis. From this perspective, endorsers are most effective when there is a match, or "fit," between said endorser and the product being endorsed (Kamins, 1990). The skill of the athlete endorser should be related to perceptions of fit, especially when promoting a sport-related product (e.g., a sports drink). In addition, attractiveness has been shown to positively influence the perceived fit of women endorsers. This is particularly the case when women athletes promote sport events. As Cunningham, Fink, and Kenix (2008) note, "it is possible that people have come to associate some sports with the attractive athletes who participate in them (e.g., tennis and Maria Sharapova)" (p. 373).

Cunningham et al. (2008) experimentally examined how expertise and attractiveness contributed to the perceived fit of a female athlete endorsing the NCAA Tennis National Championship. They found that attractiveness and expertise were both positively associated with perceived fit but that these effects were qualified by a significant expertise-by-attractiveness interaction. Specifically, among highly qualified athletes, attractive and unattractive endorsers were viewed as equally appropriate endorsers. This was not the case for unqualified endorsers, however; attractive athletes were greatly preferred over unattractive ones. In discussing their findings, Cunningham et al. noted that the findings lend support to the growing literature that suggests women athletes are rewarded more for their appearance than for their physical prowess.

As previously noted, Hosoda observed that attractiveness was positively associated with desired work outcomes for both women and men. From a different perspective, Bell and her colleagues (Bell, 2007; Bell & McLaughlin, 2007) have argued that there might be some cases in which women are actually disadvantaged by their attractiveness. Highly attractive women might be valued more for their looks than for their intellect or physical abilities, and such perceptions are likely to hurt them as they pursue upper-level positions. Bell (2007) relayed the story of Desiree Goodwin, a woman who had two degrees from Cornell University and was denied 16 promotions during her time at Harvard. In her lawsuit against the university, Goodwin relayed how her supervisors told her that she was viewed as "a pretty girl who wore sexy outfits" (p. 408).

A second way in which attractiveness might influence women is through the use of makeup (Bell & McLaughlin, 2007). Women who wear makeup at work are often viewed in a positive light, being perceived as energetic, healthy, and heterosexual. In fact, some women wear makeup only to comply with heterosexual norms, while some lesbians wear makeup only to avoid standing out from others. Bell and McLaughlin reported that one lesbian who did not wear makeup was denied a promotion for not looking feminine enough.

This same pattern has been observed among athletes. Women often feel as though they have to emphasize their attractiveness and femininity by wearing makeup and dressing fashionably. These behaviors are particularly important for women participating in masculine-type sports, such as basketball, in order to combat lesbian labels (Hargreaves, 2000). Ross and Shinew (2008), in their compelling qualitative study, found that athletes practiced "selective femininity" (p. 51). In this case, the athletes were cognizant of and tried to reinforce their femininity in select contexts, such as gymnastic competitions, but not in other contexts such as classrooms or practice. Thus, the athletes practiced femininity only on occasions that they chose. (See also the Diversity in the Field box for a discussion of how attractiveness influences the effectiveness of athlete endorsements.)

Attractiveness and Physical Activity

Research related to physical activity rates among attractive and unattractive people is scarce. There is, however, emerging research pertaining to the association of attractiveness with athleticism or physical prowess. Throughout evolutionary history, individuals with desirable traits advertise these characteristics to attract mates. For instance, peahens are attracted to peacocks with large, colorful trains, because these feathers actually indicate underlying desirable traits (i.e., large amount of caloric energy and resistance to environmental stressors). It is beneficial for the female to pass along these traits to her offspring (Williams, Park, & Wieling, 2010).

While large and colorful feathers are desired among peacocks, in humans, physical superiority and athleticism have always been important in selecting and competing for mates, especially among males (Williams et al., 2010). In many respects, the world of sport is a stage designed to advertise these characteristics (Miller, 2000), and research suggests that athletic traits are highly heritable (Missitzi, Geladas, & Klissouras, 2004). Furthermore, testosterone is an important hormone directly influencing athleticism, and it is also associated with desirable facial features in men, such as a strong jaw line and prominent brow ridge (see also Rhodes, 2006). Considering that athleticism and facial attractiveness (as a result of high testosterone) are linked to heritable fitness, researchers have begun to explore the possibility of an association between facial attractiveness and athleticism.

As far-fetched as this association might seem, there is actually evidence to support it. In one study, Park, Buunk, and Wieling (2007) examined the attractiveness ratings of professional soccer and hockey players. In both sports, the authors argued that goal keepers/goalies and strikers/forwards are likely to be the most athletic because of the skills needed to effectively compete at those positions. Defenders, on the other hand, require considerable endurance but comparatively less athleticism. Thus, if attractiveness is associated with athleticism, then the former group (i.e., goal keepers/goalies and strikers/forwards) should be rated as more attractive than the latter (i.e., defenders). Ratings of facial attractiveness from female students largely confirmed these expectations. In a later study, Williams et al. (2010) examined the linkage between facial attractiveness and performance among professional football quarterbacks. Using the NFL's quarterback rating system as the measure of performance, the authors found a positive association between attractiveness and quarterback performance.

Other measures of appearance also influence people's sport participation, as illustrated in the Diversity in the Field box.

DIVERSITY *in the field*

Women's Headscarves and Their Sport Participation. The garments people wear can influence their sport participation opportunities. For instance, many Muslin women wear a traditional hijab, or headscarf, and they desire to do so while participating in sport, as well. However, until 2007, they were unable to do this and participate in international taekwondo competitions. Recognizing that this prohibition limited women's participation in the sport, the World Taekwondo Federation (WTF) changed the rule and thereby allowed women to wear a hijab under their protective head gear. Dae Won Moon, chair of the WTF technical committee, commented that "this measure means that taekwondo is one of the few sports that treats women and men equally in the Muslim world." He went on to comment that "we believe that our respect for others' cultures and beliefs will allow taekwondo to enhance its status as an Olympic sport."

Information gathered from http://english.aljazeera.net/sport/2009/09/200991621752992657.html.

CHAPTER *summary*

The purpose of this chapter was to examine the influence of appearance on how people experience work, sport and physical activity promotion, and sport participation. As illustrated in the case of Jennifer Portnick and Jazzercise in the Diversity Challenge, appearance has the potential to shape a person's opportunities. People who do not fit the norm, either by being perceived as overweight, as too short, or as unattractive, are faced with a number of challenges. After studying this chapter, you should be able to:

1. Understand key terms and different standards related to appearance.

Three elements of appearance were highlighted in this chapter: weight, height, and attractiveness. With respect to weight, some agencies and scientists classify people based on their BMI or their percent of body fat relative to lean muscle. Activists argue against this approach and suggest that such standards ignore variations in people's bodies. In terms of height, the average height for adult women in the United States is 5'3", while the average height for adult men is 5'9". Those who deviate from this mean are considered short or tall. Finally, attractiveness is based on averageness, symmetry, and sexual dismorphism; and assessments of what is considered attractive are consistent across cultures, sexes, and ethnicities.

2. Discuss the influence of weight, height, and attractiveness on people's work outcomes.

Weight, height, and attractiveness have been shown to influence a bevy of work outcomes, including access to positions, performance appraisals, opportunities for promotion, and earnings. Persons who are considered to be overweight experience work in a negative manner, while persons who are tall and attractive are generally thought to experience work well and be privileged in their prospects for promotion.

3. Highlight the influence of appearance on exercise participation and physical activity promotion.

The available literature suggests that adults considered to be overweight are less likely to exercise than their counterparts, though no differences exist among children. Research related to physical activity levels and the other two diversity dimensions, height and attractiveness, is not available.

QUESTIONS *for discussion*

1. Some consider weight to be a function of individual choices, while others point to environmental and genetic influences. What is your position and why?

2. Why are persons considered to be overweight ascribed negative attributes? Do you think similar ascriptions occur for persons who are underweight?

3. Research suggests that people implicitly prefer leaders who are tall. Why is this the case? Has this been your experience?

4. People have been shown to interact in a positive manner with attractive people, while the same cannot be said of their interactions with unattractive people. Why do you think these differences exist?

5. Are there times when being attractive would hurt people in their job hunt? If so, when is this likely to occur?

6. Pick one of the factors discussed in this chapter and reflect upon your personal concerns and considerations of said factor. Why is this important to you, and what are its implications?

LEARNING *activities*

1. Using the Internet, identify job postings for fitness clubs. Is there language in the advertisement designed to attract persons who might be considered fit or athletic looking?

2. One could argue that attractiveness should be considered when making personal decisions since people (clients) might respond more favorably to attractive than to unattractive persons. Others might argue that such an approach is unreasonable and could be used to justify preferential hiring based on other diversity dimensions (e.g., race). As a class, divide into two teams and debate the two positions.

READING *resources*

SUPPLEMENTARY READINGS

Brownwell, K. D., Schwartz, M. B., Pugh, R. M., & Rudd, L. (2005). *Weight bias: Nature, consequences and remedies.* New York: Guilford Press. (Edited text from leading scholars in the field; explores the nature and causes of weight discrimination, as well as ways to combat the discrimination.)

Rothblum, E., & Solovay, S. (Eds.). (2009). *The fat studies reader.* New York: New York University Press. (A collection of essays addressing anti-fat bias and weight discrimination; also introduces the field of fat studies.)

Solovay, S. (2000). *Tipping the scales of injustice: Fighting weight-based discrimination.* Amherst. NY: Prometheus Books. (Provides a comprehensive, social justice-perspective of weight discrimination, and also addresses legal remedies.)

WEB RESOURCES

■ The Obesity Society (www.naaso.org): national society dedicated to the scientific study of obesity and obesity-related issues, including discrimination.

■ Rudd Center (www.yaleruddcenter.org/): an academic research center that seeks to improve the world's diet, reduce obesity, and ameliorate weight stigma.

■ World Health Organization (www.who.int): an international agency responsible for providing leadership on health matters worldwide, shaping the research agenda, setting health standards, and providing health-related support to countries.

references

Albanese, A. (2005, September 15). Dove introduces body lotions and creams with $200,000 ad and marketing campaign. *Caribbean Business, 33*(36), 46.

Bell, M. P. (2007). *Diversity in organizations*. Mason, OH: Thomson South-Western.

Bell, M. P., & McLaughlin, M. E. (2007). Outcomes of appearance and obesity in organizations. In A. M. Konrad, P. Prasad, & J. K. Pringle (Eds.), *Handbook of workplace diversity* (pp. 455–474). Thousand Oaks, CA: Sage.

Bell, M. P., McLaughlin, M. E., & Sequeira, J. M. (2004). Age, disability, and obesity: Similarities, differences, and common threads. In M. S. Stockdale & F. J. Crosby (Eds.), *The psychology and management of workplace diversity* (pp. 191–205). Malden, MA: Blackwell.

Bellizzi, J. A., & Hasty, R. W. (1998). Territory assignment decisions and supervising unethical selling behavior: The effects of obesity and gender as moderated by job-related factors. *Journal of Personal Selling & Sales Management, 18*(2), 35–49.

Bellizzi, J. A., & Hasty, R. W. (2000). Does successful work experience mitigate weight- and gender-based discrimination in face-to-face industrial selling? *Journal of Business and Industrial Marketing, 15*, 384–398.

Carron, A. V., Hausenblas, H. A., & Estabrooks, P. A. (2003). *The psychology of physical activity*. New York: McGraw-Hill.

Chambliss, H. O., Finley, C. E., & Blair, S. N. (2004). Attitudes toward obese individuals among exercise science students. *Medicine and Science in Sports and Exercise, 36*, 468–474.

Collins, L. T., Jr. (1955). Height and weight as predictors of metal polishing efficiency. *Personnel Psychology, 8*, 461–467.

Crawford, S., & Eklund, R. C. (1994). Social physique anxiety, reasons for exercise, and attitudes toward exercise settings. *Journal of Sport and Exercise Psychology, 16*, 70–82.

Cunningham, G. B., Fink, J. S., & Kenix, L. J. (2008). Choosing an endorser for a women's sporting event: The interaction of attractiveness and expertise. *Sex Roles, 58*, 371–378.

Dimmock, J. A., Hallett, B. E., & Grove, J. R. (2009). Attitudes toward overweight individuals among fitness center employees: An examination of contextual factors. *Research Quarterly for Exercise and Sport, 80*, 641–647.

Dipboye, R. L. (2005). Looking the part: Bias against the physically unattractive as a discrimination issue. In R. L. Dipboye & A. Collela (Eds.), *Discrimination at work: The psychological and organizational bases* (pp. 281–301). Mahwah, NJ: Lawrence Erlbaum.

Duncan, M. C. (2008). The personal is political. *Sociology of Sport Journal, 25*, 1–6.

Eagly, A., Ashmore, R. D., Makhijani, M. G., & Longo, L. C. (1991). What is beautiful is good, but . . . : A meta-analytic review of research on the physical attractiveness stereotype. *Psychological Bulletin, 110*, 109–128.

Finkelstein, L. M., Frautschy Demuth, R. L., & Sweeney, D. L. (2007). Bias against overweight job applicants: Further explorations of when and why. *Human Resource Management, 46*, 203–222.

Fiske, S. T., & Cox, M. G. (1979). Person concepts: The effect of target familiarity and descriptive purpose of the process of describing others. *Journal of Personality, 47*, 136–161.

Garrison, K. C. (1933). A study of some factors related to leadership in high school. *Peabody Journal of Education*, July, 11–17.

Gladwell, M. (2007). *Blink: The power of thinking without thinking*. New York: Back Bay Books.

Gortmaker, S. L., Must, A., Perrin, J., Sobol, A. M., & Dietz, W. H. (1993). Social and economic consequences of overweight in adolescence and young adults. *New England Journal of Medicine, 329*, 1008–1112.

Greenleaf, C., & Weiller, K. (2005). Perceptions of youth obesity among physical educators. *Social Psychology of Education, 8*, 407–423.

Hargreaves, J. (2000). *Heroines of sport: The politics of difference and identity*. London: Routledge.

Hebl, M. R., & Heatherton, T. F. (1998). The stigma of obesity in women: The difference is black and white. *Personality and Social Psychology Bulletin, 24*, 417–426.

Hosoda, M., Stone-Romero, E., & Coates, G. (2003). The effects of physical attractiveness on job-related outcomes: A meta-analysis of experimental studies. *Personnel Psychology, 56*, 431–462.

Judge, T. A., & Cable, D. M. (2004). The effect of physical height on workplace success and income: Preliminary test of a theoretical model. *Journal of Applied Psychology, 89*, 428–441.

Kamins, M. A. (1990). An investigation into the match-up hypothesis in celebrity advertising: When beauty may only be skin deep. *Journal of Advertising, 19*(1), 4–13.

Kava, R. (2005, March). Are our athletes fat? *CANSTATS Bulletins*. Retrieved January 20, 2006, from www.canstats.org/readdetail.asp?id=742.

Kitson, H. D. (1922). Height and weight as factors in salesmanship. *Journal of Personnel Research, 1*, 289–294.

Langlois, J. H., Kalakanis, L., Rubenstein, A. J., Larson, A., Hallam, M., & Smoot, M. (2000). Maxims or myths of beauty? A meta-analytic and theoretical review. *Psychological Bulletin, 126,* 390–423.

Langlois, J. H., Ritter, J. M., Roggman, L. A., & Vaughn, L. S. (1991). Facial diversity and infant preferences for attractive faces. *Developmental Psychology, 27,* 79–84.

Lox, C. L., Martin Ginis, K. A., & Petruzzello, S. J. (2010). *The psychology of exercise: Integrating theory and practice* (3rd ed.). Scottsdale, AZ: Holcomb Hathaway.

McDowell, M. A., Fryar, C. D., Ogden, C. L., & Flegal, K. M. (2008). Anthropometric reference data for children and adults: United States, 2003–2006. *National Health Statistics Reports,* No. 10. Washington, DC: U. S. Department of Health and Human Services.

Miller, G. (2000). *The mating mind: How sexual choice shaped the evolution of human nature.* New York: Random House.

Missitzi, J., Geladas, N., & Klissouras, V. (2004). Heritability in neuromuscular coordination: Implications for motor control strategies. *Medicine and Science in Sport and Exercise, 36,* 233–240.

Mortensen, C. (2002, July). *Seeking new image, Patriots' Weis almost loses life.* ESPN.com. Retrieved January 25, 2006, from http://espn.go.com/chrismortensen/s/2002/0724/1409547.html.

Park, J. H., Buunk, A. P., & Wieling, M. B. (2007). Does the face reveal athletic flair? Positions in team sports and facial attractiveness. *Personality and Individual Differences, 43,* 1960–1965.

Parker, S., Nichter, M., Nichter, M., Vuckovic, N., Sims, C., & Rittenbaugh, C. (1995). Body image and weight concerns among African American and White adolescent females: Differences that make a difference. *Human Organization, 54,* 103–113.

Paul, R. J., & Townsend, J. B. (1995). Shape up or ship out? Employment discrimination against the overweight. *Employees Responsibilities and Rights Journal, 8,* 133–145.

Reyes, M. (2005). Who gets better service? *Glamour, 103*(8), 125.

Rhodes, G. (2006). The evolutionary psychology of facial beauty. *Annual Review of Psychology, 57,* 199–226.

Robbins, S. P., & Judge, T. A. (2007). *Organizational behavior* (12th ed.). Upper Saddle River, NJ: Prentice Hall.

Roehling, M. V. (1999). Weight-based discrimination in employment: Psychological and legal aspects. *Personnel Psychology, 52,* 969–1016.

Roehling, M., Roehling, P., & Pichler, S. (2007). The relationship between body weight and perceived employment discrimination: The role of sex and race. *Journal of Vocational Behavior, 71,* 300-318.

Ross, S. R., & Shinew, K. J. (2008). Perspectives of women college athletes on sport and gender. *Sex Roles, 58,* 40–57.

Rudolf, C. W., Wells, C. L., Weller, M. D., & Baltes, B. B. (2009). A meta-analysis of empirical studies of weight-based bias in the workplace. *Journal of Vocational Behavior, 74,* 1–10.

Sartore, M. L., & Cunningham, G. B. (2007). Weight discrimination, hiring recommendations, person-job fit and attributions: Implications for the fitness industry. *Journal of Sport Management, 21,* 172–193.

Schwartz, M. B., Chambliss, H. O., Brownel, K. D., Blair, S. N., & Billington, C. (2003). Weight bias among health professionals specializing in obesity. *Obesity Research, 11,* 1033–1039.

Solovay, S. (2000). *Tipping the scales of injustice: Fighting weight-based discrimination.* Amherst, NY: Prometheus Books.

Stunkard, A. J., Thorkild, I. A., Sørensen, C. H., Teasdale, T. W., Chakraborty, R., Schull, W. J., & Schulsigner, F. (1986). An adoption study of human obesity. *New England Journal of Medicine, 314*(4), 193–198.

Swami, V., Furnham, A., Balakumar, N., Williams, C., Canaway, K., & Stanistreet, D. (2008). Factors influencing preferences for height: A replication and extension. *Personality and Individual Differences, 45,* 395–400.

Turner, E. T., Bounds, J., Hauser, D., Motsinger, S., Ozmore, D., & Smith, J. (1995). Television consumer advertising and the sports figure. *Sport Marketing Quarterly, 4*(1), 27–33.

Vogel, A. (1999). Female fit-body stereotype. *Fitness Management, 25,* 38–41.

Wade, T. J., & DiMaria, C. (2003). Weight halo effects: individual differences in perceived life success as a function of women's race and weight. *Sex Roles, 48,* 461–465.

Williams, K. M., Park, J. H., & Wieling, M. B. (2010). The face reveals athletic flair: Better National Football League quarterbacks are better looking. *Personality and Individual Differences, 48,* 112–116.

Woods, J., Cunningham, G. B., & Greenleaf, C. (2010, March). *Examining the influence of fitness club culture on attitudes toward joining.* Paper presented at the annual conference of the American Association for Health, Physical Education, Recreation, and Dance, Indianapolis, IN.

9

Religious Beliefs

DIVERSITY ▼ **CHALLENGE**

Anyone who is even vaguely familiar with NASCAR knows that the cars driven in the events are covered with company logos. These logos are representative of a variety of companies in various industries, including DuPont (on Jeff Gordon's #24 car), Goodwrench (on Kevin Harvich's #29 car), and Home Depot (on Tony Stewart's #20 car). In 2004, Bobby Labonte made headlines by promoting Mel Gibson's film *The Passion of the Christ*, a movie depicting the crucifixion of Jesus Christ, on his car's hood. According to Labonte, "It's a chance to get the word out. Someone who is curious about Jesus and has never been saved sees the races and says, 'Hmmm, I'd like to see what that's about.' . . . Maybe we can change their minds." Other racers also include Christian material on their racing machines. Morgan Shepherd, for example, has a Jesus decal on his racing truck, and his racing team is called "Victory in Jesus." That some drivers choose to proclaim their close links to the Christian faith is nothing new to NASCAR; its participants' strong ties to the Christian faith are long-standing. Church services often are held in the racetrack infield for the drivers, their crew, and race officials; prerace invocations are a regular occurrence; and there is a break in the racing schedule during Easter weekend.

Other sport leagues and their teams also have religious ties. The first line of the Little League pledge, which is recited by teams prior to each competition, is "I trust in God." The NBA's Portland Trailblazers had a "Family and Faith Night" at one of their 2004 contests against the Sacramento Kings. After the game, spectators stayed to listen to the Christian acappella group Rescue perform. The WNBA's Minnesota Lynx also offered a "Faith and Family Night," during which the Christian group Go Fish performed. As these examples illustrate, religious beliefs often are incorporated in sport and the entertainment associated with the events.

Information adapted from: ■ Newberry, P. (2004, February). *NASCAR mixing religion, racing.* Deseret news.com. Retrieved February 4, 2006, from http://deseretnews.com/dn/print/1,1442,590042201,00.html ■ www.blazers.com; www.littleleague.org/about/pledge.asp; www.wnba.com/lynx

LEARNING OBJECTIVES

After studying this chapter, you should be able to:

■ Define religion and spirituality, and discuss the differences between the two.

■ Provide an overview of how religious beliefs influence people's work behaviors.

■ Discuss the influence of religion among sport participants.

DIVERSITY CHALLENGE | **R E F L E C T I O N**

1. Are you aware of any other sport teams that use religious themes to attract people to the event?

2. What are the advantages and disadvantages of sport organizations' use of such marketing techniques?

3. What advantages and disadvantages are there for NASCAR drivers who have religious-themed logos or advertisements on their cars? What might be the impact on their fans? On their potential or existing sponsors?

4. How might employees' religious beliefs influence their attitudes and behaviors in the general workplace?

s the Diversity Challenge illustrates, sport and religion are often intertwined. For a host of reasons, now more than ever before, people are likely to integrate their religious beliefs into their everyday work activities; athletes are likely to use their religious beliefs to make sense of their sport participation; and sport organizations may incorporate religion and faith into their efforts to attract fans to their events. These dynamics are important because people's religious beliefs have the potential to influence their attitudes, the decisions they make at work, and how well they integrate with others in the workplace or on an athletic team. Interestingly, despite the importance of religion to many people, this topic has received little interest in the diversity literature. In fact, Hicks (2003) has commented "if the respective fields of leadership and management studies have avoided religion, the academic discipline of religious studies has overlooked the workplace" (p. 3). Consequently, sport managers must remain cognizant of how this form of deep-level diversity influences the workplace's culture, processes, and outcomes.

The purpose of this chapter, therefore, is to examine the influence of religion in sport organizations. The chapter begins with a discussion of religion and spirituality and the distinctions between those two constructs. I then highlight the influence of religion in the workplace, where both categorical and group-level effects are observed. In the final section of the chapter, I provide an overview of how athletes incorporate religion into their sport participation.

Background and Key Terms

To understand the effects of religious beliefs in the workplace, it is first necessary to define basic terms. Durkheim (1965) defines *religion* as "a unified system of beliefs and practices relative to sacred things, that is to say, things set apart and forbidden—beliefs and practices which unite into one single moral community called a Church, all those who adhere to them" (p. 62).

According to Durkheim, religion has several social functions. At the individual level, religion provides people with emotional support and an ultimate sense of meaning. Religion operates at an interpersonal level by creating a form of social bonding through the shared values and beliefs among people of a particular faith. At the institutional level, religion provides a form of social control by prescribing certain behaviors that are consistent with the values, norms, and beliefs of that faith and of society. Finally, religion provides a form of social integration, uniting people of a common faith. Religion brings together people of diverse backgrounds, reaffirms the basic customs and values of a society, and unites people in ways that transcend the individual self.

Some authors contrast religion with the concept of spirituality (e.g., Cacioppe, 2000; Mitroff & Denton, 1999). For them, *spirituality* is conceptualized as "the basic feeling of being connected with one's complete self, others, and the entire universe" (Mitroff & Denton, 1999, p. 83). Terms associated with spirituality include self-actualization, wholeness, meaning, purpose, life force, virtue, and interconnectedness, among others (Hicks, 2002). These authors who distinguish between the two concepts often view religion as being structured and organized, as providing external controls, and as being divisive. On the other hand, spirituality is viewed as being broad and inclusive, providing inner peace, and being the ultimate end in itself (Mitroff & Denton, 1999). For example, one CEO in Mitroff and Denton's study explained, "not only do you not have to be religious in order to be spiritual, but it probably helps if you are not religious, especially if you want your spirituality to grow and be a basic part of your life" (p. 87).

Although these authors distinguish between spirituality and religion, Bailey (2001) asserts that "a meaningful conversation about spirituality sans religion is dubious" (p. 367). A similar position is advocated by others (Cash & Gray, 2000; Hicks, 2002) and is adopted for use in this chapter. Consider, for example, that many of the terms associated with spirituality such as passion, self-actualization, or virtue (Hicks, 2002) are also associated with many people's religious beliefs. Furthermore, Mitroff and Denton (1999) suggest that spirituality is:

- the basic belief that there is a supreme being that governs the universe,
- the notion that the higher power affects all things, and
- the ultimate source of meaning in one's life.

Christians, Jews, and Muslims would, for the most part, make similar statements about God and their religious beliefs. Given the similarities between, and overlap of, the two concepts, the subsequent discussion uses the terms *religion* and *religious beliefs*.

The Emphasis on Religion

Interest in the mix of religion and work has increased over the past 20 years, and this proliferation can be attributed to two primary factors. First, most of the world's population subscribes to a particular religious belief or faith. Kriger and Seng (2005) report that 82 percent of all persons follow one of the five major religions: Judaism, Christianity, Islam, Hinduism, and Buddhism. Further, Spilka, Hood, Hunsberger, and Gorsuch (2003) note that "few human concerns are taken more seriously than religion" (p. 2). Across a variety of contexts and cultures, religious ceremonies are held throughout one's lifetime: for birth, for marriage, and for death (Spilka et al., 2003). In addition, religion has played a prominent role in the formation of countries such as the United States: religious freedom was a key factor in the establishment of the country (Bellah, 1988); religion has historically played a key role in the country's culture and politics (Mead, 2006); and "religious sentiment and religious activism have sparked some of our most powerful political movements, from abolition to civil rights to the prairie populism of William Jennings Bryan" (Obama, 2006, p. 199). Collectively, these factors suggest that (a) people in leadership positions are likely to subscribe to a particular religious belief system and (b) religion has the potential to meaningfully influence one's life; thus, these leaders' attitudes and behaviors are probably shaped, at least in part, by religious tenets.

The second factor, as noted in Chapter 1, is the major changes that have occurred in the workplace. Corporate scandals have eroded the trust employees have in upper management. Changing technologies and organizational restructuring have resulted in downsizing and variations in the nature of work. The loyalty previously offered by organizations to employees is perceived to be weaker than it once was, making work life uncertain. Despite these negative changes, people are spending more time at work now than they ever have before. Time spent away from home in other activities, such as attending social gatherings, has decreased, while the hours spent at work have increased. This dynamic causes people to seek greater meaning in their lives, a quest that often leads to a greater integration of religious and work identities (Cash & Gray, 2000; Jurkiewicz & Giacalone, 2004). As they seek greater meaning, employees are likely to merge their religious beliefs, values, and identities into their work. Thus, for many employees, the two identities are no longer separate, and religion is no longer viewed as something to be kept out of the workplace. For example, the Christian Faculty Network is found on many campuses and serves as a social network for university faculty and staff of the Christian faith.

Religion in the Workplace

Because religious beliefs can be important to people in their work life, it is useful to consider possible effects in the workplace. Past research shows that religious beliefs can influence a variety of work-related outcomes, including strategic decisions, ethical behavior, leadership, and stress. In addition, religion is often used as a source of categorization and, as a result, can influence how well people integrate into a group. Each is discussed in turn.

Strategic Decisions

The literature provides several examples of managers' religious beliefs influencing their strategic decisions. Malden Mills is a New England manufacturer of materials, most notably Polartec, used in winter clothing by such enterprises as Lands End and L.L. Bean. In 1995, the plant was ravaged by a fire, and many wondered whether the firm should move its operations overseas—a strategic decision that would have been economically advantageous. However, Aaron Feuerstein, the firm's owner and CEO, and a devout Jew, would hear nothing of it. He chose to rebuild the plant in the same community and, even more striking, continued to pay all of the workers for months, until the plant was again operational. When explaining his decisions, Feuerstein indicated that he felt a social responsibility to the workers—both blue- and white-collar—as well as the community, suggesting that leaving the community would have been "unconscionable." He further suggested that his religious beliefs and heritage played a significant role in his decision-making process (Shafran, 2002).

Though not always as dramatically as in the Malden Mills situation, religious beliefs impact decisions in the sport context. For example, Brigham Young University is an institution affiliated with, and named after a former president of, The Church of Jesus Christ of Latter-Day Saints. With its mission to assist individuals in their quest for perfection and eternal life, the university follows Mormon principles, which require that university athletic teams not participate in events on Sundays. This requirement certainly impacts the university's athletic scheduling practices and has influenced other entities as well. When the university's basketball teams play in the NCAA national tournament, they are always placed in those team brackets that play on Thursdays and Saturdays, as opposed to the alternative Friday and Sunday brackets.

Dunn and Stevenson (1998) in their study of a church hockey league, found additional evidence of how religious beliefs influence strategic decisions. This hockey league was designed to promote the values and norms of evangelical Christians—a design reflected in many of the league rules. For example, body contact was prohibited—rare in the hockey context. Community prayers were said prior to the games and swearing was prohibited, as was beer in the locker rooms prior to and after the games. Finally, official team standings were not maintained—all teams made the playoffs. The league's cooperative nature, as evidenced by its rules, differs markedly from other recreational hockey leagues. See the Diversity in the Field box for another example of how religious beliefs influence strategic decision making.

As a final example, several health promotion specialists have started using faith-based initiatives to encourage physical activity participation. Bopp and her colleagues (2009) examined the efficacy of this approach among a sample of African Americans. They believed that faith-based initiatives would be particularly helpful among this population, because "African Americans have high levels of religiosity, are more likely to attend church and use religion as a coping strategy, and indicate that

DIVERSITY *in the field*

Church-Organized Sport Leagues. A number of churches use sport as a way to extend their outreach efforts. As Eitzen and Sage (2009) note, "social service is a major purpose of the religious leaders who provide play and recreation under the auspices of their churches" (p. 173). These outreach programs are seen as another avenue through which the churches can "promote 'the Lord's work'" (p. 173).

One such example of this outreach program is the basketball league organized by Central Baptist Church in Bryan, Texas. According to the church website (www.cbcbryan.org), the purpose of the league is to ensure that all children are winners by:

- sharing the love of Jesus Christ with each player, coach, referee, and family member.
- helping each player grow as Jesus did—spiritually, physically, mentally, and socially.
- helping every player develop character, an understanding of fair play, and a respect for authority in any situation, on and off the court.
- helping every player develop self-esteem and a sense of personal value.
- teaching all players the fundamentals of basketball and helping them grow in their understanding and enjoyment of the sport.
- helping draw out the "winner" in every child.

religion or prayer contributes to their physical health" (p. 569). Among a sample of persons attending African Methodist Episcopal churches in South Carolina, the researchers implemented a program that incorporated elements of both the Health-e-AME Physical-e-Fit program and the *8 Steps to Fitness* program. Their program was designed to increase people's awareness of the importance of regular physical activity, their participation in physical activity programs, and the emphasis placed by church leaders on the promotion of regular exercise. In their study, Bopp et al. compared a group of people who went through the program with a control group of people who did not. They found that, compared with persons in the control group, persons who went through the program showed greater losses in their Body Mass Index, decreased blood pressure, decreased depression, and more physical activity enjoyment. These findings are encouraging and suggest that faith-based interventions can serve as potential tools to encourage physical activity and decrease obesity levels.

Ethical Behavior

Because certain forms of moral behavior (e.g., "love your neighbor as yourself") are common across the five major religions (Kriger & Seng, 2005), it might be expected that people with strong religious beliefs, irrespective of their particular religion, will behave differently than those without strong beliefs, particularly with regard to ethics. In some instances, this reasoning holds true. For example, people with strong religious beliefs are unlikely to use illicit or illegal substances (Khavari & Harmon, 1982). However, when it comes to business ethics, the picture is mixed, with some studies showing no relationship and others showing a strong relationship between religiosity and ethical behavior (see Weaver & Agle, 2002).

One potential way to understand these equivocal findings is to apply the social identity theory portion of the social categorization framework (see Chapter 2) to the issue (see Weaver & Agle, 2002). We know that people maintain various identities—student, man, golfer, Episcopalian, and the like. The salience of these identities is likely to change depending on the context. In some situations, being a fan of your favorite team is most important, and that identity shapes your attitudes and behaviors (e.g., giving a high-five to another fan at a game). For most people, however, being a fan is not the primary identity in all situations. At home, the role of being a husband or a father might be the most salient, just as at church, being an Episcopalian might be the most salient. Having a certain social identity that remains the most salient in a particular context influences the attitudes, preferences, and behaviors someone exhibits in that context.

Social identity salience is particularly important in the discussion of religious preference and ethical behavior. If a person's religious identity remains salient across most social contexts, including work, then that individual's attitudes, preferences, and behaviors are likely to be shaped by his religious beliefs. On the other hand, if the religious identity of a person is primed on Sundays, but the work identity is primed at work, then it is less likely that the attitudes and behaviors of that individual at work will be guided by religious beliefs. "The more salient religion is for a person—that is, the larger role it plays in one's self-identity—the more difficult it will be for other factors to push aside or thwart the influence of religious expectations" (Weaver & Agle, 2002, p. 85).

Of course, there are several factors that could influence the expected positive relationship between religious identity and ethical behavior, including organizational commitment and the presence of others in the workplace who share the same religion (Weaver & Agle, 2002). If one is highly committed to the organization, this commitment will tend to counteract the salience of one's religious identity while at work. One cannot serve two masters; employees will either be committed and highly identified with their work or committed and highly identified with their religion, but not both. Under such circumstances, the strong workplace commitment may negate (or at least reduce) the effects of one's religious beliefs on subsequent ethical behavior.

The presence in the workplace of others who share one's religious beliefs is likely to increase the power of those beliefs to guide subsequent actions in the workplace. For example, if a Christian has many coworkers who also identify themselves as Christians, the identity of being a Christian is likely to be reinforced at work. Furthermore, there is likely to be greater accountability for one's actions among the Christian coworkers. Because the religious salience is likely to be high in that work environment, the link between religious beliefs and ethical behavior is likely to be positive. For additional discussion of the influence of religion on ethics, see the accompanying box.

RELIGIOUS INFLUENCE ON TEACHING ETHICS

Joel Evans, Linda Trevino, and Gary Weaver are professors who specialize in the study of organizational ethics. In one of their studies, they were interested in discovering the factors that influence whether or not MBA programs include ethics in their curricula. The best predictor of that outcome was whether or not the university had a religious affiliation, with religious-based schools being more likely to require ethics training than their counterparts. They looked to professors who taught at those universities to understand their findings. One professor, who taught at a Roman Catholic–affiliated institution, commented "our commitment to ethics . . . comes from the founding fathers . . . and the tradition found in their order, which is primarily that of missionary work with a clear emphasis on social justice" (Evans, Trevino, & Weaver, 2006, p. 281). Thus, the religious institutions emphasized ethics, morality, and social justice, and as a result, the curricula reflected those forms of social controls.

Leadership

Several authors developed leadership theories based on religious and spiritual principles (Fry, 2003; Kriger & Seng, 2005; Whittington, Pitts, Kageler, & Goodwin, 2005). The theories demonstrate that people's leadership behaviors are largely contingent upon their spiritual and religious beliefs. For example, Whittington et al. (2005) developed a theory for what they termed "legacy leadership" that is based on the wisdom and behaviors of the Apostle Paul. Drawing from various biblical books written by Paul, as well as writings from more contemporary authors, Whittington et al. argue that the qualities of legacy leadership are unique and have long-lasting effects. Paul created "a self-perpetuating model of leadership" (p. 753) that impacted numerous people throughout the world, and leaders who follow this style are likely to have a similar impact on their organizations and employees. The characteristics of legacy leaders are listed in Exhibit 9.1.

Another leadership style with religious overtones is that of servant leadership (Greenleaf, 1977; Spears, 1998). Servant leaders recognize their moral responsibility not only to their organization but also to their subordinates, customers, and others having a stake in the organization. The moral compass that servant leaders use is what separates them from other leaders. As Ehrhart (2004) notes, servant

exhibit 9.1 — Characteristics of "legacy leaders."

Legacy leaders are:

- worthy of imitation
- bold in the face of opposition
- assertive of influence without being authoritative
- demonstrative and emotional
- vulnerable and transparent
- authentic in their action and motivation
- leaders by example
- focused on others, not the self
- life-changing in their effect on others

Based on Whittington et al. (2005).

leaders "want their subordinates to improve for their own good, and view the development of the follower as an end in and of itself, not merely as a means to reach the leader's or organization's goals" (p. 69). These leaders "serve" their subordinates by helping them grow and mature and, thereby, realize their full potential. This concern for others is likely to have positive effects. Ehrhart found that servant leadership was positively associated with followers' perceptions of fairness and with followers' citizenship behaviors, such as helping and being conscientious. Thus, servant leadership is likely to positively influence several aspects of the organization.

Stress

One's religious beliefs can also produce stress in the workplace. This is particularly true in sport where the emphasis is on competition, superiority, and dominating others. These characteristics often contrast with the values of many religions, including cooperativeness, humility, and helpfulness. Bennett, Sagas, Fleming, and Von Roenn (2005) found evidence of this conflict in their case study of a university baseball coach. Specifically, they found that the coach experienced three contradictions between his religious beliefs and his role as a coach at a large university. First, he acknowledged a conflict between the emphasis on winning in sport and his spiritual beliefs. Second, as a coach who had won a national championship and currently led a major university team, his social status was exalted. The exaltation he received from others resulted in a certain degree of uneasiness. Finally, he struggled with his perception that his behavior on the field was incongruent with his spiritual beliefs. This conflict produced so much angst that he sometimes wept over his behaviors, noting that his "heart's desire" (p. 295) was to not behave in that manner.

Because these incongruities produced such stress for the coach, he developed three primary ways to resolve the contradictions. First, he used disassociation techniques—when he was away from work, he tried not to think about or discuss baseball. Second, he adopted the mind-set that he could walk away from coaching if that is what he felt "led" to do. Third, he relied heavily on his faith for comfort and reassurance (Bennett et al., 2005). Although this study focused on a single baseball coach, research shows that these contradictions are also felt by others who closely adhere to their religious beliefs (see Freshman, 1999).

Religion as a Source of Categorization

In addition, people's religious beliefs can shape how they see themselves and others. Recall from Chapter 2 and our discussion of the social categorization framework (Riordan, 2000; Tajfel & Turner, 1979; Turner, Hogg, Oakes, Reicher, & Wetherell, 1987) that people categorize themselves and others into social groups. This process is based on characteristics important to the individual or that are salient in that particular context. Thus, if a person's religious beliefs are particularly important, she will use religion to identify who is similar and who is different from herself. Or, even if religion might not be particularly important to the individual, it might be salient in the context of a Fellowship of Christian Athletes meeting. In this case, religion would still be used to differentiate the self from others.

Though researchers have not often considered religion as a source of categorization, there is evidence to support this rationale. Burris and Jackson (2000), for instance, suggested that "religion has been numbered—along with gender, ethnicity and nationality—among the core social categories around which an individual's social identity is organized" (p. 257). Later, Weeks and Vincent (2007) showed empirically that people spontaneously categorize the self and others using a religious dimension. As these authors note, "an individual's religious beliefs serve as a dominant schema, acting as a filter and organizer as they view the world" (p. 318).

There are several potential outcomes associated with people categorizing the self and others based on religion. First, consistent with the relational diversity perspective outlined in Chapter 2, people who differ religiously from the majority might have poor work experiences. Cunningham (2010) examined this very issue in a study of NCAA athletic administrators. He found that people who differed religiously from others in the department also perceived that their values differed—that is, they had different ideas about what is right, good, or valuable. These effects were particularly pronounced when religion was important to the individual (i.e., when the religious personal identity was strong). Persons who perceived they differed from others based on their religion and values were also less satisfied with their jobs than were their coworkers. These outcomes were observed even after taking into account other factors such as the person's age, gender, and race.

Another outcome of religious categorization is integration into a group. Belle Rose Ragins (2008) recounts the story of a Jewish professor at a Catholic university:

> My mother told me not to take a job at a Catholic university. She told me they'd fire me once they found out I'm Jewish. I thought she was so old school, until my first day on the job. The ex-Dean told me that he moved from a neighborhood because "there were too many Jews there." I decided not to tell anyone I was Jewish. But then my colleagues became my friends, and one day I found myself putting up Christmas ornaments before they came over. I was denying who I was in my very own home. So I

DIVERSITY *in the field*

Religion and Soccer. Soccer is the most popular sport in the world, and its supporters are the most fanatical. This is especially the case in Ireland with the rivalry between Glasgow's premier soccer clubs, Rangers F.C. and Celtic F.C. *Sports Illustrated* columnist Grant Wahl described the rivalry as "a purity of hatred that involved politics, class, and above all, religion." Most Rangers supporters are Protestant while most Celtic supporters are largely Catholic, and for years, the players on the teams reflected these religious divisions. For years, violence has erupted between the rival teams' fans. In fact, stabbings and bar fights in Glasgow are routinely investigated for Celtic-Rangers links. The players also embody this disdain for the other team's religious links. Rangers forward Paul Gascoigne once celebrated a goal against Celtic by mimicking a flute player—his way of commemorating William of Orange's victory over the Catholics at the Battle of the Boyne in 1690. Similarly, Celtic players find special meaning in crossing themselves when they score against their rivals. As this case illustrates, religious affiliation and categorization influence the dynamics among soccer fans and players.

Adapted from Wahl (1999).

decided to come out of the "Jewish closet" at work. I found out later that the Provost kept a list of the Jewish faculty. He added me to the list. (p. 194)

As this story illustrates, people's religious beliefs can influence how others see them, the manner in which they interact with others, and how well they integrate into a social group.

A final way in which religious categorization can influence work outcomes is through people's support of diversity initiatives. For instance, people's religious beliefs might call on them to oppose various diversity initiatives, such as support for gay rights. This might be the case among religious fundamentalists, who view their religious beliefs as the sole source of truth. Strauss and Sawyerr (2009) observed these effects in their study of business students. Specifically, they found that religious fundamentalists, irrespective of their particular religious affiliations, expressed negative attitudes toward gays, lesbians, and bisexuals. They also found that religious fundamentalists were unlikely to embrace a universal-diverse orientation, or an attitude of acceptance of both similarities and differences among people. These viewpoints seemingly run contrary to organizational efforts to support diversity and inclusion.

See the Diversity in the Field box for an overview of how religious categorization influences the behavior of fans in the sport context.

Religion and Sport Participation

eligious beliefs affect sport participants in two ways. First, religion influences who participates in sport and their reasons for doing so. Second, some athletes rely on their religious beliefs while participating.

Influence on Sport Participation

One's religious beliefs can influence the degree of sport participation and the reasons for that participation. Eitzen and Sage (2009) provide a historical account of the issue. According to them, primitive societies used sport and physical activity to defeat their foes, influence supernatural forces, or to increase crop and livestock fertility. The ancient Greeks also used sport in a religious context. In fact, the early Olympics was actually a religious performance intended to please Zeus. Although these cultures used sport in various religious capacities, according to Eitzen and Sage, early 17th-century Puritans viewed sport as antithetical to Christian ideals. They note that no Christian group opposed sport and sport participation more than the Puritans. See the Alternate Perspective box for a different viewpoint of how the Puritans viewed sport. This view was largely maintained by Christian churches in North America until the 20th century. Subsequently, however, changes in the United States—industrialization, urbanization, and an awareness of the health benefits of sport and physical activity—resulted in a more positive relationship between sport and religion. Eitzen and Sage note that church leaders "gradually began to reconcile play and religion in response to pressure from medical, educational, and political leaders for games and sport. Increasingly, churches broadened their commitment to play and sport endeavors as a means of drawing people together" (p. 170). Consequently, some churches now include sport in their social programs, and attendees are often actively involved in sport and physical activity (see also Hoffman, 1999).

Other religions also influence decisions about who participates in sport and about the reasons for participating. For example, Walseth and Fasting (2003) found that Egyptian women's participation in sport and physical activity was largely shaped by their Islamic beliefs. The women in their study believed that Islam called for people to be physically active for various reasons, includ-

alternative PERSPECTIVES

Some Sports Are Tolerated. Some authors suggest that the Puritans were adamantly opposed to all sport and recreation (Eitzen & Sage, 2009). Rader (1999), however, feels differently. True, the Puritans prohibited sport or recreational activities held on the Sabbath or that resulted in undesirable outcomes such as drunkenness. Under other circumstances, however, sport was seen as beneficial and rejuvenating. To be "acceptable," a sport should refresh people so they could better execute their worldly and spiritual callings. Rader notes, "believing that all time was sacred (and therefore one's use of it was accountable to God), conscientious Puritans approached all forms of play with excruciating caution" (p. 7). These rigid rules did not apply to children, who played with toys and were allowed to swim and skate as long as they were orderly while doing so. Evidently, the rules also did not apply to military training. All men age 16 to 60 met regularly for required military training, engaging in jumping, foot races, horse racing, and shooting at marks (Rader, 1999). These exceptions suggest that the Puritans have often been mislabeled as "anti-sport."

ing to care for their overall health and to be ready in case of war. Because Islam says that women may participate in sport as long as the sport movements are not "exciting" for men who might watch them, the extent to which the women participated in sport and physical activity depended on whether they adopted a more modern or more traditional view of Islam. Women who adopted a more modern view of Islam considered most activities (except gymnastics, dancing, or aerobics) appropriate and not likely to excite men. Women with a more traditional view felt that all sport forms were inappropriate unless the sport was conducted in sex-segregated venues. Because such venues were limited in Egypt, so was their sport participation.

Alternatively, rather than examining the linkage between sport and religion, others suggest that sport has become a form of religion for some. The Alternative Perspectives box on the following page highlights this perspective.

Athletes' Use of Religion

Many athletes use religious beliefs, prayers, and rituals while participating in sport. Though research in this area is generally scarce, Coakley (2009) suggests that there are six reasons why athletes use religion (see Exhibit 9.2).

alternative PERSPECTIVES

Sport as Religion. Many people focus on the relationship between sport and religion. From a different perspective, some, such as Stanley Eitzen and George Sage, have argued that sport can be considered a form of religion. Consider the following parallels:

- Each religion has its deity or deities that people revere. Similarly, sports superstars are "worshipped" by adoring fans.
- Religion has priests and clergy. The equivalent persons in sport are the team coaches, who direct the destinies of their players and often play to the emotions of the fans.
- Religion has holy places, such as mosques or churches, while sport also has revered places, such as Wrigley Field.
- Religious shrines are commonplace, and they preserve sacred symbols that followers can see and admire. Similarly, sports have halls of fame where the notable achievements of teams, players, and coaches are celebrated.
- Religions sponsor a number of holidays and festivals that call for communal involvement. Within sport, the Super Bowl and the Olympics both provide similar functions, bringing people together to celebrate the pageantry.

Eitzen & Sage (2009).

Reduce anxiety

Athletes use religion as a way of coping with the anxiety-producing uncertainty that is a fact of life with many sports, whether the uncertainty pertains to the risk of bodily harm, pressure to perform well, or not knowing if they will be traded or cut from a team. Some athletes use prayer, scriptures, meditation, or other religious rituals to reduce this anxiety. For example, DeBerg (2002) examined the way athletes used their religion in their sport performance. One athlete noted, "it gives me security, especially from injuries. It means a higher power is looking out for you" (p. 11). Another athlete explained, "sometimes you get so nervous out there. I say a little prayer" (p. 11).

Avoid trouble

Athletes may also use religion as a way of keeping out of trouble (Coakley, 2009). As previously discussed, persons who hold strong religious beliefs may behave differently than those who do not. Their beliefs also provide them focus in their lives. This is certainly true for University of Southern California defensive end Jeff Schweiger. Commenting on the challenges he often faces in the "un-Christian" football environment, Schweiger said, "There's been points where I'm like, 'screw this, I can't do this, it's too hard right now.' But I always come back" (Malcolmson, 2005). Thus, even in this environment, which makes it difficult

---

exhibit **9.2**   **Using religion during sport participation.**

Athletes use religion for one or more of the following reasons:

- Reduce anxiety
- Keep away from trouble
- Give meaning to sport participation
- Gain perspective
- Increase team unity
- Achieve personal success

Based on Coakley (2009).

for the athlete to behave according to his ideals, he can return to his Christian beliefs as a source of inspiration and a guide.

Give meaning to sport participation

Coakley (2009) notes that athletes also use religion to give personal meaning to their sport participation. Athletes spend countless hours training and practicing. Even in team sports, the focus is primarily on the self and improving individual performance. How do people rationalize spending so much time focusing on the self or, from another perspective, so much time focusing on sport in general? Athletes of faith often consider sport participation an act of worship, thereby bringing glory to God. An athlete in DeBerg's (2002) study illustrated this point: "The Lord has been in my life before football, and he will be in it afterwards. Jesus gave his all for me so how can I give less?" (p. 10).

Gain perspective

Some athletes use religion to keep their sport participation in perspective (Coakley, 2009). If an athlete perceives that her participation is part of God's calling, then facing challenges in sport becomes easier. The athlete does not become so consumed by sports that she is overwhelmed by its challenges and the regular failures that occur in that context. The Egyptian women interviewed by Walseth and Fasting (2003) provided evidence of this phenomenon. One participant commented on why she participated in sport: "Islam tells us that we have got the body as a gift from God, and that we should take care of it. God tells us to do a lot of things. How much we do of these things, is what decides our place in heaven" (p. 53).

Increase team unity

Religion is often used to increase team unity (Coakley, 2009). Former NFL coach George Allen commented that religion and prayer united teammates like no other factor he witnessed as a coach (Coakley, 2009). Murray, Joyner, Burke, Wilson, and Zwald (2005) conducted a study of university softball teams to examine this very relationship. For many of the players in the team members' study, prayer and shared religious beliefs positively influenced the team's cohesiveness. One player explained, "I think team prayer is an awesome way to get people focused on the task at

DIVERSITY *in the field*

Costs of Prayer. As noted, athletes use prayer and their religious beliefs for various reasons in the sport context. The same is true for coaches: they often lead prayers prior to or after athletic events. Although this practice has occurred for some time (and continues to), not everyone considers coach-led prayer appropriate. Some people view a coach leading a team prayer as a violation of the separation of church and state requirement for public schools. This very issue came to a head in October 2005 at East Brunswick High School in New Jersey. Marcus Borden, who had compiled five conference championships and seven playoff appearances during his 23-year career as head coach, was awarded the 2004 American Football Coaches Association Power of Influence Award for his positive influence on the lives of his players. However, when told by school officials that he would have to stop leading and taking part in team prayers, he resigned his position. Borden noted that the practice of leading team prayers was not uncommon and that coaches across the state led similar prayers prior to the sport events they coached. However, many team parents and school officials had a different view. Trish LaDuca, a spokesperson for the school district, noted "a representative of the school district cannot constitutionally initiate prayer, encourage it, or lead it." Rather, any team prayer must be initiated by the students, or else the law is violated ("Coach," 2005; "Power," 2004). As this situation illustrates, one's religious beliefs and convictions can have a substantial influence on leadership behaviors and career decisions.

hand. I think it lets people know they can put their trust in God and whatever the outcome, it's okay. Faith helps you get through any obstacle and lets people bond over commonality" (p. 236).

Achieve personal success

Some athletes use religious beliefs as a means to improve performance (Coakley, 2009). Although performance is usually viewed in terms of wins and losses, Czech, Wrisberg, Fisher, Thompson, and Hayes (2004) found that prayers for performance can take several forms. Many athletes, for example, will pray that they perform to the best of their ability, and if success comes as a result, then so be it. As one wrestler commented, "I didn't really pray for victory so much as I prayed to help me give my best and to perform to the highest ability that God gave me" (p. 8). Other athletes use prayer as a way of showing their gratitude for their athletic abilities. One athlete said, "You kind of thank God for providing opportunity. You realize He did provide this opportunity" (p. 8).

CHAPTER *summary*

This chapter focused on the intersection of religion and sport. Unlike other, more visible diversity dimensions, religion is generally not known to others unless it is disclosed. Nevertheless, as the Diversity Challenge illustrates, religious beliefs have the potential to substantially affect people's actions, preferences, and beliefs. People's religious beliefs also influence strategic decision making, organizational practices, and marketing efforts. After reading the chapter, you should be able to:

1. **Define religion and spirituality and discuss the differences between the two.**

Religion is defined as a set of beliefs and practices related to sacred things that unites all those who adhere to them (Durkheim, 1965). The influence of religion is seen at the individual, interpersonal, institutional, and social integration levels. Spirituality is the feeling of connectedness and unity with others and the universe (Mitroff & Denton, 1999).

2. **Provide an overview of how religious beliefs influence people's work behaviors.**

Religion has been shown to influence people's strategic decisions, ethical behavior, leadership, and how they manage stress in the workplace. In addition, religion can be used as a source of categorization, in which case people religiously different from the majority are likely to have negative work experiences.

3. **Discuss the influence of religion among sport participants.**

Religious beliefs also influence how and why people participate in sport. Sport participants use religion to (a) reduce anxiety, (b) avoid trouble, (c) give meaning to sport participation, (d) gain perspective, (e) increase team unity, and (f) achieve personal success.

QUESTIONS *for discussion*

1. Some people distinguish between religion and spirituality. Do you? If so, what are the major differences between religion and spirituality? If not, how are the two concepts similar?
2. Is the influence of religion on organizational practices stronger or weaker in sport than it is in other contexts? Why or why not?
3. How much should one's religious beliefs influence the decisions one makes on behalf of the organization, such as its strategic path? Why?
4. Some have suggested that sport has become a religion for some. What are the pros and cons of this argument? Do you agree with that perspective?
5. In your experience, how much do athletes rely on their religious beliefs while participating in sport? What is the primary reason for this reliance?

LEARNING *activities*

1. The courts have consistently ruled that public school coaches cannot lead their teams in prayers. Divide the class into two groups and debate the issue. Would the arguments remain if the person leading the prayer was the instructor of this class?
2. As an outside assignment, interview current and former athletes about the degree to which they incorporated religion in their playing careers. If they did, in what ways was it incorporated and what were the outcomes of doing so?

READING *resources*

SUPPLEMENTARY READING

Hicks, D. A. (2003). *Religion and the workplace: Pluralism, spirituality, leadership.* New York: Cambridge University Press. (Offers one of the most comprehensive treatments of religion in the workplace.)

Putney, C. (2001). *Muscular Christianity: Manhood and sports in Protestant America, 1880–1920.* Cambridge, MA: Harvard University Press. (Provides a historical account of the relationship between the Protestant church, sports, and men in the early 20th century.)

Spilka, B., Hood, R. W., Jr., Hunsberger, B., & Gorsuch, R. (2003). *The psychology of religion: An empirical approach* (2nd ed.). New York: Guilford. (Provides a psychological approach to the study of religion; touches on many issues concerning religion, including religion in the workplace.)

WEB RESOURCES

- Athletes in Action (www.athletesinaction.org): an international organization that uses sport competition as a way for athletes to spread their Christian faith.
- Fellowship of Christian Athletes (www.fca.org): an organization that challenges coaches and players to use sport to spread their Christian faith.
- Jewish Community Center Association of North America (www.jcca.org): an organization that helps its affiliates offer education, cultural, Jewish identity-building, and recreational programs for persons of all ages and backgrounds.

references

Bailey, J. R. (2001). Book review of J. A. Conger and associates: Spirit at work: Discovering the spirituality in leadership. *The Leadership Quarterly, 12,* 367–368.

Bellah, R. N. (1988). Civil religion in America. *Daedalus, 117*(3), 97–118.

Bennett, G., Sagas, M., Fleming, D., & Von Roenn, S. (2005). On being a living contradiction: The struggle of an elite intercollegiate coach. *Journal of Beliefs & Values, 26,* 289–300.

Bopp, M., Wilcox, S., Laken, M., Hooker, S. P., Parra-Medina, D., Saunders, R., et al. (2009). 8 Steps to Fitness: A faith-based, behavioral change physical activity intervention for African Americans. *Journal of Physical Activity and Health, 6,* 568–577.

Burris, C. T., & Jackson, L. M. (2000). Social identity and the true believer: Responses to threatened self-stereotypes among the intrinsically religious. *British Journal of Social Psychology, 39,* 257–278.

Cacioppe, R. (2000). Creating spirit at work: Re-visioning organization development and leadership—Part I. *Leadership and Organizational Development Journal, 21,* 48–54.

Cash, K. C., & Gray, G. R. (2000). A framework for accommodating religion and spirituality in the workplace. *Academy of Management Executive, 14*(3), 124–134.

Coakley, J. (2009). *Sports in society: Issues and controversies* (10th ed.). New York: McGraw-Hill.

Cunningham, G. B. (2010). How closely do you identify? The interactive effects of perceived religious dissimilarity and religious personal identity on perceived value dissimilarity and job satisfaction. *Social Justice Research, 23,* 60-76.

Czech, D. R., Wrisberg, C. A., Fisher, L. A., Thompson, C. L., & Hayes, G. (2004). The experience of Christian prayer in sport: An existential phenomenological investigation. *Journal of Psychology and Christianity, 23,* 3–11.

DeBerg, B. A. (2002). Athletes and religion on campus. *Peer Review, 4*(4), 10–12.

Dunn, R., & Stevenson, C. (1998). The paradox of the church hockey league. *International Review for the Sociology of Sport, 32,* 131-141.

Durkheim, E. (1965). *The elementary forms of religious life.* New York: Free Press.

Ehrhart, M. G. (2004). Leadership and procedural justice climate as antecedents of unit-level organizational citizenship behavior. *Personnel Psychology, 57,* 61–94.

Eitzen, D. S., & Sage, G. H. (2009). *Sociology of North American sport* (8th ed.). Boulder, CO: Paradigm Publishers.

Evans, J. M., Trevino, L. K., & Weaver, G. R. (2006). Who's in the ethics driver's seat? Factors influencing ethics in MBA curriculum. *Academy of Management Learning & Education, 5,* 278–293.

Freshman, B. (1999). An exploratory analysis of definitions and applications of spirituality in the workplace. *Journal of Organizational Change Management, 12,* 318–327.

Fry, L. W. (2003). Toward a theory of spiritual leadership. *The Leadership Quarterly, 14,* 693–727.

Greenleaf, R. K. (1977). *Servant leadership.* New York: Paulist Press.

Hicks, D. A. (2002). Spiritual and religious diversity in the workplace: Implications for leadership. *The Leadership Quarterly, 13,* 379–396.

Hicks, D. A. (2003). *Religion and the workplace: Pluralism, spirituality, leadership.* New York: Cambridge University Press.

Hoffman, S. (1999). The decline of civility and the rise of religion in American sport. *Quest, 51,* 69–84.

Jurkiewicz, C. L., & Giacalone, R. A. (2004). A values framework for measuring the impact of workplace spirituality on organizational performance. *Journal of Business Ethics, 49,* 129–142.

Khavari, K. A., & Harmon, T. M. (1982). The relationship between the degree of professed religious belief and use of drugs. *International Journal of Addictions, 17,* 847–857.

Kriger, M., & Seng, Y. (2005). Leadership with inner meaning: A contingency theory of leadership based on the worldviews of five religions. *The Leadership Quarterly, 16,* 771–806.

Malcolmson, B. (2005, April). *Religion key for many USC athletes.* Daily Trojan Online. Retrieved February 8, 2006, from www.dailytrojan.com.

Mead, W. (2006). God's country. *Foreign Affairs, 85*(5), 24–43.

Mitroff, I. I., & Denton, E. A. (1999). A study of spirituality in the workplace. *Sloan Management Review, 40,* 83–92.

Murray, M. A., Joyner, A. B., Burke, K. L., Wilson, M. J., & Zwald, A. D. (2005). The relationship between prayer and team cohesion in collegiate softball teams. *Journal of Psychology and Christianity, 24,* 233–239.

Obama, B. (2006). *The audacity of hope: Thoughts on reclaiming the American dream.* New York: Three Rivers Press.

Power of influence award. (2004, October). *American Football Coaches Association.* Retrieved February 15, 2006, from http://www.afca.com/lev2.cfm/611.

Rader, B. G. (1999). *American sports: From the age of folk games to the age of televised sport* (4th ed.). Upper Saddle River, NJ: Prentice Hall.

Ragins, B. R. (2008). Disclosure disconnects: Antecedents and consequences of disclosing invisible stigmas across life domains. *Academy of Management Review, 33,* 194–215.

Riordan, C. M. (2000). Relational demography within groups: Past developments, contradictions, and new directions. In G. R. Ferris (Ed.), *Research in personnel and human resources management* (Vol. 19, pp. 131–173). Greenwich, CT: JAI Press.

Shafran, A. (2002, June). Mr. Feurstein is a legend in the corporate world: His company is now bankrupt and he doesn't regret a thing. Aish.com. Retrieved February 6, 2006, from www.aish.com/societyWork/work/Aaron_Feuerstein_Bankrupt_and_Wealthy.asp.

Spears, L. C. (Ed.). (1998). *Insights on leadership: Service, stewardship, spirit, and servant leadership.* New York: Wiley.

Spilka, B., Hood, R. W., Jr., Hunsberger, B., & Gorsuch, R. (2003). *The psychology of religion: An empirical approach* (2nd ed.). New York: Guilford.

Strauss, J. P., & Sawyerr, O. O. (2009). Religiosity and attitudes toward diversity: A potential workplace conflict. *Journal of Applied Social Psychology, 39,* 2626–2650.

Tajfel, H., & Turner, J. C. (1979). An integrative theory of intergroup conflict. In W. G. Austin & S. Worchel (Eds.), *The social psychology of intergroup relations* (pp. 33–47). Monterey, CA: Brooks/Cole.

Turner, J., Hogg, M. A., Oakes, P. J., Reicher, S. D., & Wetherell, M. S. (1987). *Rediscovering the social group: A self-categorization theory.* Oxford, UK: B. Blackwell.

Wahl, G. (1999, May). Holy war. *Sports Illustrated.* Retrieved December 1, 2009, from www.si.com.

Walseth, K., & Fasting, K. (2003). Islam's view on physical activity and sport: Egyptian women interpreting Islam. *International Review for the Sociology of Sport, 38,* 45–60.

Weaver, G. R., & Agle, B. R. (2002). Religiosity and ethical behavior in organizations: A symbolic interactionist perspective. *Academy of Management Review, 27,* 77–97.

Weeks, M., & Vincent, M. A. (2007). Using religious affiliation to spontaneously categorize others. *The International Journal for the Psychology of Religion, 17,* 317–331.

Whittington, J. L., Pitts, T. M., Kageler, W. V., & Goodwin, V. L. (2005). Legacy leadership: The leadership wisdom of the Apostle Paul. *The Leadership Quarterly, 16,* 749–770.

10

Sexual Orientation

ugby is one of the roughest, most violent sports played in the world. For those not familiar with the sport, imagine football played without the pads or helmet. Given the physical nature of rugby, it is hardly surprising that it also sets a hypermasculine context that has been described as barbaric and makes rugby one of the most macho of all male sports in the world.

While rugby has many stars, among the brightest of them is Gareth Thomas. He was captain of the 2005 Wales team that captured the Grand Slam victory. That same year, he served as captain for the British Lions squad that toured New Zealand. He has over 100 caps to his name, which makes him the most accomplished Welsh player in history and places him sixth among all Rugby Union players ever, as of 2009.

One other characteristic that sets Thomas apart from other rugby stars, or almost any other active professional athlete, is that he has publicly identified himself as gay. Some background is helpful here: Thomas realized that he was gay when he was 17, but he decided to repress those feelings and desires for the next 18 years of his life. In response to feelings of guilt and shame, he prayed that his attraction to other men would be taken away, and in 2002 he married his longtime girlfriend, Jemma. Though he loved her dearly, his affection for her did not change his desires or attraction to men. This conflict resulted in a turmoil of strong feelings and self-loathing, and he often contemplated suicide. Unable to lead a double life any longer, in 2006, he told his wife that he was gay, and the couple split thereafter.

The same year he told his wife, he also disclosed his sexual orientation to his coach and two of his teammates. He expected the worst: there were no openly gay rugby players at that time, and a culture of hypermasculinity and heteronormativity permeated the sport. Despite Thomas's trepidation, his teammates and coach reacted to the news with support and comfort. Three years later, in 2009, Thomas decided to announce his sexual orientation publicly.

LEARNING OBJECTIVES

After studying this chapter, you should be able to:

- Define sexual orientation and discuss the major historical issues associated with it.
- Discuss the effects of sexual orientation on persons working in sport organizations.
- Identify the manner in which sexual orientation affects sport participation and physical activity opportunities.

This announcement was almost unique in that very few gay male athletes who are still competing have disclosed their sexual orientation. Many factors affected the decision, including the desire to be a role model for others, especially youth, and the longing to be accepted for who he is. He noted, "I don't want to be known as a gay rugby player. I am a rugby player first and foremost. . . . I just happen to be gay. It's irrelevant. What I choose to do when I close the door at home has nothing to do with what I have achieved in rugby."

Information adapted from: ■ Weathers, H. (2009, December). British Lions rugby legend Gareth Thomas: "It's ended my marriage and nearly driven me to suicide. Now it's time to tell the world the truth—I'm gay." *Mail Online*. Retrieved December 21, 2009, from http://www.dailymail.co.uk.

DIVERSITY CHALLENGE   R E F L E C T I O N

1. Unlike Thomas, most male athletes who reveal that they are gay do so after their playing careers are over. Why do you think this is the case? Why is it the case for men and not necessarily for women?

2. How would the presence of a gay teammate influence the dynamics on the team, if at all?

3. Why do you think relatively few athletes, as compared with the general population, disclose they are gay or lesbian?

s a deep-level characteristic and possible stigma (Ragins, 2008), the sexual orientation of individuals who are lesbian, gay, and bisexual (LGB) is often not known by others. This does not mean, however, that sexual orientation does not matter in sport. Rather, sport has been described as a context where heterosexuality is the norm (Sartore & Cunningham, 2009b), and as such, people who deviate from this norm are cast as "others." The Diversity Challenge illustrates this point, establishing that Gareth Thomas hid his sexual identity from his wife, coaches, and teammates for nearly half of his life for fear of negative reprisals. His reservations were well-founded, considering that there is considerable evidence in both the popular and academic press of persons who as lesbian, gay, bisexual, and transgendered (LGBT) facing prejudice, being subjected to discrimination in the workplace and on the playing field, and in some cases, being physically abused. Luckily for Thomas, and perhaps due to the elite status he already enjoyed, reactions to his revelation that he was gay were largely supportive.

The purpose of this chapter is to examine the intersection of sexual orientation and sport. In doing so, I first provide a definition of *sexual orientation* and a historical overview of the topic. The discussion then turns to *sexual prejudice*, including a definition of the term and an overview of its antecedents and outcomes. I then focus on sexual orientation in the workplace and close the chapter by discussing the intersection of sexual orientation and sport participation.

Before proceeding, a note on terminology is warranted. Throughout the chapter, I will use the terms LGB (i.e., lesbian, gay, and bisexual) or LGBT (i.e., lesbian, gay, bisexual, and transgender). I use LGB when referring to specific populations and to the proportion of people within a given setting, such as the proportion of persons who are LGB in the United States. In all other cases, I include persons who are transgender in the grouping and use the term LGBT. I recognize that not all persons within the LGBT community have uniform desires or experiences, just as not all women or all African Americans, for example, have uniform desires. However, theorists and researchers often refer to individuals who are LGBT as a collective, and when appropriate, I will follow suit. I also use the term *sexual minority* when referring to individuals who are LGBT (see Herek, 2000). This term is preferable to "homosexual." As seen in *Publication Manual of the American Psychological Association* (2010), the latter term "has been and continues to be associated with negative stereotypes, pathology, and the reduction of people's identities to their sexual behavior" (p. 75).

Key Terms and Historical Context

According to Gonsiorek and Weinrich (1991), between 4 percent and 17 percent of the U.S. population is lesbian, gay, or bisexual. To put this figure into perspective, consider that the U.S. population in 2010 was roughly 310 million people. Thus, between 12.4 and 52.7 million U.S. citizens at that time were lesbian, gay, or bisexual. The lower estimate (4 percent) is similar to the proportion of Asian Americans, while the higher estimate (17 percent) is greater than the proportion of African Americans or Hispanics. Clearly then, individuals who are LGBT constitute a sizable segment of the U.S. population.

But how do we conceptualize what it means to be lesbian, gay, or bisexual? Historically, people viewed sexual orientation as a binary construct—one was either heterosexual or homosexual (Lubensky, Holland, Wiethoff, & Crosby, 2004). Kinsey and his colleagues challenged this assumption (Kinsey, Pomeroy, & Martin, 1948; Kinsey, Pomeroy, Martin, & Gebhard, 1953). They considered sexual orientation as existing on a continuum from completely heterosexual to completely homosexual, with various gradations between, including bisexuality. Various authors continue to consider sexual orientation in this manner (e.g., Gill, Morrow, Collins, Lucey, & Schultz, 2006).

Despite the advances of Kinsey and his colleagues, their approach is limited in some ways: their measurement focuses on sexual behavior but ignores other aspects of sexual orientation. Indeed, one's sexual orientation is complex, with dimensions beyond simply the sex of one's sexual partners, including self-image, fantasies, attractions, and behaviors (Lubensky et al., 2004; Ragins & Wiethoff, 2005). These elements can interact in seemingly contradictory ways. A person can, for example, be attracted to and have fantasies about both women and men, yet exhibit exclusively heterosexual behavior. Contradictions such as this make it difficult to obtain precise estimates of the number of persons who are LGB. The malleability of one's sexuality also makes it difficult to gauge the number of persons who are LGB. Some people do not recognize their LGB identity until late in their lives. Others form rela-

alternative PERSPECTIVES

Determining Sexual Orientation Through Implicit Tests.
Most assessments of one's sexual orientation are done through direct measures. For instance, researchers will often employ a paper-and-pencil questionnaire that requests the study participant to indicate her or his sexual orientation. However, there are other ways of assessing people's sexual orientation—or at least the degree to which they prefer same-sex partners. One such technique is to incorporate the Implicit Association Task (IAT). In this technique, a computer times how quickly people associate pictures with various terms. For instance, compared with a heterosexual man, a gay man might more quickly associate "attractive" with a picture of an attractive man. The opposite would also hold, so that the heterosexual would more quickly identify an attractive woman as "desirable" than would a gay man. Through several iterations of this process, researchers can then determine a person's preference for men or women. Snowden, Wichter, and Gray (2008) did precisely this in their study of 50 heterosexual men and 25 gay men. In fact, the IAT scores correctly predicted the participants' self-identified sexual orientation 96 percent of the time.

tionships with members of the opposite sex after years of having a same-sex partner. Lubensky et al. note that for persons who are not exclusively heterosexual or exclusively homosexual, "it may make sense to think in terms of sexual orientation as something with multiple facets that is influenced by social context" (p. 207).

Sociologist Eric Anderson highlighted these contradictions in his 2008 study. Participants in his study were 68 former high school football players who later became collegiate cheerleaders. Despite all self-identifying as heterosexuals and being attracted to women, many of the men in his research (40 percent) also engaged in sexual encounters with other men. They challenged the "one-time rule," which holds that a one-time same-sex experience categorizes one as gay; instead, the cheerleaders in his study constructed the same-sex encounters as either (a) a means to an end (i.e., the encounter led to further intimate contact with women) or (b) a form of sexual recreation. In neither case did the same-sex interactions serve to challenge their self-identity as heterosexual or to reduce their attraction to women. Thus, consistent with critiques of sexual orientation consisting solely of sexual experiences (Lubensky et al., 2004; Ragins & Wiethoff, 2005), Anderson observed that sexual orientation is a complex, multidimensional, and sometimes seemingly contradictory construct. For additional information about determining sexual orientation, see the Alternate Perspectives box.

Scientific thinking about sexual orientation has changed over the years, and so too have people's attitudes toward individuals who are LGB. As recently as 1973, the American Psychiatric Association classified individuals who are LGBT as suffering from a mental illness (Creed, 2006). That classification has since changed, and research from Herek (2009) illustrates this point.

■ Since the early 1970s, the General Social Survey has asked whether same-sex sexual relations are "always wrong, almost always wrong, wrong only sometimes, or not wrong at all." From 1973 to 1993, two of three people considered such relations to be "always wrong." Since 1993, that figure has dropped. In 1995, 54 percent of those surveyed considered same-sex sexual relations as "always wrong," and the figures have remained steady since that time.

■ Since 1982, Gallup polls have asked whether homosexuality should be considered an acceptable alternative lifestyle. In 1982, homosexuality was considered unacceptable by 51 percent, compared with 34 percent who considered it acceptable, and the gap increased to 19 points in 1993 (57 percent to 38 percent). During the 1990s, the trend reversed, and in 2003, 54 percent of those surveyed considered homosexuality as an appropriate lifestyle (43 percent did not). In 2007, the acceptability ratings increased to 57 percent.

■ As a final indicator, the ongoing American National Election Studies have asked people about their feelings toward gay men and lesbians for several decades. They use the Feeling Thermometer, where people's feelings toward a particular group range from 0 (very cold or unfavorable feelings) to 100 (very warm or favorable feelings). In 1984, the mean rating for feelings toward gays and lesbians (as a collective group) was 30. Feelings have improved since that time, from 39 in 1996 to 49 in 2004. Despite this positive trend, it is worth noting that there was still a sizable proportion of people (15 percent) who gave gays and lesbians a zero.

These figures suggest that attitudes toward homosexuality, persons who are LGBT, and the rights of people who are LGBT have become more positive over time.

Sexual Prejudice

he purpose of this section is to review sexual prejudice, its antecedents, and the manner in which it affects the lives and opportunities of individuals who are LGBT.

Background and Key Terms

Though attitudes related to persons who are LGBT have become more positive, such individuals still experience considerable prejudice and discrimination. Researchers have used various terms to describe this process, including *homophobia, heterosexism,* and *sexual prejudice. Homophobia* was coined in the 1960s by psychologist George Weinberg to describe the dread heterosexuals felt toward sexual minorities and the self-loathing individuals who were LGBT felt toward themselves (Weinberg, 1972). This term focuses on the individual and the irrational fears (hence, the use of "phobia" in the word) she or he has toward sexual minorities and their lifestyles.

Heterosexism is different from homophobia in that it focuses more on macro elements of prejudice (Creed, 2006; Herek, 2000). Specifically, *heterosexism* refers to the cultural system of arrangements that privileges heterosexuality and casts a negative light on individuals who are LGBT and their behaviors, relationships, and communities. Like other "isms," such as racism or sexism, heterosexism is socially constructed over time, specific to a particular society or context, and ingrained into the institutions (e.g., laws, religion, education) within that society.

Finally, *sexual prejudice* refers to the negative attitudes held toward an individual because of that person's sexual orientation (Herek, 2000). Like other prejudices, sexual prejudice is an attitude, directed toward people who belong (or are perceived to belong) to a social group, and it is negative, such that it encompasses hostility or dislike. Herek notes that this construct is preferred over that of homophobia for several reasons: (a) unlike homophobia, sexual prejudice conveys no a priori assumptions about the genesis of the negative attitudes; (b) the construct allows researchers to incorporate the study of anti-gay attitudes into a rich social psychological tradition that studies prejudice; and (c) using the term does not automatically assume that the anti-gay attitudes are irrational or evil, as the term homophobia does. Consistent with this perspective, throughout the chapter, I use the term *sexual prejudice* when referring to a negative attitude toward individuals who are LGBT and their behaviors, or communities, and I use the term *heterosexism* to refer to the larger, societal system that privileges heterosexuals and casts sexual minorities as second-class citizens.

The discussion now turns to the prevalence of sexual prejudice and the motivation for such negative behaviors and attitudes.

Prevalence of Sexual Prejudice

Though attitudes have improved toward individuals who are LGB, some negativity still persists. Herek (2000) notes that generally the public is reluctant to view homosexuality as being on a par with heterosexuality, and the evidence, as outlined by Meyer (2003), seems to support this contention. Persons who are LGBT are twice as likely as their heterosexual counterparts to experience some form of prejudice in their lifetime. Furthermore, these persons are likely to be victims of denigrating remarks, torture, assault, or murder. These abuses appear to be especially prevalent among LGBT youth. Most (90 percent) sexual minority youth have heard sexually prejudiced remarks at their schools, with many of these remarks (37 percent) coming from teachers or administrators. As might be expected, these effects are also evident in the workplace.

This same pattern of prejudice exists in the sport and physical activity realm—a context in which sexual prejudice is considered rampant. Anderson (2002) notes that sexual prejudice is especially prevalent among athletes on men's teams. For example, as an openly gay cross-country coach, Anderson witnessed one of his runners being beaten by a football player who assumed the runner was gay (he was not). The football player fractured four of the runner's facial bones and tried to gouge out his eyes.

Sexual prejudice also occurs in the coaching ranks. Krane and Barber (2005) interviewed 13 lesbian college coaches. The sexual orientation of only one of the coaches was known to all members of the athletic department for which she worked. The other coaches withheld this information because of the repercussions they thought would ensue if such information was made public. In fact, some of the coaches asked if the interview records could be traced back to them or if the tapes could be subpoenaed. The coaches in the study discussed many types of sexual prejudice. As one coach noted, "the coaching world is not always a kind world. . . . It's a really strange issue within coaching. . . . There are so many lesbians in coaching, and yet it's not somewhere that people can be comfortable with that being openly known about them" (p. 71). The sexual prejudice directed toward the lesbian coaches does not come only from others in the athletic department. Other coaches against whom they compete will use sexual orientation as a "chip" in the athlete recruiting process. The openly gay coach commented, "I'm the only coach that's gay, that is open, so I'm sure it's been used as a recruiting tool. . . . I'm sure kids don't come here because of that" (p. 72). Some coaches capitalize on the prejudice toward persons who are LGB by generating negative attitudes among parents and athletes toward a specific coach or team. (See the Diversity in the Field box for another example).

It is also noteworthy that people who are *presumed to be* LGB can also face prejudice. Sartore and Cunningham (2009b) developed a theoretical framework in which they illustrated how masculine norms and patriarchal ideals in sport contrib-

DIVERSITY
in the field

Sexual Prejudice Toward Coaches. Bloomburg is a small town in northeast Texas with a population of 374. The high school is too small to field a football team, so like many towns this size, basketball reigns supreme and is the source of town pride. For many years, however, the girl's team performed at subpar levels—that is, until Coach Merry Stephens arrived in 1999. Her team excelled at high levels, making the playoffs three times and reaching the state semifinals in 2004. These successes resulted in Stephens being named teacher of the year by the local Walmart and coach of the year by the district in which the team competed. However, only nine months after guiding her team to the state semifinals, Stephens was fired.

Many aspects about Stephens made her unique. She was not only the first female coach in Bloomburg history but also she was a lesbian. Her partner (who also worked at the school) was formerly married, had two children, and was a school board member's niece. When their relationship became public, the school board members, along with the school superintendent, set out to make both women's lives miserable by assigning them difficult tasks and holding them to abnormally high standards. Her partner was fired by the school's superintendent, and the school board voted to begin proceedings to terminate Stephens' contract. When Michael Shirk, a Texas State Teachers Association attorney, began to take depositions for the termination hearings, he found that the school board had no basis to fire Stephens. Unlike her partner who was an at-will

employee and could be fired without cause, Stephens was also a teacher, and in Texas, teachers cannot be fired without just cause. Shirk commented, "what doomed these administrators from the start was their hubris and obvious bigotry" (Colloff, 2005, p. 60). Ultimately, a settlement was reached that required the school board to pay Stephens' salary for the 18 months remaining on her contract in exchange for her resignation.

The actions taken by the school board and superintendent left the town divided. Some believed that Stephens and her partner were treated unfairly; one such person was the pastor of the First Baptist Church, Tim Reed. Though he preaches that homosexuality is a sin, Reed was appalled at what occurred: "unless we are going to remove every abomination from the school district, I don't see why we should focus on one at the exclusion of all others." He continued, "Maybe we should have a crusade against gossipers too. Let's cut their tongues out and run them out of town! There might be three of us left" (p. 60). Others believed that the school board was justified and supported their decision.

The competing views came to a head in 2005 when the school board elections were held. Jimmy Lightfoot, the school board member who spearheaded the move to release Stephens, was challenged by Suzanne Bishop who was critical of the way Lightfoot handled the terminations. Bishop easily won the election. Of the five persons running for the seat, Lightfoot came in a distant last (Colloff, 2005).

---

uted to women, irrespective of their sexual orientation, being subject to the lesbian label. These effects are especially likely when the women are participating in "sex-inappropriate" sports, such as ice hockey or basketball. As an illustrative example, Rene Portland, the former head coach of the Penn State women's basketball team, was charged with harassing and ostracizing players she believed to be lesbian. She was even quoted as saying, "I will not have it on my team," in reference to the presence of lesbian players (or players she presumed to be lesbian) (see Griffin, 2007).

Subsequent qualitative work from Sartore and Cunningham (2010) supported this anecdotal evidence when they observed the often stigmatizing effects of being labeled a lesbian. Participants in their study reported being relegated to out-group membership and facing discrimination in the workplace. The label also limited the interactions the women had with their coworkers. Taken as a whole, Sartore and

Cunningham's work suggests that many women in sport, regardless of their actual sexual orientation, are thought to be lesbian and treated negatively as a result.

Motivations for Negative Behaviors and Attitudes

It is important to understand the underlying motivations for the negative behaviors and attitudes directed toward persons who are LGBT. Herek (2000) outlines four primary motivations, all of which may interact with one another.

1. Sexual prejudice may have originated from an unpleasant interaction with an individual who was LGBT. For example, if an athlete has a negative experience with a gay coach (e.g., incongruence in leadership style), then the athlete might hold negative attitudes toward all other gay coaches—and even gay athletes. Generalization of this kind is more likely to occur when the gay coach is perceived as typical or representative of other gay men.

2. Fear of homosexuality itself (Herek, 2000) may develop in people who are uncomfortable with their own sexual impulses or their gender conformity. Also, a fear may arise from the perception that homosexuality challenges traditional heterosexual social structures (Lubensky et al., 2004).

3. People may express sexual prejudice when group norms mandate hostility toward individuals who are LGBT. There are many contexts, such as the military or sport, where such group norms are prevalent. Messner (1992) notes that "boys (in sports) learn early that to be gay, to be suspected of being gay, or even to be unable to prove one's heterosexual status is unacceptable" (p. 34). Messner states that sport is a place where heterosexuality is the norm and homosexuals are seen as "others." When someone holds this "other" distinction, they are likely to face negative attitudes, be trusted less, and be subjected to disapproving behaviors. To the extent that mandated precepts are maintained, the prejudice will continue.

4. Some people are prejudiced toward persons who are LGBT because homosexuality is contrary to their personal belief systems (Herek, 2000). This is especially true for those who hold conservative or fundamentalist religious beliefs (Lubensky et al., 2004), in which case sexual prejudice is justified by the religious beliefs. Research shows that such beliefs exist across a variety of religions including Christianity, Judaism, Islam, and Buddhism (Lubensky et al., 2004). For other antecedents, see Exhibit 10.1.

Effects of Sexual Prejudice

Most of the outcomes associated with experiencing sexual prejudice relate to one's health and well-being, which may in turn be associated with other outcomes, including those related to work. A meta-analysis performed by Meyer (2003) indicated that individuals who are LGB are about 2.3 times more likely than heterosexuals to experience a mental disorder (e.g., mood disorder, increased anxiety, substance abuse) during their lifetimes. Persons who are LGB are also more likely to attempt or commit suicide than their heterosexual counterparts.

Historically, people pointed to the mental health differences between heterosexuals and sexual minorities as an indicator of the mental deficiencies of the latter group. Herek and Garnets (2007) described this perspective as the illness model.

Personal characteristics predictive of sexual prejudice. *exhibit* **10.1**

Sexual prejudice can be predicted by people's personal characteristics. According to Herek (2009), persons who exhibit high levels of sexual prejudice are likely to:

- be male
- be older
- have limited formal education
- reside in the Midwest or Southern portions of the United States
- hold fundamentalist religious beliefs
- be a Republican
- demonstrate high levels of psychological authoritarianism
- not be sexually permissive
- hold traditional gender role attitudes
- view sexual orientation as a free choice
- have few or no friends who are LGBT

Although a small minority might still hold this view, a more contemporary and well-informed perspective is that any differences in mental health or well-being are due to the stress persons who are LGBT experience. This perspective, referred to as the minority stress model (Cochran, 2001; Herek & Garnets, 2007; Meyer, 2003), holds that minority group members (in this case, individuals who are LGBT) are at risk for various psychological ailments because they continually face stress resulting from their disadvantaged status in society. This stress is added to the everyday stress that all members of society experience and thus weighs heavily on the individual. To illustrate this point, Mays and Cochran (2001) found that association between mental health and sexual orientation was largely explained by the discrimination people experienced. When the authors statistically controlled for discrimination, LGBT individuals and heterosexuals did not differ in their mental health indicators.

Sexual Orientation and Work

People's sexual orientation has the potential to intersect with the way they experience work. The heterosexism pervasive across the sport industry means that, for heterosexuals, sexual identity is largely taken for granted. The same is not necessarily the case for sexual minorities because their sexual orientation potentially influences how they are treated and the way they interact with others. These dynamics are outlined in the following paragraphs.

Differential Work Experiences

Sexual prejudice and heterosexism influence a number of work outcomes for sexual minorities, including their access to jobs, the pay they receive, and their work experiences and career progression.

Access to jobs

People who are thought to be LGBT are often denied access to jobs or positions they seek—a dynamic largely explained by people's sexual prejudice. As an example, Sartore and Cunningham (2009a) found that former and current athletes' level of sexual prejudice was highly predictive of their unwillingness to play on teams coached by gay men or lesbians (Study 1). They also found that parents' willingness to let their children play on teams coached by gay men or lesbians was largely a function of the parents' sexual prejudice (Study 2). They also asked the parents to provide a rationale for their decisions. Overwhelmingly, the resistance was based on distrust of sexual minorities, the perceived immorality of persons who are LGBT, and reliance on gay and lesbian stereotypes.

Although there is some overt access discrimination, some authors suggest that people are more likely to discriminate in subtler ways. Hebl, Foster, Mannix, and Dovidio's (2002) innovative experimental study aptly illustrates this point. Supposed job applicants went into stores at a mall and inquired about employment opportunities. Some of the applicants wore hats that read "Gay and Proud" while other applicants wore hats that read "Texan and Proud," though they did not know which hat they were wearing during the study. Consistent with their expectations, there were no overt forms of discrimination against the applicants who were supposed to be LGBT. There was, however, evidence of subtle discrimination: employers were verbally negative, spent less time, and used fewer words when interacting with the applicants who were LGB than with the other applicants.

A recent study from Cunningham, Sartore, and McCullough (2010) also provides evidence of subtle discrimination. Participants in their study reviewed one of four application packets for a person who was applying for a personal trainer position at a fitness club. The packet varied by the applicant's gender and the person's supposed sexual orientation. In the supposed sexual minority condition, the applicant was a medalist in the Gay Games, while in the control (heterosexual) condition, the applicant was a medalist in Amateur Athletic competitions. All applicants were highly qualified, as evidenced by degrees in exercise science, certifications, and previous personal training experience. After reviewing the packet, participants were asked to rate the qualification of the applicant, provide attribution assessments (i.e., the degree to which the person was ethical, moral, and trustworthy), and submit hiring recommendations. All job applicants were viewed as qualified, irrespective of their gender or sexual orientation. However, male raters provided less positive attributions of sexual minorities than they did of heterosexuals. Women did not provide differential ratings. The attribution ratings were important because they were reliably related to hiring recommendations. Thus, even though the applicants who were LGBT were qualified, male raters would deny them access to the position because of more subtle biases.

Pay

In addition to facing access discrimination, employees who are LGBT also face wage discrimination. Research from Blanford (2003) illustrates this point. Men who are gay or bisexual were found to earn between 30 and 32 percent *less* than their heterosexual counterparts. These differences existed despite the greater educational attainment of the gay men. On the other hand, lesbians earn between 17 and 23 percent *more* than heterosexual women. The findings were more pronounced among lesbians who lived with a partner. Even with these differences, lesbians still earn less than men who are gay or heterosexual men.

Why do these differences occur? Blanford (2003) offers several explanations. First, men who are gay were more likely to be in female-typed professions than their counterparts, and pay is less in these jobs. For instance, an art designer (a female-typed job) will generally get paid less than an architect (a male-typed job). The opposite occurred for lesbians because they were more likely than other women to be in male-typed professions, where the pay was higher. Alternatively, it is possible that men who are gay are penalized for violating social norms about gender roles, while lesbians' violations of those roles is met with ambivalence. Research in other areas corroborates this notion: men who are gay are usually met with greater prejudice than lesbians (e.g., Gill et al., 2006; Sartore & Cunningham, 2009a). Finally, lesbians living with their partner might earn high salaries because of their high attachment to the labor market and the equitable distribution of household activities (e.g., cleaning, child-rearing) relative to heterosexual women who are married.

In addition to the wages received, persons who are LGBT are also impacted by company benefits. Heterosexuals routinely have the option of including their spouses in the benefits package. As a result, their spouses receive medical coverage, dental coverage, and life insurance, to name a few. Heterosexual men also regularly have the option of taking leave when their spouses give birth. These benefits are often taken for granted but are a rarity among employees who are LGBT. According to a report from the Human Rights Campaign (2009), only 57 percent of all Fortune 500 companies offer domestic partner benefits. This represents an increase from years past, but these figures still mean that more than four of every ten Fortune 500 companies do not offer any partner benefits. Furthermore, only 18 percent of all Fortune 100 companies provide transgender-inclusive health insurance.

Work experiences and career progression

As might be expected, persons who are LGBT face less-positive work experiences and often have shorter careers than their heterosexual counterparts. Research suggests that between 25 and 66 percent of employees who are LGBT experience sexual orientation discrimination at work (see Ragins, 2004). These figures are probably conservative because few people fully disclose their sexual orientation at work. In fact, Ragins, Singh, and Cornwell (2007) found that only 26.7 percent of the participants in their study reported full disclosure of their sexual orientation to everyone at work. If more people fully disclosed their sexual orientation, then the rates of discrimination would probably be higher.

The experience of sexual orientation discrimination can negatively impact the manner in which one experiences work. In one of the most comprehensive studies examining this issue, Ragins and Cornwell (2001) found that people who faced discrimination were likely to seek employment elsewhere and had low organizational commitment, career commitment, organizational self-esteem, and job satisfaction. They also had relatively few opportunities for promotion and had low promotion rates. Button (2001) observed a similar pattern of findings. Sexual minorities' suffer not only from negative work experiences but also from harm to their mental health: persons who face sexual prejudice at work are more likely to experience psychological distress (Waldo, 1999) and depression (Smith & Ingram, 2004).

Sexual prejudice can also influence career decisions of those in a sexual minority. Ragins (2004) argued that some organizations or occupations are safe havens that are supportive of individuals who are LGBT and serve as a refuge from sexual orientation discrimination. Obviously, safe havens are attractive to sexual minorities, so much so that they might choose to remain in that organization or occupation even when other, potentially more lucrative, offers are available. The prospect of potentially facing discrimination or having to go back to concealing one's sexual identity in the new position makes such a change undesirable.

Although the presence of safe havens is positive, the limited availability of safe havens can limit one's career progress. As a hypothetical example, consider the case of Latisha, a lesbian who serves as an assistant track and field coach. If Latisha currently works at a safe haven, then she has pleasant work experiences, is able to freely express her sexual identity, and is not subjected to sexual prejudice (see Ragins, 2004). As an assistant coach, however, her prospects for career advancement at the current institution might be limited: she can potentially earn raises but will not move into a head coaching position unless her current head coach (who is probably responsible for creating the safe haven atmosphere) leaves. Thus, the lack of other safe havens effectively limits her potential earnings and promotions.

Finally, research suggests that there are a number of organizational factors that influence sexual minorities' work experiences. Persons who are LGBT and who (a) work in organizations with formal policies and practices against sexual prejudice, (b) work alongside other sexual minorities, and (c) have supportive relationships with their supervisors and coworkers are less likely to experience sexual prejudice than their peers (Button, 2001; Huffman, Watrous-Rodriguez, & King, 2008; Ragins & Cornwell, 2001). Huffman et al. offered a number of strategies managers can employ to promote a supportive environment. These are provided in Exhibit 10.2.

---

exhibit **10.2**   **Managerial strategies for promoting LGBT inclusiveness.**

1. Provide mentoring opportunities.
2. Offer social networking events.
3. Remain cognizant of one's actions toward all employees.
4. Interact with employees from various backgrounds.
5. Offer diversity training for employees and managers.
6. Relay the LGBT-inclusive standards of the organization to job applicants.
7. Gather employee input concerning practices that are not supportive.
8. Encourage all significant others (e.g., spouses and same-sex partners) to attend social events.
9. Do not assume the sexual orientation of any employee.
10. Schedule meetings with LGBT support group or listserv members and leaders.
11. Become acquainted with LGBT organizations that monitor sexual prejudice and discrimination in the workplace.
12. Allow time off for all persons the employee considers family.
13. Use inclusive language (e.g., partner rather than spouse) and respond quickly and negatively to sexual prejudice.

Information based on Huffman et al. (2008).

Sexual Orientation Disclosure

A key decision for employees who are LGBT is whether or not to disclose their sexual orientation to others in the workplace. As might be expected, this decision, especially within the sport context, can be a life-altering choice. After all, if individuals who are LGBT are treated differently, have limited access to positions, are paid less than what they deserve, and face difficult work environments, then they may not readily wish to disclose such information. Furthermore, because sexual orientation is a deep-level characteristic, others are not aware of this potentially stigmatizing characteristic unless they are told (Ragins, 2004, 2008). However, there are advantages to disclosing this information, and sometimes the benefits outweigh the costs. In the following section, I discuss how people decide whether to disclose their sexual orientation, the antecedents of this decision, and the decision's outcomes.

Passing and revealing

Clair, Beatty, and MacLean (2005) outline various strategies people use to decide whether to *pass* or to reveal their sexual orientation. Exhibit 10.3 summarizes these concepts.

Passing. *Passing* refers to a "cultural performance whereby one member of a defined social group masquerades as another in order to enjoy the privileges afforded to the dominant group" (Leary, 1999, p. 82). In the context of sexual orientation, this refers to persons who are LGBT passing as heterosexuals. Passing can be done intentionally by deliberately providing false information or unintentionally

Passing and revealing at work.   *exhibit* **10.3**

- **Passing:** the practice of withholding or failing to reveal a personal identity that is invisible or unrecognizable to others. Passing can take several forms:
  - *Fabrication:* a type of passing that occurs when someone deliberately provides incorrect or false information about the self.
  - *Concealment:* a type of passing that occurs when people actively try to withhold information or prevent others from acquiring information that would reveal their sexual orientation.
  - *Discretion:* a type of passing that occurs when people avoid questions related to their sexual orientation.
- **Revealing:** the practice of disclosing a personal identity that would otherwise be indistinguishable to others. Revealing can take several forms:
  - *Signaling:* a type of revealing that occurs when people disclose their sexual orientation by sending messages, providing subtle hints, or giving certain clues.
  - *Normalizing:* a type of revealing that occurs when people reveal their sexual orientation to others and then attempt to make their difference from others seem commonplace or ordinary.
  - *Differentiating:* a type of revealing that occurs when people disclose their sexual orientation and highlight how it makes them different from others who do not share such preferences.

Information based on Clair et al. (2005).

by allowing a coworker to assume that a lesbian is heterosexual. Passing involves leading a "double life," so that one persona is adopted in the workplace and another in personal life.

People who are LGBT use three strategies to pass: fabrication, concealment, and discretion (Clair et al., 2005). *Fabrication* occurs when someone deliberately provides incorrect or false information about the self. For example, a coach who is gay might deny that he is gay or, more subtly, bring a woman companion, rather than a man, to an athletic department event. *Concealment* occurs when people actively withhold information or prevent others from acquiring information that would reveal their sexual orientation. An example might be an administrator who is gay and does not display a picture of his partner on his desk, thereby concealing he has a same-sex partner. Finally, *discretion* occurs when people avoid questions related to their sexual orientation. Though related, discretion and concealment differ. People who choose discretion do not hide information about their sexual orientation (as they do with concealment)—they simply sidestep the issue altogether. People who use discretion avoid conversations where their sexual orientation might become a topic or simply change the topic.

Revealing. Clair et al. (2005) refer to *revealing* as the choice to "disclose an identity that would otherwise be invisible or unrecognizable to others" (p. 82). Revealing is a general term that is used with a myriad of identities such as religious affiliation, social class, and so forth. "Coming out" is the term most often used when referring to revealing one's sexual orientation.

People who are LGBT use three different methods to reveal their sexual orientation: signaling, normalizing, and differentiating (Clair et al., 2005). People who choose the *signaling* method disclose their sexual orientation by sending messages, providing subtle hints, or giving certain clues. Sometimes, people use signals that are meaningful to insiders but are innocuous to others, thereby making their preferences known only to those they choose. For example, an athlete who is bisexual might put a rainbow sticker on her car's back window.

Normalizing occurs when people reveal their sexual orientation to others and then attempt to make their difference from the others seem commonplace or ordinary (Clair et al., 2005). People who adopt the normalizing method seek to assimilate into the dominant culture and downplay the significance of the difference. For example, a coach who is lesbian might share the everyday difficulties she and her partner have, such as mowing the grass or paying the bills, that underscore how much they have in common with heterosexual couples.

Finally, *differentiating* occurs when people disclose their sexual orientation and highlight how it makes them different from others who do not share such preferences. Clair et al. (2005) note that people who differentiate "seek to present an identity as equally valid (rather than stigmatized) and many engage in an effort to change the perceptions and behavior of the groups, organizations, and institutions that may stigmatize them" (p. 83). By doing so, people claim a certain identity at work (e.g., coach who is gay) and redefine the way their identity is understood and viewed by others in the workplace. For example, an athlete who is gay might speak up when his teammates use derogatory terms (e.g., "that is so gay").

Antecedents to passing and revealing

As the preceding discussion illustrates, the decision to disclose personal information related to sexual orientation is complex. Clair et al. (2005) outline several factors that influence the decision to pass or reveal.

Contextual conditions. Clair et al. (2005) identify three contextual conditions that are thought to influence the decision to pass or reveal: organizational diversity climate, industry and professional norms, and legal protections. These authors suggest that people view these conditions as indicators of whether they will receive support for, or be stigmatized because of, their sexual orientation.

With respect to the *diversity climate,* organizations that have formal anti-discrimination policies and procedures are transparent in their decision-making processes and have several "out" individuals currently employed. These organizations are consequently more congenial to persons who are LGB. Anderson (2002) found evidence of this in his study of athletes who are gay. For those athletes who had a supportive team environment and backing from their teammates, "coming out" was met with little or no resistance and was perceived as a generally pleasant experience. On the other hand, in organizations where support is lacking, discrimination is rampant, and no other persons are "out," then it is likely that revealing behavior will not be seen as an option (see also Griffin, 1998).

Industry and professional norms set the standard by which people can "fit in" (Clair et al., 2005). For instance, the Clinton administration implemented a "don't ask, don't tell" policy in the U.S. military, implying that soldiers and other personnel who are LGB should pass. (As of this writing this policy is under debate.) Many argue that the same policy is implicitly followed in sports (e.g., Griffin, 1998; Sartore & Cunningham, 2009b). Even if one works in a supportive organization, and thus reveals his sexual orientation, others in the sport industry might "use" that information against the person. Krane and Barber (2005) documented this occurrence, especially in recruiting battles, in their study of women coaches. Because the same is true in other aspects of sport, it explains why so few people, especially men who are gay, reveal their sexual orientation in the sport industry.

Finally, *legal protections* may impact the decision to pass or reveal (Clair et al., 2005). Although federal laws protect people from discrimination on the basis of their race, disability, and sex, there is no such protection for sexual orientation (Clair et al., 2005). Without protection, the decision to reveal one's sexual orientation becomes more difficult.

Individual differences. The decision whether or not to disclose one's sexual orientation will probably be influenced by several individual differences: willingness to take risks, self-monitoring tendencies, stage of adult development, and the presence of other stigmatizing characteristics (Clair et al., 2005).

Clearly, revealing one's sexual orientation can be a risky proposition in the sport context. Thus, people who have more *willingness to take risks* may be more willing to reveal their sexual orientation, even without other enabling contextual conditions, than others who are less willing to take risks.

Self-monitoring tendencies (Clair et al., 2005) refer to the extent to which people regulate or try to control how well they fit the social expectations of their roles within certain environments. Strong self-monitors are very cognizant of how others perceive them and try hard to "fit in." On the other hand, weak self-monitors are less concerned with how others perceive them and less likely to temper their actions. Strong self-monitors are likely to pass or reveal depending on the situation; they will pass when the social situation calls on them to do so, and reveal when it socially benefits them. Weak self-monitors may reveal regardless of the situation, if revealing is more consistent with their general character as a person.

One's *stage of adult development* should also impact the decision to pass or reveal (Clair et al., 2005). People who have higher levels of self-esteem and are more self-assured are more likely to reveal than are those who do not. The same is likely to be true for people who fully embrace their identity as an individual who is LGB.

Finally, the degree to which one has other potentially *stigmatizing characteristics* influences decisions to pass or reveal (Clair et al., 2005). If one does possess such characteristics, one already faces stress and bias at work. Further exacerbating such a situation by revealing that one is LGB is not often viewed as an appealing option. For example, women already face a gender bias in many organizational settings; hence, revealing one's lesbian identity would only amplify the bias. This might explain why men are more likely to reveal at work than women (Ragins, 2004). On the other hand, people who are not already being subjected to stigmatization might be more willing to reveal their LGB orientation.

Passing and revealing outcomes

Several studies examined the outcomes associated with passing or revealing (Button, 2001; Day & Schoenrade, 1997; Meyer, 2003). Generally, passing might be expected to achieve more positive outcomes. After all, people choose to pass, at least in part, because of a fear that they may be subjected to verbal or physical abuse or be stigmatized—all undesirable outcomes. However, research shows that passing is actually associated with more negative outcomes. People who pass are hiding something, and this leads to authenticity issues (Leary, 1999). They also might be isolated from others because of certain behaviors associated with passing, such as avoiding particular people or issues. Indeed, research shows that people who pass at work or in sport are generally less satisfied with their experiences in those contexts (Day & Schoenrade, 1997).

Those people who reveal at work, however they choose to do so, are often pleased with their choice. Of course, not all situations are pleasant. People can be ostracized or stigmatized because of their LGB identity (Anderson, 2002; Ragins, 2008; see the Alternative Perspectives box for more information). Many times, however, the choice to reveal ultimately eliminates the stress of having to live a "double life." People who disclose their LGB orientation might also feel more whole because they no longer have to hide an important part of who they are. Day and Schoenrade (1997) found that persons who are LGB and "open" at work did not differ from heterosexuals on any of the following important work outcomes: affective commitment, continuance commitment, job satisfaction, job stress, support from top management, role ambiguity, role conflict, and work–home conflict. These results suggest that employees who are openly LGB experience work the same as any other employee might, thereby demonstrating the benefits of revealing at work (see also Griffith & Hebl, 2002).

Just as with Gareth Thomas in the Diversity Challenge, Sheryl Swoopes' decision to reveal her sexual orientation illustrates this point. Swoopes, a three-time MVP of the WNBA, decided to disclose the fact that she was a lesbian in October 2005. She commented, "I'm just at a point in my life where I'm tired of having to pretend to be somebody I'm not. I'm tired of having to hide my feelings about the person I care about. About the person I love" (Granderson, 2005). As this illustrates, revealing her sexual orientation relieved some of the stress associated with passing and allowed her to be more authentic as a person.

Marketing to Customers Who Are LGB

Another way in which people's sexual orientation influences the workplace is through organizational efforts to specifically encourage people who are LGB to become customers and, possibly, employees (Lubensky et al., 2004). These organizations believe that increasing the number of employees who are LGB serves to increase the overall workforce diversity. A diverse workforce is thought to excel in certain areas—creativity, breadth of decision making, and effectiveness in confronting the challenges of a changing marketplace (see Chapter 1). Thus, the presence of employees who are LGB is highly desired.

Organizations also believe that persons who are LGB are "ripe for product marketing" (Lubensky et al., 2004, p. 213). Persons who are LGB are perceived to have considerable discretionary income and thus serve as a key demographic on which to focus marketing and promotional efforts. Because persons who are LGB have been neglected for so long, even modest attempts at marketing to the LGB community are viewed in a very positive light and result in increased sales and brand loyalty. The extant data seem to support these claims, as evidenced by Harris Interactive polls (see www.harrisinteractive.com):

- Persons who are LGBT spend over 50 percent more than heterosexuals on their travel.
- Seventy percent of gays and lesbians have switched products or services when they learned that the company engaged in actions deemed harmful to the LGBT community.
- Twenty-four percent of persons who are LGBT have switched their allegiance to an alternative brand when they perceived the company was supportive of LGBT issues.

alternative PERSPECTIVES

Negative Outcomes of Revealing at Work? A prevailing notion is that revealing one's sexual orientation to others is a liberating process and is often associated with positive outcomes. Ragins, Singh, and Cornwell (2007) challenged this line of thought. Specifically, they argue that people's fear of disclosure had a debilitating effect on their career and workplace experiences. In their study, persons who were LGB and feared the negative consequences of fully disclosing their sexual orientation had less positive work attitudes, received fewer promotions, and reported higher levels of stress than their counterparts who did not express such trepidations. The fears people experienced were the result of past discrimination and prejudice they had encountered. These findings led Ragins and her colleagues to conclude: "In contrast to the view of disclosure as a uniformly positive behavior that reflects the final stage of gay identity development . . . this study suggests that concealment may be a necessary and adaptive decision in an unsupportive or hostile environment" (p. 1114).

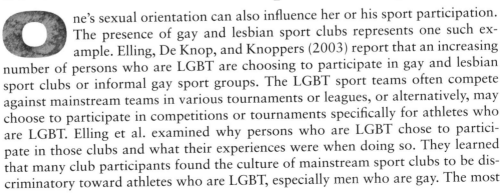

PROFESSIONAL PERSPECTIVES

Olivia Cruises and Resorts. Amy Errett is a former college athlete who earned her finance degree at the University of Connecticut and an MBA from the Wharton School at the University of Pennsylvania. She is also the CEO of Olivia Cruises and Resorts, a company dedicated to being a lesbian's lifestyle company, with a particular focus on travel and tourism. One way Olivia promotes its products is through celebrity endorsements, including Rosie Jones of the LPGA, tennis great Martina Navratilova, and Sheryl Swoopes of the WNBA. Errett notes that, "for many people, the fear of saying you're gay would then translate into nobody wanting to endorse you . . . what a great thing to have a company [such as Olivia] that wants to endorse you because you are gay." Errett believes that Swoopes serves as a good role model, especially for African American women who might be grappling with their sexual orientation. Errett also suggests that having Swoopes as a product endorser has substantially enhanced Olivia's profitability. In the weeks immediately after Swoopes signed with Olivia, the company experienced a huge upsurge in media mentions (21 million) as well as a considerable increase in sales. The same trend occurred when they signed Jones and Navratilova. Although some companies may shy away from having athletes who are LGB endorse their products, Olivia found that such spokespersons provide a meaningful benefit to the organization.

- Two of three sexual minorities will remain with a product or service when the company is considered to be friendly or supportive of the LGBT community, even when competitors offer the products and services at a lower price.

Clearly, individuals who are LGBT represent a viable demographic for sport and tourism organizations, especially ones that demonstrate support for the LGBT community (e.g., offering partner benefits).

There are several organizations specifically designed to cater to the needs and wants of travelers who are LGBT, including Rainbow Tourism (www.rainbowtourism.com). This Australia-based company was founded in 2005 and specializes in niche tourism experiences. People interested in traveling to Australia can work with Rainbow Tourism to visit locations and stay in hotels that are owned and operated by gays or lesbians or are designated as gay-friendly properties. Research from Community Marketing, Inc. (Roth, 2006) suggests that such locations are very important to tourists who are LGBT. For instance, 98 percent of those in their survey indicated that a destination's gay-friendly reputation influenced their decision to visit that destination. Further, 59 percent indicated that gay-friendly hotels were very important to them. All of these data support the notion that targeting customers who are LGBT may be financially beneficial for sport and tourism organizations (see also the Professional Perspectives box).

Sexual Orientation and Sport Participation

One's sexual orientation can also influence her or his sport participation. The presence of gay and lesbian sport clubs represents one such example. Elling, De Knop, and Knoppers (2003) report that an increasing number of persons who are LGBT are choosing to participate in gay and lesbian sport clubs or informal gay sport groups. The LGBT sport teams often compete against mainstream teams in various tournaments or leagues, or alternatively, may choose to participate in competitions or tournaments specifically for athletes who are LGBT. Elling et al. examined why persons who are LGBT chose to participate in those clubs and what their experiences were when doing so. They learned that many club participants found the culture of mainstream sport clubs to be discriminatory toward athletes who are LGBT, especially men who are gay. The most important reason, however, for joining the club was that respondents felt more at ease and believed they were better able to socialize with people like them (i.e., other persons who are LGBT) in those clubs.

The Gay Games represent another example (see also Exhibit 10.4). According to the Federation of Gay Games website (www.gaygames.com/en/; see also Waitt, 2003), the Gay Games are an international sporting event that is supportive of athletes who are LGBT. The genesis of the event began in the late 1970s when Tom Waddell, a 1968 Olympic decathlete, led a group of San Francisco residents, including Mark Brown and Paul Mart, to conjure up the idea of what is now known as the Gay Games. The group incorporated an entity called San Francisco Arts & Athletics (SFAA), and it was this organization that oversaw the planning and coordination of the first two Gay Games, both of which were held in San Francisco in 1982 and 1986, respectively. In 1987, Waddell lost his battle with AIDS, and since that time, the Gay Games have been administered by Federation of Gay Games. Today, the Games are held every four years, consist of over 30 sports, and regularly play host to 12,000 athletes from dozens of countries around the world. The Games not only attract thousands of participants and spectators but also generate considerable revenues for the host city. The 2014 Gay Games, which are set to be held in Cleveland, Ohio, are expected to generate a $50 to $80 million economic benefit for the city.

According to Krane, Barber, and McClung (2002), Gay Games participants report a number of other benefits gained by taking part in the event. Participation has continually been linked with higher self-esteem, increased self-confidence, and a sense of pride in one's sexuality. The Games also provide the athletes with an enhanced collective esteem. Collectively, these factors contribute to a number of behavioral outcomes. For instance, persons who are LGBT are more likely to reveal their sexual orientation to others (i.e., "come out") after participating in the Gay Games, and doing so has been shown to positively impact one's health and well-being. Gay Games participants are also often motivated to become more politically active in terms of educating others about tolerance and in campaigning for human rights around the world.

The mission of the Gay Games. *exhibit* **10.4**

Unlike the Olympics, where the focus of participation is on athletic excellence, Tom Waddell conceived of athletic success as doing one's best. Consistent with this belief, and the premise that the Gay Games should be a place that is supportive of athletes who are LGBT, the mission of the Gay Games is to better the lives of sexual minorities by bringing together artists and athletes from around the world to participate in this premier athletic and cultural event. Participation is open to all persons, irrespective of ability, age, sexual orientation, race, gender, nationality, political beliefs, religion, ethnicity, or HIV status. Further, participants represent their city, not their country, and as a result, the Gay Games are devoid of much of the nationalism observed at other international sport events.

Information adapted from Federation of Gay Games website, www.gaygames.com/en/.

CHAPTER *summary*

The purpose of this chapter was to explore the influence of sexual orientation on people's experiences in the workplace and their sport participation. As evidenced by the Diversity Challenge, sexual orientation, though perhaps taken for granted by some, can seriously affect one's well-being. Sexual minorities are likely to face sexual prejudice, they have varied work experiences, and they must decide when and if to disclose their sexual orientation to others. From a different perspective, some organizations opt to actively pursue consumers who are LGBT and employees, with the belief that doing so will better their business. After reading this chapter, you should be able to:

1. **Define sexual orientation and discuss the major historical issues associated with it.**

Sexual orientation is a multifaceted construct consisting of one's self-image, fantasies, attractions, and behaviors. Though sexual minorities were historically believed to suffer from a mental illness, such a perspective is no longer embraced. Finally, polling suggests that attitudes toward sexual minorities have become more positive over time, though some negative attributions still exist.

2. **Discuss the effects of sexual orientation on persons working in sport organizations.**

Employees who are LGBT regularly face discrimination in the workplace, with some estimates suggesting that two of every three employees are subjected to sexual prejudice. This prejudice negatively affects their potential to obtain jobs, their pay, and their work experiences. Furthermore, individuals who are LGBT must balance the decision of whether or not to disclose their sexual identity to others in the workplace—an anxiety-producing decision others do not encounter. Discussions of disclosure focus on the different forms of passing (i.e., fabrication, concealment, and discretion) and revealing (i.e., signaling, normalizing, and differentiating) and their antecedents and outcomes.

3. **Identify the manner in which sexual orientation affects sport participation and physical activity opportunities.**

A number of sport organizations and tourist destinations actively seek to attract employees and consumers who are LGBT, with the belief that such practices will improve their organization. Other entities, such as the Gay Games, are designed and structured specifically to support athletes who are LGBT.

QUESTIONS *for discussion*

1. Various ways of conceptualizing sexual orientation were presented in the chapter. With which approach do you most closely identify and why?
2. Many authors suggest that sexual prejudice is prevalent in the sport context. Has this been your experience? Provide some examples.

3. Research suggests that attitudes toward men who are gay are more negative than attitudes toward lesbians. Why do you think this is the case?

4. Sexual orientation disclosure in the workplace is potentially one of the most anxiety-producing decisions an individual who is LGBT can make. Do you think the same is true for persons who disclose other invisible diversity forms? Why or why not?

5. What are some of the outcomes, both positive and negative, for an organization seeking to specifically target customers who are LGB?

LEARNING *activities*

1. Visit the Federation of Gay Games website (www.gaygames.com/en/) and research the origin of the Games, the date and location of the next Games, and information about the participants.

2. While some sport organizations see tremendous value in actively recruiting employees and consumers who are LGBT, others are hesitant to adopt such an approach. Divide the class into two groups to debate the issue.

READING *resources*

SUPPLEMENTARY READING

Anderson, E. (2005). *In the game: Gay athletes and the cult of masculinity.* Albany, NY: State University of New York Press. (Book based on qualitative research with both closeted and openly gay team-sport athletes; explores the prevalence of sexual prejudice in sport and how athletes negotiate that process.)

Griffin, P. (1998). *Strong women, deep closets: Lesbians and homophobia in sport.* Champaign, IL: Human Kinetics. (Analyzes stereotypes and prejudice directed toward lesbians in the sport context; considers the influence of religion on attitudes toward lesbians; addresses identity management for lesbian coaches and athletes.)

Marcus, E. (2005). *Is it a choice? Answers to the most frequently asked questions about gay and lesbian people.* San Francisco, CA: HarperSanFrancisco. (Provides candid and well-researched responses to a variety of questions about LGBT issues.)

WEB RESOURCES

■ European Gay and Lesbian Sport Federation (http://www.eglsf.info/eglsf-about.php): Organization devoted to supporting LGB sport communities and athletes, as well as fighting discrimination.

■ OutSports (www.outsports.com): site devoted to providing the most comprehensive information related to the gay sport community.

■ The Williams Institute (http://www.law.ucla.edu/williamsinstitute/home.html): A Center at the UCLA School of Law dedicated to advancing the field of sexual orientation law and public policy.

references

Anderson, E. (2002). Openly gay athletes: Contesting hegemonic masculinity in a homophobic environment. *Gender & Society, 16,* 860–877.

Anderson, E. (2008). "Being masculine is not about who you sleep with . . . :" Heterosexual athletes contesting masculinity and the one-time rule of homosexuality. *Sex Roles, 58,* 104–115.

Blanford, J. M. (2003). The nexus of sexual orientation and gender in the determination of earnings. *Industrial and Labor Relations Review, 56,* 622–642.

Button, S. B. (2001). Organizational efforts to affirm sexual diversity: A cross-level examination. *Journal of Applied Psychology, 86,* 17–28.

Clair, J. A., Beatty, J. E., & MacLean, T. L. (2005). Out of sight but not out of mind: Managing invisible social identities in the workplace. *Academy of Management Review, 30,* 78–95.

Cochran, S. D. (2001). Emerging issues in research on lesbians' and gay men's mental health: Does sexual orientation really matter? *American Psychologist, 56,* 931–947.

Colloff, P. (2005, July). She's here. She's queer. She's fired. *Texas Monthly, 33*(7), 52–61.

Creed, W. E. D. (2006). Seven conversations about the same thing: Homophobia and heterosexism in the workplace. In A. M. Konrad, P. Prasad, & J. K. Pringle (Eds.), *Handbook of workplace diversity* (pp. 371–400). Thousand Oaks, CA: Sage.

Cunningham, G. B., Sartore, M. L., & McCullough, B. P. (2010). The influence of applicant sexual orientation and rater sex on ascribed attributions and hiring recommendations of personal trainers. *Journal of Sport Management, 24,* 400-415.

Day, N. E., & Schoenrade, P. (1997). Staying in the closet versus coming out: Relationships between communication about sexual orientation and work attitudes. *Personnel Psychology, 50,* 147–163.

Elling, A., De Knop, P., & Knoppers, A. (2003). Gay/lesbian sport clubs and events: Places of homo-social bonding and cultural resistance? *International Review for the Sociology of Sport, 38,* 441–456.

Gill, D. L., Morrow, R. G., Collins, K. E., Lucey, A. B., & Schultz, A. M. (2006). Attitudes and sexual prejudice in sport and physical activity. *Journal of Sport Management, 20,* 554–564.

Gonsiorek, J. C., & Weinrich, J. D. (1991). The definition and scope of sexual orientation. In J. C. Gonsiorek & J. D. Weinrich (Eds.), *Homosexuality: Research implications for public policy* (pp. 1–12). Newbury Park: Sage.

Granderson, L. Z. (2005, October). *Three-time MVP "tired of having to hide my feelings."* ESPN.com. Retrieved October 26, 2005, from http://sports.espn.go.com/wnba/news/story?id=2203853.

Griffin, P. (1998). *Strong women, deep closets: Lesbians and homophobia in sport.* Champaign, IL: Human Kinetics.

Griffin, P. (2007). Rene Portland resigns, lesbian athletes rejoice. Outsports.com. Retrieved May 14, 2010, from http://www.outsports.com/campus/2007/0322griffin.htm.

Griffith, K. H., & Hebl, M. R. (2002). The disclosure dilemma for gay men and lesbians: "Coming out" at work. *Journal of Applied Psychology, 87,* 1191–1199.

Hebl, M. R., Foster, J. B., Mannix, L. M., & Dovidio, J. F. (2002). Formal and interpersonal discrimination: A field study of bias toward homosexual applicants. *Personality and Social Psychology Bulletin, 28,* 815–825.

Herek, G. M. (2000). The psychology of sexual prejudice. *Current Directions in Psychological Science, 9,* 19–22.

Herek, G. M. (2009). Sexual stigma and sexual prejudice in the United States: A conceptual framework. In D. A. Hope (Ed.), *Contemporary perspectives on lesbian, gay, and bisexual identities* (pp. 65–111). New York: Springer.

Herek, G. M., & Garnets, L. D. (2007). Sexual orientation and mental health. *Annual Review of Clinical Psychology, 3,* 353–375.

Huffman, A. H., Watrous-Rodriguez, K. M., & King, E. B. (2008). Supporting a diverse workforce: What type of support is most meaningful for lesbian and gay employees? *Human Resource Management, 47,* 237–253.

Human Rights Campaign. (2009). *The state of the workplace for lesbian, gay, bisexual, and transgender Americans: 2007–2008.* Human Rights Campaign Foundation: Washington, DC.

Kinsey, A. C., Pomeroy, W. B., & Martin, C. E. (1948). *Sexual behavior in the human male.* Philadelphia: W. B. Saunders.

Kinsey, A. C., Pomeroy, W. B., Martin, C. E., & Gebhard, P. H. (1953). *Sexual behavior in the human female.* Philadelphia: W. B. Saunders.

Krane, V., & Barber, H. (2005). Identity tensions in lesbian intercollegiate coaches. *Research Quarterly for Exercise and Sport, 76,* 67–81.

Krane, V., Barber, H., & McClung, L. R. (2002). Social psychological benefits of Gay Games participation: A social identity theory explanation. *Journal of Applied Sport Psychology, 14,* 27–42.

Leary, K. (1999). Passing, posing, and "keeping it real." *Constellations, 6,* 85–96.

Lubensky, M. E., Holland, S. L., Wiethoff, C., & Crosby, F. J. (2004). Diversity and sexual orientation: Including and valuing sexual minorities in the workplace. In M. S. Stockdale & F. J. Crosby (Eds.), *The psychology and management of workplace diversity* (pp. 206–223). Malden, MA: Blackwell.

Mays, V. M., & Cochran, S. D. (2001). Mental health correlates of perceived discrimination among lesbian, gay, and bisexual adults in the United States. *American Journal of Public Health, 91,* 1869–1876.

Messner, M. (1992). *Power at play: Sports and the problem of masculinity.* Boston: Beacon.

Meyer, I. H. (2003). Prejudice, social stress, and mental health in lesbian, gay, and bisexual populations: Conceptual issues and research evidence. *Psychological Bulletin, 129,* 674–697.

Publication Manual of the American Psychological Association (2010). American Psychological Association. Washington, DC.

Ragins, B. R. (2004). Sexual orientation in the workplace: The unique work and career experiences of gay, lesbian and bisexual workers. *Research in Personnel and Human Resources Management, 23,* 35–120.

Ragins, B. R. (2008). Disclosure disconnects: Antecedents and consequences of disclosing invisible stigmas across life domains. *Academy of Management Review, 33,* 194–215.

Ragins, B. R., & Cornwell, J. M. (2001). Pink triangles: Antecedents and consequences of perceived workplace discrimination against gay and lesbian employees. *Journal of Applied Psychology, 86,* 1244–1261.

Ragins, B. R., Singh, R., & Cornwell, J. M. (2007). Making the invisible visible: Fear and disclosure of sexual orientation at work. *Journal of Applied Psychology, 4,* 1103–1118.

Ragins, B. R., & Wiethoff, C. (2005). Understanding heterosexism at work: The straight problem. In R. L. Dipboye & A. Collela (Eds.), *Discrimination at work: The psychological and organizational bases* (pp. 177–201). Mahwah, NJ: Lawrence Erlbaum.

Roth, T. E. (2006). *CMI's gay & lesbian tourism profile.* San Francisco: Community Marketing, Inc.

Sartore, M. L., & Cunningham, G. B. (2009a). Sexual prejudice, participatory decisions, and panoptic control: Implications for sexual minorities in sport. *Sex Roles, 60,* 100–113.

Sartore, M. L., & Cunningham, G. B. (2009b). The effects of the lesbian label in the sport context: Implications for women of all sexual orientations. *Quest, 61,* 289–305.

Sartore, M. L., & Cunningham, G. B. (2010). The lesbian label as a component of women's stigmatization in sport organizations: An exploration of two health and kinesiology departments. *Journal of Sport Management, 24,* 481–501.

Smith, N. G., & Ingram, K. M. (2004). Workplace heterosexism and adjustment among lesbian, gay, and bisexual individuals: The role of unsupportive interactions. *Journal of Counseling Psychology, 51,* 57–67.

Snowden, R. J., Wichter, J., & Gray, N. S. (2008). Implicit and explicit measurements of sexual preference in gay and heterosexual men: A comparison of priming techniques and the Implicit Association Task. *Archives of Sexual Behavior, 37,* 558–565.

Waitt, G. (2003). Gay Games: Performing "community" out from the closet of the locker room. *Social & Cultural Geography, 4,* 167–183.

Waldo, C. R. (1999). Working in a majority context: A structural model of heterosexism as minority stress in the workplace. *Journal of Counseling Psychology, 46,* 218–232.

Weinberg, G. (1972). *Society and the healthy homosexual.* New York: St. Martin's.

Social Class

articipation in high school athletics provides a number of potential benefits, including character development, learning how to work with others, and engaging in cross-cultural experiences. Empirical evidence of these advantages was demonstrated in a 2009 study, wherein the authors showed that students who participated in sports enjoyed better outcomes, such as academic ability, confidence, interpersonal connections, pro-social behavior, and character development, than their peers who did not engage in such activities. These effects are thought to be particularly strong among students from disadvantaged backgrounds because their participation in school-sponsored athletics provides them with after-school activities they might not otherwise have.

Despite the many positive outcomes associated with high school athletics, the economic downturn in 2008 and 2009 forced many schools to drop or scale back their sport offerings. According to the *Wall Street Journal*, the proportion of schools planning to cut their extracurricular activities for the 2009–2010 academic year almost tripled—from 10 percent the previous academic term to 28 percent. These cuts come in a variety of areas. Some districts, such as those in Dixon, Calif., eliminated all of their middle school and high school programs. Across Florida, athletic departments were asked to reduce the number of games on their schedule, sometimes by as much as 40 percent.

Another approach being advanced in a number of school districts is that of "pay-to-play," in which case students pay a fee to participate in the sport. As Vincent A. Mustaro, a senior staff associate for the Connecticut Association of Boards of Education, explains, "It's a way of meeting budget, and it's a better alternative than eliminating programs." Although this approach certainly offsets costs that the school incurs, there are also potential negative effects. Cherry Rodriguez, a student at Deer Valley High School (AZ), submitted that a "pay-to-play" plan "wouldn't be fair for us, because some students would not be able

After studying this chapter, you should be able to:

- Define key terms, including socioeconomic status, social class, and classism.

- Discuss the influence of cognitive, interpersonal, and institutional distancing on the maintenance and promotion of classism.

- Provide an overview of the effects of classism on people's education, health, and well-being including their sport participation.

- Highlight the manner in which sport involvement results in social mobility.

237

to experience a new sport or activity because some couldn't pay." Others agree, suggesting that because low income families are unable to pay such fees, "pay-to-play" programs "perpetuate the separation between the classes." Thus, despite the potential cost saving benefits, there are a number of potential drawbacks with the "pay-to-play" program.

Information adapted from: ■ "Gimme a C for cutbacks:" Schools slash sports, parents "pay to play" (2009, April). *Wall Street Journal.* Retrieved August 31, 2009, from http://blogs.wsj.com; Javier, J. (2009, March). Deer Valley Unified School District's students troubled by budget options. Retrieved August 31, 2009, from www.azcentral.com ■ Linver, M. R., Roth, J. L., & Brooks, Gun, J. (2009). Patterns of adolescents' participation in organized activities: Are sports best when combined with other activities? *Developmental Psychology, 45,* 354–367 ■ Nussbaum, D. (2006, August). Paying to play at school. *The New York Times.* Retrieved August 31, 2009, from www.nytimes.com ■ Sager, J. (2009, August). Is pay to play at public schools fair? Retrieved August 31, 2009, from www.babble.com.

DIVERSITY CHALLENGE   R E F L E C T I O N

1. Other than those listed in the Diversity Challenge, what options could school administrators pursue to balance their athletic budgets?

2. Why do opponents of "pay-to-play" programs argue that the participation fees hurt low-income students more than other students? Do you agree with this perspective?

3. Are you aware of other ways in which school financing plans tend to disadvantage low-income students or students in low-income districts?

s the Diversity Challenge illustrates, economic means and social power play significant roles in the opportunities people have for sport and physical activity opportunities. But the effects of social class, however, are not limited to the hard court or playing field. One's class affects many of the opportunities available in one's life; class ultimately may influence physical and educational opportunities, jobs held, and psychological health, including perception of one's self. Clearly, then, class is a meaningful diversity form that demands our attention.

Despite the primacy of class in people's lives, it is often neglected in discussions of diversity. Lott (2002; Lott & Bullock, 2007), for instance, highlighted how the American Psychological Association (APA) continually overlooks class in multicultural and diversity-related conferences and publications. Academic publications and course texts often follow suit. For instance, Liu, Ali, et al. (2004) found that only 18 percent of the academic articles they reviewed even mentioned class, except by way of describing the participants in a study rather than to serve as the focus of the study. Even diversity management texts are guilty of this omission, and many of them (e.g., Bell, 2007) do not include even a chapter devoted to the topic. But, large professional organizations and diversity scholars are not alone: the media have also been found to either ignore the poor or to portray them negatively and as deficient in moral character (Bullock, Wyche, & Williams, 2001).

I have experienced this trend in my own classes as well. Early in the semester, I ask students to complete the "Diversity Pie Chart" (see Powell, 2004), in which they identify group affiliations that meaningfully contribute to their self-concept. Invariably, only one or two students list class as a social identity category, and many times, no students in the class will include that diversity form in their pie chart. This trend has taken place over a number of years—with both undergraduate and graduate students. For many, then, class has a taken-for-granted nature such that people think about other characteristics, some of which might be closely linked with class (e.g., gender, race), when deciding on identity markers.

Thus, although class plays an important role in the experiences and chances one has in life, people often overlook class in their discussions of diversity. The purpose of this chapter, therefore, is to provide an overview of the influence of class and class consciousness on people's lives and in the delivery of sport. I begin by providing an overview of key terms, including *socioeconomic status* and *class*. We then turn our attention to *classism,* which involves the structures and mechanics proceeding from class consciousness, and provide an overview of this construct and a discussion of how it is manifested in everyday life, including sport systems and sport participation. The discussion then moves to the effects of classism on people's health and well-being, and the chapter concludes with a focus on the influence of sport participation on people's social mobility.

Basic Concepts

There are a number of different conceptualizations pertaining to social class. In fact, Liu, Ali, et al. (2004), in their review of over 3,900 psychology articles published between 1981 and 2000, found that nearly *500 different words* were used to either describe, conceptualize, or discuss social class and classism. Luckily, a review of all of those terms is not provided here. Instead, I highlight two primary approaches that researchers, government organizations, and policy makers have employed (see Exhibit 11.1).

Approaches to the study of economic inequality.   *exhibit* **11.1**

Socioeconomic status approach: a materialistic focus, with a particular emphasis on income, occupation, and education.

Class approach: a power and privilege focus, with particular emphasis on how power, political action, and socially constructed realities economically and socially advantage some at the expense of others.

From APA (2006), Smith (2008).

Socioeconomic Status

The first approach is what the APA (2006) and others (Smith, 2008) have termed the materialistic approach, with a focus on the material and economic resources people possess. Persons adopting this approach favor the term *socioeconomic status,* or SES, and take into account three primary factors: income, education, and occupation. Here, the fundamental focus is on one's access to resources.

Income indicators take several forms, ranging from one's yearly income to complex formulas taking into account a number of variables. For instance, in defining the poverty line, the U.S. Census Bureau considers a family's income and the family characteristics to generate a family threshold. In 2008, the poverty threshold for a single-person household was $11,201, while the same threshold for a single parent with two children under age 18 was $17,346. Others have argued that wealth, or one's private assets minus debts, is a better indicator because it reflects intergenerational transfers of resources and serves as a buffer against potential fluctuations in annual income (APA, 2006).

Education is considered a reliable indicator of desired economic outcomes, good health and well-being, and the reduction of health risk behaviors (Ross & Wu, 1995). It is important to understand, however, that incremental increases in educational attainment are not necessarily associated with more positive outcomes. Instead, the jumps are discontinuous in nature, and occur only after one is conferred an academic degree (Backlund, Sorlie, & Johnson, 1999). Thus, a student who spends four years in college but fails to earn a degree will not reap the same benefits as another student who spends the same time at college and earns a diploma. This distinction is due to the prestige associated with earning the credential or with the presumed positive characteristics (e.g., perseverance) that people associate with degree holders.

Finally, one's occupation is expected to serve as a reflection of overall SES. There are various scales that order occupations based on a number of criteria. For instance, according to the Bureau of Labor Statistics (www.bls.gov), federal agencies in the United States use the 2000 Standard Occupational Classification System to categorize workers by occupation. This process is a complicated one because people are classified into one of over *820 occupations!* These categorizations can be further broken down into either 449 broad occupations, 96 minor groups, or 23 major groups. A breakdown of the latter categorization scheme is provided in Exhibit 11.2. To illustrate the process, I draw from a category of particular relevance to our discussion: 27-0000—arts, design, entertainment, sports, and media occupations. This major group is further broken down into four minor groups:

1. 27-1000 (arts and design workers),
2. 27-2000 (entertainers and performers, sports and related workers),
3. 27-3000 (media and communication workers), and
4. 27-4000 (media and communication equipment workers).

Major group 27-2000 is further subdivided into five broad occupation categories, including

1. actors, producers, and directors (27-2010),
2. athletes, coaches, umpires, and related workers (27-2020),

| | Classification of occupations based on the Standard Occupational Qualification System. | *exhibit* **11.2** |

11-0000	Management occupations
13-0000	Business and financial operations occupations
15-0000	Computer and mathematical occupations
17-0000	Architecture and engineering occupations
19-0000	Life, physical, and social science occupations
21-0000	Community and social services occupations
23-0000	Legal occupations
25-0000	Education, training, and library occupations
27-0000	Arts, design, entertainment, sports, and media occupations
29-0000	Healthcare practitioners and technical occupations
31-0000	Healthcare support occupations
33-0000	Protective service occupations
35-0000	Food preparation and serving related occupations
37-0000	Building and grounds cleaning and maintenance occupations
39-0000	Personal care and service occupations
41-0000	Sales and related occupations
43-0000	Office and administrative support occupations
45-0000	Farming, fishing, and forestry occupations
47-0000	Construction and extraction occupations
49-0000	Installation, maintenance, and repair occupations
51-0000	Production occupations
53-0000	Transportation and material moving occupations
55-0000	Military specific occupations

Data from Bureau of Labor Statistics (www.bls.gov).

3. dancers and choreographers (27-2030),

4. musicians, singers, and related workers (27-2040), and

5. miscellaneous entertainers and performers, sports and related workers (27-2090).

Each of these occupations is associated with different wages, prestige, and power—all factors that contribute to one's SES.

The use of SES is widespread, and income, educational attainment, and occupational status have been linked to a number of important outcomes, including psychological and physical health, academic performance, and life expectancy, among others (see APA, 2006, for an overview). Nevertheless, there are a number of shortcomings with his approach. First, conceptualizations of income, education, and occupation often vary. Even in the U.S. government, the U.S. Census Bureau uses one formula for classifying poverty while the Department of Health and Human Services uses another (see Smith, 2008). There are similar ambiguities with education and occupation.

A second shortcoming is that there are considerable differences within given classifications. One can certainly envisage differences in opportunities and access to resources between a television producer and a junior high track and field coach, both of whom are included in the same major occupational category (arts, design, entertainment, sports, and media occupations). Third, and most important, discussions of SES fail to recognize the very important issues of power, privilege, control, and subjugation. As Smith eloquently notes, "creating class divisions according to SES sidesteps the issue of relationship to (or distance from) sociocultural power and carries with it the implication that class-related experiences and oppressions are similar for people who fall within the same numerical SES classification" (p. 902). Given this criticism, many sociology and social psychology researchers have turned to the concept of social class.

Social Class

Rothman (2002) defined *social class* as the positions within "the economic system of production, distribution, and consumption of goods and services in industrialized societies" (p. 6). Unlike SES, social class is more overtly political in nature, draws attention to differences in power, and focuses on the socially constructed nature of social standing, including the treatment of persons from various classes (Lott & Bullock, 2007). From this perspective, then, inequality is not only a function of differential access to valued resources but also the social (re)creation of privilege, power, and domination, particularly within capitalist societies (APA, 2006). As some illustrative examples, consider that a third of all U.S. Senators are millionaires, compared with only 1 percent of the U.S. population ("Millionaires," 2004) or that major college football coaches routinely make 100 times the equivalent compensation for players (i.e., their tuition, room, board, and stipend).

The focus on power, politics, and socially constructed realities also allows for different mechanisms of grouping classes. Smith (2008), in combining the frameworks put forth by Leondar-Wright (2005) and Zweig (2000), advanced the following typology:

■ *Poverty:* includes working-class persons who, because of various circumstances, including unemployment, low wages, or lack of healthcare, do not have the income needed to support their basic needs.

■ *The working class:* includes persons without power or authority in the workplace, who have little discretion in how they complete their work, and are marginalized when it comes to providing feedback concerning their healthcare, education, and housing. Relative to people in more powerful classes, the working class has lower income levels, less net worth, and less education.

■ *Middle class:* includes persons who are college educated, salaried, and typically work as professionals, managers, or small business owners. Relative to the working class, middle-class persons have greater job autonomy and economic security; however, they do rely on their earnings to support themselves.

■ *Owning class:* persons in this class have accumulated enough wealth that they do not need to work to support themselves; further, they generally own businesses and resources from which others make their livings. Given their power and access to resources, owning-class persons also maintain substantial social, cultural, and political clout, particularly relative to other classes.

Several points concerning the typology should be highlighted here. First, unlike SES-based distinctions, the social class–based typology overtly brings into the discussion issues of subjugation, autonomy, and politics, thereby recognizing that power and status help us to make sense of the socially constructed notion of class (Lott & Bullock, 2007; Smith, 2008). Second, poverty, as outlined in this framework, is not bound by single numerical cutoff values, but instead, the social-class perspective recognizes that persons in this class simply do not have the requisite income to consistently provide them with enough monies to cover basic individual and family needs. Finally, the framework recognizes that people living in poverty predominantly include members of the working class and, in doing so, helps to counter the classic, albeit incorrect, stereotype that poor are an "under class" of people who are either unwilling or unable to work (see also Zweig, 2000).

Classism

In building on our discussion of class, it is also important to consider *classism*. Drawing from the social categorization framework outlined in Chapter 2, we could potentially conceptualize *classism* as the differential evaluations persons from one class have toward another. Indeed, Liu and colleagues (Liu, 2002; Liu, Ali, et al., 2004; Liu, Soleck, Hopps, Dunston, & Pickett, 2004) have made similar arguments in suggesting that classism can be expressed toward persons above, below, and even within one's own social class. However, this general definition tends to de-emphasize the issues of power and subordination that are so central to our discussions of class and classism. As such, I follow Bullock's (1995) more specific definition, in which *classism* is characterized by its "oppression of the poor through a network of everyday practices, attitudes, assumptions, behaviors, and institutional rules" (p. 119). Indeed, classism is concerned with the assignment of characteristics or worth based on class standing, the attitudes and policies that are enacted to perpetuate this unequal valuing, and the subordination of certain groups by those who have access to power and resources (Collins & Yeskel, 2005). Also embedded in these dynamics is class privilege, or the "unearned advantage and conferred dominance" among those in the upper classes (Moon & Rolison, 1998, p. 132).

According to Lott (2002), classism results from three, interrelated distancing responses: cognitive distancing, interpersonal distancing, and institutional distancing. Each of these processes is outlined in the following section (see also Exhibit 11.3).

---

exhibit **11.3**   **Dimensions of classism.**

Cognitive distancing: the use of stereotypes that cast the poor in a negative light (e.g., laziness, dishonesty, and lack of initiative).

Interpersonal distancing: the discriminatory behaviors persons from more powerful classes express toward the poor.

Institutional distancing: the manner in which societal institutions and prevailing norms and values allocate positive social value to dominant, power-holding groups while disproportionately assigning negative social value to subordinates.

Adapted from Lott (2002) and Lott and Bullock (2007).

Cognitive Distancing

Cognitive distancing primarily takes the form of stereotyping (Lott, 2002), and considerable research supports Bullock's (1995) contention that "the poor are perceived as failing to seize opportunities because they lack diligence and initiative. . . . Poor people and welfare recipients are typically characterized as dishonest, dependent, lazy, uninterested in education, and promiscuous" (p. 125). For instance, Cozzarelli, Wilkinson, and Tagler (2001) found that college students in their study were more likely to attribute negative characteristics to persons in poverty than they were to persons in the middle class. Specifically, they believed the poor to be less educated, less motivated, lazier, more unpleasant, angrier, more immoral, and more violent than their counterparts. In another study, Beck, Whitley, and Wolk (1999) examined the attitudes toward the poor held by members of the Georgia state legislature. They found consensus among the legislators that people's actions serve to perpetuate their own poverty. The poor were considered to lack talent, morals, ambition, and the will to make an effort. It is not only adults who hold these views toward the poor, but children also express stereotypical, negative attitudes toward the poor relative to the rich (Woods, Kurtz-Costes, & Rowley, 2005; see also Chafel, 1997).

A provocative study from Fiske (2007) sheds light on why this takes place. Fiske and her colleagues examined the brain's responses to seeing photos of a homeless man. Two key findings were observed. First, within moments of the photo being viewed, participants' brains set off a sequence of reactions that are linked with disgust and avoidance. The area of the brain that was activated, the insula, is usually triggered when people express disgust toward *nonhuman* objects, like garbage or human waste. Also of interest was the part of the brain that was not activated: the dorsomedial prefrontal cortex. This is noteworthy because this section of the brain is usually activated when people think about other people or about themselves. Fiske explains, "in the case of the homeless . . . these areas simply failed to light up, as if people had stumbled on a pile of garbage" (p. 157). This research suggests that people are likely to dehumanize the poor—a process that potentially explains the negative attitudes expressed toward the poor or the shocking nature of certain hate crimes against the homeless. There were 142 hate crimes against the homeless in 2007 alone (Green, 2008).

The negative stereotypes associated with cognitive distancing are also directed toward elements associated with those in poverty or the working class, such as speech accents, dress, and manners. Scully and Blake-Beard (2007) note that, within the organizational context, persons from privileged backgrounds often dress, talk, and act in ways that are associated with style and success. They have the cultural capital (Liu, Soleck, et al., 2004) needed for advancement opportunities. Persons from less privileged backgrounds, however, might dress or talk "differently," thereby demonstrating that they lack this capital. As a result, the less privileged are either shunned outright or strongly "encouraged" to alter their behaviors and speech pattern and, in doing so, to leave behind the cultural remnants of their lower-class status (Scully & Blake-Beard, 2007). This process can be disheartening to disadvantaged persons, resulting in anxiety and negative emotional responses (Liu, Soleck, et al., 2004).

Interpersonal Distancing

Interpersonal distancing refers to the discriminatory behaviors persons from more powerful classes express toward the poor. Bullock (1995) noted that "poor people commonly experience face-to-face discrimination in their daily lives" (p. 142). Barriers are erected in such a way that the poor cannot enjoy full societal participation. In the workplace, this discrimination is seen in the hiring process and the placement of people into particular jobs. For example, Kennelly (1999) found that employers were sometimes reluctant to hire people who they perceived to be from a poor background, because the applicants were thought to possess a poor work ethic. When they are hired, people from poor backgrounds are likely to be placed in "class appropriate" jobs such as janitorial or parking lot attendant positions (Bullock, 2004).

Interpersonal distancing is also observed in the school setting. In one example (Borg, 2004), teachers in Rhode Island were asked to assess students' academic potential based on their economic and demographic information. Teachers believed that students from middle-class families had a much better chance of graduating college (72 percent) than their counterparts from poor families (48 percent). Given the influence of self-fulfilling prophecies, it is hardly surprising that poor students perform less well academically than their counterparts in more powerful social classes.

Institutional Distancing

Institutional distancing refers to the manner in which societal institutions and prevailing norms and values allocate positive social value to dominant, power-holding groups while disproportionately assigning negative social value to subordinates (see also Sidanius & Pratto, 1999). This form of classism punishes members of low-status groups by erecting barriers to their access to resources and full participation in society (Lott, 2002; Lott & Bullock, 2007). This is manifested primarily through the institutionalized notion of meritocracy, education, housing, healthcare, organizational structures, and sport systems, each of which is described in the following sections.

Meritocracy

Meritocracy refers to the worldview that one's social standing and the rewards received are based on individual effort and merit. This ideal is highly valued and engrained within the United States and other Western cultures, so much so that it has been referred to as America's dominant ideology (Kluegel & Smith, 1986). Key elements in American culture, including children's books (e.g., *The Little Engine That Could*), autobiographies (e.g., Iacocca & Novack, 1984), and movies (e.g., *Hoosiers*), all promote the notion that with hard work, persistence, and determination, anyone can rise from humble beginnings to overcome hurdles placed in front of them and achieve greatness. This belief system is often used, perhaps implicitly, to justify the positions of those in power (i.e., they worked hard to get there) and those in disadvantaged circumstances (i.e., they made poor choices and now must face the consequences) (see McCoy & Major, 2007).

These examples are illustrative of meritocracy's three underlying elements (Daniels, 1978). First, merit is thought to be a well-understood and measurable basis for selecting persons either for positions or promotion. Second, individuals have equal opportunities to both develop and display their talents, thereby allowing them to advance. Finally, the positions attained by people vary according to different levels of status, reward, and income.

From a different perspective, those adopting a class-based view challenge these underlying premises on a number of fronts (Scully & Blake-Beard, 2007). First, they claim that powerful persons who have access to material and economic resources are those who decide what is meritorious and what is not. Merit is socially constructed so as to privilege elites and ensure that they maintain their power and status, all the while delegitimizing the achievements of persons from disadvantaged groups. As one example, consider the requirements among many sport organizations that employees have an undergraduate, or sometimes even a graduate, degree for even a ticket sales position. As an educator, I certainly value the knowledge, understanding, and experience that people obtain through the formal educational process. I also acknowledge, however, that there are many times when this arbitrarily assigned requisite condition serves to disadvantage someone who is qualified (e.g., prior sales experience) but whose class background did not direct them to the higher education route.

Second, an individual's family class background is often a better predictor of life success than individual merit (Scully & Blake-Beard, 2007). Similar to wealth, class is transferred from generation to generation. This is meaningful because even if two people differ in class but are otherwise identically meritorious from birth, they are still likely to have different experiences and chances in life. Clearly, there are examples of persons, such as Lee Iacocca, Sam Walton, or Barack Obama, who rose from meager backgrounds to do extraordinary things in their lives, thereby supporting the "American Dream" ideal. However, these exceptional cases are just that—exceptions. As Scully and Blake-Beard note, "any meritocracy needs only just enough permeability of elite ranks to justify the possibility that 'anyone can make it'" (p. 436). Also, this anecdotal evidence does not negate the experiences of millions of others who, despite their meritorious achievements, are overlooked, bypassed, and marginalized because of their class position.

Finally, critics of meritocracy argue that the different values society places on varying jobs, coupled with the status and rewards of those jobs, can be challenged (Scully & Blake-Beard, 2007). From this perspective, wage gaps between the elite and those in the working class or in poverty come into question. These discrepancies are seen as a function of the greed and power of those at the top who pay

DIVERSITY *in the field*

Inequitable Wage Distributions in College Athletics. The worldwide economic crisis that occurred in 2008 and 2009 affected nearly every aspect of sport, including intercollegiate athletics. Cash-strapped athletic departments were forced to make tough decisions, including trimming team budgets, cutting some athletic squads, and reducing their workforce. As *Eagle* reporter Matthew Watkins (2009) outlined, this was certainly the case at Texas A&M University, where during the 2008–2009 fiscal year, the department ran a $1 million deficit, even after taking a $4.5 million loan from the university. If the business practices were left unchanged, the athletic department was projected to lose an additional $4.5 million during the 2009–2010 academic year.

Faced with these financial difficulties, the athletic director, Bill Byrne, along with the university's division of finance, identified $3 million in cuts, including the elimination of several student worker posts, cutting free tickets for families and staff, reducing the international travel that teams took during the preseason, and altering phone allowances. As another cost-cutting technique, the athletic department opted to eliminate 17 full-time positions—most through layoffs—as a way to cut an additional $1 million. Billy Pickard, who began his time at Texas A&M as a student worker during Paul "Bear" Bryant's days at the university, was among those cut from the staff.

This information alone, while disconcerting, might not be surprising, considering that many sport organizations, including several professional sport leagues (e.g., NFL), were forced to lay off employees as a way to cut costs. What makes the Texas A&M example particularly troubling, however, was that the layoffs occurred while the most powerful in the department were taking large raises. In August 2008, for instance, Byrne's salary increased over 40 percent (from $486,000 to $690,000), and this was on top of the $178,500 in performance bonuses he received that year. One month before the 17 full-time positions were eliminated, Byrne also paid out $1 million in bonuses to coaches who had participated in post-season play. What makes these bonuses noteworthy is that their contracts stipulated that they be paid *only if* the department had money available. In justifying these expenses, Byrne commented that the coaches were deserving of the extra monies because of their "great success" and as a way to keep other schools from recruiting them away from the university.

This example illustrates the abuses of power that sport organizations' elites can wield. They pay themselves high wages and bonuses, justifying them through self-made rules and flawed notions of meritocracy, all the while marginalizing and subjugating those who are in less powerful positions.

themselves exorbitant salaries that do not reflect true differences in merit or value that society places on those jobs. This disjunction was aptly observed during the financial crisis the United States experienced in 2008 and 2009, during which companies would lay off thousands of employees only to pay the executives millions of dollars in bonuses. Note, too, that these "performance bonuses" were paid out even though the companies were in financial dire straits, surviving only because of governmental assistance. Elites, of course, seek to justify their wages, arguing that their salaries are based on market demand and that their unique skills and expertise (re: meritorious achievements) call for such compensation. What else should be expected, though? After all, "every highly privileged group develops the myth of its natural superiority" (Weber, 1978, p. 437), and persons in power "use 'autobiographical reasoning' to describe their positions as the outcome of hard work and ability, extrapolating from their own experiences" (Scully & Blake-Beard, 2007, p. 437). The corollary of this argument is that those who do not earn such outstanding wages and who have not exceeded in the stratified social order are not hard working, do not possess unique skills and attributes, and are not meritorious. The clear problem with such errant reasoning is the considerable evidence to the contrary: millions of people work extremely hard completing tasks that require special skills only to be compensated with wages that do not allow them to provide for their most basic needs and for their families (Chang, 2000; Ehrenreich & Hochschild, 2004). The Diversity in the Field box on the previous page provides a detailed example of this phenomenon that occurred in the athletics setting.

Education

The second way in which institutional distancing takes place is through education. Specifically, because most schools are funded through property taxes, class inequalities and social injustices are continually reinforced. Eitzen (1996) explains the dynamics in this way:

> Schools receive some federal money, more state money, and typically, about half of their budget from local property taxes. The result is a wide disparity in per-pupil expenditures among the states and within each state. The use of property taxes is discriminatory because rich school districts can spend more money than poor ones on each student, yet *at a lower tax rate*. This last point is important—poor districts have higher mill levies than wealthy districts, yet they raise less money *because they are poor* (emphasis original, p. 102).

To further illustrate these disparities, the highest spending school district in Illinois spent $19,361 more per student in 2005 than the lowest spending school district (Urrea, 2005). These differences obviously have meaningful ramifications for quality of instruction, sport opportunities, number of teachers and coaches, and quality of facilities and equipment.

The differences in the quality of education between privileged and disadvantaged students have a number of ramifications, including the likelihood of completing school and prospects of attending college. Bullock (2004) reports that school children from the poorest 20 percent of families are *six times less likely* to finish high school than their wealthier peers. Class inequalities in primary education also impact the likelihood of pursuing higher education opportunities. Disadvantaged students are unlikely to attend the most elite institutions (Lott & Bullock, 2007) or get a degree at all. According to Brooks (2005), students from families earning over $90,000 have a 50/50 chance of completing college before turning 24. The proportion drops to only 10 percent for students from families earning between $35,000 and $60,000, and to just over 5 percent for students from families earning less than $35,000.

Krugman (2007) draws from different research to illustrate a similar point. Data were gathered from 8th graders in 1988. Based on this information, they were sorted into categories based on their intellect (as measured by mathematics performance) and the SES of their parents (as measured by income, occupation, and education). The researchers then examined whether or not the students finished college. As might be expected, students who scored well and whose parents were in the top SES quartile were very likely to finish college (79 percent), and those who were at the other end (bottom quartile in both SES and academic performance) were unlikely to finish college (3 percent). What is striking, though, is the data from those students who fell into the other categories. Among students who were in the top quartile of academic performers but whose parents were in the bottom SES quartile, only 29 percent completed college. This is *less than* the proportion (30 percent) of the students who performed poorly academically but came from affluent households. In commenting on these findings, Krugman noted, "what this tells us is that the idea that we have anything close to equality of opportunity is clearly a fantasy. It would be closer to the truth, though not the whole truth, to say that in America, class—inherited class—usually trumps talent" (p. 248).

Housing

A third way in which institutional distancing occurs is through housing. The ability to provide shelter for one's family—one of the most basic needs people have (Maslow, 1943)—is continuously listed as the most pressing concern for persons in the poverty class (Lott & Bullock, 2007). The high costs of rent and utilities support the reality of this concern. One national study found that the average cost of rent and utilities for a two-bedroom apartment was $791/month ("Housing," 2003). According to Lott and Bullock, to afford the rent, food, and other necessities, one would need to earn $15.21/hr, which is twice the minimum wage rate ($7.25/hr) in 2009. Thus, even in a household in which two persons work full time, there may not be enough money to obtain the basic necessities. These data shed light on why homelessness rates continue to increase and also illustrate that even gainfully employed individuals can lose their homes because they are not paid a living wage.

Cost is not the only way in which institutional distancing occurs in relation to housing. Low-income families are also likely to live in communities that are geographically and socially segregated from middle-class and owning-class families (Lott, 2002). Within large, urban areas, the poor are relegated to "the ghetto" while more affluent families live in high-rise apartments: the former dwelling is dangerous and poorly maintained while the latter receives around-the-clock security (Lott, 2002). Low-income neighborhoods are also more likely to be places where toxins are dumped and air pollution is high (Allen, 2001). Companies that produce environmentally hazardous waste are likely to locate in low-income communities, with the thinking that resistance to such a business move will be less than it would in other neighborhoods. As Pinderhughes (1996) commented, "to save time and money, companies seek to locate environmentally hazardous industries in communities which will put up the least resistance, which are less informed and less powerful, and are more dependent upon local job development efforts" (p. 233). Lott and Bullock (2007) refer to this practice as environmental classism.

Of course, the distancing from overcrowded, polluted urban locations occurs until the cities and sport franchises decide that the location would be an ideal site for a new stadium and urban redevelopment efforts. Once this decision is made, the poverty and working-class families who live in the area are displaced—forced to move to other locations. Efforts to clean up, revitalize, and energize the neighborhoods are then made—only after the poor are displaced and the wealthy team owners and fans move into town. This displacement process has a serious negative effect on families. Residents are forced to leave their homes, the local shops they

DIVERSITY *in the field*

Housing and the Olympics. The Olympics are often promoted as a way to showcase one's city and, at the same time, improve the supporting infrastructure. New stadiums and arenas are constructed, roads are built, new jobs are created, and urban centers are revitalized. The Olympics come at a tremendous cost, however. Most often, these costs are discussed in terms of the billions of dollars local governments and organizations spend to prepare for the Games. This does not tell the whole story, however, because the poor are disproportionately negatively affected by a city's hosting of the Olympics as well. This was particularly the case in Vancouver, host of the 2010 Winter Olympics. According to Tessa Cogman (2008), over 800 people were displaced in one area of downtown Vancouver after the 2010 Games were announced, the consequence of low-rent hotels being closed and demolished so that high-priced condominiums could be built in their place. There were no housing alternatives to be seen. Despite spending over $4.5 billion to support the Games (monies that could have made almost 2,800 housing units for the poor), government officials claimed not to have the resources to address the increased number of homeless on the streets. Cogman finds such claims particularly curious, given the fact that "the new RAV [light rail] line is being built to the Vancouver International Airport, a new highway is in the works, and condos are shooting up everywhere." This kind of displacement of the poor in favor of the Winter Olympics is nothing new. The Sydney Olympics was also accompanied by increased homelessness, an outcome caused by the skyrocketing cost of living in the city. In addressing this trend, Sydney officials literally bussed the homeless to different cities (Beadnell, 2000), presumably so they would not "interfere" with Olympics activities. In response to this disturbing but long-lasting phenomena, Cogman acutely noted that "If the homeless had an Olympic category, maybe someone would notice."

enjoy visiting, and the friends and social networks they have developed. Members of the owner class can reap more profits by placing their new stadium where the poor once lived. Consequent to the urban gentrification process, the rent and property values increase, thereby forcing local merchants to move (because they cannot afford the rent) and prohibiting them from relocating in a nearby area. It is little wonder that Carr (1994), after examining these effects on 400 families, concluded that "displacement, the act of casting out, is inescapably an assault on personhood" (p. 200).

The Diversity in the Field box provides an overview of the displacement process that occurs when communities host the Olympics. The Alternative Perspectives box then provides some of the proposed benefits to such urban revitalization efforts as well as the counterarguments to those positions.

Healthcare

Institutional distancing is also manifested through healthcare. Krugman (2007) notes that the United States is unique among wealthy nations in its failure to provide healthcare to all of its citizens. Over 46 million persons were uninsured in 2009, and it is not only those who do not work who lack health coverage. Krugman reports that, as of 2001, 65 percent of American workers had employment-based coverage—a figure that had decreased to 59 percent by 2006. Among persons who earn between $25,000 and $35,000, approximately 40 percent lack any form of insurance (Krugman, 2007). The lack of insurance is not due to a lack of money devoted to healthcare. In fact, quite the opposite is the case: the United States spends more than double per patient ($7,421 in 2007) than other Western nations, and healthcare spending represents 16.0 percent of the country's Gross Domestic Product (Health Care, 2009). The latter figure is expected to grow, so that by 2025, one of every four dollars in the United States economy will be tied to healthcare (Health Care, 2009).

Given the high costs, healthcare and health insurance have increasingly become a luxury commodity affordable only to persons with power and wealth, while less privileged persons suffer without care. Low-income wage earners represent half of the uninsured, and four of ten go without insurance (Health Disparities, 2009). This pattern led Lott and Bullock (2007) to conclude that "the resource to which low-income people in this country [the United States] have the least access is health care" (p. 65).

These figures are meaningful on a number of fronts. According to the National Coalition on Health Care (http://www.nchc.org/facts/cost.shtml) 62 percent of all personal bankruptcies stemmed from healthcare costs. Of these *80 percent had some form of health insurance*, but the insurance simply did not cover enough costs. Lack of adequate health insurance is also associated with people choosing to forgo medical treatments (Health Disparities, 2009). This means that people in poverty and working-class persons are more likely to contract illnesses and diseases that would have otherwise been prevented, treated, or cured. It is hardly surprising, then, that low-income families are more likely to suffer from a host of health ailments, including obesity, Type II diabetes, cancer, and HIV/AIDS. These data support Lott and Bullock's (2007) contention that within the United States, social class "is a strong and reliable predictor of health outcomes . . . and all causes of death regardless of ethnicity, gender, and age" (p. 68).

Given the linkage between social class and the provision of healthcare, Congress passed a healthcare reform bill, the Patient Protection and Affordable Care Act, in 2010. Among the many benefits of the reform is the promise of making healthcare more accessible for all persons, irrespective of their class. Only time will tell if the changes will result in the intended benefits.

Organizational structure

The manner in which organizations, including those in sport, are structured also reinforces institutional classism. Rothman (2002) reported that occupations linked with the middle and owning classes are at the top of the prestige hierarchy, while those occupations associated with poverty or working classes are perceived as low-status positions. Indeed, when I ask students in my sport management classes to what they aspire upon graduation, many site general manager, athletic director, or events coordinator—all high-status positions. Less common are responses related to grounds crew or concessions—positions more

alternative PERSPECTIVES

Are There Benefits to Displacement? Some argue that the potential negative effects associated with displacing families in favor of building a stadium are outweighed with the many benefits associated with the practice. After all, the stadium also brings new restaurants and shops to the neighborhood that people frequent when attending events. Collectively, this new business is thought to provide many benefits, including increased tax revenues. Coakley (2009) notes many fallacies with these arguments. For instance, officials will often give discounted tax rates to the owners and their real estate partners as enticement for choosing to build in their city. However, considering that property taxes are the primary sources of revenue for public schools, this practice actually serves to decrease the potential revenues the schools could receive. Thus, as team owners continue to increase their wealth through this public subsidization, school systems continue to fail due to poor funding.

Another argument is that the new, publicly financed stadiums and arenas create new jobs; thus, even though people might be displaced, at least they have the work opportunities that otherwise would have not been there. There are similar inconsistencies with this notion as well. First, because the new facilities sit empty for most of the year, the types of jobs that are normally created are seasonal and low paying (Crompton, 1995). Second, developing jobs through the public subsidization of sport franchises is remarkably inefficient when compared with government-assisted initiatives. To illustrate, Maryland financed a $222 million football stadium for the Baltimore Ravens in 1998. Each new job created in connection with that project cost the state $127,000. This is more than *20 times* what it costs the Maryland economic development fund to develop the equivalent job ($6,250). Put another way, for every job that was created in connection with the stadium, more than 20 jobs could have been created had the monies been invested in state development projects (Coakley, 2009). Thus, despite claims of supposed benefits of publicly supported stadiums and the displacement of persons from their homes, the evidence points to the contrary.

frequently held by the poor. Note, too, that other characteristics differentiate the two classes of positions. Athletic directors, when compared with concession workers, are likely to have better benefits, choose their work structure and hours, and travel to exciting destinations. These distinctions are important because the status of a given occupation is partly associated with the benefits thereto, including vacation time, paid leave, healthcare, salaried work, and retirement.

Class is also reinforced in the attitudes toward high-status and low-status employees' behaviors. Let us consider mobilization efforts, for instance. Unions are generally considered to be organizations formed to improve the working conditions of workers and the pay they receive (Abercrombie, Hill, & Turner, 2000).

HEALTH OUTCOMES OF CLASSISM

Given the pervasiveness of cognitive, interpersonal, and institutional classism, one should not be surprised to learn that middle- and poverty-class persons face a number of unique life difficulties. Relative to persons in other classes, the poor report higher incidents of anxiety, depression, and hostility; express less optimism and control over their lives; have poor social support; are more likely to be overweight; and are more likely to report physical illnesses, such as Type II diabetes, cancer, and heart disease (see Liu, 2002, Liu, Ali, et al., 2004, for reviews). It is important to note that these effects are not uniform, because class intersects with other diversity dimensions to differentially impact some groups over others (see Exhibit 11.4). This is also the case for conceptions of social class, as illustrated in the Professional Perspectives box on p. 254.

According to the APA (2006), social class influences health through a number of potential pathways. First, as previously outlined in the discussion of institutional distancing, the poor have limited access to healthcare, and when they do receive healthcare, it is often of poor quality. Second, poverty-class and working-class persons are more likely to encounter hazardous materials in their work settings and in their neighborhoods than their higher status counterparts. A third pathway is through health behaviors such as smoking, diet, and lack of exercise. Finally, social class might be related to health and well-being through differential exposure to stress. Poverty-class and working-class persons are more likely to experience more acute and chronic stress than their counterparts, and this repeated exposure to stress deleteriously affects the body's ability to fight off illness and disease.

Laborers benefit in many ways from unionization and have fought for rights related to fair work practices, just pay, healthcare benefits, and retirement options, among others. Despite these many benefits, Americans' attitudes toward unions have become less favorable over the years, and in 2009, fewer than half approved of labor unions (Saad, 2009). These attitudes are interesting, considering the general positive attitudes people have toward chambers of commerce and professional associations, both of which are forms of mobilization, albeit by different names, of middle and owning class persons (Smith, 2008). This hypocrisy is routinely illustrated in the media coverage of labor strife in the professional sport leagues: relative to the owners (who operate legal cartels), players unions are more likely to be vilified and characterized as greedy when there is a strike or lockout (for other examples, see Zweig, 2000).

Examples of classism within the organizational context are perhaps best illustrated through the wildly disparate pay scales. According to Smith (2008), the gap between a company's highest paid employee and the mean salary in that company has jumped from a ratio of 28 to 1 in 1970 all the way to a ratio of 369 to 1 in 2006. As previously noted, these salaries are justified through the promotion of stereotypes and through socially reinforcing belief systems such as meritocracy.

Perhaps not surprisingly, given these figures, research from Emmanuel Saez (2009) suggests that income inequalities are increasing at substantial rates. According to his calculations, the top .01 percent of Americans reaped 6 percent of the total wages in the country, a proportion that

Intersection of class and other diversity dimensions.   *exhibit* **11.4**

The influence of social class on subsequent outcomes is moderated by other diversity dimensions in such a way that the effects are stronger for some groups than for others. This is observed for the following characteristics:

1. *Race:* The legacy of slavery, prejudice, and discrimination in the United States means that racial minorities are disproportionately represented in poverty classes and middle classes. This is particularly true of African Americans, "for whom individual deprivation and poverty are compounded by residential segregation, resulting in a greater proportion of Blacks living in concentrated poverty" (APA, 2006, p. 12).

2. *Gender:* Women are more likely to be in less powerful social classes than men. Women also have lower incomes than men, even when education and experience levels are the same. These differences account, at least in part, for the strikingly high rates of poverty for children living in single-parent households headed by the mother.

3. *(Dis)ability status:* Persons with disabilities are disproportionately represented among the unemployed, underemployed, and those in the poverty class. Fewer than one in five persons with disabilities are employed, and they are twice as likely as their able-bodied counterparts to live in poverty.

4. *Sexual orientation:* Although persons who are lesbian, gay, bisexual, and transgendered (LGBT) are perceived to have considerable discretionary income, in reality they are likely to be economically disadvantaged. People who identify as LGBT earn up to 32 percent less than similarly qualified peers. Termination of employees based on their sexual orientation is legal in 31 states. Finally, the incidence of homelessness is higher among individuals who are LGBT than it is among heterosexuals, particularly with youth.

5. *Age:* Class can affect the young and the poor. Though older adults are generally not poor, there is a meaningful number (5.6 million) living at or near the poverty line. This is especially the case for older racial minorities. Among children, poverty rates are the highest in the industrialized world. Research indicates that nearly one in four (or 22.4 percent) U.S. children live in poverty—figures far greater than those in Sweden (2 percent), France (7.9 percent), Spain (13.3 percent), or the United Kingdom (18.8 percent).

Information retrieved from APA (2006).

had doubled since 2000. Furthermore, as of 2007, the top 10 percent of American earners pulled in nearly 50 percent of the total wages in the United States, a level not seen for decades. Unfortunately, similar gains were not made by the poor, and as a result, the gap between the "haves" and "have-nots" continues to grow. In explaining his findings, Saez wrote, "a number of factors may help explain this increase in inequality, not only underlying technological changes but also the retreat of institutions developed during the New Deal and World War II—such as progressive tax policies, powerful unions, corporate provision of health and retirement benefits, and changing social norms regarding pay inequality" (p. 4).

The institutionalized nature of class inequalities in organizations has a number of effects, including perceptions of opportunities among children. Bullock (2004)

PROFESSIONAL PERSPECTIVES

Alternate Conceptions of Social Class. Jacqueline McDowell is a scholar at the University of Illinois, where she studies the intersection of race, gender, and social class. According to McDowell, traditional definitions of class focus on issues of income, wealth, power, and standing in society. However, in the African American community, social class takes on a different meaning, and class is "typically defined by someone's attitude that they might have about their life, or their behavior . . . so it is actually independent of the power that they might have in the wider society." She found support for this position in her research with African American women administrators. When asked about their class background, women in her research were reluctant to pigeonhole themselves into a particular class based on their income or occupation; rather, "a lot of them actually felt that their class reflected an attitude about their life." Thus, from McDowell's perspective, ideas people have about class, including where they are situated, are likely to vary with their race.

notes that in the United States, middle-class cultural norms hold that people freely choose their occupations. For example, if you ask children what they want to be when they grow up, you will receive a myriad of responses, including the president, a firefighter, a professional athlete, and a school teacher. This freedom to explore different career options and then to choose the career one wants to pursue is encouraged by middle-class parents. This liberty to choose one's occupation also connotes the idea that one's occupation is based on personal choice, not economic factors or class-based opportunities. This belief does not factor in the demands that limit the many who live in poverty and the working-class youth: the necessity of working at an early age to provide for one's family or being unable to afford to attend college are both common to these people.

Illustrative of these dynamics, Weinger (2000) conducted a study of how school children viewed opportunities for career success of children from poor or middle-class backgrounds. She found that among both the middle-class and the poor children, persons who were poor were viewed as being least likely to obtain a job having high potential for career success. Poor children were also believed most likely to obtain working-class or blue-collar jobs, as opposed to professional or management positions. Interestingly, poor children were believed to obtain entertainment positions—such as a movie star or professional basketball player—more often than middle-class children. Finally, poor children were believed to encounter more obstacles to achieving their dreams than middle-class children. The middle-class children who participated in the study believed that dreams of poor children would be thwarted because of a lack of effort on their own part. On the other hand, the study's poor children anticipated that a poor child's dreams would be truncated because of overt prejudice and discrimination. Overall, these findings suggest that children's views of potential career success are largely shaped by social-class factors.

Sport systems

Sport also has a number of institutionalized activities that serve to reinforce classism. Differences in sport participation provide one example. Participating in sport and recreational activities takes time and money, two things that middle- and owning-class persons are likely to have more of than other members of society. People who participate in sport are most likely to be highly educated, be from a high-income bracket, and have a high-status occupation (Gibson, 1998). This pattern is evident in several segments of the sport industry, including the

Olympics, health and fitness, and recreational activities (Eitzen & Sage, 2009). For example, skiing, golf, and tennis can entail substantial costs for club dues and equipment. Therefore, persons from the elite or professional middle class are more likely to participate in these activities than those from the poor or working classes.

The structure and expectations related to corporate wellness centers also contribute to these differences (Eitzen & Sage, 2009). Companies increasingly offer on-site wellness centers and encourage employees to be physically active, but participation varies based on occupational status: powerful, salaried employees generally demonstrate enthusiasm for such programs, while reactions from hourly employees are more tempered. Eitzen and Sage (2009) provide several potential explanations for this dynamic. First, all else equal, research suggests that the middle-class and owning class are more likely to engage in healthy behaviors than persons from working and poverty classes. Second, the activities offered, such as running or Pilates, have a greater appeal to high-status employees than to their counterparts. In addition, corporate wellness centers might be viewed as something established for those in upper management, and thus, hourly workers would be considered outsiders in that context. Finally, hourly workers may resent the monies and time spent on wellness activities, especially considering that these do not address their work needs (i.e., higher wages, decreasing the danger, monotony, and lack of autonomy in their work).

In addition to participation rates, social class also influences who attends sport events. A report from the *Sports Business Journal* (Genzale, 2003) illustrates this point. This publication tracked the fan demographics of the four major professional sport leagues in the United States (MLB, NBA, NFL, and NHL) from 1995 to 2001. Across each league, the proportion of people earning $20,000 to $29,000 and $30,000 to $49,000 decreased over the seven-year span. During the same time frame, the proportion of fans who earned $100,000 or more increased by at least 50 percent. This trend is not necessarily surprising, considering the high costs of attending a professional sport event as discussed in Chapter 2. More and more, watching live sport is becoming something available only to persons in the professional middle class or the elite. The cost of attending is simply too much for persons from other social classes.

Finally, as evidenced in the Diversity Challenge, the increasing use of "pay-to-play" programs in high school athletics and other school-sponsored activities is privileging to students from families who have the economic resources for such activities and, simultaneously, is disadvantaging to students from poorer families. According to sport management professor Scott Smith of Central Michigan University, participation rates do not decline noticeably when the fees are small (e.g., $50); however, when the fees increase above the $300 range, participation rates "drop noticeably," sometimes by a third or more (as cited in Brady & Glier, 2004). Such policies guarantee that opportunities to participate in varsity programs will continue for those young people born into middle- and owning-class families or who attend wealthy school districts that can afford to finance sport teams. For those students in poor school districts or whose families cannot afford the hundreds of dollars in fees, formal sport participation opportunities are eliminated.

Sport and Social Mobility

The foregoing discussion suggests that social class plays a significant role in the education people receive, the opportunities people are afforded, the types of jobs they have, and the experiences they have in the workplace. Nevertheless, some are of the opinion that sport participation can serve to negate this pattern. For example, does being a star athlete at a major university provide a person with the capital needed to be successful throughout life? Does participating in sport and athletics in high school mean that people will be more successful later in life? There are certainly isolated examples in which this is the case. Most of us can think of people who were raised in lower-income households, and as a result of their sport participation, received the college education, met the important social contacts, or gained the confidence needed to be successful in life. Of course, this is not the case for every athlete from a low-income background. There are just as many who have not risen above humble beginnings to be successful. How then does sport contribute to occupational success or upward social mobility, if at all?

Coakley (2009) suggests that sport participation will be positively related to upward social mobility when it does the following:

- Provides the athlete with educational opportunities as well as the chance to develop skills relevant to the workplace
- Increases the support others give the athletes for their overall growth and development
- Provides opportunities to make friends and social contacts with people outside sport and sport organizations
- Provides people with the material resources necessary to create future career opportunities
- Allows the athlete to develop identities unrelated to sports through expanded opportunities and training
- Minimizes the risks of injuries that would incur substantial medical costs and rehabilitation

These predictions suggest that, under some circumstances, sport will help expand one's opportunities. This is certainly true when sport allows one to obtain education, skills, and training unrelated to sport. For example, when a volleyball player from a poor family receives a scholarship to a university, she is afforded the chance to obtain an education. To the extent that she takes advantage of this opportunity, develops her skills for the workplace, gains experiences through internships, and cultivates her social relationships, her sport participation is likely to be positively related to her upward social mobility and career success.

CHAPTER *summary*

The purpose of this chapter was to provide an overview of how class and classism affect people's lives and the delivery of sport. As evidenced in the Diversity Challenge, the decisions sport managers make concerning the structure of sport and how it is financed often serve to hurt those who are already socially and economically disadvantaged. These dynamics are observed in other ways, too, including how people interact with the poor and institutionalized practices that privilege persons from middle and owning classes. Based on this information, you should now be able to:

1. Define key terms, including SES, social class, and classism.

Socioeconomic status refers to one's economic standing, with a particular emphasis on income, education, and occupation. Social class refers to people's positions within an economic system, with a particular emphasis on how power, politics, and socially constructed realities economically and socially advantage some at the expense of others. Finally, classism describes the subjugation of the poor through stereotypes, interpersonal discrimination, and institutionalized activities.

2. Discuss the influence of cognitive, interpersonal, and institutional distancing on the maintenance and promotion of classism.

Cognitive distancing refers to the use of stereotypes that cast the poor in a negative light, such as being lazy, dishonest, and lacking initiative. Interpersonal distancing is manifested through the discriminatory behaviors persons from more powerful classes direct toward the poor. Finally, institutional distancing refers to the manner in which societal institutions and prevailing norms and values allocate positive social value to dominant, power-holding groups and disproportionately assign negative social value to subordinates.

3. Provide an overview of the effects of classism on people's health and well-being.

Classism negatively affects people's physical health, mental health, and overall well-being. These effects are augmented for women, racial minorities, individuals who are LGBT, and those who are especially young or old.

4. Highlight the manner in which sport involvement results in social mobility.

The argument that sport involvement is strongly related to social mobility is overstated. Rather, social class standing will improve only when sport participation also allows a person to obtain education, social contacts, skills, and training unrelated to sport.

QUESTIONS *for discussion*

1. What are the differences between SES and social class? Which construct do you prefer in discussions of economic inequalities?
2. Some argue that class-related stereotypes can also be directed at persons other than the poor. Is this the case, and if so, do all class-related stereotypes have the same impact on subsequent outcomes?
3. Challenging the notion of meritocracy is often a difficult task. Why is this the case, and what arguments could effectively be made to illustrate that the notion of meritocracy promotes classism?
4. Several examples were provided in the chapter illustrating how the structure and delivery of sport reinforce classism. What are other examples of how class and sport interact?

READING *resources*

SUPPLEMENTARY READING

Krugman, P. (2007). *The conscience of a liberal.* New York: W. W Norton & Company. (A provocative book from the Nobel Prize Laureate; provides an overview of economic inequalities in the United States and possible solutions to the problem.)

Lott, B., & Bullock, H. E. (2007). *Psychology and economic injustice: Personal, professional, and political intersections.* Washington, DC: American Psychological Association. (Provides an exceptional overview of the psychological dynamics of class; also provides telling life stories of the authors.)

Sage, G. H. (1998). *Power and ideology in American sport: A critical perspective* (2nd ed.). Champaign, IL: Human Kinetics. (Addresses the manner in which social, political, and economic influences shape sport in the United States today.)

WEB RESOURCES

- American Psychological Association Office of Socioeconomic Status (SES) (http://www.apa.org/pi/ses/homepage.html): An entity that focuses on the psychological dynamics of social class and SES.

- Class matters (http://www.nytimes.com/pages/national/class/): A special section of the *New York Times* that provides articles, reports, and statistical information pertaining to class in America.

- Health Reform (http://www.healthreform.gov/index.html): a website of the U.S. federal government that provides reports concerning social class and healthcare.

references

Abercrombie, N., Hill, S., & Turner, B. S. (2000). *The Penguin dictionary of sociology* (4th ed.). New York: Penguin Books.

Allen, D. W. (2001). Social class, race, and toxic releases in American counties, 1995. *The Social Science Journal, 38,* 13–25.

American Psychological Association. (2006). *Task force on socioeconomic status (SES).* Washington, DC: Author.

Backlund, E., Sorlie, P. D., & Johnson, N. J. (1999). A comparison of the relationships of education and income with mortality: The National Longitudinal Mortality Study. *Social Science and Medicine, 49,* 1373–1384.

Beadnell, M. (2000, February). Sydney's homeless to be removed for Olympics. *World Socialist Web Site.* Retrieved September 5, 2009, from http://www.wsws.org/articles/2000/feb2000/olymp-f03.shtml.

Beck, E. L., Whitley, D. M., & Wolk, J. L. (1999). Legislators' perceptions about poverty: Views from the Georgia General Assembly. *Journal of Sociology and Social Welfare, 26*(2), 87–104.

Bell, M. P. (2007). *Diversity in organizations.* Mason, OH: Thomson South-Western.

Borg, L. (2004, August 3). Less is expected of poor students. *The Providence Journal,* pp. B1, B3.

Brady, E., & Glier, R. (2004, July). To play sports, many U.S. students must pay. *USA Today.* Retrieved February 19, 2006, from www.usatoday.com/sports/preps/2004-07-29-pay-to-play_x.htm.

Brooks, D. (2005, October). Pillars of cultural capital. *New York Times.* Retrieved September 4, 2009, from http://select.nytimes.com/2005/10/06/opinion/06brooks.html?_r=1.

Bullock, H. E. (1995). Class acts: Middle-class responses to the poor. In B. Lott & D. Maluso (Eds.), *The social psychology of interpersonal discrimination* (pp. 118–159). New York: Guilford Press.

Bullock, H. E. (2004). Class diversity in the workplace. In M. S. Stockdale & F. J. Crosby (Eds.), *The psychology and management of workplace diversity* (pp. 226–242). Malden, MA: Blackwell.

Bullock, H. E., Wyche, K. F., & Williams, W. R. (2001). Media images of the poor. *Journal of Social Issues, 57,* 229–246.

Carr, L. (1994). The can't move—must move contradiction. A case study of displacement of the poor and social stress. *Journal of Distress and the Homeless, 3,* 185–201.

Chafel, J. A. (1997). Societal images of poverty: Child and adult beliefs. *Youth & Society, 28,* 432–463.

Chang, G. (2000). *Disposable domestics: Immigrant women workers in the global economy.* Boston, MA: South End Press.

Coakley, J. (2009). *Sports in society: Issues and controversies* (10th ed.). New York: McGraw Hill.

Cogman, T. (2008, December). A new Olympic legacy: Homelessness. *The Navigator Newspaper.* Retrieved September 5, 2009 from http://thenav.ca/2008/12/05/a-new-olympic-legacy-homelessness/.

Collins, C., & Yeskel, F. (2005). *Economic apartheid.* New York: New Press.

Cozzarelli, C., Wilkinson, A. V., & Tagler, M. J. (2001). Attitudes toward the poor and attributions for poverty. *Journal of Social Issues, 57,* 207–228.

Crompton, J. L. (1995). Economic impact analysis of sports facilities and events: Eleven sources of misapplication. *Journal of Sport Management, 9,* 14–35.

Daniels, N. (1978). Merit and meritocracy. *Philosophy and Public Affairs, 3,* 206–223.

Ehrenreich, B., & Hochschild, A. R. (2004). *Global woman: Nannies, maids, and sex workers in the global economy.* New York: Owl Books.

Eitzen, D. S. (1996). Classism in sport: The powerless bear the burden. *Journal of Sport & Social Issues, 20,* 95–105.

Eitzen, D. S., & Sage, G. H. (2009). *Sociology of North American sport* (8th ed.). Boulder, CO: Paradigm Publishers.

Fiske, S. T. (2007). On prejudice and the brain. *Daedalus, 136*(1), 156–159.

Genzale, J. (Ed.). (2003). *Sport Business Journal by the numbers 2003.* Charlotte, NC: Street & Smith's *Sport Business Journal.*

Gibson, H. J. (1998). Active sport tourism: Who participates? *Leisure Studies, 17,* 155–170.

Green, A. (2008, February). Attacks on the homeless rise, with youths mostly to blame. *New York Times.* Retrieved September 3, 2009, from http://www.nytimes.com/2008/02/15/us/15homeless.html?_r=2&ref=us&oref=slogin.

Health care. (2009, September). *White House.* Retrieved September 7, 2009, from http://www.whitehouse.gov/issues/health_care/.

Health disparities: A case for closing the gap (2009, June). *Healthreform.gov.* Retrieved September 7, 2009, from http://www.healthreform.gov/reports/healthdisparities/disparities_final.pdf.

Housing too high for many. (2003, September). *The Providence Journal,* p. A3.

Iacocca, L., & Novack, W. (1984). *Iacocca: An autobiography.* New York: Bantam.

Kennelly, I. (1999). "That single-mother element": How White employers typify Black women. *Gender and Society, 13,* 168–192.

Kluegel, J. R., & Smith, E. R. (1986). *Beliefs about inequality: American's view of what is and what ought to be.* Hawthorne, NJ: Aldine de Gruyer.

Krugman, P. (2007). *The conscience of a liberal.* New York: W. W Norton & Company.

Leondar-Wright, B. (2005). *Class matters.* Gabriola Island, Canada: New Society Publishers.

Liu, W. M. (2002). The social class-related experiences of men: Integrating theory and practice. *Professional Psychology: Research and Practice, 33,* 355–360.

Liu, W. M., Ali, S. R., Soleck, G., Hopps, J., Dunston, K., & Pickett, Jr., T. (2004). Using social class in counseling psychology research. *Journal of Counseling Psychology, 51,* 3–18.

Liu, W. M., Soleck, G., Hopps, J., Dunston, K., & Pickett, Jr., T. (2004). A new framework to understand social class in counseling: The social class worldview and modern classism theory. *Multicultural Counseling and Development, 32,* 95–122.

Lott, B. (2002). Cognitive and behavioral distancing from the poor. *American Psychologist, 57,* 100–110.

Lott, B., & Bullock, H. E. (2007). *Psychology and economic injustice: Personal, professional, and political intersections.* Washington, DC: American Psychological Association.

Maslow, A. H. (1943). A theory of human motivation. *Psychological Review, 50,* 370–396.

McCoy, S. K., & Major, B. (2007). Priming meritocracy and the psychological justification of inequality. *Journal of Experimental Social Psychology, 43,* 341–351.

Millionaires fill U.S. Congress halls (2004, June). Retrieved September 2, 2009, from http://www.commondreams.org/cgi-bin/print.cgi?file=/headlines04/0630-05.htm.

Moon, D. G., & Rolison, G. L. (1998). Communication of classism. In M. L. Hecht (Ed.), *Communicating prejudice* (pp. 122–135). Thousand Oaks, CA: Sage.

Pinderhughes, R. (1996). The impact of race on environmental inequality: An empirical and theoretical discussion. *Sociological Perspectives, 39,* 231–248.

Powell, G. N. (2004). *Managing a diverse workforce: Learning activities* (2nd ed.). Thousand Oaks, CA: Sage.

Ross, C. E., & Wu, C. (1995). The links between education and health. *American Sociological Review, 60,* 719–745.

Rothman, R. A. (2002). *Inequality and stratification: Race, class, and gender* (4th ed.). Upper Saddle River, NJ: Prentice Hall.

Saad, L. (2009, September). Labor unions see sharp slide in U.S. public support: For first time, fewer than half of

Americans favor unions. *Gallup.* Retrieved September 7, 2009, from http://www.gallup.com/poll/122744/Labor-Unions-Sharp-Slide-Public-Support.aspx.

Saez, E. (2009, August). Striking it richer: The evolution of top incomes in the United States (updated with 2007 estimates). Retrieved September 7, 2009, from http://elsa.berkeley.edu/~saez/saez-UStopincomes-2007.pdf.

Scully, M. A., & Blake-Beard, S. (2007). Locating class in organizational diversity work: Class as structure, style, and process. In A. M. Konrad, P. Prasad, & J. K. Pringle (Eds.), *Handbook of workplace diversity* (pp. 431–454). Thousand Oaks, CA: Sage.

Sidanius, J., & Pratto, F. (1999). *Social dominance: An intergroup theory of social hierarchy and oppression.* New York: Cambridge University Press.

Smith, L. (2008). Positioning classism within counseling psychology's social justice agenda. *The Counseling Psychologist, 36,* 895–924.

Urrea, L. A. (2005, October). City of the big gaps. *The New York Times.* Retrieved September 4, 2009, from http://www.nytimes.com/2005/10/02/opinion/02urrea.html.

Watkins, M., (2009, August). A&M athletics reworks budget to pay loan. *The Eagle.* Retrieved August 26, 2009, from http://www.theeagle.com/PrinterFriendly/A-amp-amp-M-athletics-reworks-budget-to-pay-loan.

Weber, M. (1978). *Economy and society: An outline of interpretive sociology.* In G. Roth & C. Wittich (Eds.). Berkeley, CA: University of California Press.

Weinger, S. (2000). Opportunities for career success: Views of poor and middle-class children. *Children and Youth Services Review, 22,* 13–35.

Woods, T. A., Kurtz-Costes, B., & Rowley, S. J. (2005). The development of stereotypes about the rich and poor: Age, race, and family income differences in beliefs. *Journal of Youth and Adolescence, 34,* 437–445.

Zweig, M. (2000). *The working class majority.* Ithaca, NY: Cornell University Press.

PART III

Managing Workplace Diversity

CHAPTER 12

Legal Aspects of Diversity   281

CHAPTER 13

Managing Diverse Organizations   289

CHAPTER 14

Managing Diverse Groups   315

CHAPTER 15

Diversity Training   339

261

12

Legal Aspects of Diversity

LEARNING OBJECTIVES

Sport participation by women has increased dramatically over time, and this trend is particularly true in university athletics. The average number of women's teams sponsored by NCAA universities has increased from two to eight since 1972, and similar trends are present in other contexts. During the same time frame, however, many men's teams were cut, those teams usually falling in the "Olympic sports" category (e.g., swimming, gymnastics, and wrestling). For example, since 1972, 441 universities have stopped sponsoring varsity wrestling programs.

What accounts for these practices? The answer depends largely on who is asked. Some people, such as Donna Lopiano (considered one of the most influential people in sports today) of the Women's Sport Foundation, suggest that the "arms race" in "big-time" college sports is to blame. Lopiano notes that Division II and III universities—schools with the smallest budgets and fewest revenues—generally do not drop men's sports, as might be expected; rather, these sports are most often cut by Division I programs, which have the largest budgets and most lucrative revenue streams of all athletic departments. Title IX and the associated mandates requiring equal participation opportunities are usually pitted as the culprits when such cuts are made. Lopiano contends that monies *are* available to support those sports, but college presidents and athletic directors spend lavishly and foolishly. The following is a list of actual events that occurred at schools claiming not to have the budget to carry Olympic sports any longer:

- A university spent $300,000 on lights for a football practice field, but the lights were never used. The coach claimed they were needed for recruiting purposes.

- A football team spent the night in a hotel the night prior to a *home* game so the coaches could monitor the players' behaviors. In addition to the 50 rented rooms and meals, the team also rented a movie theater for entertainment purposes.

After studying this chapter, you should be able to:

- Discuss the major equal employment opportunity laws and their influence on workplace diversity.

- Describe the steps people can take if they face discrimination in the workplace and the defenses employers have against such charges.

- Discuss the basic tenets of Title IX and the law's impact on sport and physical activity.

■ After a football season in which the team won seven games, the head coach treated the entire coaching staff, including the coaches' wives, to a trip to the Bahamas.

Citing these and other examples, Lopiano contends that fiscal irresponsibility is to blame for the cuts to men's Olympic sports, not Title IX mandates. Her position is supported by Walter Byers, the former head of the NCAA.

Not all people, however, agree with Lopiano and Byers. For example, columnist George F. Will referred to Title IX as a "train wreck" because of what is perceived to be discrimination against men and men's teams. Researchers have statistically demonstrated that men's access to athletics realized a net decrease after the implementation of Title IX, leading to the conclusion that "men have been disenfranchised—we contend, from a disregard of demand." Sport economists Howard and Crompton argue that Title IX caused inordinate spending increases by university athletic departments. The spending increases are viewed as problematic because "women's sports at most institutions currently contribute no more than 5 to 10 percent of the total revenues generated by average collegiate athletic programs." Thus, there continues to be two sides to the Title IX debate—a debate that has been hotly contested and undoubtedly will continue for years to come.

Information adapted from: ■ Byers, W. (1995). *Unsportsmanlike conduct: Exploiting college athletes.* Ann Arbor, MI: The University of Michigan Press ■ Howard, D. R., & Crompton, J. L. (2004). *Financing sport* (2nd ed.). Morgantown, WV: Fitness Information Technology ■ Lopiano, D. (2001, May). The real culprit in the cutting of men's Olympic sports. *Women's Sports Foundation.* Retrieved January 3, 2006, from www.womenssportsfoundation.org/cgi-bin/iowa/issues/opin/article.html?record=76 ■ McBride, D. K., Worcester, L. L., & Tennyson, S. L. (1999). Women's athletics and the elimination of men's sports programs: A reevaluation. *Cato Journal, 19,* 323–330 ■ Will, G. F. (2002, May 27). A train wreck called Title IX. *Newsweek, 139,* 82.

DIVERSITY CHALLENGE   REFLECTION

1. What are some of the arguments for and against the position that cuts to men's sports can be attributed to fiscal irresponsibility by university athletic departments? Which side is more compelling? Why?

2. What are some of the arguments for and against the position that cuts to men's sports can be attributed to discrimination resulting from Title IX mandates? Which side is more compelling? Why?

 s the Diversity Challenge illustrates, sport managers and administrators may be confronted with various legal issues. Local, state, and federal laws impact organizations' employment and human resource decisions. The way employees are treated, the compensation they receive, and how employees are hired and fired are governed by various legal mandates. Within U.S. athletic departments, the sports that are offered, the scholarships that are allocated, and the distribution of resources must comply with federal mandates concerning gender equity. The degree to which an organization complies with these laws can have a meaningful impact on the organization's overall effectiveness (Wright, Ferris, Hiller, & Kroll, 1995).

This chapter provides an overview of several legal issues related to diversity in sport organizations. After discussing the evolution of employment discrimination law, I then outline how the equal employment opportunity laws influence hiring and other personnel decisions. Employment discrimination claims are addressed in the third section. In the last section, I provide an overview of Title IX—a law that substantially influences virtually all aspects of American sport today.

Evolution of Employment Discrimination Law

Though many might believe that diversity-related legislation is a recent phenomenon, it is not. For example, the 5th Amendment to the U.S. Constitution (ratified in 1791) gave *all* persons the right to due process. The 13th Amendment, which was ratified in 1865, outlawed slavery, and the courts have ruled that it prohibits racial discrimination. The 14th Amendment (ratified in 1868) prohibits states from making or enforcing laws that abridge the privileges and immunities of any U.S. citizen. This amendment prevents states from denying citizens due process and equal protection. Thus, as Dessler (2003) notes, there are over 200 years of legislation outlawing various forms of discrimination.

In this section, I discuss the evolution of employment discrimination law. In doing so, I draw partly from Dessler (2003), who outlined how various court cases have influenced the way equal employment laws are applied.

Title VII of the Civil Rights Act of 1964

Title VII of the Civil Rights Act of 1964, later amended by the Civil Rights Act of 1991, protects individuals against employment discrimination on the basis of race, color, religion, sex, or national origin. It applies to employers who are involved in interstate commerce with 15 or more employees, including federal, state, and local government; educational institutions; labor unions; and players associations. Title VII and the 1991 amendments are discussed in more detail later in this chapter.

Section 703 of Title VII states that it is unlawful employment practice for an employer: (1) to fail or refuse to hire or to discharge any individual, or otherwise to discriminate against any individual with respect to his compensation, terms, conditions, or privileges of employment, because of such individual's race, color, religion, sex, or national origin; or (2) to limit, segregate, or classify his employees or applicants for employment in any way which would deprive or tend to deprive any individual of employment opportunities or otherwise adversely affect his status as an employee, because of such individual's race, color, religion, sex, or national origin.

Griggs v. Duke Power Co.

The earliest landmark court case was *Griggs v. Duke Power Co.*, 401 U.S. 424 (1971). Duke Power Company required all employees to have a high school diploma. Lawyers for Willie Griggs argued that this policy was discriminatory because (a) possessing such a degree was not necessary to perform the required duties at the power plant and (b) the requirement's effect discriminated against African Americans because they were more often denied employment than Whites. Writing the decision for a unanimous Supreme Court, Chief Justice Warren Burger provided three guidelines affecting equal employment opportunities:

1. **Discrimination need not be intentional.** The power plant was not accused of intentionally discriminating against African Americans; rather, the policies unintentionally discriminated. Thus, employees need only show that discrimination occurred—not that it was deliberate.

2. **Employment practices must be job-related.** When certain employment practices have an adverse effect on members of a protected class, then the employer must show that the policy is directly related to how well people can perform the job. In *Griggs,* having a high school diploma did not influence how well people worked at the power plant.

3. **The burden of proof is on the employer.** It is up to the employer to show that a certain policy or test is job-related.

Albemarle Paper Co. v. Moody

Another case that had a meaningful impact on equal employment laws is *Albemarle Paper Co. v. Moody,* 422 U.S. 405 (1975). In its ruling, the Court specified the steps employers should take to use screening tools: a company must carefully analyze and document the specific job duties and responsibilities. The performance standards used to evaluate people currently on the job should be clear and unambiguous so the employer can identify who is the most qualified.

Price Waterhouse v. Hopkins

For over three decades, as seen in the above cases, the courts supported protected persons in employment cases; however, in 1989 two Supreme Court decisions changed this practice (Dessler, 2003). In *Price Waterhouse v. Hopkins,* 490 U.S. 228 (1989), the plaintiff (a woman) sued her employer for being passed over for promotion. She showed that her sex was a contributing factor in the decision, while the firm demonstrated that her "abrasiveness" was a factor as well. The Court, in finding for the employer, ruled that although sex was a factor, she would not have been promoted anyway because of her abrasiveness.

Wards Cove Packing Co. v. Atonio

The second influential decision came in *Wards Cove Packing Co. v. Atonio,* 490 U.S. 642 (1989). In this case, the company was sued because racial minorities were overrepresented in lower-level positions while Whites were overrepresented in upper-management positions and received better housing. Ever since the *Griggs* decision, the employee only had to demonstrate statistic evidence of discrimination, and then the burden of proof shifted to the company. The *Wards Cove* court ruled that the employee had to demonstrate statistical evidence of discrimination *and* prove that the underrepresentation was the result of a policy or practice by the employer. This ruling substantially shifted the burden of proof in employment discrimination cases and placed the expense and onus of proving the case on the employee.

Civil Rights Act of 1991

The *Wards Cove* and *Price Waterhouse* rulings limited the protection that minority group members had under Title VII and prompted Congress to pass new legislation: the Civil Rights Act of 1991 (Dessler, 2003). This Act had the following major provisions:

- **Burden of proof.** The Act shifted the burden of proof back to the employer —a company must show that a test or policy is a business necessity.
- **Money damages.** The Act allows those persons who have been intentionally discriminated against to sue for both compensatory and punitive damages. To recover punitive damages, the employee must show that the employer acted with malice or reckless disregard for the rights of the aggrieved employee.
- **Mixed motives.** Recall in the *Price Waterhouse* case, the court ruled that although sex discrimination was a contributing factor, the plaintiff would have been passed over for promotion in any event because of her abrasive behavior. The Civil Rights Act of 1991 overturned this ruling by making it unlawful for discrimination to have any bearing on employment decisions. That is, the employee's sex cannot impact any part of the decision.
- **Normed tests.** The Act also forbids adjusting test scores to equalize groups, a practice known as within-group norming (Ployhart, Schneider, & Schmitt, 2006). Prior to the Act, some employers hired a minority at one test score (e.g., 80) and a White applicant at another test score (e.g., 90), thereby holding persons from different racial groups to different standards. The Civil Rights Act of 1991 makes this practice unlawful.

The Civil Rights Act of 1991 returned employment discrimination laws to where they were prior to *Wards Cove,* at least with respect to the protections employees have.

Equal Employment Opportunity Legislation

Unfortunately, people still face discrimination today. As discussed in previous chapters, there are substantial differences among various social groups in (a) hiring decisions, (b) compensation, (c) opportunities for training and advancement, and (d) the overall incidence of discrimination in the workplace. Although such differences exist, they are still illegal under most circumstances. In the following sections, I discuss the major equal employment laws as they relate to the various diversity forms. Unless otherwise indicated, the information was gathered from the Equal Employment Opportunity Commission (EEOC) website, www.eeoc.gov.

Title VII of the 1964 Civil Rights Act is the primary law prohibiting employment discrimination on the basis of race or color, national origin, sex, or religion. This law applies to (a) all organizations with at least 15 employees, including state and local governments, (b) labor unions, (c) employment agencies, and (d) the federal government.

Race

Title VII protects people from discrimination based on their race or skin color in hiring and firing decisions, promotions, compensation, and training opportunities. This law also prohibits people from making employment decisions based on the stereotypes associated with people from a particular race—assumptions about people's work ethic, personal traits, or their overall abilities. The law also forbids employers from making employment decisions based on a spouse's race, membership in or affiliation with race- or ethnic-based organizations (e.g., the Black Coaches and Administrators), or attendance at schools or places of worship that might be associated with a particular racial group (e.g., having attended a Historically Black College or University, such as Grambling State University).

Title VII prohibitions also include the following:

- **Race-related characteristics and conditions.** Discrimination based on a characteristic often associated with a particular race (e.g., specific hair texture, skin color) is unlawful. Organizations cannot make employment decisions based on conditions that predominantly affect members of one race more than they do members of other races unless it can be conclusively demonstrated that such practices are job-related and are a business necessity. For example, a fitness club that has a policy of not hiring people with sickle cell anemia discriminates against African Americans because that condition is predominantly found among members of that race and is not job related.

- **Harassment.** Harassment takes many forms, including racial slurs, racial jokes, comments that could be deemed offensive, and other verbal or physical contact that is based on one's race.

- **Segregation or classification of employees.** An organization may not physically isolate members of a racial minority group from other employees or from customers. This prohibition also relates to the assignments people receive. It is unlawful, for example, to assign Hispanics to a mostly Hispanic division or geographic region. Finally, it is also illegal to group people from a protected class into certain positions. Suppose an athletic department always assigns African American employees to life skills coordinator or academic advisor positions, as opposed to positions dealing with development or finances, based on the assumption that people in those positions have the most contact with the athletes, many of whom are also African American. Classifying employees in this manner is unlawful. Based on NCAA data (DeHass, 2007), this actually does occur frequently.

- **Preemployment inquiries.** With a few exceptions, it is always unlawful to ask job applicants what their race is. Employers that use affirmative action in the hiring process or track applicant flow may ask for information on race. Under these circumstances, it is best to use a separate form to keep the information separate from the application. This ensures that the information will not be used in the remainder of the selection process.

According to the EEOC, 33,579 complaints of racial discrimination were reported in 2009. In that same year, the Commission recovered $82.4 million in damages for the charging parties and other aggrieved persons. This figure does not include the additional monies obtained through litigation. In addition to race discrimination, color discrimination charges are prevalent. For information related to national origin discrimination, see Exhibit 12.1.

National origin discrimination.   *exhibit* **12.1**

A topic related to racial discrimination is national origin discrimination. Persons of different ancestries have historically added value to the United States. As EEOC Chairperson Carli M. Dominguez notes, "Immigrants have long been an asset to the American workforce. This is more true than ever in today's increasingly global economy." As with racial discrimination, Title VII prohibits discrimination on the basis of national origin. Treating people differently because they come from a different country or region, have a different accent, or are believed to have a different ethnic background is forbidden. The law prohibits hiring, firing, or promoting people on the basis of national origin. Ethnic slurs and jokes about a person's homeland are prohibited because they can create a hostile work environment. Employers are also barred from making employment decisions based on one's accent or English proficiency, unless they substantially influence the manner in which people perform in their job. Incidents of national origin discrimination are widespread. In 2004, the EEOC fielded 8,361 complaints, and the people who brought these claims recovered over $22 million.

Information gathered from EEOC website (www.eeoc.gov).

Sex

Title VII prohibits discrimination based on one's sex. It is unlawful to make employment decisions related to hiring, firing, compensation, the availability or type of training, or any other term, condition, or privilege of employment based on an employee's sex. Employment decisions that are based on gender stereotypes concerning traits, abilities, or performance are also forbidden. This law prohibits employers from intentionally or unintentionally creating policies that disproportionately exclude people on the basis of sex and that are not related to the job.

Title VII prohibitions also include the following:

■ **Sexual harassment.** The term *sexual harassment* covers a variety of behaviors, including requesting sexual favors and creating a hostile work environment. A hostile work environment exists "when an employee is subjected to repeated unwelcome behaviors that do not constitute sexual bribery but are sufficiently severe and pervasive that they create a work environment so hostile that it substantially interferes with the harassed employee's ability to perform his or her job" (Sharp, Moorman, & Claussen, 2010, p. 137). People of either sex can be sexually harassed. This prohibition also covers same-sex harassment. This concept is discussed in greater detail in the box on the following page.

■ **Pregnancy-based discrimination.** Title VII was amended by the Pregnancy Discrimination Act. Pregnancy-related protections include hiring, pregnancy and maternity leave, health insurance, and fringe benefits. Exhibit 12.2 (page 271) provides an overview of these protections.

Another issue related to sex discrimination is inequality of compensation for women and men. The Equal Pay Act of 1963 requires that women and men in the same organization receive equal pay for equal work. The jobs do not have to be identical; rather, the jobs have to be substantially equal. For example, if a kinesiology department hires two professors, a woman and a man, who have the same

SEXUAL HARASSMENT IN THE WORKPLACE

According to the EEOC, sexual harassment is a form of sex discrimination that violates Title VII. This type of discrimination can take several forms: unwanted sexual advances, solicitation of sexual favors, and other forms of sexual conduct, verbal and physical, that implicitly or explicitly influence one's continued employment, negatively influence performance, or create a hostile, intimidating workplace environment. The harassers can be either men or women, and they do not have to harass members of the opposite sex. In 2004, for example, over 15% of all charges of sexual harassment were made by men. The harassment may be inflicted by peers, subordinates, customers, or other nonemployees. Sexual harassment victims are not always the particular person who is being harassed; a victim may be someone who is otherwise negatively affected by the direct harassment of others.

Fitzgerald and her colleagues developed an instrument designed to measure the incidence of sexual harassment in the workplace (Gelfand, Fitzgerald, & Drasgow, 1995; Fitzgerald et al., 1988). They identified three behavioral dimensions: (a) gender harassment, which consists of those behaviors that connote a negative or hostile view toward women but are not necessarily aimed at seeking sexual cooperation; (b) unwanted sexual attention, which is conduct that is explicitly sexual in nature such as requesting dates or discussing one's sex life; and (c) sexual coercion, which consists of demands for sexual favors backed by either a threat or a promise of future rewards.

The effects of being harassed can be detrimental to one's career. Research shows that women who are harassed report decreased morale on the job, are absent more frequently, and generally have negative experiences in the workplace. Women may leave their job after experiencing harassment—they resign, are transferred to another work environment, or are even fired. There are also psychological costs associated with harassment. Clinical studies show that women who have been harassed have greater levels of fear, anxiety, and depression than those who have not been harassed (see Marshall, 2005, for a review).

Sexual harassment is seen in all work contexts, including sport. United States Olympics coach Tim Nardiello was suspended from his skeleton team coaching position because of sexual harassment charges ("Accused," 2006). Jean Brooks, who was the women's basketball coach and a part-time instructor at the Southern University at New Orleans, recovered over $275,000 in damages for the years of sexual harassment to which she was subjected (Matisik, 2005).

Because of the frequency of sexual harassment in sport, many professional organizations adopted official statements and positions against that form of discrimination. For example, the National Association for Sport and Physical Education issued a statement in 2000 titled "Sexual harassment in athletic settings," outlining the issues related to sexual harassment; examples of the discrimination; and the steps that coaches, players, and administrators can take to confront it. Other entities such as WomenSport International developed similar statements.

rank, roughly the same experience, and perform the same duties, both professors must be paid the same salary even though they may teach different courses.

Five factors are applied to determine violations of the Equal Pay Act:

1. **Skill.** The pay may differ between women and men if the two people have dissimilar job-related skills. For example, a coach with 500 career wins has more skill than a coach with only 42 career wins, because the number of games won is a job-related skill. Two ticket-clerk jobs at a professional sport franchise are considered equal even if one of the clerks has a master's degree, because the advanced degree is not required for the job.

2. **Effort.** Compensation can vary if there are differences in the physical or mental efforts needed to complete a certain task or hold a particular job. For example, an employee at a fitness club who is charged with moving the

| Pregnancy-based discrimination in the U.S. population. | *exhibit* **12.2** |

The Pregnancy Discrimination Act, an amendment to Title VII, applies to all organizations with at least 15 employees, including state and local governments, employment agencies, labor unions, and the federal government. In general terms, this Act requires that women who are pregnant or who are affected by related conditions be treated the same as their colleagues who have comparable abilities or limitations. Pregnancy-related protections include:

- **Hiring.** Organizations cannot refuse to hire a woman solely because she is pregnant, because she has a pregnancy-related condition, or because of any prejudices that her coworkers, clients, or customers might have. For example, a pregnant woman who applies for a position with an athletic shoe company may not be denied employment merely because the manager believes that the company's clients will not respond well to a pregnant salesperson.

- **Pregnancy and maternity leave.** If a woman is unable to perform her job because of her pregnancy, the employer must treat that condition as any other temporary disability. For example, if employees with temporary disabilities are able to modify the way they accomplish their tasks, the pregnant woman must be permitted to modify her tasks. In addition, employers must hold open a job for a woman who is absent because of her pregnancy the same length of time the employer would for a person who is sick or on disability leave.

- **Health insurance.** If an employer provides medical insurance, then pregnancy must be covered. The charges for pregnancy-related expenses must be at the same rate as other illnesses. Employers must provide the same health benefits for spouses of male employees as they do for spouses of female employees.

- **Fringe benefits.** The same pregnancy-related benefits provided to married women must be available to single women. If an employer provides benefits for people who are on leave, the benefits must also be given to women on leave for pregnancy-related conditions. Finally, women on pregnancy leave must be treated the same as people on other types of leave when it comes to issues such as seniority, vacation calculation, pay increases, and temporary disability benefits.

In 2009, the EEOC received 6,196 complaints of pregnancy-based discrimination. In that same year, the Commission recovered $16.8 million for the people who brought the claims (this figure does not include money recovered through litigation).

Information gathered from EEOC (www.eeoc.gov).

weight machines around the facility exerts considerably more physical effort than the employee who checks the membership status of patrons when they enter the facility. Thus, the former employee may be paid more than the latter, regardless of the employee's sex.

3. **Responsibility.** People who hold more meaningful responsibilities may be paid more than their counterparts. A regional salesperson who also coordinates the efforts and responsibilities of other salespeople earns a greater salary because of the extra responsibilities. It should be noted, however, that the increased responsibilities must be meaningful.

4. **Working conditions.** Two factors are considered with respect to working conditions: the physical surroundings and hazards. People with more challenging or difficult work conditions may be paid more than others.

5. **Establishment (place of employment).** The Equal Pay Act applies only to differences in compensation among employees of the same organization.

Based on the number of complaints filed with the EEOC (28,028 in 2009), it appears that incidents of sex discrimination are rather common. Companies that discriminate based on sex receive severe financial punishments. In 2009 alone, over $121.5 million in damages were collected for persons who made complaints (this figure does not include damages recovered through litigation).

Religion

Discrimination on the basis of religion is also prohibited by Title VII. Under Title VII:

- Employers cannot treat people more or less favorably because of their religious affiliation.

- Employees cannot be forced to participate in religious ceremonies or prayers as a condition of employment. As discussed in Chapter 9, this issue often arises in the context of team prayers.

- Employers must accommodate their employees' sincerely held religious beliefs unless doing so would cause undue hardship to the employer. Reasonable accommodations include flexible work hours and the ability to change working assignments with other employees. Unreasonable accommodations are those that impose hardships on other employees, jeopardize workplace safety, or decrease efficiency.

- Employers cannot restrict an employee's religious expression any more than other forms of expression that might have a comparable effect. For example, an employer may not restrict personal, silent prayers when they do not negatively impact performance.

- Employers must take all reasonable steps to prevent religious harassment in the workplace.

Charges of religious discrimination are not as prevalent as other forms. In 2004, the EEOC received 3,386 complaints. This is only a fraction of the racial (10 percent), sex (12 percent), age (15 percent), or disability (16 percent) claims. In 2009, the EEOC recovered $7.6 million in damages for those claiming religious discrimination.

Age

People over age 40 are protected from discrimination by the Age Discrimination in Employment Act of 1967 (ADEA). This law protects both current employees and job applicants. Employers cannot discriminate against people because of their age with respect to any aspect of employment, including hiring, firing, promotion, compensation, benefits, and the quality of job assignments. It also protects people from retaliation if they do file a complaint. The ADEA applies to all organizations with at least 20 employees, including state and local governments, employment agencies, labor unions, and the federal government. Protections under the law also include the following:

- **Apprenticeship programs.** Under most circumstances, it is unlawful for apprenticeship programs to set age limits.
- **Job notices and advertisements.** When advertising for a position, it is unlawful to include age preferences or limitations. The only exception to this policy is when age is a bona fide occupational qualification.
- **Preemployment inquiries.** Although it is *not* unlawful to ask prospective employees for their age or date of birth, the EEOC has indicated that the requests will be closely scrutinized to ensure that they are made for lawful purposes.
- **Benefits.** Some older employees may need more medical care than their younger counterparts. Because this costs money, it may serve as a disincentive to hire older employees or provide them with benefits—both of which are unlawful. The Older Workers Benefit Protection Act of 1990 amended the ADEA to guarantee these rights.
- **Waivers of ADEA rights.** Some organizations offer special early retirement packages to their older employees for a variety of cost-saving and human resource reasons. The ADEA and the Older Workers Benefit Protection Act of 1990 allow for early retirement if the employee willingly chooses to waive his rights. A valid waiver must
  - be written and understandable by all parties;
  - explicitly refer to ADEA rights and claims;
  - not surrender future rights or claims;
  - be in exchange for something that is valuable (e.g., a retirement package worth more than a standard retirement);
  - recommend that the employee seek legal advice before signing; and
  - provide the employee with at least three weeks to consider the agreement and one week to revoke the agreement, even after the document is signed.

Though not as commonplace as sex or racial discrimination, age discrimination is still prevalent in the workplace. In 2009, the EEOC received 22,778 claims of age discrimination. Not including other money awards from litigation, the EEOC recovered $72.1 million from organizations that were found to discriminate on the basis of age.

Ability

The Americans with Disabilities Act of 1990 (ADA) prohibits private organizations; local, state, and federal government entities; employment agencies; and labor unions from discriminating against persons with disabilities (either mental or physical). As outlined in Chapter 7, people are considered to have a disability when they possess an impairment (whether physical or mental) that significantly restricts one or more major life activities. A major life activity, as defined in the ADA, is an activity that is fundamental to human life—"caring for oneself, performing manual tasks, walking, seeing, hearing, speaking, breathing, learning, and working" (ADA, 1985). Within the sport as well as other business contexts, a qualified person with a disability is one who can perform the basic elements of the job with reasonable accommodations.

Reasonable accommodations are those that the employer can make without undue hardship and may include restructuring the nature of the job (e.g., modifying the work schedule), making existing facilities readily accessible by persons with a disability, or modifying equipment.

Employers are not required to lower the job standards. If a person with a disability cannot perform the basic job functions with reasonable accommodations, then the person need not be hired. The employer is also not required to provide employees with items such as glasses or hearing aids.

The ADA covers medical examinations and inquiries as well as drug and alcohol abuse. Employers cannot ask job applicants if they have preexisting medical conditions, but they can ask if the applicants are able to perform the basic duties related to the job. Medical examinations are permissible when they are required of *all* job applicants. The examinations must be job related and consistent with the employer's overall business needs. With respect to drugs and alcohol, the ADA does not apply to people who take illegal drugs. Mandatory drug testing is legal, and employers can hold substance abusers to the same performance standards as other employees.

In 2009, the EEOC received 21,451 claims of disability discrimination, recovering over $67.8 million in damages. For sport industry examples, see the Diversity in the Field boxes.

Obesity

As of 2010, there are no laws in place that specifically address the issue of obesity discrimination. This does not mean, however, that people have not successfully sued on the basis of such differential treatment. These suits are usually brought under the Rehabilitation Act of 1973, which prohibits discrimination on the basis of disability alone (Bell, McLaughlin, & Sequeira, 2004). In *Cook v. Rhode Island*, 10 F.3d 17 (1st Cir. 1993), Cook was denied employment at a state facility because it was believed her obesity would limit her job performance even though Cook had performed at high levels in her previous job. The employer also believed that Cook would miss more time from work and that the state would face more compensation claims because of her condition. The court, in finding in Cook's favor, ruled that obesity was a disability because it (obesity) resulted from a metabolic dysfunction.

Because most suits similar to Cook's are not successful, various groups advocate the adoption of laws and ordinances prohibiting weight discrimination (Bell et al., 2004). Local ordinances in San Francisco and Santa Cruz, California, and the District of Columbia prohibit discrimination

---

DIVERSITY *in the field*

ADA Compliance in Fitness Organizations. A 2003 report in the periodical *Club Industry* (Cardinal, 2003) suggested that fitness clubs are not doing all they should to comply with ADA guidelines. Investigations of 84 facilities in two demographic regions (Kansas City, Missouri, and Western Oregon) found that *not a single facility* was ADA compliant! Within the clubs, the poorest compliance involved accessibility to and around the exercise equipment, access to the customer service desk, and accommodations in restrooms and locker rooms. Facility and telephone access received the highest marks. According to Marc D. Spaziani, many of the problems are easily addressed—such as reducing the thickness of the rubber mats so they can be accessed by persons in wheelchairs. Other problems, though, are more perplexing. "Many of the problems related more to a lack of space," Spaziani noted. "A club will add new equipment or cardio machines and cram them into existing space—and suddenly there's no room to maneuver anymore." Despite these issues, there are some fitness clubs that are very "disability friendly." Crosstrainers Fitness Forum, which is located in Clinton Township, Mich., boasts full access for persons with disabilities. These efforts have not gone unrecognized, and 10 percent of all members are persons with disabilities. Thus, it is possible for the fitness industry to excel in the area of ADA compliance.

on the basis of weight. As noted in the Diversity Challenge in Chapter 8, these laws and ordinances have helped people such as Jennifer Portnick fight discrimination and overcome the barriers they encounter because of their weight.

Sexual Orientation

As of 2010, no federal laws prohibited sexual-orientation discrimination. According to the U.S. Office of Personnel Management (www.opm.gov), Executive Order 13087, issued by President Clinton on May 28, 1998, explicitly forbids sexual-orientation discrimination in Executive Branch civilian employment.

According to the Human Rights Campaign (www.hrc.org), as of 2010, only 20 percent of states provided protection against sexual-orientation discrimination. Several of the states provided protection based on sexual orientation and gender identity (see Exhibit 12.3 for an overview). Some major cities, such as Atlanta, have local ordinances barring such discrimination. Many of the larger U.S. firms also have such policies, including IBM and the Marriott Corporation (Hayes-Thomas, 2004).

DIVERSITY *in the field*

Casey Martin and the PGA. Casey Martin is a person with a severe circulatory disorder in his legs, prohibiting him from walking long distances without stopping to rest. He is also a golfer who is good enough to compete at the highest levels. Because of his condition, he needs to ride in a golf cart during play. This became an issue when Martin tried to qualify for the Professional Golf Association (PGA) Tour, as Tour rules prohibit participants from riding in carts. Martin sued the PGA Tour under the ADA. In 2001, the Supreme Court ruled in favor of Martin (*PGA Tour, Inc. v. Martin,* 532 U.S. 661), saying that allowing Martin to ride a cart during an event would not fundamentally alter the nature of the game (Sharp, Moorman, & Claussen, 2010).

exhibit **12.3** — Laws addressing discrimination based on sexual orientation and gender identity.

STATE/DISTRICT	ADDRESSES SEXUAL ORIENTATION	ADDRESSES GENDER IDENTITY
Alabama		
Alaska		
Arizona		
Arkansas		
California	X	X
Colorado	X	X
Connecticut	X	X
Washington, DC	X	X
Delaware	X	
Florida		X
Georgia		
Hawaii	X	X
Idaho		
Illinois	X	X

(continued)

exhibit **12.3** Continued.

STATE/DISTRICT	ADDRESSES SEXUAL ORIENTATION	ADDRESSES GENDER IDENTITY
Indiana		
Iowa	X	X
Kansas		
Kentucky		
Louisiana		
Maine	X	X
Maryland	X	
Massachusetts	X	X
Michigan		
Minnesota	X	X
Mississippi		
Missouri		
Montana		
Nebraska		
Nevada	X	
New Hampshire	X	
New Jersey	X	X
New Mexico	X	X
New York	X	X
North Carolina		
North Dakota		
Ohio		
Oklahoma		
Oregon	X	X
Pennsylvania		
Rhode Island	X	X
South Carolina		
South Dakota		
Tennessee		
Texas		
Utah		
Vermont	X	X
Virginia		
Washington	X	X
West Virginia		
Wisconsin	X	
Wyoming		

Data from Human Rights Commission (www.hrc.org).

Section Summary

For most forms of diversity, federal laws protect people against discrimination. In general, employers cannot use demographic characteristics, ethnic background, or religious preferences in employment decisions. The two notable exceptions are weight and sexual orientation.

Employment Discrimination Claims

n this section, I highlight the steps involved when charges of discrimination do arise. This issue is addressed from both the employee and employer perspectives.

Employee Perspective

Discrimination in the employment context can take two forms: disparate treatment and disparate impact. *Disparate treatment* occurs when an employer intentionally discriminates against persons from various groups (e.g., women, racial minorities). As noted in the *Griggs* case, however, not all forms of discrimination are intentional. *Disparate impact* occurs when some neutral company policy results in discrimination. For example, some employment policies or tests negatively impact one group relative to another even though that is not the employer's intent.

Employees must establish a prima facie case (i.e., plaintiff's evidence is sufficient to prevail unless controverted by defendant's evidence) of discrimination by demonstrating that a certain policy had an adverse impact on members of a protected group. For example, if 80 percent of men pass an employment test, but only 10 percent of women pass the same test, then this test has an adverse impact on women, who are a protected group. After the prima facie case is established, the burden of proof then shifts to the employer to demonstrate the legality and validity of its actions.

What steps, then, can employees take to show disparate impact? Although a variety of methods are available (see Bobko & Roth, 2004), the EEOC applies the "four-fifths rule." As Mathis and Jackson (2006) explain, "if the selection rate for a protected group is less than 80 percent (four-fifths) of the selection rate for the majority group or less than 80 percent of the majority group's representation in the relevant labor market, discrimination exists" (p. 116). For example, suppose an athletic sporting goods company has 1,000 job applicants, 800 of whom are White and 200 of whom are African American. If 450 Whites and 80 African Americans are hired from that pool, the "four-fifths rule" is violated.

80/200 = .40
450/800 = .56
.40 / .56 = .71
.71 < .80

The burden then shifts to the employer to show that the selection rate differences are legally justified (discussed next). (See the box on p. 278 for the steps for filing a discrimination complaint with the EEOC.)

FILING A COMPLAINT WITH THE EEOC

According to the EEOC, *any* person who believes her or his employment rights have been violated can file a charge of discrimination.

- The complaint must be filed either by mail or in person at the nearest EEOC Office (see www.eeoc.gov/offices.html for a list of offices nationwide).

- The following information must be provided in the complaint:

  (a) the name, address, and telephone number of the complainant;

  (b) the name, address, and telephone number of the entity charged with discriminating; and

  (c) a brief description of the alleged discrimination including when it occurred.

- All Title VII complaints must be filed within 180 days of the discriminating event.

Employer Perspective

If a prima facie case is established, the burden then shifts to the employer to show that there was no discrimination. There are several defenses available to an employer (Dessler, 2003).

Business necessity

One defense to an allegation of discrimination is to demonstrate that there was an overriding business purpose or necessity for a policy or test, thereby warranting its use. Dessler (2003) notes that proving a business necessity is often difficult. The courts have dismissed the notions that inconvenience, annoyance, or expense to the employer qualify as a business necessity. Those jobs that require minimal training as preemployment standards are usually closely scrutinized by the courts.

Bona fide occupational qualification

Another defense available to employers is that a particular employment practice is a bona fide occupational qualification (BFOQ) for performing the job. Dessler (2003) notes that the BFOQ defense is most often used in cases of intentional discrimination, not in cases of disparate impact. One's age, sex, religion, and national origin may all be considered BFOQs under certain circumstances. For example, age is often a BFOQ for persons involved in transportation (e.g., bus drivers, pilots) or acting. Sex can be a BFOQ for some jobs such as acting, modeling, or locker room attendants. One's religious beliefs might be a BFOQ when it involves jobs with religious-based societies or organizations—the position's tasks must be related to the particular religion. For example, a physical educator's religious preferences might be a determining factor in whether or not she receives a position at a private, religious-based high school, because a physical educator at this school is expected to incorporate religious principles in her or his classes. Finally, there are some cases in which one's national origin might be considered a BFOQ. For example, an employer who is running a Korean Sport Forum might prefer persons of Korean heritage as employees. Title VII prohibits the use of other characteristics (e.g., race) as BFOQs.

Title IX

The previous sections outlined equal employment opportunity laws and how they influence employment decisions. These laws have a substantial impact on the way *all* business in the United States is conducted today. A law that significantly influences sport organizations is Title IX, which states:

No person in the United States shall, on the basis of sex, be excluded from participation in, be denied the benefits of, or be subjected to discrimination under any educational program or activity receiving Federal financial assistance. (Title IX of the Education Amendments of 1972, P.L. 92-318, 20 U.S.C.S § 1681)

Note that the words "sport," "athletics," "physical education," and "recreation" are not included in the law. Nevertheless, this legislation impacts sport perhaps more than any other. In essence, it requires that equal opportunities be provided to women and men participating in activities that receive federal financial assistance. Because almost every high school and institution of higher education in the United States receives some federal financial assistance, either directly or indirectly, the law influences almost all aspects of amateur athletics. In the following sections, I give a brief historical overview of Title IX and then discuss the law's influence on sport today. Unless otherwise noted, the information was gleaned from Carpenter and Acosta's (2005) comprehensive and authoritative text, *Title IX*.

History of Title IX

Title IX was passed in 1972 as part of the Education Amendments. The law provided little direction to administrators about how to provide equal opportunities for men and women in educational settings. Thus, the Office of Civil Rights (OCR) developed regulations that "would breathe an enforceable life into Title IX" (Carpenter & Acosta, 2005, p. 6). Congress approved these regulations in 1975, giving them the force of law. The regulations are used by organizations and the courts to interpret, measure, and enforce Title IX.

Of particular application to athletics are the following regulations:

■ **Section 106.37:** When athletic scholarships are offered, they must be offered to both women and men in proportion to the number of women and men participating in athletics overall.

■ **Section 106.41(a):** No person shall, on the basis of sex, be excluded from, denied the benefits of, or be discriminated against in any form of athletics (e.g., interscholastic, intercollegiate, club, or intramural).

■ **Section 106.41(b):** Separate athletic teams can be formed for women and men. If a school supports a men's team but does not offer a similar sport for women, then women must be allowed to try out for the men's team. The exception to this is contact sports such as rugby, ice hockey, football, and basketball.

■ **Section 106.41(c):** Schools that support athletic teams should provide equal opportunities to both women and men. To do so, the athletic director should consider 10 factors:

1. whether the teams are congruent with the interests and abilities of members of both sexes;
2. the provision of equipment and supplies;
3. the manner in which games and practices are scheduled;
4. travel and per diem;
5. coaching and academic counseling;
6. compensation of the coaches and academic tutors;
7. the provision and quality of locker rooms and facilities (both practice and game);

8. the provision of medical and training staff and their facilities;
9. the provision of housing, dining facilities, and dining services; and
10. overall publicity.

Later policy interpretations identified two additional factors: recruitment and support services. Thus, the financial aid regulations identified in Section 106.37, the 10 regulations in Section 106.42(c), and the two factors identified in the policy interpretations established 13 areas to consider when enforcing Title IX.

Institutions had until 1978 to comply with the law, but few met the deadline (Carpenter & Acosta, 2005). In 1984, a meaningful blow was dealt to Title IX by the Court's decision in *Grove City College v. Bell,* 465 U.S. 555. The U.S. Supreme Court addressed two issues:

1. Does the word "program" refer to the institution as a whole or to individual programs within that entity?
2. Does an institution have to receive direct federal funding in order for it to be subject to Title IX guidelines?

With respect to the first issue, the Court found that only those units receiving federal monies were included in the term "program." Therefore, if an athletic department did not receive federal funds, it was not bound by Title IX regulations. However, with respect to the second issue, the Court ruled that an institution did not have to receive direct federal funds to be subject to the Title IX regulations.

The effects of the *Grove City* decision were severe. Because many (if not most) university athletic departments did not receive federal monies, they were now not subject to Title IX. As a result, many schools immediately cut women's scholarships and selected women's teams to be cut at the end of the academic year. In addition, all complaints that had been filed with the OCR were closed, and Title IX lawsuits were dismissed.

According to Carpenter and Acosta (2005), Congress considered the Supreme Court's interpretation of "program" to be incorrect. To remedy this situation, the Civil Rights Restoration Act of 1987 was passed over President Reagan's veto in 1988. This Act clarified issues surrounding the word "program." According to the Civil Rights Restoration Act, the term "program" refers to the entire institution, not just individual programs within that entity. Most physical education departments and athletic departments do not receive federal funds; however, the universities in which they are housed *do* receive such funds. Thus, every entity within a university now fell under Title IX guidelines.

Two other cases of particular relevance to the history of Title IX are *Franklin v. Gwinnett County Public Schools,* 503 U.S. 60 (1992) and *Jackson v. Birmingham Board of Education,* 544 U.S. 167 (2005). The key issue in *Franklin* was whether or not monetary damages could be awarded to persons who successfully sued under Title IX. In this case, a student who had been sexually harassed filed a Title IX lawsuit, but neither the statute nor the regulations contained any language related to monetary damages. The Supreme Court unanimously ruled that monetary damages could be awarded under Title IX. As a result of this ruling, Title IX enforcement changed dramatically. It is now in the best financial interest of institutions to comply with Title IX mandates. Failing to do so means losing potentially large sums of money—money the institutions could ill afford to relinquish. The *Jackson* case is also relevant. Roderick Jackson, a male coach of a girls' high school basketball team, alleged that the girls on the team were discriminated against. He complained to the board about this discrimination and was subsequently fired. He sued the Board of Education claiming that his termination was in retaliation for complaining about the discrimination. The Supreme Court ruled that Title IX whistle-blowers who were subjected to retaliation for filing a Title IX claim could recover damages.

Much of the Title IX discussion thus far has focused on the athletics context; however, the law impacts all educational activities. For information related to the influence of Title IX on physical education and recreation, see the Diversity in the Field box on the following page.

Title IX Compliance

The 1979 policy interpretations, together with a 2003 letter of clarification, established a three-prong test for evaluating Title IX compliance by universities and colleges (Carpenter & Acosta, 2005). According to this framework, often referred to as *the three-prong test,* a school must select one of the following in order to be compliant with the law:

1. Provide participation opportunities for female and male athletes that are in proportion to their respective enrollments at the university (referred to as substantial proportionality).

[Note that the numbers need not be equal; they need only be in proportion. Consider the following examples using data obtained from the Equity in Athletics website (http://ope.ed.gov/athletics/). In 2009, women represented 45 percent of the athletes at both the University of Utah and Virginia Commonwealth University. During that same year, women constituted 45 percent of the undergraduates at Utah and 57 percent of the undergraduates at Virginia Commonwealth. Using these data, we can conclude that the University of Utah was in compliance with Title IX, while Virginia Commonwealth University was *not*. The two schools had different compliance outcomes even though they provided the same opportunities for female athletes.]

2. Demonstrate a history and continued practice of program expansion for athletes of the underrepresented sex.

[Under this condition, the school need not be compliant at the time of its evaluation; rather, it only has to demonstrate that it has continually strived to be more equitable and provide opportunities for persons of the underrepresented sex to develop their skills and compete in athletic events.]

3. Effectively demonstrate that the programs and opportunities offered are congruent with the interests and abilities of the underrepresented sex (referred to as the accommodation of interest and ability test).

[Critics from both sides have weighed in on this. If women are the underrepresented sex and do not have an interest in playing varsity sports, why should the athletic department spend the time and money to field a team? On the other hand, interest in sports may wane if opportunities are not provided. How can an athletic

DIVERSITY
in the field

THE INFLUENCE OF TITLE IX ON
PHYSICAL EDUCATION AND RECREATION

Physical Education. Within the sport context, Title IX is most often discussed in relation to athletics; however, the law also impacts physical education (Carpenter & Acosta, 2005). According to Title IX, schools may not:

- Treat males and females differently when determining whether they satisfy necessary requirements or conditions prior to receiving physical education services. For example, a teacher may not require girls to pass a skills test if such screening is not also required of boys.

- Provide differing physical education benefits or services to boys and girls. For example, it may be improper to group students in a class by sex, or to hire experienced teachers for boys' classes and novices for the girls' classes.

- Deny students of one sex access to the benefits or services associated with physical education. Weight rooms, for example, were traditionally reserved for boys. This practice is unlawful because it denies girls access to the facilities.

- Subject students to a different set of rules based on their sex. Behavioral issues might fall under this category. It is not uncommon for teachers to punish girls for misbehaving in class but attribute similar behaviors on the part of boys to the notion that "boys will be boys."

- Apply different rules concerning the residence of a student or an applicant. It is a violation of Title IX to enroll an out-of-district male student because he might be an asset to the basketball team and then deny a similar request by a female student.

- Aid or assist discrimination by providing help to an entity that discriminates on the basis of sex. A school may not allow an all-male tennis league to use its facilities, because the league discriminates on the basis of sex by not allowing girls to participate.

- Otherwise limit the students' enjoyment of their rights and privileges as they relate to physical education. For example, if boys are allowed to use a gym after school for "free play" basketball, girls must be given the same opportunity.

Recreation Programs. Title IX impacts those recreational activities that meet the three requirements for Title IX jurisdiction:

1. Sex discrimination occurs.
2. The activity is educational in nature.
3. The entity sponsoring the activity receives federal financial assistance.

The first two of these conditions are usually easily demonstrated because recreation and sport activities are generally considered educational. If the discrimination occurs on a college campus, the third condition is met, because most universities receive federal funding of some form. Outside the school context, however, demonstration of the third condition may be more difficult.

Carpenter and Acosta (2005) discuss several scenarios that, as of 2005, had not been decided by the courts but may provide evidence of federal financial assistance. First, if an entity does not receive federal monies directly, but its member organizations do, is Title IX triggered? Suppose a governing body (e.g., National Intramural-Recreational Sport Association, NIRSA) is a private organization but some of its institutional members receive federal funding. These institutions pay dues to the governing body; thus, some argue that federal monies are, in an indirect fashion, being received by the governing organization. If this is true, then the organization is subject to the Title IX requirements. Second, what if an organization is tax-exempt? Is the federal government supporting the organization by not collecting taxes, thereby activating Title IX? These issues do raise the possibility of bringing Title IX claims against sport organizations that might not otherwise fall under the jurisdiction of the law.

department claim in good faith that women are not interested in participating in sports if few women's sports are offered? If sports are offered, perhaps they would attract women to the campus who might not otherwise have come.]

In its 2003 letter of clarification, the OCR notes that, traditionally, schools have viewed substantial proportionality (i.e., the first prong) as a "safe harbor" for Title IX compliance. That is, they primarily sought to satisfy this requirement to the neglect of the other prongs. This is unnecessary. According to the OCR, each of the three tests is a viable option for Title IX compliance, and no single test is preferred over the others.

Title IX Outcomes

The final section examines three relevant Title IX outcomes: increased participation by girls and women in sport, increased prestige of women's sport, and the effects on women coaches and administrators. For additional information, see the Professional Perspectives box on the following page.

Participation

One of the primary purposes of Title IX is to create equal opportunities for women and men to participate in educational activities, including sport and recreation. By all measures, the law has achieved this goal. Carpenter and Acosta (2005) note, "The often heard phrase 'if you build it, they will come' is true of females and sport opportunities. Indeed, they have come. Each year the participation of females in sport breaks new records" (p. 168).

This growth of female participation in sport is seen in several areas. Carpenter and Acosta (2005) indicate that one of the largest increases has been in the high school context. In 1972, girls represented only 5 percent of all high school athletes. This proportion increased to 32 percent by 1978 (the first year of mandatory compliance) and to 41 percent by 2002. During this time, the number of girls participating in high school sports increased by over 900 percent (from 294,015 to 2,856,358).

Similar increases have been seen at the university level (Carpenter & Acosta, 2005). Results from their longitudinal work show many advances, including the following:

- When Title IX was passed in 1972, the average number of women's teams offered per university was 2.50. By 2004, this figure increased to 8.32.
- From 1998 through 2004, 1,155 new teams for females were added.
- In 1977, less than 3 percent of all schools offered women's soccer. By 2004, this figure increased over 4,000 percent to 88.6 percent of all schools.

These data indicate that more girls and women are participating in sport today than ever before. These trends have also spilled over to other types of sport and recreation. There are many female professional sport leagues, such as the WNBA, today—something that many thought impossible prior to Title IX. Girls and women are also regular participants in such recreational activities as running and weight training. The sport opportunities made available by Title IX are a primary reason for these increases.

PROFESSIONAL
PERSPECTIVES

Title IX. Lori Miller, a former Professor of Sport Administration and Associate Dean in the College of Education at Wichita State University, has written numerous articles and coauthored a book about legal issues in the sports world. Miller suggests that Title IX has "had a tremendous impact" on all aspects of education. In the sport context, Title IX created additional opportunities for girls and women to participate in sport. Similar effects are seen in other contexts. According to Miller, prior to Title IX, only 9 percent of all law degrees were awarded to women. The equal opportunities for men and women resulting from Title IX changed these figures substantially.

Though strides have been made in terms of gender equity as a result of Title IX, Miller contends that there is "still a lot of territory to cover." For example, she notes that only 2 percent of all claims with the EEOC are Title IX–related, meaning that either the agency does not take the claims seriously, or people are not filing charges under this law. When charges are made, many schools use the accommodation-of-interests-and-abilities defense under the three-prong test. Miller notes, however, that this defense is inherently flawed because it does not address the history of inequality between men and women. "What really needs to be addressed is accommodation at lower levels," Miller argues. This means bringing suits against high schools and elementary schools for not providing equal opportunities for girls and women in the sport context. If lawsuits are initiated, they might increase the interest in sport and physical activity among younger girls. As Miller explains, "there needs to be litigation at the lower levels so we can start addressing the needs of the young girls."

Increased prestige

Title IX requires schools to provide equal opportunities for men and women in sports; this means sponsoring teams, hiring coaches and support staff, paying for scholarships, building facilities, and publicizing the teams—all of which take time, effort, and money. With the monetary resources now available to female athletes and their teams, the prestige of women's sport also increased. As noted in Chapter 5, coaches for and players on women's teams are still paid less than men; however, the salaries they do receive are substantially higher than the salaries prior to Title IX. Furthermore, recruiting budgets, scholarship allocations, and monies spent on facilities are all greater than they would be had Title IX never been enacted.

Leadership effects

The increased prestige and attention accorded to female athletes and their teams has, in many respects, been positive, but there have also been problems. One drawback of the increased prestige is the decline of women in leadership positions (Carpenter & Acosta, 2005). Although more women's teams were formed after Title IX was enacted, the coaching vacancies for these teams are usually filled by men. For example, in 1972, about 90 percent of all coaches of women's teams were women. This figure dramatically declined in the first years after Title IX (58 percent in 1978) and has continued to do so over time. In 2010, only 42.6 percent of all coaches of women's teams were women (Acosta & Carpenter, 2010).

A similar trend has occurred with administrators, with more drastic effects (Acosta & Carpenter, 2010). In 1972, 90 percent of the administrators of women's programs were women, a figure that dropped to 20 percent by 1980 and was at 19.3 percent as of 2010. As with coaching, there are more men serving as administrators in women's sports than women.

Recall that the reasons for these declines were discussed in Chapter 5. First, the increased prestige of women's sport made coaching females and their teams a viable option for men; thus, men became more apt to seek positions coaching women's teams than in the past. Second, women are likely to leave coaching at an earlier age than men. This results in fewer women in the field and, consequently, a supply-side shortage (Hasbrook, 1988). Finally, among assistant coaches, men have a greater interest and desire to become a head coach (Cunningham & Sagas,

2002; Cunningham, Sagas, & Ashley, 2003). When positions do become available, men are more likely to apply for the openings than their female counterparts.

The second and third reasons for the underrepresentation of women in leadership positions seem to place the blame on the women. As noted in Chapter 5, there are structural forces in place (e.g., access and treatment discrimination) that affect the selection and careers of female coaches. There are also gender roles and norms that influence ideas about what women "can" and "should" do with their careers, families, and friends. All of these factors interact to influence who seeks leadership positions, who is selected for these roles, and how long they remain in them.

CHAPTER *summary*

This chapter focused on diversity laws as they affect sport organizations. As noted in the Diversity Challenge, these laws have a substantial influence not only on an organization and its practices but also on its employees and customers. Who is hired or fired, who receives training, and the level of compensation they receive are all influenced by employment discrimination laws. Within the sport, recreation, and physical education context, laws govern the opportunities provided to people and the monies and facilities allocated to them. The laws impact virtually every aspect of organizational life. After reading the chapter, you should be able to:

1. **Discuss the major equal employment opportunity laws and their influence on workplace diversity.**

Employment laws protect against discrimination on the basis of race (Title VII of the Civil Rights Act of 1964), color (Title VII), national origin (Title VII), sex (Title VII, Title IX of the Education Amendments, Equal Pay Act of 1963), age (Age Discrimination in Employment Act of 1967, Older Workers Benefit Protection Act of 1990), disability (American with Disabilities Act of 1963), and religion (Title VII). There are no federal laws barring discrimination based on weight or sexual orientation.

2. **Describe the steps people can take if they face discrimination in the workplace and the defenses employers have against such charges.**

A person must file a charge with the EEOC prior to instituting any legal action in the courts. Once a lawsuit is initiated, the employee must establish a prima facie case by demonstrating that organizational policies or behaviors had an adverse impact on members of a protected group. The onus is then on the organization to prove that the adverse impact was based on legitimate reasons. They can do so by proving that the policies or behaviors relate to a business necessity or a bona fide occupational qualification.

3. **Discuss the basic tenets of Title IX and the law's impact on sport and physical activity.**

Title IX requires that educational programs receiving federal funds provide equal opportunities for males and females. Athletic departments must abide by one of three standards to comply with the law. The standards are aimed at providing athletic opportunities and funding for members of the underrepresented sex, which is most often women. The effects have been substantial: The number of females participating in sport has increased, as has the prestige of and funding for these activities. On the negative side, however, the proportion of women in leadership positions has decreased as more men assumed these roles.

QUESTIONS *for discussion*

1. The ADA is the primary legislation protecting persons with disabilities. Think about a health and fitness organization with which you are familiar. In what ways is that organization not ADA compliant? Are there steps the managers can take to become compliant?
2. What are the primary defenses against discrimination available to an organization? In your estimation, is one defense better than the other? Why?
3. What are the basic tenets of Title IX, and what are the steps an athletic department can take to comply with the law?
4. What are the various outcomes of Title IX, both good and bad?

LEARNING *activities*

1. Interview a manager of a sport organization. Ask her about the collective impact of equal employment legislation on her staffing and employment decisions. Based on the interview, do you think that this legislation will be needed in the future? Why or why not?
2. Though federal mandates outlawing weight and sexual orientation discrimination do not exist, various cities and municipalities have adopted their own ordinances. Use the Internet to identify some of these cities and municipalities. Compare the ordinances. Which do you think will prove most effective and why?

READING *resources*

SUPPLEMENTARY READINGS

Carpenter, L. J., & Acosta, R. V. (2005). *Title IX*. Champaign, IL: Human Kinetics. (Most comprehensive text related to Title IX available; examines the law as applied to numerous areas; considers the influence of the law on subsequent outcomes, such as participation and coaching.)

Landry, F. J. (Ed.). (2005). *Employment discrimination litigation: Behavioral, quantitative, and legal perspectives*. San Francisco: Jossey-Bass. (Edited text that provides scenarios from the perspective of both the plaintiff and the defendant; includes questions related to race, sex, disability, and age.)

Sharp, L. A., Moorman, A. M., & Claussen, C. L. (2007). *Sport law: A managerial approach*. Scottsdale, AZ: Holcomb Hathaway. (Approaches legal issues in sport from a managerial perspective; sections on Title IX, sexual harassment, and disabilities.)

WEB RESOURCES

- Department of Justice (www.usdoj.gov/crt/emp/faq.html): answers frequently asked questions related to employment discrimination.

- National Women's Law Center (www.titleix.info/): site devoted to Title IX issues.

- U.S. Equal Employment Opportunity Commission (www.eeoc.gov/): contains guidelines, facts, and figures.

- WomenSport International (www.sportsbiz.bz/womensportinternational/task forces/wsi_position_statement.htm): position statement on sexual harassment and abuse of girls and women in sport.

references

Accused skeleton coach's suspension upheld. (2006, January 10). MSNBC.com. Retrieved March 22, 2006, from www.msnbc.com/id/10658008/print/1/displaymode/1098/.

Acosta, R. V., & Carpenter, L. J. (2010). *Women in intercollegiate sport: A longitudinal study—thirty-three year update—1977–2010.* Unpublished manuscript, Brooklyn College, Brooklyn, NY.

Americans with Disabilities Act, 45 C.F.R. 843(j)(2)(i) (1985).

Bell, M. P., McLaughlin, M. E., & Sequeira, J. M. (2004). Age, disability, and obesity: Similarities, differences, and common threads. In M. S. Stockdale & F. J. Crosby (Eds.), *The psychology and management of workplace diversity* (pp. 191–205). Malden, MA: Blackwell.

Bobko, P., & Roth, P. L. (2004). The four-fifths rule for assessing adverse impact: An arithmetic, intuitive, and logical analysis of the rule and implications for future research and practice. In J. Martocchio (Ed.), *Research in personnel and human resource management* (Vol. 23, pp. 177–198). Oxford, UK: Elsevier.

Cardinal, B. J. (2003). Fitness for all: Is your club ADA compliant? *Club Industry, 19*(5), 31–34.

Carpenter, L. J., & Acosta, R. V. (2005). *Title IX.* Champaign, IL: Human Kinetics.

Cunningham, G. B., & Sagas, M. (2002). The differential effects of human capital for male and female Division I basketball coaches. *Research Quarterly for Exercise and Sport, 73,* 489–495.

Cunningham, G. B., Sagas, M., & Ashley, F. B. (2003). Coaching self-efficacy, desire to head coach, and occupational turnover intent: Gender differences between NCAA assistant coaches of women's teams. *International Journal of Sport Psychology, 34,* 125–137.

DeHass, D. (2007). *2005–06 ethnicity and gender demographics of NCAA member institutions' athletics personnel.* Indianapolis, IN: The National Collegiate Athletic Association.

Dessler, G. (2003). *Human resource management* (9th ed.). Upper Saddle River, NJ: Prentice Hall.

Fitzgerald, L. F., Shullman, S. L., Bailey, N., Richards, M., Swecker, J., Gold, Y., et al. (1988). The incidence of dimensions of sexual harassment in academia and the workplace. *Journal of Vocational Behavior, 32,* 152–175.

Gelfand, M. J., Fitzgerald, L. F., & Drasgow, F. (1995). The structure of sexual harassment: A confirmatory analysis across cultures and settings. *Journal of Vocational Behavior, 47,* 164–177.

Hasbrook, C. A. (1988). Female coaches: Why the declining numbers and percentages? *Journal of Physical Education, Recreation, and Dance, 59*(6), 59–63.

Hayes-Thomas, R. (2004). Why now? The contemporary focus on managing diversity. In M. S. Stockdale & F. J. Crosby (Eds.), *The psychology and management of workplace diversity* (pp. 3–30). Malden, MA: Blackwell.

Marshall, A. M. (2005). *Confronting sexual harassment: The law and politics of everyday life.* Burlington, VT: Ashgate.

Mathis, R. L., & Jackson, J. H. (2006). *Human resource management* (11th ed.). Mason, OH: Southwestern.

Matisik, E. N. (2005, January 21). Men's basketball coach sexually harassed women's basketball coach. *College Hoopsnet.* Retrieved March 22, 2006, from www.collegehoopsnet.com/specials/050121.htm.

NASPE (2000, Fall). Sexual harassment in athletic settings. Naspe@aahperd.org. Retrieved November 7, 2006, from www.aahperd.org/naspe/pdf_files/pos_papers/sex-harr.pdf.

Ployhart, R. E., Schneider, B., & Schmitt, N. (2006). *Staffing organizations: Contemporary practice and theory* (3rd ed.). Mahwah, NJ: Lawrence Erlbaum.

Sharp, L. A., Moorman, A. M., & Claussen, C. L. (2010). *Sport law: A managerial approach* (2nd ed.). Scottsdale, AZ: Holcomb Hathaway.

Wright, P., Ferris, S. P., Hiller, J. S., & Kroll, M. (1995). Competitiveness through management of diversity: Effects on stock price valuation. *Academy of Management Journal, 38,* 272–287.

13

Managing Diverse Organizations

A boriginal, or First Nations, people in Canada are disadvantaged in many ways. Consider the following statistics: the poverty rate is comparable to that in developing nations, 25 percent of all adults are unemployed, the suicide rate among youth is 500 percent greater than non-Aboriginals, and the incidence of alcohol and drug abuse is high. Aboriginal persons also have several barriers to sport and physical activity participation, including:

- a general lack of awareness of sport opportunities,
- economic difficulties,
- insensitivity to Aboriginal culture and traditions,
- a lack of Aboriginal coaches and/or coaches who are cognizant of the Aboriginal culture,
- the substantial distance of many villages from sport venues,
- lack of governmental financial support,
- racism, and
- an inadequate sport infrastructure.

Because of these issues, the Canadian federal government took several steps to improve the quality of life among Aboriginals. Together with economic and social policies, the government is using sport as a way to achieve this goal. Sport is viewed as a tool for economic development and as a mechanism that engages citizens, overcomes social constraints, and contributes to cohesion among people in a community. Sport Canada, the sport governing body in Canada, is on record as being "committed to contributing, through sport, to the health, wellness, cultural identity, and quality of life of Aboriginal Peoples."

Sport Canada actively works with governmental agencies, Aboriginal communities and leaders, and other entities to achieve the following goals:

- *Enhanced participation.* Sport Canada is increasing the participation of Aboriginal peoples in sport at all levels by providing equitable access,

After studying this chapter, you should be able to:

- Discuss the four models for managing diversity in sport organizations.

- Outline the methods managers can use to implement diversity management strategies.

- Provide an overview of the leadership competencies necessary in diverse organizations.

developing programs that meet their unique needs, involving Aboriginal persons in the planning and development of sport, and encouraging youth participation.

■ *Enhanced excellence.* Sport Canada creates an environment that welcomes Aboriginal peoples to national teams and encourages high performance levels by increasing the number of qualified Aboriginal athletes, coaches, and officials by providing access to and support for quality facilities, training, and development.

■ *Enhanced capacity.* Sport Canada seeks to improve the capacity of individuals, groups, and communities in support of Aboriginal sport in Canada by identifying the needs of Aboriginal people, providing facilities, promoting Aboriginal leaders, and maintaining cultural sensitivity.

■ *Enhanced interaction.* Sport Canada increases the levels of communication and interaction among Aboriginal peoples and other sport and governmental entities at the federal, provincial, and local levels.

The Canadian government recognizes that for Canadian sport to be successful, all people must have access to it and be provided an opportunity to achieve excellence. Sport Canada's policies are aimed at driving "the actions necessary to create and maintain an inclusive Canadian sport system that supports Aboriginal participation in sport from playground to podium."

Information adapted from: ■ *Sport Canada's Policy on Aboriginal Peoples' Participation in Sport.* Retrieved March 28, 2006, from www.canadianheritage.gc.ca/progs/sc/pol/aboriginal/2005/1_e.cfm.

DIVERSITY CHALLENGE   **R E F L E C T I O N**

1. In your opinion, how viable is sport as a vehicle for creating social change? Explain.

2. How effective are the goals outlined by Sports Canada? Are there any you feel might be especially effective? Less effective?

3. What are other sport-related strategies that could be implemented to decrease the disparities Aboriginal peoples face?

4. Are you aware of other instances wherein sport has been used as a vehicle for promoting change among members of a social group?

---

s the Diversity Challenge illustrates, organizations or governmental entities will often implement strategic initiatives aimed at diversity issues. Here, Sport Canada's strategies sought to (a) decrease the negative effects of diversity in a particular context by improving the quality of life of a certain group of people and (b) capitalize on the unique cultural attributes that Aboriginal peoples and their sports could bring to the overall fabric of Canadian sport. These strategies are referred to as diversity management.

Recall from Chapter 1 that diversity management involves proactive, strategic actions aimed at capitalizing on the benefits diversity brings to organizations. In its ideal form, diversity management emphasizes the manner in which managers realize the advantages of diversity and minimize its potential disadvantages.

The purpose of this chapter is to provide an overview of strategies that can be used to manage diversity in sport organizations. The focus here is largely macro, and we will consider the top leaders within the organization and the organization as a whole. Chapter 14 deals with more micro issues related to diversity management at the group level. The first section of the present chapter discusses four primary models for managing diversity in sport organizations. The next two sections consider how organizations implement diversity strategies and how managers can ensure the success of their diversity management efforts. The final section discusses the influence of leadership in diverse organizations.

The notion that persons from diverse backgrounds desire diversity management is implicit in the arguments presented in this chapter. However, this notion might not always be true. It is possible that such strategies may be perceived as providing remedial training for racial minorities, women, and so forth. For example, a special program designed to provide racial minorities with leadership opportunities may create the perception they are deficient in that area and thus need additional training. Fitzgerald Hill effectively articulates this point in the accompanying Professional Perspectives box. However, the diversity management initiatives described in this chapter are aimed at capitalizing on the positive effects of diversity and minimizing its potential disadvantages. Capitalizing on the positive effects of diversity entails providing an equitable workplace for all people, irrespective of their surface- or deep-level differences.

PROFESSIONAL PERSPECTIVES

Potential Unintended Effects of Diversity Management Programs. Fitzgerald Hill is the President of Arkansas Baptist College, located in Little Rock. He earned a Ph.D. in Higher Education Leadership from the University of Arkansas in 1997, served as the assistant head football coach at the University of Arkansas from 1998 to 2000, and was the head football coach at San Jose State University from 2000 to 2004.

Hill participated in many conferences and programs while coaching in the NFL (prior to college coaching) and NCAA. Reflecting on those experiences, he suggested that the diversity management programs in place in these sport organizations, as well as others like them, may have unintended effects. These entities often have special programs to provide extra training for minority coaches. According to Hill, these programs, in essence, suggest to African American coaches that they are not qualified, so they need extra training. The same message, however, is not conveyed to White coaches, as no special programs exist for them. "They are saying we are not qualified or that we are inept," Hill explained. "This can be dehumanizing in nature."

As Hill's comments suggest, the diversity programs in the NFL and NCAA may have negative effects on those they are intended to benefit. It is important to remain cognizant of these potential effects when implementing such initiatives.

Diversity Management Strategies

Many examples are presented throughout this book of insensitivity toward others or a general lack of understanding of cultural differences that resulted in negative outcomes for organizations. Yet another example is found in the Diversity in the Field box on the next page. Often these problems can be avoided by using appropriate diversity management strategies. Although many

DIVERSITY
in the field

A Little Diversity Management Would Have Helped.
The NFL's San Francisco 49ers created a video that was shown to the players as part of a diversity training seminar. The video was supposed to illustrate how the players should handle the media in a town as diverse as San Francisco. Although the film was intended for diversity purposes, its "over the top" content had the opposite effect—it was offensive to many who viewed it. The film included racial slurs, a spoof of an Asian man trying to translate the sports section of a newspaper, a lesbian wedding followed by the two women engaging in heavy petting, and considerable profanity, and it ended with a man and three topless women engaging in a four-way hug. The video, intended only for the players, was secretly released to the media. As a result, many in the 49er organization spoke out against it, arguing that it was "absolutely contradictory to the ideals and values" of the sports franchise. The person who made the video, Kirk Reynolds, subsequently left the franchise (Matier & Ross, 2005). As this situation illustrates, even people who are charged with developing diversity initiatives may need diversity training themselves.

diversity management models exist, both in the general business and psychology literature (e.g., Cox, 1991; Thomas, 1996), this section focuses on four models that are specific to the sport context.

DeSensi's Model

DeSensi (1995) developed one of the earliest models for managing diversity in the educational and sport context. Her model was built on the notion that managing diversity "involves increasing the consciousness and appreciation of differences associated with heritage, characteristics, and values of different groups" (p. 35). She adopted the term *cultural diversity* to refer to both the surface- and deep-level differences discussed in earlier chapters. DeSensi suspected that effective diversity management strategies would provide many benefits to organizations, such as an increased understanding of different people and cultures and a reduction or elimination of prejudice and discrimination.

Drawing from various sources (e.g., Chesler & Crowfoot, 1990; Cox, 1991), DeSensi (1995) has proposed that diversity revolves around five organizational dimensions: mission, culture, power, informal relations, and major change strategies. These dimensions determine an organization's level of multiculturalism with reference to these three stages:

■ **Monocultural:** Diversity and diverse people are either ignored or deliberately excluded in articulations of the organization's mission. The organization's culture revolves around the norms and mores of those people who traditionally have been in charge—that is, White men. These organizations are likely to be hierarchical in nature, with power residing at the top with White men. Communication patterns are likely to be segregated, so that people are more likely to communicate with others who are similar to the self. Diversity initiatives in these organizations usually result only from litigation, demands placed on the organization by external constituents, or in rare cases, actions of elite people within the organization.

■ **Transitional:** There is a stated desire to increase organizational diversity. Though gains are made, some of the remnants of the monocultural organization remain: (a) aspects of discrimination are still present, albeit in lesser forms; (b) the norms of White men dictate the organizational culture, though they may be challenged; (c) the power is still primarily in the hands of White men, though a few women and minorities may rise to the top; (d) informal communications may cross social group boundaries, but discussions of very important issues are held only with like others; and (e) some diversity initiatives are present (e.g., administrative mandates, affirmative action programs, "awareness" training).

■ **Multicultural:** Diversity is valued and viewed as contributing to the organization's overall effectiveness. The organization's culture values diverse perspectives, and prejudice and discrimination are largely nonexistent as a result of stiff sanctions imposed for such actions and beliefs. A multicultural team holds the power. The organization has a sense of community, and communication lines cross race, gender, and other cultural boundaries. These organizations actively combat external social oppression and have performance appraisal systems in place that reward people for multicultural work.

DeSensi's (1995) work is significant for several reasons. First, it was the earliest theory-based conceptualization of diversity management in the sport context. Although others have since followed suit, DeSensi's work provided the groundwork. Second, she specifically identified many organizational factors that she perceived as contributing to workplace diversity. Such specification allows managers to focus on key areas in the organization to implement their diversity strategies. For these reasons, DeSensi's model is valued.

Doherty and Chelladurai's Model

Doherty and Chelladurai (1999) define cultural diversity as "the unique sets of values, beliefs, attitudes, and expectations, as well as language, symbols, customs, and behaviors, that individuals possess by virtue of sharing some common characteristic(s) with each other" (p. 281). They began with the premise that aligning diversity with organizational objectives creates synergy for the organization, thereby improving the overall effectiveness. They also suggest that it is the *management* of diversity—not just diversity itself—that results in positive outcomes for the organization.

Doherty and Chelladurai (1999) believe that organizations can be characterized as either those with a culture of similarity or those with a culture of diversity. Organizations with a *culture of similarity* are generally rigid, avoid risks, are intolerant of uncertainty, are task-oriented, and view differences as deficits. As a result, these organizations are likely to have closed communication lines, a process-based performance appraisal system, one-sided decision making, and closed group membership. Organizations with a *culture of diversity* have very different values, assumptions, and outcomes—they are characterized by a respect for differences, a tolerance of risk and ambiguity, are people- and future-oriented, and acknowledge that there are often many ways to accomplish tasks. The organization's communication lines are likely to be open, and they are likely to have outcome-based reward systems, multilevel decision-making systems, and open group membership.

Drawing from this dichotomy, Doherty and Chelladurai (1999) identify cultural diversity outcomes that result from each type of organizational culture—similarity or diversity. See Exhibit 13.1. Their two-by-two framework is as follows:

■ **Low cultural diversity, organizational culture of similarity:** The organization is unlikely to realize any benefits of diversity.

■ **High cultural diversity, organizational culture of similarity:** The organization is unlikely to realize any benefits of diversity; negative outcomes may result.

■ **Low cultural diversity, organizational culture of diversity:** The organization *may* realize some benefits of diversity, but not many because of the low cultural diversity.

exhibit **13.1** Doherty and Chelladurai's model.

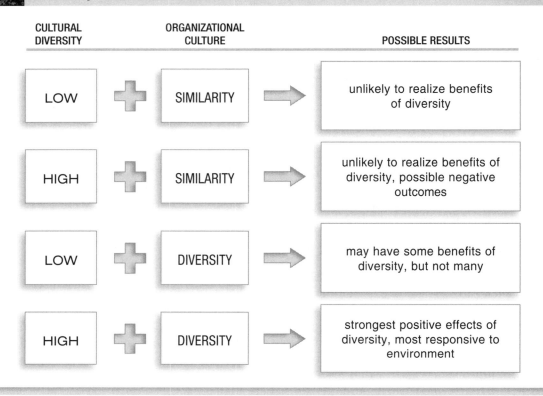

CULTURAL DIVERSITY	ORGANIZATIONAL CULTURE	POSSIBLE RESULTS
LOW	SIMILARITY	unlikely to realize benefits of diversity
HIGH	SIMILARITY	unlikely to realize benefits of diversity, possible negative outcomes
LOW	DIVERSITY	may have some benefits of diversity, but not many
HIGH	DIVERSITY	strongest positive effects of diversity, most responsive to environment

■ **High cultural diversity, organizational culture of diversity:** The positive effects of cultural diversity are likely to be strongest, and the organization is most responsive to its environment.

Doherty and Chelladurai's (1999) work is significant for several reasons. First, it has a strong theoretical foundation. As discussed in Chapter 2, models with such a grounding are likely to be the most useful for sport organization managers. Second, Doherty and Chelladurai explicated on both the values and assumptions underlying a particular culture and manifestations of that culture, allowing us to decouple the intricate effects of culture on subsequent outcomes. Third, their model specifically considers context. Cultural diversity is not expected to result in positive effects in all situations. Rather, there must be a fit, or a match, between the diversity level and the organization's culture for the positive effects to be realized.

Fink and Pastore's Model

Fink and Pastore (1999) drew extensively from the business literature to develop their model of diversity management. They support the social need for diversity in organizations and the moral obligation to provide an equitable workplace for *all* people. They recognize, however, that not all organizations will embrace the social aspects of diversity; rather, a business reason provides a stronger rationale. They note, "while it would be wonderful for all of those in positions of power to recognize the moral and social advantages of diversity, it may not be a realistic goal. Thus, for diversity initiatives to be truly embedded within the organization, those in power must be convinced of diversity's relationship to organizational effectiveness" (p. 315).

Using these ideas, Fink and Pastore (1999) propose four categories of organizations: noncompliance, compliance, reactive, and proactive. They realize that an organization may not fall neatly into one category or another; nevertheless, it is useful, for clarity purposes, to discuss them in isolation. Further, Fink and Pastore suggest that the strategies can be viewed on a continuum and that an organization is likely to move through a compliance stage before becoming reactive. The specific categories are as follows:

- **Noncompliance:** Noncompliant organizations are monocultural in nature (DeSensi, 1995) and do very little to follow state and federal guidelines related to diversity. Employees view diversity as a liability or a deficit (Doherty & Chelladurai, 1999), and those in power seek to keep the organization as homogeneous as possible. Lines of communication are rigid, and there are few prospects for voluntary change.

- **Compliance:** Compliant organizations still view diversity as a liability, but efforts are made to comply with equal employment opportunity laws—probably from a feeling of "having to" do so. This obligation to comply with diversity regulations may breed resentment among Whites and among men in the organization toward persons unlike them or toward diversity in general. Persons from diverse backgrounds may be employed, but little is done to help them succeed in the "majority" culture. Lines of communication are rigid, and the power is held by a select few.

- **Reactive:** Reactive organizations are viewed as a "big leap" (Fink & Pastore, 1999, p. 323) from compliance organizations because diversity is deemed an asset, not a liability. Top decision makers acknowledge that diversity and its effective management can result in greater organizational success. Therefore, efforts are made to create a diverse work environment, one that gleans the positive effects of employee differences. Because of their reactive nature, however, attempts at effective diversity management may be sporadic (e.g., once-a-year diversity seminar). If these attempts fail, then other efforts may be thwarted. Furthermore, as with compliance organizations, diversity initiatives are sometimes met with resistance, and a backlash is felt from those who traditionally have held the power.

- **Proactive:** Only proactive organizations realize the full benefits of diversity. These entities take a broad view of diversity and value diversity to its fullest extent. Company policies, procedures, and practices are all focused on developing a diverse workforce and effectively managing differences. Because all employees benefit from the positive outcomes associated with diversity, the backlash against such initiatives seen in other organizations is not present. These organizations generally have a different structure than their counterparts—one that is flexible, with open lines of communication, and where the power is shared by diverse persons.

Although there are many similarities between Fink and Pastore's (1999) model and the models proposed by DeSensi (1995) and Doherty and Chelladurai (1999), only Fink and Pastore's model was empirically tested, allowing us to determine whether their propositions materialize in real-life settings.

All studies were conducted in the athletic setting. The first study, by Fink, Pastore, and Riemer (2001), involved collecting data from persons in NCAA Division I athletic departments. Their results revealed that most athletic departments employed compliance strategies, followed by proactive strategies, and finally, reactive strategies. They also examined the strategies' outcomes. Both the compliance and proactive strategies significantly contributed to desired organizational outcomes such as attracting and retaining talented workers, employee satisfaction, employee involvement in decision making, the presence of a creative workplace, and overall workplace diversity. These findings largely support their proposed model.

In a subsequent study, Fink, Pastore, and Riemer (2003) focused on the diversity management strategies in NCAA Division III athletic departments because of the major differences between Division I and Division III departments. Because the former have more employees, larger budgets, and are generally more diverse than the latter, they serve as an interesting contrast. The study's results identified interesting similarities to and differences from their previous work. As in their Division I study, Fink et al. found that compliance strategies were more characteristic of Division III programs, followed by proactive strategies and reactive strategies. However, the effects of using proactive strategies were stronger in the Division III context than in the Division I setting. Among Division III universities, only the proactive strategies held a significant association with the recruitment of talented workers, the existence of a diverse fan base, the presence of a creative workplace, and overall workplace diversity. These results suggest that because Division III universities are generally not known for their diversity, those departments that do employ proactive strategies are better able to realize the strategies' benefits.

Finally, Cunningham (2009a) examined how the diversity of the department intersected with the diversity strategy to predict objective measures of performance in NCAA Division I athletic departments (i.e., Director's Cup points). In drawing from managerial theories of diversity (see Chapter 2), he argued that racial diversity would be positively associated with performance. These effects were expected to be heightened when the department coupled employee diversity with a proactive diversity strategy. Note that these predictions combine elements of both Doherty and Chelladurai's (1999) and Fink and Pastore's (1999) models. After controlling for the size of the department and its expenditures, racial diversity was positively associated with Director's Cup points earned. These main effects were qualified by the moderating effects of diversity strategy: athletic departments that coupled high racial diversity with a proactive strategy far outperformed their peers. Interestingly, diverse departments that did not have a proactive strategy did not perform any better than their non-diverse counterparts.

Chelladurai's Model

The final model was developed by Chelladurai (2009). In addition to being the most contemporary, it is perhaps the most comprehensive macro-level model developed for the sport context. Chelladurai's model primarily differs from the three models discussed previously in its explicit emphasis on competence, a point also emphasized by others (Lawson & Shen, 1998; Thomas, 1996). From his perspective, employers will be able to attract a diverse workforce if the primary focus of all hiring decisions is the applicants' competency. As Lawson and Shen argue, "no one group of members has a monopoly on competence; rather, different persons have different competencies" (p. 80). Employers who focus on competency first should attract a wide variety of people, all of whom, though they may have a similar level of competency, may differ in other respects. See the Alternative Perspectives box for a discussion about focusing *solely* on competency.

Chelladurai (2009) adopts a different approach to classifying the various diversity forms (recall the discussion of surface- and deep-level characteristics in Chapter 1) by identifying four categories:

- *Appearance or visible features* refer to such characteristics as sex, race, age, or skin color—surface-level attributes.
- *Behavioral preferences* refer to penchants for things such as certain foods or clothing.
- *Values and attitudes* are forms of deep-level differences that can be ascertained only through interaction with a person.
- *Cognitive orientations* are forms of how people differ at a deep level and relate to one's technical, human, and conceptual skills.

Chelladurai suggests that the four categories are expressed in one of two ways: symbolically or substantively. *Symbolic expressions* are identified by symbols such as Muslims' clothing preferences or Catholics' food preferences during Lent. *Substantive expressions* are related to people's values, attitudes, preferences, and orientations.

Chelladurai (2009) suggests that all management efforts begin with valuing diversity—that is, an awareness of the personal differences among employees, an acknowledgment of such differences, and an understanding that they can add value to the workplace.

Managers who value diversity use one of two management strategies—accommodation or activation. *Accommodation* occurs when managers permit symbolic expressions of diversity as long as the expressions do not interfere with task performance. For example, it is reasonable to allow a woman from India to wear a sari or a Christian to wear a cross necklace because neither expression impedes the work process. Setting aside a room for the Muslim employees to use for their daily prayers is another accommodation strategy.

alternative PERSPECTIVES

The False Hope of Competency. Chelladurai (2009) and others (Lawson & Shen, 1998; Thomas, 1996) emphasize the need to focus on competency when making employment or other similar decisions. On the surface, this idea has considerable merit because it potentially diminishes the influence of biases and other factors not directly pertinent to the job. In some situations, however, this practice can have an adverse impact on members of particular social groups. For example, consider a university that uses only academic competence to select its students. This is seemingly a sound selection technique because universities typically try to select the brightest students for their programs. By using such an admission standard, we might expect that those students who attend prestigious high schools, who take college preparatory courses, or who receive private tutoring have the best chance for admission. Of course, these options cost money and require resources—something available only to certain people. This selection technique, therefore, has a disparate impact on racial minorities, persons from lower socioeconomic circumstances, and persons in rural settings. It is not that these other people cannot learn or lack motivation; rather, they simply were given different opportunities in their lives. In most cases, when these students attend universities, they excel in the classroom. This example illustrates the problem with focusing solely on competency—it ignores situational and historical factors that influence one's outcomes. Although competence should be a cornerstone, other factors must be considered, such as one's ability to learn or be trained, motivation, personality, and overall fit with the organization.

Activation strategies are concerned with more substantive expressions and involve intentionally bringing employees with divergent values or perspectives together to work in groups on projects because such heterogeneous perspectives produce better decision making and more creative solutions—a position consistent with the managerial theories discussed in Chapter 2 (Phillips, Northcraft, & Neale, 2006; Pelled, 1996).

It is hard to envisage a time when accommodation strategies should not be permitted; however, activation strategies might work better in some situations than in others. Chelladurai (2009) recognized this and identified two key moderating variables: task complexity and task interdependence. For simple tasks, activation strategies are not necessary and may even impede the process. When activities are simple and straightforward, employees can rely on past experiences or organizational procedures to guide their actions (Jehn, Northcraft, & Neale, 1999). With more complex tasks, however, it is desirable to have many perspectives in the group. Complex tasks are not routine, and a good outcome is likely to be a function of the various group ideas and preferences.

Task interdependence, or the degree to which employees work closely with one another, is also thought to influence the usefulness of activation strategies. When employees do not work closely with one another, the effects of diversity are likely to be neutralized. When employees work closely and rely on one another to complete their tasks, the effects of diversity are likely to be realized (see also Doherty & Chelladurai, 1999).

Chelladurai's (2009) model draws from previous works in the sport context to provide a comprehensive integrated model. This is a user-friendly model because it considers the four diversity forms, acknowledges that the ways in which people differ are not the same, and uses moderators to determine whether and when particular strategies should be implemented.

Sport Industry Support for Diversity Management

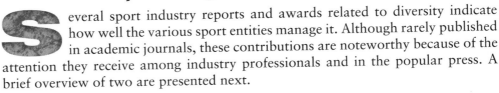 everal sport industry reports and awards related to diversity indicate how well the various sport entities manage it. Although rarely published in academic journals, these contributions are noteworthy because of the attention they receive among industry professionals and in the popular press. A brief overview of two are presented next.

Racial and Gender Report Card

Richard Lapchick, often referred to as the "racial conscience of sport," is the founder of the Institute for Diversity and Ethics in Sport, an organization that regularly publishes reports focusing on racial equality issues and/or student-athlete education. Perhaps the most influential of these publications is the semi-annual *Racial and Gender Report Card*. This comprehensive report outlines the racial and sex distribution of administrators, employees, and athletes in virtually every segment of American sports, including all of the professional sport leagues, university athletic departments, and the NCAA. Scores are assigned based on the proportion of persons from various social groups relative to their representation in the general U.S. population. The *Report Card* also outlines the major diversity initiatives each sport entity has initiated. Without doubt, Lapchick's publications are regarded as the most authoritative works related to diversity in the sport context. Exhibit 13.2 offers an overview of diversity initiatives among the major professional sports and the NCAA.

Diversity initiatives among the major sport entities in the United States.	*exhibit* **13.2**

Diversity management strategies used by major sport entities.

- **Major League Baseball:** This league seeks diversity not only in its employees but also in a wide range of product and service offerings. The league has initiatives in place to ensure diversity in the following areas: suppliers, player development, community relations, education, and philanthropic awards.

- **Major League Soccer:** The league adopted a Diversity Initiative that guarantees a focus on diversity throughout league operations. In 2008, the league conducted training on such topics as different management styles, communicating with co-workers, and the importance of diversity with MLS. There is also a Diversity Committee that consists of administrators from each team who share best practices in diversity management. MLS Futbolito (MLSFutbolito.com), which targets Hispanic youth, is the largest grassroots diversity strategy among any of the professional sport leagues.

- **National Basketball Association and Women's National Basketball Association:** The NBA has mandatory diversity training for all employees. The program must be completed by the employee within the first three months of employment. In addition the NBA and WNBA collaborate on a number of NBA and WNBA Cares initiatives, including ones related to education, health-related causes, and youth and family development.

- **National Football League:** At the NFL, diversity is viewed as a business imperative, essential to the growth of the sport, the strength of the clubs, and to league leadership and innovation. In 2002, the league established the NFL Diversity Council to design and implement programs for building diversity awareness and establishing an inclusive work force. In 2004, it created the NFL Special Teams Initiative. Teams of employees from various occupations, departments, and levels of employment worked on such projects as NFL network programming for Black History Month, increasing the number of female fans, and marketing to Hispanics.

- **National Hockey League:** The NHL has many policies in place aimed at improving the diversity within the league. NHL Diversity was founded in 1995 and serves as the league's group that focuses on diversity (nhl.com/nhlhq/diversity). The annual Willie O'Ree All-State Game, named after the NHL's first African American hockey player, puts 14–16-year-old inner-city hockey players together to participate in an East versus West hockey game. The league also sponsors a "Hockey Is for Everyone Month" when the teams provide tickets to those inner-city youth who want to attend games. Finally, there are scholarship and equipment programs, both of which are aimed at inner-city youth.

- **Professional Golf Association:** In an effort to increase diversity within the golf industry, the PGA established the Diversity Internship Program in 1992. The program is available to racial minority students of African American, Hispanic, Asian, Pacific Islander, and Native American descent, providing the participants with internships in marketing, communications, information systems, and event management, among others. The PGA partnered with industry leaders (e.g., Nike Golf, Titleist) to help them diversify their workforces.

(continued)

exhibit **13.2** Continued.

■ **United States Tennis Association:** The USTA views diversity as essential to achieving its overall goal of promoting and developing the growth of tennis. To this end, the organization created a Multicultural Participation Committee. Its goals include (a) identifying multicultural barriers to participation; (b) developing programs to increase multicultural participation in the USTA; (c) ensuring that tennis has the appropriate links to multicultural communities; and (d) monitoring and evaluating multicultural participation in USTA programs. In addition, the USTA also promotes an adaptive tennis program (usta.com/news/fullstory.sps?iType=946&inewsid=33099).

■ **NASCAR:** NASCAR's Executive Steering Committee for Diversity has implemented both on- and off-track initiatives to diversify the sport. For example, the Drive for Diversity program seeks to develop drivers and crew members from diverse backgrounds. NASCAR also has diversity internship programs, an urban youth racing school, and scholarship programs at Historically Black Colleges and Universities.

■ **National Collegiate Athletic Association:** Steps taken by the NCAA to improve the diversity and its related outcomes in college athletics include providing postgraduate scholarships for racial minorities and women, developing internship programs aimed at racial minorities and women who want to work in university athletics administration, providing matching funds to Division II and III universities that hire full-time administrators to increase the department's sex and racial diversity, giving matching grants for minority women coaches, creating a leadership institute for racial minority males, and requiring diversity education.

Adapted from *2009 Gender and Racial Report Card,* www.nhl.com, www.usta.com, www.pgatour.com, www.work placefairness.com, and www.ncaa.org.

Diversity in Athletics Award

The Laboratory for Diversity in Sport, in collaboration with the NCAA, presents the Diversity in Athletics Award on an annual basis. The award's purpose is to recognize NCAA athletic departments that excel in eight diversity-related categories:

1. diversity strategy,
2. sex diversity of department employees,
3. racial diversity of department employees,
4. value and attitudinal diversity of department employees,
5. graduation of African American male student-athletes,
6. graduation of African American female student-athletes,
7. Title IX compliance, and
8. overall excellence in diversity.

A list of the 2009–2010 Division I award recipients for each category is found in Exhibit 13.3.

The Diversity in Athletics Award differs from Lapchick's *Report Card* in several respects. First, it examines the diversity within each department rather than

2009–2010 Diversity in Athletic Award Recipients, NCAA Division I.

exhibit 13.3

OVERALL EXCELLENCE IN DIVERSITY

DePaul University

Drexel University

Georgia State University

Indiana University–Purdue University, Indianapolis

Indiana University–Purdue University, Fort Wayne

Loyola Marymount University

Northern Illinois University

San Jose State University

University of Connecticut

University of Houston

University of South Alabama

University of Texas at El Paso

DIVERSITY STRATEGY

Duke University

Georgia State University

Jacksonville State University

Loyola Marymount University

St. Francis College (New York)

The Ohio State University

University of California, Davis

University of Connecticut

University of San Francisco

GENDER EQUITY COMPLIANCE

Bucknell University

Radford University

San Jose State University

University at Buffalo

University of Kansas

University of Maryland, College Park

University of Michigan

University of South Alabama

University of Vermont

AFRICAN AMERICAN GRADUATION: FEMALE STUDENT ATHLETES

Eastern Michigan University

Iona College

Long Island University–Brooklyn Campus

Morehead State University

University of Akron

University of Northern Iowa

Wright State University

AFRICAN AMERICAN GRADUATION: MALE STUDENT ATHLETES

Austin Peay State University

Coastal Carolina University

Fairleigh Dickinson University, Metropolitan

Georgia State University

Indiana University–Purdue University, Fort Wayne

Northern Illinois University

University of Arkansas, Little Rock

University of New Orleans

University of Wisconsin, Milwaukee

Youngstown State University

GENDER DIVERSITY

Ball State University

California State University, Fullerton

DePaul University

East Tennessee State University

Texas A&M University–Corpus Christi

University of Central Florida

University of Missouri, Kansas City

University of North Carolina, Asheville

University of San Francisco

RACIAL DIVERSITY

New Mexico State University

San Jose State University

Seton Hall University

University of Arizona

University of California, Irvine

University of Hawaii, Manoa

University of Houston

University of Miami (Florida)

University of Texas at Austin

University of Texas at El Paso

University of Texas, Pan American

VALUE AND ATTITUDINAL DIVERSITY

California State University, Fresno

Drexel University

Eastern Washington University

Florida Atlantic University

Indiana University–Purdue University at Indianapolis

Northwestern State University

University of Delaware

University of Wyoming

Source: Laboratory for Diversity in Sport, Texas A&M University, www.diversityinsport.com.

college sports overall. Second, although the award does consider the proportion of racial minorities and women in the individual departments (as does the *Report Card*), it also includes other variables thought to impact the department diversity, including Title IX compliance, graduation of minority athletes, and the overall diversity strategy implemented. Even though the award focuses on a much narrower sector of the sport industry—university athletics—it provides a more in-depth analysis of the entities.

Diversity Management Processes

As you may have noticed, the theoretical models and the reports and awards by and large focus on the desired ends. They describe what an organization using, for example, a proactive strategy looks like and some of the strategy's expected outcomes. What is missing from the earlier discussions is the process of achieving those ends. Even in the Chelladurai (2009) model, which indicates when to use certain diversity management strategies, the process organizational leaders may use to achieve a diverse workforce is not explicitly described. This critique applies to most diversity management strategies in all of the management literature (Agars & Kottke, 2004), not only those in the sport context. It is important to understand, therefore, the process organizations use to successfully implement a desired diversity management strategy. Cunningham and his colleagues (2008b, 2009b; Cunningham & Sartore, 2010; Cunningham & Singer, 2009) have devoted considerable time to understanding the diversity-related change process, and the key findings from their research are discussed below.

Factors Influencing Change

As previously noted, most sport organizations are *not* characterized by diversity and inclusion. The exclusion of persons who differ from the typical majority has been the norm for decades—a point aptly illustrated by considering who serves in leadership positions (Acosta & Carpenter, 2008; DeHass, 2007). Furthermore, as illustrated throughout the preceding chapters, racial minorities, women, sexual minorities, religious minorities, persons with disabilities, and the poor, among others, have routinely been marginalized and relegated to "other" status within the sport context. Thus, in many ways, cultures of similarity and exclusion have become institutionalized, meaning that through habit, history, and tradition, they have become unquestionably accepted as "how things are done" (see also Scott, 2001). Institutionalized practices are highly resistant to change (Zucker, 1987) and are maintained over time without objection, seen largely as the "legitimate" modus operandi.

If cultures of similarity and exclusion are firmly engrained and legitimated within the sport context, then what factors would spur organizations to change? That is, what prompts sport organizations to seek a culture of diversity and inclusion? In drawing from institutional theory (Dacin, Goodstein, & Scott, 2002; Oliver, 1992; Scott, 2001), Cunningham (2008b, 2009b) points to three primary factors: political pressures, functional pressures, and social pressures.

Political pressures

Political pressures arise when there are mounting performance deficits, the presence of conflicting interests among stakeholder groups, increasing pressures for innovation, and changing reliance upon external constituents (Oliver, 1992). As Dacin et al. (2002) note, these pressures "result primarily from shifts in the interests and underlying power distributions that have supported and legitimated existing institutional arrangements" (p. 46). Cunningham (2009b) observed the influence of political pressures in his study of an intercollegiate athletics department undergoing a diversity-related change process. Specifically, the organization sought to attract diverse fans to the events as a way to generate more revenues. As another example, though use of sexist language is prevalent throughout much of the sport industry, various educators and activists have challenged its use (e.g., Blinde, Greendorfer, & Shanker, 1991; Messner, Duncan, & Jensen, 1993). As a result of these political pressures, Parks and Roberton (2002) designed an educational program that effectively curbed the use of sexist language among those who underwent the training.

Functional pressures

Functional pressures manifest when there are concerns about organizational effectiveness or the utility of a given practice (Oliver, 1992). These pressures are associated with environmental pressures, such as competition for scarce resources (Dacin et al., 2002). Perhaps the best example of functional pressures comes from what Ladson-Billings (2004) refers to as the "Bear Bryant/Adolph Rupp epiphany" (p. 10). Bryant, the head coach of the University of Alabama football team, saw his all-White University squad be soundly beaten by the University of Southern California—a game in which USC's African American tailback, Sam (Bam) Cunningham, ran for 135 yards and 2 touchdowns on just 12 carries. Likewise, Rupp was the head coach of the University of Kentucky's all-White men's basketball team when his squad was beaten in the championship game by a Texas Western team that started five African Americans. Ladson-Billings suggests that both victories "made clear to big-time college athletics that winning required recruiting players from beyond all-White prep fields" (p. 12). Not surprisingly, both Bryant and Rupp fielded racially integrated teams soon after those defeats.

Social pressures

Finally, social pressures result from differentiation among groups (e.g., increasing employee diversity), disruptions in the organization's historical continuity (e.g., when mergers take place), or changes in laws or social movements that might disrupt the continuation of an institutionalized practice (Scott, 2001). Cunningham (2009b) observed these pressures at the university where his study was conducted. Many in the community perceived that the athletic department had a history of excluding racial minority coaches and administrators, and they made their concerns known through various mechanisms; for example, an open letter decrying the abysmal hiring practices was penned by former players and circulated on national websites. In addition, the athletic department's mascot had long been a Native American—a practice viewed as hostile and offensive by many (e.g., Staurowsky, 2007). Collectively, these issues resulted in mounting concerns from a myriad of external stakeholders, and in response to these concerns, the athletic department sought to change their otherwise institutionalized activities.

Implementing Change

When organizations respond to these pressures for deinstitutionalization, they will then seek to implement diversity-related change. Sport managers can engage on several different fronts and use various methods to ensure the success of the organizational transformation. Among the most important are valuing diversity, conducting an organizational analysis, using education, activating top management support, using proactive hiring procedures, and integrating diversity into all organizational activities (i.e., systemic integration; Cunningham, 2008b, 2009b; Cunningham & Singer, 2009).

Valuing diversity

In valuing diversity, people sense a moral obligation to provide opportunities to all people, irrespective of their individual differences. This also means that employees will appreciate learning from others and will value the different perspectives and beliefs people bring to the organization. This view of diversity is quite different from the view that seeks a diverse and inclusive workplace only for the benefits it brings to the organization. The latter approach is akin to "using" diversity for organizational gain, and researchers have shown that external stakeholders are cognizant of such approaches and resentful of them (Cunningham, 2009b). Thus, as Cunningham and Singer (2009) noted, "employees must value diversity—that is most critical to creating and sustaining a workplace of diversity and inclusion" (p. 17).

Organizational analysis

In addition to valuing diversity, managers must gain an understanding of how diversity impacts the workplace. This comprehension comes through an organizational analysis. Preliminary steps in conducting an organizational analysis often entail examining the proportion of different groups at various levels of the department (e.g. proportion of women coaches). However, if the gathering of this data is not followed by further analysis, it falls far short of what is needed, because it "ignores the complex power and political relationships that are inherent in considering the intersectionality of marginalized and underrepresented groups" (Shaw, 2007, p. 426). As such, Cunningham and Singer (2009) recommend undertaking an extensive analysis that supplies an understanding of the underlying values that guide the organization—the "deep structure" of the workplace that shapes how and why activities take place, including the existing, taken-for-granted power and political structures. Without undertaking this process, subsequent efforts to implement diversity changes are likely to be misguided.

Education

Employees might resist diversity-related change. As is seen in Exhibit 13.4, much of this apprehension comes simply from not understanding, or being misinformed about, how the change will affect people on an individual level. For example,

| Forms of resistance to diversity-related change. | *exhibit* **13.4** |

INDIVIDUAL RESISTANCE

- **Prejudice:** People may prefer a homogeneous workplace. This preference may come from a strong liking of in-group members or disliking out-group members.

- **Habit:** People use habits to reduce uncertainty in their lives and to increase efficiencies. The same is true for organizational policies and procedures. When diversity-related strategies are implemented, they might represent a departure from a habit and, therefore, be met with resistance.

- **Security:** People with a high need for security may resist any and all efforts toward change because the changes might impact the power they have, the roles they assume, and so forth—all of which decreases the security people have at work.

- **Economic factors:** Some people resist change that they perceive will negatively affect them monetarily. For example, if a diversity strategy meant (or was perceived to mean) that some people would receive reduced pay increases, then they would probably resist the initiative.

- **Fear of the unknown:** People generally prefer to have an understanding of what the future holds for them, and change alters those perceptions. When diversity management strategies are implemented, people may be unsure of how the strategies will affect their jobs, the relationships they have with others, and their overall standing in the organization. If this is true, they are likely to resist any efforts toward change.

- **Selective information processing:** Once people form perceptions of their world, they are unlikely to change them. This unwillingness to change may result in people selectively interpreting some information, while ignoring other input. For example, people may ignore arguments as to how diversity will improve the organization, because the arguments are counter to their current perceptions of the organization and how it functions.

ORGANIZATIONAL RESISTANCE

- **Limited focus of change:** Because organizations are comprised of interrelated systems, changing one part requires changing another if the change is to have a lasting effect. Diversity initiatives often have a narrow focus that is nullified by the larger organizational system.

- **Inertia:** Organizational inertia is the tendency for organizations to resist change and remain in their current state. Even if certain people want the change, the organizational norms and culture may act as constraints.

- **Threat to expertise:** Changes that threaten the expertise of particular groups cause resistance. For example, hiring a diversity officer to oversee the organization's diversity efforts might be resisted by the human resource staff because that threatens their expertise in the area of hiring and employee relations.

- **Threat to established power relationships:** In proactive organizations, the power is held by a multicultural group of people. In other organization types, the power rests primarily with White males. To the extent that diversity is viewed as disrupting established power relationships, it may face resistance.

- **Threat to established resource allocations:** Those groups that control sizable resources may view efforts toward change as threatening. For example, in university athletics, men's teams traditionally have received the lion's share of the budget. Thus, moves to increase the gender equity might be met with resistance by these players or coaches, if they believe it means they will receive fewer resources.

Adapted from Robbins (2003).

how does an organizational focus on diversity influence the way people complete their work, the power they maintain, and the organization's outcomes? How will working with people different from the self impact such work outcomes as satisfaction, identification, or commitment? Organizational efforts to educate people about the proposed change can serve to allay these fears of the unknown (Robbins, 2003). Managers should use memorandums, leader speeches, change teams, and seminars to educate employees. Regardless of the method used, it is imperative that people are apprised of *what* the change means for them and *why* it is taking place.

Top management support

Top management support is also needed to ensure the transformation into an organization of diversity and inclusion (Cunningham, 2008b; Cunningham & Singer, 2009). In providing that support, managers set the examples for the behaviors and attitudes expected from others in the organization. Bandura (1986) noted the benefits of such actions in commenting that "virtually all learning phenomena, resulting from direct experience, can occur vicariously by observing other people's behaviors and the consequences for them" (p. 19). Indeed, several researchers have found evidence for the primacy of top management support (Cox, 2001; Jayne & Dipboye, 2004). In Gilbert and Ivancevich's (2000) study, the CEO led the charge for diversity efforts, and his enthusiasm spread throughout the organization. This strong enthusiasm was also noted in Cunningham and Singer's (2009) research, and they noted that by exuding such passion, the leaders exemplified the attitudes and behaviors expected from others in their workplace. Leaders in Cunningham and Singer's study went through same training as everyone else in the department and held people accountable for how they contributed to the department's efforts. These authors noted that "absent strong leadership, diversity initiatives are doomed" (p. 33).

Proactive hiring process

Another step to ensure that the workplace is one of diversity and inclusion is to engage in a proactive hiring process (Cunningham & Singer, 2009). Members of underrepresented groups are typically hired into peripheral positions such as assistant coaches rather than coordinator, human resource manager rather than business manager, or life skills coordinator rather than development officer (see Anderson, 1993; DeHass, 2007; McDowell, Cunningham, & Singer, 2009). These distinctions are important because the latter positions are typically the areas that set employees on the career track to become a senior administrator. Thus, to have a workplace that is truly diverse and inclusive, *all people* should have access to key organizational positions. Further, managers should be diligent in the recruitment and selection of members from underrepresented groups, approaching the process with the same vigor as they do when recruiting student athletes.

Systemic integration

Finally, to truly realize the benefits of diversity, the diversity initiatives must be integrated throughout the entire organization (Cunningham, 2008b, 2009; Cunningham

& Singer, 2009). In this way, diversity and inclusion are seen as contributing to the success of all organizational activities. Furthermore, when diversity is integrated into all organizational activities, then ensuring that the workplace is one characterized by diversity and inclusion becomes the duty of *all* employees. In short, this means making diversity a central part of the structure, strategy, and mission of the workplace. By doing so, employees will come to see organizational activities through a diversity lens and, as a result, will identify the diversity-related implications and opportunities in all they do.

Contrary to systemic integration, some sport managers will seek to integrate diversity into some organizational activities but not others. For example, some athletic departments will set up diversity committees or localize diversity efforts to a specific position, e.g., the Senior Woman Administrator (Cunningham, 2009b). Doing so results in several problems. First, diversity becomes "somebody else's problem," and the responsibility for ensuring that the workplace is one of diversity and inclusion is deflected from the self to others. Second, and related to the first point, activities in some organizational subunits might seem to conflict when diversity and inclusion are not systemically integrated. As a result, external constituents might receive a mixed message concerning the organizational image. Indeed, researchers have shown that failing to systemically integrate diversity and inclusion initiatives severely thwarts the effectiveness of those activities (Agars & Kottke, 2004; Cunningham, 2009b).

Commitment to and Behavioral Support of Diversity

For diversity and inclusion to be enmeshed into all organizational activities, sport managers must continually reinforce the aforementioned activities. This task becomes easier when employees have a commitment to and behaviorally support diversity and inclusion.

Commitment to diversity

In drawing from Meyer and Herscovitch (2001), Cunningham (2008a) defined commitment to diversity as "a force or mindset that binds an individual to support diversity" (p. 178). He further suggested that the mindset could be reflected in one of three ways: (a) affective commitment, which represents a desire to support diversity because of the value of diversity; (b) continuance commitment, or the support of diversity because of the costs of not doing so; and (c) normative commitment, or the felt obligation to provide support for diversity.

Research suggests that commitment to diversity is needed among employees of a sport organization to realize diversity's benefits. Cunningham (2008a) found that departments that merged a diverse staff with a strong collective commitment to diversity (i.e., high in all mindsets) outperformed their peers in terms of attracting diverse fans, achieving employee satisfaction, and encouraging employee creativity. Departments with high commitment but lack of employee diversity were unable to realize these benefits. These findings suggest that employees should not only recognize the benefits of diversity (affective) but also adopt a sense of obligation to support it (normative), recognizing that not doing so will adversely affect the workplace (continuance).

Behavioral support

In addition to demonstrating a commitment to diversity, employees should also exhibit behavioral support for the diversity-related initiatives (Dass & Parker, 1999). According to Herscovitch and Meyer (2002), behavioral support can take two forms: focal or discretionary. Focal behaviors are those to which employees are bound based on their involvement and association with the organization. Thus, employees have to demonstrate these behaviors because they are employed by the organization. On the other hand, discretionary behaviors represent an effort on the part of the employee to go above and beyond what is required. The most helpful and desired form of discretionary behavior is called *championing,* and this entails employees making specific sacrifices and exerting considerable effort to support the change. Champions of change persuade others inside and outside the organization as to the value of the change (Herscovitch & Meyer, 2002). Similarly, diversity scholars, such as Holvino, Ferdman, and Merrill-Sands (2004), argue that champions "promote successful diversity initiatives" by "building alliances and coalitions among diverse internal constituencies and networks to support change" (p. 272).

Given the critical role that champions play in promoting diversity-related change in the workplace, Cunningham and Sartore (2010) examined factors that influence whether or not people engage in championing behavior. They found that women, racial minorities, sexual minorities, people who have an extraverted personality, and people who expressed low levels of racial and sexual prejudice were all likely to champion diversity. In addition to these personal characteristics, Cunningham and Sartore also found that people who worked with others who also supported diversity were engaged in championing behaviors. These findings have implications for sport managers seeking to transform their workplace into one of diversity and inclusion.

Diversity and Leadership

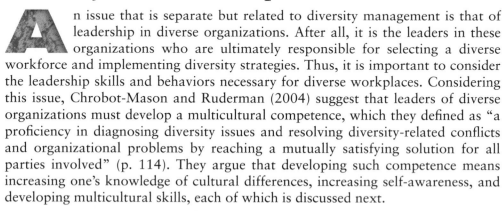

An issue that is separate but related to diversity management is that of leadership in diverse organizations. After all, it is the leaders in these organizations who are ultimately responsible for selecting a diverse workforce and implementing diversity strategies. Thus, it is important to consider the leadership skills and behaviors necessary for diverse workplaces. Considering this issue, Chrobot-Mason and Ruderman (2004) suggest that leaders of diverse organizations must develop a multicultural competence, which they defined as "a proficiency in diagnosing diversity issues and resolving diversity-related conflicts and organizational problems by reaching a mutually satisfying solution for all parties involved" (p. 114). They argue that developing such competence means increasing one's knowledge of cultural differences, increasing self-awareness, and developing multicultural skills, each of which is discussed next.

Knowledge of Cultural Differences

Effective leaders have an awareness of the differences in values, beliefs, and norms across various cultures (Chrobot-Mason & Ruderman, 2004). Having such knowledge allows for an organizational culture that respects differences among people.

Without an awareness and understanding of the dissimilarities, it is likely that some behaviors may be offensive to others. For example, when the former San Jose MLS team moved to Houston, Texas, officials originally renamed the team Houston 1836. This was the year that Texas won its independence. What team officials failed to consider, however, is that the name might be offensive to the area's large Hispanic population because it was from Mexico that Texas won its independence (Trecker, 2006). Hispanics represent a large portion of MLS fans, so the team changed the name to the Dynamos. A greater knowledge of cultural differences by the Houston team officials would have enabled them to avoid this public relations problem.

Increased Self-Awareness

Chrobot-Mason and Ruderman (2004) suggest that, in addition to a knowledge of cultural differences, leaders of diverse organizations also must increase their self-awareness. Effective leaders interact with their followers on an interpersonal level. To have meaningful interactions, leaders must be aware of their own biases, prejudices, and attitudes toward those who differ from themselves. This understanding helps leaders to reduce or rid themselves of such biases, thereby improving their interactions with others.

Multicultural Skills

Effective leaders develop such important multicultural skills as conflict management, interpersonal communication, feedback seeking, and role modeling (Chrobot-Mason & Ruderman, 2004).

Conflict management

Many conflicts arise because of multicultural differences between people, and it is often incumbent upon the leader to resolve the conflicts. Haslam (2000) believes that conflicts are best resolved when the values and preferences of both sides are considered. Therefore, managers must not only understand these issues but also develop techniques to reduce destructive forms of conflict between employees (Chrobot-Mason & Ruderman, 2004).

Interpersonal communication

Effective leaders often interact with people on an interpersonal level (Chrobot-Mason & Ruderman, 2004). For these interactions to be useful, leaders must develop effective communication skills and encourage trust, honesty, and openness with their followers. This is challenging in diverse organizations, where differences in power, demographic characteristics, or deep-level attributes make meaningful interactions with some followers difficult. There may be times when leaders have not had the same life experiences as their diverse followers; this is especially true when the leader is a White male. Despite these potential hurdles, effective leaders find ways to develop a closeness with their followers. As Chrobot-Mason and Ruderman note, "although it is easier to understand and empathize with people who are similar, multiculturally competent leaders will listen to dissimilar others with an open mind and attempt to understand the issues that minority members face in the workplace, even if they have never shared or witnessed this experience" (p. 119).

Feedback seeking

Effective leaders constantly seek feedback from sources internal and external to the organization in order to evaluate their own leadership as well as the organization's policies and procedures (Chrobot-Mason & Ruderman, 2004). It is often necessary to explicitly seek feedback from diverse constituents so that they may provide unique perspectives concerning diversity issues. This feedback is acquired through interviews, questionnaires, focus groups, or informal conversations with others. For example, a manager at a city recreational center might ask local diversity leaders, the NAACP, or other entities for feedback on how well the organization is performing in such areas as staffing, the provision of recreational opportunities, and community outreach. The insights received are then used to shape future decisions.

Role modeling

Effective leaders show a commitment to diversity. This is perhaps best accomplished through role modeling behaviors (Chrobot-Mason & Ruderman, 2004). For example, leaders should be actively involved in recruiting and hiring diverse employees, developing congruent missions and goals that emphasize diversity, and initiating and developing relationships with people from diverse backgrounds. Leaders should expand their comfort zone by placing themselves in situations where they might be the minority, thereby increasing their understanding of the experiences of dissimilar others.

CHAPTER *summary*

This chapter provided an overview of macro-level diversity management strategies, those aimed at the organization as a whole as opposed to specific groups or individuals. As illustrated in the Diversity Challenge, there is often a need to employ specific strategies to provide equal opportunities to all parties. Without such strategies, dissimilar others may have negative work experiences. Effective diversity management strategies generate positive outcomes for the organization as a whole. After reading the chapter, you should be able to:

1. Discuss the four models for managing diversity in sport organizations.

Four primary diversity management strategies are used in the sport context. DeSensi (1995) described three stages of organizational multiculturalism: monocultural, transitional, and multicultural. Organizations were classified based on five organizational dimensions: mission, culture, power, informal relations, and major change strategies. Doherty and Chelladurai (1999) proposed a model that characterized organizations as having either a culture of diversity or a culture of similarity. They expected that an organization's diversity-related outcomes would be a function of the level of its employee diversity and the specific culture. Fink and Pastore (1999) categorize organizations as noncompliant, compliant, reactive, or proactive, with the latter category being the most desirable. Finally, the Chelladurai (2009) model is based on the manifestations of diversity (i.e., symbolic or substantive) and the specific strategies a manager could employ (i.e., accommodation or activation). The choice of strategy is dependent upon the manifestation of diversity, the task complexity, and group interdependence.

2. Outline the methods managers can use to implement diversity management strategies.

Implementing any change initiatives can be a challenging process. Managers must ensure that employees value diversity, conduct an organizational analysis, provide education, demonstrate clear support, engage in proactive hiring, and integrate diversity into all organizational activities. They should also promote employee commitment to diversity and encourage organizational members to champion diversity and inclusion.

3. Provide an overview of the leadership competencies necessary in diverse organizations.

Leaders of diverse organizations must develop a knowledge of culture differences, increased self-awareness, and multicultural skills, including skills in conflict management, interpersonal communication, feedback seeking, and role modeling.

QUESTIONS *for discussion*

1. Why do organizations need diversity management plans? Isn't the presence of a diverse workforce sufficient to realize positive organizational outcomes?

2. Four diversity management models were discussed in the chapter. What are the models' similarities? What are the major differences?

3. Refer to the forms of resistance listed in Exhibit 13.4. Which one might be the most prevalent in sport organizations? Which one is the most difficult to overcome?

4. Are there any methods not discussed in the chapter that managers could use to decrease resistance to diversity management programs?

5. Of the competencies that leaders of diverse organizations must have, which is likely to be most important and why?

LEARNING *activities*

1. Suppose you are hired to manage a recreational sport facility. Which diversity management strategy would you implement? Would a combination of two or more strategies be the best fit? Develop a written plan for the strategy (or strategies) you select, and include the rationale for your decision.

2. Suppose you are trying to implement a particular diversity management strategy in your organization. Develop a written action plan outlining the steps you would take to ensure the success of the program. Address the steps necessary to present the desirability of the program to your employees and to overcome any opposition to it.

READING *resources*

SUPPLEMENTARY READING

Cunningham, G. B., & Singer, J. N. (2009). *Diversity in athletics: An assessment of exemplars and institutional best practices.* Indianapolis, IN: National Collegiate Athletic Association. (A best practices manual based on extensive qualitative research with NCAA athletic departments from across the nation.)

Mor Barak, M. (2005). *Managing diversity: Toward a globally inclusive workplace.* Thousand Oaks, CA: Sage. (Provides an overview for establishing inclusive diversity management perspectives; adopts a global perspective of diversity.)

Stockdale, M. S., & Faye, F. J. (Eds.). (2004). *The psychology and management of workplace diversity.* Malden, MA: Blackwell. (An edited text that provides several informative chapters related to transforming the workplace into one of diversity and inclusion.)

WEB RESOURCES

- Bernard Hodes Group (www.hodes.com): consulting agency whose purpose is to develop and institute diversity management plans.

- Catalyst (www.catalyst.org): leading research and advisory organization whose aim is to help organizations build inclusive, diverse work environments.

- Diversity, Inc. (www.diversityinc.com): provides a "best practices" page for diversity management.

references

Acosta, R. V., & Carpenter, L. J. (2010). *Women in intercollegiate sport: A longitudinal study—thirty-three year update—1977–2010.* Unpublished manuscript, Brooklyn College, Brooklyn, NY.

Agars, M. D., & Kottke, J. L. (2004). Models and practice of diversity management: A historical review and presentation of new integrated theory. In M. S. Stockdale & F. J. Crosby (Eds.), *The psychology and management of workplace diversity* (pp. 55–77). Malden, MA: Blackwell.

Anderson, D. (1993). Cultural diversity on campus: A look at intercollegiate football coaches. *Journal of Sport and Social Issues, 17,* 61–66.

Bandura, A. (1986). *Social foundations for thought and action: A social cognitive theory.* Englewood Cliffs, NJ: Prentice-Hall.

Blinde, E. M., Greendorfer, S. L., & Shanker, R. J. (1991). Differential media coverage of men's and women's intercollegiate basketball: Reflection of gender ideology. *Journal of Sport and Social Issues, 15,* 98–114.

Chelladurai, P. (2009). *Managing organizations for sport and physical activity: A systems perspective* (3rd ed.). Scottsdale, AZ: Holcomb Hathaway.

Chesler, M., & Crowfoot, J. (1990). Racism on campus. In W. May (Ed.), *Ethics and higher education* (pp. 195–230). New York: Macmillan.

Chrobot-Mason, D., & Ruderman, M. N. (2004). Leadership in a diverse workplace. In M. S. Stockdale & F. J. Faye (Eds.), *The psychology and management of workplace diversity* (pp. 101–121). Malden, MA: Blackwell.

Cox, T. (1991). The multicultural organization. *Academy of Management Executive, 5*(2), 34–47.

Cox, T. H., Jr. (2001). *Creating a multicultural organization: Theory, research, and practice.* San Francisco, CA: Jossey-Bass.

Cunningham, G. B. (2008a). Commitment to diversity and its influence on athletic department outcomes. *Journal of Intercollegiate Sport, 1,* 176–201.

Cunningham, G. B. (2008b). Creating and sustaining gender diversity in sport organizations. *Sex Roles, 58,* 136–145.

Cunningham, G. B. (2009a). The moderating effect of diversity strategy on the relationship between racial diversity and organizational performance. *Journal of Applied Social Psychology, 36,* 1445–1460.

Cunningham, G. B. (2009b). Understanding the diversity-related change process: A field study. *Journal of Sport Management, 23,* 407–428.

Cunningham, G. B., & Sartore, M. L. (2010). Championing diversity: The influence of personal and organizational antecedents. *Journal of Applied Social Psychology, 40,* 788–810.

Cunningham, G. B., & Singer, J. N. (2009). *Diversity in athletics: An assessment of exemplars and institutional best practices*. Indianapolis, IN: National Collegiate Athletic Association.

Dacin, M. T., Goodstein, J., & Scott, W. R. (2002). Institutional theory and institutional change: Introduction to the special research forum. *Academy of Management Journal, 45,* 45–57.

Dass, P., & Parker, B. (1999). Strategies for managing human resource diversity: From resistance to learning. *Academy of Management Executive, 13*(2), 68–80.

DeHass, D. (2007). *2005–06 ethnicity and gender demographics of NCAA member institutions' athletics personnel*. Indianapolis, IN: The National Collegiate Athletic Association.

DeSensi, J. T. (1995). Understanding multiculturalism and valuing diversity: A theoretical perspective. *Quest, 47,* 34–43.

Doherty, A. J., & Chelladurai, P. (1999). Managing cultural diversity in sport organizations: A theoretical perspective. *Journal of Sport Management, 13,* 280–297.

Fink, J. S., & Pastore, D. L. (1999). Diversity in sport? Utilizing the business literature to devise a comprehensive framework of diversity initiatives. *Quest, 51,* 310–327.

Fink, J. S., Pastore, D. L., & Riemer, H. A. (2001). Do differences make a difference? Managing diversity in Division IA intercollegiate athletics. *Journal of Sport Management, 15,* 10–50.

Fink, J. S., Pastore, D. L., & Riemer, H. A. (2003). Managing employee diversity: Perceived practices and organizational outcomes in NCAA Division III athletic departments. *Sport Management Review, 6,* 147–168.

Gilbert, J. A., & Ivancevich, J. M. (2000). Valuing diversity: A tale of two organizations. *Academy of Management Executive, 14*(1), 93–105.

Haslam, S. A. (2000). *Psychology in organizations: The social identity approach*. Thousand Oaks, CA: Sage.

Herscovitch, L., & Meyer, J. P. (2002). Commitment to organizational change: Extension of a three-component model. *Journal of Applied Psychology, 87,* 474–487.

Holvino, E., Ferdman, B. M., & Merrill-Sands, D. (2004). Creating and sustaining diversity and inclusion in organizations: Strategies and approaches. In M. S. Stockdale & F. J. Crosby (Eds.), *The psychology and management of workplace diversity* (pp. 245–276). Malden, MA: Blackwell.

Jayne, M. E. A., & Dipboye, R. L. (2004). Leveraging diversity to improve business performance: Research findings and recommendations for organizations. *Human Resource Management, 43,* 409–424.

Jehn, K. A., Northcraft, G. B., & Neale, M. A. (1999). Why differences make a difference: A field study of diversity, conflict, and performance in workgroups. *Administrative Science Quarterly, 44,* 741–763.

Ladson-Billings, G. (2004). Landing on the wrong note: The price we paid for *Brown*. *Educational Researcher, 33*(7), 3–13.

Lawson, R. B., & Shen, Z. (1998). *Organizational psychology: Foundations and applications*. New York: Oxford University Press.

Matier, P., & Ross, A. (2005, June). 49ers' personal foul: Team's in-house training video includes lesbian porn, racial slurs, and barbs at Newsom. *SFGate.com*. Retrieved April 13, 2006, from www.sfgate.com/cgi-bin/article.cgi?f=/c/a/2005/06/01/mnghqd1iot1.dtl.

McDowell, J., Cunningham, G. B., & Singer, J. N. (2009). The supply and demand side of occupational segregation: The case of an intercollegiate athletic department. *Journal of African American Studies, 13,* 431–454.

Messner, M. A., Duncan, M. C., & Jensen, K. (1993). Separating the men from the girls: The gendered language of televised sports. *Gender & Society, 7,* 121–137.

Meyer, J. P., & Herscovitch, L. (2001). Commitment to the workplace: Toward a general model. *Human Resource Management Review, 11,* 299–326.

Oliver, C. (1992). The antecedents of deinstitutionalization. *Organization Studies, 13,* 563–588.

Parks, J. B., Roberton, M. A. (2002). The gender gap in student attitudes toward sexist/nonsexist language: Implications for sport management education. *Journal of Sport Management, 16,* 190–208.

Pelled, L. H. (1996). Demographic diversity, conflict, and work group outcomes: An intervening process theory. *Organization Science, 7,* 615–631.

Phillips, K. W., Northcraft, G. B., & Neale, M. A. (2006). Surface-level diversity and decision-making in groups: When does deep-level similarity help? *Group Processes & Intergroup Relations, 9,* 467–482.

Robbins, S. P. (2003). *Essentials of organizational behavior* (7th ed.). Upper Saddle River, NJ: Prentice Hall.

Scott, W. R. (2001). *Institutions and organizations* (2nd ed.). Thousand Oaks, CA: Sage.

Shaw, S. (2007). Touching the intangible? An analysis of *The Equality Standard: A framework for sport*. *Equal Opportunities International, 26,* 420–434.

Staurowsky, E. J. (2007). "You know, we are all Indian": Exploring White power and privilege in reactions to the NCAA Native American mascot policy. *Journal of Sport & Social Issues, 31,* 61–76.

Thomas, R. R., Jr. (1996). *Redefining diversity*. New York: AMACOM.

Trecker, J. (2006, February). Report: *Houston 1836 close to name change*. Foxsports.com. Retrieved April 13, 2006, from http://msn.foxsports.com/soccer/story/5331940.

Zucker, L. G. (1987). Institutional theories of organizations. *Annual Review of Sociology, 13,* 443–464.

14

Managing Diverse Groups*

Melaleuca Elementary School is less than 10 miles from Palm Beach, Florida, where multimillion-dollar mansions line the beachfront. Most of its students, however, do not come from high-income families or live in luxurious homes; rather, most students come from working-class families, and 70 percent are racial minorities. Two of every three students receive free or reduced lunches.

Despite the class-related dissimilarities, these students have at least one thing in common with students from the more affluent neighborhoods: lacrosse. It is the working together toward a common goal—winning—that brings the students together. Claire Lawson, a midfielder on the team, explains, "when we're on the team, we're not focused on color or ethnic background. We're just focused on playing as a team." Though the potential for race-related or social class-related friction certainly exists, sport brings this diverse collection of athletes together.

In a similar fashion, in Seattle, Washington, efforts are under way to make rowing more accessible to everyone. Those students who participate learn several life lessons, such as the importance of working together. Steve Gerritson, who serves as the Executive Director of the George Pocock Rowing Foundation, notes: "It teaches values that are important no matter what you are doing. . . . If you can't cooperate, you don't stay dry." It is lessons such as these that demonstrate to people the importance of teamwork and of overlooking differences in the interest of the team.

Information adapted from: ■ Sharp, D. (2003, June). *High-brown sports seek diversity*. USAToday.com. Retrieved April 15, 2006, from www.usatoday.com/news/nation/2003-06-15-croquet-usat_x.htm.

*Portions of this chapter are adapted from Cunningham (2004).

LEARNING OBJECTIVES

After studying this chapter, you should be able to:

■ Discuss the conditions of contact under which prejudice should be reduced.

■ Discuss how categorization-based strategies are used to manage diverse groups.

■ Explain the integrated model of managing diverse groups.

1. In your experience, does sport serve to bring people together in such a manner that any differences are ignored? If so, explain why this occurs.

2. Have you had experiences where team member dissimilarities remained the primary focus instead of team cooperation? If so, why did this happen?

3. Does sport serve to unify other people, not just the athletes? If so, what are some examples?

s the Diversity Challenge illustrates, some groups' dynamics assuage any potential negative effects of member differences. This is often seen in the sport context because demographics sometimes do not matter on the playing field. This is not true of all athletic teams, however, and we can all think of situations when differences among team members were too great to overcome. The likelihood that individual differences will subvert an otherwise positive group dynamic is even greater when we move away from the athletic context and consider work groups in the organizational setting, thereby suggesting that strategies must be used at the group level to reduce the potentially negative effects of diversity.

I begin this chapter with an overview of the early perspectives upon which more contemporary theories were built. The focus then turns to the social categorization perspective, with the suggestion that the key to reducing the negative effects of diversity in the group setting is to adjust the categorization process. This can be done in one of three ways: breaking down the categories, differentiating between the groups, or building up a superordinate identity. This chapter concludes with a discussion of an integrated model that combines the three categorization-based strategies. For other approaches to prejudice reduction in the group setting, see Paluck and Green (2009).

The Contact Hypothesis

llport's (1954) contact hypothesis is among the earliest and most influential theories related to reducing prejudice. Most of the contemporary theories on bias reduction are grounded in his work (Brewer & Gaertner, 2001), and many scholars and practitioners still incorporate his original piece in their efforts to reduce prejudice (Binder et al., 2009; Pettigrew & Tropp, 2006). The basic premise underlying Allport's *contact hypothesis* states that prejudice is sustained against others because of unfamiliarity and separation; thus, the key to reducing prejudice is to enable members of various social groups to have contact with one another under the right conditions (see also Exhibit 14.1).

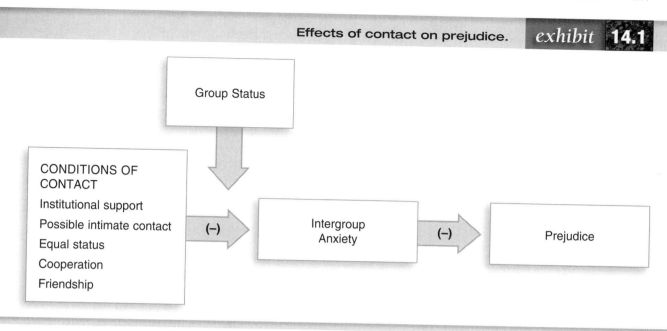

Conditions of Contact

As suggested earlier, Allport's contact hypothesis recognized that contact may not under *every* circumstance reduce prejudice, and in fact, in some situations it might exacerbate it. Thus, contact between dissimilar people improves intergroup relations under the five conditions presented in Exhibit 14.1 and discussed below.

Availability of social and institutional support

Institutional support, such as support from top administrators, should lead to social norms that favor intergroup interaction, tolerance, and acceptance (Allport, 1954). Early research focusing on people in housing projects demonstrated this effect (Deutsch & Collins, 1951; Wilner, Walkley, & Cook, 1955). Prejudice was higher among Whites in segregated housing projects than it was for Whites in integrated projects. For the latter group, bias was especially low when the Whites believed that interactions with racial minorities would be viewed as acceptable and normal.

This idea is certainly applicable to the organizational context. Group leaders often set the norms for the group, thereby prescribing acceptable modes of behavior. If the leader endorses interaction among members from different social groups (e.g., Hispanics and Whites), then that becomes the accepted way of doing things in that group. This available support, coupled with the other conditions, reduces bias among group members.

Possibility of intimate contact

Allport (1954) suggests that close, intimate contact is more effective in reducing bias than brief, impersonal encounters for two reasons. First, developing friendships is usually rewarding and provides a pleasurable affective experience. Second, if people interact with one another on a close, intimate level, then it is likely that this contact will result in stereotype disconfirmation. Stereotypes are largely based on faulty information (Allport, 1954); thus, close interaction with someone will expose the faulty information as such. The housing project research mentioned earlier supports Allport's contention. Those White families who lived close to African American families reported more interaction and significantly more favorable attitudes toward them, relative to the other White families (Wilner et al., 1955).

This principle is applicable to the sport organization context. Consider, for example, groups working on a project in a physical education or kinesiology class. Many times projects require students to work closely with each other over an extended period of time, allowing them to get to know one another on a more personal level. During this process, friendships may be formed, or at the very least, preconceptions and stereotypes may be discredited.

Equal status

Prejudice is more likely to be reduced when the various social groups have equal status (Allport, 1954). If some members are in a subordinate role, then it is likely that stereotypes will be reinforced and strengthened (Cohen, 1984); however, if everyone is on a "common ground," then the interaction is likely to result in bias reduction.

Applying this principle to sport organizations, interaction with dissimilar colleagues on the same hierarchical level is more likely to reduce bias than interaction between a supervisor and a subordinate. For example, bias held by a White assistant athletic director toward Asians is reduced more when his interaction is with an Asian assistant athletic director than with an Asian student worker. The interaction with the Asian assistant director involves two people who have the same power and organizational rank; hence, the equal status might result in reduced bias and prejudice. With the Asian student worker, power differences are still present between the two, so stereotypes may remain.

Necessity for cooperative interaction

Prejudice is thought to be reduced when the situation requires cooperative interdependence among group members (Allport, 1954). Prejudice directed toward out-group members is likely to be reduced when members of separate groups have to work together in order to accomplish the task. Without the others' contributions, the task cannot be completed.

Brewer and Gaertner (2001) suggest that this is the principle that has received the greatest attention and support since the 1950s. This awareness was spurred in large part by Sherif's (Sherif, Harvey, White, Hood, & Sherif, 1961) Robbers Cave study, which involved 22 boys who signed up for three weeks of summer camp. They were randomly assigned to groups of 11 and subsequently named themselves the Eagles and the Rattlers. During the camp's first week, the boys participated in activities with members of their own group, not knowing that the other group even existed. During the second week, the two groups competed against each other in a series of activities such as touch football, resulting in intergroup competition and bias. Previous laboratory settings have shown in-group favoritism to be common; however, in the camp-competition setting, the boys displayed out-group derogation, harboring negative feelings toward the out-group to the extent that there were hostile relations between the two groups (Gaertner et al., 2000). During the third week, the campers were brought together under noncompetitive conditions, but the hostility remained. It was not until the two groups worked together under cooperative conditions (e.g., working together to fix a truck) that the bias between the two groups began to subside. The results of this study, and the studies that support its results (e.g., Johnson, Johnson, & Maruyama, 1984), suggest that cooperative interdependence among group members can decrease levels of intergroup bias.

The efficacy of cooperative interdependence is routinely seen in sport organizations. Recall that in the Diversity Challenge, one of the players commented that her teammates' demographics did not matter while they were playing, because all members focused on the team. In a highly interdependent sport such as lacrosse, teammates must cooperate in order for the team to be successful. Therefore, it is understandable that the team, not the individual differences among the members, becomes the focus of attention, thereby reducing intergroup bias.

Friendship

In addition to the four conditions of contact originally proposed by Allport (1954), there is growing evidence that friendship potential is a key condition for reducing prejudice (Pettigrew, 1998). Consider, for instance, that when people develop friendships with others, they learn information about, change their attitudes toward, generate affective ties with, and change their evaluations of those persons. All of these factors are critical to reducing prejudice (Ellers & Abrams, 2003).

Various studies have provided evidence for the benefits of friendships. Herek and Capitanip (1996) found that people with friends who had confided their sexual minority identity to them had more positive attitudes toward sexual minorities than people whose friends had not revealed a sexual-minority identity. In a longitudinal study of international students participating in a study program abroad, Cunningham, Bopp, and Sagas (2010) found that students who developed intergroup friendships were also likely to reduce their prejudice toward out-group members in general. Finally, Cunningham (2008b) observed that friendship potential, rather than developing actual friendships, was sufficient to positively influence people's general affective reactions to the group. These studies point to the efficacy of emphasizing friendships, or the potential thereof, in intergroup interactions.

Intergroup Anxiety

Initially, researchers assumed that the aforementioned conditions of contact had a direct effect on prejudice reduction. More recent research suggests that the effects probably occur through a reduction in intergroup anxiety (Binder et al., 2009; Brown & Hewstone, 2005; Pettigrew & Tropp, 2006). Intergroup anxiety refers to feelings of unease or apprehension when visualizing or being in contact with out-group members. This anxiety arises from the misunderstanding and rejection people anticipate when interacting with people different from themselves. As a result of this anxiety, people are likely to harbor negative feelings toward out-group members and, in turn, exhibit prejudice.

Research suggests that the presence of these conditions for contact should reduce intergroup anxiety and, ultimately, prejudice. In an examination illustrative of these effects, Ellers and Abrams (2003) conducted a study of Americans studying Spanish in Mexican language institutes. They observed that friendship with out-group members was reliably related to a variety of outcomes, including reduction of anxiety directed toward the out-group and reduction of social distancing. Binder et al.'s (2009) longitudinal study of European school children yielded similar findings.

Influence of Status

Thus far, I have argued that the five conditions of contact should result in decreased intergroup anxiety, which as a result, will reduce prejudice. Contemporary research suggests that these effects are not uniform. Instead, the aforementioned relationships are stronger for majority members than for minority members (Binder et al., 2009; Tropp & Pettigrew, 2005). There are several possible explanations for these findings. From one perspective, majority members have higher status in society, and they might seek to avoid displaying discrimination against minority members because this would be socially unacceptable. Among minority members, these concerns would be trumped by the distress associated with facing discrimination from majority members (Tropp & Pettigrew, 2005).

From a different perspective, it is possible that minority members, because they usually represent the numerical minority in social situations, are more accustomed to interacting with majority members. Thus, the effects of contact would be minimal. For majority members, however, contact with minority members can largely be avoided by, for instance, living in certain neighborhoods, attending particular schools, shopping at a certain supermarket, and the like (for related discussions, see McIntosh's 1990 discussion of White privilege). Thus, contact with minority members, because it is less common, would have a meaningful effect for majority members. This rationale is consistent with Tsui, Egan, and O'Reilly's (1992) non-symmetry hypothesis.

Contact Hypothesis Limitations

Although Allport's (1954) contact hypothesis has been used extensively throughout the years, it does have three primary limitations (Brewer & Gaertner, 2001). First, most of the research was conducted in laboratory settings where contact conditions are controlled. It is possible that the expected contact outcomes may not occur when there is a history of hostility between the groups. For example, would the contact conditions reduce the biases between Palestinians and Jews? In the context of sport organizations, biases might not be as strong as those in the Middle East, but strong prejudicial attitudes exist nonetheless.

Second, bias reduction in one context might not translate to a corresponding reduction in another—it might not generalize to other contexts. For example, suppose players on a boys' basketball team experience a reduction in racial bias because the contact conditions are met. Does this mean that bias is reduced toward *all* racially different people in *all* subsequent situations? That is not likely. A White player's reduction in bias toward racial minority teammates in that situation does not mean that bias toward racial minority students in the classroom context will

GENERALIZING THE EFFECTS OF CONTACT

When bias is reduced, it may be only for that specific situation, or it may be transferred to other situations. The latter circumstance is termed *generalizability* and is more desirable because it means bias is reduced in more than a single situation. Pettigrew (1998) identified three forms of generalization: across situations, from the individual to the entire out-group, and from the immediate out-group to other out-groups.

1. *Generalization across situations.* This form refers to the reduction in bias toward an out-group member in multiple contexts. If diversity strategies are applied in only one context (e.g., workplace training center), then bias toward specific out-group members will likely be reduced in that specific setting, but not others. When the bias reduction is generalized across settings, this means that the strategies were effective in that specific setting (e.g., workplace training center) as well as other settings (e.g., a place outside work).

2. *Generalization from an individual to the entire out-group.* Bias reduction might also be transferred from

an individual to all other members of an out-group. Suppose that, as a result of a diversity training seminar, a White male coach expresses less bias toward the two African Americans in his work group—a good result. A better result is if the training results in the White coach expressing less bias toward all African Americans in all situations.

3. *Generalization from the immediate out-group to other out-groups.* To extend the previous example, the best result is when the White coach not only expresses less bias toward individual African American coaches and African Americans in general but also expresses less bias toward *all* racial minorities. This is what is meant by generalizing from the immediate out-group to all out-groups. Though seldom observed, this form of generalization has occurred in some studies (Pettigrew, 1998). As might be expected, those diversity strategies and training endeavors that have this effect are the most desirable.

also be reduced. Thus, the effects might be context-specific. See the sidebar for additional information related to generalization.

Third, Brewer and Gaertner (2001; see also Pettigrew, 1998) suggest that subsequent studies related to the contact hypothesis placed many boundary conditions on the general theory, resulting in the attachment of an inordinate number of qualifiers. As noted in Chapter 2, boundary conditions can be useful because they indicate when and where certain effects are thought to occur. However, when too many conditions are placed on a theory, it is essentially rendered useless. Commenting on these conditions, Pettigrew believes it is important to distinguish between factors essential to bias reduction and factors that facilitate the process of bias reduction. For our purposes, the first four conditions we described are considered essential, while any remaining boundary conditions (see Brewer & Gaertner, 2001) are facilitators.

Social Categorization Strategies for Reducing Bias

The limitations of the contact hypothesis meant that more sophisticated conceptualizations were needed. As Brewer and Gaertner (2001) note, "contact researchers needed a more elaborate theory of what the underlying processes are and how they mediate the effects of intergroup contact under different conditions" (p. 456). The social categorization framework (Tajfel & Turner, 1979; Turner, Hogg, Oakes, Reicher, & Wetherell, 1987) provides one such perspective. Although this approach was discussed at length in Chapter 2, it is instructive to recall the following two points:

1. In an attempt to organize their social world, people will categorize themselves and others into social groups, and this process minimizes differences *within* groups while heightening differences *between* groups; and

2. People who are similar to the self are considered in-group members and are afforded more positive affect and trust than those who differ from the self—out-group members. The end result is intergroup bias—in-group members are viewed in a more positive light than out-group members.

This theory suggests, therefore, that the potential negative effects of diversity are a function, at least in part, of the intergroup bias that exists between groups. Tsui, Egan, and O'Reilly (1992) argue that the social categorization process is "fundamental to the formation of in-groups and the widely documented tendency of individuals to prefer homogeneous groups of similar others" (p. 522). Williams and O'Reilly (1998) arrived at similar conclusions after reviewing over 40 years of diversity research. They note that "it is clear that there are potentially negative consequences from social categorization processes operating in groups" (p. 118).

This literature suggests that the key to reducing the potentially negative effects of diversity in the group setting is to adjust the categorization process. Indeed, researchers have drawn from the contact hypothesis and social categorization's basic tenets to develop three strategies—decategorization, recategorization, and intergroup contact—thought to overcome categorization boundaries (see Exhibit 14.2). For yet another approach, see the Alternative Perspectives box.

Decategorization

Decategorization seeks to reduce intergroup bias by breaking down the categorization boundaries between interacting groups (Brewer & Miller, 1984). This strategy holds that repeated, individualized interactions among members of different groups

---

exhibit **14.2**   **Categorization-based strategies for managing diverse groups.**

- **Decategorization.** Reduces bias by breaking down categorization boundaries through repeated individualized interactions with out-group members.

- **Recategorization.** Reduces bias by building up a superordinate group identity that is inclusive of all groups.

- **Intergroup contact.** Reduces bias by emphasizing both the categorization boundaries and the unique contributions of each subgroup to the overall group.

Adapted from Brewer & Gaertner (2001).

alternative
P E R S P E C T I V E S

Cross-Categorization Strategies for Managing Diverse Groups. It is possible for people to maintain several identities, but each identity may simply be salient at different times and in different contexts. For example, a person might hold the identity of coach in the workplace, husband at home or during time spent with his family, Christian at church or when religious questions arise, and son when in the presence of his parents. Clearly, not all of these identities hold equal weight across all situations. Within a particular situation, each may serve as the source of categorization. At work, the person might consider other coaches as in-group members and therefore hold those coaches in higher regard than other persons in the organization. This is consistent with the categorization process outlined throughout this book.

We have been working with the assumption that people's identities are orthogonal, so that when one is important in a certain context, others are not. What would happen, however, if one could blur the distinctions of categorization boundaries? What if a person could concurrently trigger multiple identities in a specific social context, so that for example, the categorizations of being a coach and being a male were both salient in the work context? The answer is that the prejudice and bias normally resulting from a particular category distinction may be reduced. This is the essence of the *cross-categorization*

argument. As Brewer and Gaertner (2001) note, "there are reasons to expect that simultaneous activation of multiple ingroup identities both is possible and has potential for reducing prejudice and discrimination based on any one category distinction" (p. 463).

There are several reasons why this might be true. First, when multiple identities are activated in a specific context, the significance of in-group and out-group distinctions become blurred. Second, the bias toward out-group members in one category is thought to be lessened when that person is an in-group member in another category. Finally, cutting across categorization boundaries allows for increased interactions with former out-group members—something that should ultimately reduce the level of bias toward that person (Brewer, 1999).

To illustrate, suppose the coach in the earlier example attends the same church as an opposing coach. In this situation, two categories are crossed—that of a Christian and that of a coach. In this context, the distinction of the opposing coach as an out-group member may be blurred because the coach attends the same church and is thus an in-group member in that regard. Because of the cross-categorization, the coaches are likely to spend more time with one another than they otherwise would, and biases might be reduced. Thus, the cross-categorization decreased the intergroup bias.

will ultimately reduce bias. This is accomplished in two ways. First, recall that through the categorization process, all members of a specific social group are perceived as largely homogeneous (e.g., "all women act *that* way"), and distinctions are not made between members of the group. Decategorization allows one to make distinctions between out-group members, a process called *differentiation*. Second, when people interact on a personal level with others, they compare others to themselves. This results in a process called *personalization*, in which out-group members are viewed "in terms of their uniqueness and in relation to the self" (Hewstone, Rubin, & Willis, 2002, p. 589). Both processes allow one to see oneself and the other person as *individuals*, not as members of homogeneous in-groups or out-groups. To the extent that these interactions are repeated over time, this breaking down of categorization boundaries might also be applied in new situations or to hitherto unfamiliar out-group members (Gaertner et al., 2000).

Research support

Considerable laboratory research supports this rationale (Bettencourt, Brewer, Croak, & Miller, 1992; Gaertner, Mann, Murrell, & Dovidio, 1989; Marcus-Newhall, Miller, Holtz, & Brewer, 1993). Gaertner et al. (1989) found a reduction in bias when members of separate groups came to conceive of themselves as separate individuals as opposed to members of differing social groups. They also identified the manner by which the bias was reduced—decategorization resulted in less attraction toward former in-group members, or reduced in-group favoritism (see also Brewer, 1999). Jones and Foley's (2003) experiment focused on the degree to which decategorization reduced bias among school children. Students were assigned to one of two conditions: (a) the experimental condition, in which students heard a presentation emphasizing anthropology (e.g., origin of humans, the spread of humans across the globe), problems associated with depending on physical biological characteristics to determine differences among people, and the idea that most persons in the United States have common ancestry; and (b) the control condition, in which students heard a reading of Dr. Seuss's *Oh, The Places You'll Go!* The researchers found that those in the experimental condition were more likely to perceive similarities between themselves and others, and as a result, their formerly held prejudice toward out-group members was reduced.

Application

Although it may not be referred to as decategorization, this approach is often used in organizational and team settings. For example, many organizations use rope courses or other adventure escapes, such as those offered by Adventure Associates (www.adventureassoc.com) as methods to build a team. These programs allow people to become acquainted outside the office, build communication skills among team members, and strengthen interpersonal relationships. It is expected that boundaries among team members will be reduced, thereby increasing the team's effectiveness.

As another example, the Dallas Cup, a competitive weeklong soccer tournament held in Dallas, Texas, is designed to host youth teams from around the world. To attract these teams to the tournament, housing must be provided. This is accomplished by having those area athlete participants host several international players for the week. According to tournament organizers, the local players are initially apprehensive about hosting players so different from themselves. However, by week's end, the players have become so close to each other that tears often accompany the goodbyes. Tournament organizers attribute this closeness to the fact that the players get to know one another on a very personal level during that week and grow quite fond of each other (personal communication, Gordon Jago, November 15, 2005).

Potential limitations

Despite the support of decategorization by various studies and its use in professional settings, the approach does have limitations. First, it is unclear how well decategorization is maintained over time or across situations (Brewer & Gaertner, 2001). For example, a common criticism of ropes courses and other adventure activities is that they might reduce bias only in that specific context, but the effects may not transfer back to the workplace or athletic team. The fact that two people learn information about one another and come to like each other in an adventure-course setting may not be sufficient to carry those same feelings over to another context. On the contrary, it might be more likely that once they're back in the workplace—a setting to which the parties are accustomed—the usual routines, behaviors, preferences, and biases will recur. Even if the bias reduction is sustained for a short time, it is unclear whether the effects will last.

Second, even if bias is reduced toward specific individuals, it is unclear whether this effect can be transferred to similar persons (Brewer & Gaertner, 2001). For example, suppose that a Jew and a Muslim share personal information about one another over a period of time, lessening the categorization boundaries. Because this occurred with these two people, does that mean that the categorization boundaries that might exist between the Jew and other Muslims in other contexts will also be reduced? Although that is possible, it is more likely that the bias reduction was directed toward a specific person; consequently, the same process would have to occur with other individuals.

Despite these limitations, decategorization is an effective strategy for reducing bias in the group setting.

Recategorization

According to Gaertner and Dovidio (2000), who developed the Common Ingroup Identity Model, the purpose of *recategorization* is to encourage "members of both groups to regard themselves as belonging to a common superordinate group—*one group* that is inclusive of both memberships" (p. 33, emphasis in original). If members of different groups consider themselves members of a single, common group, then former membership boundaries become less important because all are now members of the same in-group. It serves to replace the "us" and "them" dynamics with a more inclusive "we." Suppose members of a racially diverse sport marketing team considered themselves as *all* belonging to a common in-group—for example, the organization's "sport marketers." If this is the primary identity source in that organization, then the group members would consider themselves "sport marketers" first and perceive other attribute differences (e.g., race) second.

Note the differences between this approach and decategorization. In the latter, the focus is on breaking down categorization boundaries. The goal is to recognize that not all out-group members are the same and, in fact, some out-group members have characteristics similar to the self (Brewer & Miller, 1984). With recategorization, the focus is on creating a new, more inclusive category that encompasses *both* in-group *and* out-group members. Although bias is reduced through decategorization by devaluing former in-group members (Gaertner et al., 1989), bias is reduced through recategorization by bringing former out-group members closer to the self through a process known as pro–in-group bias (Gaertner & Dovidio, 2000; Gaertner et al., 2000). Former out-group members are now afforded in-group status, and because in-group members are generally viewed in a positive light, the former out-group members are now viewed that way as well.

Research support

Several studies lend support to this model, both in the laboratory and the field context. One of the earliest laboratory studies was conducted by Gaertner et al. (1989). They designed an experiment whereby they could manipulate the conditions under which groups worked with one another. They found that when two groups came together and considered themselves members of a single, common group, then intergroup bias was reduced. In line with their theoretical predictions, the bias was reduced because attitudes toward former out-group members became more positive. This supports the notion that bias in recategorized groups is reduced through the pro–in-group bias process. Subsequent laboratory research shows that recategorization is associated with an increase in helpful behaviors directed toward out-group members (Dovidio et al., 1997), satisfaction with the group (Cunningham & Chelladurai, 2004), and preference to work with the group in the future (Cunningham & Chelladurai, 2004).

Terry and O'Brien (2001) conducted a field study involving people who had recently experienced an organizational merger. They found that people who perceived a common identity with the employees with whom they recently merged also expressed higher levels of satisfaction. Nier, Gaertner, Dovidio, Banker, and Ward (2001, Study 2) conducted a field study related to helpful behaviors directed toward African Americans by Whites. They found that Whites were more likely to help African Americans when the African Americans rooted for the same team the Whites did than when they did not. Finally, Cunningham (2005) conducted a field study of NCAA Division I track and field coaches. He found that coworker satisfaction among people who differ racially from their colleagues was higher when they were on staffs characterized by a common in-group identity than when they were not.

All of these studies suggest that developing a common in-group identity among group members helps to reduce the potential negative effects of diversity.

Application

Gaertner and Dovidio (2000) propose several methods a group leader can use to form a common in-group identity, including

- spatial arrangement,
- common threat,
- common fate, and
- common goals.

Spatial arrangement. Gaertner and Dovidio (1986) found that the *spatial arrangement* of group members could influence perceptions of a common in-group identity—members from various groups sit together rather than with members of their own group. Sitting only with in-group members reinforces categorization boundaries; however, sitting with people from other groups, while still in the context of a work group, team, or classroom, reinforces the perception that all of the people are members of a common group, not separate groups. See the Professional Perspectives box on the following page for another example.

Common threat. Establishing a *common threat* is another method to engender a common in-group identity (Rothgerber, 1997). This is perhaps best illustrated by the September 11 terrorist attacks on the United States. After the attack, people from all backgrounds, irrespective of race, religion, sex, or other characteristics, joined together to form a united front against those who attacked the United States. The same principle applies in work groups. When there is a common enemy or common threat, people in the group will unite together to combat that threat. From a managerial standpoint, it is important to explicitly identify the threat and the danger it poses to the group or organization. For example, employees at adidas might view other sporting goods companies such as Nike as a threat to the company's economic well-being. To the extent that the adidas employees all perceive the threat, they are likely to be united in confronting the competitor in the marketplace.

Common fate. Groups that share a common fate are also likely to form a common in-group identity (Gaertner & Dovidio, 2000). *Common fate* means that if the group does well, then all group members are rewarded. Similarly, if the group performs poorly, then all members suffer. This is often seen in highly interdependent athletic teams when, despite individual performances, if the team loses, then all team members suffer the effects. A common fate has a way of bringing the team together and forming solidarity among the members. It is interesting that this same principle is often ignored in the organizational context (DeNisi, 2000). For example, people who work on a team and are collectively responsible for a particular product are often erroneously compensated and evaluated on an individual basis. A work group whose members are dependent upon each other to complete their tasks are collectively responsible for the group's outputs (e.g., the products or services produced); thus, it is reasonable to reward all group members the same for the group's outputs (see Cunningham & Dixon, 2003). Managers or group leaders who adopt this approach are not only likely to incorporate effective performance appraisal systems but are also likely to create a common identity among the group members.

Common goals. The presence of common goals is also likely to create an in-group identity (Gaertner & Dovidio, 2000). *Common goals* have a way of unifying efforts among the group members toward a singular objective. When this occurs, the members are likely to work together for the sake of the team, thereby overlooking individual differences in the interest of the team. This phenomenon is seen on athletic teams when the

PROFESSIONAL PERSPECTIVES

Recategorization on a Soccer Team. Stoney Pryor, the head coach of the A&M Consolidated High School varsity girls' soccer team, observed that the team is diverse in many ways. First, the players differ in ability, so one of his primary tasks is "to get these girls of varying abilities to work together." Second, the levels of motivation differ across the team—some players participate in the hope of playing at the college level, some play to win, and others play for the mere enjoyment of doing so; thus, the girls' work ethic may not be uniform. Third, the players have varying personal styles (e.g., aggressive, offensive-minded, defensive-minded). Fourth, socioeconomic differences among the girls influence the team dynamics. Finally, the attitudes on the team can (and frequently do) vary, thereby opening the possibility of cliques.

In light of these differences, it is imperative that Pryor develop strategies that help the girls work together as a team. He accomplishes this team-building by emphasizing the common group identity and conducting team-building activities throughout the year. For example, team goals (e.g., district championship) are established prior to the season to ensure that the players "are working on the same goals as a team." In addition, the team members participate in considerable group work during practice to reinforce the team concept. This concept of a team is also carried outside the playing field—players regularly have team dinners (usually organized by the seniors) that encourage additional bonding and team-building.

All of these activities focus on reducing the potential negative effects of differences and working together as a team. As Pryor explains, "Some differences are good. We need different positions and different personalities. But, in order for a team to work effectively, we must embrace our particular role, perform it well, and enable those around us to perform their roles. Then, we can begin to achieve the goals set forth as a team. Individual goals are fine, but in team sports, success is generally measured in how the team achieves its goals."

primary objective, winning, brings the players together, and a common identity is formed. The common identity is not only likely to reduce bias but also likely to create more positive outcomes for the group (Murrell & Gaertner, 1992).

Potential limitations

As with decategorization, there are limitations to the recategorization approach. Perhaps the most substantial question is whether a common identity is possible when the opposing groups have a history of strong animosity toward each other (Hewstone et al., 2002; Pettigrew, 1998). For example, would the formation of a common in-group identity be possible between Serbians and Croatians? Most would suspect not. Of course, not all intergroup bias is as pronounced as that example. Even in sport organizations, however, there may be a history of ill will between groups. If the bias is strong enough, if there are substantial differences in group size, or if variations exist in the status, power, or resources allocated to the groups, then efforts to recategorize might be thwarted (Brewer & Gaertner, 2001).

Even though members may conceive of themselves as belonging to a single, common in-group, this does not guarantee that bias will be reduced. Cunningham (2006) conducted an experiment in which demographically diverse students were randomly assigned to three-person groups. All groups worked on projects independently and then came together to form six-person groups. The six-person groups then worked on projects under conditions of interaction, common goals, and common fate. Subsequent checks indicated that the group members believed that the six-person group represented a single, common group, inclusive of both three-person groups. Though all groups recategorized, not all groups experienced the same level of bias reduction. Homogeneous three-person groups that merged with other homogeneous three-person groups experienced substantial bias reduction, as did diverse groups that merged with other diverse groups. However, the bias reduction was not as great when a homogeneous group merged with a diverse group. Cunningham's study showed that even when recategorization occurs, the bias reduction might be dependent upon the diversity of the groups merging together.

Finally, some critics argue that creating a single, common group forces people to give up their other identities (Swann, Polzer, Seyle, & Ko, 2004). For example, if people's strongest identification is with their organization, work group, or athletic team, this implicitly means that their other identities (e.g., race or sex) must be secondary or nonexistent. Such a group structure is akin to the cultures of similarity (Doherty & Chelladurai, 1999) or monocultural organizations (DeSensi, 1995) discussed in Chapter 13 and is not considered desirable. Gaertner and Dovidio (2000) counter that the formation of a common in-group identity does *not* require one to give up other identities; rather, it is possible for people to have multiple identities, all of which are important to them. In the context of academics, for example, it is possible for people to strongly identify with their functional background (e.g., sport management, biomechanics) *and* their academic department. A coach might identify as a Hispanic, a male, and a coach—three salient identities.

The limitations associated with recategorization do not necessarily negate the approach's effectiveness. Many groups successfully recategorize and reduce the level of intergroup bias and poor group dynamics.

Intergroup Contact

Intergroup contact (Brown & Hewstone, 2005; Hewstone & Brown, 1986) represents a third strategy for reducing prejudice in groups. This approach is sometimes referred to as mutual differentiation or salient categorization. Recall that the previous strategies for prejudice reduction sought to alter categorization boundaries. Distinctly different from these perspectives, intergroup contact theory holds that intergroup salience should be maintained. From this perspective, the conditions of contact (i.e., equal status, common goals, cooperation, institutional support, friendship potential) should yield the greatest reduction in prejudice when the contact is with typical out-group members. If the contact is with out-group members who are not typical, then people might dismiss information designed to deconstruct stereotypes and consider them as outsiders (Allport, 1954). If this occurs, then positive attitudes are directed to the individual but not the group as a whole. On the other hand, when group identities are salient and out-group members are viewed as typical of that group, then reduced prejudice should be both individualized (i.e., to the specific out-group member) and generalized (i.e., to other out-group members).

Research support

Empirical support for intergroup contact theory is impressive (see Brown & Hewstone, 2005, for an overview). Binder et al.'s (2009) multinational study of school children provides one of the best illustrations. They found that contact with out-group members was predictive of reduced prejudice six months later. Consistent with the theoretical predictions, prejudice reduction was stronger when interactions were with typical out-group members.

In addition, earlier conceptualizations of the theory (Hewstone & Brown, 1986) pointed to the importance of mutual group differentiation in reducing prejudice as people realize the strengths and superiorities of other groups. Several researchers have extended this line of thinking by arguing that diversity mindsets play a critical role in the relationship between group diversity and subsequent outcomes. The underlying premise is that "the effects of diversity should be more positive in contexts where individuals, groups, and organizations have more favorable beliefs about and attitudes toward diversity, are more focused on harvesting the benefits of diversity, and have a better understanding of how to realize these benefits" (van Knippenberg & Schippers, 2007, p. 531).

There is considerable evidence to support the notion that pro-diversity mindsets will result in better intergroup processes and outcomes. In a laboratory study, Homan, van Knippenberg, Van Kleef, and De Dreu (2007) investigated the manner in which diversity beliefs influenced interactions among people working in diverse groups. When group members held pro-diversity beliefs, the interactions were more positive and the task performance of the group was superior to their counterparts. In a different set of studies, one set in the field and another in the laboratory, van Knippenberg, Haslam, and Platow (2007) observed that people were more closely identified with diverse groups when they believed that diversity added to the value of that group. Cunningham's (2008a) work in the athletic context confirms these views, with his research showing that departments that couple a high commitment to diversity with high employee diversity enjoy a number of benefits, including employee satisfaction.

Application

Intergroup contact theory can certainly be applied to diverse groups. First, managers should seek to create favorable conditions of contact (Allport, 1954; Pettigrew, 1998) and also maintain the saliency of the categorizations. Doing so will ensure that the positive effects of contact are transferred to other out-group members.

Second, past research shows that prejudice is reduced when out-group members' contributions are mutually valued (Dovidio, Gaertner, & Validzic, 1998; Homan et al. 2007; van Knippenberg et al., 2007). Thus, managers should emphasize the benefits that group members' divergent perspectives and varying backgrounds bring to the group. This can be achieved by summarizing research findings in lay terms or offering anecdotes of how diversity positively influenced the group's past performance.

Potential limitations

As with the other approaches, there are shortcomings associated with intergroup contact theory. One of the most recognizable is that emphasizing categorization boundaries might actually have a *negative* effect. Recall that this approach holds that emphasizing group boundaries might be beneficial if both (or all) groups see the value that the out-group brings to the entity. However, there may be situations in which one group might not bring value to the larger group, or the contributions might not be perceived to be as important as the other group's contributions. As Brewer and Gaertner (2001) note, "by reinforcing perceptions of group differences, the differentiation model risks reinforcing negative beliefs about the outgroup" (p. 462). Under these circumstances, emphasizing the differences among the groups actually does more harm than good.

The limitations associated with the mutual group differentiation model do not negate its effectiveness; rather, they simply inform managers and group leaders when it is best to use the strategy and when it should be avoided.

Integrated Model

At first glance, the three strategies for reducing intergroup bias may seem to conflict with one another. One approach calls for reducing categorization boundaries, another calls for creating a common identity, and the third calls for emphasizing the differences among the groups. Which is correct? How can they be reconciled? Pettigrew (1998) and Cunningham (2004) answer these questions. An integrated model is presented in Exhibit 14.3 and is discussed next.

General Principles

Pettigrew (1998) suggests that Allport's (1954) conditions of contact, the potential for friendships to be formed, one's personal characteristics, and one's previous experiences all influence the initial contact between in-group and out-group members. This contact should then initially result in *decategorization,* increasing the level of liking and positive affect directed toward out-group members. This is then followed by established contact between former in-group and out-group members.

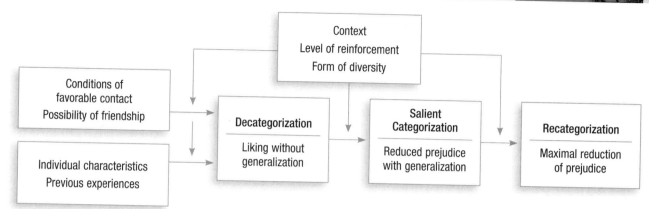

exhibit **14.3**

Integrated model of categorization-based diversity management strategies.

Pettigrew calls this the *salient categorization* stage, which is similar to Hewstone and Brown's (1986) intergroup contact model. This contact between in-group and out-group members leads to a reduction in prejudice with some degree of generalization to others. The reduction of bias toward out-group members is thought to be generalized to all other members of the out-group. In the final stage, members of the various groups are *recategorized* so that a common in-group is formed. Pettigrew believes that in this stage a maximal reduction in bias and prejudice is observed. Ellers and Abrams (2003) provide general support for this model, particularly with respect to the importance of friendships in reducing bias.

Moderators

Cunningham (2004) added to this model by emphasizing the importance of context as a moderator. Other potential moderators are the level of reinforcement and form of diversity.

Context

Context plays an important role in discussions of bias and prejudice because one's identity is often context specific. As Oakes (2001) notes, "we know that meaning varies with context—tears at a wedding are not the same as tears at a funeral" (p. 9). For example, an in-group member at the office might be an out-group member in another context. The same is true for diversity and categorization-based strategies in groups. Efforts to recategorize members of an athletic team, for example, may reduce racial bias among members of that specific team but not in other contexts such as athlete interaction with members of other teams or students at the school.

It is important for managers and group leaders, therefore, to realize that categorization-based diversity strategies may be effective only in specific contexts. Usually, this is not an issue, because the purpose of implementing the strategy is to reduce intergroup bias *in that context*. However, when the purpose is to generalize the reduction of bias to other contexts, strategies may have to be reinforced in those specific contexts.

Level of reinforcement

As with the diversity strategies described in Chapter 13, the categorization-based strategies require continual reinforcement to be effective (Tsui & Gutek, 1999). This is especially true if the effects are to be long-lasting. Consistent with the discussion in Chapter 13, managers and group leaders must continually monitor the diversity climate in the group and reinforce the categorization-based strategies that were implemented. Without doing so, the short-term reduction in intergroup bias is not likely to last.

Form of diversity

As previously discussed, the efficacy of categorization-based strategies may vary depending on the form of diversity. Consider the following:

- The importance of various forms of diversity might change over time. For example, Harrison, Price, Gavin, and Florey (2002) found that demographic differences were important at the beginning of a group's formation, but deep-level diversity became more prominent as the group members remained together.

- Some diversity forms may have historically been a source of categorization and conflict within particular organizations or work groups. For example, one's race is highly salient because of its visibility, and race issues have historically been at the forefront in society (Feagin, 2006).

- Still other forms of diversity might be so intrinsic to one's identity that efforts to alter the categorization process associated with that form of diversity might be met with strong resistance or even hostility. For example, sexual orientation may be so important to an individual that efforts either to downplay or to underscore that form of identity might be met with considerable resistance.

CHAPTER *summary*

This chapter outlined several diversity management strategies that are used at the group level to reduce bias. As demonstrated in the Diversity Challenge, it is possible for members of diverse groups to work effectively with one another. To facilitate the groups' ability to work together, it is incumbent upon managers and team leaders to create team dynamics that alter the otherwise negative effects of social categorization. After reading the chapter, you should be able to:

1. Discuss the conditions of contact under which prejudice should be reduced.

According to the contact hypothesis (Allport, 1954; Pettigrew, 1998), prejudice will be reduced when the following conditions of contact exist: social and institutional support is available, there is a possibility of intimate contact, members of the various groups have equal status, cooperative interaction is required, and there is a potential to develop friendships.

2. Discuss how categorization-based strategies are used to manage diverse groups.

There are three primary categorization-based strategies for reducing the potential negative effects of diversity in the group context. Decategorization focuses on reducing bias by breaking down categorization boundaries through repeated individualized interactions with out-group members. Recategorization focuses on reducing bias by building up a superordinate group identity that is inclusive of in-group and out-group members. Intergroup contact focuses on reducing bias by emphasizing categorization boundaries and the unique contributions of each subgroup to the overall group.

3. Explain the integrated model of managing diverse groups.

Pettigrew (1998) suggests that the three categorization-based strategies could be integrated into a single model. Allport's (1954) conditions of contact, the potential for friendships to be formed, one's personal characteristics, and one's previous experiences all influence the initial contact between in-group and out-group members. This contact should then initially result in decategorization, which is expected to influence salient categorization (i.e., mutual group differentiation) and then recategorization. Three moderators were explicated: context, the level of reinforcement, and the form of diversity.

QUESTIONS *for discussion*

1. Are there situations when asking in-group and out-group members to interact, even under the conditions of contact, might result in negative outcomes? If so, why would this happen?

2. If the conditions of contact reduce bias in one situation, will that transfer to bias reductions in other situations? Why or why not?

3. Three categorization-based strategies for reducing bias in diverse groups were discussed. Which of the three do you believe is the most effective? Why?

4. How does decategorization reduce bias between in-group and out-group members? What are the limitations of this approach?

5. How does recategorization reduce bias between in-group and out-group members? What are the limitations of this approach?

6. How does intergroup contact reduce bias between in-group and out-group members? What are the limitations of this approach?

LEARNING *activities*

1. Suppose you are selected as a leader of a diverse group at a sporting goods company. While working in student groups, decide which of the categorization-based strategies is the best to manage the diversity within the group. Be sure to identify the advantages and disadvantages of the selected strategy.

2. Interview a coach at your university or a local high school about the strategies she uses to manage differences on her team. How do her strategies compare with those outlined in the chapter?

READING *resources*

SUPPLEMENTARY READING

Allport, G. W. (1954). *The nature of prejudice.* Cambridge, MA: Addison-Wesley. (The classical work on which much of the theories and perspectives espoused in this chapter are based.)

Gaertner, S. L., & Dovidio, J. F. (2000). *Reducing intergroup bias: The common ingroup identity model.* Philadelphia: Psychology Press. (Provides an excellent overview of the recategorization process, including research and practical examples.)

Paluck, E. L., & Green, D. P. (2009). Prejudice reduction: What works? A review and assessment of research and practice. *Annual Review of Psychology, 60,* 339–367. (Offers a comprehensive review of various strategies to reduce prejudice in group settings.)

WEB RESOURCES

- Diversity Australia (www.diversityaustralia.gov.au/index.htm): Australian agency that promotes the benefits of diversity to various entities.

- Program of Intergroup Relations (www.umich.edu/~igrc/): program at the University of Michigan aimed at promoting an understanding of intergroup relations.

- Society for Human Resource Management (www.shrm.org/diversity/): site related to various human resource issues, including the management of diversity in work groups.

references

Allport, G. W. (1954). *The nature of prejudice.* Cambridge, MA: Addison-Wesley.

Bettencourt, B. A., Brewer, M. B., Croak, M. R., & Miller, N. (1992). Cooperation and the reduction of intergroup bias: The role of reward structure and social orientation. *Journal of Experimental Social Psychology, 28,* 301–319.

Binder, J., Zagefka, H., Brown, R., Funke, F., Kessler, T., Mummendey, A., Maquil, A., Demoulin, S., & Leyens, J-P. (2009). Does contact reduce prejudice or does prejudice reduce contact? A longitudinal test of the contact hypothesis among majority and minority groups in three European countries. *Journal of Personality and Social Psychology, 96,* 843–856.

Brewer, M. B. (1999). The nature of prejudice: Ingroup love or outgroup hate? *Journal of Social Issues, 55,* 429–444.

Brewer, M. B., & Gaertner, S. L. (2001). Toward reduction of prejudice: Intergroup contact and social categorization. In R. Brown & S. L. Gaertner (Eds.), *Blackwell handbook of social psychology: Intergroup processes* (pp. 451–472). Malden, MA: Blackwell.

Brewer, M. B., & Miller, N. (1984). Beyond the contact hypothesis: Theoretical perspectives on desegregation. In N. Miller & M. B. Brewer (Eds.), *Groups in contact: The psychology of desegregation* (pp. 281–302). New York: Academic Press.

Brown, R., & Hewstone, M. (2005). An integrative theory of intergroup contact. *Advances in Experimental Social Psychology, 37,* 255–343.

Cohen, E. G. (1984). The desegregated school: Problems in status power and interethnic conflict. In N. Miller & M. B. Brewer (Eds.), *Groups in contact: The psychology of desegregation* (pp. 77–96). New York: Academic Press.

Cunningham, G. B. (2004). Strategies for transforming the possible negative effects of group diversity. *Quest, 56,* 421–438.

Cunningham, G. B. (2005). The importance of a common in-group identity in ethnically diverse groups. *Group Dynamics: Theory, Research, and Practice, 9*, 251–260.

Cunningham, G. B. (2006). The influence of group diversity on intergroup bias following recategorization. *The Journal of Social Psychology, 146*, 533–547.

Cunningham, G. B. (2008a). Commitment to diversity and its influence on athletic department outcomes. *Journal of Intercollegiate Sport, 1*, 176–201.

Cunningham, G. B. (2008b). The importance of friendship potential in reducing the negative effects of group diversity. *The Journal of Social Psychology, 148*, 595–608.

Cunningham, G. B., Bopp. T. D., & Sagas, M. (2010). Overcoming cultural barriers in sport management study abroad programs: The influence of extended inter-group contact. *International Journal of Sport Management, 11*, 347–359.

Cunningham, G. B., & Chelladurai, P. (2004). Affective reactions to cross-functional teams: The impact of size, relative performance, and common in-group identity. *Group Dynamics: Theory, Research, and Practice, 8*, 83–97.

Cunningham, G. B., & Dixon, M. A. (2003). New perspectives concerning performance appraisals of intercollegiate coaches. *Quest, 55*, 177–192.

DeNisi, A. S. (2000). Performance appraisal and performance management: A multilevel analysis. In K. J. Klein & S. W. Kozlowski (Eds.), *Multilevel theory, research, and methods in organizations: Foundations, extensions, and new directions* (pp. 121–156). San Francisco: Jossey-Bass.

DeSensi, J. T. (1995). Understanding multiculturalism and valuing diversity: A theoretical perspective. *Quest, 47*, 34–43.

Deutsch, M., & Collins, M. E. (1951). *Interracial housing: A psychological evaluation of a social experiment.* Minneapolis: University of Minnesota Press.

Doherty, A. J., & Chelladurai, P. (1999). Managing cultural diversity in sport organizations: A theoretical perspective. *Journal of Sport Management, 13*, 280–297.

Dovidio, J. F., Gaertner, S. L., & Validzic, A. (1998). Intergroup bias: Status, differentiation, and a common in-group identity. *Journal of Personality and Social Psychology, 75*, 109–120.

Dovidio, J. F., Gaertner, S. L., Validzic, A., Matoka, K., Johnson, B., & Frazier, S. (1997). Extending the benefits of recategorization: Evaluations, self-disclosure, and helping. *Journal of Experimental Social Psychology, 33*, 401–420.

Ellers, A., & Abrams, D. (2003). "Gringos" in Mexico: Cross-sectional and longitudinal effects of language school-promoted contact on intergroup bias. *Group Processes & Intergroup Relations, 6*, 55–75.

Feagin, J. R. (2006). *Systematic racism: A theory of oppression.* New York: Routledge.

Gaertner, S. L., & Dovidio, J. F. (1986). Prejudice, discrimination, and racism: Problems, progress, and promise. In J. F. Dovidio & S. L. Gaertner (Eds.), *Prejudice, discrimination, and racism* (pp. 315–332). Orlando, FL: Academic Press.

Gaertner, S. L., & Dovidio, J. F. (2000). *Reducing intergroup bias: The common ingroup identity model.* Philadelphia: Psychology Press.

Gaertner, S. L., Dovidio, J. F., Banker, B. S., Houlette, M., Johnson, K. M., & McGlynn, E. A. (2000). Reducing intergroup conflict: From superordinate goals to decategorization, recategorization, and mutual differentiation. *Group Dynamics: Theory, Research, and Practice, 4*, 98–114.

Gaertner, S. L., Mann, J., Murrell, A., & Dovidio, J. F. (1989). Reducing intergroup bias: The benefits of recategorization. *Journal of Personality and Social Psychology, 57*, 239–249.

Harrison, D. A., Price, K. H., Gavin, J. H., & Florey, A. T. (2002). Time, teams, and task performance: Changing effects of surface- and deep-level diversity on group functioning. *Academy of Management Journal, 45*, 1029–1045.

Herek, G. M., & Capitanio, J. P. (1996). "Some of my best friends": Intergroup contact, concealable stigma, and heterosexuals' attitudes toward gay men and lesbians. *Personality and Social Psychology Bulletin, 22*, 412-424.

Hewstone, M., & Brown, R. (1986). Contact is not enough: An intergroup perspective on the "contact hypothesis." In M. Hewstone & R. Brown (Eds.), *Contact and conflict in intergroup encounters* (pp. 1–44). Oxford, England: Basil Blackwell.

Hewstone, M., Rubin, M., & Willis, H. (2002). Intergroup bias. *Annual Review of Psychology, 53*, 575–604.

Homan, A. C., van Knippenberg, D., Van Kleef, G. A., & De Dreu, C. K. W. (2007). Bridging faultlines by valuing diversity: Diversity beliefs, information elaboration, and performance in diverse work groups. *Journal of Applied Psychology, 92*, 1189–1199.

Johnson, D. W., Johnson, R. T., & Maruyama, G. (1984). Goal interdependence and interpersonal attraction in heterogeneous classrooms: A meta-analysis. In N. Miller & M. B. Brewer (Eds.), *Groups in contact: The psychology of desegregation* (pp. 187–212). New York: Academic Press.

Jones, L. M., & Foley, L. A. (2003). Educating children to decategorize racial groups. *Journal of Applied Social Psychology, 33*, 554–564.

Marcus-Newhall, A., Miller, N., Holtz, R., & Brewer M. B. (1993). Cross-cutting category membership with role assignment: A means of reducing intergroup bias. *British Journal of Social Psychology, 32*, 125–146.

McIntosh, P. (1990). White privilege: Unpacking the invisible knapsack. *Independent School, 49*, 31–36.

Murrell, A. J., & Gaertner, S. L. (1992). Cohesion and sport team effectiveness: The benefit of a common group identity. *Journal of Sport and Social Issues, 16,* 1–14.

Nier, J. A., Gaertner, S. L., Dovidio, J. F., Banker, B. S., & Ward, C. M. (2001). Changing interracial evaluations and behavior: The effects of a common ingroup identity. *Group Processes and Intergroup Relations, 4,* 299–316.

Oakes, P. (2001). The root of all evil in intergroup relations? Unearthing the categorization process. In R. Brown & S. L. Gaertner (Eds.), *Blackwell handbook of social psychology: Intergroup processes* (pp. 3–21). Malden, MA: Blackwell.

Paluck, E. L., & Green, D. P. (2009). Prejudice reduction: What works? A review and assessment of research and practice. *Annual Review of Psychology, 60,* 339–367.

Pettigrew, T. F. (1998). Intergroup contact theory. *Annual Review of Psychology, 49,* 65–85.

Pettigrew, T. F., & Tropp, L. R. (2006). A meta-analytic test of intergroup contact theory. *Journal of Personality and Social Psychology, 90,* 751–783.

Rothgerber, H. (1997). External intergroup threat as an antecedent to perceptions of in-group and out-group homogeneity. *Journal of Personality and Social Psychology, 73,* 1206–1212.

Sherif, M., Harvey, O. J., White, B. J., Hood, W. R., & Sherif, C. (1961). *Intergroup conflict and cooperation: The Robbers Cave experiment.* Norman: University of Oklahoma Book Exchange.

Swann, W. B., Polzer, J. T., Seyle, D. C., & Ko, S. J. (2004). Finding value in diversity: Verification of personal and social self-views in diverse groups. *Academy of Management Review, 29,* 9–27.

Tajfel, H., & Turner, J. C. (1979). An integrative theory of intergroup conflict. In W. G. Austin & S. Worchel (Eds.), *The social psychology of intergroup relations* (pp. 33–47). Monterey, CA: Brooks/Cole.

Terry, D. J., & O'Brien, A. T. (2001). Status, legitimacy, and ingroup bias in the context of an organizational merger. *Group Processes and Intergroup Relations, 4,* 271–289.

Tropp, L. R., & Pettigrew, T. F. (2005). Relationships between intergroup contact and prejudice among minority and majority status groups. *Psychological Science, 16,* 951–957.

Tsui, A. S., Egan, T. D., & O'Reilly, C. A., III. (1992). Being different: Relational demography and organizational attachment. *Administrative Science Quarterly, 37,* 549–579.

Tsui, A. S., & Gutek, B. A. (1999). *Demographic differences in organizations: Current research and future directions.* New York: Lexington Books.

Turner, J., Hogg, M. A., Oakes, P. J., Reicher, S. D., & Wetherell, M. S. (1987). *Rediscovering the social group: A self-categorization theory.* Oxford, UK: B. Blackwell.

van Knippenberg, D., Haslam, S. A., & Platow, M. J. (2007). Unity through diversity: Value-in-diversity beliefs, work group diversity, and group identification. *Group Dynamics: Theory, Research, and Practice, 11,* 207–222.

van Knippenberg, D., & Schippers, M. C. (2007). Work group diversity. *Annual Review of Psychology, 58,* 515–541.

Williams, K. Y., & O'Reilly, C. A., III. (1998). Demography and diversity in organizations: A review of 40 years of research. In B. M. Staw & L. L. Cummings (Eds.), *Research in organizational behavior* (Vol. 20, pp. 77–140). Greenwich, CT: JAI Press.

Wilner, D. M., Walkley, R. P., & Cook, S. W. (1955). *Human relations in interracial housing.* Minneapolis: University of Minnesota Press.

15

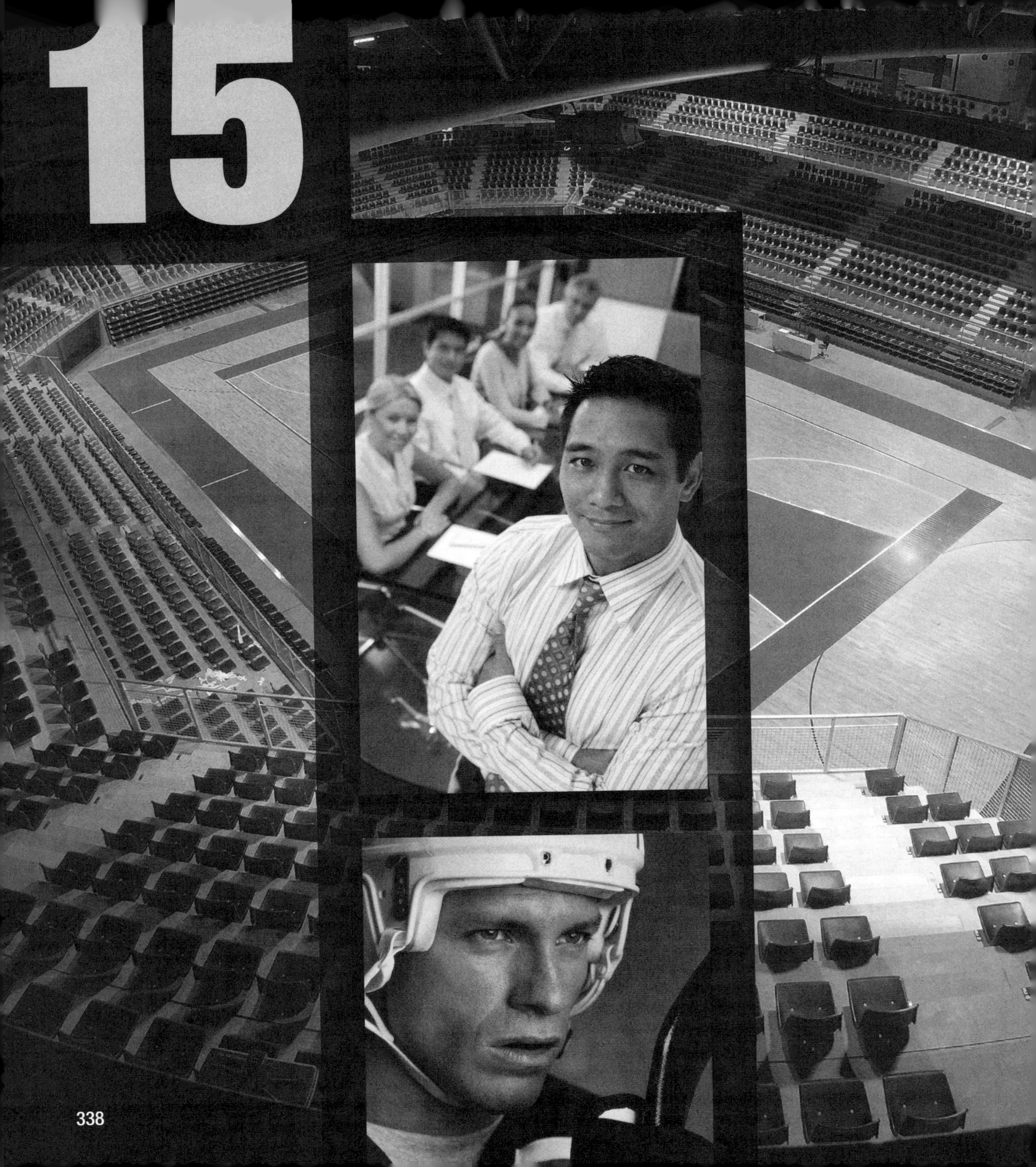

Diversity Training

DIVERSITY CHALLENGE

D iversity is a significant issue in sport organizations today, and college sports is no exception. In fact, the major governing body of college sports in the United States—the NCAA—mandates diversity training for its member institutions. Noncomplying colleges and universities cannot be certified to participate in athletic competition. Such educational endeavors are aimed at providing "a positive learning environment that teaches the values of diversity and maximizes team effectiveness."

The training sessions, however, are met with mixed reviews. In one situation, all members of the 41 varsity teams at Harvard University were required to attend a training session entitled "Community Building and Diversity for Athletes." The session featured Elaine Penn, who is a motivational speaker as well as a former athlete. Penn discussed various issues related to tolerance, gender stereotypes, and racism. Although well-intentioned, the training session was viewed in a negative light. Some athletes believed that the speaker "overestimated the level of prejudice" among the athletes, while others questioned why they were required to attend the session at all. "In general sports break down stereotypes," opined one athlete. "We're exposed to a very diverse mix of people. The meeting would've been better geared toward the rest of the student body, who are exposed to much less diversity than we are." Many of the athletes left the training session feeling frustrated, claiming that the meeting was not necessary and, at times, even insulting.

Although the diversity training at Harvard had a negative effect, others hail the positive effects of these educational programs. Critical Measures, LLC, is an organization that specializes in cultural diversity, with the mission of "offering the finest and most authoritative diversity-related expertise in the U.S." According to this company, a myriad of benefits are to be gained from diversity training in the university athletics setting, including:

LEARNING OBJECTIVES

After studying this chapter, you should be able to:

- Discuss the positive and negative effects of diversity training.

- Discuss the essential elements of effective diversity training programs.

- the ability to recruit and retain top athletes, coaches, and administrators from a variety of backgrounds,

- better team chemistry and performance,

- the creation of a market for women's sports, thereby potentially increasing ticket sales, and

- the reduction of both public relations and legal quandaries.

Critical Measures suggests that diversity training can positively influence an athletic department's staff, players, and overall effectiveness.

Information adapted from: ■ www.criticalmeasures.net ■ www.ncaa.org ■ www.thecrimson.com.

DIVERSITY CHALLENGE   R E F L E C T I O N

1. Have you attended a diversity training program? If so, what were your impressions of it?

2. The Diversity Challenge suggests that diversity training sessions can have both positive and negative effects. Which are more likely and why?

3. What are some of the reasons that people such as the athletes at Harvard University would oppose the diversity training? How would you address their concerns?

iversity training is the educational process whereby people acquire skills, knowledge, attitudes, and abilities about diversity-related issues. The training is used to glean various benefits, both for the organization and the individuals in it (Kulik & Roberson, 2008), and some have suggested that diversity training should be mandatory for aspiring managers (Bell, Connerley, & Cocchiara, 2009). However, training does not always have its intended benefits, and this is certainly true with diversity training as seen in the Diversity Challenge. Equivocal results have spurred criticisms of diversity training (e.g., Kalev, Dobbin, & Kelly, 2006). Some question why it is necessary, others feel they are being singled out, while still others believe that it does more harm than good. What, then, are the actual effects? Further, how do organizations that are required to conduct such training (e.g., NCAA member institutions) provide programs that generate the intended benefits? Are there steps managers can take to institute effective diversity management sessions?

The purpose of this chapter is to address these issues. The first section notes the prevalence of diversity training among organizations today. The potential positive and negative effects of such programs are then discussed. The third section discusses the four steps involved in designing effective diversity training programs: conducting a needs analysis, evaluating antecedent training conditions, selecting the training methods, and ensuring effective post-training conditions. The final section addresses general program considerations. This chapter is designed to introduce managers of sport organizations to the tools needed to conduct effective diversity training.

Prevalence of Diversity Training

Organizations routinely implement training programs to educate and develop their employees. Industry estimates suggest that companies spend between $55.3 billion and $200 billion annually to provide training for their employees (see Salas & Cannon-Bowers, 2001). Mathis and Jackson (2006) report that the typical organization spends about 1.5 to 2 percent of payroll costs on such training. This means that the average organization spends over $600 per employee on training and development activities. For some organizations—those that believe training is integral to their competitive advantage—the costs can rise to $1,665 per eligible employee!

These figures are related to all forms of training—new employee orientation, technology training, and so forth. The figures for diversity training are considerably lower, though they are growing. A 1988 study of medium and large firms showed that diversity was not included among the 40 most common topics covered in training sessions (Gordon, 1988). By 2005, Esen reported that 67 percent of U.S. companies used diversity training in the workplace. Large companies are more likely to implement diversity training than smaller ones, and the former are more likely to employ a diversity manager (Rynes & Rosen, 1995). These figures represent data available for all organizations, not just those related to sport and physical activity. Data pertaining to the prevalence of diversity training in sport and physical-activity organizations do not exist.

Effects of Diversity Training

At first glance, instituting a diversity training program would seem very beneficial. Providing people with necessary knowledge, skills, attitudes, and abilities about diversity would seem to be the first step toward a workplace where the positive effects of diversity are realized. However, there are some instances when these educational programs are met with resistance and actually do more harm than good, as illustrated in the Diversity Challenge. This section outlines both the positive and negative effects of diversity training in the organizational context.

Positive Effects

A review of the literature (Bendick, Egan, & Lofhjelm, 2001; Holladay, Knight, Paige, & Quinones, 2003; Kulik & Roberson, 2008; Mathis & Jackson, 2006; Plummer, 1998; Rynes & Rosen, 1995; Wentling & Palma-Rivas, 1999) suggests that diversity training can have many positive effects (see Exhibit 15.1).

- **Attract and retain a diverse set of employees:** Organizations that have diversity training programs show a commitment to diversity and the inclusion of all peo-

exhibit **15.1**   Positive and negative effects of diversity training programs.

POSITIVE EFFECTS

- Attract and retain a diverse set of employees
- Maintain high worker morale
- Foster understanding among groups
- Curb lawsuits
- Contribute to organizational success

NEGATIVE EFFECTS

- Uneasiness over discussion of sensitive issues
- Code for affirmative action
- White men feel singled out
- Reinforce stereotypes and categorization boundaries
- Sensitize trainees to existing problems
- Lack of positive organizational effects

ple irrespective of their individual differences. This commitment is a source of organizational attraction for potential job applicants from diverse backgrounds. Diverse job holders who react positively to such efforts strengthen their attachment to the organization and tend to stay in the organization longer.

- **Maintain high worker morale:** Diversity training programs can reduce friction among in-group and out-group members. If this occurs, then the overall morale may be strengthened.

- **Foster understanding among groups:** Diversity training sessions are usually designed to identify the fallacies of stereotypes. At the same time, they give people from various groups an appreciation of how out-group members experience work and interact with others. These factors should result in a greater understanding and harmony among members of various groups.

- **Curb lawsuits:** Diversity training can reduce the number of lawsuits brought against the organization. When employees have a greater understanding and knowledge of equal employment, discrimination, and harassment laws, it is likely that the incidence of diversity-related lawsuits will decline.

- **Contribute to organizational success:** The purpose of all training programs is to ultimately contribute to the organization's success by generating greater financial returns, reducing turnover, and so forth.

This review suggests that diversity training can bring real benefits to an organization. The positive outcomes can be seen in human resource issues, legal issues, and overall firm effectiveness.

Negative Effects

Although diversity training can positively benefit the organization, there are times when the programs are actually detrimental. A review of the diversity training literature (Arai, Wanca-Thibault, & Shockley-Zalabak, 2001; Bendick et al., 2001; Hemphill & Haines, 1997; Holladay et al., 2003; Jackson, 1999; Kalev et al., 2006; Karp & Sammour, 2000; Lindsay, 1994; Plummer, 1998; Tallarigo, 1998; Thomas, 1996) identifies several potential drawbacks (see Exhibit 15.1).

- **Discussion of sensitive issues:** Subordination, lack of opportunity, prejudice, discrimination, sexual harassment, and other related issues are sometimes viewed as "hot button" issues. Those issues, along with politics and religion, are generally considered to be outside the realm of polite conversation. Lindsay (1994) equated diversity training to discussing the "undiscussable" (p. 19). Training session conversations can create a tense environment, one in which people either do not feel open to freely convey their thoughts or feel obliged to express thoughts that they would rather not. Such contexts are generally not enjoyed.

- **Code for affirmative action:** Occasionally diversity training initiatives are viewed as efforts by the organization to implement affirmative action strategies. White men often view such actions in a negative light and ultimately reduce their support for these programs.

- **White men feel they are being "blamed":** Some White men who participate in diversity training may feel that they are singled out in the training or that they are being blamed for any negative effects of diversity. This is especially true when the training focuses on topics such as prejudice and discrimination. When White men have these perceptions, they are unlikely to support the training.

- **Reinforcement of stereotypes and categorization boundaries:** Many diversity training sessions focus on relevant stereotypes intending to expose employees' faulty perceptions of out-group members. Unfortunately, the training may have the opposite effect: rather than break down categorization boundaries between in-group and out-group members, the sessions may reinforce or even create boundaries.

- **Sensitization of trainees to existing problems:** Diversity training programs make people more aware of diversity-related issues, of the prejudice in organizations and society at large, and of the inequitable distribution of resources and opportunities. Trainees become more attuned to such issues and take special note of their work experiences, intent upon discovering whether discrimination is taking place. If this occurs, the incidence of diversity-related lawsuits and grievances may actually increase rather than subside, thereby having the opposite effect of what was intended.

- **Lack of positive organizational effects:** When poorly designed, diversity training has a null or negative effect on the organization's overall effectiveness.

These findings suggest that such training might create friction and discomfort among the trainees, and it might actually *increase* the number of diversity-related grievances and negatively influence organizational processes and outcomes.

Making Sense of the Effects

As discussed above, the literature reviews provide conflicting information about the effects of diversity trainings. How, then, do people make sense of these varying effects? The answer lies not only in the design and implementation of the diversity training but also in whether or not the lessons are actually applied to the workplace setting—a process known as *transfer of training*. When the training sessions are ill-conceived, held simply for the sake of satisfying external constituents, or do not have the support from important organizational decision makers, they are unlikely to be successful. When the training is designed for the organization's specific needs, is a central part to the organization's mission, and has top management support, it is likely to benefit the trainees and the organization as a whole. Therefore, it is important to learn how to design and deliver effective diversity training programs. This is discussed in the next section.

Designing and Delivering Effective Diversity Training Programs

When developing a diversity training program be aware that *there is no one model that is best for all organizations* (Plummer, 1998; Sussman, 1997). Many consulting organizations offer the same "cookie cutter" diversity training program to every organization they serve. Some administrative bodies require that certain elements be covered in the training held by its institutions. Many university systems offer the same training (usually in an electronic format that takes several *minutes* to complete) on all of their campuses. There are several reasons why such standardization occurs, including issues related to consistency, reliability, and cost effectiveness. Nevertheless, most, if not all, of these programs fail to deliver the genuinely positive effects that diversity training offers.

To truly realize the benefits, it is imperative that the training be tailored to the needs of the specific organization. For some organizations, issues related to sexual orientation or religious differences may be most salient. For others, harassment of and discrimination against women may be the source of stress and friction. For still other organizations, diversity issues may not be a source of consternation; the organization may simply be seeking to reinforce principles and values. Because the list of potential diversity issues relevant to a specific organization is virtually endless, it is foolish and irresponsible to offer the same training to all organizations. Instead, the training must be personalized for each organization. Designing and delivering an effective diversity training program requires managers to conduct a needs analysis, examine the pre-training conditions, decide on the specific training topics and methods, and consider various post-training factors (e.g., training evaluation, transfer of training). Each of these issues is discussed in turn (Mathis & Jackson, 2006; Salas & Cannon-Bowers, 2001). An illustrative summary is presented in Exhibit 15.2.

exhibit **15.2** **Designing effective diversity training programs.**

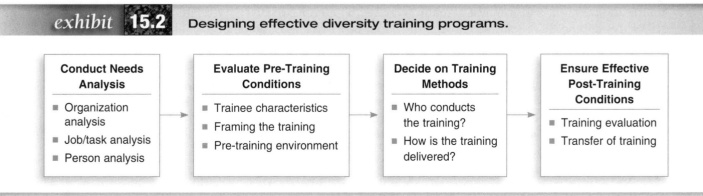

Conduct Needs Analysis	Evaluate Pre-Training Conditions	Decide on Training Methods	Ensure Effective Post-Training Conditions
▪ Organization analysis ▪ Job/task analysis ▪ Person analysis	▪ Trainee characteristics ▪ Framing the training ▪ Pre-training environment	▪ Who conducts the training? ▪ How is the training delivered?	▪ Training evaluation ▪ Transfer of training

Needs Analysis

Salas and Cannon-Bowers (2001) note that "it is well acknowledged that one of *the most* important steps in training development is conducting a training needs analysis" (p. 475, emphasis added; see also the Diversity in the Field box on the next page for related information). Unfortunately, there is some evidence that preliminary analyses are not conducted (Arthur, Bennett, Edens, & Bell, 2003). This is disappointing because a *needs analysis* is instrumental in understanding *where* training is needed, *who* needs the training, and *what* material should be included in the training (Goldstein, 1993).

When conducting a needs analysis, remember that not all deficiencies are training-related problems. For example, poor customer relations may be due to a lack of cultural awareness on the part of the service provider. It could also be, however, that the method of providing the services is flawed, that the service provider simply lacks the motivation to provide high-quality services, or that the support needed to provide the service is lacking. Obviously, these latter issues pertain more to structural or managerial factors than to diversity issues; thus, once a problem is identified, managers must critically analyze the source of the problem and take appropriate action.

A needs analysis covers three areas: the organization, the jobs tasks, and the people. See Exhibit 15.3 for the four primary motivations organizations have for conducting diversity training.

Organizational analysis

The organizational analysis requires managers to examine all of the elements of an organization that may affect the training's effectiveness (Salas & Cannon-Bowers, 2001). This includes the congruence of the training with the organization's overall mission and strategy, the monies available to deliver the training, and the level of support from top management. This is a critical first step in the overall needs-analysis process because it will identify any constraints or barriers to delivering an effective training program. Salas and Cannon-Bowers note that too many organizations neglect this step; consequently, the training is not as successful for them as it is for those organizations that do the analysis.

Motivations for diversity training.   *exhibit* **15.3**

Researchers have identified four primary motivations for initiating diversity training programs:*

- To increase productivity and improve customer relations (82.1%)
- To comply with federal, state, and local mandates related to equal employment opportunity and prevent related lawsuits (37.4%)
- To enable an organization to effectively operate in the international business arena (27.2%)
- To fulfill requirements associated with a diversity-related lawsuit (4.8%)

*Respondents could choose more than one response.

Adapted from Bendick et al. (2001).

DIVERSITY
in the field

How a Needs Analysis Shows the Need for Diversity Training. Kemp Elementary School is a public school located in Bryan, Texas. The students are largely economically disadvantaged (97 percent receive free or reduced lunches), and the racial composition of the student body is an interesting mix, with 45 percent African American, 50 percent Hispanic, and 5 percent White. The staff recently conducted an organizational needs analysis to assess how well the school was serving the students' needs. According to school principal Kellie Deegear, several of the findings pointed to the need for diversity training. First, the staff is comprised predominantly of White females and thus does not match the demographic composition of the students. Second, African American students are overrepresented in special education, alternative education, and in-school suspension, while being underrepresented in the gifted and talented programs and on the honor roll. Third, the top 12 most challenging students from a discipline standpoint are all African American males. Fourth, there are large gaps between African American test scores on standardized tests and the scores of students of other races. Deegear notes, "as a staff, we believe we need to change so we can meet the needs of all students." She also notes that the following quote from Lisa Delpit, director of the Center for Urban Educational Excellence and the Benjamin E. Mays Professor of Urban Educational Leadership at Georgia State University, serves to guide their diversity efforts: "The key here is not the kind of instruction but the attitude underlying it. When teachers do not understand the potential of the students they teach, they will under-teach them no matter what methodology."

Research suggests that the organizational climate is particularly important to the training process (Rouiller & Goldstein, 1993; Wentling & Palma-Rivas, 1999). Organizations with a culture of diversity (Doherty & Chelladurai, 1999) are likely to have more supports in place to allow the trainees to apply the information they learn in the training session to the workplace. Because diversity and individual differences are valued in these organizations, the importance attached to the training is likely to be amplified.

Top management support is also key. Without management backing, employees might question how important diversity and the related training really is, potentially undermining the training's overall effectiveness.

Job/task analysis

A job/task analysis entails collecting information related to the specific duties of each job; the conditions under which employees complete the job; and the specific knowledge, skills, and abilities necessary to complete the tasks (Salas & Cannon-Bowers, 2001). The job and task requirements are then compared to the existing performance level, and if a discrepancy exists, training might be needed (Mathis & Jackson, 2006). This analysis is useful because it identifies areas where the employee training can be made more effective.

A job/task analysis is certainly necessary to forecast accurately what skills will be needed for future jobs (Arvey, Salas, & Gialluca, 1992), but it is also useful in developing diversity training for existing employees. For example, the level of interaction with others probably varies from job to job within most sport organizations. Employees in customer service, public relations, and marketing have the most interaction with a sport organization's customers and clients. Thus, it is more useful to tailor their diversity training to fit the customers rather than other organization employees. Although this example is somewhat simplistic, it does show how conducting a job/task analysis is beneficial in developing the training program.

Person analysis

The third prong of the needs analysis involves the organization's people (Salas & Cannon-Bowers, 2001). Analyzing the people can be accomplished by examining employees' performance appraisals and focusing on those portions that highlight deficiencies (Mathis & Jackson, 2006). Although some organizations include diversity-related criteria on their performance appraisals (Gilbert & Ivancevich, 2000), most do not. Thus, managers must develop alternative methods to identify the employees' specific needs. One option is to distribute an organization-wide questionnaire that assesses employee attitudes (and potentially behaviors) toward diversity issues. A sample item might be, "All employees within the organization, irrespective of their differences, are treated fairly" (agree or disagree). Another option is to purposefully observe employees and their interactions with others and with clients.

Regardless of how the information is collected, it is imperative that managers understand the training needs of each employee. As is discussed through this book, each person brings different diversity-related experiences, attitudes, preferences, and behavioral tendencies to the workplace. These differences influence the employees' attitudes toward work, the manner in which they interact with their colleagues, and the way they serve the customers. Where deficiencies exist, training is needed to achieve the desired behaviors and attitudes.

Pre-Training Conditions

Before designing and implementing the training program, it is important to ensure that optimal training conditions are in place. Salas and Cannon-Bowers (2001) argue that "events that occur before training can be as important as (and in some cases more important than) those that occur during and after training" (p. 447). Managers should be particularly mindful of three pre-training conditions: the trainees' characteristics, the framing of the training, and the pre-training environment.

Trainee characteristics

Four characteristics influence the trainees' readiness to learn the material: (1) ability to learn, (2) self-efficacy, (3) motivation to learn (Mathis & Jackson, 2006; Salas & Cannon-Bowers, 2001), and (4) learning style.

Ability to learn. Not all employees have the same ability to learn the training material. For some, a lack of overall cognitive ability may impede their capacity to learn new material. Many studies show that one's general cognitive ability is a reliable predictor of training effectiveness and knowledge acquisition (see Colquitt, LePine, & Noe, 2000; Kaemar, Wright, & McMahan, 1997). For other trainees, there may be language differences that inhibit the learning process. Still other trainees might simply lack the reading and writing capabilities necessary to learn the material. To correct these deficiencies, Mathis and Jackson (2006) suggest three options:

- Offer remedial training to current employees who lack those skills.
- Knowingly hire people who are deficient in those skills and provide specific training in the workplace.
- Work with local schools and agencies to better educate future employees.

These recommendations are global and, for some companies (e.g., smaller sport organizations), might represent unrealistic demands. The key is to ensure that employees have the ability to learn. For example, if the majority of the workforce is Spanish speaking, then perhaps the training should also be presented in Spanish, or at least the option should be available. If the workforce is not computer-savvy, then develop the training in both an electronic and a paper-and-pencil format. The point is to guarantee that employees at least be capable of learning the material.

Self-efficacy. Bandura (1986) defines self-efficacy as "people's judgments of their capabilities to organize and execute courses of action required to attain specific types of performances" (p. 391). Self-efficacy is related to a variety of behaviors, such as the choice of activities and the effort expended in those activities. Within the training context, self-efficacy refers to a belief in one's own *ability* to learn the material presented. Research in this area shows that the self-efficacy people possess prior to the training session is reliably related to their performance (i.e., knowledge acquisition) in the training and their ability to apply the concepts to the work context (Colquitt et al., 2000).

What steps can managers take to increase trainees' self-efficacy? The extant literature (Colquitt et al., 2000; Gist & Mitchell, 1992) points to several possibilities, including:

- Showing that people with characteristics similar to the trainee have successfully completed the training session. For example, a manager of a group of older employees could provide data illustrating the high percentage of people of a similar age who successfully completed the training.
- Explaining why the training is needed and the possible benefits. A manager of an inner-city recreational facility might demonstrate how multicultural training will help employees reach, communicate with, and positively affect the organization's clientele.
- Persuading trainees that they have the skills and capabilities necessary for knowledge acquisition. Trainers might make the initial training sessions easy to ensure early success among the participants. This success is then used to convince the trainees that they have the ability to complete the training.

Motivation. Noe and Schmitt (1986) define training motivation as the "specific desire on the part of the trainee to learn the content of the training program" (p. 501). Trainees must have not only the capacity to learn but also the desire to learn. Without the latter, even the best-developed program will be for naught (Tannenbaum & Yulk, 1992). Indeed, research shows that training motivation is positively associated with a variety of important outcomes, including learning outcomes (Mathieu, Tannenbaum, & Salas, 1992; Tracey, Hinkin, Tannenbaum, & Mathieu, 2001), affective reactions (Quinones, 1995; Tracey et al., 2001), post-training self-efficacy (Cunningham & Mahoney, 2004), and perceived training transfer (Facteau, Dobbins, Russell, Ladd, & Kudish, 1995). Furthermore, Colquitt et al. (2000) found that training motivation predicted important training outcomes even beyond the effects of one's general mental ability.

Research identifies various factors that influence training motivation. One factor is personality: people who are conscientious are more likely to have confidence in their capacity to learn the material (Martocchio & Judge, 1997) and are likely to possess a strong desire to do so (Colquitt & Simmering, 1998). Others found that organizational attachment positively relates to training motivation (Cunningham & Mahoney, 2004)—those people who are vested in the organization and strongly identify with it will want to learn the material for the good of the organization. Furthermore, people are likely to be more motivated to learn when they see the value in the learning (Colquitt et al., 2000; Cunningham & Mahoney, 2004). Managers should demonstrate how diversity training benefits not only the individual trainees but also the organization as a whole. Finally, people's general attitudes toward diversity influence their attitudes toward diversity training. For example, Wiethoff (2004) argues that people who have experienced discrimination in the past might be more likely to express a motivation to learn in diversity training sessions. We might expect similar trends with people who strongly value fairness or who believe that diversity is beneficial to the organization and its employees.

Learning style. Because people learn in different ways, it is important for managers to understand the differences before designing and implementing a training session. Mathis and Jackson (2006) suggest that there are three primary learning styles: auditory, tactile, and visual. *Auditory* learners retain the most information when they can hear the instructions or material. *Tactile* learners prefer to touch and experience things directly; thus, they should be given hands-on type instruction. Finally, *visual* learners retain more when they can watch or see the material. Although it may be difficult to individualize the material for each trainee, all three learning styles should be incorporated into the material. Part of the training may be presented using a lecture format, another portion delivered electronically, and a final portion through hands-on activities such as role-playing. This approach provides the most effective training by diversifying the training techniques to allow for different learning styles.

Framing the training

Managers must consider how they frame or depict the training. Research across a variety of disciplines shows that the manner in which an event or behavior is framed substantially influences people's behaviors and attitudes. Framing is particularly important when it involves "hot button" issues (Holladay et al., 2003). For example, people's view toward affirmative action often depends on how those policies are framed (Crosby, Iyer, & Sincharoen, 2006). People are more likely to favor affirmative action when it is viewed as a way organizations reach out to traditionally disadvantaged groups than when it is perceived as a quota system. The way a policy is framed or contextualized influences subsequent reactions to it.

In the context of diversity training, considerable research suggests that pre-training attitudes and beliefs influence subsequent motivation and performance (Hanover & Cellar, 1998; Holladay et al., 2003). Holladay et al. explicitly considered the effects of two aspects of framing on trainees' subsequent attitudes: the title of the training ("Diversity Training" versus "Building Human Relations") and the scope of the training (a focus only on racial issues versus a broad focus on race, sex, personality, and lifestyle differences). They found that these two factors interacted to predict backlash to the training and likelihood of training transfer. Training that had a direct title (e.g., "Diversity Training") and a broad focus received less backlash than the other training formats. The same was true for the likelihood of transfer—trainees in a program that had a direct title and broad focus were the most likely to use the information in their work. Thus, the manner in which managers frame the training is likely to substantially influence the way people view the training and the likelihood that they will use the information in the future.

Pre-training environment

The last antecedent of which managers must be mindful is the pre-training environment. Several factors contribute to the pre-training environment: support for the training from both managers and coworkers, the training's (in)voluntary nature, and the link between the material and subsequent job-related behaviors.

Support. As previously noted, support is one of the most important factors contributing to the training's success (Wentling & Palma-Rivas, 1999; Wiethoff, 2004). This support comes from supervisors and coworkers. Wiethoff argues that, although support can positively influence people's training motivation, this effect is likely to be moderated by the extent to which employees are motivated to comply with their supervisors and coworkers. Trainees who believe there is support for the training and who are highly motivated to act in accordance with their coworkers and supervisors are more likely than their counterparts to reap the benefits of diversity training.

(In)voluntary nature of training. There is some debate as to whether diversity training should be mandatory or voluntary. As you recall from the Diversity Challenge, the athletes at Harvard resented being required to attend the diversity training. Wiethoff (2004) suggests that mandatory training might be counterproductive because it may result in less positive attitudes among the trainees. On the other hand, others argue that mandatory training conveys the message that the training is important to upper management (Bell et al., 2009; Cunningham & Mahoney, 2004). This is especially true when the top management team members attend the training session (Cunningham & Singer, 2009).

Link between the training and other outcomes. Trainees are likely to be motivated to learn and apply the information when doing so is linked to subsequent job performance and evaluations (Bendick et al., 2001; Wiethoff, 2004). If people believe that they can use the information in their jobs, that their performance evaluations will be tied to doing so, and that their pay raises to some extent will be linked to applying the information to their everyday work, then the training is likely to be successful. If employees do not make such causal links, then the motivation to learn and transfer the information is likely to be low, thereby limiting the training's effectiveness. After presenting information related to multicultural competence, a manager might ask the trainees to role-play situations and apply the recently learned knowledge in a scenario they are likely to encounter in their everyday work settings.

Training Methods

The next steps in designing a diversity training program are to consider who will conduct the training and how the material will be delivered. Exhibit 15.4 provides information about the topics that are routinely covered in diversity training sessions.

| Topics typically covered in diversity training programs. | *exhibit* **15.4** |

- Issues of discrimination, prejudice, and stereotypes in the workplace
- Ways in which diverse groups can work well with one another
- Explanation of how a diversity training program contributes to organizational effectiveness
- Explanation of the client organization's policies relative to diversity issues
- Fair and nondiscriminatory processes for recruitment, hiring, performance appraisals, and promotion
- Backlash from White males
- Cultures of various demographic groups (e.g., employees, customers/clients, community)
- Using the training on the job

Adapted from Bendick et al. (2001).

Conducting the training

Although many people can conduct the training program, it is necessary to determine whether the training is done by someone within the organization or by an outside consultant. The advantages and disadvantages of each alternative are presented next.

Internal training. It is usually advantageous for the diversity training to be conducted by a person within the organization. Some sport organizations may have human resource personnel on staff who are specifically trained in this area. When there is no staff person available, persons with an expertise in diversity issues or who have had diversity training could lead the sessions. Using in-house personnel reduces the costs associated with training. Because an in-house trainer probably has a working knowledge and understanding of the specific diversity issues facing the organization, the training can be made more individualized.

Despite these advantages, there are potential drawbacks with an internal approach. First, the scope of diversity issues is broad, and the trainer's expertise might be limited in some areas. Second, many sport organizations do not have a full-time human resource professional on staff, and others who might conduct the training may have had limited training. Thus, the training's effectiveness may be reduced. Third, trainees might be reluctant to discuss issues or disclose certain information to trainers with whom they work—another factor that can limit the program's overall success.

Outside training. There are many advantages of hiring an individual or firm to conduct the training session. Many organizations offer these services, such as Withycombe Consulting (www.withycombeconsulting.com). These firms specialize in diversity training and have the knowledge and expertise necessary to conduct high-quality programs. Outside trainers are detached from the organization and therefore from the emotional baggage that might accompany some of the diversity issues. They can, therefore, provide a more objective assessment of the diversity issues and effectively train the employees from a third-party perspective.

Employees may be more inclined to discuss sensitive diversity issues with people outside the organization.

Using outside personnel, however, also has its disadvantages. The costs may be substantial, consuming a substantial portion of a small organization's training and human resource budget. In addition, some outside agencies standardize their training, presenting the same information to every organization with which they consult. Although efficient, this practice is not likely to benefit the sport organization, because it has specific diversity-related needs that must be addressed.

Training delivery

If an in-house trainer will be used, the next consideration is how the training will be delivered. (If the training is conducted by an external agent, that person or organization will design the delivery.) Mathis and Jackson (2006) identify four delivery methods: cooperative training, instructor-led classroom, distance training, and simulations.

Cooperative training. This approach blends classroom training with on-the-job experience and usually involves a school-to-work transition, internships, or apprenticeship training. It is most often used with new employees, combining the classroom learning with the real-life experience on the job.

Among the many advantages of this approach, perhaps the greatest is the opportunity for the trainee to combine the theories and principles learned in the classroom with the work context, gaining practical firsthand experience. This approach is more useful in some situations, such as with new employees, than in others, such as when knowledge acquisition is the primary desired outcome of the training.

Instructor-led classroom. The most widely used form of training involves a presentation of the material primarily using a lecture format, discussions, case studies, and videos. The use of several methods in delivering the information accommodates the trainees' various learning styles.

This approach has several advantages. First, the information can be conveyed to a relatively large group of people. Second, this approach lends itself to the presentation of diversity issues aimed at providing factual information or, in some instances, to programs aimed at changing attitudes. A disadvantage is that trainees may be averse to listening to a straight lecture, especially if it lasts for an extended period of time. Also, trainees get little hands-on experience with this method.

Distance training. Distance training is one of the newest and fastest growing forms of training delivery. This training can be delivered using correspondence packets, video conferencing, Internet classes, and voice-over PowerPoint presentations. Software such as Blackboard (www.blackboard.com), Camtasia (www.techsmith.com), Impatica (www.impatica.com), and Adobe (www.adobe.com) offer many options that sport organizations and universities can use for distance training and education.

As with the other training designs, this approach also has its advantages and disadvantages. Distance training allows an expert speaker in one location to reach thousands of people around the world. This is especially useful for multinational corporations like Nike and adidas. Technological advances allow for more innovative, high-tech forms of delivering information. Unfortunately, the lack of interaction that typically accompanies distance courses limits their effectiveness. Not every organization can afford the initial start-up costs, even though the future cost savings may compensate for the large up-front costs. In addition, not all trainees will be sufficiently technologically savvy to effectively use the materials.

Simulations. Many organizations use simulations for various training needs, with the military and aviation sectors using them most often (Salas & Cannon-Bowers, 2001). This training form uses computer-supported games and scenarios that reflect many of the psychological and behavioral requirements of the general work environment. In the context of diversity training, trainees might work through a computer-based simulation related to hiring and recruiting a diverse workforce. CBT Planet (www.cbtplanet.com) offers a training session that lasts two to four hours. Trainees work through five simulations that teach them about (a) the general principles related to diversity, (b) cultural differences, (c) overcoming barriers to diversity, (d) communicating with a diverse workforce, and (e) managing workplace diversity. The advantages and disadvantages of this method are generally the same as with distance education.

The specific delivery method choice should be driven by the specific training needs, the trainees' learning styles and preferences, and the organization's budgetary constraints (see also Arthur et al., 2003). See Exhibit 15.5 for other training design principles.

Post-Training Conditions

The final part of designing an effective diversity training program pertains to the two post-training factors that impact the program's long-term effectiveness: training evaluation and ensuring the transfer of training (Mathis & Jackson, 2006; Salas & Cannon-Bowers, 2001).

Effective diversity training principles.   *exhibit* **15.5**

Research suggests that the most effective training programs are centered around four basic principles:

1. *Present pertinent information and material about the training.* Trainees should know what they are expected to learn and how they will do so.

2. *Demonstrate the knowledge, skills, and abilities the trainees are expected to learn.* Trainers must demonstrate to the participants what is to be learned. Simply telling them is often insufficient, especially when physical or behavioral skills are involved.

3. *Create environments for people to practice the skills.* Provide trainees many opportunities to actually practice each skill themselves.

4. *Provide feedback during and after the training.* Trainees must have corrective feedback so they can practice the skills properly. Feedback is important not only during the actual training but also after the training when the trainees are expected to apply the material they learned to their everyday jobs.

Adapted from Salas and Cannon-Bowers (2001).

Training evaluation

When evaluating the training's effectiveness, managers must consider what should be evaluated and the method for doing so.

Evaluation content. Kirkpatrick (1976) developed a framework for assessing training effectiveness. He argues that training outcomes can be grouped into one of four categories (see also the Alternative Perspectives box on page 356 for another method of evaluating training effectiveness):

1. **Reactions.** Sport organizations can evaluate trainees' reactions to the session by interviewing them or asking them to complete post-training questionnaires. The questions might relate to trainees' perceptions about the overall value of the training, how well they liked the instruction style or the trainers, or how useful they believe the training will be in their work. Most often, trainee reactions are gathered immediately after the training; however, data can also be gathered weeks or months after the training takes place to assess how useful the information has been in their everyday job duties.

2. **Learning.** Sport organizations can assess how well the trainees learned the material by asking the trainees to complete a simple test on the material covered in the session. This method is particularly useful when the subject matter is primarily factual (e.g., legal issues related to Title IX, sexual harassment, or equal employment opportunity laws).

3. **Behavior.** A third outcome to be evaluated is actual behavior. Suppose a sport organization is subjected to claims of discrimination in the hiring and promotion process arising from differential evaluations of racial minorities and Whites. Teaching the evaluators how to construct and implement objective evaluations should reduce or eliminate this problem. The trainers can assess the training's effectiveness by tracking the behavior prior to the training and again at several points after the training.

4. **Results.** The final issue to be analyzed is how well organizational objectives have been realized. Some desired results of interest are the retention of employees, decreased absenteeism, increased customer satisfaction, increased level of positive employee affect, and increased financial gains. Managers should compare the level prior to training with the level after training to determine whether the training was effective.

Which outcome should be assessed? The answer is largely driven by the training content. In general, it is easy to assess the reactions and difficult to assess the results. What is interesting, however, is that the results data are usually the most important to the organization and the reaction data usually least important (Mathis & Jackson, 2006). Thus, managers must make trade-offs and weigh the training content against outcomes the organization wishes to achieve.

Evaluation designs. Managers can choose from among many designs to assess the training's effectiveness. In increasing order of the design's effectiveness, they include a post-training-only design, pre- and post-training design, pre- and post-training design with a control group, and a post-training-only design with a control group (see Exhibit 15.6 for an illustration).

| Evaluation designs for assessing training's effectiveness. | *exhibit* **15.6** |

POST-TRAINING

| Training Group | | T | | E |

PRE- AND POST-TRAINING

| Training Group | E | T | | E |

PRE- AND POST-TRAINING WITH A CONTROL GROUP

| Training Group | E | T | | E |

| Control Group | E | | | E |

POST-TRAINING ONLY WITH A CONTROL GROUP

| Training Group | | T | | E |

| Control Group | | | | E |

T = Training   E = Evaluation

With a *post-training-only* design, data is collected from the trainees after the training. Trainees can take a test or complete a questionnaire. This approach is easy to design and administer; however, there are no data to which the results can be compared. It is impossible to determine whether the trainees improved over the course of the training or how they compare with people who have no training.

The *pre- and post-training* design evaluates the trainees prior to and after the training. If an increase in, for example, knowledge related to diversity laws is observed, then it might indicate that the training was effective. Because there is no control group, it is impossible to determine whether the increase would be greater than that observed of people who had not received the training.

The third evaluation design—*pre- and post-training with a control group*—addresses the issue of comparing the trained people with people who have not received the training. Managers randomly assign people to one of two groups—the training group or the control group, whose members do not receive the diversity training. Members of both groups are then evaluated both prior to and after the training. Because the members are randomly assigned to the training or control group, differences between the groups are not expected for the pre-training scores. After the training, however, we would expect those people who went through the training to score higher (or have more positive reactions or more desired behaviors) than people who did not complete the training. This design is desirable because it addresses the issues of (a) improvement after the training and (b) improvement

Evaluating Diversity Training Effectiveness. Kirkpatrick's (1976) model is the most popular method of evaluating training effectiveness. Salas and Cannon-Bowers (2001) note that although the method is useful and provides a firm foundation, newer and more elegant models are needed. Kraiger, Ford, and Salas (1993) developed a three-component model of training effectiveness. The first component, *cognitive outcomes,* includes such outcomes as the development of verbal knowledge, organization of knowledge, and cognitive strategies. Understanding laws that impact diversity in the workplace is an example of a cognitive outcome. *Skill-based outcomes,* the second component, pertain to skill compilation—the continued practice of a skill beyond initial success—and skill automaticity—the practice of a skill in a fluid, accomplished, and individualized manner. For example, managers who can develop and administer fair performance appraisals have learned skill-based outcomes. Finally, *attitudinal outcomes* encompass two elements—affective outcomes (e.g., group norms) and motivational outcomes (e.g., motivational disposition, post-training self-efficacy, and goal setting). If trainees reduce their level of bias toward out-group members as a result of the training process, this is an attitudinal outcome. Although there are similarities to Kirkpatrick's model, Kraiger et al.'s framework is a possible alternative.

relative to a control group. A design drawback is that it can be cumbersome and time-consuming to collect data prior to and after the training.

The final design—*post-training-only with a control group*—is the most desired. Here, managers randomly assign people to one of two groups: training or control group. An evaluation is made after the training, and any differences between the groups would suggest that the training was effective. The pre-training evaluation is not needed, because theoretically, the randomly assigned group members should not differ in their scores prior to training. Of course, this assumption rests on the complete random assignment of employees to the two groups. If this cannot be achieved, then a pre-test is required.

In two of the designs, the control group did not receive diversity training, but would we not want those persons to ultimately do so? One way to address this issue is to evaluate the training's effectiveness with small pilot test groups before administering it to the entire organization. If the training is effective, then require *all* employees to complete it.

Ensuring a transfer of training

Lim and Morris (2006) note that one of the most important goals of training should be the application of the knowledge, skills, and abilities to the workplace setting. Research, however, suggests that this transfer of training often does not occur: the material learned in the training session is not used in the work setting (Kupritz, 2002). Why provide diversity training if the trainees do not use the information in their work lives? Fortunately, recent research points to several factors that can improve the transfer of training (Colquitt et al., 2000; Lim & Morris, 2006; Salas & Cannon-Bowers, 2001).

Organizational climate. The organizational climate can have a substantial influence on whether people apply the information from the training to their work. As Salas and Cannon-Bowers (2001) note, the organizational climate can shape "motivations, expectations, and attitudes for transfer" (p. 489). Transfer of training is likely to take place in sport organizations that (a) encourage employees to try new things, (b) promote continuous learning by employees, (c) do not punish people when they are not immediately successful in implementing the information they learned, and (d) reward people for the transfer of training (see also Roberson, Kulik, & Pepper, 2009).

Applicability. Trainees are most likely to actually use the information in their lessons when they believe it is applicable to their work. If they cannot see the connection between what was presented in the training and their job performance, then the information, no matter how valuable it is perceived to be by the organization, is unlikely to be used. Thus, trainers must not only present the information so it can be understood but must also explicitly outline how the information benefits the trainees in their everyday job.

Support. One of the most influential factors involved in the transfer of training is the support trainees receive from their peers and supervisors to actually make the transfer. Research shows that the influence of peers is especially important in the transfer process (Colquitt et al., 2000). Much of what people do is influenced by those people who are important to them. If one's peers and supervisors show support for the training, think it is important, try to transfer the information to their own work, and are supportive of others who are doing the same, then transfer of training among employees is likely to be successful.

General Principles

In this final section, general principles that should be considered when delivering a diversity training program are discussed. Wentling and Palma-Rivas (1999) interviewed a panel of diversity experts from across the United States, all of whom had published extensively in the diversity literature and had consulted with public and private entities about diversity and diversity training. Wentling and Palma-Rivas asked the experts what they considered to be the primary components of an effective diversity training program. After analyzing the experts' responses, the following themes emerged (see Exhibit 15.7).

Effective diversity training program components.   *exhibit* **15.7**

- Demands commitment and support from top management
- Includes diversity training as part of the overall strategic plan
- Meets the sport organization's specific needs
- Uses qualified trainers
- Combines the training with other diversity programs
- Makes attendance mandatory
- Creates inclusive programs
- Ensures trust and confidentiality
- Requires accountability
- Evaluates the training

Adapted from Wentling & Palma-Rivas (1999).

- **Ensure commitment and support from top management.** Effective diversity training programs must have support from top management. Top management should be actively involved in the training process and convey to employees how important the training is to them and the organization as a whole.

- **Include diversity training as part of the overall strategic plan.** The training must be linked to the overall goals, needs, and objectives of the sport organization. Effectiveness is likely to be highest when the training is linked to the overall business strategy.

- **Ensure training meets the sport organizations' specific needs.** The most successful training programs are those that are based on the results of a needs analysis. Without such an assessment, "training may focus on issues that are not real problems in the organization, which may result in a waste of resources without achieving desired results" (Wentling & Palma-Rivas, 1999, p. 222).

- **Use qualified trainers.** Qualified trainers are essential. The best trainers are those who have a good mix of professional and academic skills, coupled with a dynamic personality. Because diversity training often touches on sensitive issues, trainers should not only be well-versed in the subject matter but should also be skilled at diffusing disruptive forms of conflict.

- **Combine the training with other diversity programs.** Diversity training works best when it is introduced as one of several diversity-related initiatives (e.g., the organization also has an overall strategy aimed at diversifying the workforce and clientele). If conducted in isolation, the training is likely to have only a minimal impact, if any. In addition, "linking diversity training to existing training programs such as leadership training, team building, total quality management, and employee empowerment and participation will increase its effectiveness" (Wentling & Palma-Rivas, 1999, p. 222).

- **Make attendance mandatory.** Diversity training is most successful when attendance is mandatory. The requirement for attendance demonstrates organizational seriousness and commitment to the program. Mandatory attendance should apply to *all* people—including top management. Requiring top managers to attend the training may result in their setting examples of the desired behaviors for their employees to model.

PROFESSIONAL PERSPECTIVES

Diversity Behind the Face. Cheryl Kravitz is a diversity training consultant who uses an interesting technique to create empathy and understanding in the programs she delivers. She calls the technique "The Person Behind the Face." In this exercise, participants receive a piece of paper with balloons drawn all over it. They then use as many balloons as they deem necessary to define their personal identities. As the exercise facilitator, Kravitz goes first. She describes herself as "a young mom and an old mom" because she had a child at age 16 and adopted her second child at age 40. She also reveals other bits of information about herself: that she is Jewish, her mother has Alzheimer's, she was once in a coma, and she almost died at the hands of her abusive ex-husband. Revealing such personal information is beneficial, Kravitz notes, because people will then share information about themselves. Revealing such information has a way of creating empathy among the trainees and sometimes results in bonds being forged among otherwise different people. For example, another woman in the group might reveal that she too was a battered wife, or another group member might identify with having an ill parent. Thus, people come to realize that although they differ physically, they might share common deep-level characteristics. The exercise "can help unfreeze people's preconceptions of others and help melt prejudice and stereotypes" (Koonce, 2001, p. 30).

- **Create inclusive programs.** The best diversity training programs are those that are inclusive of all people because they avoid the "us" versus "them" dynamics. Also, White males are more likely to support the diversity initiatives if they believe it is inclusive of all people and does not single them out for "blame."
- **Ensure trust and confidentiality.** Establishing trust and confidentiality ensures a safe training environment and minimizes risks to the employees and the organization. Setting guidelines early in the training process, such as "respect other people's opinions" and "keep the conversations here confidential," helps to establish these norms.
- **Require accountability.** Holding people accountable provides a means for the trainees to actively advance diversity in the workplace. Accountability practices include establishing a link between what is learned in the session and work performance, including diversity in performance appraisals and merit raises, and associating diversity performance with the organization's overall objectives.
- **Evaluate the training.** "Evaluation is one of the most important ways of providing accountability and support for continuing with diversity programs" (Wentling & Palma-Rivas, 1999, p. 223). Indeed, evaluating the program demonstrates its success, provides information about trainees' reactions to the training, and informs the design and implementation of subsequent training sessions.

Managers should use these principles as a guide when designing and implementing diversity training programs to ensure greater success with the initiative.

CHAPTER *summary*

As illustrated in the Diversity Challenge, diversity training can be, and has been, met with mixed emotions: some oppose such programs, while others argue that the training will result in positive outcomes for employees, work groups, and the organization as a whole. Implementing diversity training can be a complex undertaking because many factors must be considered in the program's design, implementation, and evaluation. The time, resources, and effort associated with designing and delivering a diversity training program are worthwhile because effective programs, when coupled with other diversity initiatives, positively influence a sport organization. After reading the chapter, you should be able to:

1. Discuss the positive and negative effects of diversity training.

The positive outcomes include attracting and retaining a diverse set of employees, maintaining worker morale, fostering understanding among groups, curbing lawsuits, and contributing to organizations' overall effectiveness. Negative effects include the uneasiness associated with discussing sensitive issues, the belief that diversity training is "code" for affirmative action, the incidence of White men feeling singled out, the reinforcement of stereotypes and categorization boundaries, the sensitization of trainees to diversity issues, and a potential lack of organizational effects.

2. Discuss the essential elements of effective diversity training programs.

There are several factors that must be considered when delivering diversity training. Organizations must first conduct a needs analysis, which includes an organizational analysis, a job/task analysis, and a person analysis. The antecedent training conditions must be examined, including trainee characteristics, the manner in which the training is framed, and the pre-training environment. Next, the training methods, such as who should deliver the training and which delivery method should be used, must be addressed. Finally, post-training conditions—training evaluation and ensuring the transfer of training—must be completed.

QUESTIONS *for discussion*

1. The incidence of diversity training has increased in Fortune 500 companies over the past decade to the point that more companies conduct this training than those that do not. Do you believe there has been a corresponding increase in the number of sport organizations that provide diversity training? Why or why not?

2. Companies that view diversity training as a central part of their strategic plan spend almost three times more per employee on training than other organizations. Why is there such an increase in spending, and do you think the organizations receive the benefits of the spending?

3. How does one conduct a needs analysis, and why is it important to do so?

4. Several trainee characteristics influence training effectiveness. Of those listed in the chapter, which do you think is the most influential and why? What can managers do to improve these characteristics?

5. Several training delivery options were discussed. What are the advantages and disadvantages associated with each approach? Which is your preferred approach and why?

6. Trainees bring differing needs, attitudes, preferences, and learning styles to the diversity training session. What steps can trainers take to ensure that *all* trainees learn the material?

7. Several factors were identified that could help with the transfer of training. Which of these factors is likely to be most influential and why?

LEARNING *activities*

1. Using the Web, identify companies that specialize in diversity training. Which of these companies do you believe would provide the best training and why?

2. Working in small groups, consult the Lambert and Myers book (listed in the Supplementary Reading), and try one of the diversity training activities. Present the activity to the class, and evaluate its effectiveness. Which were the most successful and why?

READING *resources*

SUPPLEMENTARY READING

Clements, P., & Jones, J. (2002). *The diversity training handbook: A practical guide to understanding and changing attitudes* (2nd ed.). London, UK: Kogan Page, Ltd. (Offers practical advice for implementing diversity training programs, with many evaluation models and learning points.)

Katz, J. H. (2003). *White awareness: Handbook for anti-racism training* (2nd ed.). Norman: University of Oklahoma Press. (Provides a detailed analysis for designing training aimed at reducing racism and creating change in the White community.)

Lambert, J., & Myers, S. (2005). *Trainers' diversity source book: 50 ready-to-use activities, from ice breaker through wrap ups.* Alexandria, VA: Society for Human Resource Management. (Provides trainers with a variety of exercises to use during a training session to actively engage the participants.)

WEB RESOURCES

- Diversity Builder (www.diversitybuilder.com/diversity_training.php): provides diversity training in a variety of areas; provides specialized programs for each client.

- Diversity Training Group (www.diversitydtg.com/): specializes in providing diversity training workshops for organizations.

- Scottsdale National Gender Institute (http://gendertraining.com/): helps organizations to provide diversity training, with an emphasis on gender issues.

references

Arai, M., Wanca-Thibault, M., & Shockley-Zalabak, P. (2001). Communication theory and training approaches for multiculturally diverse organizations: Have academics and practitioners missed the connection? *Public Personnel Management, 30,* 445–455.

Arthur, W., Jr., Bennett, W., Jr., Edens, P. S., & Bell, S. T. (2003). Effectiveness of training in organizations: A meta-analysis of design and evaluation features. *Journal of Applied Psychology, 88,* 234–245.

Arvey, R. D., Salas, E., & Gialluca, K. A. (1992). Using task inventories to forecast skills and abilities. *Human Performance, 5,* 171–190.

Bandura, A. (1986). *Social foundations of thought and action: A social cognitive theory.* Englewood Cliffs, NJ: Prentice Hall.

Bell, M. P., Connerley, M. L., & Cocchiara, F. K. (2009). The case for mandatory diversity education. *Academy of Management Learning and Education, 8,* 597–609.

Bendick, M., Jr., Egan, M. L., & Lofhjelm, S. M. (2001). Workforce diversity training: From anti-discrimination compliance to organizational development. *Human Resource Planning, 24*(2), 10–25.

Colquitt, J. A., LePine, J. A., & Noe, R. A. (2000). Toward an integrative theory of training motivation: A meta-analytic path analysis of 20 years of research. *Journal of Applied Psychology, 85,* 678–707.

Colquitt, J. A., & Simmering, M. J. (1998). Conscientiousness, goal orientation, and motivation to learn during the training process: A longitudinal study. *Journal of Applied Psychology, 83,* 654–665.

Crosby, F. J., Iyer, A., & Sincharoen, S. (2006). Understanding affirmative action. *Annual Review of Psychology, 57,* 585–611.

Cunningham, G. B., & Mahoney, K. L. (2004). Self-efficacy of part-time employees in university athletics: The influence of organizational commitment, valence of training, and training motivation. *Journal of Sport Management, 18,* 59–73.

Cunningham, G. B., & Singer, J. N. (2009). *Diversity in athletics: An assessment of exemplars and institutional best practices.* Indianapolis, IN: National Collegiate Athletic Association.

Doherty, A. J., & Chelladurai, P. (1999). Managing cultural diversity in sport organizations: A theoretical perspective. *Journal of Sport Management, 13,* 280–297.

Esen, E. (2005). *Workplace diversity practices report*. Alexandria, VA: Society for Human Resource Management.

Facteau, J. D., Dobbins, G. H., Russell, J. E. A., Ladd, R. T., & Kudish, J. D. (1995). The influence of general perceptions of the training environment on pretraining motivation and perceived training transfer. *Journal of Management, 21*, 1–25.

Gilbert, J. A., & Ivancevich, J. M. (2000). Valuing diversity: A tale of two organizations. *Academy of Management Executive, 14*(1), 93–105.

Gist, M. E., & Mitchell, T. R. (1992). Self-efficacy: A theoretical analysis of its determinants and malleability. *Academy of Management Review, 17*, 183–211.

Goldstein, I. L. (1993). *Training in organizations: Needs assessment, development and evaluation* (3rd ed.). Monterey, CA: Brooks/Cole.

Gordon, J. (1988). Who is being trained to do what? *Training, 25*(10), 51–60.

Hanover, J. M., & Cellar, D. F. (1998). Environmental factors and the effectiveness of workplace diversity training. *Human Resource Development Quarterly, 9*, 105–124.

Hemphill, H., & Haines, R. (1997). *Discrimination, harassment, and the failure of diversity training: What to do now*. Westport, CT: Quorum Books.

Holladay, C. L., Knight, J. L., Paige, D. L., & Quinones, M. A. (2003). The influence of framing on attitudes toward diversity training. *Human Resource Development Quarterly, 14*, 245–263.

Jackson, L. C. (1999). Ethnocultural resistance to multicultural training: Students and faculty. *Cultural Diversity and Ethnic Minority Psychology, 5*, 27–36.

Kaemar, K. M., Wright, P. M., & McMahan, G. C. (1997). The effects of individual differences on technology training. *Journal of Managerial Issues, 9*, 104–120.

Kalev, A., Dobbin, F., & Kelly, E. (2006). Best practices or best guesses? Assessing the efficacy of corporate affirmative action and diversity policies. *American Sociological Review, 71*, 589–617.

Karp, H. B., & Sammour, H. Y. (2000). Workforce diversity: Choices in diversity training programs and dealing with resistance to diversity. *College Student Journal, 34*, 451–458.

Kirkpatrick, D. L. (1976). Evaluation of training. In R. L. Craig (Ed.), *Training and development handbook* (2nd ed., pp. 301–319). New York: McGraw-Hill.

Koonce, R. (2001). Redefining diversity. *Training & Development, 55*(12), 22–33.

Kraiger, K., Ford, J. K., & Salas, E. (1993). Application of cognitive, skill-based, and affective theories of learning outcomes to new methods of training evaluation. *Journal of Applied Psychology, 78*, 311–328.

Kulik, C. T., & Roberson, L. (2008). Common goals and golden opportunities: Evaluations of diversity education in academic and organizational settings. *Academy of Management Learning & Education, 7*, 309–331.

Kupritz, V. W. (2002). The relative impact of workplace design on training transfer. *Human Resource Development Quarterly, 13*, 427–447.

Lim, D. H., & Morris, M. L. (2006). Influence of trainee characteristics, instructional satisfaction, and organizational climate on perceived learning and training transfer. *Human Resource Development Quarterly, 17*, 85–115.

Lindsay, C. (1994). Things that go wrong in diversity training: Conceptualization and change with ethnic identity models. *Journal of Organizational Change Management, 7*(6), 18–33.

Martocchio, J. J., & Judge, T. A. (1997). Relationship between conscientiousness and learning in employee training: Mediating influences of self-deception and self-efficacy. *Journal of Applied Psychology, 82*, 764–773.

Mathieu, J. E., Tannenbaum, S. I., & Salas, E. (1992). Influences of individual and situational characteristics on measures of training effectiveness. *Academy of Management Journal, 35*, 828–847.

Mathis, R. L., & Jackson, J. H. (2006). *Human resource management* (11th ed.). Mason, OH: Southwestern.

Noe, R. A., & Schmitt, N. (1986). The influence of trainee attitudes on training effectiveness: Test of a model. *Personnel Psychology, 39*, 497–523.

Plummer, D. L. (1998). Approaching diversity training in the year 2000. *Consulting Psychology Journal: Practice and Research, 50*, 181–189.

Quinones, M. A. (1995). Pretraining context effects: Training assignment as feedback. *Journal of Applied Psychology, 80*, 226–238.

Roberson, L., Kulik, C. T., & Pepper, M. B. (2009). Individual and environmental factors influencing the use of transfer strategies after diversity training. *Group & Organization Management, 34*, 67–89.

Rouiller, J. Z., & Goldstein, I. L. (1993). The relationship between organizational transfer climate and positive transfer of training. *Human Resource Development Quarterly, 4*, 377–390.

Rynes, S., & Rosen, B. (1995). A field survey of factors affecting the adoption and perceived success of diversity training. *Personnel Psychology, 48*, 247–270.

Salas, E., & Cannon-Bowers, J. A. (2001). The science of training: A decade of progress. *Annual Review of Psychology, 52*, 471–499.

Sussman, L. (1997). Prejudice and behavioral archetypes: A new model for cultural-diversity training. *Business Communication Quarterly, 60*, 7–18.

Tallarigo, R. (1998). Book review of *Discrimination, harassment, and the failure of diversity training: What to do now*. *Personnel Psychology, 51*, 749–752.

Tannenbaum, S. I., & Yulk, G. (1992). Training and development in work organizations. *Annual Review of Psychology, 43,* 399–441.

Thomas, R. R. (1996). *Redefining diversity.* New York: AMACOM.

Tracey, J. B., Hinkin, T. R., Tannenbaum, S., & Mathieu, J. E. (2001). The influence of individual characteristics and the work environment on varying levels of training outcomes. *Human Resource Development Quarterly, 12,* 5–23.

Wentling, R. M., & Palma-Rivas, N. (1999). Components of effective diversity training programmes. *International Journal of Training and Development, 3,* 215–226.

Wiethoff, C. (2004). Motivation to learn and diversity training: Application of the theory of planned behavior. *Human Resource Development Quarterly, 15,* 263–278.

Author Index

Abercrombie, N., 54, 71, 81, 103, 252
Acosta, R. V., 35, 54, 57, 111–112, 115, 119, 284, 302
Adler, N. E., 72
Agars, M. D., 302, 307
Age Discrimination in Employment Act, 272
Agyemang, K., 70, 72
Aitchison, C., 115
Albanese, A., 182
Allen, D. W., 249
Allen, J. B., 117
Allison, M. T., 88
Allport, G. W., 51, 54, 62, 316, 317, 318, 319, 320, 329, 330, 332, 333, 334
American Psychological Association, 239, 240, 242, 253
Americans with Disabilities Act, 155, 273, 274
Ancona, D. G., 32
Anderson, D., 78, 80, 306
Anderson, E., 38, 216, 218, 227, 228, 233
Anderson, K., 115, 116, 117, 118
Antonioni, D., 61
Applebaum, B., 80
Arai, M., 342
Armstrong, K. L., 91, 122, 123
Arthur, W., Jr., 345, 353
Arvey, R. D., 346
Australian Sports Commission, 111
Avery, D.R., 28

Bacharach, S. B., 29, 43
Backlund, E., 240

Bailey, J. R., 197
Baldridge, D. C., 161
Bandura, A., 59, 306, 348
Barney, J., 33
Beadnell, M., 250
Beatty, P. T., 149
Beck, E. L., 244
Bell, M. P., 5, 6, 22, 28, 72, 136, 141, 142, 155, 156, 165, 177, 178, 179, 188, 238, 274, 340, 350
Bellah, R. N., 198
Bellizzi, J. A., 178, 181
Bem, S. L., 104, 105
Bendick, M., Jr., 341, 342, 345, 350, 351
Bennett, G., 147, 202, 203
Bettencourt, B. A., 324
Beyer, J. M., 82
Binder, J., 316, 319, 320, 329
Birrell, S., 36
Blake-Beard, S. D., 28
Blanford, J. M., 222, 223
Blinde, E. M., 303
Bobko, P., 277
Bopp, M., 199
Borg, L., 245
Bowker, A., 105
Brady, E., 255
Bray, C., 76
Brewer, M. B., 51, 54, 316, 318, 320, 321, 322, 323, 324, 325, 328, 330
Brittain, I., 168
Brooke, L., 139
Brooks, D., 22, 95, 248
Brown, G. T., 18, 78, 84, 86

Brown, K., 34
Brown, R., 63, 319, 329
Brownwell, K. D., 191
Bruening, J. E., 37, 56, 117, 120
Buffington, D., 80
Bullock, H. E., 239, 243, 244, 245, 248, 253–254
Burden, J. W., Jr., 88
Bureau of Labor Statistics, 240, 241
Burris, C. T., 203
Burton, L. J., 114
Butler, J. A., 123
Button, S. B., 50, 59, 223, 224, 228
Byers, W., 264
Byrne, D., 41, 57, 146

Cacioppe, R., 197
Caldwell, A. A., 3
Callahan, J. S., 143
Campbell, A. A., 82
Cardinal, B. J., 274
Carpenter, L. J., 107, 279, 280, 281, 282, 283, 284, 286
Carr, L., 250
Carron, A. V., 119, 147, 182, 183
Cash, K. C., 197, 198
Catalyst Institute, 111
Chadiha, J., 142
Chafel, J. A., 244
Chamberlain, J., 135
Chambliss, H. O., 179
Chan, S., 144
Chang, G., 248
Chattopadhyay, P., 41
Chelladurai, P., 9, 79, 90, 296, 297, 298, 302, 310

Chesler, M., 292
Chrobot-Mason, D., 308, 309, 310
Clair, J. A., 225, 226, 227, 228
Clements, P., 361
Coaching Association of Canada, 111
Coakley, J., 29, 36, 44, 71, 72, 80, 120, 205, 206, 207, 208, 251, 256
Coates, R. D., 80
Cochran, S. D., 221
Cogman, T., 250
Cohen, E. G., 318
Cokley, K., 78
Colella, A., 63, 159, 160, 163
Collins, C., 243
Collins, L. T., Jr., 184
Collins, P., 37
Colloff, P., 219
Colquitt, J. A., 347, 348, 349, 356, 357
Covell, D., 93
Cox, T. H., 19
Cox, T., 292, 306
Cox, T., Jr., 6, 7, 27, 44
Cozzarelli, C., 244
Cramer, J. A., 107
Crandall, C. S., 51, 52
Crawford, S., 183
Creed, W. E. D., 216, 217
Crompton, J. L., 81, 251
Crosby, F. J., 349
Cuneen, J., 107
Cunningham, G. B., 6, 9, 10, 33, 34, 41, 42, 52, 55, 56, 57, 59, 75, 78, 79, 81, 82, 83, 84, 85, 86, 87, 107, 115, 116, 118, 119, 125, 136, 146, 188, 222, 284, 285, 296, 302, 303, 304, 306, 307, 308, 312, 315, 319, 326, 327, 328, 330, 331, 348, 349, 350
Czech, D. R., 208

Dacin, M. T., 302, 303
Daddario, G., 57
Daniels, N., 246
Danylchuk, K. E., 112
Dass, P., 308
Day, N. E., 228
DeBerg, B. A., 206, 207
DeBerry, F., 90

DeHass, D., 75, 76, 77, 78, 79, 84, 85, 112, 122, 268, 302, 306
DeNisi, A. S., 327
DePauw, K. P., 156, 157, 165, 166, 167, 168, 170
DeSensi, J. T., 17, 292, 293, 295, 310, 328
Dessler, G., 265, 266, 267, 278
Deutsch, M., 317
DiMaggio, P. J., 80
Dimmock, J. A., 179
Dipboye, R. L., 186, 187
DiTomaso, N., 6, 15
Dixon, M. A., 15, 104, 117
Doherty, A. J., 15, 17, 29, 86, 114, 293, 294, 295, 296, 298, 310, 328, 346
Dovidio, J. F., 51, 53, 63, 82, 83, 326, 330
Dowden, S., 52, 82
Duncan, M. C., 178
Dunn, R., 199
Durkheim, E., 196–197, 208

Eagly, A. H., 51, 186
Eastough, K., 109
Ebenezer, S., 154
Eccles, J. S., 106
Ehrenreich, B., 248
Ehrhart, M. G., 201–202
Eitzen, D. S., 34, 35, 36, 38, 71, 89, 108, 120, 199, 204, 205, 206, 248, 255
Ellers, A., 319, 320, 331
Elling, A., 230
Esen, E., 341
Evans, J. M., 201
Everhart, B. C., 75

Facteau, J. D., 348
Feagin, J. R., 70, 80, 95, 332
Fernandez, E., 176
Feyrer, J., 134
Fink, J. S., 6, 7, 17, 50, 54, 56, 57, 58, 86, 107, 124, 125, 294, 295, 296, 310
Finkelstein, L. M., 141, 143, 181
Fiske, S. T., 162, 163, 186, 244
Fitzgerald, L. F., 270
Fitzgerald, M.P., 3
Florey, A. T., 161

Freeman, R. E., 81
Freshman, B., 203
Frey, D., 53
Fry, L. W., 201
Fulks, D. L., 82
Funk, D. C., 124

Gaertner, S. L., 51, 53, 54, 82, 83, 319, 323, 324, 325, 326, 327, 328, 334
Garrison, K. C., 184
Gelfand, M. J., 270
Genzale, J., 255
Gibson, H. J., 254
Gilbert, J. A., 306, 347
Gill, D. L., 56, 215, 223
Gioia, D. A., 29, 43
Gist, M. E., 348
Giulianotti, R., 44
Gladwell, M., 185
Goffman, E., 161
Goldstein, I. L., 345
Gonzales, G. L., 89
Gordon, J., 341
Gordon, R. A., 138
Gortmaker, S. L., 179, 180
Gosiorek, J. C., 215
Gouke, C. G., 91
Graen, G. B., 159
Granderson, L. Z., 229
Green, A., 244
Greenhaus, J. H., 54, 56, 59, 62, 83, 84, 85, 117
Greenleaf, C., 179
Greenleaf, R.K., 201
Gregory, R.F., 149
Griffin, P., 219, 227, 233
Griffith, K. H., 229
Gruenfeld, D. H., 32

Hallinan, C., 89
Hamilton, B. H., 55, 74
Hamilton, D. L., 137
Hanover, J. M., 349
Haq, R., 14, 134, 135, 156
Hargreaves, J., 188
Harrison, D. A., 7, 8, 21, 332
Hart, B. A., 119
Hasbrook, C. A., 284
Haslam, S. A., 309
Hayes-Thomas, R., 5, 6, 7, 275

Healy, M. C., 144
Hebl, M. R., 180, 222
Hedge, J. W., 140, 141
Hemphill, H., 342
Henderson, K. A., 122, 123
Herek, G. M., 53, 215, 216, 217, 218, 220, 221, 319
Herring, C., 17
Herscovitch, L., 308
Hewitt, P., 14
Hewstone, M., 323, 328, 329, 331
Hibbler, D. K., 89
Hicks, D. A., 196, 197, 209
Highhouse, S., 18
Hodge, S. R., 88
Hodson, G., 83
Hoffman, L. W., 106
Hoffman, S., 205
Holladay, C. L., 341, 342, 349
Holvino, E., 308
Homan, A. C., 329, 330
Hosoda, M., 187
Howard, D. R., 92
Huffman, A. H., 224
Human Rights Campaign, 223
Human Rights Commission, 276
Humphreys, B. R., 110
Hums, M. A., 35, 55, 166, 171
Hylton, K., 37, 58, 70, 71, 80

Iacocca, L., 246
Ilgen, D. R., 60
Inglis, S., 56

Jackson, L. C., 342
Jackson, S. E., 5, 146
Jago, G., 324
Jayne, M. E. A., 306
Jehn, K. A., 8, 21, 298
Johnson, C. D., 28
Johnson, D. W., 319
Jones, E., 159, 161, 162, 164, 170
Jones, L. M., 324
Joplin, J. R. W., 5
Joshi, A., 5
Judge, T. A., 184
Jurkiewicz, C. L., 198

Kaemar, K. M., 347
Kalev, A., 340, 342
Kamins, M. A., 188

Kamphoff, C., 86
Kane, M. J., 106
Karp, H. B., 342
Katz, J. H., 361
Kava, R., 177
Kennelly, I., 245
Kerlinger, F. N., 29, 43
Khavari, K. A., 200
Kikulis, L. M., 80
Kilty, K., 116, 117, 118
Kinsey, A. C., 215
Kirchmeyer, C., 116
Kirkpatrick, D. L., 354, 356
Kitson, H. D., 184
Kling, K. C., 106
Kluegel, J. R., 246
Knight, J. L., 53
Knoppers, A., 36, 54, 56, 58, 114, 115, 118
Konrad, A. M., 127
Koonce, R., 358
Korman, A. K., 15, 140
Kossek, E. E., 145
Kozlowski, S. W. J., 79
Kraiger, K., 356
Krane, V., 56, 218, 227, 231
Kriger, M., 197, 200, 201
Krugman, P., 248–249, 250, 258
Kulik, C. T., 340, 341
Kupritz, V. W., 356

Ladson-Billings, G., 37, 70, 71, 80, 303
Lambert, J., 361
Landry, F.J., 286
Langlois, J. H., 185–186
Lantz, C. D., 105
Lapchick, R. E., 74–75, 76, 77, 82, 298, 299, 300
Lavigne, P., 87
Lavoie, M., 89
Lawrence, B. S., 144
Lawrence, S. M., 84
Lawson, R. B., 297
Lazarus, R. S., 163
Leary, K., 225, 228
Legg, D., 157, 166
Lent, R. W., 59, 86
Leondar-Wright, B., 242
Levenson, M., 58
Levinson, D.J., 143

Lewin, K., 29
Lichtenstein, R. A., 146
Lieber, L. D., 134
Lim, D. H., 356
Lindsay, C., 342, 343
Linver, M.R., 238
Littlefield, A., 71
Liu, W. M., 238, 239, 243, 245, 252
Long, J., 80
Longley, N., 55
Lopiano, D., 264
Lorbiecki, A., 6, 7
Lord, R., 85
Lott, B., 238, 242, 243, 244, 245, 248, 249, 250, 251, 258
Lovett, D. J., 54, 55, 115, 116
Lowry, C. D., 115
Lox, C. L., 181
Lubensky, M. E., 215, 216, 220, 229
Lumpkin, A., 107
Lytton, H., 106

Malcolmson, B., 206
Mannix, E., 18
Marcus, E., 233
Marcus-Newhall, A., 324
Marks, M. A., 15
Marshall, A. M., 81, 270
Martocchio, J. J., 348
Maslow, A.H., 249
Mathieu, J. E., 348
Mathis, R. L., 14, 277, 341, 344, 346, 347, 349, 352, 353, 354
Matier, P., 292
Matisik, E. N., 270
Mays, V. M., 221
McBride, D. K., 264
McCoy, S. K., 246
McDowell, J., 37, 79, 80, 306
McDowell, M. A., 183, 184
McGraw, D., 35
McIntosh, P., 80, 320
McKelvey, S., 92
McLaughlin, M. E., 161, 162, 164, 165
Mead, W., 198
Mehrotra, C. M., 135, 136, 137, 147, 148, 149
Messner, M. A., 52, 104, 127, 220, 303

Meyer, I. H., 218, 220, 221, 228
Meyer, J. P., 307
Miller, G., 189
Missitzi, J., 189
Mitroff, I. I., 197, 208
Moon, D. G., 243
Moore, K., 69
Mor Barak, M., 312
Mortensen, C., 180
Murray, M. A., 207
Murrell, A. J., 328

NASPE, 270
National Collegiate Athletic Association, 111
Newberry, P., 41, 195
Ng, T. W. H., 138
Nguyen, H. D., 90
Nier, J. A., 326
Noe, R. A., 348
Nussbaum, D., 238

Oakes, P., 331
Obama, B., 198
Ogmundson, R., 81
Oliver, C., 302, 303
Olkin, R., 165
Ordish, R., 92
Ostroff, C., 140

Paetzold, R. L., 161
Palmer, F. R., 117
Paluck, E. L., 316, 334
Paraschak, V., 92
Park, J. H., 189
Parker, S., 180
Parks, J. B., 103, 111, 303
Pattnayak, S. R., 74
Paul, R. J., 178
Pelled, L. H., 31, 32, 34, 298
Perry, E. A., 141, 142, 144
Perry, E. L., 145
Pettigrew, T. F., 316, 319, 321, 330, 332, 333
Phillips, K. W., 32, 85, 298
Pinderhughes, R., 249
Pingitore, R., 180
Pitz, W., 156, 157
Ployhart, R. E., 14, 267
Plummer, D. L., 342, 344
Pomerleau, A., 106

Posthuma, R. A., 134, 138, 139, 140, 141, 145
Powell, G. N., 103, 104, 105, 106, 127, 239
Powell, S., 84
Prasad, P., 6, 17
Prenda, K. M., 138
Pryzgoda, J., 104
Putney, C., 209

Quinones, M. A., 348

Rader, B. G., 80, 205
Ragins, B. R., 204, 214, 216, 223, 224, 225, 228, 229
Ren, L. R., 160, 164
Reyes, M., 181
Reynaud, C., 128
Rhodes, G., 186, 187, 189
Richard, O., 33, 34
Richard, O. C., 33, 34
Ridinger, L. L., 15
Riordan, C. M., 5, 29, 39, 203
Robbins, S. P., 184, 305, 306
Roberson, L., 356
Robidoux, M. A., 93
Robinson, G., 7, 17, 19
Robinson, J., 80
Roehling, M. V., 178, 180
Rosen, B., 138, 139
Rosenberg, M., 82
Rosette, A. S., 85
Ross, C. E., 240
Ross, S. R., 188
Roth, T. E., 230
Rothblum, E., 191
Rothgerber, H., 326
Rothman, R. A., 242, 251
Rouiller, J. Z., 346
Rovell, D., 16
Rudman, L. A., 51, 53
Rudolf, C. W., 179, 181
Ruuskanen, J., 147
Rynes, S., 341

Saad, L., 252
Sack, A. L., 80, 89
Saez, E., 252
Sagas, M., 56, 58, 84, 107, 116, 118, 119
Sage, G. H., 36, 70, 255, 258

Sager, J., 238
Saguy, A. C., 81
Sailes, G. A., 80, 90
Salas, E., 341, 344, 345, 346, 347, 353, 356
Sartore, M. L., 56, 58, 60, 61, 84, 114, 115, 118, 178, 179, 180, 181, 214, 218, 219, 222, 223, 227
Schein, E., 86
Schein, V. E., 113
Schnittker, J., 72
Schwartz, M. B., 178–179
Scott, W. R., 80, 302, 303
Scully, M. A., 245, 246, 247
Sefko, E., 102
Seibert, S. E., 116
Shafran, A., 199
Shakib, S., 106
Shaoa, C. Y., 124
Sharp, D., 315
Sharp, L. A., 269, 275, 286
Shaw, S., 114, 304
Sherif, M., 52, 318
Shifflett, B., 107
Shore, L. M., 140, 141–142, 144
Siciliano, J. I., 146
Sidanius, J., 245
Simons, T., 146
Simpson, P. A., 142
Singer, J. N., 37, 58, 80, 91
Smith, L., 239, 240, 242, 243, 252
Smith, N. G., 223
Snowden, R. J., 216
Solovay, S., 177, 191
Son Hing, L. S., 51, 54, 83
Spears, L. C., 201
Spence, J. T., 104
Sperber, M., 82
Spilka, B., 197, 198, 209
Sport England, 111
Stangl, J. M., 54, 55, 115
Stauffer, J. M., 60
Staurowsky, E. J., 93, 118, 303
Stephens, D. L., 168
Stevens, J., 147
Stockdale, M. S., 22, 312
Stone, D. L., 162, 163, 164
Stone, J., 90
Stone-Romero, E. F., 160
Strauss, J. P., 204
Stroh, L. K., 111, 112

Stunkard, A. J., 178
Sum, A. M., 137
Sussman, L., 344
Swami, V., 183
Swann, W. B., Jr., 72, 328
Swanson, S. R., 124

Tajfel, H., 39, 57, 146, 203, 322
Tallarigo, R., 342
Tannenbaum, S. I., 348
Tate, W. F., 37, 70, 71, 80
Taylor, H., 158
Terry, D. J., 326
Thomas, D. C., 9
Thomas, D. R., 71
Thomas, K. M., 139, 160
Thomas, N., 157, 168, 171
Thomas, R. R., 15, 292, 297, 342
Thorsteinson, T. J., 15
Tracey, J. B., 348
Trail, G., 124
Trecker, J., 309
Tropp, L. R., 320
Tsui, A. S., 13, 17, 39, 41, 87, 116, 322, 332
Tuggle, C. A., 107
Turner, C. S. V., 87–88
Turner, E. T., 188
Turner, J., 39, 57, 146, 203, 322

Unger, R. K., 103

Urrea, L. A., 248
U.S. Census Bureau, 13, 14, 35, 73, 109, 155, 156, 158, 159
U.S. Department of Labor, 121

van Knippenberg, D., 5, 6, 16, 18, 32, 34, 39, 329, 330
Van Sickle, G., 107
Vogel, A., 179

Wade, T. J., 181
Wahl, G., 204
Waitt, G., 231
Waldman, D. A., 138
Waldo, C. R., 223
Walseth, K., 205, 207
Wann, D. L., 124
Ward, M., 109
Watkins, M., 247
Weathers, H., 214
Weaver, G. R., 200, 201
Weber, M., 247
Weeks, M., 203
Weihenmayer, E., 154
Weinberg, G., 217
Weinberg, S., 93
Weinger, S., 254
Weiss, E. M., 139
Wentling, R. M., 341, 346, 350, 357, 358, 359
West, A., 81

West, C., 95
Whisenant, W. A., 36, 56
Whittington, J. L., 201, 202
Wiersema, M. F., 146
Wiethoff, C., 349, 350
Will, G. F., 264
Willams, S., 50
Williams, D. R., 72
Williams, J., 80
Williams, K. M., 189
Williams, K. Y., 39, 40, 322
Wilner, D. M., 317, 318
Wilson, T. D., 53
Wink, P., 147
Wixon, M., 77, 87
Wojciechowski, G., 84–85
Wong, E., 82
Woodhill, B. M., 105
Woods, J., 181–182
Woods, T. A., 244
Woodward, J. R., 80
Wright, P., 265

Young, I. M., 102

Zenger, T. R., 146
Zimbalist, A., 110–111
Zinn, H., 70
Zucker, L. G., 80, 302
Zweig, M., 242, 243, 252

Subject Index

A&M Consolidated High School, 327
Aaron, Hank, 53
Abbott, Jim, 165
ABC, 36
Ability, mental and physical, 153–171 (*see also* Disability)
Ability to learn, age and, 138, 139–140
Aboriginal peoples of Canada, 289–290
Academic advising, 90
Academic performance, gender and, 106
Access, to sports, 289–290
Access discrimination, 54, 55
  outcomes related to, 59
  sports and, 57
  theories related to, 56–57
Accessibility, disability sport and, 167–168
Accommodation, diversity management and, 297
Accommodations, ADA and, 160–161
Acquisitions, corporate, 16
ACT exam, 69
Activation, diversity management and, 298
Adidas, 16
Administration, racial minorities in, 76–78 (*see also* Management)
Adventure Associates, 324
Advertisements:
  disability and, 168–169
  sport and, 125, 188
  weight and, 182
Advisors, academic, 90

Aerobics and Fitness Association of America, 176
Aerobics certification, 175
Affective commitment, 307
Affective conflict, 31
Affirmative action, 342, 343, 349
African Americans, 5
  academic advising and, 90
  academic standings and, 90
  as high school coaches, 77
  as sport consumers, 91–92
  athletes and fines, 49–50
  coaches, 18, 69–70, 77, 79, 268, 291
  disability and, 157
  earnings and, 73–74
  earnings influenced by sex, 121
  employment discrimination and, 265–266
  feminist theory and, 37
  graduation rates and, 69
  Hall of Fame players, 53
  increase in population, 11
  needs analysis and, 346
  positions played in MLB, 89
  racism toward, 51, 53, 55
  religion and, 199–200
  underrepresentation as coaches, 79 (*see also* Underrepresentation)
  weight and, 180–181
  women and sport participation, 122–123
African Methodist Church, 200
Age, 133–149
  ability to learn and, 138, 139–140

  caring for elderly, 145
  college athletics and, 144
  defining, 134–136
  disability rates and, 155–156
  discrimination, 59
  discrimination protection and, 272–273
  effect of in work groups, 146
  employment and, 137–146
  increase in median, 10, 12
  intersection with class, 253
  mentoring and, 143
  moderators and, 144–146
  NFL and, 142
  performance and, 137–139, 143–144
  physical activity and, 133
  poverty and, 136–137
  promotion potential and, 143–144, 145
  relative to coworkers, 144–145
  resistance to change stereotype, 138, 139
  sport consumption and, 147
  sport/leisure participation and, 147–148
  stereotypes and, 137–141
  tenure and, 140
  training/development and, 142–143, 145
  volunteering and, 147–148
Age Discrimination in Employment Act of 1967 (ADEA), 272–273
AIDS, *see* HIV/AIDS
Albemarle Paper Co. v. Moody, 266
Alumni expectations, 81–82

Amenorrhea, 183
American Heart Association, 133
American National Election Studies, 217
American Psychiatric Association, 216
American Psychological Association, 238
Americans with Disabilities Act (ADA), 155, 160–161, 168, 273–274, 275, 286
  compliance and, 273–274
Ancestry, discrimination and, 269 (*see also* Race)
Anderson, Eric, 216
Androgyny, 105
Anxiety:
  disability and, 163–164
  intergroup, 317, 319–320
  religion and, 206
Apostle Paul, 201
Appearance, 175–191, 297
  attractiveness, 185–189
  height and, 183–185
  weight and, 177–183 (*see also* Weight)
Application, of diversity training, 356–357
Apprenticeship, age and, 273
Arkansas Baptist College, 291
Asian Americans, 5, 14
  earnings and, 73–74, 121
  increase in population, 11
  poverty rates, 137
  prejudice and, 318
  sexual orientation and, 215
  underrepresentation in coaching, 59
  volunteering, 148
Athletes:
  attractiveness of, 125, 188, 189
  disability and, 153–154 (*see also* Disability)
  elite, 117
  endorsements and, 188
  fines and, 49
  gay/lesbian, 230–231
  graduation rates of, 91
  obesity and, 177
  treatment of, 91
  use of religion, 205–208

Athletics:
  college, *see* College athletics
  high school, 237
Attendance/accountability, diversity training and, 358–359
Attitudes:
  as category of diversity, 297
  changing toward work, 10, 14–15
Attitudinal outcomes to diversity training, 356
Attractiveness, 185–189
  defining, 185–186
  discrimination and, 59
  in the workplace, 187–188
  influence on sport marketing, 188
  makeup and, 188
  physical activity and, 188
Auditory learners, 349
Augusta National country club, 57
Australia, women as coaches in, 111
Australian Sports Commission, 122
Aversive racism, 53, 82–83
Award, for diversity in athletics, 300–302

Baby boomers, 12
Balance, work-life, 15
Bally Total Fitness, 175
Barnes, Rick, 110
Barnett, Joe, 77
Barriers, disability sport and, 167–168
Basketball, racism and, 55
BBC, 168
Bear Bryant/Adolph Rupp Epiphany, 303
Beauty, defining, 187 (*see also* Attractiveness)
Behavioral preferences, as category of diversity, 297
Behavioral support, of diversity, 307–308
Behaviors:
  championing, 308
  changed by diversity training, 354
  role modeling, 310
Bench press, disability and, 165

Benefits (*see also* Earnings):
  age and, 273
  pregnancy and, 271
Bias (*see also* Discrimination; Prejudice):
  context and, 331–332
  decategorization and, 322–325
  performance appraisal, 60–61
  racial, 98 (*see also* Discrimination; Prejudice)
  recategorization and, 322, 325–328
  social categorization approach to reducing, 321–330
Bilingualism, 88
Black coaches, 18, 69–70, 77, 79, 29
Black Coaches and Administrators, 268
Black feminist theory, 37
Black History Month, 299
Blood pressure, 133
Bloomsburg, Texas, 219
Body mass index (BMI), 177, 179
Body type, "ideal," 179
Bona fide occupational qualification (BFOQ), 278
Boston Marathon, 166
Boston Red Sox, 76
Bottom line, diversity management and, 19
Boundaries, categorization, 325
Boundary conditions, 29, 321
Bowl Championship Series, 36
Braathen, Daniel, 52
Bridge employment, 136
Brigham Young University, 199
Brooks, Jean, 270
Brown, Mark, 231
Brown, Maureen, 175–176
Bryant, Bear, 303
Budgetary constraints, training and, 353
Burden of proof, employment discrimination and, 266
Bush, George W., 81
Business ethics, 201
Byers, Walter, 264

Canada:
  Aboriginal people and sport, 289–290

native persons and sport experiences, 92–93
women as coaches in, 111
Carew, John, 52
Categorical approach to studying diversity, 42
Categories, of diversity, 297
Categorization:
    boundaries, 325, 342, 343
    forms of diversity and, 332
    process, 186
    religion as source of, 203–204
Categorization-based diversity management, 331
Categorization-elaboration model, 32
CBT Planet, 353
Center for the Study of Sport in Society, 22
Centers for Disease Control (CDC), 177, 178
Central Baptist Church, 199
Cerebral palsy, 165
Championing, of diversity, 308
Change, diversity management and:
    champions of, 308
    factors influencing, 302–304
    forms of resistance to, 305
    implementing, 304–307
    limited focus of, 305
    resistance to based on age, 138, 139
Change-process, diversity related, 302–308
Chelladurai's model for diversity management, 296–298
Children:
    decategorization among, 324
    intergroup contact and, 329
China, sports and, 92
Christian Faculty Network, 198
Civil rights, 37
Civil Rights Act of 1964, 50, 56, 81, 108, 265, 267, 268 (see also Title VII)
Civil Rights Act of 1991, 267
Civil Rights Restoration Act of 1987, 280
Claims, legal, based on employment discrimination, 277–278
Class:
    definitions of groupings, 242–243

social, see Social class; see also Classism
Classicism, 243–255
    cognitive distancing and, 244–245
    defined, 243
    education and, 248
    housing and, 249–250
    institutional distancing, 245–255 (see also Institutional distancing)
    interpersonal distancing and, 245
    meritocracy and, 245–248
    sport systems and, 254–255
Clinton, Bill, 275
Coaches:
    African American, 18, 69–70, 77, 79, 268, 291
    discrimination and, 66
    discrimination against women as, 115–116
    expectations/intentions, 86–87
    human capital and, 89–90
    lesbian, 66, 218, 219
    male hiring male, 54
    NCAA Division I, 70
    NFL minority, 75–76
    representation of racial minorities as, 75–76
    salaries of university basketball, 110
    sexual prejudice and, 218–219
    track and field, 146
    underrepresentation of women as, 111–112, 115–117
    weight and, 180
    White, 291
    women for women's sports, 58
    women's attitudes toward being, 117–119
Cognitive:
    distancing, 244–245
    orientations, 297
    outcomes, to diversity training, 356
College athletics:
    age discrimination in, 144
    bridge employment in, 136
    diversity in, 300–302, 303
    diversity training and, 339–340

race and employment outcomes, 82–86
    racial integration of, 303
racial representation and, 75, 76
    wage distributions and, 247
Color barrier, breaking, 57
Commitment:
    to diversity, 307–308
    to diversity training, 358
Common Ingroup Identity Model, 325
Common threat/fate, 326–327
Communication:
    barriers to, 18
    interpersonal, 309
Compassion, 162–163
Compensation:
    disability and, 165
    height and, 184–185
    men and, 109–111
    race and, 73–74
    women and, 109–111
Competency:
    as factor for decisions, 297
    false hope of, 297
Compliance, organizational diversity and, 295
Compositional approach to studying diversity, 42
Concealment, 225, 226
Confidentiality, diversity training and, 359
Conflict:
    affective, 31
    management, 309
    substantive, 31
    theory, 35–36
    work-family, 10, 15
Conradt, Jody, 110
Construct, defined, 29
Consultant, diversity training and, 351–352
Consumers (see also Marketing):
    anti-fat attitudes and, 181
    who are LGB, 229–230
Contact:
    effect on prejudice, 317
    generalizing effects of, 321
    intimate, 317–318
Contact hypothesis, 316–321
    limitations of, 320–321

Context, bias and, 331–332
Continuance commitment, 307
Cook v. Rhode Island, 274
Cooperative diversity training, 352
Cooperative interaction, among groups, 318–319
Cordellos, Harry, 165–166
Costs, of diversity training, 341
Couples, Fred, 107
Cox, Jr., Taylor, 27
Cox, Michael, 58
Creighton University, 69
Critical Measures, 339–340
Critical race theory, 37
Critical theory, 36–37
    critical race theory, 37
    feminist theory, 36
    hegemony theory, 36
Cross-categorization, managing diversity and, 323
Cultural differences, 308–309 (*see also* Diversity)
Cultural diversity, *see* Diversity
Cultural norms, and sport/leisure participation, 89
Culture of diversity vs. culture of similarity, 293
Culture, organizational, 86, 292, 293–294
Cultures, attractiveness and, 186
Customer service, 124–125
Customers, anti-fat attitudes and, 181

Dallas Cup, 324
Daniels, Jon, 76
Davenport, Lyndsay, 117
Davie, Bob, 144
Davis-Todd, Benjamin, 51
Deaflympics, 166
Decategorization, 322–325, 330–331
Decisions, influence of religion on, 198–200
Deegear, Kellie, 346
Deep-level diversity, 8–10, 15, 16, 18, 21, 39, 297, 309 (*see also* Religion; Sexual orientation; Social class)
    job satisfaction and, 29
    sexual orientation and, 196, 225

similarity-attraction paradigm and, 41
Delpit, Lisa, 346
Demographics:
    changes in racial composition, 10–12
    changing, 10–14
    disability and, 164–165
    global changes, 14
    median age and, 10, 12
    weight and, 180–181 (*see also* Weight)
Demonstrations, of diversity knowledge and skills, 353 ??
DeMoss, Mickie, 118
Dependability, age and, 138, 141
DeSensi's model for diversity management, 292–293
Designs, of diversity training evaluation, 354–356
Diabetes, 73, 155, 157
Differences (*see also* Diversity):
    cultural, 308–309
    perceived, 5–6
Differential treatment, 55–56, 58 (*see also* Treatment discrimination)
Differentiating, 225, 226
Differentiation, 323
Director's Cup, 296
Disability, 55, 153–171
    anxiety and, 163–164
    barriers to inclusion in sports, 167
    defined, 155–157
    discrimination and, 161–164
    discrimination protection and, 273–274
    education and, 157–158
    incidence, 155–157
    intersection with class, 253
    language and, 157
    marketing and, 168–169
    media and consumers, 168–169
    moderating variables, 164–165
    pay and, 158–159
    perception based on type of, 164
    pity and, 162–163
    sport, *see* Disability sport
    stigma and, 161–162
    supervisor relationships and, 159

work experiences and, 159–165
work performance and, 160
Disability sport, 153–154, 165–168
    accessibility and, 167–168
    attitudes toward athletes, 167
    barriers to inclusion, 167
    events, 166
    history of, 166
    trends and issues, 167
Disclosure of sexual orientation, 225–229
Discretion, 225, 226
Discretionary support, of diversity, 308
Discrimination, 54–61
    access, *see* Access discrimination
    age and, 272–273 (*see also* Age)
    anxiety and, 163–164
    as influence on women advancing, 113, 115–116 (*see also* Gender; Women)
    assessment of intention, 266
    athletes with disabilities and, 167
    based on language, 56
    based on race, 268–269
    based on sex, 269–272
    claims based on, 277–278
    definitions, 54–55
    disability and, 161–164, 273–274
    employment, legislation concerning, 265–286 (*see also* Employment discrimination law)
    forms of, 55–61
    hiring process and, 59 (*see also* Access discrimination)
    national origin, 269
    obesity and, 274–275
    outcomes, 58–61
    performance appraisals and, 60–61
    pity and, 162–163
    pregnancy and, 269, 271
    prima facie case, 277–278
    questioning differing work experiences, 58
    religion and, 272
    sexual orientation and, 217–221, 275–276 (*see also* Sexual orientation; Sexual prejudice)

state laws addressing sexual orientation/gender identity, 275–276
stigma and, 161–162
theoretical explanations for, 56–58
treatment, *see* Treatment discrimination
underrepresentation and, 83–85
Disparate impact, 277
Disparate treatment, 277
Displacement, 251
Dissimilarity, overcoming, 41 (*see also* Diversity management)
Distance education, diversity training and, 352–353
Diversity:
  age, 133–149 (*see also* Age)
  appearance and, 175–191 (*see also* Appearance)
  approaches to studying, 42
  attractiveness and, 185–189
  categorical approach, 42
  Chelladurai's categories of, 297
  classifying, 9
  compositional approach, 42
  deep-level, *see* Deep-level diversity
  definitions, 4–7
  forms of, 7–10, 332
  forms of resistance to, 305
  height and, 183–185
  importance of in sport, 19
  importance of theory in studying, 29–30
  information, 8, 9
  initiatives in major league sports, 299–300
  interest in, 10–19
  intersection with class, 253
  leadership and, 308–310
  legal aspects of, 10, 16–17, 263–286 (*see also* Legislation)
  management of organizations and, 289–312 (*see also* Diversity management)
  management strategy approach, 42
  managerial theories, *see* Managerial theories
  multiculturalism and, 292

organizational culture and, 293–294
organizational effectiveness and, 19
overview of, 3–22
potential negative effects of, 10, 17–18
prejudice and, *see* Prejudice
race and, 69–95 (*see also* Race)
relational approach, 39, 42
religion and, 195–209 (*see also* Religion)
sexual orientation and, 212–233 (*see also* Sexual orientation)
social class and, 237–258 (*see also* Social class)
social pressures and, 17
social responsibility for, 17
sociological theories, *see* Sociological theories
surface-level, *see* Surface-level diversity
theoretical tenets of, 27–44
theories used to understand, 30–42
understanding the emphasis on, 10–19
value, 8, 9
value-in hypothesis, 10, 18–19
valuing, 304
weight and, 175–183
Diversity Council, in NFL, 299
Diversity in Athletics Award, 300–302
Diversity Inc., 22
Diversity Internship Program, in PGA, 299
Diversity management:
  accommodation and, 297
  activation and, 298
  as strategic action, 7
  Chelladurai's model for, 296–298
  commitment to change, 307–308
  cross-categorization and, 323
  defined, 6–7
  DeSensi's model, 292–293
  discrimination and, *see* Discrimination
  Doherty and Chelladurai's model, 293–294

factors influencing change and, 302–304
Fink and Pastore's model, 294–296
implementing change, 304–307
integrated model of, 330–332
leadership and, 308–310
legal aspects of, 263–286 (*see also* Legislation)
of diverse groups, 315–334 (*see also* Groups)
prejudice and, *see* Prejudice
proactive hiring and, 306
processes, 302–308
promoting LGBT inclusiveness, 224
racial issues and, 70–95 (*see also* Racial minorities; Race)
religion and, *see* Religion
resistance to change and, 305
sexual orientation and, 212–233 (*see also* Sexual orientation)
social class and, 237–258 (*see also* Classism)
sport industry support for, 298–302
strategies (models) for, 291–298
systemic integration and, 306–307
training, 339–360 (*see also* Diversity training):
Diversity pie chart, 239
Diversity training, 339–360
  application of, 356–357
  benefits of, 339–340
  conducting, 351–352
  delivery of, 352–353
  developing effective programs, 344–357
  effective principles of, 353
  effects of, 341–344
  evaluating effectiveness of, 356
  evaluation of, 344, 354–356
  "framing" the training, 349
  general principles of, 357–359
  internal employee vs. outside consultant, 351–352
  lack of positive results, 342, 343
  linked to other outcomes, 350
  making sense of effects, 343–344

motivations for, 345
NCAA and, 339–340
need for, 346
needs analysis, 344, 345–347
options for, 347–348
post-training conditions,
362–366
pre-training conditions and, 344,
347–350
pre-training environment, 350
prevalence of, 341
topics typically covered, 351
training methods, 344, 350–353
voluntary/involuntary nature of,
350
Doherty and Chelladurai's model
for diversity management,
293–294
Donor expectations, 81–82
Dove marketing campaign, 182
Drive for Diversity program, in
NASCAR, 300
Dual-career families, 15
Dyad, comparisons and, 5, 6

Earnings:
differences based on sex and
race, 121
disability and, 158–159, 165
employees who are LGBT,
222–223
height and, 184–185
of men in workforce, 109–111
of women in workforce,
109–111
race and, 73–74
social class and, 240
Eating disorders, 183
Economic development, sport and,
289–290
Economic factors, and resistance to
change, 305
Education:
age and, 136–137
as a method to implement
change, 304, 306
classism and, 248–249
disability and, 157–158
social class and, 240
EEOC, see Equal Employment
Opportunity Commission

Effectiveness of diversity training,
356
Effort, as factor for Equal Pay Act,
270–271
Egyptian women, sport and, 205
Eight Steps to Fitness Program, 200
Elderly, caring for, 145
Empathy, creating, 358
Employee satisfaction, commitment
to diversity and, 329
Employees, ability to learn,
347–348
Employees (see also Diversity
training):
age and selection, 141–142
age and turnover, 144
age stereotypes and, 137–141
attitudes and behaviors of, 347
educating about change, 306
retaining diverse, 341, 342
Employers, negative feelings
regarding diversity, 17–18
Employment:
age and, 137–146
"bridge," 136
decisions and race, 78–79
earnings, see Earnings
race and, 73–88 (see also
Underrepresentation)
training and, see Diversity
training
Employment discrimination law,
265–286
Age Discrimination in Employment Act of 1967 (ADEA),
272–273
claims and, 277–278
early court decisions, 265–267
equal opportunity legislation,
267–277
Equal Pay Act, 270–271
Title VII, 265, 267
Endorsements, 125, 188
England, gender stereotypes in, 111
English, required, 18, 56
Environment, pre-diversity training,
350
Epstein, Theo, 76
Equal Employment Opportunity
Commission (EEOC), 267,
268, 269, 277

filing a complaint with, 278
Title IX claims and, 284
Equal opportunity legislation,
267–277
Equal Pay Act of 1963, 270–271
Equity in Athletics website, 281
ESPN, 36
ESPN Desportes, 92
Ethics:
religion and, 200–201
teaching, 201
Ethnicity, defining, 71–72
Evaluation of diversity training,
344, 354–356
Executive Order 13087, 275
Executive Steering Committee for
Diversity, in NASCAR, 300
Explicit racism, 82
Expressions, of diversity, 297

Fabrication, 225, 226
Faculty, minority representation
and, 87–88
Fatness, 177–178 (see also Obesity)
Fear of unknown, 305
Feedback:
during training, 353
seeking, 310
Female Athlete Triad Coalition,
182
Femininity, 105–107 (see also
Gender)
Feminist theory, 36, 57–58
Black, 37
Feuerstein, Aaron, 198
Fifth Amendment, 265
Financial aid, Title IX and, 280
Fink and Pastore's model for diver-
sity management, 294–296
First Nations people of Canada,
289–290
Fitness:
industry, 175–176
movement, 120
organizations, ADA compliance
and, 274
promotion of and weight,
181–182
Florida State University, 93
Focal support, of diversity, 308
Football Bowl Subdivision, 82

Four-fifths rule, 277
Fourteenth Amendment, 265
Franklin v. Gwinnett County Public Schools, 280
Franks, Laurence, 75
Free time, age and, 147 (*see also* Leisure)
Friendships, reducing prejudice and, 317–318, 319
Frisby, Wendy, 38
Functional pressures, as change factors, 303
Functionalism theory, 34–35
Funk, Fred, 107

Gallup polls, sexual orientation focus, 216–217
Garcia, Gabriela Deyanira Martinez, 119
Gay Games, 231
Gender:
    defined, 103–104
    identity, 104–107
    in sport context, 107–108
    influence on sport marketing, 123–125
    intersection with class, 253
    media influence on, 106–107
    origin of socialization, 106–107
    parental influence on, 106
    roles, 106–107
    schools influence on, 106
    sport organizations and, 101–128
    sport participation and, 120–121, 122–123
    state laws addressing gender identity, 275–276
    stereotypes, 107, 113–115
Gender and Diversity in Organizations, 44
General Social Survey, 216
Generalizability, 321
Generalization, of effects of contact, 321
Generation Y, 147
Generational differences, 135 (*see also* Age)
Genetics, obesity and, 178
George Pocock Rowing Foundation, 315

Gerritson, Steve, 315
Gilbert, Bil, 120
Gini Index, 14
Glass ceiling, 112
Globalization, 15
Goals, common, 327–328
Godfrey, Phil, 133
Gold's Gym, 175
Gordon, Jeff, 195
Graduation rates, racial minorities and, 91
Grant, Christine, 116
Gravity Games, 147
Greeks, sport and, 204
Griffey, Jr., Ken, 117
Griggs v. Duke Power Co., 265–266
Group dynamics, compositional approach and, 42
Groups:
    comparisons and, 5, 6
    contact hypothesis and, 316–321
    cross-categorization and, 323
    decategorization and, 322–325
    differences between and among, 321–330
    equal status of, 318
    fostering understanding among, 342
    heterogeneity of, 42
    integrated model for managing diverse, 330–332
    intimate contact and, 317–318
    managing diverse, 315–334 (*see also* Diversity management)
    need for cooperative interaction, 318–319
    recategorization and, 322, 325–328
    support for interaction among, 317
    work, age and, 146
Grove City v. Bell, 280
Guttman, Sir Ludwig, 166

Habit, and resistance to change, 305
Harassment:
    race and, 268
    sexual, 269–270
Harvard University, diversity training and, 340

Hate crimes, 73, 218
Haves and have nots, 253 (*see also* Classism)
Headscarves, sport participation and, 189
Health, African Americans and, 72
Healthcare, social class and, 250–251
Health-e-AME, 200
Health insurance, pregnancy and, 271
Hegemony theory, 36
Height, 183–185
Heterosexism, 217–218
Hill, Fitzgerald, 291
Hiring:
    discrimination in, 59 (*see also* Access discrimination)
    pregnancy and, 271
    proactive, 306
Hispanics:
    disability and, 157
    earnings and, 73–74
    earnings influenced by sex, 121
    increase in population, 11
    marketing and, 92
    positions played in MLB, 90
    tennis and, 3–4
Historically Black Colleges and Universities, 300
Hitting like a girl, 107
HIV/AIDS, 73, 155, 162, 164, 231, 251
Hockey Company, The, 16
Home Depot, 195
Homophobia, 217
Homosexuality, 212–233 (*see also* Sexual orientation)
    disclosure of, 225–229
Hot-button issues, discussion of, 342–343, 349
Housing, social class and, 249–250
Houston 1836, 309
Houston Dynamos, 309
Howard, Kristi, 175
Human capital, 89–90
    theory, 89–90
Human resources, competition for, 19
Human Rights and Equality Commission, 63

Human Rights Campaign, 223, 275

Identity, in-group, 326–328
If-then conditions, 29
Illiteracy, athletes and, 69–70
Implicit racism, 82
Inactivity, costs of, 133
Income:
    changes, 13–14
    disability and, 158–159, 165
    employees who are LGBT,
        222–223
    height and, 184–185
    influenced by sex and race, 121
    of men in workforce, 109–111
    of women in workforce,
        109–111
    race and, 73–74
    social class and, 240
    wage gaps and, 246–248
Individual merit, success and, 246
Individual resistance, to change,
    305
Inertia and resistance to change,
    305
Information diversity, 8, 9
Information/decision-making theory,
    32–33
In-group identity, forming,
    326–328
In-house personnel, diversity train-
    ing and, 351
Institute for Diversity and Ethics in
    Sports, 63, 298
Institutional distancing, 245–255
    education and, 248–249
    healthcare and, 250–251
    housing and, 249–250
    meritocracy, 245–248
    organizational structure,
        251–254
Institutional support, for intergroup
    interaction, 317
Institutionalized practices, 80
Instructor-led diversity training,
    352
Integrated model of diversity man-
    agement, 330–332
Interaction, cooperative among
    groups, 318–319
Interactionist theory, 38–39

Intercollegiate athletics, see College
    athletics
Interdependence, cooperative,
    318–319
Intergroup:
    anxiety, prejudice and, 317,
        319–320
    bias, 39
    contact, 322, 329–330
International Association of Athlet-
    ics Federations, 153
International sport, 92
Interpersonal communication,
    309
Interpersonal distancing, 245
Intervening process theory, 31–32
Islam, sport and, 205
Israel and Pakistan, 41
Issues, sensitive, 342–343

Jackson, Roderick, 281
Jackson v. Birmingham Board of
    Education, 280, 281
Jazzercise, 175–176
Jeter, Derek, 60
Job notices, age and, 273
Job performance, diversity training
    and, 350, 357
Job relatedness, 31, 32
Job type, gender stereotypes and,
    114–115
Job/task analysis, diversity training
    and, 346
Jobs:
    access to by persons who are
        LGBT, 222
    "old-type" vs. "new-type," 145
Johnson, Lyndon, 81
Johnson, Magic, 19

Kane, Mary Jo, 115
Kava, Ruth, 177
Kearse, Jevon, 177
Kemp Elementary School, 346
Kinnick Stadium, 108
Kinsey, Alfred, 215
Kravitz, Cheryl, 358
Ku Klux Klan, 51

Laboratory for Diversity in Sport,
    44, 300, 301

Lacrosse, diversity and, 315, 319
Lands End, 198
Lang, Tian, 92
Language:
    and disability, 157
    discrimination based on, 56
    sexist, 103
Lapchick, Richard, 74–75, 82,
        298–300
Lawson, Claire, 315
Lawsuits, curbing through diversity
    training, 342
Leader-member exchange theory,
    159, 163
Leaders:
    intergroup interaction and, 317
    skills and behaviors of,
        308–310
Leadership:
    diversity and, 308–310
    legacy, 201–202
    religion and, 201–202
    representation by women in
        positions, 111–112 (see also
        Underrepresentation)
    servant, 201
    stereotypes regarding women
        and, 113–115
    stereotypes, underrepresentation
        and, 85–86
    support for change and, 306
    Title IX effects on, 284–285
    women and transformational,
        114
Leagues, church-organized, 199
Learn, ability to, 347–348
Learning:
    application of, 356–357
    from diversity training, 354
    styles, 349, 353:
Legacy leadership, 201–202
Legal aspects of diversity, 263–286
    (see also Legislation)
Legal mandates, 10, 17
Legislation:
    Age Discrimination in Employ-
        ment Act of 1967 (ADEA),
        272–273
    Americans with Disabilities Act,
        see Americans with Disabili-
        ties Act

Civil Rights Act of 1964, *see* Civil Rights Act of 1964; *see also* Title VII
Civil Rights Act of 1991, 267
claims based on employment discrimination, 277–278
employment discrimination law, 265–286 (*see also* Employment discrimination law)
Equal Pay Act, 270–271
Pregnancy Discrimination Act, 271
state laws addressing sexual orientation/gender identity, 275–276
Title IX, *see* Title IX
Title VII, *see* Title VII
Leisure:
    age and participation, 147–148
    race and participation, 89
Lesbian:
    coaches, 56, 218, 219
    sport clubs, 230
    earnings and, 222–223
LGB (lesbian, gay, bisexual) sexual orientations, 212–233 (*see also* Sexual orientation)
    targeting as employees/customers, 229–230
LGBT, definition of terms, 215–217
Lieberman, Nancy, 101–102
Little League, 195
    communication issues and, 18
L.L. Bean, 198
Lopiano, Donna, 263, 264

Macro-level factors, 79, 80–82
Major League Baseball (MLB), 35, 36
    diversity in, 15–16
    diversity initiatives in, 299
    earnings gap and, 255
    Hispanic audience and, 92
    race and positions played, 89
    racial representation and, 74, 76
Major League Soccer (MLS):
    diversity initiatives in, 299
    racial representation and, 75, 76
    team names and, 309
Makeup, attractiveness and, 188
Malden Mills, 198–199

Management:
    commitment to/support of diversity, 307–308
    commitment to diversity training, 359
    conflict, 309
    implementing change, 304–307
    of diverse organizations, 289–312 (*see also* Diversity management)
    organizational analysis and, 345–346
    reducing intergroup bias and, 330–332
    representation by women in, 111–112
    representation of racial minorities in, 121–122
    support for change, 306
    systemic integration and, 306–307
Managerial theories, 30, 31–34
    implications of, 33–34
    information/decision-making theory, 32–33
    intervening process theory, 31–32
    resource-based theory, 33
Managers:
    "framing" diversity training, 349
    diversity training for, 340
Manley, Dexter, 69–70
Marketing:
    athlete endorsements and, 125, 188
    disability and, 168–169
    NASCAR and, 195
    of sport, 123–125, 147, 188
    racial influences on, 91–92
    to customers who are LGB, 229–230
Mart, Paul, 231
Martin, Casey, 275
Marx, Karl, 42
Mascots, Native American, 93
Masculinity, 105–107 (*see also* Gender)
MasterCard, 91
Masters Golf Tournament, 57
Maternity leave, 271

McDowell, Jacqueline, 254
Media:
    disability and, 168–169
    influence on gender socialization, 106
    influence on sport participation, 106–107
Median age, increase in, 10, 12
Melaleuca Elementary School, 315
Men (*see also* Gender):
    earnings and, 109–111
    motives for sport consumption, 124
Mentoring, age and, 143
Mergers, diversity and, 16
Meritocracy, 245–248
Merritt, LaShawn, 153, 154
Meso-level factors, 79, 82–86
Mexico, women's work experiences in, 119
Micro-level factors, 79, 86–87
Middle class, defined, 242
Miller, Kendall, 77
Miller, Lori, 284
Minorities (*see also* Race; Racial Minorities):
    defining, 71–72
    underrepresentation in employment areas, 79–87
Models for diversity management, 291–298
Moderation, of activation strategies, 298
Moderators:
    age and, 144–146
    integrated model and, 331–332
    weight and, 180–181
Money damages, Title VII and, 267
Monocultural organizations, 292
Moore, Joe, 144
Morale, maintaining through diversity training, 342
Mothers, elite athletes as, 117
Motivation, diversity training and, 348–349
Motives, discrimination and, 267
Multicultural organizations, 293
Multicultural Participation Committee, in the USTA, 300
Multicultural skills, leadership and, 309–310

Mutual group differentiation, 329–330

Nardiello, Tim, 270
NASCAR, 19, 195–196
    diversity initiatives in, 300
NASPE statement regarding sexual harassment, 270
National Basketball Association (NBA), 15–16, 19, 35
    as international sport, 92
    Development League, 101
    diversity initiatives in, 299
    earnings and, 74
    earnings gap and, 255
    obesity and, 177
    promotions and, 195
    racial representation and, 74, 75, 76
National Collegiate Athletic Association, *see* NCAA
National Football League (NFL), 15, 35, 36
    attractiveness and performance, 189
    diversity initiatives in, 299
    diversity programs training and, 291, 292
    earnings gap and, 255
    obesity and, 177
    racial representation and, 74, 75, 76
    youth movement in, 142
National Hockey League (NHL), 35, 55
    diversity initiatives in, 299
    earnings gap and, 255
    gender stereotypes and, 107
National Institutes of Health, 178
National origin discrimination, 269 (*see also* Race)
National Senior Games Association, 133
Native American:
    women and sport participation, 123
    disability and, 157
    mascots and, 93
    sport experiences of, 92–93
NCAA, 57, 263, 264
    Director's Cup points, 296

disability and, 167
Diversity in Athletics Award, 300–302
diversity initiatives in, 300
diversity training/management/ programs, 291, 296, 339–340
Football Bowl Subdivision, 82
graduation rates and, 69
Native American mascots and, 93
report on graduation rates, 69
sports, racial representation and, 76
Sunday games and, 199
women as coaches for women's teams, 111–112
Needs analysis, diversity training and, 344, 345–347
Networks:
    creating/maintaining, 85
    women and, 116–117
New Jersey Nets, 75
Nike, 16
Noncompliance, organizational diversity and, 295
Normalizing, 225, 226
Normative commitment, 307
Normed tests, discrimination and, 267
North American Society for the Sociology of Sport, 44
Notre Dame, 144

Obama, Barack, 81
Obesity (*see also* Weight):
    athletes and, 177
    defining, 177–178
    discrimination protection and, 274–275
Occupation, social class and, 240
Occupational segregation, 78–79, 94
Occupational turnover, women and, 119
Ochoa, Lorena, 117
Office of Civil Rights (OCR), 279–280, 283
Old Dominion University, 101
Older Workers Protection Act of 1990, 273
Old-type vs. new-type job, 145

Olivia Cruises/Resorts, 230
Olympic Games, 168, 204, 231
    cut to school-based sports, 263–264
    disability and, 154
    housing and, 250
Oppression, racial, 70–71
Organization:
    implementing change in, 304–307
    management's support for change, 306
    success of, 342
    systemic integration of, 306–307
Organizational:
    climate, 356
    culture, underrepresentation and, 86
    dimensions of diversity, 292–293
    effectiveness, diversity and, 19
    resistance, to diversity-related change, 305
    structure, classism and, 251–254
Organizational analysis, 304
    diversity training and, 345–346
Organizations:
    diversity training and, *see* Diversity training
    level of diversity in, 292–293, 294–296
    management of diverse, 289–312 (*see also* Diversity management)
    pressures to change, 303–304
    resistance to change and, 305
Osteoporosis, 183
Outcomes:
    associated with prejudice, 53–54
    diversity training and, 356
    passing/revealing and, 228–229
Out-groups, prejudice and, 319–320
Overweight, defining, 177–178
Owning class, defined, 242

Pakistan and Israel, 41
Paralympic Games, 156, 166, 169
Parents:
    role in gender socialization, 106
    single, 15

Participation:
limited access to, 57
Title IX outcomes and, 283–284
Participatory action research, 38
Passing/revealing:
antecedents to, 227–228
LGB persons and, 225–229
outcomes, 228–229
Pay to play sports, 237–238, 255
Pay, *see* Earnings
Peers, influence of, 357
Penn, Elaine, 339
Perceived differences, 5–6
Performance:
age and, 137–139, 143–144 (*see also* Age)
appraisals, discrimination and, 60–61
bonuses, 247
disability and, 153–154 (*see also* Disability)
evaluation, disability and, 165
expectations for persons with disabilities, 160
self-limiting behavior and, 60–61
Person analysis, diversity training and, 346–347
Person Behind the Face technique, 358
Personalization, 323
Perspective, gaining through religion, 207
PGA, 275
Championship, 57
diversity initiatives in, 299
PGA Tour, Inc. v. Martin, 275
Physical activity:
attractiveness and, 188
faith-based initiatives and, 199
patterns of, 133
weight and, 181–183
Physical education, Title IX and programs, 282
Pistorius, Oscar, 153–154, 165
Pity, discrimination and, 162–163
Pizza Hut, 160
Political climate, underrepresentation and, 81
Political pressure, as a change factor, 303

Portland, Rene, 219
Portnick, Jennifer, 175, 275
Positions held, race and, 74–78 (*see also* Underrepresentation)
Positions played, racial influence on, 89–90
Poverty:
age and, 136–137
defined, 242
Power:
and resistance to change, 305
women advancing and, 115
Practicality of theory, 29–30
Prayer, 200
athletes' use of, 205–206, 208
community, 199
costs of, 207
Preconceptions, diminished by intimate contact, 318
Preemployment enquiries, 268
Pregnancy, discrimination and, 269, 271
Pregnancy Discrimination Act, 271
Prejudice, 50–54 (*see also* Discrimination; Racism)
and resistance to change, 305
classism and, *see* Classism
contact hypothesis and, 316–321
defined, 51
explicit, 51–52
implicit, 52–53
outcomes associated with, 53–54
racism and, 51–53 (*see also* Racism)
reduction of, 317–319
sexual orientation and, 217–221 (*see also* Sexual orientation; Sexual prejudice)
socially permissible, 52
strategies for reducing, 321–330
underrepresentation and, 82–83
Pressures, as change factors, 303–304
Prestige, Title IX and, 284
Pre-training conditions, diversity training and, 344, 347–350
Price Waterhouse v. Hopkins, 266
Proactive hiring, ensuring diversity and, 306
Proactive, organizational diversity and, 295

Professional sports, diversity initiatives in, 299–300
Project Implicit, 63
Promotion:
age and, 143–144, 145
employees who are LGBT, 223–224
of sport, attractiveness and, 188
Property taxes, 248
Proposition, defined, 29
Pryor, Stoney, 327
Purdue University, 117
Puritans, sports and, 204–205

Quadriplegic, 164

Race, 69–95
and sex, 120
and sport participation, 122–123
as influence on participants' experiences, 88–91
defining, 71–72
defining ourselves in terms of, 72
disability and, 156–157
discrimination protection and, 267–269
earnings and, 73–74
employment decisions and, 78–79
in employment context, 73–88
intersection with class, 253
leisure and, 89
positions held, 74–78 (*see also* Underrepresentation)
sport participation and, 88–91
Title VII protection and, 267–269
trends and, 72
volunteering and, 148
Racial and Gender Report Card, 74–75, 298–300, 302
Racial integration, of college athletics, 303
Racial minorities:
academics and sports, 69–70
as faculty members, 87–88
effect of race on participatory experiences, 88–91
effect of race on positions played on teams, 89–90
experiences of relative to Whites, 70–95 (*see also* Race)

graduation rates and, 91
health issues and, 72
in administration, 76–78 (*see also* Management)
increase in U.S., 10–12, 72
occupational segregation and, 94
reasons for underrepresentation, 79–87
representation as coaches, 75–76
representation in sport organizations, 79–87
stereotypes as influence on participatory experiences, 90
treatment by coaches/administrators, 90–91
treatment of athletes and, 91
Racial oppression, 70–71
Racism:
    aversive, 53, 82–83
    critical race theory and, 37
    implicit/explicit, 82
    institutionalized, 70, 80
    soccer and, 52
Rainbow Tourism, 230
Reactive (organizational category), 295
Reagan, Ronald, 81
Recategorization, 322, 325–328, 331
Recreation, Title IX and programs, 282
Reebok, 16
Rehabilitation Act of 1973, 274
Reinforcement, level of, 337
Relational approach to studying diversity, 39, 42
Religion, 195–209
    and soccer, 204
    and sport participation, 204–208
    as source of categorization, 203–204
    as way to avoid trouble, 206–207
    athlete's use of, 205–208
    defined, 196–197
    discrimination protection and, 272
    emphasis on, 197–198
    ethical behavior and, 200–201
    in the workplace, 198–204

influence on strategic decisions, 198–200
    leadership and, 201–202
    personal success and, 208
    prayer and, *see* Prayer
    sexual prejudice and, 220
    social functions of, 197
    stress and, 202–203
    team unity and, 207–208
Research:
    participatory action, 38
    pertaining to categorical approach, 42
    pertaining to compositional approach, 42
    pertaining to diversity management study approach, 42
    pertaining to relational approach, 42
Resistance, forms of, 305
Resource allocation, and resistance to change, 305
Resource-based theory, 33
Responsibility, as factor for Equal Pay Act, 271
Results, from diversity training, 354
Retirement:
    early, 273
    leisure and, 147
Revealing, LGB persons and, 225–229
Reynolds, Kirk, 292
Richardson, Nolan, 69
Rieke, Ann, 175
Risks, passing/revealing and, 227
Robbers Cave Study, 318–319
Robinson, Jackie, 53, 57
Robinson, Mike, 77
Roby, Peter, 19
Role modeling, 310
Ross, Kevin, 69–70
Rowing, diversity and, 315
Rugby, 213
Rupp, Adolph, 303

Safe harbor schools, 283
Safe havens, for employees who are LGBT, 224
Sailes, Gary, 85
Salary, *see* Compensation; Earnings

Salient categorization, 329, 331
San Francisco 49ers, 292
Satisfaction, of employees, 329
Scholarships, Title IX and, 280
School children, *see* Children
Schools, role in gender socialization, 106
Section 106.37 of Title IX, 279
Section 106.41 of Title IX, 279
Security, and resistance to change, 305
Segregation, 268
    occupational, 78–79, 94
Selective information processing, and resistance to change, 305
Self-awareness, increased, 309
Self-categorization theory, 39
Self-efficacy, diversity training and, 348
Self-limiting behavior, bias and, 60–61
Self-monitoring tendencies, 227–228
Senior Games, 133
Senior Woman Administrator, 112, 122, 307
Sensitive issues, discussion of, 342–343
Sensitization, to problems of diversity, 342, 343
Separation, prejudice and, 316
Servant leadership, 201
Sex (*see also* Gender; Masculinity; Women):
    age and, 137
    changes in composition of, 13
    defined, 103–104
    disability and, 164
    disability rates and, 155–156
    discrimination protection and, 269–272
    influence on sport marketing, 123–125
    objects, females as, 53
    sport participation and, 120–121, 122–123
    Title VII protection and, 269–272
Sex/gender, workplace and, 108–119

Sexist language, 103, 303
Sexual harassment, 269–270
Sexual orientation, 212–233
    changing attitudes and, 215–217
    coaching and, 218–219
    defining terms, 215–217
    determining through tests, 216
    disclosure of, 225–229
    discrimination protection and,
        275–276
    historical context, 215–217
    intersection with class, 253
    passing/revealing, 225–229
    prejudice and, 217–221 (see also
        Sexual prejudice)
    work and, 221–229
Sexual prejudice:
    prevalence of, 218–220
    characteristics predictive of, 221
    coaches and, 218–219
    defined, 217–218
    effects of, 220
    motivation for, 220
Shaw, Sally, 30
Shoal Creek, 57
Signaling, 225, 226
Similarities, perceived, 5–6
Similarity-attraction paradigm, 41
Simulations, diversity training and,
    353
Skill, as factor for Equal Pay Act,
    270
Skill-based outcomes, to diversity
    training, 356
Slavery, 70
    13th Amendment and, 265
Soccer (see also Major League
    Soccer):
    racism in, 52
    religion and, 204
Social categorization framework,
    39–41, 55, 57, 60, 62, 115,
    182, 243
    decategorization and, 322–325,
        330–331
    for reducing bias, 321–330
    intergroup contact and, 329–330
    recategorization and, 328
    religion and, 200, 203–204
Social change, sport as a tool for,
    289–290

Social class, 237–258 (see also
        Classism)
    alternate conceptions of, 254
    defined, 242–243
    education and, 248–249
    heath care and, 250–251
    housing and, 249–250
    social mobility and, 256
    socioeconomic status, 239–242
    sport and, 256
Social closure theory, 89
Social economic status:
    education and, 248–249
    housing and, 249–250
Social identity, 200
Social identity salience, 200
Social networks, women and,
    116–117
Social outcomes, poor group dy-
        namics and, 146
Social pressures, 10, 17–18
    as change factors, 303–304
Social psychological theories, 30,
        38–41
    similarity-attraction paradigm,
        41
    social categorization framework,
        39–40
Social support, for intergroup inter-
        action, 317
Social unit, studying using composi-
        tional approach, 42
Social-identity theory, 39
Socioeconomic status (SES),
        239–242 (see also Social
        class)
    and sport/leisure participation,
        89
    changes in, 13–14
Sociological theories, 30, 34–38
    conflict theory, 35–36
    critical theory, 36–37
    functionalism theory, 34–35
    implications, 38
    interactionist theory, 38–39
Sorenstam, Anika, 107
Spanish-speaking, employment and,
    88
Spatial arrangement, in-group iden-
        tity and, 326, 327
Special Olympics, 162, 166

Special Teams Initiative, in NFL,
    299
Spinal Injuries Center at Stoke,
    166
Spirituality, 197 (see also Religion)
Sponsorship, NASCAR and, 195
Sport:
    age and consumption of, 147
    age and participation, 147–148
    and religion, see Religion
    as religion, 206
    as tool for development and so-
        cial change, 289–290
    church-organized leagues, 199
    classism and, 254–255
    consumption of, 124
    cost of enjoying, 35–36
    disability and, 153–154, 165–168
        (see also Disability sport)
    earnings gap and, 255
    equal access to, 289–290
    gender and, 107–108 (see also
        Gender)
    importance of diversity in, 19
    industry support for diversity
        management, 298–302
    influence of race on participa-
        tion, 88–91
    international, 92
    marketing of, 123–125, 147,
        188 (see also Marketing)
    motives for consumption, 124
    participation and gender, 120–
        121, 122–123
    participation and race, 122–123
    participation and sex differences,
        120–121, 122–123
    promoting, 125 (see also
        Marketing)
    promotion and attractiveness,
        188
    religion and, 204–208 (see also
        Religion)
    sexual orientation and, 230–231
    sexual prejudice and, 218–219
    social mobility and, 256
    women's, 123–125
Sport Canada, 289
Sport consumption, racial influ-
        ences on, 91–92
Sport England, 122

Sport organizations:
    ADA compliance and, 273–274
    age and, 133–149 (*see also* Age)
    customer service and, 124–125
    disability and, 153–171
    diversity management and, *see* Diversity management
    diversity training and, *see* Diversity training
    fan loyalty, 124–125
    globalization and, 15
    management of diverse groups, 315–334
    occupational segregation, 78–79
    pay to play, 237–238, 255
    race and sex and, 119–123
    race as influence on participants' experiences, 88–91
    race issues in, 69–95 (*see also* Race; Racial minorities)
    reasons for underrepresentation of racial minorities, 79–87
    representation of racial minorities in management roles, 121–122
    representation of racial minorities, 79–87
    representation of women in leadership positions, 111–112 (*see also* Gender; Women)
    sex and gender in, 101–128
    structure and classism, 251–243
    underrepresentation in, *see* Underrepresentation
Stacking, 90
Stakeholder expectations, 81–82
Standard Occupational Qualification System, 241
Status:
    equal among groups, 318
    influence of, 320
Stephens, Merry, 219
Stereotypes (*see also* Discrimination):
    about athletic performance, 90
    age and, 137–141 (*see also* Age)
    as influence on participatory experience, 90
    diminished by intimate contact, 318
    gender, 107, 113–115

    leadership, 85–86
    regarding persons with disabilities, 160
    reinforcing, 342, 343
    women in leadership and, 113–115
Stereotyping, cognitive distancing and, 244–245
Stigma:
    discrimination and, 161–162
    passing/revealing and, 228
    weight and, 179
Stigmatizing characteristics, 228
Stoke-Mandeville Games, 166
Stress, religion and, 202–203
Structural forces, advancement of women and, 113, 115–117
Substantive conflict, 31
Substantive expressions, of diversity, 297
Success:
    individual merit and, 246
    religion and, 208
Summit, Pat, 117
Supervisors, relationships with disabled employees, 159
Support:
    diversity training and, 350, 357
    for intergroup interaction, 317
Surface-level diversity, 7, 8, 9–10, 15, 17, 21, 39, 41, 297
Swoopes, Sheryl, 229, 230
Symbolic expressions, of diversity, 297
Systemic integration, of an organization, 306–307

Tactile learners, 349
Task:
    analysis, training and, 346
    complexity, 298
    interdependence, 298
Team building, 324–325
Team Marketing Report's Fan Cost Index, 36
Team unity, religion and, 207–208
Teams, race and positions played, 89–90
Tennis, 3–4, 49–50
Tenure, age and, 140
Testosterone, 189

Texas A&M University, 247
Texas Christian University, 90
Texas Rangers, 76
Texas Western University, racially integrated teams in, 303
Theory:
    defining, 28–30, 35–36
    discrimination and, 56–58
    diversity and, 27–44
    feminist, 57–58
    importance of in studying diversity, 29–30
    practicality and, 29–30
    used to understand diversity, 30–42
Thirteenth Amendment, 265
Thomas, Gavin, 213–214
Thomas, R. Roosevelt, 27
Threat, and resistance to change, 305
Three-prong test, 281, 283
Title IX, 17, 50, 81, 101, 108, 111, 120, 123, 126, 140, 263, 264, 278–285
    compliance with, 281–283
    history of, 279–281
    influence on physical education, 282
    influence on recreation programs, 282
    leadership effects, 284–285
    outcomes, 283–285
    safe harbor schools, 283
    three-prong test for compliance, 281, 283
Title VII of CRA of 1964, 56, 265
    Pregnancy Discrimination Act, 271
    protection on basis of age, 272–273
    protection on basis of race, 267–269
    protection on basis of religion, 272
    protection on basis of sex, 269–272
Titleist, 33
Toyota, 169
Track and field, coaches, 146
Trainee characteristics, diversity training and, 347–349

Trainers, qualified, 358
Training and development, disability and, 165
Training, employees over 50, 143, 145
Training/development, age and, 142–143, 145
Transfer of training, 343–344
Transformational leadership, 114
Transitional organizations, 292
Treatment discrimination, 54, 55–56, 91
  outcomes related to, 59–61
  theories related to, 57–58
  underrepresentation and, 84
Trust, diversity training and, 359
Tucker Center for Research on Girls and Women in Sport, 115
Turnover:
  age and, 144
  intentions, 87
  occupational, for women, 119

Underrepresentation:
  discrimination and, 83–85
  expectations/intentions of coaches, 86–87
  in administrative positions, 76–78
  institutionalized practices, 80
  leadership stereotypes and, 85–86
  macro-level factors, 79, 80–82
  meso-level factors, 79, 82–86
  micro-level factors, 79, 86–87
  of women as coaches, 111–112
  of women in leadership roles, 113–119
  organizational culture, 86
  political climate and, 81
  prejudice, 82–83
  stakeholder expectations, 81–82
  Title IX and, 284–285 (see also Title IX)
  treatment discrimination and, 84
  turnover intentions, 87
Unfamiliarity, prejudice and, 316
United States Tennis Association (USTA), 3, 4, 20
  diversity initiatives in, 300
Unity, religion and, 207–208

University athletics, diversity in, 300–302, 303
University athletics, see College athletics
University of Alabama, 303
University of Kentucky, 303
University of Southern California, 303
University of Texas, 110
University of Utah, 281
Unknown, fear of, 305

Value diversity, 8, 9
Value-in-diversity hypothesis, 10, 18–19
Values, as category of diversity, 297
Valuing diversity, as a method to implement change, 304
Virginia Commonwealth University, 281
Visibility, level of, 31, 32
Visible features, as category of diversity, 297
Visual learners, 349
Volunteering, age and, 147–148
Voting Rights Act of 1965, 81

Waddell, Tom, 231
Wage gaps, 246–248
Wards Cove Packing Co. v. Atonio, 266–267
Warmth/competence, disability stereotypes and, 162–163
Weight, 175–183
  effect of in workplace, 178–181
  female athlete triad and, 183
  fitness promotion and, 181–182
  genetics and, 178
  moderators of effects, 180–183
  negative perceptions and, 179–180
  physical activity and, 181–183
  stigma and, 179
  type of job as moderator, 181
Weihenmayer, Erik, 153–154
Weis, Charlie, 180
Wellness centers, classism and, 255
Whistle-blowing, 281
Whites, decreasing proportion, 72
Will, George F., 264

Williams, Serena, 49–50, 125
Williamson, Nancy, 120
Willie O'Ree All-State Game, 299
Withycombe Consulting, 351
Women:
  as coaches, 111–112, 115–117
  as sex objects, 53
  attitudes toward being head coaches, 117–119
  disability and, 164
  discrimination and, 269–272
  discrimination and advancement, 115–116
  earnings and, 109–111
  Equal Pay Act and, 270–271
  feminist theory and, 36
  headscarves and sport, 189
  in key leadership roles, 101–102 (see also Gender)
  leadership stereotypes and, 113–115
  occupational turnover and, 119
  of color in leadership roles, 142–143
  percentage in workforce, 108–109
  personal characteristics and coaching, 117–119
  reasons for underrepresentation in leadership roles, 113–119
  representation in management positions, 111–112
  sport consumption and, 123–125
  structural forces and advancement, 113, 115–117
  transformational leadership and, 114
  underrepresentation in leadership positions, 284–285
  weight and, 179, 180 (see also Weight)
  work-family conflict and, 117
Women's American Basketball Association, 101
Women's National Basketball Association (WNBA), 101, 230
  diversity initiatives in, 299
  promotions and, 195
  racial representation and, 75
Women's Sport Foundation, 101, 123, 263

Women's sports, increase due to Title IX, 283–285 (*see also* Title IX)

Women's Sport Services, 59

WomenSport International, 270

Woods, Tiger, 107

Work:
    changes in nature of, 10, 15–16
    changing attitudes toward, 10, 14–15
    experiences, experiencing different, 58
    groups, effect of age in, 146
    outcomes, 6

Work-family conflict, 10, 15, 117

Workforce (*see also* Workplace):
    changing demographics of, 10–14 (*see also* Demographics)

    men and women in, 108–119

Working class, defined, 242 (*see also* Social class)

Working conditions, as factor for Equal Pay Act, 272

Work-life balance, 15

Workplace:
    age and employee selection, 141–142
    age and opportunities, 141–144
    age stereotypes and, 137–141
    application of diversity training in, 356–357
    attractiveness in, 187–188
    disability and, 157–165
    diversity's impact on, 304
    effects of height in, 183–184
    effects of weight in, 178–181

    men and women in, 108–119
    nature of regarding disability, 165
    religion in, 198–204
    sexual harassment in, 269–270
    sexual orientation and, 221–229

World Cup, 147

World Health Organization, 133, 178, 181

World Series, 147

Wright-Eger, Cathy, 117

X Games, 147

YMCA, age and, 146